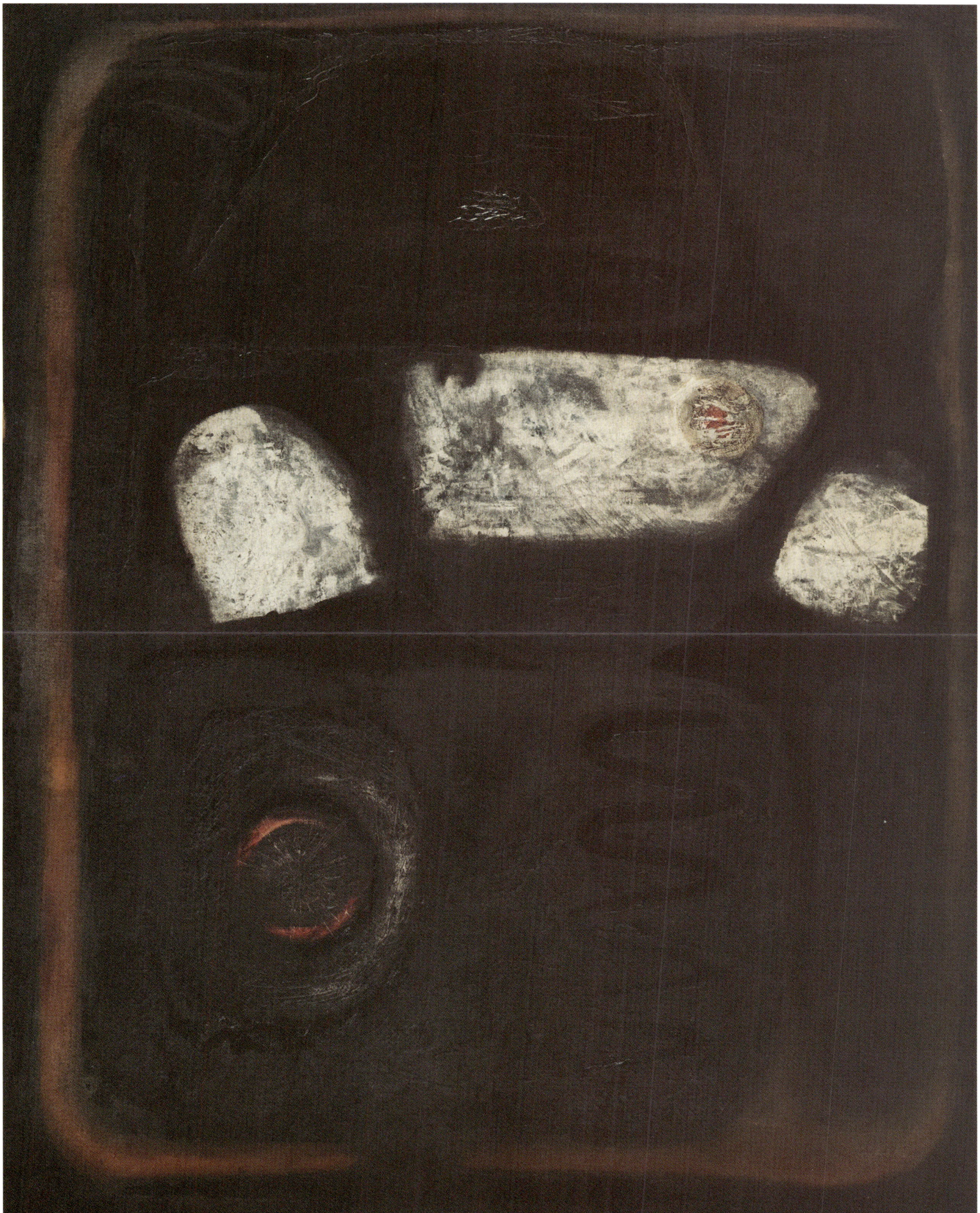

J. Swaminathan
Untitled, 1963, oil on canvas and mixed media, 48 x 60 inches
Collection: S. Kalidas and Harsha Vardhana Swaminathan
Exhibited in 'Group 1890', Lalit Kala Akademi, New Delhi, October 1963

KB GOEL

CRITICAL WRITINGS ON ART

1957–1998

KB GOEL

CRITICAL WRITINGS ON ART

1957–1998

edited and introduced by
Shruti Parthasarathy

SHER-GIL SUNDARAM ARTS FOUNDATION
Tulika Books

First published in India in 2020 by
SSAF–Tulika Books

Sher-Gil Sundaram Arts Foundation (SSAF)
3/9 (first floor), Shanti Niketan, New Delhi 110 021, India | ssaf.in

Tulika Books
44 (first floor), Shahpur Jat, New Delhi 110 049, India | tulikabooks.in

ISBN: 978-81-9373299-1 (hardback)

Design: Alpana Khare

Printed at Chaman Enterprises, Delhi 110 002

CONTENTS

FOREWORD

From the 1960s through the '90s, *Link* and *The Patriot* (sometimes *Mainstream* and much later, *The Economic Times*) carried the voice of a maverick art critic, K.B. Goel.[1] This was a voice not heard with any real attention, both because it was featured in media linked to the Communist Party (supposedly addressing only comrades) and because it spoke in an idiom that was often *tendentious* in the Marxist sense of that term. But the neglect of K.B. Goel by the art discourse in Delhi has been a loss that we must now repair.[2]

This book is a substantive compilation of Goel's numerous articles and reviews (from 1957 to 1998). The Editor, Shruti Parthasarathy, has selected, configured, sequenced and annotated Goel's articles. Her Introduction offers a close reading of Goel's texts and she is able to place this otherwise 'random' mass of articles (written as and when a review was due for publication) in both art-historical retrospect and contemporary context.

In the last two decades there has been an advance in both retrieving and formulating critical accounts of modern and contemporary art in India. Placed within this process, K.B. Goel emerges as a critic who recognized, as early as in the 1960s, how practice and theory were abutting each other in art history discourse – and even within the art review.

In this same period there are new vectors of critique envisioned by a Third World; here artists, like citizens, begin to see themselves as coeval *and* contestatory in relation to the Western canon. Interestingly, Goel remained less interested in post-colonial terminology and more in an untethered contemporary. He conducted his solitary 'research' in the many libraries of Delhi – desiring to engage with the most advanced debates in international avant-garde art. We are especially beholden to Shruti's Introduction for bringing out this strand, including especially Goel's (sometimes laboured) effort at decoding Marcel Duchamp.

By the 1960s, the international canon was pronounced by New York (the School of Paris, fully hegemonic in the first half of the twentieth century was waning in the post-war period). The New York School was constituted by major artists but also major critics, and it was these figures that attracted Goel: he admired, for instance, Michael Fried and the formidable Rosalind Krauss. We again owe it to Shruti for focusing on this forgotten aspect of Goel. I would add, however, that his tracking of the New York axis was both provocative and unsystematic. A left-oriented critic in India was more likely to consider American art as imperialist in its cultural triumphalism; and the formalist approach predominantly favoured by American critics should have seemed inappropriate before the more content-led concerns of Indian artists.

What Goel's writing does yield is theories of perception and analyses of form within the larger quest to grasp – as a self-taught critic – the terms advanced by the major movements of modern art after Cezanne.

Thereon, he chose to pursue the formal logic of paint, surface, structure and flat support; the sheer opticality and pristine *presentness* whereby late modernist painting gains its 'sovereign' status.

This book reproduces as a frontispiece, J. Swaminathan's large, heavily encrusted, near-black painting with obscure markings displayed at the Group 1890 exhibition in 1963. Swaminathan's paintings from this show are mostly 'lost'; the reappearance of this one complements what we hope will also be posthumous recognition of the critic K.B. Goel.

Goel developed his perceptual and writing skills in tandem with his friend and 'comrade' Swaminathan, in the early 1960s, when both artist and critic were relative 'amateurs'. Goel would certainly have been inspired by the ingeniously polemical 'Manifesto' written by Swaminathan on behalf of his fellow artists in the folder-catalogue of the Group 1890 exhibition. Swaminathan's tactics of argument were to get his point across every which way, allowing a simultaneous repudiation and valorization of ideologies that would gain him the status of difference and alterity. Goel was in no way as shrewd as Swaminathan, but he was better read in art history texts and often brought an erudite slant to his maverick position.

Goel developed a phenomenological and semiotic reading of painting through his textual forays into contemporary international art; this was complemented, fortuitously, by Swaminathan's own early preference to treat the painting surface as an opaque 'wall' rather than a picture-window. Goel wrote about this concurrence: 'The indeterminacy of experience is an obstacle and Swaminathan enjoys this game of our trying to scale an invisible wall. His art . . . presents the . . . puzzle recently posed by America's single-colour giant-size canvases covering the whole wall of a gallery; their enormous expanse forced the spectator through colour dynamics alone to feel as though he was inside the picture and yet conscious of the fact that he was outside it' ('Scaling the Invisible Wall', p. 108 of this volume; all page numbers at the end of quotations from Goel's writings refer to this volume).

In 1988, Swaminathan 'returned' – after two decades of mystical-lyric paintings of metaphoric 'landscape' – to non-representational language. Goel wrote: 'Earlier the paint soaked in and became part of picture's life: now the canvas has a life of its own. . . . Similarly Swaminathan's concept of totality in which parts were all fitted into what is called a composition has gone: now, colour implicates not only surface values, texture and tone but the responsive echo of the presence of the other' ('Africa of the Rational Mind', p. 402).

In 1991, Goel reiterated this aesthetic: 'With this, it seemed, Swaminathan returned to the point from where he had started. The position between the eye and the hand hardened into a resolve. . . . In the new paintings, the vision does not organize the visible, nor does it bestow meaning upon it, constituting it into a sign. . . . In the new mode, the surface becomes an arena within which to act and from which the creative act and its material world arise' ('The Painter in His Labyrinth', p. 118). Further: 'Because the Swaminathan world remains nascent, in a permanent state of gestation, it is like an apparition that never reaches the threshold of reality' (ibid., p. 119).

Once Goel had brought to the fore mediumistic renderings of colour-saturated picture surfaces and the perceptual protocols that the viewer must uphold in the act of looking at modernist painting, he gave Swaminathan's dilemmas an existential bearing: 'The desire for a world other than he was born into made him in his youth a Utopian socialist, a trade unionist, a journalist. . . . But a desire for a self-made world led him to painting. Which, in the long years of struggle, became his other . . .' (ibid.).

Although Goel was often blunt in his prejudice against the iconic status assumed by the Bombay-based Progressive Artists' Group, he wrote often and very well on M.F. Husain. And when, from the 1970s, Souza decided to 'return' to India almost every year, Goel became a close friend and wrote about this provocative artist with fervour and forthright confidence: 'Souza's frontier-jumping acts, his extremisms, his readiness to shock the audience, and if the audience is ready for it, his readiness for the next: so his antics, the love of the irony and his Dali-like bluntness and cantankerous honesty. Souza's egotistical, almost condescending superiority exhibits the old kind of consciousness which is princely as if it were part of a throne, issuing from a centre without a margin' ('The Fall of Man and Other Images', p. 68). Also: 'The subject of a Souza painting is Souza himself and the expressionist sensibility gives vent to its emotion by spontaneously loaded brushwork. Souza does it with unfettered egomania, almost to the point of being blind to form: and yet there is evidence of rational control. His painting is a site of visual frenzy and yet it is marked by excessive stillness. His iconography is original . . . it does not suffer from the presence of the ethnic' ('Superbly Self-Conscious', p. 79).

If Goel offered allegiance to the principles of modernist painting, he also recognized the political timeliness and vigour of its opposite: the 'theatric' mode of installation art which developed in India in the 1990s. He was among the first critics to theorize installation art. Because he already had an interest in phenomenology, he could appreciate the relationship between the subject-position of the spectator, the art object and the occupied space in installatory practice. This staging of *presences* Goel theorized as an encounter at once risky and disjunctive. He recognized that installation art in India was a political – an avant-garde – move. And he engaged with Vivan Sundaram (the first artist, alongside Nalini Malani, to make the break) with keen, if also critical, commitment. About Sundaram's first installation, *Memorial*

(1993), he wrote: 'Vivan uses barricades that were erected at Ayodhya as self-referential interpretation of Duchampian 'facticity' (the subject-less art). They have what may be called phenomenological intent. The attempt is to indicate the . . . problem inherent in Duchampian aesthetic – answering the problem of a conceptual art that looks like art' ('When Art Only Looks Like Art: A review of Vivan Sundaram's solo exhibition from 1993 in response to the pogrom following the Babri Masjid demolition of 1992', pp. 140–41).

Noting the elaborate layout of Sundaram's installation, Goel wrote: 'The impression created is that the installation is structured on a central axis with a specific geographical metaphor' (ibid., p. 141). And: 'Vivan is totally unconcerned with the conventional manipulation of the limits that art installations offer. He is rather conscious that photographs can be offered as counterparts to the four axial divisions of space. They exist at several removes from the original fallen mortal, these having been replaced by photographs. The photographs, too, seem an auxiliary effort: they have been erased just like Duchamp's readymades. The similarity to Duchamp's readymades may appear tenuous: the link is their repetition and virtual obliteration of legibility (ibid., pp. 142–43).

The Indian art scene was changing significantly in the mid-1990s and thereon we have several trajectories of art practice and critical exegeses mapping the field. Goel's agitated passion in the act of looking and his attempt at a hermeneutical reworking of the 'truth' value in art demonstrate that he was trying, perhaps at best only trying, to search for a method whereby established forms of philosophy come to be both tested and unravelled in the practice of art.

During his last days, when he was very frail, Goel 'concluded' a lifetime's reading with something so riddled as the 'optical unconscious' explored by Rosalind Krauss, and with Bataille's 'base materialism' that was surrealism's working premise.[3] If he could have developed this trail, there would be yet another digression of consciously obscure thought attributable to Goel.

What this book's fresh perspective should do is to recognize that K.B. Goel brought to the understanding of contemporary Indian art a peculiar kind of *discomfort* which is crucial as a marker of change.

In 'The Painter in His Labyrinth', Goel, referring to Swaminathan, wrote: 'The reply to a question like "Am I still myself?" is difficult. But it presumably lies in the recognition of sociality which is at the heart of desiring – the desire for the "other". For, a relationship with the other empties me of myself and calls me into question' (p. 115). But here, then, is also The Critic in His Labyrinth: Kanha Babu Goel. This book plots his meanderings through the labour of its tenacious Editor, Shruti Parthasarathy.

20 November 2019, New Delhi GEETA KAPUR

1 Some parts of this text were first tested in an article on K.B. Goel: Geeta Kapur, 'The Critic in His Labyrinth: K.B. Goel on Swaminathan', *TAKE on Art*, TAKE Critic, vol. 4, issue 15, 2014.

2 The only other art critic to be substantially represented through a compilation of his writing oeuvre is Richard Bartholomew, a contemporary of K.B. Goel. It was the voice of Richard Bartholomew, his elegant poetics, that set the standards for art writing in the decades from the 1950s to the '80s (Bartholomew died prematurely in 1985). See my essay, 'A Bard's Puzzle', in homage to Bartholomew, in *An Art Critic: Richard Bartholomew*, edited by Rati Bartholomew *et al.*, New Delhi: BART, 2012. As scholarship expands, we expect to see the retrieval of diverse critical vocabularies.

3 Rosalind E. Krauss, *The Optical Unconscious*, Cambridge, Mass.: MIT Press, 1993.

PREFACE

Delhi-based art critic K.B. Goel began writing on art in the 1950s and did so for a period of forty years till the late 1990s. He wrote for a variety of left newspapers and art journals, and was soon recognized as a prominent critic in Delhi's art circles. In the late 1990s, he stopped writing, for reasons ranging from a decision to stop reviewing to shrinking avenues for art writing *per se* and, perhaps, a wish to retire.

The project of compiling K.B. Goel's select writings on art has been intense for those involved, as well as long in the making. Some time in the early 2000s, Goel himself decided to publish such a volume, and, towards this end, put together a fairly large and representative body of his writings. The project was apparently taken up by multiple agencies over time but did not proceed far, and the book languished. In late 2016, the newly founded Sher-Gil Sundaram Arts Foundation (SSAF) decided to take on the project as a part of its publications programme in association with Tulika Books. I was asked to come on board as Editor, tasked with organizing a volume of K.B. Goel's art writings and bringing to it a critical perspective. This book, comprising a selection of Goel's critical writings over a period of forty years, is a result of all these efforts.

The manuscript that I began work on contained articles chosen by Mr Goel himself – classified under four thematic categories. As I began reading, I was enthused to learn about the artists and exhibitions of Indian art he had covered over the decades of the 1960s–90s, crucial to Indian modernism. Prior to this, I had read very little by him – only a couple of articles on the artist and critic J. Swaminathan, which are perhaps the best known of K.B. Goel's writings. There was in them an acuity of perception and a confidence relatively rare among Indian art critics; and a rhetorical style that reminded one of Swaminathan's own writing. It soon became clear to me that this was no 'ordinary' critic reviewing exhibitions week after week like a seasoned hack; instead, the writings brimmed with a cerebral response to the art under review, tracing and providing art-historical contexts, elucidating and interrogating the concepts as also theory that informed artworks, even if unevenly.

My first task was to do a close reading of the articles and examine their classification as received: despite the author's hand in it, it did not always work across the range of his writings. So, a new classification and text selection were devised, even while retaining one or two of the old categories, to showcase the range of K.B. Goel's writings as well as create a logical structure for the reader. I also decided to annotate the large number of references to books, concepts and philosophies that Mr Goel brought to his writing – to help the reader navigate the frequently complex intellectual terrain charted by his criticism. It took me several months to locate, research and annotate the references traversing the gamut of writings by art historians and critics, theoreticians and philosophers, social scientists, artists and writers of the twentieth and nineteenth centuries – work that remained, in many ways, ongoing till the end. Their sheer range brought a renewed respect for what K.B. Goel had seemingly set out to do as an art critic. Meanwhile, I also sought to trace and include a few significant writings of the critic that did not form a part of his selection, and thus added quite a few articles from external sources and the K.B. Goel archive.

As this process was under way, I visited Mr and Mrs Goel at their home in August 2017, to seek answers to some of the questions the reading had prompted, and to gain insight into him as a critic and person. Mr Goel was ailing and fragile by then, and unable to speak much. During this warm meeting, it was Mrs Premlata Goel who largely spoke for him, giving me biographical details and a sense of his life of nearly half a century as a critic; Mr Goel too joined in a few times, wishing to speak at greater length about his work. That was the only time I met him.

During the course of his long career, K.B. Goel wrote (predominantly) art reviews, reflective essays, articles on individual artists and themes, and also a few catalogue essays to accompany exhibitions. The original manuscript revealed several gaps: missing dates/years and significant exhibition reviews, some of which I had already sourced from elsewhere. At this meeting, therefore, I went through the archive of Mr Goel's writings and, with valuable help from Mrs Goel, was able to make several additions to the existing manuscript.

The existing manuscript also had a large number of typographical and other errors, necessitating a line for line comparison of each article with the original newspaper/magazine cutting or scan, reconciling misprints, stray punctuation marks and missing text. This was perhaps the most time-consuming stage of the process of preparing the manuscript, given its length. As this process wound down and as I felt I had a near-final manuscript, came the blow of Mr Goel's passing in early January 2018. In February, the Raza Foundation, New Delhi, held a memorial meeting for Mr Goel as part of an art criticism workshop, where I made a brief presentation on the book under preparation. It was at this meeting that Mrs Premlata Goel revealed that there still remained a large batch of Mr Goel's writings – particularly on photography – that he had not included in his original manuscript. This led to the further inclusion, in this volume, of a significant number of additional writings: reflections on contemporary international art in the 1970s and 1980s, and articles on contemporary photography.

STRUCTURE OF THE BOOK

K.B. Goel's writings in this volume are organized into five broad sections, and arranged chronologically within each. The first of his writings is from 1957 (an interview with the artist K.S. Kulkarni) and they span forty years from 1957 to 1998, when we have the last of his published writings. A review discovered late, written in ill-health in 2017, is included at the end of the section 'Artists'. As a newspaper columnist, reviews constitute the majority of K.B. Goel's writings, though he also wrote a large number of reflective, explicatory articles on an art style or movement. The five thematic sections under which the writings in this volume have been organized are:

1. Artists: this includes reviews of solo exhibitions, reflections on individual oeuvres and styles, and interviews
2. Institutions: on India's art institutions, divided into two sub-sections:
   Lalit Kala Akademi: Art Infrastructure, Politics and Reforms
   Triennale-India: on the Triennale-India events held since 1968
3. Art and Ideas: on individual art trends, movements and styles; and within it a sub-section on Photography, comprising articles from the 1970s to late 1990s
4. Reviews: of group art exhibitions as well as a few book reviews
5. Catalogues: introductory texts or curatorial notes in exhibition catalogues of group and solo exhibitions.

Despite being written in newspapers and magazines for lay readers, K.B. Goel's articles often contain dense references that are not always pointed out expressly. These have been elaborated through annotations and citations of sources, contexts, meanings or theoretical explications, to aid the reader's understanding and improve access to his writings. They are also accompanied by illustrations of the original newspaper/magazine articles written by Goel, wherever available. The main body of K.B. Goel's writings in the book is accompanied by a critical introduction that presents the key ideas, concerns and themes that run through them, and seeks to locate his importance in Indian art criticism; a brief biography provides an account of his life as a critic; and art critic Geeta Kapur has written the Foreword.

Acknowledgements are due to Mrs Premlata Goel for the invaluable help given by her in tracing articles, for sharing her knowledge and close understanding of Mr Goel's work, and, above all, for her tenacious spirit that has indeed spurred this project; and to Brij Goel (their son) for helping with high-quality scans and all manner of logistical assistance. My deep thanks, too, to Geeta Kapur, Vivan Sundaram and the editorial team at SSAF–Tulika Books, particularly Nilanjana Dey.

As a critic, K.B. Goel's work has not received sufficient attention. Geeta Kapur has acknowledged the general silence and erasure his work has suffered (see 'The Critic in His Labyrinth: K.B. Goel on Swaminathan', *TAKE on Art*, vol. 4, issue 15, 2014, pp. 36–40), and this book project seeks to address this erasure by bringing his writings to a wider audience. Hopefully, it will create a new appreciation for K.B. Goel's writings and position as a critic, and deepen our collective understanding of twentieth-century Indian art criticism and through it, Indian art itself.

K.B. GOEL: A CRITIC'S ENQUIRY

Shruti Parthasarathy

In Indian modern art, the recovery of significant but lesser known moments, voices and narratives from under the shadow of a few dominant ones is an ongoing project that has been effected only in recent times. And within it, the field of art criticism, its chroniclers and, in many ways, conscience keepers have borne even greater neglect. There is little contemporary appreciation of the historicity or tenor of the project of Indian art criticism, which goes back a century. Only since the last two decades have significant attempts been made towards examining and consolidating its history.[1] The mapping, still preliminary, has focused on the more influential voices, largely impeded as any such enterprise is by the relative lack of documentation. The paucity of original material has kept in obscurity many other deserving voices.[2]

This volume seeks to recover one such significant voice and accord it belated recognition: that of the Delhi-based art critic K.B. Goel (1930–2018), who wrote on Indian art for four decades, from the 1950s to the 1990s. A substantial body of his writings covering a formative half-century of Indian art is included in this volume, and it is hoped that this will gain us a sense of its journey, open up implications via Goel's concerns as a critic for the next generation of readers, and inform our contentious present.

When K.B. Goel began his art career in the mid-1950s in Delhi, besides the senior critic Charles Fabri who had migrated to Delhi from Lahore, there was the key figure of Richard Bartholomew, who remained a focal point of reference in matters of Indian art criticism until his death in 1985. There was also, for a short period, the vivid presence of J. Swaminathan, who moved from active politics to journalism and art criticism to becoming an artist. At a broader level, there were critics such as the Santiniketan- and US-educated Jaya Appasamy, who edited the Lalit Kala Akademi's journal, *Lalit Kala Contemporary*, and newspaper reviewers like Krishna Chaitanya, Santo Dutta and Keshav Malik. A number of critics operated in the other urban centres of Bombay, Calcutta and, to a lesser extent, Madras, while reviewers and critics in Delhi certainly benefited from the larger number of 'national-level' exhibitions held in the national capital.

Beginning to write in 1953 in *Thought* magazine, both under his own name and using pseudonyms such as 'Vimarshak' (critic), on cinema, issues of cultural interest and art, Goel moved to the leftist newspaper *The Patriot* as resident art critic in the early 1960s, writing there for two decades alongside its sister-concern *Link*. He also wrote intermittently for a number of Delhi-based publications: the magazines *Caravan, Mainstream, Design, Shankar's Weekly* and *Commerce*; the newspapers *Indian Express* and, from 1990 to 1996,

The Economic Times. From around 1988, he wrote select commissioned texts for catalogues of solo and group exhibitions. As a respected critic, he also served on a few national and international juries: notably, for the Madhya Pradesh government's highest honour, the Kalidas Samman, in 1985, and in 1991, as commissioner of the Indian art section at the Havana Biennial.

K.B. Goel covered art exhibited in Delhi over a forty-year period and yet he was not just a local art critic. From the 1960s through the 1990s, he was seen as a significant critic covering national-level exhibitions and reviewing major artists from around the country who exhibited in the capital. His visibility also came from writing for the Lalit Kala Akademi's publications. And thanks to the Triennale-India that regularly brought world art to Delhi from 1968, he was also able to view a great deal of international art. Singular to his position as an Indian art critic is the writing he devoted to contemporary world art. This reflected an internationalist outlook that was intrinsic to his vision of art, and which he assiduously cultivated as a critic.

Theoretical sources and critical apparatus

As a critic, Goel possessed extraordinarily wide reading, his interests ranging as far afield as art history, art theory, aesthetics, literary theory, semiotics, linguistics, media and technology, literary fiction, and philosophy. He adapted this extensive array of conceptual frameworks to approach and view art. Unlike most of his generation of critics of the 1950s, it was not Europe but America, then a rising new power centre, that set the tone for his intellectual engagement in art. Accordingly, his eclectic reading, which moved between intellectuals, theorists, philosophers, historians, critics and writers, witnessed a move from Europe to America. Beginning in the 1950s with established European names like Apollinaire, Andre Malraux, Herbert Read, Ernst Gombrich, Ernst Fischer, Kenneth Clark and John Berger, Goel's references in the 1960s as cited in his writings increasingly drew from America: names such as long-term Museum of Modern Art (MoMA) director and art historian Alfred Barr, Meyer Shapiro, Clement Greenberg, Harold Rosenberg, Leo Steinberg, Michael Fried, Michael Kerby, Marshall McLuhan, Robert Hughes, Susan Sontag and Rosalind Krauss. Another significant presence was that of Marcel Duchamp, who rejected modernist easel painting and the canon, and was centrally positioned in Goel's landscape as a French émigré artist in mid-century America. In many of Goel's writings, Duchamp is seen to signal 'new' art; he becomes a source and an inspiration moulding Goel's ideas on art.

Philosophy, which he read at university, became a significant base for Goel's thinking. The major, sustained influences throughout his life were the philosophers Ludwig Wittgenstein and Maurice Merleau-Ponty, while an engagement with the ideas of Descartes, Hegel and Nietzsche also appears in his writings. He read and applied in his criticism the ideas of post-structuralists like Roland Barthes, Michel Foucault, Jacques Derrida,

Jean-Francois Lyotard and Jean Baudrillard at a time when no art writer in India was thus engaged. It is especially interesting to find in his writings the notable theoretical presence of the formalist art critic Michael Fried. Fried's books, *Theatricality and Absorption* and *Art and Objecthood*, mediated Goel's critical formulations but in contrarian ways. Goel took seriously Fried's trenchant criticism of the minimalists; recognized the aspects of 'theatricality' and 'performativity' as being central to their object-based aesthetic.[3] Yet he saw this very shift to a post-painting realm as being central for the 1960s' avant-garde, or in some way as being their marker.

K.B. Goel's true significance as a critic comes from his choice of critical apparatus, his engagement with theory and his attempts to develop a conceptual framework. Compared to the then prevailing norm of descriptive–interpretive art writing, the art review mode, his insistent desire to formulate a theoretical basis for his encounter with the art object was neither wholly understood nor accepted, sometimes even derided. Not always entirely cogent in his formulations, he remained somewhat an outsider in the critical scenario of Indian art in the decades from the 1960s to the 1990s.

Philosophy, to which he was introduced early in life, remained a guiding principle of his critical practice. Seeing himself as a philosopher-interlocutor, he adopted a phenomenological basis, particularly as evolved by Merleau-Ponty in *Phenomenology of Perception*: human perception, intrinsically linked to or based in the sensory body, implies that the world is not objective/empirical but as perceived, particularly in aesthetic experience, as arising from within the 'scope of experience'.[4] This concept of subjectivity is central to Goel's art criticism, with *interpretation* being key to the positions of Merleau-Ponty and Wittgenstein, and aligned him, as seen later, to a Duchampian worldview.[5]

Writing style

Goel's reliance on concepts and referencing of philosophic texts within the art review mode makes his critical bid unique. However, his writing style is not always accessible, nor his tone gentle. He can be bracing, polemical, sometimes outright dismissive. A frequent difficulty posed by his writing is that in his attempt to navigate conceptual territory, the main thread is abandoned for an exploration of a tangential idea which ends inconclusively. Another is an instructive or revelatory article or passage coming to an abrupt end, leaving the reader to grapple with multiple ideas that remain unresolved. Some of the confusion, of course, may be attributed to editorial intervention in the magazines/newspapers he wrote for.

In his best articles, however, Goel comes through as a critic who builds a historical context for an art style, raises significant questions, points out curatorial oversights and provokes thought. Averaging around 1,500 words, his reviews were much longer than the typical ones of the time, gaining him ample space to place his arguments. The granting of such space also points to the esteem he was held in as a critic, and attests to the existence of a newspaper readership that was willing to read lengthy, conceptual expositions on art.

Legacy

The first reckoning of Goel's criticism, though brief, came in 1992 from his younger colleague Uma Nair, who, within a larger reflection on what art criticism ought to be, termed him a 'philosophical critic' that 'revelled in the art of reflection', so his 'commentaries . . . verge on . . . the precise precipice of symphonic cerebralization'.[6] The only other assessment is by the art critic and cultural historian Geeta Kapur in 2014; she attempts to locate Goel as a critic, takes stock of his enterprise with respect to his theoretical sources, and notes his sizeable achievement – of having been able 'to complicate issues around contemporary art' – within a larger exploration of his writings and critical position on the artist J. Swaminathan.[7] Unfortunately, Goel achieved nowhere near the prominence that a commitment to creating an intellectual ambience for art ought to have garnered. The reasons may be complex, but, as Kapur observes, some of it had to do with publishing in left-leaning newspapers/journals that were not the staple of popular reading.[8]

As evidenced by the relatively small number of books on Indian art produced in the twentieth century, circuits of publication that offered a writer the space to conduct deep analysis were limited. Yet critics who were K.B. Goel's contemporaries did author book-length works. And art historians emerging in the 1980s and '90s conducted (art-) historical assessments of Indian modernism, examining specific strains and periods.[9] Working amidst them, Goel could not do so: his analytical mode of writing and conceptual explication remained scattered across reviews. He did embark on two book projects – one, a biography of the artist J. Swaminathan; and two, a volume titled, promisingly, 'Postmodernism and Regional Styles' (an area addressed later and only by far younger critics) – but unfortunately, neither saw the light of day.

The present volume is an attempt to bring to a wider readership, K.B. Goel's art writings over the period 1950s–90s. Even as these writings provide a ringside view of Indian art, they enrich art discourse with potentially instructive modes and manoeuvres unique to Goel's art criticism.

THE AVANT-GARDE AND THE POSTMODERN

Engaging with the avant-garde

Where K.B. Goel stands unique in Indian art criticism is in his ability to respond to the avant-garde and the postmodern. He did so from as early as the 1960s, writing with assurance on Western avant-garde forms such as minimalism, technological art, environmental art and new forms of sculpture, and current trends and debates in Western art. When the postmodern moment arrived in India in the 1990s, it is no surprise that he was able to articulate it.

While some of his early contemporaries such as Jaya Appasamy and Richard Bartholomew did not live to see this shift in Indian art, Goel was the only one of his generation to effortlessly make the transition, possessing the tools to theorize on it – doing so specifically in the case of installation art as it emerged in the 1990s, even if with reference to only one artist, Vivan Sundaram, who was perhaps the first to develop its concept and form in Indian art. Goel's career can thus be said to mirror Indian modernism's own trajectory, beginning with the modernist enterprise and ending at a crucial juncture in its narrative when it goes into a postmodern, avant-garde space.

For Goel, the term 'avant-garde' appears to have been both significant and familiar, and there was a ready embrace of it even in its early phase. It appears in his reviews and reflections of the 1960s, a decade of volatile politics in the global arena that seeded many changes in art practice: decolonization movements, renewed military incursions in Southeast Asia and, most prominently, the anti-imperialist war in Vietnam. And equally, the resistance: the 1968 student protest movements in Paris and other European countries, as also the American civil rights and anti-war movements. His choice of the term avant-garde was concurrent with its use in the West, which is surprising given that it was either ignored or opposed in Indian art criticism even as late as the early 1990s.

The term comes from French military usage, of the 'forward guard'; its earliest use in the arts appeared in this sense and for Goel, too, its resonance is as a vanguard of change and the new – the artist seen as a 'precursor', as the maker of an art that 'prepares the future'.[10] It is a chief criterion attributed to the avant-garde myth, constituting calls to 'revolutionary action and moral renewal' in early twentieth century,[11] and later as *anti*-art: disdainful, wry, some of it anarchist and opposed to the bourgeois, capitalist-mercenary art establishment.

From the 1960s through subsequent decades, contemporary Indian artists began to respond to local issues as well as to international imperatives that impacted local politics. Goel began to use the term avant-garde for those Indian artists he regarded as invested in the new, both via and independent of their engagement with Western avant-garde art. This could take a turn towards an irreverent and kitsch-based aesthetic or a politically confrontational position.

Goel's desire for an Indian avant-garde stemmed as much from his conversance with contemporary Western art as the avant-garde's history of innovation challenging the canon. He foresaw the declared break with the modernist, painting-based mode and the desire to evolve a new art language suited to a particular cultural context. Championing a daring among Indian artists from the 1960s on, he went so far as to say: 'It is perhaps natural to be looking around for signs of an avant-garde, for without its existence it is as good as not having the arts at all.'[12]

A brief detour here on the concept of the avant-garde itself. *Re*-entering art criticism in the 1960s, the term avant-garde (or, often, the neo-avant-garde) eluded a settled definition and even now continues to be brought into question. Theorists and critics like Peter Bürger, Paul Mann and Hilton Kramer of the 1970s and '80s noted its 'failure' to fully resist appropriation and assimilation by the establishment, and pronounced its destiny: redundant, toothless, 'dead'.[13] And with 'no revolutionary power left', as Robert Hughes defined it.[14] In her 1986 book, *The Originality of the Avant-Garde and Other Myths*,[15] Rosalind Krauss critically examined the somewhat readily accepted premise of the avant-garde's 'originality'. Reading the grid form adopted by many 1950s–'60s abstract (avant-garde) artists, she noted its non-referential, non-naturalistic and non-mimetic premise in relation to the real world, and thereby qualified the notion of 'originality'. The grid offered a double or binary construct: originality/repetition, where art in its non-referentiality and 'self-formedness' drew on the self as source and sought the repetition of a linear unit or motif. Extending the discourse to reproduction and the copy, Krauss made a case for the avant-garde as not modernist but postmodernist: operating in the space of reproduction, simulacrum, and thus opposed to the (modernist) cult of the original.

In the Indian context, a recent exchange reflects on the use and renewal of the term in spaces of the global South: the critic Geeta Kapur reformulated a proposition in 2014 and suggested that 'a new avant-garde' be conceptualized so as to offer resistive expression at social, ethical, political levels within a new world order.[16] Kapur wrote of her own adoption of the term 'avant-garde' after she encountered its use at the 1989 Havana Biennial, seeing how it had been re-imagined positively and specifically in the post-colonial discourse of Latin America. In the face of its rejection in Indian art criticism as also its claimed obsolescence in the West, her usage of the term is, she stated, an anachronistic *and* provocative gesture. She proposed continuance of its use to expand its key premise of a 'dialectic between "art and life"'; to forge alliances and pose a collective voice of resistance to statist violence, as also to create 'radical disruption'[17] along the route of social inequities.

K.B. Goel's critical practice operated from a recognition of the avant-garde's art–life dialectic and essential contentiousness. Perhaps the only Indian critic of that time to be committed to such revelatory, re-inventive possibilities, whether via confrontation or negotiation with the past, and with modernism, Goel could certainly be said to be the critic who (acknowledging a post-painting position) pointed to the avant-garde as a challenger, in defiance and circumvention of the museum–gallery establishment – though he remained keenly aware of the dangers of its appropriation by the same establishment.

The other realm Goel was alive to is postmodernism, and we should note that the two terms, avant-garde and postmodern, became nearly synonymous in his understanding and were used interchangeably. In this, a key influence for him was the Australian art critic Robert Hughes's book, *The Shock of the New*, where the avant-garde is contextualized against nineteenth- and twentieth-century movements and styles (and traced from Gustave Courbet to 1960s' body art).[18] In the wake of Hughes's deconstruction of the term and reading down *avant-gardism*, Goel followed a long-term engagement with the avant-garde to report on the increasing pronouncements of its demise.

As we examine Goel's writings, it soon becomes apparent that international art was not a mere point of reference for the critic but something he approached in its own right. From the early 1960s till the end of his career, he wrote on contemporary world art movements, many of which made their influence felt in India. These writings took the form of surveys of various art movements. He wrote on art shown at the international forum of Triennale-India (beginning in 1968), but also, unexpectedly, exhibitions held in the West – on art movements whose emergence and syntax he attempted to decode, often via a close reading of Western critics and theorists – notwithstanding his own geographical or even intellectual distance.

Goel's references are almost entirely the mid-century avant-garde, but he also makes frequent references to innovators who could be seen as their predecessors, providing context to the present – for example, Courbet and Cezanne and Picasso. Similarly, in his tribute to the great Mexican muralist David Siqueiros at his passing in 1974, Goel eschews the interpretive mode to write in a biographical style, locating Siqueiros's place in Mexican muralism: the revolutionary fervour he called for in artists; his influence on Jackson Pollock that gave to American modernism a truly original turn; his political work and commitment to art in the service of social revolution.

Taking his lead from Michael Fried, the theorist of 'late' modernist painting and sculpture, Goel wrote: 'Modernism defines itself by the theoretical project of an absolute self-absorption.... That which is theatrical is not modern, because theatrical implies the presence of the beholder, while modernism demands complete absorption of the beholder in the painting.'[19] Admiring Fried's stern consistency of argument, Goel found a retroactive consonance with Brecht and Duchamp: that a work of art is made equally by the beholder. In this strain, he discussed the postmodern aesthetic in terms of a Brechtian approach: revealing or making apparent the art (making) apparatus, the artifice, which modernism sought to hide in its insistence on the viewer's complete immersion. Goel applied his ideas to Indian painters committed to the modernist aesthetic of the School of Paris, and he then turned it on its head and engaged postmodernism, as Geeta Kapur observes in her assessment of Goel. She points to the incongruity of Goel thus using formalist criticism while not being a formalist, and suggests we read this as a subversive, 'innovative inflexion' by those outside Western canons.[20]

However, it is with Duchamp that Goel found his consonance, and before a discussion of the key international avant-garde art forms he wrote on, a brief look at Duchamp whose abiding influence mediated Goel's positions.

Marcel Duchamp

Marcel Duchamp's influence on twentieth-century art and on formulations of the avant-garde has been foundational. His 'discovery' of readymades, a concept in which he used a mass-produced object, offered the first serious challenge to art conventions: the 1917 *Fountain*, rejected at the Society of Independent Artists, New York,[21] became the best known instance. The uncrafted, unoriginal object – mass-produced and easily available – posed a rejection of the conventional art object. Art now lay in the 'idea' or the concept behind it. Duchamp's challenge to modernism through his readymades, and the irreverence, parody and eroticism they staged, inspired the 'neo-Dada' movements of the 1960s. To Goel, Duchamp signified a 'break with tradition . . . from vision to the perceptible thing'.[22]

Duchamp refuted the modernist ideas of beauty and originality, and the aura of the artist as creator. He relegated the artist's role to that of a mere conduit, insisting that art lay not in the 'making' but in what the spectator made of it – what he termed, in later years, the 'de-deifying of the artist'.[23] (An idea that John Berger took further in tracing *how* the spectator saw: an act that was political with social and cultural conditions impinging upon it.) In later years, while discussing his readymades, Duchamp spoke[24] of an 'art coefficient' that came via the 'transference . . . of an [a]esthetic osmosis' from artist to spectator.[25] This insistence on the spectator's defining role in making meaning implied multiple subjective readings.[26] The idea of *interpretation*, thus, is central to Duchampian thought and elementally informed Goel's art criticism, connecting too with Wittgenstein's privileging of subjectivity.

It was Duchamp's rejection of the narrow purview of modernism and its painterly, material-based aesthetic that provide for Goel an initiation into the avant-garde and thence postmodernism. Dada and Duchampian acts offered the jester's or romantic's challenge to the establishment – thus becoming 'anti-art' and defying the capitalist/bourgeois system.[27] Goel credited Duchamp with initiating this key shift in world art: from art as craft and object to art as idea and experience, rejecting art's 'retinal' value and visual content in favour of the idea. And it is via him that Goel argues such significant aspects of art as the artist/signature cult, or its institutional life – the art object gaining legitimacy from being displayed in a gallery or museum setting, i.e. the art institution.

Duchamp's 'irreverent eccentricity explodes the conventional source of meaning', Goel writes in one place.[28] Duchampian rhetorics and his early art practice, which earned him the art establishment's opprobrium, formulated for Goel what the avant-garde could stand for. Not the anarchic Dada antics, even as Goel recognized Dada performances filled with unpredictability as orchestrated by Dada ideologue Tristan Tzara, as the progenitors of the 1950s' Happenings.

Cubism, Pop, Happenings

Goel's earliest response to the 'avant-garde' is to pop art of the 1960s, in a discussion bookended by cubism and Duchamp. He traces pop as inheriting the avant-garde spirit of cubism and Dada; their radical, disruptive and anti-art spirit. He argues that cubism is central in marking a significant breach with preceding art, and also significant as avant-garde art. He argues this as not just a revolution in planes and therefore in seeing, as understood via John Berger's discussion of Picasso,[29] but a watershed moment of change reflected equally in philosophy and literature, ushering art 'as a critical discourse between man and man'.[30]

Cubism's momentum was broken by a thirty-year period of 'subjective emotionalism' in art, Goel writes, jettisoned only by pop's arrival that returned art to a state of 'non-involvement'. We should note that he missed out the major intervention by the Russian/Soviet avant-garde, what is known as the historical avant-garde including constructivism and suprematism, decidedly *not* based on the kind of emotional subjectivism of expressionism and surrealism he references.

Pop practitioners regarded Duchamp as their predecessor; Goel terms him 'the grandfather of pop realism', though Duchamp himself remained ambivalent on this as seen in later interviews.[31] Even as they favoured the kitsch aesthetic of advertising, this brought up the idea of reproduction – in the Walter Benjaminian sense. Goel reads pop as advertisement's twin, similarly didactic but differing in being a 'comment', the essence of which was a Duchampian 'non-involvement' calling for both the artist's and the viewer's detachment. However, few pop artists – even well-known ones like Jasper Johns or Robert Rauschenberg or Andy Warhol – could achieve this in the manner the Duchampian readymades did, he declares. Goel also sees in 1960s' neo-Dada/pop a return to a kind of 'realism', social realism: 'Neo-dada pop artists are the social realists of the Thirties [1930s].'[32]

Drawing on multiple sources, Goel sometimes made odd connections in art: as, for instance, between pop art and an artist like Fernand Leger, via the plastic possibilities the latter saw in the machine. He reads Leger's 'isolating' of an object or individual fragment on the cinema screen in his film *Ballet Mecanique* as anticipating pop.[33] Leger's celebration of human solidarity focused on the working class and was altogether serious, and thus removed from pop's irreverent and kitsch aesthetic based in reproduction. Goel, while acknowledging their wide differences, compares Leger nonetheless to a pop icon like Roy Lichtenstein.[34]

Happenings, a phenomenon that emerged in the late 1950s, held Goel's interest and recurs in his writings. He saw its Indian offshoot in the event staged by artist Bhupen Khakhar and his artist-critic friends at his exhibition opening in 1970.[35] Though Goel considered it to be mostly gimmicky, he examined via this event the original Happenings of the 1950s as significant 'gestures aimed against the all-powerful museums', a 'heroic attempt to construct a mirage-like experience', for 'art's ultimate aim was to provide an intimate experience'.[36]

Minimalism and 'theatrical' art

Emerging in the early 1960s, minimalism soon became a compelling movement that challenged the basic conventions of art. The context for Goel's review-like discussion was an important exhibition of American minimalism, 'Art of the Real', in London's Tate Gallery in 1969. Despite having no access to the show itself, Goel wished to introduce this key arrival in world art to Indian readers, and drew, presumably, on the exhibition catalogue or reviews. In his discussion of the exhibition and the works of key American minimalists on display, he attempts to convey the *experience* of beholding the gigantic works, central to the minimalist doctrine. Marked by an extreme, pared-down simplicity and the absence of any expressive content, minimalism privileged formal characteristics. This confirmed Goel's own preferred conceptual engagement, writing of its scale as content and theatrical presence as form. Minimalism was assuredly for him an avant-garde movement in its rejection of painting's two-dimensionality, breaking the rules of modernist art.

Borrowing the exhibition curator E.C. Goossen's title, 'Art of the Real', Goel writes about minimalist works presented as a form of realism, an antithesis of the representative kind and condensed now, in the curator's words, to the 'simple, irreducible, irrefutable object'.[37] Goel establishes for the readers, the key aspects of minimalism: 'macroscopic and gigantic' size that provokes the viewer's confrontation; the 'experience' of being forced to step back and behold the work and walk around it, thus creating a heightened encounter between the object and the self. He discusses the large scale and immersive experiences of the objects in this early phase of some minimalist work: John McCracken's large planks that could barely be accommodated in a Parisian gallery; Donald Judd's painted, hollow wooden cubes; and Carl Andre's row of 'bricks' laid on the ground to form a 'carpet' and Morris's white slabs at the Tate exhibition. Morris wrote about the large, reflective surfaces of the objects creating an immersive, 'entire situation'.[38] (Having begun with fibreglass irregular polyhedrons in the 1960s, Robert Morris, retaining the viewer's experientiality and sensory experience as the strongest drive, began in some years to work with strips of felt, creating large 'sculptures' with soft texture and organically flowing contours – the opposite of the forbidding, hard-edged, stolid immovability and fixed 'object-type' of cubes, slabs and blocks.)

Goel's theorizing on minimalism uses a key frame of reference provided by the formalist critic Michael Fried. In a 1967 essay, 'Art and Objecthood', that became contentious in contemporary art discourse, Fried discussed the display and reception of minimalist art as theatrically drawing attention to itself and thus contributing to its 'objecthood'. In a sharp attack on minimalism, Fried termed it 'literal' art that was also inversely theatrical in its self-positioning. And, as with theatre, it needed the building of an audience for art: one that will decide 'whether a particular work can stand comparison with the painting of the past whose quality is not in doubt'.[39]

Goel engages with the phenomenological 'presence' of minimalist works, and the subjectivity and *experientiality* of their reception. Their objecthood also had him recognize minimalist works as the earliest 'installation art', though the term did not come into use until almost a decade later. Also, while artists and critics did discuss minimalism as 'conceptual art', the artist was now a 'designer' using industrial material, conceiving the conceptual ecosystem around art.

Interested as he was in art-historical explanations, Goel questions the curatorial premise of the exhibition under discussion, 'Art of the Real', where minimalism's antecedents were sought to be traced to abstract expressionism and also to 'freehand semi-automatic abstraction', such as that of Jackson Pollock or Morris Louis. Instead, for Goel, the Duchampian idea of the artist *not* handcrafting the work was a key factor in conceptual and minimal art; as also its use of repetition and reproduction, and the conscious desire to leave the work's meaning entirely in the space of the viewer's reception/experience. This certainly made Goel's surmises belong properly within art-historical logic.

Goel expresses faint hope of viewing these works, given their scale, which no gallery could hope to accommodate, and due to the absence of the 'electronic technology' needed, presumably, for the objects' manufacture and display. Minimal or conceptual art never did move to India in its original sense, certainly not until much later. Goel rued the absence of any local practitioner or response to the style even as many Indian painters, he writes, became 'minimal minded'.

When Carl Andre came to Delhi for the 1971 Triennale-India, Goel sought him out for an interview citing the former's radical, anti-bourgeois stance and identification with the working class. Here was an artist with little or no attachment to his work, disinterested in the gallery–museum–exhibiting–sale circuit (though, as Robert Hughes pointed out, Andre's art object, otherwise an everyday article, gained its art status wholly from the gallery–museum context).[40] Goel quotes Andre's interest in 'place' instead of 'object' from his published conversations with the critic Hollis

Frampton. Always alert to the political, Goel concludes with the incongruity of Andre's sympathy with the protesting Indian artists at the Triennale as, notwithstanding his political past and opposition to MoMA, his presence as part of the (ironically, MoMA-led) official American delegation only affirmed the establishment.

Art, technology and capitalism

The incipient move towards use of technology in art in the 1970s–80s, particularly 'computer art', fascinated Goel. The French artist Jean Dupuy's use of technology to help the spectator make meaning in art (via a pre-fed computer programme) was read by Goel in Duchampian terms: as conceptual, with the onus of interpretation on the spectator. The possibilities of technology as art producer drew him – less the (ethical) concerns around the implied pre-programming, and more the precision and control involved. This is revealed by the frequent analogy he employs: of the relationship between the married couple in the novel *End of the Road*, whose lives purportedly run on such a well-oiled set of rules as to seem mechanistic – with human parallels for the controller and controlled of technological art.

Elsewhere, Goel discusses anxieties around the use of computers in art: the possibilities of a 'personal style', creation of 'instrument-objects in place of objects' and the aspect of 'play'. He takes stock of its anticipated dangers in an article titled 'Fascist Games' on the 'Art and Technology exhibition' held in 1971 in Los Angeles, which resulted from a four-year project that brought together avant-garde artists and technology corporations to make technology-mediated art.[41] Goel reads it politically: the new obsession with technology and its deployment in art. He examines ethical concerns, the connections between state, war, corporations and imperialism as central to how technology was being deployed, even in the arts, (already) in the 1970s. And reports on the protests against this by several artists (notable among them, Richard Serra and R.B. Kitaj) in highly volatile political times for America: the Vietnam War, the Cambodian invasion and political assassinations in the face of the still simmering bogey of 'communism'.

Another frequent conceptual reference for Goel was the work of media theorist Marshall McLuhan, the first to explore technologies and their 'effect' on human society. His core idea was that technologies – for which he coined the term 'media', bringing into its fold print, television, speech, the press, visual arts – have been the greatest influences in shaping society, an idea propounded in his famous and ill-understood maxim, 'the medium is the message': that the 'message' of a medium or technology lay in its own form regardless of its content, of what it said.

Highly controversial in the two active decades of his life, the 1960s–70s, McLuhan made pronouncements on advertising's effect on consumer psyches that are today *de rigueur*. He termed print-dominated modern culture as 'visual', dominated by sight and led by reason and logic, while pronouncing older cultures 'acoustic', in which all senses participated. As early as the mid-1960s, he spoke of the West and the East assimilating great parts of one another in a 'global village' and of an 'information overload' to come in the 'electric age', presaging present-day media studies and scholarship.

Much of Goel's McLuhan references were made in the above two contexts of message and technology, but a strong engagement remained via the works of the Indian artist P. Mansaram who came to have a close association with McLuhan, and adopted his ideas in his work.[42] Goel reviewed Mansaram's *Rear View Mirror* series (mid-1960s–72) based on McLuhan's ideas: that the rear view mirror shows what is to come, i.e. the future. The series comprised collages on paper, bringing together disparate elements from advertising, palmistry, calendar prints, to popular erotica and Indian traffic. Here, Mansaram was drawing on McLuhan's writings on the collage form as 'particularly relevant to our times' with its 'mosaic or field approach', where 'perpetually interacting forms' underwent a 'kaleidoscopic transformation'.[43]

Going wider afield, Goel quotes the American intellectuals Herbert Marcuse and Carl E. Schorske,[44] informing his Indian readers of the existence of a Weimar-like polarization in American society and the resultant fears, as reported by American publications and artists. He cites the Happenings author Michael Kirby's fear of a new art that has become 'electronic theatre' and a 'consciousness expanding game' – a time of the avant-garde's 'death' in its appropriation by the capitalist bourgeois value system.[45] It is with reference to technology's highly manipulative face that Goel uses the term 'Pavlovian' – James Turrell's coinage for technologically programmed and manipulated human behaviour, as did Pavlov his dog.[46] Goel cites Turrell's artwork of an anechoic chamber isolated from all outside sounds, and Wesley Duke Lee's plastic birth chamber that 'recreated' sounds and sights of a traumatic birth. In response to the ethical dilemmas these works stirred, each artist walked away from his project. Goel's review informs us of similar Indian plans with the Lalit Kala Akademi proposing to mount such an exhibition on technology, inviting Turrell himself and the same artwork he had left incomplete in Los Angeles.[47]

Goel was able to address the cutting-edge concerns of several contemporary non-canonical moments/movements. Under a heading titled 'Destructive Art' within his assessment of John Berger,[48] who proposed resisting capitalist forces within the art system with an 'aesthetics of impermanence', Goel does not mention the eponymous movement created by artist and holocaust survivor Gustave Metzger in 1959 – which sought to create just such an impermanent art that would destruct with little artistic control, in a rejection of capitalist consumerism and the dominant gallery–museum system. He quotes Berger's hopes for these new avant-garde forms to defy their propertyhood by defeating the art market and its gallery-museum nexus. While this remains a strong concern for Goel even in later writings, he does not follow up on the reckoning by Hilton Kramer and Robert Hughes that these seemingly incorruptible forms too would be subsumed and absorbed, in time, by the institutions.

Broadly speaking, Goel was aware of the waves of avant-garde movements that emerged in the 1960s, such as, for instance, Environment art and Land art with which he was considerably taken up: the artist Christo's work of 'wrapping' the Australian coast in the 1960s, drawing attention to the coastal formations through their altered visual appearance; and, perhaps best known, Robert Smithson's 1970 *Spiral Jetty*, which rejected the gallery in favour of site-specific installations fronting political and ecological concerns.

The avant-garde in India

Bringing the context back to India, interested as he was in Indian reinventions, K.B. Goel sought to examine how such art could travel here. This sets him apart from much of the Indian art world where the general grain of response to current Western art was one of conscious disinterest or distancing, if not antipathy, particularly out of fear of its 'influence' and the charge of 'derivation' applied to non-Western artists.

It should be said that Goel's theorizing of the avant-garde in Indian art was based on the idea of an original voice and a new language evolved by Indian artists as fitting their times and temperament. His use of the term avant-garde was eclectic and, in fact, too general to be art-historically valid. He went across from artists who are more characteristically modernist to those that might be called avant-garde, to those who transit to the postmodern – each a distinct, if often overlapping, category.[49]

Goel's first encounter with what may be called an Indian avant-garde was with Group 1890, a collective of artists that, in 1963, sought a radical repositioning of Indian art. Their distinct challenge to the canon could be seen as encapsulated in the work of three distinctly original artists: Jeram Patel, with a singular aesthetic and encrypted language rare even in world art; Himmat Shah, with his intuitive rejection of history, his erotic practice; and J. Swaminathan, who too rejected Western historicist pressures and sought to arrive at a modernity in dialogue with the (deconstructed) 'primitive' – these were artists who construed a liberating ground for contemporaneity. Eric Bowen's constructivist-like wall reliefs of the mid-1960s and the use of industrial material and junk by Raghav Kaneria were other features that gave the members of Group 1890 unique individual positionings, as did the evolving vocabularies of Ambadas, Gulammohammed Sheikh and Jyoti Bhatt. In his review of their inaugural (and only) show, Goel termed the Group 'maverick', and registered their bid to usher an indigenous and modernist vocabulary; he framed their emergence against the global 'back to roots' movement by terming them 'modern primitives'.[50]

Rosalind Krauss lists the historic presence of the avant-garde artist as having essayed the roles of the 'revolutionary, dandy, anarchist, aesthete, technologist, mystic',[51] while Octavio Paz had characterized those of 'libertine, saint, buffoon' for the modern artist.[52] Many of these personas certainly fit exemplars in India, whether Souza, Husain, Swaminathan or Jeram Patel, and, to an extent, something of Group 1890's collective character. The Group member that Goel was deeply impressed by at the very outset was Jeram Patel, who, he wrote, had 'expanded the vocabulary of painting' with his blowtorch works. For Patel's later solo exhibition, Goel wrote a catalogue text declaring his work to be 'ineffable' with a quality of 'self-referentiality', bearing a sign that referred to nothing.[53] Recalling fellow-critic Richard Bartholomew's parley to the reader of how one was to relate to Patel's work that bore no coordinates to the real world, Goel responded with the following advice: 'catch the play between the work's . . . articulate principles of presence, and . . . that which leads us to make lyrical self-celebrations in the midst of a critical climate'.[54]

Other than the avant-garde initiative of Group 1890, Goel seems to have thought there was little follow-up response to the 1960s' Western avant-garde movements – hardly any emulation or radical repositioning. He noted Group 1974's varied political–personal stances, and credited Bhupen Khakhar's reinvention of pop's influence as significant. He noted the changed art practice from the 1990s, honing in especially on Vivan Sundaram, with whom emerged the first installations proper. Goel employed the terms avant-garde and 'postmodern' for them, and in fact theorized his own position in this new field via Sundaram's work. Artists that Goel wrote about repeatedly, attributing progressive, maverick, avant-garde and postmodern criteria to their practice, are discussed in greater detail later in this text. They are J. Swaminathan, F.N. Souza, Bhupen Khakhar and Vivan Sundaram.

Provincialism as a countering strategy

A concept K.B. Goel was particularly partial towards and wont to judging most art by, post the late 1960s, was 'provincialism': the dynamic of a 'centre' and a periphery tied in a dependent and subordinate relationship. The periphery performed a 'satellite' role to the metropolitan centre which, as the wellspring of cutting-edge avant-garde, dictated trends. First entering Western art consciousness in the 1960s, it came to prominence through a 1974 article titled 'The Provincialism Problem' by a (then) young Australian art critic and artist, Terry Smith, in the influential American art magazine, *Artforum*.[55]

In this 'accelerated avant-gardism', the centre – which remained New York for as long as the next thirty years – made the rules; the provincial artist *cannot choose his provinciality* (emphasis Smith's) or influence the centre: s/he can only imitate, satisfy a local audience but remain, at best, 'amusingly exotic' to the metropolitan centre. Smith wrote in the context of Australian art, which evolved in relation to the art of Britain, its former colonizer. But he found the situation replicated in every country/region. Influences travelled at second remove: of distance from the centre, but also at a delay – what the periphery received was not the exciting early phases of innovation of a new style, he wrote, but its mature form, encountering reproductions that caused further distortion in the reception.

Smith's article, resonating with a wider cross-section of the post-colonial world, was re-issued in the Brazilian conceptual art journal, *Malasartes*.[56] By the 1970s, New York was the avant-garde nerve centre to not just remote locations and former colonies, but also, surprisingly, to artists in First World Europe and major American cities. Provincialism pervaded New York itself, with thousands of artists in a 'satellite relationship' to a few star artists, galleries, publications, critics and collectors. Igniting a debate in Australia and to an extent globally,[57] Smith revisited the article in 2017 and found the 'problem' alive, alarmingly so now, liberalized and globalized.[58]

New York's ascendance grew post the two World Wars,[59] and Smith saw it being dismissive of art produced anywhere else as provincial/irrelevant.[60] As a regular visitor to the American Centre library in Delhi, Goel likely read the *Artforum* article soon after publication. Given the long colonial encounter,[61] Goel recognized provincialism's presence in Indian modernism from the outset; he saw the condition mirrored in Indian art's star system, of a few artists in Bombay and Delhi (bearing the influence of the Paris or New York Schools) that most others in the country maintained a provincial relationship with, and the expatriate artist whose success abroad ensured acceptance at home. Thus, he adopted the term provincialism as a useful framework to theorize Indian art emerging in interaction with the West – vividly manifesting for him in the Triennale-India: 'Our desire for a strong showing in these international shows is evidence of our surrender to what is called mainstream tendencies in art.'[62]

Indian modernists had questioned this strong 'Western influence', traced first to the Paris and later the New York School since the days of the Progressives, and it harked, too, to the early century anxiety around Western art hegemony which had birthed the Indian revivalist movement.[63] Goel also saw resistance to it from the 1960s onward, when Indian artists seeking a two-way engagement with Indian visual traditions 'stopped looking towards the West'[64] and made a push towards indigenism.[65] He saw a rejection of the hegemonic metropolitan influences towards evolving a relevant native modernism. In this narrative, he saw Bhupen Khakhar as a key figure, terming his participation in the 1968 Triennale 'a turning point in India's provincial history'. He appreciated Khakhar's modern-day reworking of traditional Indian idioms, his drawing upon miniature painting, his amalgam of nineteenth-century Company School painting – and how he enlivened these references with 'humour and satire'.[66]

Khakhar was a strong influence and presence among figurative painters of the 1970s–80s, and Goel's reading of him was as a 'provincialist' evolving a contemporary and postmodern idiom.

Khakhar broke important taboos and became something of a symbol for a new generation of artists confident in the assertion of their own cultural roots as artistic sources of a modern Indian art they would usher. Adopting a deliberately naïve style, Khakhar's tributes to the unsung heroes of Indian life, such as watchmakers, shopkeepers, tea stall/*dhaba* owners, immortalized the Indian street and its public spaces where classes and castes, otherwise segregated, interacted. His significant contribution, too, was to bring the focus on the otherwise effaced presence of the ordinary homosexual Indian man and the staging of his desire in bold scenes of homoeroticism. Unique in Indian modernism, Khakhar's paintings did not hide behind euphemisms. Their pictorial and narrative power derived from their autobiographical confessional mode with the artist's own key placement.

In dealing with Khakhar's Indianization of pop art – adopting its irreverence and playfulness to represent Indian social reality and street life expressed in a bazaar aesthetic – Goel saw him as an Indian Henri Rousseau.[67] Unlike Rousseau's posthumous recognition, Khakhar became something of a star on the Indian art scene soon after his entry in the 1960, championed by a new generation of fellow artists and critics. Given his naïve style, Goel feared his 'cooption' by friends from the art world,[68] but Khakhar continued to play agent provocateur through the adopted persona of a poseur, employing mockery and parody in his staged advertisements and exhibition openings: an unctuous, tongue-in-cheek pantomime in various guises and 'roles'.

For Goel, it is Khakhar's 'showbiz values' that make him a pop artist,[69] the way he made 'pop's readymades with a primitivist's innocence'.[70] He frequently refers to a 'Happening' event Khakhar staged at his 1970 Delhi exhibition, opening it with his friends 'performing their roles in Khakhar's scene paintings'. Unimpressed with the theatrics, Goel is nonetheless alert to the politics of the Khakhar image, noting his modernization of the early, folk-based aesthetic of calendar art as radical in its upstaging of 'highbrow' art and the gallery-museum-sale circuit.[71]

Goel's understanding of provinciality must also be examined against the artistic practice of J. Swaminathan, who 'rejected' history and (even as he remained with easel painting) any reference at all to Western art history in his art. He proclaimed a personal mythology, calling himself a pure biological product.[72] He achieved a contemporaneity in his art whose emotional-aesthetic sources maintained an affinity with ancient scriptures, primitive art and Indian visual traditions from miniature painting to folk art, and would seem to have escaped the provincial bind entirely. Goel does not state it so explicitly, but his reading of Swaminathan gestures to such a feat; we return to his complex position on Swaminathan later.

WIDER INTERESTS

Throughout his writings, K.B. Goel navigates in the Indian art context key ideas that held currency in the then international art discourse, and polemicizes on this basis. Below is a brief discussion of some of them.

Photography

Goel's writings that cover Indian and international photography from the 1960s to the 1990s stand out for their keen engagement. He used Walter Benjamin's ideas of reproduction central to thinking about photography and other advances in the field until the 1980s. The material and the references are numerous: Andre Bazin, Roland Barthes, Susan Sontag, Rosalind Krauss, Stanley Cavell, Hollis Frampton, Max Kozloff.

Goel seeks to reflect – in the manner Sontag does in *On Photography* (1973) – what it means to take and view photographs, what the photographic image says of how we view the world, our self-image and our aesthetic, while he wagers for photography the status of an art form. Frequently seeking to differentiate between a photograph – possessing 'an entirely separate sign system of its own' – and a 'picture' – its effect not 'exhausted by its indicative function' – Goel's writing on photography seeks to present both a historicist narrative and a philosophical position for it, repeatedly returning to the question, 'Is photography art?'

Many of his ideas on photography come together in a couple of texts.[73] Beginning with Benjamin's reflections on the loss of 'aura' in photography and cinema (given the image's disembodied nature[74]), Goel traverses through Baudelaire's response to the figure of the 'dandy', whose mix of immersion/absorption in the world and detachment – as also of the *flâneur* who passes through the world unnoticed – is similar to that of the photographer. Revisited here are some of his favoured themes: a questioning of the artist's art-making ability (made keener in photography since anyone possessing a camera can create an image), or the idea of '"play[ing]" to the spectator'.

Via thinkers like Bazin – photography as 'recording' the world, Cavell – a seeing of the world through 'absence' where the photographer engages with the world but does not appear in the images created and cannot see herself,[75] and the Cartier-Bresson 'decisive moment' school of photography, Goel explores photography's indexicality, mimesis and 'detachment'. He resists, and indeed refutes, this professed indexicality with assertions of photography's subjectivity (aware, too, of the manipulation inherent to its practice) via voices such as, for instance, Sontag: photography captured not just the object/the world but *how* a person saw it, of photographs as interpreting the world.[76]

In the hierarchy Goel creates of photographers, the photo-taker 'snap-shooters' are at the bottom, above them 'photographers' who work on achieving photography's finer technical aspects, interested in its indexical abilities (though, oddly, not the work of a photographer like Lazlo Maholy-

Nagy[77]), and right on top, the pictorialists.[78] The partisan position on pictorialism derives from Goel's definition: where a photographer uses the (the mechanical) camera to fuse with it intention, the pictorialist worked towards a 'metamorphosis of the mechanical' – the dominant perception of photography as 'mechanical' held by even an avant-garde writer such as James Joyce. The 'atmospheric' effects and sensuous visuality achieved by the early pictorialists – Edward Weston, Paul Strand and Alfred Stieglitz – expand to a widened ambit for later pictorialists, as Goel cites Susan Sontag via Lyotard's literary quotation, 'to make seen what makes one see and not what is visible'.[79]

Writing on key Indian photographers, Goel sees Raghu Rai as a 'photo taker' with 'always the grand view' tempered by a 'baroque quality'[80] that brings him closer to the pictorialists. He credits S. Paul, Rai's older brother with a discerning following of his own, with a painterly sensibility, his elusive image quality lying in the tonal balance he achieves.[81] Reviewing the retrospective mounted as a tribute to the widely respected photojournalist Kishor Parekh a year after his sudden death in 1982, Goel praises his bringing to photojournalism's 'casualness' the 'discipline of the darkroom', i.e. technical mastery even as the images could 'open a nerve of memory'.[82] Instead of the expected 'truth' value or indexicality in Parekh's famed Bangladesh pictures during the 1971 war, praised for their 'dramatic mode and a fine sense of timing' by a critic such as Richard Bartholomew,[83] Goel reads the choice of the 'enemy shoe',[84] 'half-way between the function of a sign and . . . a symbol', as pointing to the absent soldier.

He sees the Indian pictorialist as the inheritor of early Indian photographers who brought to the mechanical medium their own way of seeing and rendering the world – placing the camera at the service of the individual eye as opposed to indexical recording.[85] He writes of the 'innovation' and a photograph's affective quality, its 'emotional tone', as being central to the work of a few Western pictorialists;[86] of the American pictorialist Jerry Uelsmann's philosophy of being open, like a painter, to 'the unexpected image' and to move away from a 'literal image' to a 'metamorphosis' of the qualities a photographer seeks, as constituting his photographer-as-artist credo.[87]

Goel has written extensively on the Delhi pictorialists, led by O.P. Sharma, whose mastery of technical effects includes pronounced contours, complex tonal gradations with solarized negatives in his variation of the 'G-effect'[88] and his op-like patterns. Beyond the formal effects, it is the 'presence' of sitters in Sharma's portraits, reminiscent of Paul Strand, that strike Goel – the remarkable ability, as Berger wrote, to 'invite the narrative'.[89]

Institutional theory of art

A concept that centrally informs K.B. Goel's art criticism is 'institutional theory', so named by the critic George Dickie in his 1971 book, *Aesthetics:*

An Introduction.[90] Dickie traced such authority to a social institution that would confer upon an object the status of an artwork, which he termed an 'artefact'. It took forward the Duchampian proposition that any found or mass-produced object could be deemed an artwork if an artist pronounced it so. The implication was that endorsement by an art-institutional setting – museum, gallery, or the art ecosystem made up of institutions, public, critics, publications – lent the entity the status of 'art'. 'Outside the museum, a Duchampian object has no desire',[91] Goel stated, discussing the 'impossibility' of creating art 'independent of the context of an art institution'.[92]

In several articles he wrote on this theory, including a long eponymous catalogue text,[93] Goel examined the concept extensively, keenly interested in this system that clashed with the autonomy sought by the artist. Duchamp flatly refuted and denied this very power to the artist as the 'creator' or maker of art, leaving it firmly in the space of viewership. Goel pursues, by turn, the championing of Duchampian nihilism of artistic dominance, and, contrarily, the questioning of the determinist idea of power wielded by institutions over the individual (artist) and art discourse via the art market. In the latter position, his key interlocutor is John Berger's idea of art as 'property', with the contingent hope that the various modes of conceptual art emerging in the 1960s would resist and sidestep the museum–gallery culture that monetized art – particularly those such as Environmental or Destructive art with their stated extra-gallery premise.

Goel followed this line of argument in many articles on the 1960s' avant-garde, and in a long catalogue text devoted to the theory, he concludes that it holds true, with the new centres of power able to subsume even the avant-garde when they assume or become the canon themselves, that art institutions go on to become the 'dominant forms of interdisciplinary discourse'. At its heart, he writes, 'art is a historically situated set of social processes and not a basic human orientation'.[94]

Art institutions in India

A significant part of K.B. Goel's writings is devoted to the politics of Indian art centred around the state art institution, Lalit Kala Akademi. The 1960s and '70s were intense years marked by nation-wide protests by the artist community against the Akademi. Goel followed these in his writings closely, from a position of idealistic investment in the creation of a vibrant art system in the country.

Founded in 1955 to envision and develop the emerging art scene of the recently independent nation, the national academy played a central role up to the 1970s. The Lalit Kala Akademi was important as a state-funded institution in the years before India developed an art market and alternative spaces. Its Rabindra Bhavan Galleries were the site of the most prominent national and international exhibitions, while the Garhi Studios, initiated by Sankho Chaudhuri, provided space to artists for practice and discussion. Today, the Akademi has been relegated to a position of insignificance. Accused of opaque functioning and failure to develop the right vision for Indian arts, the Akademi has bred mistrust and indifference in the art community at large.

Charting this shifting landscape of Indian art and its institutionalization, Goel's writings trace in particular the international initiative termed Triennale-India envisioned by the Lalit Kala Akademi's then chairman, the writer Mulk Raj Anand, in 1968. Triennale-India, established in conjunction with the global phenomenon of art biennales and triennales,[95] was conceived as a grand event that allowed India to stake a claim to international art by inviting the world and staging in Delhi what was termed a 'Triennale of Contemporary World Art'. Opened in a highly celebrative spirit by the Indian President, Dr Zakir Husain, with a commemorative postage stamp issued on the occasion, it featured participation by thirty-one countries. Anand's opening address extolled 'The Artist as Hero' – a figure of ceaseless experimentation and innovation.[96]

The biggest contingent to the first edition of Triennale-India was that of the Americans; their presentation came on the heels of the 1967 touring exhibition, *Two Decades of American Painting*, sent by the Museum of Modern Art, New York to Delhi (and accompanied by Clement Greenberg).[97] The commissioner for the first edition, Ellen Johnson, wrote about bringing 1960s' avant-garde art[98] – Donald Judd's cubes, Joseph Cornell's boxes, Robert Morris's sculpture of felt strips, Stanley Landsmann's light work with bulbs, Claes Oldenberg's soft sculptures of everyday, domestic objects – in short, the contemporary avant-garde that Goel championed.

Circa 1970, a battle began around the Akademi's institutional lapses and lacunae, where an important rallying point for debate and dissension was the Baroda-based arts journal *Vrishchik*, edited by Gulammohammed Sheikh and Bhupen Khakhar. Protest and a protracted battle ensued that brought together and, equally, divided the art community. These years of protest against the Akademi were reported faithfully by critics such as Goel, and the least it did was to bring to the fore artists' working situation and their agency in demanding standards of institutional probity.

Meanwhile the Triennale-India, held with a gap of three to five years, was beset by frequent delays and controversies – changing selection criteria, artist protests, seminars and even parallel exhibitions – to which there was some institutional response; however, overall disaffection among the artist community grew. Goel covered the first to fourth editions and then the seventh. While the Triennale retained some importance for international artists till its fourth edition in 1978, it soon faded to relative insignificance.

The now globalized art world has taken forward the internationalism the Lalit Kala Akademi had sought to spearhead through Triennale-India in the previous decades. K.B. Goel's coverage of international art events includes, too, the quadrennial exposition Documenta held in Kassel, Germany; he was perhaps the only Indian critic to do so (despite not attending). Goel's reflection on the Documenta emerges on the occasion of the issue of the 'Triennale Special' number of the Akademi's journal in 1991, a time for 'self inspection and . . . critical assessment of the show [Triennale]', noting that the 'internationalism' of such events have only promoted a kind of provincialism and 'an attitude of subservience to an externally imposed hierarchy of cultural values'.[99] Despite its ambitions of curating the best tendencies of world art, free from market pressures, the Documenta, he writes, succumbed over the decades to the growing clout of American institutions (including the gallery system); that it propagated an eventual (New York-centred) American domination of art trends and operated in Orientalist modes when representing Asian or Latin American art. The event held in parallel to it, Stoffwechsel, whose members came to India in 1991 to choose works for the upcoming edition, he reports, reveals a similar Western exoticized search for a region's (India's) modernity – defined as 'untouched' by Europe or the West. 'We do not regard this as a form of manipulation but as a form of protection for individual freedom', Goel quotes the group, reflecting on how such terms of engagement demanded the third world artist to continually perform a cultural uniqueness.[100]

In these writings, Goel captured the clash of value systems in the formative years of art in independent India, a debate that galvanized early protests by artists seeking institutional support for modern art. But even as he threw his weight behind the moral battle of artists against the hegemonic status of the institution, he was keenly attuned to dissonances within the community itself. He reported with dismay the writ of an influential few within the campaigns of dissent that were fought on idealistic grounds, demanding transparency, merit and equality. Revisiting the debate in 1990, he notes: 'Against all imaginative provocations, those who sought positions of power . . . have remained the dominant power group.'[101]

While many Indian critics reported on the Akademi and the Triennales, Goel's commitment remained with excavating larger connections, such as the impact of interactions with contemporary Western art within the skewed provincialist framework and other inequities in global art.

SELECTIVE PREFERENCES AND BLIND SPOTS

K.B. Goel's relationship to India's pre-Independence art – to questions of tradition, lineage and social meaning – was a vexed one. He had a deep admiration for Amrita Sher-Gil from the immediate past, and forthright engagement with modernist figuration, especially that of Husain and Souza. But within the contemporary context, his appreciation of the figurative idiom, especially as it related to social ethics, remained doubtful. That he saw contemporary figuration as a kind of anomaly remains an intriguing prejudice. I would like to register the back-and-forth between Goel's eager endorsements and his blind spots.

The generation of artists from the 1950s, especially Souza, had dismissed Amrita Sher-Gil as a 'European hybrid'; and her efforts to adopt the language of Ajanta and the miniatures were seen as a forced attempt at accessing a lost past which they, the Progressive Artists' Group, rejected as stagnant. Goel, on the other hand, writes about Sher-Gil's bold break with Western salon art and engagement with select aspects of Indian traditional art, and acknowledges her as having evolved a modern 'Indian' idiom. He considers her to be Indian art's first modernist who 'heralded an entire genre and style in painting'.[102] While he sees her as an innovator with an 'avant-garde' spirit, his admiration comes as much from finding her well-schooled in what he sought in an artist and termed *an art-historical consciousness.* Discussing her journey, Goel brings in Western art history, including especially Gauguin and Cezanne; at the same time, he discusses Sher-Gil's immense appreciation of the wealth of ancient art, Asian but particularly Indian, which she claimed as her heritage and saw as the necessary setting for her work to flower. He mentions her understanding of 'internationalism', the self-aware distance from India that allowed her to value and approach her Indian heritage. She also recommended to Indian modernists this path of exposure to the West, to better articulate their cultural individuality.

Goel wrote on Amrita Sher-Gil's 1972 Retrospective (held at the National Gallery of Modern Art and Lalit Kala Akademi, New Delhi); his reflective assessments deepened twenty years later, the distance of time enhancing his appreciation of her enterprise, at her 1993 exhibition.[103] He looks specifically at the narrative emerging from her many self-portraits, analysing how they chart both an early, self-aware narcissism and her journey to a nuanced understanding of what painting could be – as she moved away from perspectival Western painting, allowing 'for a relativity of interpretation in relation to a beholder'.[104] Goel rues the myth that revolved more around her celebrity and less on the merits of her work, concluding with regret that Indian artists had disregarded her initiative, her artistic search and its significance for the journey of Indian art.

An aside: Sher-Gil's famous criticism of the dominant revivalist aesthetic of the Bengal School as a watered-down derivative of Ajanta (and miniature painting), and thus lacking in vitality, had certainly much to do with making the Bengal School the favourite whipping boy of Indian art – and this included Goel. But while Goel shared the collective, often misinformed prejudice of his generation of critics and artists against the Bengal School: one also notices a redeeming quality – remarkable in a critic with a history of such rigid positions – where he demonstrates a willingness to pause and be open to changing his mind. In a later article, while not changing the epithets 'weak', 'romanticized' and 'revisionist', Goel traces the origins and constituents of the Bengal School.[105] He examines the work of the style's founder, Abanindranath Tagore, and his brother, India's first cubist-modernist, Gaganendranath Tagore, and presents a more nuanced understanding of the Bengal School style and the kinds of experiments that emerged from Bengal. (In this context, it should be noted that Amrita Sher-Gil as well as the Progressives, and artists and critics of Goel's generation, frequently conflated Abanindranath Tagore's revivalism with the indigenous modernism that arose from Santiniketan, which included Nandalal Bose, and, more importantly, Benodebehari Mukherjee and Ramkinkar Baij, terming them all 'Bengal' School of Art. Their understanding of Indian modernism would arguably have been different had they been acquainted with the wellspring of knowledge and language that developed in Santiniketan from the 1930s onwards.)

In continuation of his interest in the origins of Indian modernism, Goel reads Husain's encounter with the aesthetic of the Mathura sculptures on view at the 1948 exhibition in Delhi of Indian art[106] as highly significant to the evolution of individual style: the strength of his line - discontinuous, sculpturesque - and the use of colour and form seen in relation to the artist's love for Urdu poetics. He writes about the 'rich associative imagery',[107] the metaphoric possibilities and symbolic content in Husain's work.[108] And further, about Husain's creation of a 'native sensibility' that calls for not 'categories of art criticism' but some affinity with which to respond to his work. If these artists created new possibilities in Indian art within the terms of modernism, Goel goes on to designate certain practices as postmodern, as for example, the paintings of pedagogue-artist K.G. Subramanyan.[109] Using the artist's own definition of modernism as some kind of 'purism' based on the notion of originality, Goel sees Subramanyan's paintings (for example, the series made in response to the Mughal miniatures of Mansur) as reflecting a postmodern attitude.

Goel notes that Amrita Sher-Gil's position gained credence during the 1960s and '70s, following a growing consciousness of roots and artistic traditions among Indian artists, many of whom sought art-historical knowledge, artistic indigenism and a consequent individuality. Yet he sustained a scorn for the figurative and narrative movement that emerged precisely at the time. It foregrounded subjective realism in conjunction with social engagement and sought to place art practice within discernible aspects of the political in contemporary India. Goel was unsympathetic to this new wave of figurative artists from Baroda, Bombay and Delhi, who staged the seminal 1981 exhibition, 'Place for People'.[110] It remained for Goel an area he would neither write about nor acknowledge. Thus, while Goel wrote on the work of artists bearing allegiance to the figural mode, from the pedagogue-postmodernist K.G. Subramanyan to Bhupen Khakhar with his pop assertion and provocative provincialism, and Vivan Sundaram fronting the avant-garde, oddly, he would not engage with their narrative works or this movement, heavily critical of the 1978 'Pictorial Space' exhibition. Like any art critic with a long-term presence and investment in the art space, K.B. Goel, too, had his blind spots.

AND SOME PARTISAN POSITIONS

J. Swaminathan

The artist on whom Goel wrote the most, who moulded and, to an extent, embodied his ideas on art, was the critic, painter and poet, Jagdish Swaminathan. Their three decades-long association began after the Group 1890 exhibition of 1963, which catapulted Swaminathan to national prominence. Swaminathan's preparation for this role began in the 1950s, but as an astute art critic familiar with contemporary art, pictorial language and its sources. Most remembered for his polemical stances, the draw of his personality was paradoxical: inspiring contention, but also enormous loyalty and affection in the Delhi art scene. Artists and critics in the 1980s formed a circle around him, among whom K.B. Goel was a prominent presence.

If, predominantly, it is the critics who have mentored young artists, showing ways of arriving at the style best suited to their artistic talents (Walter Langhammer–S.H. Raza, Rudy von Leyden–K.H. Ara), with Goel and Swaminathan the dynamic may have been the reverse. Only slightly older than Goel, Swaminathan was decidedly more worldly-wise and suited for mentorship: he had an original intellect, an instinctive insight into the identity he wished to forge as an artist, and he deployed his 'artist' persona with force and flamboyance to great effect. His propositions on Indian art vis-à-vis Western art history, his stance on issues of authenticity, his insistence on the merits of an ahistorical consciousness – these decidedly influenced Goel's approach towards the modern and the avant-garde.

Principally, Swaminathan rejected Western ideas of linearity, teleology and temporal progression – categories within which he saw trapped Marxist criticism. He emphasized the falseness of colonial binaries – 'modern' (Western) as civilized and advanced, versus pre-modern or 'primitive' cultures as that of the tribals, the Adivasis. Goel saw in his art a refreshing 'counter discourse to primitivism',[111] and, further, a simultaneous, intermingled existence of the primitive and the modern.

Goel's earliest writing on Swaminathan is from 1970, post the *Colour Geometry of Space* series, but he looked back to the early work (c. 1958–63) termed 'primitivist'. He ascribes to it a radical vision, a 'time of pre-culture and pre-aesthetic perception',[112] hailing Swaminathan as a 'tantric frontliner'.[113] Goel's otherwise contemptuous dismissal of what he terms 'tantric bizarerrie' is converted in this case to a venture arising from an art-historical awareness, where he traces Swaminathan's *tantra* works to the recent Western art development of minimalism.[114] A surprising position, as otherwise he praises Swaminathan's ahistorical consciousness.

'It is only by subjecting our pictorial attitudes to relentless criticism that we can expose ourselves to the possibility of creative accident', Swaminathan wrote.[115] Goel sharpened his critical faculties post-1970 in emulation of Swaminathan's style of polemics, and this brought about a visible change in his writings. The article 'Revolt',[116] for instance, bristles with diatribes against the redundancy of the (mostly expatriate) 'Western art historical values' of painters of the 1950s, followed by a forceful defence of Group 1890's quest, lauding it for staging a 'revolt' against the art canon's 'axiomatic superiority'.[117]

Goel divides Indian art of the 1960s between the representational conventions of Bhupen Khakhar on the one hand, and Swaminathan's 'continual level of signification' on the other, which bore 'no obvious levels of meaning'.[118] In subsequent years, he is struck by the spatial quality and sophisticated manipulation of colour and picture surface in the two decades-long metamorphoses of Swaminathan's *Bird Mountain Tree* series. Goel sees in this series a simultaneous evocation of immersion and distance; their large scale and colour absorption stand parallel, he believes, to the 1960s' single-colour canvases of American painters.

Reading Swaminathan's artistic approach as one 'arisen in a moment of time', Goel positioned him as a mystic, the canvas as a means for 'transcendental meditation'.[119] He frequently quotes Swaminathan's preferred *Ishopanishad shloka, 'Om poornamidah poornamidam* . . .', on the indivisible wholeness of existence. Noting the 'noumenal agency of intuition' brought to the imaginary released by the landscape, Goel sees Swaminathan as the first Indian modernist to rework the genre of landscape in a substantial way and with distinct difference from its history in the West.[120] Enthused by Swaminathan's 'sensuous' deployment of colour, he writes of it as 'evoking a mystic mood in a very high degree of concentration'.[121] He sees Swaminathan's last phase as coming full circle and merging with the internal sources of his earliest work: the painting surface is now 'an arena', 'the image in mind yields to the materials in hand'.[122] There is now the *ecriture*, the palm print; a wholesome investment in the symbol; and a dissociation from 'signature'.[123]

Around 1993, Goel began work on an extensive critical biography of Swaminathan. This was with the latter's involvement, but it was never finished, due to Swaminathan's passing in April 1994. In the critic's personal archive survives the draft of a letter he wrote to the Ministry of Culture, the book's commissioning body, *c.* 1995–96. In it, Goel discusses his abandoned enquiry and reveals how, at the painter's request, he had planned to examine Swaminathan as a modern-day Malevich. He writes movingly of losing purpose in the wake of Swaminathan's death – and though Goel was hardly ever a sentimental writer or traded in common hyperbole, he writes: 'The loss of Swaminathan's presence absorbed all ambient oxygen. . . . Being robbed of life and air, I felt that Swaminathan was one subject of which I can no longer speak.'[124]

Offering to resume work after a long hiatus, Goel writes about presenting Swaminathan as a counter to primitivism's othering discourse. And of Swaminathan's last work featuring concentric rectangles, as making for a 'yet to be determined stage' of his work – one that remains unknown. The book contract was presumably not renewed and no manuscript survives. In its lieu is available a compact synopsis, 'J. Swaminathan: His Art and Context', published in *Lalit Kala Contemporary* (issue 40: 'Swaminathan Special') in 1995, and featured in this volume.[124]

F.N. Souza

Goel's writings on Souza, the self-proclaimed *'enfant terrible'* of Indian art, trace a more surprising arc. Until the late 1960s, the Progressive Artists Group – of which its founder, Souza, was a chief representative, both aesthetically and politically – was a marked target of Goel's attack, in alignment with Swaminathan rhetoric over the group's canonical position. But in the 1970s, towards the end of his Western success – when Souza began to visit and exhibit in India frequently, seeking an audience and a validation from his country in his waning years – Goel, wholly unexpectedly, became something of his champion. He wrote several reviews of Souza's work, the 'chemical alterations', finding in them reminders that 'an image is not a sacred object but belongs to a space of language'[126] achieving a new personal content, and reading it as a 'play of graffiti space'.

Reviewing the exhibition held *c.* 1980s of Souza's early work from the mid-late 1940s, Goel notes their 'expressionist' style which, while not consciously drawing on recent German expressionism, did respond to the destruction, despair and alienation of the war years. He traces in them an expression of fantasy that goes beyond direct socialist concerns to express itself in a naturally adopted cubistic distortion. Goel now appreciates the significant contribution of Souza and the Progressives to Indian art. With little local referent, Souza developed an expressionist idiom that came from a personal vision. This expressionist mythology gives an 'attention-calling armature to his images of suffering', Goel declares, comparing the Christian imagery and the deeply expressive colour application to the universality and compelling appeal of Van Gogh.[127]

Goel characterizes Souza's narcissistic outbursts as 'frontier-jumping acts', and reads his blustering tirade against Group 1890 in terms of the provincialism debate. Souza's 'egotistical, almost condescending superiority', general misanthropy or 'Dali-like bluntness and cantankerous honesty' are criticized but almost excused as aristocratic![128] Souza mythologized 'his personal struggles against false consciousness', Goel observes, tracing his chafing against the conformism expected of artists as the germ for the rebellious formation of the Progressive Artists Group.[129] Souza's intentionally provocative, shockingly sexual and often misogynist images are attributed by Goel to the artist's compulsion to both express his interest in the erotic and shock bourgeois viewers, even as he cannot resist the temptation to play up to their voyeurism.

A later piece on Souza and Husain reveals Goel's insight into the work of the two painters without recourse to any theory or conceptual framework.[130] Colour is the 'life source' of Husain's art, 'electrified to be transmitters of volatile stimuli', he writes, while Souza's sexual imagery and colour application follow the European expressionists but via the painter's force of personality. If 'the medium of the self' orders the viewer's perception in Souza's art, with Husain it is the 'medium of the work', particularly his manipulation of line and colour. Goel comments on the still-towering presence of the two artists in the 1980s, remarking on the absence of a parallel or worthy successor in Indian art even three decades since the 1940s.

In later years, Goel and Souza came to be personally close: the artist stayed with the critic on his annual visits to India, gifted him works or left them in his safekeeping. And the two maintained an extensive correspondence. Perhaps getting to know Souza the man so well allowed Goel to deconstruct the built persona of misogyny and vaulted superiority, and even prompted his 'defence' of Souza's perceived lack of relevance in the 1970s and '80s – convinced, certainly, of the artist's brilliance.

Vivan Sundaram

The Indian artist K.B. Goel regards as expressly 'avant-garde' is Vivan Sundaram. Writing on him from the 1960s to the '70s, Goel recognized Sundaram's marked political stance, his social comment and his allegorical proclivity, and lauded him through the 1990s. Sundaram's drawings made in response to Neruda's long poem, *The Heights of Macchu Picchu*, Goel praised as 'visual synaesthesia'.[131] He read semiotically the artist's mockery of India's economic-cultural elite as 'made from within the class'.[132] Beginning then, Sundaram's narrative works of the 1980s took on the increasingly political approach of a commentator and activist. Goel never wrote on the artist's narrative style whose aesthetic concerns he disfavoured, and he returned to writing on Sundaram when he shifted to non-painting modes of art-making – specifically, installation art.

The years building up to the demolition of the Babri Masjid in December 1992[133] brought forth a generation of politically responsive Indian artists, mainly from Delhi and Bombay. Besides Vivan Sundaram, who now ventured into full-fledged installation art, there was the introduction of video, performance art, photography by Nalini Malani, Navjot Altaf and Rummana Hussain – all women, a fact urging closer examination. This move away from painting modes into vibrant new territory registered a distinct shift in Indian art from the modern to the postmodern. Of them, however, Goel wrote only on Sundaram's installations, perhaps reviewing what he could view in Delhi. It remains a loss, nonetheless, if we anticipate the imaginaries and analytics he may have summoned to a reading of these nascent arts given his long familiarity with avant-garde positions in minimalism, technology-driven art and media theory. However, even when writing on one artist, Sundaram, Goel's writing helped contextualize this new turn in Indian art. Appearing now in a more mainstream newspaper with a wide reach, *The Economic Times*, his writings created visibility and perhaps helped expand the field. Certainly, more art writers and artists began to register the shift in the years to follow.

One of Goel's first articles, 'Forms with a Hidden Dialectic' (1992), reviews Sundaram's exhibition 'Collaboration/Combines', featuring large mixed media installations using 'combines' of paper and engine oil trays, stone columns and photography.[134] These, he writes, operate in a dialectic between the elements. Goel deploys his familiarity with forerunners of installation art, the minimalists, in noting the 'theatrical presence' of the tray which established the work as an object, and then argues, via Fried, how the Combines defeat this theatricality 'through an implicit appeal to the richness of their surface' so that only the surfaces spread across multiple combinations are 'combined'. Goel notes that two early works reveal the artist's familiarity with kitsch and pastiche, and thus unconsciously operate on 'theoretical grounds of postmodernism'. Reading the installations in phenomenological terms, he theorizes that with the Combines, Sundaram has moved into new (postmodern) territory.

Around Sundaram's 1992–93 exhibition 'Riverscape',[135] Goel constructs a dense, illustrative discussion dealing with ideas on the aesthetic, phenomenological/experiential planes of an installation. He deconstructs Sundaram's celebrated installation *Memorial* (constituted with photographs and sculpture), a political work made in response to the Babri Masjid demolition, as an existential expression of pain – of the victims, of the narrator – and the history of art as protest and as a mirror to mass violence. He reads the use of the photograph's multiple versions in the sense of the minimalists' use of the 'square, seriality and the monochrome', of repetition, simplification and multiplication, to create the impact of an idea.

Goel's writings on Sundaram's political work mark the first robust articulations in Indian critical discourse of conceptual art – announcing the arrival of the artist as activist, thus marking the need for political engagement. With his three decades-long investment in the avant-garde, this arrival of conceptual art must have seemed like a long-realized dream, to the explication of which Goel brought his favoured theoretical bases.

However, it is at this time, around 1993, that K.B. Goel stopped writing reviews, for a number of reasons, and wrote only sporadic catalogue texts on commission until 1997–98, marking the conclusion of his career. Goel's withdrawal from writing on art remains a significant loss for a critical understanding not only of installation art, but also new media, lens-based work, performance and other new art forms. His daring had been his willingness and ability to transcend modernism, and an openness to what postmodernism could bring. Had he continued writing on these new art forms, evolving suitable interpretive frameworks even at the moment of their emergence in India, his voice would have resonated amidst younger critic-colleagues. As a witness to the previous era and its transition to the next, it would decidedly have given him a new role and readership.

In lieu of any conclusive assertions, I would like to end with a few closing remarks. This introduction to the writings of K.B. Goel has sought to bring to the reader a survey of his critical practice. It has attempted to map and investigate the broad territories of his critical interest and enquiry, and in doing so, locate the more prominent and significant of the positions he took, his pronouncements and omissions. Goel was one among the critics of a significant generation, which, arriving on the art scene in the early years of the nation's independence, built its art discourse through dedicated engagement over the next fifty years. Among them, his voice is decidedly distinctive, choosing (and sustaining) a critical practice within art review that was built on conceptual explication via other contemporary thinkers. He did not always succeed - due to his arc of interests being too wide to accord him a cogent vision, or in conveying to the reader the tricky conceptual terrain and complex ideas he was grappling with - but he became an exemplar of such a mode of criticism as an untrained scholar.

In an art discourse fraught with contesting identities and agendas, Goel's choice of Western thought, philosophy and art history as guiding lights - whether or not it was always understood, or dismissed as irrelevant - certainly contributed to the diversity of the said discourse. Writing within the Indian context, from an awareness not only of contemporary global trends and debates but also of conceptual/theoretical interventions in the art discourse, Goel's criticism provided useful and instructive ways to understand the local situation - see, for instance, his reading and incorporation of the debates around provincialism and art institutionalization. These are certainly issues no one else was discussing then in Indian art. Goel's great interest in the avant-garde places him among the early critics in India to herald the arrival of conceptual and installation art in India in the early 1990s - yet, ironically, these years also mark the waning of his singular and contrarian voice.

K.B. Goel leaves Indian art (and criticism) on the threshold of an important shift he had anticipated and awaited, some of which he elaborated on with excitement. His writings now remain - to be read, engaged with and built upon, and thus to formulate a distinct critical self in the world of art.

I would like to gratefully acknowledge the invaluable help of Ms. Geeta Kapur in restructuring this essay, and in clarifying and fleshing out many of my arguments and historical contexts. In particular, I owe to her entirely the nuanced insights into K.B. Goel's liberal, though not always consistent, use of the term avant-garde and his understanding of its Indian context.

Notes

1 The first such significant attempt is a case study of five significant Indian art critics spanning the entire twentieth century, conducted by Vidya Shivadas: *Mapping the Field of Indian Art Criticism* (New Delhi: AAA Research Grant 2009–10, 2010). The other is the compilation of the writings of the Indian art critic Richard Bartholomew, titled *Richard Bartholomew: The Art Critic* (New Delhi: Bart, 2012). Since 2000, external agencies such as the Hong Kong-based Asia Art Archive (AAA) has collated and digitized extensive archives of a few significant artists and art critics from Delhi and Baroda, the first of an ongoing project to create a substantial archive of Indian modern art linked to a wider archive of Asian art. Newer research is being supported from outside the region by those such as the Tate Foundation, while, more recently, Indian art publications/magazines have been focusing on Indian art criticism as a field, interested particularly in its history.

2 Here, I would also briefly draw attention to the neglect, in ways greater, that regional-language art writing and criticism have borne in India. These voices writing in the vernacular languages have kept alive and moulded a vibrant regional art discourse, and they need to be traced, compiled and studied with as much urgency if not more, in parallel with the present-day revisionist efforts in English art criticism.

3 In her brief assessment of and tribute to K.B. Goel, critic Geeta Kapur reads this incongruity of using Fried-led formalist criticism while not being a formalist, and applying it to the Paris School-descended Indian art scene, as a subversive 'innovative reflexion by artists and thinkers functioning outside Western canons', an act of resistance. See Geeta Kapur, 'The Critic in His Labyrinth: K.B. Goel on Swaminathan', *TAKE on Art*, vol. 4, issue 15, 2014, pp. 36–40.

4 E. Louis Lankford, writing on Merleau-Ponty's position, in 'A Phenomenological Methodology for Art Criticism', *Studies in Art Education*, 25 (3), 1984, p. 152.

5 With the wide berth that the term 'interpretation' offers, the philosopher Ludwig Wittgenstein – who opined there could never be a firm position on anything with regard to human perception, whether in the realm of linguistics, spoken language, or even something as intensely corporeal and 'individual' as bodily pain – and his doctrine of open-endedness centrally informed Goel's critical frameworks.

6 Uma Nair, 'More than a Mere Verbal Acrobat', *The Economic Times*, New Delhi, 11 October 1992. Nair's reckoning of K.B. Goel was brief, in a larger article on art criticism that also examined the work of Goel's fellow art critics, Keshav Malik and Krishna Chaitanya.

7 Geeta Kapur, 'The Critic in His Labyrinth'.

8 Ibid.

9 These would comprise critics such as Jaya Appasamy, Richard Bartholomew, Shiv Kapur and P.R. Ramachandra Rao in the 1960s and '70s; Santo Datta, Sandip Sarkar, Manasij Majumder in the 1980s–2000s. Younger colleagues would include Geeta Kapur, who authored works in 1978 and 2000 critically examining modern and contemporary Indian art, while art historians such as Partha Mitter and Tapati Guha-Thakurta became prominent from the 1990s.

10 Robert Hughes, 'The Future that Was', in *The Shock of the New*, New York: Alfred A. Knopf, 1980, pp. 365–66.

11 Ibid., p. 371.

12 'Exhibition of British Prints', in the 'Reviews' section in this volume, pp. 340–41.

13 Paul Mann's 'The avant-garde is dead, long live the avant-garde' is the most quoted declaration of the avant-garde's 'death'. See *Paul Mann, The Theory-Death of the Avant-Garde*, Bloomington: Indiana University Press, 1991, p. 33; Peter Bürger, *Theory of the Avant-Garde*, translated by Michael Shaw, Minneapolis: University of Minnesota Press, 1984; Hilton Kramer, 'The Age of the Avant-Garde', *Journal of Aesthetic Education*, April 1973, pp. 35–51.

14 Hilton Kramer was perhaps the first to declare the 'death' of the avant-garde in his 1973 essay cited above. In 'The Future that Was', in his book *The Shock of the New* (New York: Alfred A. Knopf, 1980, pp. 365–66), Robert Hughes discusses Kramer's pronouncement of this death.

15 Rosalind Krauss, 'The Originality of the Avant-Garde', in *The Originality of the Avant-Garde and Other Modernist Myths*, Cambridge, Mass.: MIT Press, 1986.

16 Geeta Kapur, 'Proposition Avant-Garde: A View from the South', *Art Journal*, May 2018, pp. 87–89.
17 The exchange was between her and two art historians, Saloni Mathur and Rachel Weiss. Her two respondents welcome her bid as potentially revitalizing to the discourse, a hopeful philosophical project that asks to put to use the avant-garde's unsettled(ing) and disruptive abilities in moulding a new art discourse at a time when it appears entirely consumed by capitalist–statist market liberalization and supported by right-wing conservatism and majoritarian threat in every realm: political, social, cultural, economic and aesthetic. See Saloni Mathur, 'A Response to Kapur's "Proposition Avant-Garde"', *Art Journal*, May 2018, pp. 90–94; Rachel Weiss, 'Some Thoughts after Kapur and Mathur', ibid., pp. 95–10.
18 In his book (*The Shock of the New*), Hughes defines the avant-garde as spanning the period from Gustave Courbet's realism in the nineteenth century up until the arrival of abstract expressionism in the 1950s; the 'avant-garde' defined principally as a gesture of resistance to the status quo, societal norms and expectations. Goel's discussion of the avant-garde too borrows this trajectory, as starting from Courbet whom he sees as the first original, 'individual' artist, followed by several mediations to Duchamp.
19 'Ambivalent Terrain', in the section 'Reviews' in this volume, p. 360. Goel's words here draw on the ideas in Michael Fried's impactful essay, 'Art and Objecthood' (1967) and his later book where he expanded on these ideas: *Absorption and Theatricality: Painting and Beholder in the Age of Diderot*, Chicago: University of Chicago Press, 1988.
20 Geeta Kapur, 'The Critic in His Labyrinth', p. 37.
21 *Fountain* was rejected by the Society (the New York equivalent of the Parisian Salon des Independants) despite a mandate to accept every entry sent with application fee paid. Duchamp was a member of its organizing body, and the work – signed R. Mutt, whose artistic creation he later acknowledged – was rejected on grounds of 'vulgarity' and immorality, and as not a work of art but 'submitting a piece of plumbing'. In the Dada journal *The Blind Man* (no. 2, May 1917), Duchamp refuted the immorality charge and wrote: 'as for the plumbing barb, why plumbing and bridges had been America's singular contribution!'
22 'Institutional Theory of Art', in the section 'Catalogues' in this volume, p. 375.
23 '"I Propose to Strain the Laws of Physics": Interview with Marcel Duchamp', *ARTnews*, December 1968; available at http://www.artnews.com/2019/01/18/archives-interview-marcel-duchamp-1968/
24 In his talk to the Museum of Modern Art in 1961, 'Apropos of Readymades'.
25 In 1959, at a 'session on the creative act' attended by art historians and critics, where Duchamp spoke on his art, representing himself as a 'mere artist'.
26 On his famous work, *Large Glass* (1915–23), for instance, Duchamp spoke in later years of 'learning from' the multiplicity of interpretations and meanings that were read into it, and thus acceptance of it as his preferred mode of artmaking – leaving the meaning to (be made by) the spectator.
27 Duchamp's position with respect to the establishment certainly remained one that sufficiently shocked the bourgeois art value system. In his 1961 address to MoMA, he stated that his battle was against the two faces of establishment: the institutions that decreed or pronounced what was art and judged it, i.e. accepted or rejected something as art, and the artists who thought they made art or who believed their consciousness contributed predominantly to the artwork.
28 'Institutional Theory of Art', in the section 'Catalogues' in this volume, p. 375.
29 John Berger, 'The Moment of Cubism', *New Left Review*, March–April 1967, and *The Success and Failure of Picasso*, Vintage, 1993.
30 'Pop or Advertisement Art?', in the section 'Art and Ideas' in this volume, pp. 219–21.
31 Goel's quotation source: ibid. While rejecting any claims of being a predecessor to pop artists, Duchamp did not speak expressly on (any) connection between pop and his work, but did acknowledge that the (1960s) pop artists were perhaps not retinal, a key Duchampian requirement for art. He conveyed this in his last interviews; see, for instance, Dore Ashton, 'An interview with Marcel Duchamp', *Studio International*, June 1966. Duchamp passed away in 1968.
32 'Art as a Weapon', in the section 'Art and Ideas' in this volume, p. 265.

33 Fernand Leger made a post-cubist film called *Ballet Mecanique* in 1924 whose driving elements were the aspects of fragmentation seen in the filmic 'cut', and the isolation of an object or detail as shown through the close-up. Via these experiments, so central now to cinema, Leger sought to alter visual response in his viewers. The two aspects, quite central to pop, thus has Goel connect Leger to pop.

34 'Berger, Art and Property', in the section 'Art and Ideas' in this volume, p. 229.

35 At New Delhi's Kunika Chemould Gallery.

36 'The Provincial Bind', in the section 'Art and Ideas' in this volume, pp. 278–79.

37 Source: E.C. Goossen's catalogue text when the exhibition was first mounted at MoMA, New York: E.C. Goossen, *The Art of the Real: An Aspect of American Painting and Sculpture 1948–1968*, New York: Museum of Modern Art, 1968, p. 7.

38 Minimalist sculptor Robert Morris discussed the 'new sculpture' emerging in the 1960s in his still remarked upon article, 'Notes on Sculpture', appearing in the February and October 1966 issues of *Artforum*. He spoke of this new sculpture as consciously opposed to painting. With (large) scale as a primary criterion, it sought to include the viewer in its space, allowing her/him to take in this 'object'. The full text is available at http://arts.berkeley.edu/wp-content/uploads/2016/01/robert-morris-notes.pdf

39 Michael Fried, 'Art and Objecthood', *Artforum*, vol. 5, no. 1, Summer 1967.

40 Hughes, 'The Future that Was'.

41 'Fascist Art Games', in the section 'Art and Ideas' in this volume, pp. 240–47.

42 Mansaram's McLuhan-inspired 'Happenings' project, *East-West Intersect*, featured performances, a 16-mm film and spontaneous audience response. The two even collaborated on an artwork in 1969, with images by Mansaram and text by McLuhan. His text, 'Help beautify junkyards – throw something lovely away today' came from a junkyard advertisement McLuhan had spotted in Toronto and been struck by enough to mention it during a television conversation with the writer Norman Mailer and Malcolm Muggeridge. Mansaram exhibited this work in his 1974 show and again in 2012, at his retrospective of sorts, now with additions of more current technology: an image of the first generation iPhone. Mansaram's chosen images in the *Rear View Mirror* collages gesture to the fragmentation of identity in our times in a globalized (West-dominated) world, which, as McLuhan rightly notes, had already begun in the late 1960s.

43 Marshall McLuhan, *The Gutenberg Galaxy: The Making of Typographic Man*, Toronto: University of Toronto Press, 1962, Prologue.

44 Goel's text source: 'Fascist Art Games', in the section 'Art and Ideas' in this volume, pp. 240–47. Herbert Marcuse was a philosopher aligned to the Frankfurt School whose ideas were influential during the student movements of 1968 and subsequent years. Ironically, both he and cultural historian Carl E. Schorske had served earlier in the CIA. In Goel's quotation, both thinkers warn of American state fascism.

45 Claes Oldenberg's *Store Days* (1961) was perhaps one of the first to make this declaration of the avant-garde's 'death', which caught on among critics in the early 1970s. This discussion on Oldenberg appears in the already cited article, 'Fascist Art Games'.

46 Goel explores the territory of 'computer art' again in a 1980 article titled 'Pavlovian Links' (in the section 'Art and Ideas' in this volume, pp. 273–76). 'Pavlovian' refers to a now well-understood condition involving stimulus and a reflex response, first developed by the Russian I.P. Pavlov working with his do.

47 'The Sense of Reality', in the section 'Art and Ideas' in this volume, pp. 236–39. James Turrell has since gone on to make works that manipulated light and space, creating intense sensory experiences for the spectator.

48 See 'Berger, Art and Property', in the section 'Art and Ideas' in this volume, p. 227.

49 I owe this reading entirely to Geeta Kapur.

50 'Enter: The Modern Primitives', in the section 'Reviews' in this volume, p. 333.

51 Krauss, *The Originality of the Avant-Garde and Other Modernist Myths*, Introduction.

52 Octavio Paz, 'Surrounded by Infinity', *Group 1890 catalogue*, 1963, Introduction.

53 'Jeram Way of Seeing', in the section 'Catalogues' in this volume, pp. 422–24.

54 Ibid., p. 422.

55 Terry Smith, 'The Provincialism Problem', *Artforum*, vol. 12, no. 1, September 1974; available at https://arthistoriography.files.wordpress.com/2011/05/smith-provincialism-problem-1974.pdf

56 *Malasartes*, no. 1, October–November 1975.

57 Smith's article followed Ian Burn's 1973 article titled 'Provincialism', published in the somewhat theory-heavy journal brought out in New York by Australian artists and critics, called *Art Dialogues*. Smith's article was published multiple times and remained a topic of debate in many places, but decidedly in Australia for thirty years (see note 58 below).

58 Terry Smith, 'The Provincialism Problem: Then and Now', *ARTmargins*, vol. 6, No. 1, February 2017. Contemporary Australian response has ranged from endorsing Smith's assertion to disagreement – with not just provincialism's persistence post the 1970s, but also Australian art's historical exclusion from the mainstream of world art. See Rex Butler and A.D.S. Donaldson, 'Was Australian Art Ever Provincial? A Response to Terry Smith's "The Provincialism Problem: Then And Now"', *ARTmargins*, vol. 6, no. 1, February 2017, pp. 6–32.

59 New York's ascendance began with migrations from Europe linked to the two World Wars, from Duchamp's time in the 1910s to the large influx of artists and intellectuals fleeing Nazi persecution in the 1930s and '40s. After that, the investment in building art infrastructure in terms of state-funded and privately endowed museums and galleries, alongside control of the art discourse with the emergence of highly influential art critics like Greenberg and Rosenberg and their respective schools of followers, and establishment of art journals and magazines that set the tone of global art debates, made New York the coveted centre that everybody began to take their cue from. This dominance also took hold, as Smith noted, via the imperializing drive of travelling exhibitions of American institutions such as MoMA to many countries.

60 An American review of P.R. Ramachandra Rao's book, *Contemporary Indian Art*, for instance, blandly expressed surprise at the absence of any reference to current American styles, 'sensing a time lag . . . as there is no sign [in the works] of Action painting, let alone op and pop' – Alfred Werner, 'P.R. Ramachandra Rao: Contemporary Indian Art', *Art Journal*, vol. 30, issue 2, 1970.

61 The colonial powers had, for the most part, rubbished Indian art and cultural practices before paying obeisance to its ancient heritage.

62 'The Provincial Bind', in the section 'Art and Ideas' in this volume, p. 277.

63 Indian art from the 1930s had allegiances to the School of Paris, from Amrita Sher-Gil to prominent 1950s' modernists such as Akbar Padamsee, S.H. Raza, Ram Kumar and Laxman Pai who, choosing to live and work in Paris from brief to sustained periods, bore its marked influence – as did a number of artists over the 1960s–'70s visiting on yearly scholarships, to whom Paris continued to be the referent.

64 'Art Without Heroes', *Link*, 26 January 1973; not included in this volume.

65 'Point of Departure', in the section 'Artists' in this volume, pp. 151–53.

66 'Contemporary Trends in Indian Painting', in the section 'Art and Ideas' in this volume, p. 257.

67 Painting at the turn of the twentieth century, Rousseau was seen as a 'primitivist' painter and bore ridicule and rejection of his work for his childlike style – extending to his paintings being slashed at an exhibition in Paris.

68 In a now well-known anecdote, Picasso came across and bought Rousseau's *Portrait of a Woman* and threw a grand party for the much older Rousseau to honour him, to Rousseau's great pleasure, but which reports suggest was a mocking inside joke that Picasso later laughed about. Goel's fears that Khakhar's theatrics were at the behest of his art world friends who 'used' him for their ends, as he writes, can be countered by the fact that the theatrics were of Khakhar's ingenious making and an important part of his response to the art world in the 1970s and '80s.

69 'Juke-Box Rousseau', in the section 'Artists' in this volume, p. 148.

70 Ibid., p. 149.

71 Ibid. Goel writes: 'The down to earth and matter-of-fact qualities of the Khakhar genre have a universal appeal; they are besides, compositions illustrating our daily mythologies, which Khakhar cleverly surrealizes in the bazaar manner and not according to some aesthetic mantra relevant only to the aesthete.'

72 J. Swaminathan, 'Form, Contemporaneity, Me', *Contra '66*, no. 1, p. 10.

73 'Seeing through Photographs', a long text, is not included in this volume but a shorter version of it with these ideas appears in 'The Hidden Text in Photography' (in the section

'Catalogues' in this volume, pp. 425–28). Goel borrows for his title Susan Sontag's phrase in her influential work, *On Photography,* which he reads as a key text. 'Despite the illusion of giving understanding, what seeing through photographs really invites is an acquisitive relation to the world that nourishes aesthetic awareness and promotes emotional detachment.' Susan Sontag, *On Photography,* New York: Farrar, Straus and Giroux, 1977, p. 87.

74 This is a Walter Benjamin insight, from his famous text, 'The Work of Art in the Age of Mechanical Reproduction' (1935). Unlike in a traditional work of art and the stage (theatre), where an actor's aura is indescribably linked to her or his physical presence, in a photograph or the cinema – where the camera replaces the live audience – the aura is lost.

75 Stanley Cavell, *The World Viewed: Reflections on the Ontology of Film,* Viking Press, 1971. Andre Bazin, 'The Ontology of the Photographic Image', translated by Hugh Gray, *Film Quarterly,* vol. 13, no. 4, Summer 1960, pp. 4–9.

76 Susan Sontag, 'In Plato's Cave', in *On Photography,* Penguin Classics, 2008, p. 4 (first edition, New York: Farrar, Straus and Giroux, 1977).

77 Maholy-Nagy was an early voice to speak of photography's indexicality and to even argue against its status as 'art'; see his book, *Painting, Photography, Film,* London: Lund Humphries, 1967 (originally published as *Malarei, Fotografy, Film,* vol. 8, Bauhausbücher series, 1925).

78 At the extreme end of this spectrum could also be staged photography, which Goel does not discuss – often seen as a 'lesser' form for precisely this distance/rejection of the found moment and purported indexicality, though, as Sontag writes, the latter can actually be more 'exploitative'.

79 Jean-Francois Lyotard, 'The Sublime and the Avant-Garde', in *The Inhuman: Reflections on Time,* English translation, California: Stanford University Press, 1991, p. 102. See Goel's quote from Lyotard in 'The Hidden Text in Photography', in the section 'Art and Ideas' in this volume, p. 427.

80 'Raghu Rai', *Link,* 4 October 1970; not included in this volume.

81 'Humanist Eye-View', in the section 'Art and Ideas' in this volume, pp. 328–29.

82 'Kishor Parekh's Lens: A Retrospective', in the section 'Art and Ideas' in this volume, p. 325.

83 Richard Bartholomew, 'Retrospective of Kishor Parekh's work', in *Richard Bartholomew: The Art Critic,* New Delhi: Bart, 2012, pp. 629–30.

84 Goel, 'Kishor Parekh's Lens: A Retrospective'. In Parekh's well-known news image of the 1971 Bangladesh war, which shows an abandoned lone soldier's boot in the foreground and two Bangladeshi militiamen at the back with guns on the move.

85 'Pure Photograph Wasn't True Enough', in the section 'Art and Ideas' in this volume, pp. 318–21.

86 On T.F. Geti whose image offers an 'invitation to fantasy, speculation and above all innovation', 'Geti's Prints', *Link,* 1974. The phrase 'emotional tone' is Herbert Read's: 'In art . . . is an aesthetic quality . . . every part as well as whole becomes suffused with an emotional tone'; see Herbert Read, *The Meaning of Art,* UK: Penguin Books, 1951, p. 49. Goel's quotation appears in an article titled 'Photographs with an Emotional Tone', *Patriot Magazine,* 25 August 1982. Both articles are not included in this volume.

87 'The Magical Box', in the section 'Art and Ideas' in this volume, pp. 307–09.

88 The 'G effect' refers to multiple solarized photographic prints. See endnotes to 'From Image to Icon', in the section 'Art and Ideas' in this volume, pp. 297–99, for a discussion.

89 John Berger, 'Paul Strand', in *Selected Essays of John Berger,* edited by Geoff Dyer, New York: Vintage, 2001.

90 George Dickie, *Aesthetics: An Introduction,* Indianapolis: Bobbs-Merrill, 1971.

91 'The Institutional Theory of Art', in the section 'Catalogues' in this volume, p. 375.

92 Ibid., p. 379.

93 Ibid., pp. 375–82.

94 Ibid., p. 379.

95 Seeking to expand artistic horizons via an exchange over art between nations and regions – events such as the Venice Biennale (the earliest, 1895), the Paris Biennale and Documenta soon expanded to the third world with the inauguration of the Sao Paulo Biennale in Brazil (1951).

96 Mulk Raj Anand, prefatory note for the Triennale catalogue, *Lalit Kala Contemporary*, nos. 7 and 8, pp. 1–6, and *Lalit Kala Contemporary*, Triennale special, 1990.
97 The scale of art in *Two Decades* had staggered audiences in New Delhi, Kyoto, Melbourne and Sydney the previous year, and had much to do with establishing American dominance in world art. But despite this 'shock and awe', evidently an old American tactic, and the undoubted impact in bringing contemporary art to audiences, the impact of the American avant-garde on artists of the three countries remains questionable, as art critics Charles Green and Heather Barker write in the context of Australia, where 'these styles arrived too late to have any genuine influence on the advanced Australian artists except at the level of measuring size and ambition'. See Charles Green and Heather Barker, 'The Watershed: Two Decades of American Painting at the National Gallery of Victoria', National Gallery of Victoria, May 2011, available at https://www.ngv.vic.gov.au/essay/the-watershed-two-decades-of-american-painting-at-the-national-gallery-of-victoria/
98 Ellen Johnson, 'Continuity in American Modern Art', *SPAN*, April 1968, New Delhi.
99 'Provincial Bind', in the section 'Art and Ideas' in this volume, p. 277.
100 'Stoffwechsel: Interpreting Modernism', in the section 'Institutions' in this volume, pp. 183–86.
101 'Closed Society', 'Artscape', *The Economic Times*, 30 April 1990; not included in this volume.
102 'Some Women Artists', in the section 'Art and Ideas' in this volume, p. 268.
103 'The Image Freed of the Mirror', in the section 'Artists' in this volume, pp. 16–20.
104 Ibid.
105 'A Disciplined Journey', in the section 'Art and Ideas' in this volume, pp. 289–91.
106 'An Exhibition of Indian Art' held in New Delhi in 1948, comprising ancient Indian art from several Indian museums. It led to the formation of the National Museum in India in 1949. See particularly Goel's article on M.F. Husain: 'Husain Sugar', in the section 'Artists' in this volume, pp. 47–50.
107 Ibid.
108 See other articles by Goel on Husain in this volume: 'The Husain Mystique', in the section 'Artists' in this volume, pp. 57–58; 'Birth of Many Husains', in the section 'Artists' in this volume, pp. 51–53; 'Husain Retrospective', in the section 'Artists' in this volume, pp. 54–56.
109 K.G. Subramanyan initated the 'craft mela' at Baroda in the 1960s which sought to bring together craftsmen and art school-trained artists together on the same platform, triggering collaborative and interactive art experiences. See 'A Post-Modern Symbol', in the section 'Artists' in this volume, pp. 35–37.
110 'In Bondage to a Narrow Self', in the section 'Institutions' in this volume, pp. 208–11.
111 'J. Swaminathan: His Art and Context', in the section 'Artists' in this volume, pp. 120–24.
112 'The Painter in His Labyrinth', in the section 'Artists' in this volume, pp. 115–19.
113 'Tantric Put-On', in the section 'Artists' in this volume, p. 103. He does so echoing the artist's unabashed self-assessment in his 1960s memoirs, *Autobiography of a Cygan*.
114 The critic Geeta Kapur, too, saw a connection with minimalism, but made the distinction of their strong rooting in materiality being absent in Swaminathan who sought to 'dematerialize' the image. See Geeta Kapur, *Contemporary Indian Artists*, New Delhi: Vikas Publishing House, 1978, p. 198.
115 'The Cube and the Rectangle', 1967; extract published in S. Kalidas, *Transits of a Wholetimer*, New Delhi: Gallery Espace, 2012.
116 'Revolt', in the section 'Catalogues' in this volume, pp. 397–400.
117 Ibid., p. 397. While enthused by Group 1890, in his review of their show, however, Goel left out Swaminathan altogether, perhaps unconsciously. But the absence is pronounced, not only because of the importance he later came to give Swaminathan, but also from Swaminathan receiving considerable attention at the time from all Indian critics, including someone like Richard Bartholomew who wrote on him from a position of contestation which yet revealed a keen insight into Swaminathan's work and personality.
118 'J. Swaminathan: His Art And Context', *Lalit Kala Contemporary*, no. 40, 1995; in the section 'Artists' in this volume, p. 123.
119 'Scaling the Invisible Wall', in the section 'Artists' in this volume, p. 106.
120 'The Painter in His Labyrinth', in the section 'Artists' in this volume, pp. 115–19.
121 'Revolt', in the section 'Catalogues' in this volume, p. 400.

122 'The Painter in His Labyrinth', in the section 'Artists' in this volume, p. 118.
123 'Scaling the Invisible Wall', in the section 'Artists' in this volume, pp. 106–08.
124 Source: K.B. Goel personal archives, New Delhi.
125 In the section 'Artists' in this volume, pp. 120–24.
126 'Study in Disguises', in the section 'Artists' in this volume, p. 76.
127 'Expressionism, Worlds of Husain and Souza', in the section 'Artists' in this volume, pp. 73–75.
128 'The Fall of Man and Other Images', in the section 'Artists' in this volume, p. 68.
129 Ibid., pp. 64–69.
130 'Expressionism, Worlds of Husain and Souza', in the section 'Artists' in this volume, pp. 73–75.
131 'Art of Substitution', in the section 'Artists' in this volume, p. 131.
132 Vivan Sundaram's 1976 solo exhibition held in New Delhi, 'The Discreet Charm of the Bourgeoisie'.
133 In the late 1980s began a strident movement of right-wing Hindu forces that resulted in the vandalism and demolition of a sixteenth-century mosque in Ayodhya, the Babri Masjid, on 6 December 1992. The destruction led to an intense and horrific period of communal riots in many parts of India, the worst being an anti-Muslim pogrom in the city of (then) Bombay in December 1992–January 1993. These sparked bomb blasts in Bombay that year, sharply polarizing India along communal/religious divides; and this renting of a formerly syncretic social fibre provoked a substantial outpouring of creative responses in the arts.
134 'Forms with a Hidden Dialectic', in the section 'Artists' in this volume, pp. 135–39.
135 'Riverscape', in the section 'Catalogues' in this volume, pp. 416–21.

K.B. GOEL: A LIFE IN THE ARTS

Shruti Parthasarathy

Kanha Babu Goel, the full name, is possibly unfamiliar to the closest associates of the art critic K.B. Goel - known only as Goel to his contemporaries and Mr Goel to younger colleagues - a relatively unsung but nonetheless significant critical voice in Indian modern art. He closely witnessed Indian art as it evolved over a phenomenal fifty-year writing career, even as he confined himself almost entirely to art developments unfolding in Delhi.

Born in 1930 in pre-Independence India in the small town of Deeg, in Rajasthan's Bharatpur district, to a family of grain stockists, K.B. Goel made his own, determined way to the life he wanted: a life of the mind. Much of this, even if indirectly, he owed to his remarkable father, who, disinterested in the mercantile life of money and increasing profits that was prescribed for him, was seen as otherworldly - 'squandering' away his wealth towards altruistic causes, giving generous loans to poor customers who came from far-flung villages or selling off ancestral property to finance a wedding. Even as he remained within a life circumscribed by his inherited vocation, his father's detachment from the usual bourgeois materialist concerns inspired K.B. Goel's own outlook to life. Some of this came, too, from the early loss of his mother and his father's rejection of social expectations by not remarrying - these seemed to temper Goel's approach to life with a certain acceptance of its vicissitudes and the choice of the dignity one could bring to it.

The town's public library was opposite the family shop; so visits there with his father meant, for Goel, spending the day among books. Besides his early love of reading, he was also a natural painting talent as a young boy, routinely winning prizes for his drawing. This led him to pursue art after school. Looking to enrol in art college, his options were the Bombay or Agra universities - visiting each, he came away dissatisfied, unsure about his ability to do the full course. He then decided to move to Jaipur and enrolled at the Maharaja's College in a Bachelor's course in literature, where he came under the influence of a charismatic teacher, Baba Govind Das, who was not an ascetic but a renunciate, and an intellectual with great belief in a disciplined life. Das's advice to young Goel was that if he wanted to study art, he ought to study philosophy first. This not only propelled Goel to begin to read philosophy, but the advice possibly laid the foundation for the philosophical basis of his understanding of art and art criticism, and provided the supportive framework for his writing. The teacher's influence also set in place a lifetime's love of reading and ideas.

Taking his graduation degree at the very young age of seventeen or eighteen, Goel got a job at the Imperial Bank in Jaipur. As the eldest child, he was determined to support himself and his siblings; so he brought them, a sister and two brothers, to live with him in Jaipur where they could study. His immediate younger brother finished his schooling and joined the magistrate's court as a reader, but his sister, soon married off under social pressure, could not study further. Goel then took his youngest brother under his wing and supported his schooling and college education. In him, Goel appears to have poured the academic ambitions he may have entertained for himself had circumstances permitted. When his brother wished to find work upon finishing graduation, Goel would hear none of it and urged him to do a Master's instead, and then aim to do a PhD. With favourable circumstances – namely the winning of a scholarship – Goel's brother was indeed able to pursue a doctorate in Canada in Economics and Industrial Relations, where he retired as a professor and still teaches as emeritus – his intellectual life and career made possible by Goel who himself walked the more uncertain life of a newspaper art critic in India.

While working in Jaipur, Goel enrolled to study art at a college where his teacher was the well-known painter, Ramgopal Vijaivargiya, who had trained in the 'Bengal School' style at Jaipur's Maharaja College of Arts under Sailendranath De, a student of the style's founder, Abanindranath Tagore. Vijaivargiya was an early and much-lauded talent, but Goel's growing interest in Western modernism acquired through reading made him question the curriculum's focus on the Bengal School mannerisms and the absence of any modernist contemporary developments had him abandon the course midway. He was also involved then in leftist student groups and his interests – under Govind Das's influence and fed by a great amount of reading on art – now began to veer more consciously towards art history, analysis and theorizing around art, and painting began to recede.

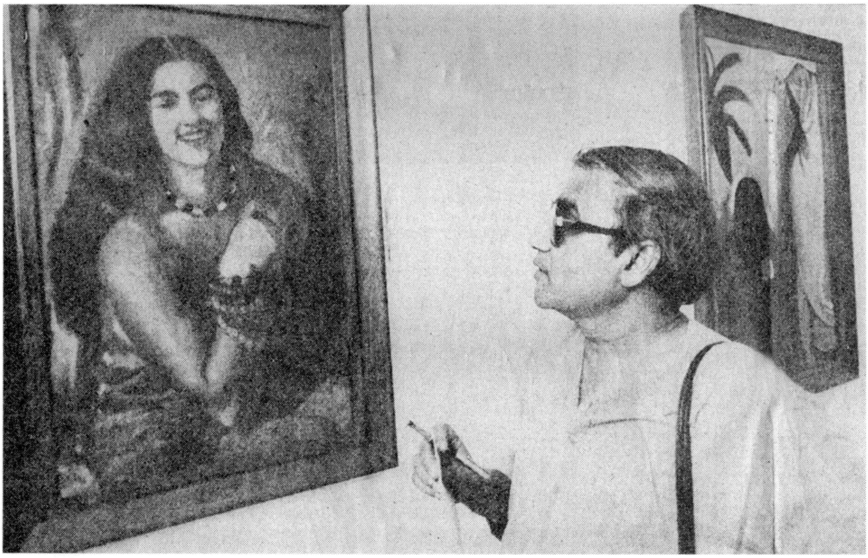

K.B. Goel at an Amrita Sher-Gil exhibition in New Delhi

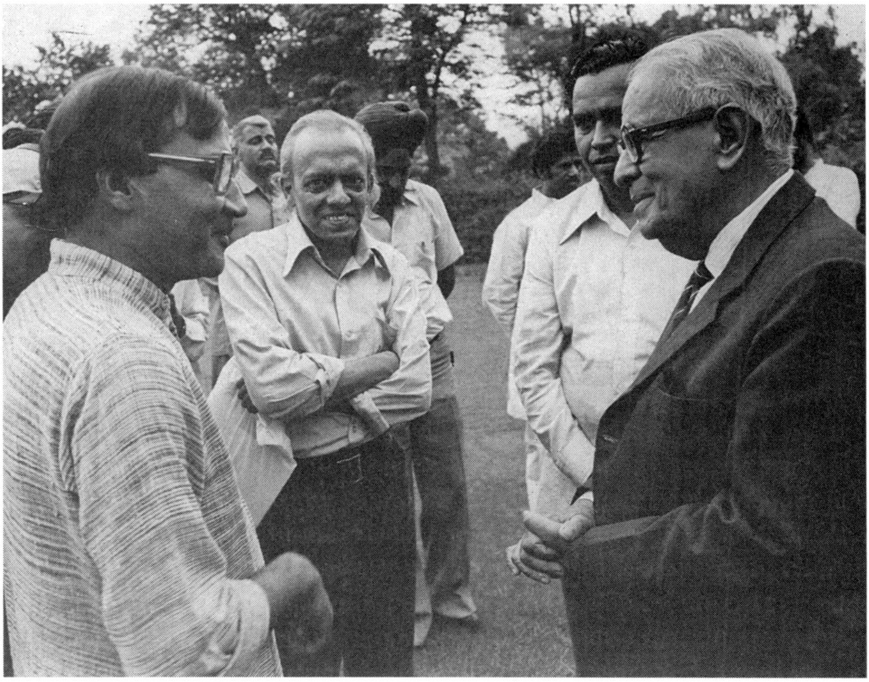

K.B. Goel (left) and artist F.N. Souza (centre) with Vice President Hidayatullah (right), New Delhi

In 1948, he happened to be in Delhi and attended the now famous exhibition on Mathura sculptures, where he met M.F. Husain and F.N. Souza who had both come from Bombay to see the exhibition. 'Though no one talked about painting as such', he felt that the two artists gained much from the 'narrative sculpture of Mathura relief', as Goel offered in halting speech when this writer met him in August 2017. Around 1951, Goel moved to Delhi, and a year or so later was employed in the leftist magazine *Thought*. In the following years, he wrote for a number of publications and newspapers, then being established in the somewhat buoyant atmosphere of the post-Independence years among a group of writers on art and culture, the coterie being a small one. He began by writing cinema reviews of Hindi films and a few art features, and he also took on odd jobs like composing bogus 'letters to the editor', ostensibly from readers.

Meanwhile he kept up his reading on art, educating himself, and became a regular at the American Center library, which received the latest American books and journals on art. At *Thought,* colleagues such as the poet and journalist Rakshat Puri and art critic Keshav Malik came to be good friends, and they urged him to write seriously on art. By the mid-1950s or so, K.B. Goel had moved towards a nearly wholehearted focus on art writing, in the different publications he wrote and worked for; these included *Caravan, Design, Shankar's Weekly, Century, Mainstream, Link* and *The Statesman*. In 1958, he joined *The Indian Express,* working there

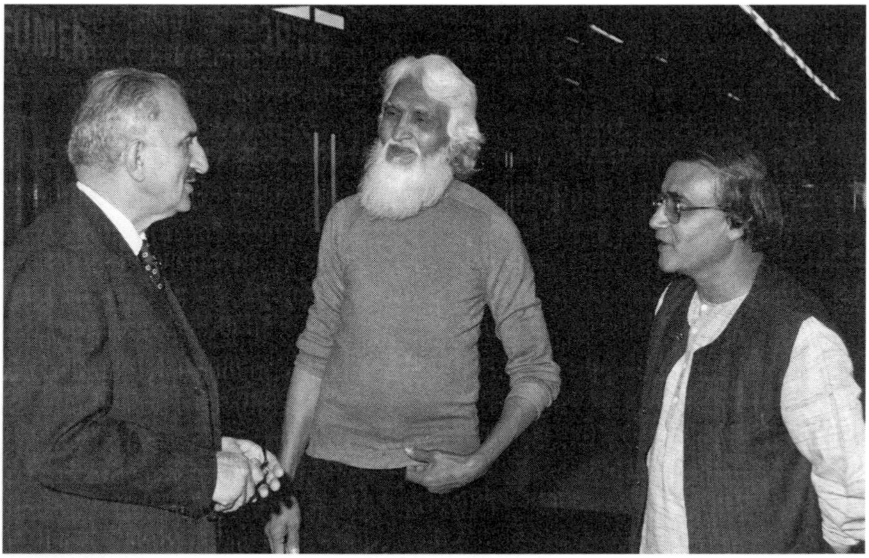

K.B. Goel (right) with artist M.F. Husain (centre), at the Festival of India, Paris

till 1963. Around 1958, too, he began to write intermittently in the leftist newspaper *Link*.

It was only in 1964 that he joined full time the *Patriot Magazine*, another leftist daily and a sister concern of *Link*, brought out by Link House. Through the 1960s–70s, Goel wrote in both these spaces, and was often given substantial front page space in *Patriot*, as evidenced by some of the writings featured in this volume. He remained with the publication, writing a regular column for twenty-five years, until his retirement in 1989. Offered an extension for only a year and no new contract, he resigned and was without work for some time. *The Political and Economic Observer* then offered him the role of a senior art critic, a position to oversee 'Page 3' and he naturally refused. His wife, Premlata Goel, recounts that the loss of his column, coupled with his not-unreasonable demand of a car to attend gallery openings in order to write a review, meant that his invitations to gallery exhibitions too dwindled soon to nothing, and Goel then drasti cally reduced writing reviews.

It was then that he received the fortuitous offer of a regular fortnightly column in the 'Artscape' section of *The Economic Times*, from the newspaper's arts editor, Sadanand Menon. Goel came on board on the condition that he would write articles of a fair length on topics of his choice, and the familiar but mostly unsuccessful quest of every writer: 'not a line must be cut'. Recognizing the value of such a critic, Menon was happy to oblige and the few years that followed at the newspaper saw Goel write some interesting articles, among them several on Vivan Sundaram and installation art; he was finally able to write in a longer form than the dictates of routine newspaper reviewing had previously permitted. A change of editorial guard in 1996 brought that relationship to a close, and in the next two years or so, Goel wrote the last of his art criticisms.

PERSONAL LIFE

K.B. Goel married Premlata in 1961, and his wife was no ordinary woman. Many wives or partners of male artists and critics in the Indian art scene of the 1950s–90s – some of them well-educated women and even art school-trained – essentially played second fiddle to their male spouses, their own work taking a back seat as they kept house and raised children. Premlata Goel is one of the exceptions and the assertion of her individuality goes back to her teens, when she insisted on intellectual and financial independence and self-reliance even within her modest professional ambition of being a teacher. Hailing from tradition-bound Rajasthan, where she was expected to marry early and where getting to finish college itself was a victory, Premlata first studied at a college in a town away from home and then insisted upon working after graduating, in English literature. Her act was in response, in particular, to the example of her oldest sister who was extremely bright but never allowed to express her talents or access opportunities. Overcoming her family's strong resistance, Premlata's very first job, around 1957, was teaching English literature in a boy's college in Ajmer/Udaipur. She followed this with a second teaching stint in another town in Rajasthan and around that time, came into Goel's acquaintance. They decided to marry, mutual respect and egalitarianism marking the modernity of their marriage.

After marriage, Premlata began working at Dayal Singh College, Delhi University, teaching English literature to undergraduates. Their well-matched personalities and Goel's own feminist ethos are reflected in his acceptance of a full-time position at *Thought* in 1964, the year their first child was born, on condition that he would come to the office only in the afternoon after his wife returned from college, as he looked after the baby until then – and this, at a time when he desperately needed full-time employment. Through the vicissitudes of his work, it was Premlata's support that got him by. In our conversation, it is him she talks about: his immense dedication to his craft; how he would sit up nights reading – almost always philosophy and frequently his favourite, Wittgenstein – to evolve a framework for his writing that was due the next morning, as in the 1960s–80s, the practice was to have the reviews published the day after the exhibition opening; and their domestic adjustments that accommodated his writing and her own work.

She also revealed that for years, he urged her to pursue a doctorate even as she vacillated, doubting her ability to find time for it; eventually, at his insistence, she did enrol in Delhi University for a PhD and completed it. Her dissertation was on Samuel Beckett's novels and Goel helped her enthusiastically, bringing her books and discussing her subject and putting her in touch with poet- and scholar-friends. Premalata Goel remained a close confidante and associate of her partner, and in the later years when he was incapacitated, it is she who put together his work. In 2014, she authored a brief biography of the critic for *Critical Collective* – an online journal dedicated to Indian art and criticism. She not only provided biographical details of K.B. Goel's career, but also contextualized his work for readers thus: 'Goel's critical enterprise, which has about it a formal precision and a philosophical framework, has been highly acclaimed and appreciated by discerning artists, art lovers and critics.'

ART-WORLD ASSOCIATIONS

Over the years, as K.B. Goel closely witnessed and commented on the evolving Indian art scene as it unfolded in Delhi, he became a significant member of its art circles. He developed close friendships and associations particularly with artists such as J. Swaminathan and F.N. Souza, and came to be seen as one among the more serious art critics. As we see from his writings, he wrote some of his keenest criticism on these two artists and while the draw of charismatic Swaminathan seems natural to Goel and helped mould his ideas, particularly with respect to Western modernism that he was so personally invested in, the connection with Souza seems more surprising. Goel and Souza's three-decades-long close friendship, maintained till the latter's death in 2002, began in the 1970s when the artist began to regularly show his works in India – a time that marked the flagging of his social currency in New York, no longer the prominent and feted artist he had been in London in the 1950s and 60s. The two also maintained an extensive correspondence and the Goel family has a substantial collection of Souza's letters to the critic. In 2012, at the end of long personal legal troubles that had cost him financially at a time when he was no longer working or writing, Goel donated fifty valuable works of Souza to a charity auction in Delhi to raise funds for an NGO in Patna that worked towards the removal of social stigmas attached to one of the lowest Dalit castes in India, the Moosahars, forced for centuries to subsist by hunting and eating rats (see http://timesofindia.indiatimes.com/city/delhi/Art-to-raise-funds-for-musahar-kids/articleshow/12285508.cms).

For those in the know within the art circles of the 1960s–90s, K.B. Goel was known for a life of integrity and, equally, an uncompromising critical stance that often had him mince no words in judgements in his writings. As Premalata Goel writes, he consistently refused to ingratiate himself with any powers that be that would put him on judging committees or juries or win him curatorial or writing commissions. And so, the first such body he was a part of was in *c*. 1985–86, when he served on the jury for the Kalidas Samman, a national-level honour in the visual arts instituted by the Madhya Pradesh government, and he participated the following year in seminars at the Swaminathan-instituted Bharat Bhavan. His first official trip abroad as part of an Indian art delegation was only in 1990, when he visited Paris as part of the Festival of India, an initiative of the

Indian government; and the following year, he served as the commissioner of the Havana Biennial in Cuba. The few catalogue texts he wrote for solo and group exhibitions were also only from the late 1980s until 1998, which marked the last year of his writing.

For close to two decades after he stopped writing, K.B. Goel maintained close ties with the world of art and critical thought – right up to reading, as Geeta Kapur notes in her Foreword, Rosalind Krauss's 1990s' work, *The Optical Unconscious*. His health deteriorated and remained indifferent from around 2000, though he retained a great enthusiasm for reading, and a proprietorial hold over his extensive and carefully collected books.

It was our great hope to publish this book in K.B. Goel's lifetime so he could have seen it but he passed away in January 2018; hence, in more ways than one, this volume is also a tribute to the critic.

The photographs featured in this biographical note are all courtesy the K.B. Goel family collection.

SECTION ONE

ART

STS

This section presents K.B. Goel's writings on a large number of artists whose work spanned much of the twentieth century. The articles consist of reviews of solo exhibitions as well as reflections on the art, style and themes of individual artists. While all the other sections in this volume are presented in chronology of the published articles, this section presents artists in the chronology of their emergence on the Indian art scene and the most dominant years of their work. Thus, it begins with an article on Raja Ravi Varma, active from the late nineteenth century to the first decade of the twentieth century, and end with artists working in the 1990s, the last of K.B. Goel's years as a critic. Also included is the very last article the critic wrote in 2017, in infirm health.

1

OF FIGURES AND MIRRORS ON THE WALL

An article on the innovations and influential aesthetics Raja Ravi Varma ushered in Indian art

'Artscape', *The Economic Times*, New Delhi, 15 June 1993

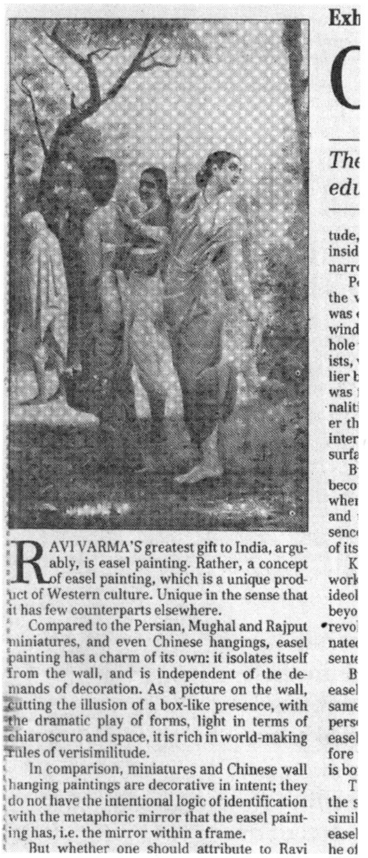

RAVI VARMA'S greatest gift to India, arguably, is easel painting. Rather, a concept of easel painting, which is a unique product of Western culture. Unique in the sense that it has few counterparts elsewhere.

Compared to the Persian, Mughal and Rajput miniatures, and even Chinese hangings, easel painting has a charm of its own: it isolates itself from the wall, and is independent of the demands of decoration. As a picture on the wall, cutting the illusion of a box-like presence, with the dramatic play of forms, light in terms of chiaroscuro and space, it is rich in world-making rules of verisimilitude.

In comparison, miniatures and Chinese wall hanging paintings are decorative in intent; they do not have the intentional logic of identification with the metaphoric mirror that the easel painting has, i.e. the mirror within a frame.

But whether one should attribute to Ravi

Ravi Varma's greatest gift to India is, arguably, easel painting. Rather, a concept of easel painting, which is a unique product of Western culture. Unique in the sense that it has few counterparts elsewhere. Compared to the Persian, Mughal and Rajput miniatures, and even Chinese hangings, easel painting has a charm of its own: it isolates itself from the wall, and is independent of the demands of decoration. As a picture on the wall, gutting the illusion of a box-like presence with the dramatic play of forms and of light in terms of chiaroscuro and space, it is rich in world-making rules of verisimilitude. In comparison, miniatures and Chinese wall-hanging paintings are decorative in intent; they do not have the intentional logic of identification with the metaphoric mirror that the easel painting has, i.e. the mirror within a frame.

But whether one should attribute to Ravi Varma the distinction of giving us the art of easel painting is in itself debatable. The more legitimate claimants for this honour would be the many 'unknown' artists whose works we associate with what is called Company Art, which flowered in the feudal courts of India in the early nineteenth century.[1] Their works created the conditions for legitimization of easel painting.

When easel painting arrived in the country through royal portraitists working in the medium of oil, it was looked down upon as inferior in sensibility to the portraits done in miniature style and remained an alien presence in India until the arrival of Amrita Sher-Gil on the Indian art scene in the 1930s. Indian aesthetic never subscribed to any form of perspectival seeing, and hence a window view of the world, however rich in verisimilitude, was rejected for it divided the world into inside and outside, limiting the outside to the narrow angle the perspective permitted.

Perhaps our sensibilities helped us to reject the window aesthetic. For, when Ravi Varma was engaged in working out its mechanics, that window - conceived as a hole in the wall in the land of its origin, if not closed forever by the cubists - was screened by a transparent material earlier by Manet and the impressionists. The cavity was filled by them with colour and textural tonalities and other effects of reflected light. Rather than exploring objects in depths, they were interested in emphasizing the frontality of the surface for the sake of decorative structure.

By the 1970s, the future of easel painting had become problematic for it no longer was a site where a work of art was woven into a tight mesh, and the formal unity contained so that the essence of the whole work was found in every one of its parts. Kinetic art, conceptual art, body art, earthworks and happenings - the ruling ideologies in the late 1960s - were intended to go beyond the private space the easel provided. The revolt was against the universality of a hallucinated space of uniformity that the easel represented. But painters in India continue to set up their easels and apply colour on the canvas in the same old conventional ways - and with amazing perseverance. The painter still stands before the easel as the first Aryan *rishi* might have stood before the rising sun to experience how a painting is born in him.

The artist's act of hallucination is shared by the spectator who too imagines undergoing a similar experience as the painter. For the easel painting invites him to see something that he often does not see. It is entirely another matter that he rarely sees the painting; he passes by it as if in a trance. He feels that he is at an arm's length of the enigma of vision which easel painting celebrates. In the moments of simulated transcendence, the viewer realizes that painting is not so much about the enigma of vision as it is about the enigma of appearing.

In relation to Ravi Varma, there are some other aspects of easel painting that need elaboration. Only easel painting kept up the tradition of handicraft to which painting provides an individual frame of reference - a concept and category of interpretation not available to handcrafted art objects. For painting claims that it has its origin within; that is, painting is not about representation but is itself an example of interpretation. Interpretation demands a reflection on reflection. This is true when painting has the ontology of a mirror, not that of a window. In other words, a mirror within a frame. Inside this, a consciousness is confronted and trapped within the impossibility of a unified image. For there is always a split between the implicit 'to be determined' and the explicit which is 'already determined'. In a portrait, this is inscribed as the impossibility of homology.

Among the early founders of modernist sensibility in India, only Amrita Sher-Gil understood the nature of this split. And it is in her work – and not in Ravi Varma's – that the split as in-between space is clearly visible. The distinction between the figurative and figural was of central importance to her. Between these two positions of the figurative and figural,[2] Lyotard builds his aesthetics. The figurative, according to Lyotard, implies translation from a model, Platonic or otherwise. The resultant pictorial object is derived from its 'real' model (real for Plato is what is inside the mind), whereas the figural is a pictorial property relative to the demands of representation.

In more general terms, the two terms can be described as the two opposite poles of reference: one represents what is called literal and the other, the figural. There is no evidence in Ravi Varma's work of a movement from the literal pole towards the figural, from the figurative to the figural, or from the model to the perception of a plastic object beyond the limits of mimesis. The dependence of the figurative on (almost photographic) representation is absolute, which prevents him from evolving a vocabulary of his own, within which – and in the movement away from the literal – he could situate his imagination.

Only the mirror allows the presence, elsewhere, of the 'real' mirror. Ravi Varma, who had access to only a few British sources on contemporary art, was denied acquaintance with the mirror which the impressionists had discovered and framed as a mirror of reflected light. Or, perhaps, he had no use for such a mirror, self-taught as he was, and his horizon reached the upper limits of art approved by the British Royal Academy of Art. And for the Royal academicians, as for Ravi Varma himself, the daguerre mirror was the only mirror available.[3] The eye of the daguerre mirror is the dominating presence in the portraits exhibited in the National Museum show. The opulent Louis XVth frames seem to have a symbolic relationship with the portraits: the frame, it seems, is the dividing line between art and non-art. The frame makes a daguerre a picture – a picture that is freely transportable into any world. The frame marks the difference of the picture itself from copies of it.

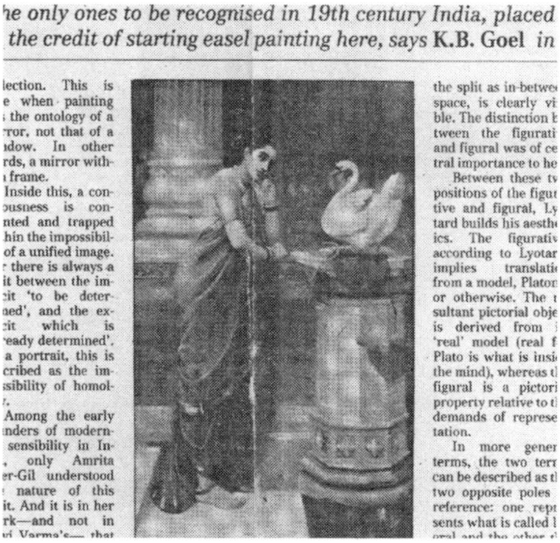
he only ones to be recognised in 19th century India, placed the credit of starting easel painting here, says **K.B. Goel** *in*

lection. This is e when painting the ontology of a ror, not that of a dow. In other rds, a mirror with a frame.
Inside this, a consciousness is contented and trapped hin the impossibility of a unified image. there is always a it between the im- it 'to be determined', and the ex- it which is eady determined'. a portrait, this is cribed as the impossibility of homol-
Among the early nders of modern- sensibility in In- , only Amrita er-Gil understood nature of this it. And it is in her rk—and not in vi Varma's— that

the split as in-betwe space, is clearly vi ble. The distinction b tween the figurati and figural was of ce tral importance to he Between these tv positions of the figur tive and figural, Ly tard builds his aesth ics. The figurativ according to Lyotar implies translati from a model, Plator or otherwise. The r sultant pictorial obje is derived from 'real' model (real f Plato is what is insi the mind), whereas t figural is a pictori property relative to t demands of represe tation.
In more gener terms, the two terr can be described as t two opposite poles reference: one repr sents what is called l

For the historical daguerre, as for Ravi Varma, the virtual image in a mirror is in one sense, an ideal copy, for what we see in a mirror is an image, not a copy or a picture. A copy has a life of its own, is useful because it does not depend, like

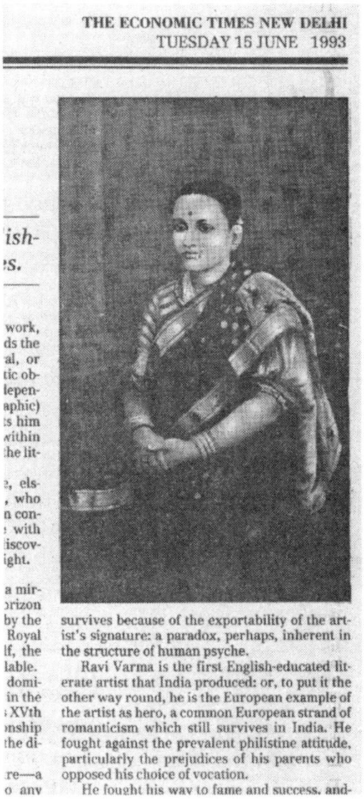

THE ECONOMIC TIMES NEW DELHI
TUESDAY 15 JUNE 1993

survives because of the exportability of the artist's signature: a paradox, perhaps, inherent in the structure of human psyche.

Ravi Varma is the first English-educated literate artist that India produced: or, to put it the other way round, he is the European example of the artist as hero, a common European strand of romanticism which still survives in India. He fought against the prevalent philistine attitude, particularly the prejudices of his parents who opposed his choice of vocation.

He fought his way to fame and success, and-

a mirror, on the presence of the original. It is self-effacing. Why then are Ravi Varma's signatures not so? An upper-class educated painter, part of the colonial establishment, a Raja – these cannot be self-effacing. Besides, Ravi Varma's signatures were the only ones to be recognized by the Victorian, colonial India of the nineteenth century. And it is because of this fact, it can be argued, that easel painting was born in India with Ravi Varma. His signatures indeed go far beyond the private space of which easel painting is its ontological truth; it is indeed the subject of the work itself. Like Husain's signature today, which is the subject of his work.

With it, in existential terms, emerges what [Karl] Jaspers calls 'the cipher of transcendence'.[4] It is a fact and not mere sophistry that easel painting survives because of the exportability of the artist's signature: a paradox perhaps inherent in the structure of human psyche. Ravi Varma is the first English-educated literate artist that India produced: or, to put it the other way round, he is the European example of the artist as hero, a common European strand of romanticism which still survives in India. He fought against the prevalent philistine attitude, particularly the prejudices of his parents who opposed his choice of vocation. He fought his way to fame and success and lived without his family's support in all the years of oblivion when he was learning to paint. His only guide in those days were the works published in the Royal Academy journal, and he closely followed them. When he first saw reproductions of paintings in the collection of the Maharaja of Baroda, he rejected the Victorian philistinism of Company Art. It seemed to him that what was produced by these colonial European artists was contrived.

Rabindranath Tagore testifies to the popularity of Ravi Varma: 'In my childhood, when Ravi Varma's age arrived in Bengal, the reproductions of European paintings on the walls were quickly replaced with oleographs of his works'.[5] The Bengal intelligentsia, used to seeing only Ravi Varma's opulent versions of Radha and Krishna, rejected Abanindranath's first major work entitled *Radha and Krishna*. As against this, Ravi Varma's famous work, *Shakuntala*, met with disapproval at the hands of Margaret Noble (a product of the Irish Revival who became Swami Vivekanand's favourite disciple).[6] She thought it was not a true representation of Shakuntala, but 'a fat woman lying on a lotus leaf'.

Editor's Notes

1 And in the works of the travelling Western painters of the eighteenth and nineteenth centuries who painted in the classical realist mode in oils.

2 Literary theorist Jean-Francois Lyotard and philosopher Gilles Deleuze, among other thinkers, draw on the fundamental distinction between the two terms, both of which derive from the word 'figure' – to indicate figurative as representative, palpable aspects of figure, while 'figural' suggests more symbolic aspects. Lyotard's *Discours, Figure* is a complex work that discusses the essentially representative role of discourse and discursive exploration – in particular, its homogenous nature as offset by the sort of multiplicity of meanings that the word 'figure' holds – bringing into text the dimension of seeing and vision, which 'figure' implies.

3 This refers to the highly mirrored metal surface of daguerreotypes invented in *c.* 1839 that involved a highly polished, silvered copper plate that captured the image. Any rubbing or scratching could damage the image surface and so the early daguerreotypes were encased in individual frames behind glass.

4 Philosopher Karl Jaspers speaks of the experience of 'transcendence' encountered 'as a cipher' in the foundering or failure of human thought when it reaches the limits of the 'unthinkable'; the failure being different from Heidegger's 'Fall', and this failure is a sign of the limit of what Jaspers calls *Existenz*. See Hannah Arendt's explication of Jasper's ideas in 'What is Existenz Philosophy?', *Phenomenology Reader*, 2002 and Oswald Shrag, *Existence, Existenz and Transcendence: An Introduction to the Philosophy of Karl Jaspers*, Duquesne University Press, 1971.

5 The art historian Partha Mitter quotes Rabindranath Tagore thus in his book, *The Triumph of Modernism: India's Artists and the Avant-Garde 1922–1947*, Oxford University Press, 2006, p. 169.

6 Better known by the Hindu name she adopted, Sister Nivedita. Nivedita was a significant figure in the Orientalist movement in late nineteenth-century Calcutta and soon after, in the Indian nationalist movement.

2

'I DON'T SEEK, I FIND'

An assessment of Pablo Picasso in his birth centenary year, examining the revolution he brought to painting and his original talent

'Complementarities', *Patriot Daily*, New Delhi, 19 October 1981

> Carried out programmatically in a few works of heroic dimensions (*Sacre du Printemps, Ulysses, The Waste Land, Guernica*), the great modern achievements were wagers which made gestures, invented methods, but laid no foundations for a future literature. They led in the direction of an immensity from which there was bound to be a turning back, because to go further would lead to a new and complete fragmentation, utter obscurity, form (or, rather formlessness) without end.
>
> – Stephen Spender, *Struggle of the Modern*

Picasso, had he lived a few more years, would have been 100 on 25 October [1981]; and in focus should be the fact that he is the first among the moderns who came to the frontline in 1908 with the showing of *Demoiselles d'Avignon* – a painting as famous as *Guernica* and a history-making gesture because it heralded the birth of cubism. The success of *Demoiselles* was of such immensity 'from which there was no turning back' for Picasso: besides, it laid the foundation for a truly modernist sensibility representing an about-face leading to 'a new and completer fragmentation' as witnessed in the cubist methodology.

Picasso made several studies for this painting: from these preliminary studies, it is clear that the painting drew for inspiration upon Cezanne's late composition of bathers; decidedly its architectonic space is Picasso's contraption as are its expressive, more artificial colours. When George Braque, Picasso's collaborator in cubism, saw it, he said: 'It is as though we were supposed to exchange our usual diet for one of two and paraffin.' The key words 'our usual diet' are very expressive indeed: the squat, angular, primitive-looking figure, heavily pigmented until the paint stood out in relief, have sculpturesque dimensions – and that was a new experience. Not the usual diet Braque expected.

It was the first avant-garde gesture of modern sensibility: how firm are its foundations? Or rather how relevant today are cubist distortions? In relation to Jean Tinguely's *Homage to New York* – which presupposed its death, for it was designed to commit suicide publicly[1] – *Demoiselles* stands as a homage to the non-beautiful, representing a shift from an aesthetic of 'an unchanging and transcendent ideal of beauty'. The non-beautiful element in *Demoiselles* is its African mask-like stare: the violent, abrupt cutting and interesting planes, flattened inasmuch as a rectangular pictorial structure would permit, are also suggestive of what may be called the collageist approach. Which is the more authentic? Tinguely's *Homage to New York* or *Demoiselles*: one leading to death as a categorical imperative of modernism and the other to a journey through the unknown lands for painting unbeauty in the round. It is no less a trap than illusionism as a necessary component in optical naturalism.

Now the modern has become popular, even if it is rooted in the death wish: it evokes a kind of nostalgia and from the vantage point of 1981, it looks very much like old furniture. Where does the break occur between the traditional and the modern, between the modern and the popular, or, say between art and entertainment? And what about Spender's pessimism about art's newer territories: that 'to go further would lead to a new and completer [sic] fragmentation, utter obscurity, form (or rather formlessness) without end?' Isn't the self-negating tradition of the new in the avant-garde responsible for the art scene of the Seventies getting bogged down in such muddy territories of what came to be known as conceptual art; the new links connecting photo realism or the earth projects depending for their status upon documentary presentation and the artist's involvement with video?

Demoiselle reminds one of [Ezra] Pound's cantos: fragments of Eastern, Western, present and past civilization, as well as Eliot's mildly hinted sympathies with the East: what he has said in another context can well be applied to a reading of *Demoiselles*: the shifter here is at work from the literary to the pictorial. The following passage from *Tradition and Individual Talent* [T.S. Eliot 1919] reads well in *Demoiselles*'s context:

> It involves in the first place the historical sense . . . and the historical sense involves a perception, not only of the pastness of the past, but of its presence; the historical sense compels a man to write not merely with his own generation in his bones but with a feeling that the whole of the literature of Europe from Homer, and within it the whole of the literature of his country, has a simultaneous existence and composes a simultaneous order.

The modern has come to be associated with a cultural phenomenon where the two opposites - the East and the West - seem to be closer, leading European culture away from its sharpened historical awareness. Kipling must have had his best laugh - the 1890s trends as impressionism, realism, expressionism and symbolism were accelerated in the first decades of this [twentieth] century with such immense speed that modern has become today synonymous with supra-national. This was due to cultural imperialism inherent in the technological advance Europe has had over the

Eastern world. At what point the modern became synonymous with the popular is hard to locate; perhaps a technology, inherently expansionistic, demands enlargement of its numbers. The popular is modern, even contemporary, but it is not art: it is something like Richard Wilbur's lines from the poem, *Museum Piece* –

> Edgar Degas purchased once
> A fine El Greco, which he kept
> Against the wall beside his bed . . .
> To hang his clothes on while he slept.

Picasso is perhaps the only artist who has not only been modern (a founder-artist of modernist sensibility he is) but always in healthy competition with his contemporaries, for he has always been inventing newer and newer forms and modes of expression. He has led painting to 'a new and completer fragmentation', but never to 'utter obscurity', he invented 'forms without end', but never joined in the self-negating exercise of Tinguely. He was with the dadaists and surrealists, but he always stopped at a point where the surreal would get the features of the ridiculous. Today, dada and surreal aesthetics look rooted in some form of a cultural yesterday but Picasso's pictorial language has never become hackneyed – in fact, his closed energy system has, since the creation of *Demoiselles*, been elementary: the two-faced negative and positive ones, this is as elementary as the principles of electricity.

Let us apply the electrical metaphors, not the value judgements, to our experience of looking at paintings. The positive element, let us say, constitutes the referents; that is to say, our awareness of something represented in a painting – say the presence of bathers and the hills beyond and a clear sky above. At the negative end, there is the co-presence of several other things: our awareness of the canvas, its shallow depth, its tonality of coloured surface, the atmospheric brushwork, the absence of line and hence a presentation in round rather than in flat – all these elements constitute the picture's form.

In a conventional sense, looking at a picture means an existential involvement between form and its referents, between the positive and the negative poles and between presence and absence. If the referent is weak, if the bathers do not look like bathers being distorted to the extent of having become part of the emergent pattern, then the picture is decorative, lending itself to the charge of so much paint on canvas: but if the tension constitutes a felt experience, the picture is right. The picture with a strong referent, putting more emphasis on its documentary value, its recognition pleasures, has no or little tension. While most modernist painters have eliminated all traces of a referent in their picture, Marcel Duchamp attempted to fog the frontier between objects and art objects:

he brought in readymades which eventually went inside the museums. [Joan] Miro, has been perceptive in lamenting the fate of a painter who is 'already a figure of history, destined, to disappear. There will no longer be painters, but rather men who express themselves by three-dimensional means and who participate in other arts such as architecture, which are more direct in their effects, more in contact with society.'

Picasso remained a traditionalist-modern in the sense he kept the tense between form and referent always alive: the referent in Picasso's paintings can, in most cases, be located in his immediate environment - it may be either a painting by another master (whether a contemporary of his or an old master, it hardly interests him) or a toy or a found object - anything that catches his attention. He says,

> To my misfortune and probably to my delight, I use things as my passions tell me to. What a miserable fate for a painter who adores blondes to have to stop himself putting them into a picture because they do not go with the basket of fruit! How awful for a painter who loathes apples to have to use them all the time because they go so nicely with the cloth! I put all the things I like into my picture so much the worse for the things they just have to get on with it.[2]

Picasso's famous remarks 'I find, I don't seek', has wider implications: it surely is linked to the middle space between the two poles - form and referent. For a painter who has arrived with the kind of Napoleonic thunder there is nothing to seek; there is everything to find.

Editor's Notes

1 Artist Jean Tinguely created a performance event, somewhat like a Happening, in the Sculpture Garden of the Museum of Modern Art, New York, titled *Homage to New York*. The work consisted of a 27-feet-high machine Tinguely built with many collaborators, which had moving parts, made noise and emitted smoke - a cacophonous 'performance' lasting 27 minutes in front of a live audience after which it was meant to destroy itself but didn't entirely, stopped as it was by the fire department. Guests then examined and took home as souvenirs its remnants, with the work's destruction and notion of rebuilding itself being a homage to New York's city's energy. Small fragments of the filming of the performance can be viewed online at https://vimeo.com/8537769.

2 This quotation is available at multiple sources. But the original is from interviews conducted by Christian Zervos, *Conversations avec Picasso*, that appeared in the journal *Cahiers d'Art*, vol. X, nos. 7–10, 1935, pp. 173–78.

3

AMRITA SHER-GIL

An assessment of Amrita Sher-Gil's art on the occasion of the first retrospective of her work held in New Delhi in 1972

Link, New Delhi, 9 April 1972

Amrita Sher-Gil, who became a legend in her lifetime, is a complex of riddles for painters, critics and art historians. There is no single key which can open all the doors. The exhibition of Amrita Sher-Gil's works spread over two galleries, the National Gallery at Jaipur House and Lalit Kala at Rabindra Bhavan, is an attempt to view them from the perspective of the Sixties when Indian artists became conscious of their roots. Besides the rich collection of the National Gallery of Modern Art, the exhibition displays many more works which have not been shown previously. Also displayed are some drawings and biographical material which help us understand better many of the works. The organizing committee (Karl Khandalavala, Vivan Sundaram, Mulk Raj Anand, K.G. Subramanyan, Krishen Khanna, Geeta Kapur, Gulammohammed Sheikh and Manu Desai) deserve our gratitude for putting up a show, the kind of which has never been organized in India before. We are also indebted for the book published to coincide with the show. The book contains, besides the probing articles by Geeta Kapur, [K.G.] Subramanyan and Gulam Sheikh, most of the letters and articles written by Amrita Sher-Gil.

Note the remarks of painter A. Ramachandran: 'Unfortunately, after Sher-Gil's death, many Indian painters copied what was genuine in her style – so ruthlessly that ultimately it ended in Vakil's greeting cards.[1] And so I lost interest in Sher-Gil's painting and avoided thinking of her work as one avoids thinking of Gandhiji when one sees a Gandhi cap.[2] Sher-Gil knew her destiny lay in India. She even compared herself with such European greats as Picasso, Matisse and Braque: 'Europe belongs to Picasso, Matisse, Braque and many others. India belongs only to me.'[3] During her lifetime, her works tended to develop into a myth; housed now in the national gallery, the myths of those in private collections are being revived.

RELEVANCE

Why this sudden interest in Sher-Gil? Painter Gieve Patel has part of the answer:

> Padamsee and Tyeb Mehta . . . have painted faces, bodies, sometimes clothing but have painted them as though Sher-Gil never existed. In doing

> so they have created an area in time between Sher-Gil and now in which one swims freely with no nationalist obsessions . . . Amrita Sher-Gil paints her servants, Khakhar paints his relatives. And I? If I were to paint those who appear in Amrita's paintings, for no reason other than that they happen to be around in millions, I might reveal that to me, twenty years after Amrita, they are still servants. For the present, Amrita leaves me with the happier option of painting their bosses – the statesman, the star . . .[4]

The Seventies, it seems, will be the decade of figure painting and who, indeed, is a bigger painter than Sher-Gil to guide this new wave of figuration? More painters in the Sixties became conscious of their roots – as Gulam Sheikh says,

> . . . there is a nostalgic cry for the lost tradition, which has again grown emphatic since the Sixties. Positively, the conflict (the oscillating positions between the alluring magnetism of traditional Indian art and the dynamism of modern European art) should lead to vital dialectics and produce a dynamic movement of art; but unfortunately a lack of coordination of potential talent has made such possibilities remote. Against this background, Amrita Sher-Gil is a symbol of this unique but partially explored potential . . .[5]

THE CULT

So Amrita Sher-Gil, in the words of Prof. Subramanyan, becomes

> . . . sharply prototypical of the modern Indian artist-intellectual whose one foot is in the West and one in the East and who is trying hard to fight out of his alienation by tugging either at his environment or his history, frustrated in the former by an in-built skepticism and in the latter by its impalpability and in both by an inordinate desire for global contemporaneity.[6]

Husain puts this more forcefully in a poem:

> Destiny cuts short the distances of her voyages
> The dialogue between landscape and figure
> Man and his soul: had just commenced
> In terms of contemporary Indian paintings[7]

The exhibition is not intended to build up a Sher-Gil cult: it is merely to open a dialogue to resolve the East-West dilemma which many painters face today. The contours of the dilemma are well sketched by Subramanyan's article, but it does not go deeper. Perhaps the two traditions are so fundamentally opposite to each other that no reconciliation is possible: the

West looking at reality with wide open eyes but the Buddha closes his and looks inward. In other words, it is a conflict between the eye and the hand, between the representational and conceptual images. Under the influence of such gurus as Cage and McLuhan,[8] the eye of the Western artist may be half-closed, hidden or veiled, but it is still the eye that determines the aesthetics of his art, the eye that is always open physically.

Paul Klee attempted to paint with closed eyes. Klee's *Drummer* [*Kettledrummer* 1940] - two arms and an open eye and roughly executed in heavy black - for instance, summarizes the dilemma of the Western artist who looks to the orient for inspiration. In India, in its miniatures and sculpture, the hand speaks with authority, the gesture carries the message. The preoccupation is with line, decoration and symbolism. Towards the end, Sher-Gil too came very close to understanding the power of the hand but she painted with the eyes of the West, a vision of the flatness of canvas, and nothing more.

Sher-Gil, to be sure, was more of an 'expatriate' artist even though she belonged to India and she suffered disproportionately, it seems, in her quest for the real India. The discovery came rather late and towards the end of her very short life, she created images of the Indian poor, those melancholic, sad faces which we have now invested with a national memory. They became identical with India, giving rise to the Sher-Gil myth. The myth is as powerful as Ajanta and as all the miniature schools, which some regard are the only available authentic modes of Indian pictorial tradition. Together, they mirror our group mind, the special genius of India. In assessing the Sher-Gil tradition of figuration are we not attempting to give a cultural status to the coming thing - the figure painting?

Editor's Notes

1 A commercial greeting-card company that used artists' artworks, among them Amrita Sher-Gil's, and active to the present day.

2 A. Ramachandran, 'Brief Statements', in *Amrita Sher-Gil*, New Delhi: National Gallery of Modern Art, 1972, p. 83.

3 Amrita Sher-Gil in a letter to Karl Khandalavala (April 1938), in *Amrita Sher-Gil: a self-portrait in letters and writings*, vol. 2, introduced, annotated and edited by Vivan Sundaram, New Delhi: Tulika Books, 2010, p. 491.

4 Gieve Patel, 'Brief Statements', in *Amrita Sher-Gil*, p. 78.

5 For a slightly altered version, see Gulammohammed Sheikh, 'Amrita Sher-Gil: Dialectics of Academicism and Pictorial Situation of Traditional Indian Art', in *Amrita Sher-Gil*, p. 55.

6 K.G. Subramanyan, 'Amrita Sher-Gil and the East-West Dilemma', in *Amrita Sher-Gil*, p. 63.

7 M.F. Husain, 'Brief Statements', in *Amrita Sher-Gil*, p. 84.

8 Radical music composer John Cage championed the innovative and experimental in music, open to being led by 'chance', an aspect which influenced an array of avant-garde art movements, not the least led by Cage's own collaboration with artists such as Robert Rauschenberg. Marshall McLuhan was a media theorist whose focus on the medium being the message in his famous dictum and writings on technological forms foresaw much of the present-day technological revolution.

4
THE IMAGE FREED OF THE MIRROR

Review of an exhibition of Amrita Sher-Gil's work held in 1993 in New Delhi

'Artscape', *The Economic Times*, New Delhi, 6 March 1993

The Amrita Sher-Gil exhibition held recently at the Hungarian Centre, New Delhi, filled one with nostalgia. It reignited the old ardour as if 80 years are merely a brief chronicle of the times, as if our separation from the artist was for a few seasons and not for decades. Her wonderfully expressive, large, dark eyes grow larger and larger until they cover the whole face. The strange, equivocal power of her face and her Botticelli features, like the flicker technique used in silent films, create the illusion of continuity as they keep feeding the memory.

'I have just completed a lovely, sugary self-portrait,' she wrote, 'that will make the public mouth water.' She knew, even as a child, that her presence was spellbinding. She knew this best when she did self-portraits. Standing before a mirror she would complain that it was all a fault of the mirror, for it is not multi-dimensional and thereby incapable of reflecting several images of her simultaneously because with the mirror, every reflection is perspectival. Perspectivism implies not the negation of meaning but the impossibility of a totalization of meaning. Every interpretation of the image is limited, but in painting - particularly in self-portraits - an interpretation is not about the effect of perspectival seeing but consists in imposing a code, the limits of which are drawn by coincidence between the discursive whole and the rules of the code.

Because of the presence of the code, one can speak of a portrait as if it were a text with a code. Text, however, differs from discourse in that where discourse is understood as a signifying whole - a univocal link between the signifier and the signified (for the link is regulated by a code) - a text is not controlled by a code. This means the portrait as text should be interpreted and not explained away as one does a mirror image, depending as it does for meaning on a point of view.

Against the located reality of a point of view, Sher-Gil attempted - and quite successfully - to discover in her portraits a relation between the empirical reality conditioning the perspective and the reality of the text which denies its perspectivist relation. Her self-portraits - and there are many - lead her to go beyond the limits imposed by perspectival seeing and achieve a relativity of interpretation in relation to the beholder. Each of her self-portraits represents a passage from one perspective to another. It involves us seemingly into a contradiction which the meaning of the words might pro-voke, but that is not the case. For the secret of her success lies in the fact that her self-portrait simultaneously affirms itself as a limited perspectival image as well as hints at going beyond a perspectivist reference.

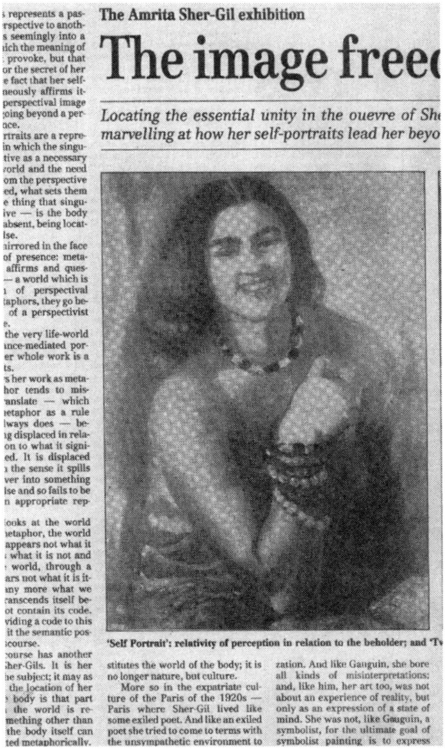

The Amrita Sher-Gil exhibition

The image free(

Locating the essential unity in the ouevre of Sh(
marvelling at how her self-portraits lead her beyo(

'Self Portrait': relativity of perception in relation to the beholder; and 'T(

stitutes the world of the body; it is no longer nature, but culture.

More so in the expatriate culture of the Paris of the 1920s — Paris where Sher-Gil lived like some exiled poet. And like an exiled poet she tried to come to terms with the unsympathetic environment to

zation. And like Gauguin, she bore all kinds of misinterpretations; and, like him, her art too, was not about an experience of reality, but only as an expression of a state of mind. She was not, like Gauguin, a symbolist, for the ultimate goal of symbolist painting is to express

These self-portraits are a repres-entation of life in which the singularity of perspective as a necessary relation to the world and the need to cut itself off from the perspective are set out. Indeed, what sets them apart – and the thing that singularizes perspective – is the body which is always absent, being located somewhere else.

The body is mirrored in the face as a metaphor of presence; a metaphor that both affirms and questions the world – a world which is a contradiction of perspectival 'seeings'. As metaphors, they go beyond the world of a perspectivist succession in life. Metaphor is the very life-world of Sher-Gil's resemblance-mediated portraits. In fact, her whole work is a series of portraits. And as always, her work as metaphor tends to mistranslate – which, metaphor as a rule always does – being displaced in relation to what it signified. It is displaced in the sense it spills over into something else and so fails to be an appropriate representation.

When one looks at the world with the eyes of a metaphor, the world splits itself and appears not what it is, but becomes what it is not and what it is [sic]. The world, through a metaphor, appears not what it is itself, nor is it any more what we make of it; it transcends itself because it does not contain its code. Sher-Gil, by providing a code to this world, offers to it the semantic possibilities of a discourse.

But the discourse has another space in the Sher-Gils. It is her body that is the subject; it may as well be seen as the location of her femininity. The body is that part through which the world is revealed to be something other than what it is, for the body itself can only be designated metaphorically. Better still, it should be treated like a text, because the text, in its singularity, points outside of itself towards meanings. The body insists, as good metaphor does, on the irreducibility of the singular and, it is in this sense that the metaphor constitutes the world of the body; it is no longer nature, but culture.

More so in the expatriate culture of Paris of the 1920s where Sher-Gil lived like some exiled poet. And like an exiled poet, she tried to come to terms with the unsympathetic environment to which fate had cast her. Or more like a bird hopping from plant to plant but always ready for homeward flight.

Or perhaps she was a female version of the artist Gauguin, wanting to 'escape' from Western civilization. And like Gauguin, she bore all kinds of misinterpretations; and, like him, her art too, was not about an experience of reality but only as an expression of a state of mind. However, she was not, like Gauguin, a symbolist, for the ultimate goal of symbolist painting is to express ideas through a special kind of language that allows the artist to distort reality according to his or her individual inclinations. It is because of Gauguin's influence that she decided to return to India. And what is the quintessential Gauguin style? Primitive simplification of forms and colours and the flattening of space. All this which Gauguin had in his style was there for her in India. She wrote to her father:

> Modern art has led me to comprehension & appreciation of Indian painting & sculpture. It seems paradoxical, but I know for certain, that had we not come away to Europe I should perhaps never have realized that a fresco from Ajanta or a small piece of sculpture at Musee Guimet is worth more to me than the whole Renaissance![1]

This is not an instance of misplaced enthusiasm. We know with what passion she studied the art of Gauguin. Gauguin saw colours flat as we find them applied in Indian miniatures. Like Gauguin, she simplified her forms and the outlines of figures. *Brahmacharis* is the quintessential representation of the Gauguin lesson: the painting has acted as a paradigmatic influence on Indian art. The work is best described in Sher-Gil's own words. 'The other picture,' (she wrote to her critic friend, Karl Khandalavala, she was in two minds whether to call this picture *Discussion* or *Brahmacharis*)

> . . . has a far simpler colour scheme. The deep red ochre background (in parts verging on a blackish red) is uniform throughout, the awful white patch, due to some bad lighting arrangement I presume, on the part of the photographer, does not exist. The figures are all clothed in white dhotis. The variations of white, although all of them different, really, are so subtle as to give an impression of <u>uniformity</u> throughout. My chief object in painting this picture was <u>uniformity</u>: a 'leit motif' of forms and postures. Although I have brought in a variety of colour in the flesh tints (the

> figures from left to right are deep green, orange-brown, light yellowish, burnt sienna and ochre colours, respectively), they don't disturb the calm of the picture – I was anything but calm, though, while I was painting it! I scratched the head of the central figure about six times, and struggled and struggled before I got it as I wanted it), not to speak of the rest! But don't you think I have learnt something from Indian painting & sculpture?[2]

This 'something' from Indian painting came from what may be called inner experience. And inner experience, Nietzsche teaches us, enters our consciousness only when it has found a language that the individual understands. Sher-Gil understood what represented core Indian sensibility and was able to express what was new in *Brahmacharis* in the language of Gauguin and of Indian miniatures. The new now had the stamp of a style to which Gauguin must [would] have paid handsome accolades. What is more, with *Brahmacharis* came her liberation; the fixed forms, representing her schooling in Paris, were broken up: images now signified one thing and, at the same time, another.

What did she demand of herself while painting *Brahmacharis*? To overcome her time in herself, to become 'timeless'. Earlier to this painting, she was a child of her time; though she was already engaged in the hardest struggle against decadence which, through her schooling in Paris, had entered her soul. She wrote:

> Were our artists to seek inspiration from modern Western art – just as the moderns discovered a new means of self-expression through the study of Eastern sculpture and painting, not only would they infuse new life into Indian painting but it would help them really to understand the underlying principles of the ancient art of their country.[3]

Her role in shaping Indian sensibility towards modernism is very much like that of Cezanne's. Like Cezanne, she knew what she wanted to do. And this is what marks her out as a genius. For example, Cezanne knew that there was something wrong with Delacroix, and set about correcting it in his work. Similarly, she knew what was right about Gauguin and what was 'wrong' with flat colours in Indian miniatures.

The point she sought to drive home was that art is a system: paintings owe more to other paintings than to wishful theorizing on art. The truth of the proposition can be illustrated with the example of Constable [late eighteenth century] who saw the English landscape in terms of Gainsborough [early 18th century]. But what about Gainsborough himself? Well, he saw the lowland scenery of East Anglia in terms of Dutch paintings of 16th–17th centuries. And from where did the Dutch get their vocabulary, their inspiration? One can go on investigating in this manner. But we have learnt nothing from Sher-Gil. Perhaps seeing art in terms of art history as a method of clarifying the intent of the artist is not for us. Like the mythical innocent eye, even criticism in India prefers to remain innocent. Perhaps some kind of an inbuilt distrust of the West comes in our way of drawing proper lessons from Sher-Gil's example.

The painters of the 1940s, for one, did not learn anything from Sher-Gil. They kept working with the wash technique much favoured by the Bengal School painters. Some took to tempera, which the colour miniaturists used, while some attempted to provide a fine art context to folk forms; it resulted in Kalighat *pats* being revived by Jamini Roy. His style became an instant success because in the 1940s, his was the most sought-after work by Western tourists. It is a pity that till now no serious study has been made of Sher-Gil's work to bring out a unity between her oeuvre and Gauguin's, to allow us to know how each helps to explain the qualities of the other.

Editor's Notes

1 Amrita Sher-Gil in a letter to her father, as cited by Salman Rushdie in his Foreword to *Amrita Sher-Gil: a self-portrait in letters and writings*, introduced, annotated and edited by Vivan Sundaram, vol. 1, New Delhi: Tulika Books, 2010, p. xi.

2 Amrita Sher-Gil in a letter to Karl Khandalavala, 15 June 1937, in *Amrita Sher-Gil: a self-portrait in letters and writings*, vol. 1, p. 379.

3 Amrita Sher-Gil, 'Indian Art Today', *The Indian Listener*, 19 August 1941, in *Amrita Sher-Gil: a self-portrait in letters and writings*, vol. 2, p. 731.

5

REVOLUTIONARY MIDWIFE

Review of a major Jamini Roy exhibition held in New Delhi in 1990

'Artscape', *The Economic Times*, New Delhi, 17 December 1990

Galerie Romain Rolland in the capital recently mounted the works of Jamini Roy, our version of the European avant-garde. Roy was not a pale version of what existed in Europe during the closing decades of the nineteenth century, but distinctly Indian and in many ways still relevant for the contemporary art scene. He was an artist who thought art was greater than how one lived. And he did not paint for a living. He wanted to paint in a manner which was new, something that no one had done before; something indulged in for personal satisfaction.

The exhibition of the works of such a painter should have been mounted on a larger scale with attention to detail. Instead, what we were offered was merely a 'put-together' effort. However, a talk by Siddhartha Roy that accompanied the exhibition compensated for the poor display. Siddhartha Roy spoke at the Alliance Francaise auditorium on the influence of the early Bengal School of painting on Jamini Roy. But the talk show was on conventional lines; it failed to bring home the relevance of Jamini Roy for our times.

Jamini Roy did not submit to the demands of any academy; he preferred to walk alone and quietly worked in the oblivion of his studio. He was a lonely, desperate man in love with his marginalized existence. He had no heroes to follow. He chose to work as a plate retoucher in some obscure studio at Allahabad but did not do any commissioned portraiture for money. He liked the anonymity of a commercial artist doing the job of drawing and painting greeting cards for a local trader in Calcutta for a payment of sixty paise per hundred cards.

Of the many commercial jobs he did, one that he enjoyed most was to apply colour on cheap woodcuts used for making greeting cards. What he wanted to do was art with a capital A: art as a form of challenge for which he was willing to suffer privations and public neglect. He knew that his was a lone voice of dissent against the revivalist tendencies of the Bengal School of art; his dissension was seconded by Amrita Sher-Gil who appreciated his work.

The Bengal School, in the opinion of Amrita Sher-Gil, was responsible for stagnation in Indian painting because it was miles away from the original sources of Indian aesthetics despite its claim of having Indian miniatures as its source of inspiration. The painters of the Bengal School developed a

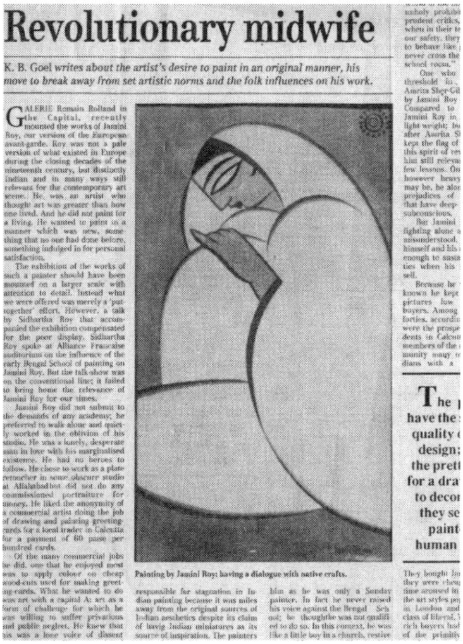

Revolutionary midwife

K. B. Goel writes about the artist's desire to paint in an original manner, his move to break away from set artistic norms and the folk influences on his work.

GALERIE Romain Rolland in the Capital, recently mounted the works of Jamini Roy, our version of the European avant-garde. Roy was not a pale version of what existed in Europe during the closing decades of the nineteenth century, but distinctly Indian and in many ways still relevant for the contemporary art scene. He was an artist who thought art was greater than how one lived. And he did not paint for a living. He wanted to paint in a manner which was new, something that no one had done before, something indulged in for personal satisfaction.

The exhibition of the works of such a painter should have been mounted on a larger scale with attention to detail. Instead what we were offered was merely a 'put-together' effort. However, a talk by Sidhartha Roy that accompanied the exhibition compensated for the poor display. Sidhartha Roy spoke at Alliance Francaise auditorium on the influence of the early Bengal School of painting on Jamini Roy. But the talk-show was on the conventional line; it failed to bring home the relevance of Jamini Roy for our times.

Jamini Roy did not submit to the demands of any academy; he preferred to walk alone and quietly worked in the oblivion of his studio. He was a lonely, desperate man in love with his marginalised existence. He had no heroes to follow. He chose to work as a plate-retoucher in some obscure studio at Allahabad but did not do any commissioned portraiture for money. He liked the anonymity of a commercial artist doing the job of drawing and painting greeting-cards for a local trader in Calcutta for a payment of 60 paise per hundred cards.

Of the many commercial jobs he did, one that he enjoyed most was to apply colour on cheap wood-cuts used for making greeting-cards. What he wanted to do was art with a capital A: art as a form of challenge for which he was willing to suffer privations and public neglect. He knew that his was a lone voice of dissent

Painting by Jamini Roy: having a dialogue with native crafts.

responsible for stagnation in Indian painting because it was miles away from the original sources of Indian aesthetics despite its claim of havig Indian miniatures as its source of inspiration. The painters

him as he was only a Sunday painter. In fact he never raised his voice against the Bengal School; he thoughthe was not qualified to do so. In this context, he was like a little boy in a church, restive

liking for Indian miniatures. The poet Rabindranath Tagore, in his own manner, wanted to correct the distortion in the thinking of the Bengal School painters, but he did not succeed; for no one listened to him as he was only a Sunday painter. In fact, he never raised his voice against the Bengal School; he thought he was not qualified to do so. In this context, he was like a little boy in a church, restive but unable to say anything for fear of committing a sacrilege. 'Let us take heart and make daring experiments,' the poet-painter appealed to the painters working in Santiniketan. 'Venture out into the open road in the face of all risks, go through experience in the great world of the human mind, defying unholy prohibitions preached by prudent critics, laughing at them when in their tender solicitude for our safety, they all ask our artists to behave like good children and never cross the threshold of their school room.'[1]

One who dared cross the threshold in the 1930s was Amrita Sher-Gil. She was followed by Jamini Roy and George Keyt. Compared to Amrita Sher-Gil, Jamini Roy in those days was a lightweight; but it was he, who after Amrita Sher-Gil was gone, kept the flag of revolt flying. And this spirit of revolt is what makes him still relevant for us; it has a few lessons – one of which is that however heavyweight an artist may be, he alone cannot fight the prejudices of those institutions that have deep roots in a nation's subconscious.

But Jamini Roy did not mind fighting alone and suffered being misunderstood. He believed in himself and his cause and that was enough to sustain him in the 1940s when his pictures began to sell. Because he was relatively unknown, he kept the prices of his pictures low which attracted buyers. Among his buyers then according to W.C. Archer, were the prosperous British residents in Calcutta and other rich members of the cosmopolitan community, many of whom were Indians with a Western outlook. They bought Jamini Roys because they were cheap and at the same time aroused in them nostalgia for the art styles popular in those days in London and Paris. This new class of liberal, Western, educated, rich buyers had heard of the love of the primitive as one of the dominant tendencies in modern arts; for them the primitive represented the heart of the Jamini Roys. Among the many high-society admirers of his work was the wife of the then Bengal Governor, Sir Casey. This also contributed to Roy's popularity: one has to consult the old issues of *Anand Bazaar Patrika* to find out how nationalist Bengali bhadralok hated Jamini Roy for his popularity among the Western bourgeoisie. He became a legend in his lifetime; indeed, innumerable romantic myths were built around his life and career.

The greatness of Jamini Roy consists in this: he saw, as no painter could see before him, the false traps Ajanta and Indian miniatures had laid for the contemporary painter. George Keyt is an example; he failed because he could not make the tail ends of the east and west meet in his painting. Jamini Roy, like Gauguin, turned to his home environment for inspiration; but, unlike Gauguin, he was not in love with the primitive; Gauguin's style, for instance, remained unaffected by what he saw and painted when he made the discovery of primitivism.

Jamini Roy, on the contrary, was a product of a dialogue with his native crafts; his work calls attention to the folk sources which were as far wide as the *patuas* of Kalighat, the sculpture of Bankura and the *kanthas* of the rural housewives. If Gaugin's work is soaked in passion, Jamini Roys are cool and highly decorative; they lack passion. Unlike Gaugin, he did not go far enough in working out the aesthetics of the folk idiom; instead he got stuck with its decorative intent, introducing for the first time in Indian painting arbitrary colours and art nouveau patterns.

The Jamini Roys have the spread-out quality of a textile design; they are the prettiest things for a drawing room to decorate with: indeed so overtly decorative are they that they seem to be painted by a human machine and not by a human hand which has trained itself in the folksy ways of making art. And the result was paradoxical: he destroyed the Bengal School and drew attention to a past which was equally romantic.

His influence on the painters of the period of transition to modern art is sizeable: one cannot imagine the birth of K.K. Hebbar, Shiavax Chavda, B.C. Sanyal and, to a lesser extent, Sailoz Mukherjea without the midwife role of Jamini Roy and his discoveries of the effects and techniques of folk ways of making pictures. His contribution to the evolution of Indian paintings is a reminder that what is permanent in a Jamini Roy painting is the feeling that decorative qualities in Indian art – the one single element that dominated the Indian painting scene until the mid-Fifties – represent the signature of a modern Indian style. It was forged by collaborative efforts and needs no justifying.

Editor's Note

1 Rabindranath Tagore in a lecture given in Santiniketan in 1921, titled 'The Meaning of Art', published by Visva-Bharati. The lecture was reissued as a booklet by the Lalit Kala Akademi, New Delhi, in 1969.

6

A GOLDEN CROP OF IMAGES

An assessment of Ramkinkar Baij's art and the innovation he brought to Indian sculpture on the occasion of his first major retrospective in New Delhi

'Artscape', *The Economic Times*, New Delhi, 28 November 1990

Ramkinkar Vaij[1] has, at last, got the attention of the official art establishment: 260 of his works – paintings and sculptures – are on display at the National Gallery of Modern Art, New Delhi. The exhibition that is on till the end of November is likely to be extended. Considering the fact that the exhibition pays homage to the solitary genius India has produced in the field of visual arts in this century, the opening ceremony was a small affair with hardly 50 people attending it.

The exhibition was inadequately advertised, the invitations failed to reach on time and the accompanying talk show was missing. The least the National Gallery could have done was to screen the film on Ramkinkar made by Ritwik Ghatak. This neglect seemed to be a part of the larger conspiracy, for, all his life Ramkinkar lived in comparative oblivion.

Ramkinkar Vaij was never a part of the bandwagon of the Bengal School of Art. In the sixty years he spent at Santiniketan, he remained an outsider. As an alien element representing a form of moral nihilism, he remained an insubstantial influence on his students. He merely did his duty in the spirit of errands. The errands were run not for others; they were to protect himself from the stagey acts the community of puritans was fond of enacting. The puritans had turned all the footlights on themselves and spoke from the pedestal: the pedestal called Gurudev and Master Moshai.[2]

The pedestal was a discovery of the clerical language which the community of puritans have perfected to the Euclidean universality of mathematical truth. Surrounding the pedestal were complicated ceremonial rituals for expressing cultish affinities. Everything depended on seeing one's position in terms of one's destiny: he who did not acknowledge this remained an outcast. In an India still struggling to discover its roots of visual culture, Santinketan became a grand symbol of culture and spoke with the academic authority of a university.

Into this closed world of Santiniketan, Ramkinkar entered as a village boy with the status of an OBC. He was unacceptable, although the academia was a divided house and the gurus lived as separate cult figures. His was essentially an alien presence, for he had no guru; nor was he in need of one. But according to one of the songs of the Santiniketan mythology, he was groomed by Master Moshai and Nandalal Bose. Prof. Sankho Chaudhuri admits as much when he says that 'Ramkinkar walked out of the puritan and elite society of Santiniketan.' If you are not a fellow-traveller, if you do not belong to the brotherhood of the faithful, you remain an outsider.

'In more ways than one the prodigal never returned home,' according to Sankho Chaudhuri. 'His roots found all the food they needed in the dry rubble of Bolpur and produced a golden crop of images in sculpture.' And his coloured sketches of the sunburnt torsos of the Santhals are like the songs of mendicant Bauls. They are an expression of an unquiet soul that braved all and said nothing. Standing before them, the grand symbolism withers; the riot of allegorical forms dies down. The work is perceived as a single phenomenon: there is no evidence of a division between springtime and time of the vanished glories. There is organic connectedness: 'His art seems to have sprung spontaneously,' not from knowledge 'but from the irrational sources of power.'

The irrational was expressed in the balance of priorities. He found his rustic ears responding to Western music: he read Shaw and Nietzsche, but he found nothing of value in the Santiniketan environment; living and learning seemed an unending errand into wilderness since he had nothing to learn in terms of discovering the actual 'tooth' of the canvas.

He shared the same fate as Gaganendranath Tagore. Gaganendranath, a brother of Abinindranath, failed because he dared to attempt an extreme Western style: he experimented with cubism between 1923 and 1928 and produced works that were inspired variations on the works of Braque and Picasso. These works were rejected without a second look because they were thought to be un-Indian. Havellian aesthetics has made the discovery of modern art by an Indian into an exercise in triviality. The prevailing tone of active hostility to whatever seemed an imitation of a Western mode of art is evident from the following semi-humorous passage written by O.C. Gangoly in 1922:

> Some of my friends have a nodding acquaintance with Massacio and probably some of them are at the present moment balancing El Greco and Cezanne, Holbein with Anup Chatar[3] and Chinese grotesque sculptures with the daring creations of Boccioni and Brancusi. I am here concerned only with the catholicity of modern Indian aesthetics. We find new thrills in Maurice Denis and Pierre Bonnard. *La Danseuse* of Van Dongen gave me shocks which I never received from any bronze figure of Nataraja. Rousseau's *Centenary of Independence* has for me transcended the 'rasa' of Botticelli's *Spring*. I have a secret sympathy with the latest Parisian craze over Negro sculpture. I can recall the new 'rupollasa'[4] which I experienced when they brought to me their Polynesian image when I first set foot on Java-dwipa. I can therefore sympathize with Picasso, Matisse and Derain in their first thrills with the Tami masks from New Guinea and share their

> new joys with the Kilamantan charms from Borneo. We are not forever chained to the beauties of Persian carpets. We can slowly respond to the charms of Peruvian textiles.[5]

That is to say, a bronze figure of Nataraja was a self-declaration of aesthetic ends towards which Indian sensibility should bend itself. And Master Moshai, lodged in his Santiniketan monastery and dazzled by his own light, insisted on the sophisticated 'knowingness' about the roots of Havellian inspiration. In a similar vein, [art historian] Herbert Read has argued in favour of the Havellian aesthetic. 'We cannot escape,' he says, 'our mental climates, for they are in a literal sense the creation of our prevailing winds and the chemistry of our soils. It is inconceivable that English art should decisively be influenced by Indian art or French art by African art.' In short, his argument betrays a romantic bent of mind in asserting that art is an expression of a regional sensibility and its 'style of expression determined, we must assume, by ethnic and geographic factors'.[6]

In talking about the conditioning of art's inner life by ethnic and geographic factors, one of the central truths of aesthetic judgement is forgotten, which is that the meaning of a painting is another painting. As Graf Yorck has put it: 'Comparison is always aesthetic, it is always concerned with the form'.

One cannot explain Ramkinkar's work by the comparative method, for he is not even a pale version of the European avant-garde: he painted like Matisse did without having ever met him. He was an Indian growth. Whatever he learnt, he assimilated by making his imagination an agent for creating a 'second nature' out of the materials he used. He invented his own rules for doing art, but never advertised his powers of invention. Perhaps he was born with a genie since the word genie is derived from genius: genie is a spirit given to a man at birth.

Editor's Notes

1 The spelling Vaij for Baij, used by K.B. Goel, is a frequent form of address for the artist in publications and art-historical references in both Bangla and Hindi from the 1930s.

2 The reference is to Rabindranath Tagore and Nandalal Bose, the founder of Santiniketan and the first principal of its art department, Kala Bhavana, respectively.

3 Anup Chatar: miniature painter of the late Mughal period. Holbein: sixteenth-century painter renowned as a portraitist.

4 Aesthetic term connoting thrill, pleasure when encountering an art object.

5 Possible source: the art journal *Rupam*, edited by Gangoly, that routinely featured his writings.

6 Herbert Read, *Contemporary British Art*, London: Penguin, 1951, pp. 38–39.

7

THE LAST PAINTER-REVOLUTIONARY

A reflection on the work of one of the leaders of the Mexican modernist revolution, the celebrated muralist David Siqueiros, on the occasion of his death

Patriot Magazine, New Delhi, 13 January 1974

David Alfaro Siqueiros, the last of Mexico's three great revolutionary artists, died on 6 January of cancer. He was given the highest funeral honours, his body lay in state for twenty-four hours at the Palace of Fine Arts in downtown Mexico City and was buried in the Dolores cemetery. The three great artists produced the greatest national school of painting since the Italian Renaissance. Under the leadership of Siqueiros, a new style of painting developed which was independent of contemporary developments in the school of Paris. These artists, particularly, Siqueiros and [Jose Clemente] Orozco (since [Diego] Rivera had remained safely abroad until the danger was over), created a monumental style as compelling in power as religion.

The significance of the new Mexican style was that it was the first humanist revolt against academism in painting. This revolt was very different from what was happening in Europe - a mere formalist revolt to be seen in the works of Gauguin, Seurat and Picasso. These two revolutionary artists who participated in the Mexican Revolution of 1917 were indeed far away from Europe although in 1913 Mexico had discovered the modern art of Europe at the Armory show and Alfredo Ramos Martinez in Mexico had begun instructing the technique of impressionism in the open air [*plein air*].

THEORETICIAN

The mural renaissance of 1922 was a new style of painting; it was far enough from Europe to borrow what was needed for the style to grow. Being the product of the social revolution, its basic direction was clear. In fact, it was Siqueiros who gave it its grammar as Orozco was then in the apprentice stage. Siqueiros led the art students and stoned the professors of art and this resulted in his arrest: the demonstration was against 'a new French system of teaching children to draw abstractly'. Orozco stood rather aloof from the revolutionary events of 1910 to 1920 as he had lost the use of his left arm and in part his eyesight as a result of an experiment with gunpowder. Siqueiros was a communist, more concerned with making the socialist message popular among artists: he was more of a theoretician than a painter.

Siqueros's role in the revolution is portrayed by Malraux in his novel *Men's Hope*. The painter-hero, Lopez, tells his sceptical friends:

> What have I been crying for these last fifteen years? A renaissance of art. See? Everything here is ready for it. That wall over there for instance. All those fools go trotting their shadows over it, and never give it a look. We have such a mob of painters, they sprout between the paving stones. . . . Yes, sir, we'll give our painters bare white walls. 'Get work! Draw! Paint! The people who are going to pass this way want you to tell them something – see? You can't fake an art that means something to the masses when you've nothing to say to them. . . .' Art isn't a matter of subjects. There's no great revolutionary art, and why? Because they're always wrangling about its tendencies rather than its function.

NOT WORKS OF ART BUT ART

Lopez, who not only shares Siqueiros's passion for politicalizing art but also shares some of his characteristics, is, in effect, telling his colleague in the revolution that we have been rating works of art too high: it was not true that Siqueiros (as portrayed by Lopez) had no faith in art – 'Not in works of art but art'. And that explains the absence of revolutionary art because the artists quarrel about its tendencies, its modes, its formal justifications, but forget about its function. Lopez therefore asks his colleague to do as they please: he would allow them 'fixing it up your own way' and for a certain amount of freedom from revolutionary themes. What he says sounds like Siqueiros telling the American artists at the 1935 Artists' Congress who had worked with him in his studio in Union Square:

> It's unthinkable that, given people who have something to say and people who are willing to listen, we won't create a style. Just give them a free hand, give them all the air-brushes and spray guns, all the modern contraptions they can want, and, after that, a chunk of modelling clay – and then you will see.

Siqueiros's central message is this: the artist should free himself from the one-dimensionality of European painting modes, and it is only then that the art could be saved in the moral sense. He had irrepressible faith in man's creative instinct. He wanted artists to shun innovation – that doctrine of style which runs in a straight line: the younger generation artists are forced to innovate in order to achieve a breakthrough and in the end innovating something that is wholly their own. It has become difficult for an artist to free himself from this prison, the inventive preoccupations of his age. So, his advice was to shun, first of all, the artful studio constructions and the fractured clowns symbolizing individual private terror.

And such lofty aloofness, even disdain, Siqueiros and Orozco had for the

European masters that when a projected contemporary show of French art was to be organized in Mexico City, Orozco asked painter Tamayo: 'Who is Picasso?' And after seeing the Picassos, he said in a rather apologetic tone: 'Picasso . . . Drawings. Figure copied or so it seems from Greek vases seen in museums . . . he distorts, disquiets, wounds, impresses, repulses, only to suddenly attract forcefully. One cannot forget him . . . Picasso is like a glassful of water, cool, limpid, but oh! so desirable . . .'. He added that appreciating French art is like going into a garden with a girlfriend for the five-o'clock tea. 'A drawing room with good society, good drinks and a good bed. As for us, we are the revolutionaries, the cursed ones, the hungry ones.' About the impressionists, for instance, the master has said: 'Impressionists are increasingly hard to suffer. I agree they have a place in art history, but do they have any place whatsoever in Art [sic]?'

No wonder Siqueiros and his friend Orozco remained indifferent to landscape and nature; they were contemptuous of the decorative in art or adapting murals to architecture. They discovered El Greco's baroque extravagance and re-invented folk forms of Mexican art using the drawing methods of Goya and Daumier. During the revolution, when other Mexican artists had betrayed their revolutionary leader, Siqueiros, only Orozco was there on the scene, painting prostitutes, drunken half-breeds, and generals gambling with government funds. He even painted the incorruptible Zapata,[1] and it was a caricature because, according to the master, 'everything was the same and remained the same as before the uprising'. The subject of their art was the human body, tortured by ignoble ambition or warped by disease, as the vehicle of expressing rage and pity in the face of man's inhumanity. They were the 'insider' artists who were moved by the human condition and drawn to values outside art to examine them in terms of art.

POLITICAL COMMITMENT

What mattered most to Siqueiros is political commitment. He said 'a truly great artist has always a truly great political conviction: the greater the conviction the greater the art'. Siqueiros, however, was tolerant when the new generation of Mexican painters abandoned him and the tradition of mural art he had inaugurated as these young artists were preoccupied with 'formal problems independent of social content'. He yet believed that they were still sympathizers of revolution. But Siqueiros's influence is still felt and young artists who want an escape from bourgeois influence look to him and his writings. The problem of self-identity which had become such a pressing issue for the Indian painters of the Sixties is perhaps more compelling today than it was for the American painters like Jackson Pollock who was one of his favourite students at his Square studio. The search for self identity with the Americans had been a live issue until Pollock invented Action painting. What Paul Burlin, a highly sophisticated painter, said in 1950 sounds very much like what Swaminathan is saying today. This is what he wrote:

> . . . My introduction to the art of the Indian stirred up strange conflicts. I was ignorant of the Indian and knew nothing of his work. . . . Mayan architecture and sculpture overwhelmed me. I wished to understand these configurations that were indigenous to the character of the land. How could I translate them? . . . Why was a bowl decorated in this abstract fashion? By contrast, all other picture making seemed like storytelling trivia. These disturbing factors, none of which had anything to do with "representation" were the vague beginnings of an aesthetic credo . . .

LESSONS FOR THE THIRD

The great Mexican has taught the artists of the Third World that if they want to free themselves of European values they should plumb their own heritage and integrate with their society. Certainly there would have been no Jackson Pollock without his schooling in the Mexican mural art he learnt at the Siqueiros studio. As a student, he had been a radical – mentioned in his school report as 'a rotten rebel from Russia'. While at school, he attended communist meetings and had read the manifesto which the three Mexican masters had issued. Siqueiros told Pollock that on the traditions of Europe he could not develop an original style nor could the new art take root in America in the aboriginal traditions represented by the remains of ancient Indian peoples. The new painting and sculpture should follow the Mexican path. And the highest, the most logical, the purest and strongest form of painting is the mural. In this form alone, it is one with the other arts – with all the others. It is, too, the most disinterested form, for it cannot be made a matter of private gain: it cannot be hidden away for the benefit of a certain privileged few. It is for the people, it is for all.

Orozco and Rivera had made Siqueiros's figure so popular that when he was exiled from his native Mexico and arrived in Los Angeles to settle there, he was warmly received by the movie colony. He made a giant mural outside the film producer Dudley Murphy's house which was a mixture of fairyland Hollywood and revolution: an essay into Hollywood venality and most of his admirers were rather disappointed. Siqueiros's presence gave a new impetus to American art. When he went to Chouinard[2] he formed a team consisting of himself and six assistants who were called 'Mural Block painters'. The murals this painter team did have been described by critic-historian Dore Ashton thus:

> The surface at his disposal was small and irregular; an outer wall six and nine metres broken by three windows and a door. As the cement surface cracked almost immediately, Siqueiros decided to use spray guns, used for applying quick-drying paint to furniture and cars.[3]

Siqueiros's career has been divided between revolutionary politics and painting. He was always busy organizing movements, issuing manifestos while his friend Orozco devoted himself exclusively to mural painting. At the age of fifteen, he [Sequieros] joined San Carlos Academy and left painting the next year and joined Venustiano Carranza's forces in the Mexican revolution. He was not only a good soldier but a good military strategist, and later wrote a book on guerilla warfare recognized as a text book in the military college of Mexico. From 1919 to 1922 he was in Spain as Cultural Attache and wrote his famous *Manifesto of Mural Painting*. On his return to Mexico, he organized a Painters' Syndicate, the government-sponsored group of painters, and executed a number of murals in the National Preparatory school. The 1922 mural movement was launched but he was so busy organizing the Artists' syndicate that the first mural he undertook was not completed for several years.

The story goes that one night someone finished the mural for him. When Siqueiros saw the mural the next morning, he could not believe it: it was done exactly in the manner he would have done it. He told Satish Gujral, who was his student in Mexico in the early Fifties, that that was one occasion when he believed in a miracle. His friend Orozco would often tease him for that, often quarrelling with him for wasting his time in political work. When the 1922 mural manifesto was written, he took it to Orozco, who was working on a mural scaffold. On Orozco's insistence, he read out the manifesto which meant almost shouting from the ground. When Siqueiros was able to persuade his friend to come down from the scaffold and sign the document which was to be issued jointly in their name, since Rivera was away in Europe, Orozco signed it with the brush.

Since 1922, until his arrest in 1930 and exile from Mexico, Siqueiros was deeply involved in left-wing politics, helping to organize labour unions, publishing labour papers and attending international syndicalist and communist congresses in Moscow, Buenos Aires, Montevideo and New York. Most of his work was done in jail in 1930 to 1931 when he was confined within the city of Taxco where he did a number of woodcuts and lithographs. After time in New York and Los Angeles, in 1936, he went to Spain and joined the Loyalists in the Spanish Civil War.

The giant mural that Siqueiros completed a few years ago at the Ministry of Education, Mexico, magnified the human material into an image of universal significance that makes Picasso's *Guernica* look almost like a game with cutouts. The human images, far from losing their identity as in the *Guernica* painting, become more personal as they become more heroic. He was able to create a mirage of objective art drawing many painting conventions from the pop and op art of the Sixties in America. However, few critics talk about his inventive methods – the use of airbrush for instance, which has become now a common painting tool. Similarly, he invented new methods of creating depth and popularized a theory of dynamic symmetry, which most painters of the Seventies use today. Through dynamic symmetry a new tactile sensation can be created which is as powerful as one feels before a sculpture: it was also a new method to measure the depth dimensions created by the relationship between static and dynamic forms. There could be no subjectless object for Siqueiros: mere form was simply not interesting enough to engage his attention. He had grown up in a milieu where sound doctrine had to be the basis of a painting – at least the intention should be visible. Otherwise, painting becomes another form of entertainment.

Although Siqueiros had been a communist all his life, he fell back on traditional Christian iconography, but this was done to involve the viewer as he was more familiar with those Christian symbols. In one mural, he painted Christ destroying his cross in despair because his followers, and most of all painters, have misused the symbol. In another mural, Christ emerges from a landscape of tanks, shattered idols and axe in hand, the right fist clenched like the destroyer of Michelangelo's *Last Judgement*. These are the images of spiritual truth. Siqueiros, in fact, played the same role as Michelangelo did for the Renaissance.

Editor's Notes

1 Revolutionary leader, Emiliano Zapata.

2 Neil Murphy Chouinard was an American artist who set up an art school in the 1920s in Los Angeles called the Chouinard School of Art, and which gained immense popularity and state support over the next decades. When Siqueiros was in America in the 1930s, he formed a collective of mural painters and the first mural he made, *Street Meeting* (later painted over and effaced for being communist), was for the Chouinard School of Art.

3 Dore Ashton, *The New York School: A Cultural Reckoning*, University of California Press, 1972, p. 41.

8

AN EXPERIENCE NOT FOR SHARING

An article in memoriam of the artist and teacher Sailoz Mukherjea, written for the catalogue of a commemorative exhibition of his works held in New Delhi in 1986

Exhibition catalogue, New Delhi, 1986

The art of the Fifties was dominated by the naughty children who thought they could play at trains without seeing a locomotive, and they played at trains as most children do, without seeing them. It was a make-believe world more artificial than that of children who have seen a real locomotive, without having seen a train and playing at trains for Indian painters. It was a necessary colonial projection of modernism. As if to convince themselves, some (like Souza and Raza, for instance) left their land to look at real engines, and they did not return - such was their fascination with the machine. As expatriates, their playing at trains seemed more authentic to the local artists; they rushed with accolades to signify their approval. For those who have not seen the real, locomotive works of the expatriates seemed as mysterious as the colonnaded space of a Greek temple.

They turned imitators and imported the Western engine by imagination through the work of the expatriates; they reconstructed it according to their mechanical insights and, in doing this, they displayed a refined sense of their knowledge of mechanics. They could make the engine run and with the help of their expatriate brothers could even check on the engine's working. This engine never saw decomposition as everyone was engaged in the task of repairing it. The result was death-like repetitions of the game of train playing, whether the name of the game was abstract expressionism or some other pontification of the mechanical.

One painter who never joined his contemporaries in playing at trains was Sailoz Mukherjea, and that was considered an act of great betrayal, for he refused to build an indigenous engine even though he had seen the real locomotive, having lived in Paris for two years in the late 1930s. Sailoz was a born rebel for he was in love with himself doing his own thing; in his life as a painter, there was no room for disaffection, deprivations or any form of internal darkness. Neither did he care like his contemporaries for the ways of polite society, of which art has now become a drawing-room decoration: bourgeois culture came to India after independence, as some rightly believe.

He lived in a time that was his, of small laughter between long afternoon walks in Connaught Place - which stretched like a child's dream - and the warm reality of a wet evening. In those moments, an encounter with him might confound the actual with the fanciful, for the ultimate vision was the dialogue with the fairies for a soul growing heavy with loneliness. That was an experience as important as the non-practical, disinterested but sympathetic attention his painting demanded. Attention paid, let us say, to words in poetry that carry a certain atmosphere within them; the mind lost in exploring some half-shades of meaning. Or, imagine two lovers talking, for the referents are internal to love's grammar.

Love's grammar does not need the glitter of linguistic correlates; it is transparent. Like music, his art was about communicating pure experience. All that he demanded of his viewers was a contemplative seeing of a castle in a cloud. Which means that he or she functions as part of the original picture for it is only this way that he or she can experience its stillness.

That is to say, he demanded of his viewers, eyes that were capable of having deep experience, eyes eager to learn that in confronting his paintings he or she is face to face with knowledge as mysterious as the ear's knowledge of a tune: an experience which is not for sharing. Standing before his painting, you cannot even speak to yourself. For those sensitive to the music of sight, what Sailoz offered was the unity of image and its signification, a sense of bewitchment that waits for the redeeming world. The redemption never comes.

The experience of a Sailoz painting is always more than what a spectator's cultural screen will allow him to have: we experience an increase of our being as we linger over it, our attention never knowing any shifts in the direction of meaning. What we experience is a fire burning. This fire illuminates the darkness within me as I remember Sailoz's *Forest* he painted a year before his death. It was exhibited at his last one-man show at Dhoomimal's. He now seems beyond the reach of time, being a journeyman. For him, painting was no goal, only a path across the field. With ethical behavior one's act is either good or bad: so with painting, either it is well painted or it is not. It seems almost an alien horizon now – a horizon which covered vast areas of unit spaces into which he would urge us to be walkers-indefatigable.

9

A POST-MODERN SYMBOL

Review of K.G. Subramanyan's exhibition of miniature paintings inspired by the Mughal painter, Mansur

'Artscape', *The Economic Times*, New Delhi, date unknown, *c.* 1990s

K.G. Subramanyan, whose works in miniature format (done on primed paper in gouache) are displayed at the Centre for Contemporary Art, New Delhi is a teacher of artists; a status no painter can claim since the death of Nandalal Bose. After Bose, only Subramanyan assumed the role of teacher and savant whose influence on the art scene of the Seventies and Eighties is comparable to that of Bose's during the 1930s and early 1940s. It will be adequate to draw a parallel in terms of the symbolic equation between these two teacher-savants.

Today, Subramanyan has become the true symbol of the post-modern condition, the symbolic equation between the role of a savant and the uncertainties that engulf him as a painter. In the context of the 1990s, this is seen in constant translation of the truth embodied in the symbol. And the theory of the symbol implies as much: as a constant translation the symbol, read as a representation of the unconscious, implicates a static model for there is a constant drive towards identification of the sources of the unconscious with the symbol. This is the kind of identification Dora had to go through during analysis by Freud and suffered much because identification with the analyst obstructed her emotional progress. Perhaps Subramanyan did not suffer the way Dora suffered, because he had a similar relationship with Nandalal Bose, his teacher at Santiniketan. He was saved because his identification was not total and hence he could cut out the process of infinite substitutions by replacing the need for the subconscious symbol by another idea. He split the symbol from within and became free from the schema's powerful set of conventions.

Modernism undermined his links with the symbolic order as represented by Santiniketan – that view of modernism was very much about the unintelligibility of experience as it was actually felt to occur. He embraced the implied insecurity of modernism; a more recent response to this insecurity has been christened 'post-modernism' because modernism failed in its attempts at devising a total aesthetic erasure of the symbolic. The post-modern exists in the real time of experience, which is open-ended and basically incomplete; it believes in the manifest intelligibility of surfaces. Subramanyan admits as much: 'As you grow old, the world grows over you, becoming more precious. Its open face is its own mystery.

You need not seek it within.' For, according to him, the fact of it being a mystery is the fable. Which is to say that claims of originality are as much a fiction as the origin of this earth – originality conceived as an absolute beginning, the moment before which nothing happened?

'The common is not so common. It is a simple enough vision, but it reconciles the near and the far. You cannot catch it with a standard sleight of hand,' says Subramanyan. So he is given to inventing devices. This long background is necessary in order to understand the devised technique of this great devisor. The works displayed provide an eloquent insight into the grammar of post-modernism according to the artist who identifies modernism with 'that push towards purism, that sense of creative exclusiveness or starting on a clean slate . . . the great wave of modernism is over'. The slate was never as clean as modernism claims it was. For, as Subramanyan says, 'What you do is never so novel except at the time of doing,' because at the end of the process one meets only anxiety, the fear that what one has done might have been done already by others.

The source of the anxiety is this; it is the same self that one falls back upon, the same sources of creativity. What is different are the moments of transition, the temporal reorganization of the past experience. A self that has identified itself with the present looks at the past as a work of memory. The present is always a source of anxiety, the awareness of being in a condition of instability, the past, a source of stability.

The stability-instability syndrome has its fable-like weave in the midlife crisis, of which the ideal representation is Samuel Beckett's career. A way out of the crisis situation for him was to resort to autobiographical writing. The reading of the past became, in the new mode, a method for achieving stability in the present. Reading and writing became a correlated activity, a form of dialogue between two versions of the authorial self. Like Beckett, for whom reading meant considering or explaining something obscure or mysterious, Subramanyan looked at the works constituting his tradition. He re-appropriated them through interpretation into his work. For him, art is seen as a form of dialogue between two authorial selves. With the overarching mental faculty of imagination mediating between them, re-appropriation of the old master and assimilation of him into his work are now not two activities but an interdependent one. We call this inter-dialogue the mediation between an earlier and a later self; and the four works, all of them called *Homage to Mansur*, are the product of this inter-dialogue.

The inter-dialogue with an old master gives these paintings a historical dimension. The results are pleasantly eccentric, but they open up a new episteme in the Foucauldian sense of the term.[1] Subramanyan is attracted to Mansur, the Persian painter who came to India at the invitation of Emperor Jehangir. 'I want to bring together the icon and the real thing,' says Subramanyan, drawing attention to two references. Mansur is denotative of the painter who came to Jehangir's court; his work is identified

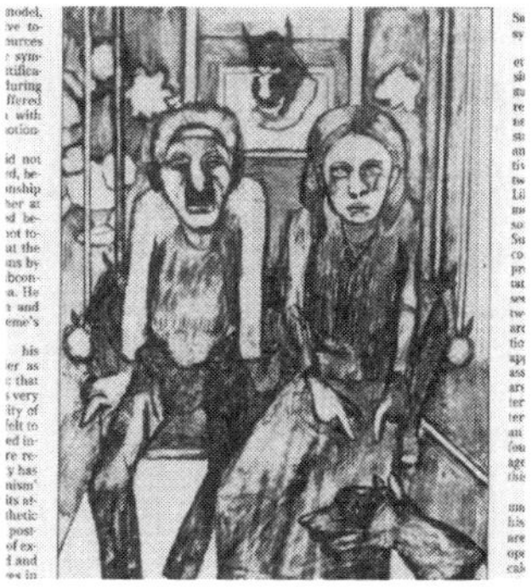

with naturalistic painting which he first introduced in India. The iconic reference is to the denotative form of naturalism. This is the subject of Subramanyan's paintings on the Mansur theme.

The Mansur paintings are acts of erasure and yet the historical iconological reference remains. For the functional essence of an icon is that it should be interpretable on the basis of recognitional abilities alone. *Acrobat,* another painting by him [Subramanyan], illustrates this well; we could recognize Picasso and the acrobats in the picture. The historical reference is obvious; Picasso painted several pictures on the theme of acrobats and circus clowns before he arrived at cubism.[2]

Similarly, he presents three versions of Premchand's Urdu short story, *Shatranj Ke Khiladi.* While in the Mansur paintings, the central focus is erasure of naturalism, in *Shatranj Ke Khiladi* the focus is on the degree of cultural relativity and decadence one associates with the game. The decadence weaves itself into images with a life of their own but the mode of narration used is to make the miniaturist context explicit - the mode of metonymy sets up an interaction between part and whole. What appears composed in one self-interior is decomposed or re-composed in another.

The strategy is to delay the progress of metonymy by a long detour; the quest becomes a labyrinth, for it is about something which does not exist in the referential outside world. The narration seeks to invalidate any insight into a personal past, for the quest is for a subject-oriented intention which is the source of personal presence. It focuses attention on the act of painting and the picture disappears behind its non-referential signifiers. This is because, for Subramanyan, there is no finished picture that would imply both the end of the project and the last word that can be said about it.

The work thus remains in process, unfinished, tentative. It refuses to realize its full meaning because with every correction, the final erasure draws nearer. The surrealists had a similar project; they sought to destroy the distinction between art and reality and they thought they had succeeded in their mission. As a final gesture, they turned the process of destruction against surrealism itself. Subramanyan, I am sure has no such surrealistic ambitions but his art comes close to a neo-surrealistic aspect of post-modernism.

Editor's Notes

1 Loosely explained, episteme as defined by Foucault refers to the rules of formation that allow the functioning of multiple discourses at a given point of time. Louis McNay, 'Introduction', in Louis McNay, ed., *Foucault: A Critical Introduction,* Cambridge: Polity Press, 1994.

2 Post-Picasso, this theme has been explored extensively by several artists in world art, as also in Indian modernism.

10

SANKHO RETROSPECTIVE

Review of the sculptor and teacher Sankho Chaudhuri's retrospective held in New Delhi in 1971

Link, New Delhi, 23 May 1971

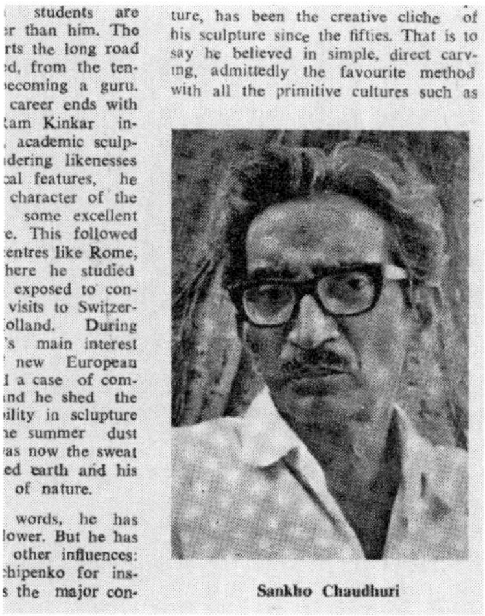

students are
er than him. The
rts the long road
ed, from the ten-
becoming a guru.
career ends with
Ram Kinkar in-
academic sculp-
ndering likenesses
cal features, he
character of the
some excellent
e. This followed
entres like Rome,
here he studied
exposed to con-
visits to Switzer-
olland. During
's main interest
new European
l a case of com-
and he shed the
ility in sclupture
ne summer dust
as now the sweat
ed earth and his
of nature.

words, he has
lower. But he has
other influences:
chipenko for ins-
s the major con-

ture, has been the creative cliche of his sculpture since the fifties. That is to say he believed in simple, direct carving, admittedly the favourite method with all the primitive cultures such as

Sankho Chaudhuri

The Sankho Chaudhuri retrospective (1949–71) exhibition at the National Gallery of Modern Art (Jaipur House) is the biggest art event of the season, and for several reasons. Prof. Chaudhuri, who teaches at the Faculty of Fine Arts, Baroda University, proves that he is a better artist than a teacher although he has spent more time teaching. This, at least, is the impression one gets from the retrospective exhibition. Prof. Chaudhuri has been showing his works in national exhibitions and other important group shows but he did not make the kind of impact he does now which may be because we missed the scale of his monumental creativity. Besides, Chaudhuri was better known by the works of his students, some of whom are now leading sculptors. Everyone is familiar with the works of Narendra Patel, Raghav Kaneria, R.R. Panchal, Nagji Patel, Ramesh Pateria, Balbir Singh Katt, Sarbari Roy Chowdhury and Raghunath Singha – all students of Chaudhuri.

LONG ROAD

A good guru is indeed one who produces disciples who better him. Chaudhuri proves this. For instance, he proved a better sculptor than his Santaniketan guru, Ramkinkar, and some of his own students are now doing much better than him. The retrospective show charts the long road Chaudhuri has travelled, from the tentative beginnings to becoming a guru. The first phase of his career ends with his rejection of the Ramkinkar influence, that is to say, academic sculpture.[1] Rather than rendering likenesses of the subject's physical features, he got involved with the character of the subject and produced some excellent expressionistic sculpture. This followed his visits to world art centres like Rome, Paris and London where he studied sculpture. He was also exposed to constructivism, during his visits to Switzerland, Belgium and Holland. During these years, Chaudhuri's main interest was the epistemology of new European sculpture. It was indeed a case of complete metamorphosis, and he shed the so-called Indian sensibility in sculpture which vanished like the summer dust after the rain. There was now the sweet smell of the rain-soaked earth and his sculpture became part of nature.

MUSICAL

In other words, he has become a Brancusi follower. But he has not closed his eyes to other influences: Arp, Picasso and Archipenko for instance. But Brancusi's is the major contribution in his growth with sight and touch becoming inseparable coordinates of his sculpture. Sculptural volume is now self-contained, achieving a full spatial completeness. His sculpture now has an abstract quality, a certain feeling which is closer to music, and Chaudhuri's love for classical music has become part of the new sensibility. However, the sculpture of this period is now wholly abstract: one can always link it up with the natural objects which he has sought to transform. But in the process of transformation, the starting point becomes insignificant, rather lost in the self-referring sculptural form and totally unrecognizable. The final culmination of Chaudhuri's search for non-objective abstract sculpture has ended with achieving the condition of music. This is indeed a dateless work and will survive the artist no doubt.

What Chaudhuri told an art critic in 1955 is worth quoting because it shows how influenced he was by the European masters. 'The various materials had their intrinsic and specific quality and character which finally determined the life and expression, the very structure of the sculpture.' 'Truth to material,' the credo of recent sculpture, has been the creative cliché of his sculpture since the Fifties. That is to say he believed in simple, direct carving, admittedly the favourite method with all the primitive cultures such as early Greek, Sumerian and Mexican. It indeed extended until the medieval Romanesque. No doubt, the truth-to-material obsession was carried to ridiculous limits - extending to junk assemblage. It became so very fashionable with both the sculptors and critics that they dismissed a work lightly if it tried to impose a form on the material.

MATERIAL

We refer to the role of material in sculpture because Chaudhuri went beyond the truth-to-material cliché, accepting at the same time the valid aesthetic behind it. And this he learnt in Europe with direct exposure to the then contemporary sculpture. He knew that sculpture displayed both the sensory and structural properties of the material: indeed, good sculpture involves both the visual and tactile properties of perception. Marble, for instance, has a translucency which reflects light from under its surface, giving to the carved forms a new source of light and glow. Indian sandstone

– which seems a Chaudhuri favourite – has a warm, erotic pink, like the dry earthiness of terracotta, with its sensuality which most primitive cultures have used to good effect. Like the hard blackness of old oak, the polished granite gleams with rich colours which sometimes match well with the soft of polished lead. Indeed, the impact of the material is so seductive that one really admires the beauty of the material rather than the sculpture proper. The assembled – mostly junk sculpture – is such a favourite with the sculpture of the Fifties; one of Chaudhuri's students, Raghav Kaneria is famous for his assemblages of junk. As a teacher at Baroda, Chaudhuri brought a new vision of Western technology and engineering and passed this on to his students who experimented with the industrial throw[aways] in the spirit of scientific experimentation. None of this constructivist nitty-gritty is displayed in this show. So we can conclude that he never gave the same importance to assemblage that his students did but it speaks volumes of his liberalism too.

WISE

Last year, Sankho Chaudhuri resigned from Baroda University to take up sculpture as his whole-time occupation. Ten works which he has executed in the last year are evidence that it was a wise decision. Indeed, Indian sculpture is the poorer in a way because this genius spent more time in teaching than working out its own destiny. Of the ten, the four shell-form sculptures in white marble are the most impressive. The white marble

sculpture. He knew that sculpture displayed both the sensory and structural properties of the material: indeed good sculpture involves both the visual and tactile properties of perception. Marble,

that it was a wise decision. Indeed, Indian sculpture is the poorer in a way because this genius spent more time in teaching than working out its own destiny. Of the ten the four shell-form

thing is also
have a limitl
convex to sp
the best of S
feeling, essent
but more ero

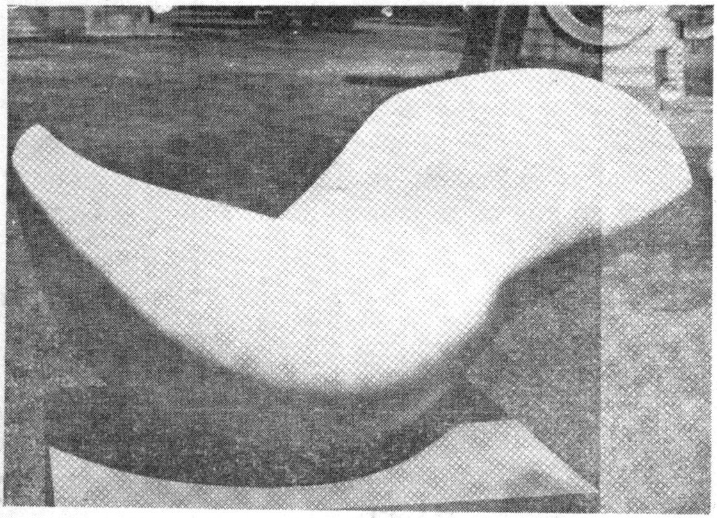

Reclining Form (White marble) by Sankho Chaudhuri

THEATRE

Black

Nabodoy G
unit in the
with the stag
kare". The s
based on th
Case which st
thirties. The
sing on raci
the judiciary
prove that th
United States
1933.

The death
Haywood Pat
borough Case
of two white
main Rolland
Thomas Man
Gorky were
demned the
District court
argued for th
against Patter

does not only transform itself into shell form with double-curved surfaces but the polished surface gets the factuality of shell itself. These are the most plastic expressions of sculptural surfaces. The curves bend and fold and glide into one another with the ease of a snake's body. Their structure is natural, resembling botanical growth so much that its geometry does not register easily on the mind. Most of the sculptures, displayed on the lawns of Jaipur House, form part of the landscape of trees and running fountains and the rich green spreads below. They get a new value because concave surfaces get easily related to the space outside.

The system of wholes makes the relationship with the outer space complete. It gives them an architectural elegance. Like a beautiful building, it is continuous, keeps extending. Another interesting aspect is the play of shadow and the varying sources of light which create its own optical areas of interest.

Indeed this is nothing new because curved surfaces allow greater plastic freedom for the sculpture. The eye, indeed, is very sensitive to the slightest curvature, the sagging or bulging surfaces have greater tactual stimulation than is possible with plain surfaces which are equally flat all over. Another thing is also important: curved surfaces have a limitless range, from spherical convex to spherical concave. Indeed, the best of Sankho's have a Barbara [Hepworth, sculptor] feeling, essentially a feminine sensibility but more erotic, more Indian.

Editor's Note

1 To clarify, Ramkinkar Baij never worked in the academic manner. Chaudhuri's own work explored sleek, smooth textures and curvaceous geometry in more 'conventional' material such as wood or bronze, which was a departure from the Giacometti-inspired Ramkinkar aesthetic of heavily textured, 'rough' and distinctly earthy, and the use of unconventional material such as concrete.

11
GREY, DARK LANDSCAPE

Review of a solo exhibition of Jehangir Sabavala in 1972

Link, New Delhi, 17 December 1972

Jehangir Sabavala got into the cubist orbit even while he was a student at the J.J. School of Art, Bombay in the early 1940s and never came out of it. Over these thirty years, he has been struggling to smudge the cubist edges but the traces remain. So also the mechanics of cubist composition, although he has now evolved a style of his own – especially in the landscape genre where his achievements are indeed considerable. Sabavala's mode of landscape composition has a touch of primitivism, a pre-cubist flair both in scale and in space-construction methods.

PLASTIC WRITING

He came to cubism by conviction after a good deal of study of the linguistic conventions of the art. His explorations, therefore, were never imitative in decorative effects as in the case of his contemporaries in the early stages of their career. But the explorations had always missed that cubist energy that could give birth to a masterpiece, remaining forever a form of cubist grammar – a manipulative game of formal grace, never a plastic writing of emotions. The viewer does not experience, standing before a Sabavala, the kind of relaxation he feels before a Braque.

Many Indian painters have attempted to come to terms with the cubist logic but their high aspiration could not win a single prize and they most often turned away defeated. Perhaps that is the reason why we have not had a single cubist painting, even an overstatement, which is self-referring and a valid expression in the cubist syntax. Cubism has been a movement, not a style, more of a methodology which has been defined as a means of depicting the modalities of depiction.

Cubism indeed is not a philosophy but a system of logic, and one learns to see and appreciate and compose rather than arrive at pictorial statements valid in themselves: few have achieved a matrix of sensation, feeling, the possibility of discovering a meaning in its net of planes. Braque, no doubt, died painting cubist pictures but he died too early: only Leger of those early cubist masters is still alive who has used cubist logic in art . . . 'which has the possibility of giving order to sensations'. Otherwise, for most practitioners of cubism, it has been like a bathtub 'with both the tap on and the drain open'.

CUBIST LOGIC

Jehangir Sabavala, who shows about thirty landscapes at Kunika-Chemould gallery, has come a long way from the canvases he showed about a decade ago in New Delhi which were too rigid even for cubist logic. Now the landscape has a relative ease, the flattened colour planes stand out sharply and also merge into a fine tonality of a weaved surface.

It is indeed a new language and the cubist elements are hardly visible: the landscape does not depict an external reality (though the external reality is highly readable): that is to say the external has been interiorized, the depiction of technology is replaced by signification, the object turned into a metaphor. What remains of the old cubist order is the frontality of composition and its formal grammar. The objective landscape, however, remains and this is what makes Sabavala a significant painter. So, the present work is merely one aspect of the results of thirty years of search for a personal style. It is not a new beginning, only a milestone on a long journey. Sabavala's landscape, however, does not have a local reference, so one cannot say that it is an observed landscape. Nor is there a hint of Indian light: it is dark, cold and windy - a mythical landscape saturated by literary references, all about a medieval darkness, grey land and brown substances which, no doubt, have recognizable human features but are less relevant to a gay, fun-loving Hindu mind.

The dull browns immediately put us off - especially when one encounters them in a landscape which is familiar in its topographical features. The formalized analytical mode makes them difficult to respond to favourably if it is accepted that in a landscape visual exhilaration is the only sensation that one seeks and responds to. The metaphysical intent, and what Adil Jussawalla calls 'the poetry of desolation, of purgatory, of the after-life and of angst' has over-heavy visual features.

12
SABAVALA MYSTERY

Review of a 1976 solo exhibition of Jehangir Sabavala

Link, New Delhi, 25 April 1976

Jehangir Sabavala, one of our elder artists and a contemporary of Husain and Souza, exhibits his landscapes at the Shridharani Gallery. The exhibition is of interest because for the first time, there is the presence of a human element in his landscape. Yet, the landscape has its familiar cubistic perceptions and their many-faceted implications have the mark of the painter's signature. This has the same thrill of discovery as when he launched himself more than three decades ago on an art career. The cubist perceptions, deployed with such meticulous craftsmanship, seem now something of a uniquely Sabavala mystery: and it is no doubt receptive to his inner voices. Because of Sabavala's dedication to his work, the apparent ease with which he composes – or rather builds in the literal sense of the metaphor – without any suggestion of effect the intricate sequences of his landscape, his painting has been mistaken for an attitudinizing direction. This response is wholly wrong; here our own conditioning is to blame as we always tend to play down the honest craftsmanship in favour of some undefined 'creative perceptions' which we have identified with good art. This has misled even such a sensitive critic as Adil Jussawalla to seek metaphysical insides in a Sabavala landscape [from the introduction in the exhibition catalogue]: (there is a goal that) 'lies beyond some of the paintings and it is not at all easy to define it. In part, at least, it would seem to be metaphysical, with the paintings as steps in a difficult, highly formalized pilgrimage towards a metaphysical "truth"'.

DIALECTICAL

The Sabavala landscape fills our mind and the successive appearances, which seem vestiges of bits and parts of an outside world, blend together into a single image to give us the kind of typical Sabavala landscape. A more successful exemplification of this landscape is *The Radiant Cloud*. This landscape seems to deny its material environment and we encounter it as more of an experience of light. The expressive element in this is neither the cubist perceptions which Sabavala so dexterously weaves with subtle colour gradations nor the vital impulses of lines which seem to have been freed of the dictates of the landscape's material environment: this expressive element represents a dialectical tension between the painter's routine and free-spirited development. In a formal sense, drawing and an art career. The cubist perceptions, deployed with such meticulous craftsmanship, seem now something of a uniquely Sabavala mystery: and it is no doubt receptive to his inner voices. Because of Sabavala's dedication to his work, the apparent ease with which he composes—or rather builds in the literal sense of the metaphor—without any suggestion of effect the intricate sequences of his landscape, his painting has been mistaken for an attitudinizing direction. This response is wholly wrong; here our own conditioning is to blame as we always tend to play down the honest cratfsmanship in favour of some undefined 'creative perceptions' which we have identified with good art. This has misled even such a sensitive critic as Adil Jussawalla to seek metaphysical insides in a Sabavala landscape: (there is a goal that) "lies beyond some of the paintings and it is not at all easy to define it. In part, at least, it would seem to be metaphysical, with the paintings as steps in a difficult, highly formalised pilgrimage towards a metaphysical 'truth'."

DIALECTICAL

The Sabavala landscape fills our mind and the successive appearances which seem vestiges of bits and parts of an outside world blend together into a single image to give us the kind of typical Sabavala landscape. A more successful exemplification of this landscape is "The Radiant Cloud." This landscape seems to deny its material environment and we encounter it as more of an experience of light. The expressive element in this is neither the cubist perceptions which Sabavala so dexterously weaves with subtle colour gradations nor the vital impulses of lines which seem to have been freed of the dictates of the landscape's material environment: this expressive element represents a dialectical

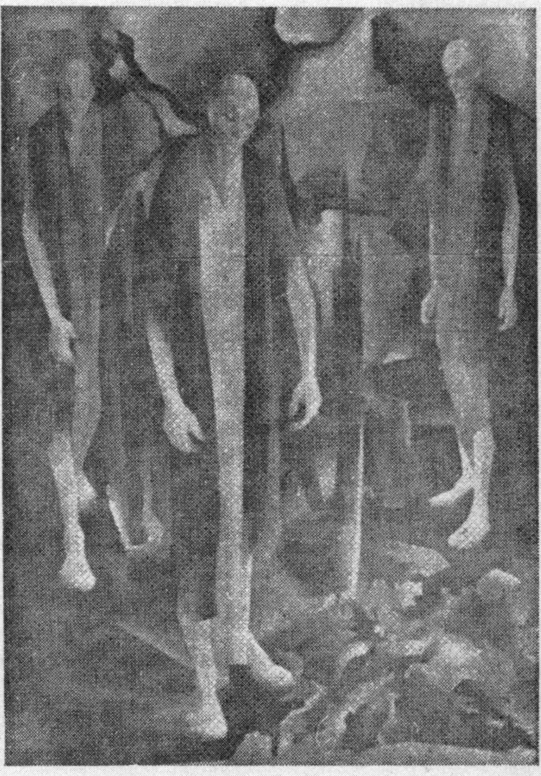

"The Sorrowing Men" by Jehangir Sabavala.

colour are unified and the landscape finds its being by an intuitive path. This was also one of Cezanne's anxieties: how to use colour to replace the procedure of drawing in line.

This brings us to Delaunay's method of simultaneous rapports of colour:[1] he gave a new direction to painting by insisting that it was light (and distinguishing light by means of colours) that gave mobility and not the introduction of several viewpoints as the cubists did by means of displacing of objects. Drawing, in the sense the cubists used, to separate line from colour, obtaining volume by means of chiaroscuro, is still an important component of Sabavala's landscape; and it is in *The Radiant Cloud* alone that light breaks the continuity of forms. The perception of a new element in this painting is not the perception of light in the sense light was interpreted by the impressionists in their paintings; it is more of a hint that the vital rhythm of colours is the key to the composing of movement. Delaunay's observation is relevant: 'The eye is our most elevated sense, that which communicates most strictly with the brain, the consciousness. The idea of the vital movement of the world and its movement is simultaneity. Our comprehension is correlative to our perception. . . .'

CONFIGURATIVE

That is to say, there are as many images of an object as there are eyes: an object does not have a fixed absolute form and so our perceptions cut the physical object into several parts. We arrange and rearrange these parts, their successive appearances, that is, to arrive at a single image. And here the perspective of light, of duration, is important. The landscape for Sabavala is not the representation of a sight seen: it is a painter's surface, and in part 'dubitative' built as it is part by part, section by section by means of lines, revealing to us the imagined sequences of a landscape which involves us by its configurative organization of lines and masses. Colour hardly has a role in this configuration: it is the light value scale of his pigments that he is most interested in. The scale is dominated by the intermediate terms and their gradations have been explored with the cool of a scientist. Sabavala has acquired the ingenuity to conceal the limitations of his chosen scale. Because of this limited scale, he is able to achieve a lyrical clarity, an order of construction through colour which is architectural.

The human figure has the same make-up as that of his landscape: that is to say, they [the landscapes] are not static and their lines of force, though seem to be intersections of the space they occupy, consisting in extracting movement. *The Sorrowing Men* is composed with such [tremendous] lines of force; space is a live experience, of the sensations of interpenetrating planes that indirectly make us aware of the possible thousand perceptions of their images. The result is that these seem to have been carved rather than painted; the intention is to render the whole surrounding atmosphere active. There is the same opacity of bodies we find in sculpture.

Sabavala's self-conscious style, the cubist-like interpenetration of planes and the sensation of a shallow depth have made him a unique painter among his contemporaries.

Editor's Note

1 Robert Delaunay wrote, 'Movement is produced by the rapport of *odd elements*, of the contrasts of colours between themselves which constitutes *Reality*' (emphasis author's): 'La Lumiere' (1912), in *Du Cubisme d l'Art Abstrait*, translated by Paul Klee, Paris: SEVEPEN, 1957, pp. 146–47.

13
HUSAIN SUGAR

Review of an M.F. Husain exhibition, with a discussion of what drove his prodigious art, his celebrity and commercial success

Link, New Delhi, 4 January 1970

The Husain painting is not for judging because judging implies comparison which divides opinions. It is also because Husain has very little objective visual wisdom, although his painting looks concrete, well-drawn and sweetly painted. It is glossy like the toy, the rocking horse of childhood, and its gleaming surface, the brilliance of colours and the decisive outline are very nostalgic. (Incidentally, it is the most expensive toy which Baudelaire also wanted to have as a child but could not and so became an object of deep admiration.) The Husain hobby horse is, then, all the more sweet because it is so readily recognizable and very Indian in its make-up and yet subjective enough for anyone to ride. It has a magical effect on the senses and the eyes that cannot think but fall in love with it and remain blind forever. That is why every Husain exhibition divides critical opinion with clearly drawn lines: either you like it or you don't.

The current exhibition of his thirteen paintings at Dhoomi Mal Gallery [later, Dhoomimal] is no exception. From the press notices, it is clear that he is fast losing his rather narrow circle of admirers. They are not to be blamed; no one can consume that much of Husain sugar. Enough is enough and they cannot have more of it. But the rocking horse of childhood is all sweet and honey, a visual presence which can be enjoyed only through a ruminative indulgence of images and Husain has attempted to make them a part of the national nostalgia. Of course, this sounds ridiculous but go and see the tourist who buys Husain blindly and believes that he is really buying not only art but 'Indian art'. The tourist, of course, has no time to measure the sugar content in the Husain painting because he is having it for the first time.

MONARCH OF MARKET

In the art market, Husain, until recently, reigned like a monarch keeping the market always in bullish fever because only his painting had that touch of national nostalgia which the tourist collects as an Indian souvenir to write home about. Husain, to be sure, never starves the market and paints as fast and in as much time as you will take in making a cup of instant coffee. Not even the current wave of tantrism has affected his sales because he can always paint symbolic stuff with intricate dance *mudras* and this goes more with the new market trends than the obscure symbology of tantric bizarrerie. So he manages to be always one-up on the latest avatars of art, whether Indian or foreign.

Why does Husain succeed and not the others? The question has been a subject of debate since Husain entered the market in the early Fifties and so far no convincing answer has been found, and as is most often the case with all stable successes, the Husain success brought forth a host of national pastiches as well as pure jealousy and even some wickedness. But we are concerned with neither, for we do not believe that Husain is a case of stable success, nor do we think that jealousy can ever produce a healthy challenge, let alone art. Husain's popularity can be understood only in the context of Indian art history because his painting demands less of judgement than identity. If one wants art to be a tradition-bound and locally produced commodity then purely formal premises of judging art are not enough. So we have first to define our sensibilities, not in terms of formally satisfying aesthetics but in terms of national heritage and adjustments made accordingly. Unless this is agreed upon, no discussion on Husain will ever make sense. And here we face a genuine dilemma because sensibilities are rooted in the experience of one's growth and cannot be discussed in abstract categories; they have to be understood in relation to other things than the categories of art criticism. Most critics who stand outside the charmed circle make this mistake and judge him by pure art critical terms as if there is some kind of a computer operating for them to predict the ratio of success or failure of a work of art. For the art market there may exist some such invisible computer which keeps the art goods in a constant grading system.

MATHURA SCULPTURE

Now, Husain's genius in creating a native sensibility has been mistaken for the presence of an ethic and he has been eulogized for this reason. It is based on the mistaken notion that the sense of tradition governs Husain's conception of form while we all know that there was no such tradition in India, at least a meaningful one in the context of easel painting. Husain built his forms not on any awareness of a local tradition, but arrived at them in much the same way as Matisse discovered the beauty of Oriental art through the Japanese prints and schematic colours in Persian carpets. For Matisse, the experience of the Islamic art exhibition in 1910 was a turning point in his artistic career. So was the case with Husain; he was a different painter ever since he saw the exhibition of Mathura sculpture in 1948 in Delhi.

Indeed, we might well extend the parallel between Matisse and Husain's careers to know the range of influence of what they saw in the exhibitions which changed the whole conception of their art. Matisse, for example, before his encounter with the 1910 exhibition, was obsessed with the problems of form simplification. The terms of this obsession were simple: it was a search to combine the geometrical forms (such as the oval, the ellipsoid and the sphere) and the feeling of sensuality which he associated with the female form. This he sought in the earlier phases of Greek tradition of which *La Danse* and *La Musique* are the better known exemplifications. For completing the famous *Pink Nude*, it is said, he took some eighteen photographs but neither the Greek tradition nor the help of photographic technology provided him with any significant insights. Similarly, Husain before the experience of the 1948 exhibition of Mathura sculpture was making and painting toys, but the toys did not give him the feel of sensuality, later to become the basis of his aesthetics.

There is yet another aspect to the Husain painting and that is his being a poet before he became the famous painter. His ideal painting is closer to the lyrical tone of the Urdu ghazal which he attempted to translate in the visual medium of painting. The implications of this are clear; more than form he is devoted to shape and colour and they make the line of beauty in his painting. Shapes, like words, have rich associative imagery and at times can suggest metaphoric meanings but [are] on the whole malleable, like photographic images. After a great many trial-and-error experiments, he evolved a system of form construction which combined sex and geometry at the same level of feeling which informs Mathura sculpture. Mathura sculpture had been a working model for Husain for a long time until he started to stuff his women with pseudo-symbology.

NOT NEW

But there is more to it because as much was achieved by Keyt who, in fact, had Indianized Matisse. Still he could not provide a lead to Indian painting. He actually missed, in a way, the hardcore of twentieth-century art or rather its starting point, which is well represented by two paintings (incidentally both painted in 1907) - Matisse's *Le Nu Bleu* and Picasso's *Demoiselles d'Avignon*. Husain was indeed the first Indian painter who learnt the proper lesson of these two historically significant paintings. He got from Picasso's painting of the prostitutes the cubistic method of building forms, and on the basis of Matisse's painting of the blue nude, he formed his painterly insights into what is called 'significant form'. Now Husain must have seen these paintings much earlier, perhaps when he was a student at the Indore School of Art but the understanding of epistemology of modern art he got only after seeing the exhibition of the Mathura sculpture. Now he was able to formulate the terms and conception of his art. Like Matisse, Husain enjoys continuous surfaces but unlike Matisse he does not believe in easy transitions and delicate modelling. Like Picasso, he is violent and aggressive and indulges in pictorial acrobatics and yet the total effect of his painting is closer to that of Matisse. His painting is indeed more like the Baudelaire rocking horse, fascinating for its 'glossy purity, the brilliance of his colours, its violent movements and decisive outline'.

All this detailed comparison of Husain with Matisse and Picasso is necessary because we tend to expect things from Husain which he is incapable of giving. For instance, it is wrong to expect more than a visual pattern from his painting and that is why his play with shapes and colours looks repetitive to us. In a painting based purely on the principle of pleasure and aimed at providing an armchair as it were for us to relax, visual technology is everything. Actually, such a painting mistakes the means for the ends. What Husain does therefore is not new.

The point is that when we view a master like Husain, we should not counterpoint it with our false expectations; rather, we should read a work by placing it in the total repertoire of Husain, for it is by knowing the whole range of expression of the artist that we can interpret a single work. And, to be sure, Husain's range of expression is limited; nevertheless, it is rich and unique. Perhaps he knows this well. Whenever he attempts a departure from the essential Husain (the pattern-making artist) and includes in his repertoire themes expressive of the human condition, he fails because it is not within his power to do so without changing his present style. Of course, he is capable of doing this and can choose any day a different way of doing things but he would not, perhaps, out of deference to the tourist tastes of his patrons.

MASTER STILL

In the present exhibition, his two paintings, both called *Men Unidentified,* are painted in a grand design, seldom seen in his painting; the range of his expressive intent is clearly blown up to giant proportions and the surprise is that his painting can accommodate such varied things. It is a landscape of images with clearly defined spatial movements; it has no illusionistic persuasions, only psychological implications. Its expressiveness and pictorial power, however, should not be viewed in isolation or in the context of the works he is exhibiting now but in totality, talking with landscape implications. He has indeed painted many landscapes since his visit to Banaras in 1957 but none contain such diverse elements as are seen in the *Men Unidentified 1.*

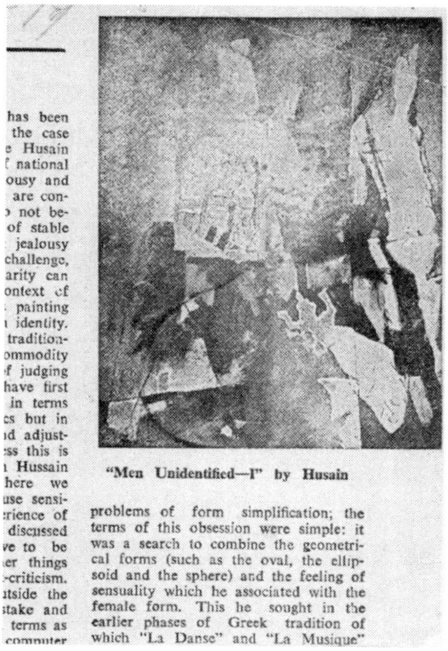

"Men Unidentified—I" by Husain

problems of form simplification; the terms of this obsession were simple: it was a search to combine the geometrical forms (such as the oval, the ellipsoid and the sphere) and the feeling of sensuality which he associated with the female form. This he sought in the earlier phases of Greek tradition of which "La Danse" and "La Musique"

Husain undoubtedly is a master and a master is never dead. He may be for a while out of his elements or choose to lie low, but from this we should not infer that he is dead and that he can never regain his old strength. The present exhibition proves that Husain is in full command of his powers.

14

BIRTH OF MANY HUSAINS

An assessment of the art of the painter M.F. Husain as a flag-bearer of India's modernism in the twenty-fifth year of its Independence

Link, New Delhi, 15 August 1972

It may sound odd to talk about the bridge-builders in the arts but in this jubilee year of independence, it may perhaps be legitimate to be nostalgic about them. Of the many bridge-builders, M.F. Husain is an eminent patriarch. And not only that: he could be the last of the bridge-builders who have helped to finally usher into Indian painting finally into modernist sensibility. Significantly enough, he first exhibited his paintings in 1947, and so in a way his art began to flower in the climate of freedom, in the year India became independent. He carried forward the tradition of Rabindranath Tagore, Amrita Sher-Gil, Jamini Roy and George Keyt. As Shiv Kapur, in the latest book on Husain (Abrams) says of him –

> Freed of the bitterness of political subjugation and of the nagging urge towards establishing a collective national identity, Husain is the harbinger of a new mood in Indian art. This is a mood at once self-assured in its use of universal idioms of artistic expression, contemporary in outlook and experience, socially committed and deeply humanistic in its exploration of the nature of reality.[1]

It is indeed not far wrong to say that with Husain modern art finally arrived in India. Or was it because of the first avant-garde group – the Progressive Painters Group in Bombay of which Husain was a leading member? This is indeed difficult to answer, as difficult as speculating on Husain's development without his membership of the group. Joining it was advantageous for him in a way; it helped him to become his own critic and judge himself as austerely as he would others' works.

Those were great days, says Husain when we fought, quarrelled and even showered imprecations at each other – but always with understanding, without meaning to cause hurt and without ill feeling. The group disintegrated in a few years when most of its members (especially Raza and Souza) left to settle abroad. The final disintegration came in 1965 when former members of the by-then moribund group held a show of drawings in New Delhi's Shridharani Gallery. This was the last time Husain ever participated in any group activity. Husain recalls with a sad, lost look that that was also the time of his total isolation – everyone talking about art, with New York or London as the main referents and not their own visions. 'We fought like children and we agreed that there was nothing common which can bind us into even a loose group.' How very different was it from those heated debates amongst members of the Progressive Artists Group which went on till dawn broke and ended because no one had energy left to talk. The long years of neglect made him hard enough to take criticism in his stride but never did anybody doubt the premises of his art sketched out in the days of the Progressive Group.

For the first time then, he was confronted with a new attack, and he had no defences except his own energy and faith. Everyone was against him because

> I did not follow the fashion of the day, because I was painting those same old things which I had been painting since my first show. I was played out, they thought. There was no hope for me. So I turned to the epic themes, went mystic, as it were, to rediscover myself in painting the human drama of the Mahabharata. I was at it for three years.

The 1965 exhibition would not have proved such a bitter experience if he had not heard the familiar criticism from critics outside the country. A reputed New York critic was very cold towards his work because it seemed old-fashioned stuff. He wanted to know why Husain did not go abstract. Husain merely said, 'How can I, or anyone in India, when we live amongst 500 million people. How can I deny those people?'

Husain may very well be the only frontliner who has never attempted anything consciously avant-gardeish. Perhaps because of this, he never got into those muddy foreign waters enough to soil his work. He has been and still is proud of what he can do with the hand than invent intellectual games for his art. Today, he prefers to show his paintings at village fairs because, there, no one asks him the 'silly' questions which people in the metropolitan art galleries do. Nothing for him is more depressing to hear than criticality in the old art history jargon. In the finest traditions of Indian art he expects nothing from his audience except the joy in their eyes.

A Husain painting is indeed made for the eye, like the best music for the ear. And yet his is art with a capital A – art which is meant to give joy and is addressed to the eye even when it is loaded with symbolic content and images that have freed themselves from logic, time and place: images which are, however, linked with their own time. Saying it another way, his work may not be defined with any reference to the ideas of art in general. What Husain's twenty-five years as a successful artist affirm is a simple truth – that there is no progress in art. And this makes it so different from every other way of achieving the truth.

How has Husain not lost his way when most of his contemporaries at one time or another were out on a limb of the current of art history?

The answer is simple: he never cut himself loose from his own moorings, tradition. Maybe the other artists attempted to replace tradition by art history consciousness. This confusion is not peculiar to Indian artists. Everywhere, the modernist artist has faced the same dilemma and wasted his whole energy in choosing between one aesthetic school and another. Each such choice has been a matter of professional life and death.

This confusion hit Husain indirectly - when the shifting aesthetic premises affected the sale of his work! He has come into his own again because most young painters have begun looking for roots in their own environment. And this may prove to be the biggest breakthrough for Indian art, promising the birth of many Husains.

Editor's Note

1 Shiv S. Kapur and Richard Bartholomew, *Maqbool Fida Husain*, New York: Harry N. Abrams, 1972.

15
HUSAIN RETROSPECTIVE

A reflection on M.F. Husain's art on the occasion of his retrospective in New Delhi in 1978

Link, New Delhi, 17 December 1978

It is a rare experience, this Husain retrospective mounted by Art Heritage at the Lalit Kala Gallery where over 100 Husains fill the first floor as well as the foyer space. Indeed, not an ordinary exhibition, this is the first retrospective New Delhi art lovers are exposed to. (Two other Husain retrospectives were held in Calcutta in 1969 and in Bombay in 1973.) Most of the paintings on display are from private collections, a large number of them from the collection of Badrivishal Pitti, an industrialist from Hyderabad. And many of them are being exhibited for the first time in New Delhi. For putting up this impressive, well-structured retrospective of Husain, we should be grateful to the Alkazis.

Since Husain has become part of Indian painting's folklore and has been written about so much, the importance of the retrospective has nothing to do with either the worth or the value of the exhibits. He has the same appeal as a film star for the popular imagination. Indeed, he can very well be called the patriarch of the modernist sensibility in Indian art. As Shiv Kapur in his book on Husain says, 'Freed from the bitterness of political subjugation and of the nagging urge towards establishing a collective national identity, Husain is the harbinger of a new mood in Indian art.' Putting it another way, one might say that with Husain what is called modern art finally arrived in India.

The Husain retrospective brings home the truth that there is no progress in his art: the essential Husain has not changed a bit - the Husain who discovered himself when he first encountered Mathura sculpture in 1948. And ever since he has been translating the language of sculptural form in his painting. The result of this media mix was a new composition - movement of forms in space. In painterly language, one might say that modelling lines in a Husain painting achieve the same high degree of visibility we find in Indian relief sculpture. A close look at a Husain will, for instance, show that the contours modelling the interior forms are frequently broken and at different depths: they do not form a continuous outline. That is to say, the internal structure of Mathura sculpture is ever present in his work. Of course, the medium is two-dimensional and the way he uses a line makes explicit the operation of these internal forces: the changes in the surface are connected through line which defines both volume as well as the surface. This linear feature which, in the language of sculpture is known as modelling lines, is the one single component of his painting that carries his signature.

SIGNATURE

The signature quality did not come easy; he continued playing variations on the tactile qualities of line until he painted his famous canvas, *Between the Spider and the Lamp* in 1956. Between 1947 (when he first won an award at the Bombay Art Society annual) and 1956, he went through many influences: reworking his style based on Picassos, Rouaults, Beckmanns and Noldes from the visual discoveries he made in the big-breasted *yakshinis* of Mathura sculpture, particularly of the Kushan period. But Husain has never been art-history conscious as his contemporaries were and for this reason alone he has never lost sight of his way when most of his contemporaries at one time or another were out on a limb of the current of art history. It is a measure of his faith - even energy - that he never cut himself loose from his moorings, tradition. Tactile sensations, and not any devotion to an idea, is what has obsessed him, ever interested as he is in a sensory mix.

The sensory mix in Husain's images is heightened by the sense of discontinuity, which produces a feeling of self-alienation. And in the act of painting, the object almost fades away as if it were a product of the successive ensemble of colour patches which most people have mistaken for a cubist methodology. But this is as much to clarify the movement of surfaces as to create the impression of depth. The feeling of movement is central to Husain's intention, it seems.

This is not an easy task. Take for instance, the many self-portraits Husain has been doing since 1956. It would seem that he is not interested in the depiction of the being but the exterior time when each moment must have been felt as one of illumination and fullness. These are indeed records of the passage of time, his confrontation with the self and the moments: of detachment, of discontinuity, of self-doubt and self-alienation; as if to show that he has painted the self-portraits for the darker purpose of seizing himself in the act of painting. This linking device, these assemblages of one instant of time in concatenation with another is to assure us that the intention behind these self-portraits is to depict the passage and not the being.

TERROR OF FAILURE

Moreover, there is the terror of failure of not being able to seize the being in time, of not being able to provide a bridge between this instant and the following instant. One feels this terror of failure as also the anxiety to succeed, in the portrait of Jawaharlal Nehru done in 1962. He has concentrated - it is obvious - on visual quantifications to recover the unified field of being in time. But in portraiture the method of pure spontaneity is indeed not the sure method: therefore the portrait of Nehru leaves much to be desired. But as an experience of segmental time, as a method of snap shooting moments the portrait is a unique creation: he has captured a kind of consciousness which is kingly, that is to say, getting hold of a centre without a margin.

This suggests a cinematic experience for us looking at these portraits where every touch of brush and line has been laid with a view to its effect, not at the instant of time - at the moment of applying paint that is - but with a view to its effect in futurity. About Husain's colour application methods, one is always in doubt: which deceives us most - sight or touch.

Husain has never played intellectual games in his painting, perhaps, because he is a born painter for whom the visual field (the world of light and space) is the mode of perceiving things. Putting it in another way, the visual field is not the product of stimulus-response determinism; it is the condition of the mind, of seeing the world as a picture. For ordinary perception, it is difficult to see the world as a picture although it is not difficult for a person with ordinary eyes to see some flat pictures as looking like the world. Husain is a born painter because he never sees the world of appearances as it looks to the eye but as they can be represented. Although Husain is obsessed with the creation of visual metaphors, interpreting the symbolic language of dance which frees his images from the logic of time and place, his paintings are indeed explorations into the realm of touch and sight; they educate, they modify our sensibility and consciousness.

16
THE HUSAIN MYSTIQUE

A reflection on what makes the maverick painter M.F. Husain tick, and his continued popularity

Commerce magazine, New Delhi, 9–15 November 1988

Painter M.F. Husain, believe it or not, has an uncanny news sense, next only to Dali, perhaps. This is not to say we are not upset by his humiliation by Bombay's Willingdon Club. Mulk Raj Anand, the famous novelist, has in a letter (*Times of India*, 1 November) asked the club authorities 'to tender a public apology for their atrocious anti-national behaviour towards Husain'. Which means, 'dishonouring' Husain is humiliating India; that is one extreme of the episode. Another extreme is to cite (another letter appearing in the same issue) that Husain is 'a crafty self-publicist (going about barefoot is of a piece) who thrives on "incidents"' and that 'no self-respecting club should admit him'.

These two extremes of reaction represent indeed the two faces of our club-going elite: the surrogate face is more representative, for there is always a need for the surrogate to belong to two nationalities. In this, he is like the non-resident Indian, the chosen expatriate, who seeks to negate the sin of belonging to the class of natives by seeking membership of a white man's club: art for him is a means of seeking liberation from that part of his being which is rooted in decay, personal terror, degradation and savage poverty. As a means of negation of one's original nationality, art is a true Utopia of a future promise with its nucleus of security enabling the expatriate-artist to become, if not actually a member of the white or proto-white club, an important personage at the various Willingdons of India.

Husain has never aspired for membership at the white or proto-white club; nor, as a leading artist, has he attempted anything consciously avant-gardeish. He has been, still is, proud of what he can do with his hand, rather than any ability to invent intellectual games for his art. He would, indeed, prefer to show his works at a small village fair because there he would not be thought a crafty self-publicist.

A Husain painting is indeed made for the eye: it contains images that have freed themselves from logic, time and place, but are yet linked with our time; they are indeed so well-crafted, well-drawn and delightfully painted that they look like glossy toys. It is the most expensive toy, this Husain rocking horse of childhood, its brilliance of colour and the alluring nostalgia. Yes, a Husain is always sweet, its sugar content always high; yet no one has accused him of causing nausea. It is this native appeal of Husain, which has enabled him to rule the Indian art market like a monarch; and Husain, to be sure, has never starved the market. If one wants one's art to stay within the bounds of recognizable tradition, an art produced with the imprint of local sensibilities rooted in one's experience, such an art would not be in terms of formally satisfying aesthetics, but would nevertheless be strong enough to awaken the sleeping myths of the past. The kind of images one goes to experience in a museum.

A Husain painting is thus a deeper kind of aesthetic experience, an awareness of our passionate assertion of what might be called ethnic memories. We look at his work in wonder: a work of art wrapped in a myth. Because of this particular quality no amount of critical noise has been able to distract Husain-hero-worship: and Husain is aware of the spell his work has cast on the public – not only on the educated urban sophisticates but on villagers as well.

A Husain turns us into mirrors of a group mind, into temples dedicated to some anointed myths. It is a complex of riddles, and art-historical methods would be poor and inadequate tools in the hands of a Husain-admirer for solving the riddles his art constructs. The admirer succumbs to its spell; he refuses to or cannot see: one would rather have faith in an illusion than have no faith at all. This does not mean that Husain's works have not been examined with critical attention. But despite all the critical attention bestowed on them, the Husains remain unexplored. Perhaps it is the presence of an ethnic element that has enabled the Husains apparently to transcend their historical limited context. This strong element of the ethnic, this particular way of looking compactly at life, that we find in a Husain painting has lent to his art a higher value.

The rest is a series of equivocations, in which one may say, 'metaphorical' habits of seeing have excluded all attempts at 'critical' seeing. Husain has become the name of a 'style', a 'manner', for the time being providing a contemporary focus on our art of the past. For Husain has brought to Indian painting all those innovations that we think are his, though these may have in fact been borrowed from the pictorial language of European art. In his work, these have been assimilated and metamorphosed into his own style. Of all contemporary artists in the country, he alone seems to be able to hold the terror of modernity firmly in his art.

17
LAST OF THE ROMANTIC ARTISTS

A reflection on the abstract painter V.S. Gaitonde, on the occasion of a solo exhibition

Shankar's Weekly, New Delhi, 25 February 1973

A rose is a rose. And call it by any other name, it remains a rose. So it is with Gaitonde's painting, which is as natural as perhaps nature is. Speaking of a rose in relation to Gaitonde's work, the analogy is right in so far as it relates to colour. For instance, we never say of a rose that its colour is this or that, or its colour is more or less because colour in a rose is intrinsic and cannot be separated from the fact of its being. To judge colour in a rose is to deny the rose itself. That is to say, the colour of a rose cannot be wrong. Similarly the Gaitonde painting cannot be wrong in terms of its colour because it is the thing itself.

This may sound a bit of overpraise. Maybe it is – the relationship part of the analogy at any rate because colour in a painting has reference to a particular norm, a particular quality which inheres it. And so it seems wrong to deduce from it the fact of its being: that is, colour in the Gaitonde painting is not the same thing as colour is in a rose. In painting – not even in a Rothko – colour is never ontologically self-evident. What seems a more intelligent proposition about the Gaitonde approach to colour is that it is the very substance of his painting, that it has a certain ease, grace and unity of perception which we associate with great art.

The impact of colour is so overpowering indeed that it produces a certain 'unthink', the perspectual mechanism comes to a stop and our responses are controlled as if we have reached the end of some kind of an absolute consciousness. Gaitonde absolutism therefore leads to a metaphysical yearning, a knowledge of the void, a range of music not limited by the sensory experience alone and finally an experience poised between magic and rational. It is always to something else rather than to colour that his paintings lead us to. That is why nearly every critic sees his work in terms of the literary images of his own feelings. A well-known critic writes:

> His work is before you. You may not see all that I imagine I see. I try and hear what I have seen, as Gaitonde paintings say things to me . . . At the heart of that canvas environment there is that superb physical and metaphysical quality of sight, sound and sensations melting into air.

A second critic, on the other hand, imagines Gai's paintings to be in link with some ancient cryptic walls where 'the secret meaning is only an appearance, for Gaitonde does not indulge in symbols even inadvertently'. Even a historical reference does not yield much information and Santo Datta resigns to the view that Gaitonde is more like an island adrift which 'seems to have moved away from the continental shelf of modern Indian art. . . . He is not there in the exhibition of the young artists.'

That turns him into an enigma: the painter who represents in his art the unbroken link with two decades of Indian art, in which rhetorics of the 1950s and 1960s are kept alive despite the fact that the absolute art of all-colour painting is now a nostalgia for another time and space. So Gaitonde is the last of the romantics, his art still reminding us of the good old days of the bohemia. It was more like Pollock's attempts of writing on the inner wall of the mind. As the last of the romantic artists, Gaitonde is indirectly asserting the fact that he is the artist with a magic wand, creating through colour a universe of extra-visual resonance, of numinous surfaces that should produce eye fatigue were it not for the fact that the mind translates everything that tires him into 'something else', i.e., the sensual colour becomes the source of mystery. And the instantaneity of effect forces us to construct a dialectic, enabling us to transfer experience from one channel to another, so that we do not regret if we fail to define our responses because we always return to the land of 'something else' by our own constructed, permutational ingenuities.

Gaitonde also reminds us of the difficulties in communicating emotional states accompanying our reaction to colour which is as difficult as communicating the experience of a dream and we know how wide is the disparity between the effect and the evidence. To put it another way, it is one of those fallacies of naming what is unnamed. Gaitonde is able to keep alive many of the old myths because he is like a Spartan who exhibits only when he must and his art essentially remains passive, inviting contemplation. He exhibited last year in New Delhi after a decade or so: this is his second exhibition, no doubt representing the work of the year 1972 he has spent in Delhi. He now goes back to Bombay because New Delhi is certainly a vulgar place for his intuitive way of responding to environment.

The exhibition at Gallery Chanakya has the same scale, the same level of professionalism and the same ability to mix colours as flat on the canvas as is optically possible. He is so particular about flatness of the effect that he divides the canvas into overlapping inner squares. The effect of these variations leads to some kind of instability, so that the eye hovers all over the place and is held firmly only by the edges of the framed canvas. Similarly, he introduces a line structure to activate the eye-fatiguing overall-ness of colour, but the line structure never gets mixed up with the action of colour. The reduction of every element in painting to its essential minimum has led Gaitonde to increase the warmth of his colours but it never leads to such gimmicks as recessions, enclosures, 'windows into space,' pattern formations and clusters. It is music of a kind for the eyes.

18

NEW LANDSCAPE

Review of a solo exhibition of landscapes by Akbar Padamsee

Patriot Magazine, New Delhi, 23 March 1969

It is indeed difficult not to take Akbar Padamsee seriously, although his paintings (on show at Kunika-Chemould gallery) look rather unserious, utterly simple, as if they were another variety of visual landscapes. No doubt, they have great visual charm. One does not have to go looking for modern painting theories to appreciate them. They are rich, both craft and composition wise, and what more should one expect if these two things are there in a modern work of art.

Here is the rub. A modern painting does not become modern; a painter does not become a serious proposition for art collectors and gallery owners, if there are only craft and composition aspects to his work. The painting has to be more seriously involved, though this may be noticeable only to a close circle of critics and painters, with aspects that are more like picture-puzzles. So what we should always take for granted whenever we go to an exhibition is this fact: a painter can qualify himself for inclusion in the category of the serious only when he gives the impression of working at some painterly problems. The critic or gallery man then comes into his own. He puts his own interpretations and solutions on these painting puzzles.

CRITIC'S THEORY

A visitor is in for difficulties if he wants to see more into these latest Padamsees: there is no catalogue, no captions to paintings and no guide to give information about them. For this economy in verbal information, Padamsee has a simple reply: you have paintings before you, if you have chosen to spend the evening with them; captions might mislead you into imagining something which is not there at all. Even numbering them (they are nine in all) would not be of much use. As for the critic, he might say: well you know all the trade tricks, so why bother about captions; say what you want to say and be done with it.

Yet, he is justified when he says that the critics have not done justice to his paintings. In fact, he is angry with them. He expects them to be 'critic-philosophers', who should not only talk like gurus of aesthetics but should be able to guide the painter also. This is indeed expecting too much. But about one thing he is right: the critics should not miss the obvious or say things, if they have missed the obvious, which might mislead others.

Funny though it is, one misled critic has misled others. This critic has quite cleverly sought to corelate the drawings with paintings, both exhibited side-by-side, and has come out with an interesting theory that Padamsee's latest landscapes are 'colour drawings'.

This is not something wholly unexpected. Padamsee's paintings are not as simple as they look; in fact, the simpler ones are the more difficult. A painter should never be judged by what he exhibits. Rather his whole development should be talked about, especially so when he is as well known as Padamsee.

MASS AND VOLUME

So while reviewing his current exhibition, it is necessary to see these works in comparison with what he showed in 1962. In the same gallery, he had come home for a visit from Paris and naturally showed his works here [New Delhi] as well as in Bombay. Those, too, were landscapes except that in some, a solitary human figure was also there. Those landscapes were painted in black-and-white, greys, being tertiary colours. As now, in those works also, his preoccupation in landscape was with mass and volume and not with landscape sequences proper. In short, they were space compositions; if they looked like landscapes – and not the non-object paintings – it was because he used some architectural and tree motifs besides the human figure which was always tucked into a corner of the canvas.

Those landscapes did not have the same visual appeal as the present ones have, primarily because of the lack of colour. Secondly, they were painted after the Cezanne geometry of landscape – but with one very important difference. Cezanne did not reduce landscape to an abstract composition; the landscape sequences were defined in terms of picture planes, while Padamsee reduced landscape to something of the mental furniture of space-geometry composition. So those landscapes had sharp edges and clearly defined volume masses. Being nothing more than exercises in volumetric painting in black-and-white with pleasing greys, they had no emotion, no mood, because they were display pieces of his mental furniture, arranged and rearranged in terms of plane structures. If there was any element of emotion in them, it was confined to the human figure. Their appeal consisted in a display of aesthetic balancing acts, significant only for their formal properties.

DEPARTURES

The present work is conceived more or less in the same mould. The significant departures from the 1962 landscape are: first, the edgy plane composition of space is given up; second, in place of black-and-white with greys he paints in a single hue and prefers greens to other colours; and third, the architectural motifs have a definite function: they make up a kind of associative imagery, speaking in hints and leaving more room for the spectator's imagination to work on them. Sometimes, the green mass is broken by a line in the Miro manner and sometimes it is used as an extra aid for defining the density of the surrounding masses. The line invariably always is in neutral colour. The volume, however, is defined in the naturalistic manner; he follows the natural contours of a landscape rather than impose his own arbitrary sequences for the sake of composition. The result is they look like aerial views of some hilly lands. It would be quite interesting to see his aerial landscapes of plain, even land.

His drawings, too, are an attempt at defining volume through line. These are, indeed, exemplifications of his craft discipline and show with what passion he explores a problem. It is indeed sad that these have been displayed rather badly as if to prove that colour is superior to line, that what matters is the size of a canvas not the discipline and insight behind a work.

19

THE FALL OF MAN AND OTHER IMAGES

Review of F.N. Souza's 1976 solo exhibition in New Delhi, and on the artist's contentious place in Indian art

Patriot Magazine, New Delhi, 8 February 1976

It indeed is a fabulous show but not quite the show to match Francis Newton Souza's genius. The enthusiasm it has generated is also not wholly unexpected; the provincial world of art has a special relationship with its expatriate artists, and for an expatriate there is a 'ready' and 'dynamic' audience which goes to his show with lewd, voyeuristic eyes. Of course, Souza does not provide cleft trees but his 'garden' is laden with 'desirable' fruits, big apple breasts and genitals, and there may not be much oral sin to 'devour' some of these with hungry eyes. And since he knows his audience, his Adam has only a passive role: he has been buried like so many irrational beliefs in the power of witches.

The Adam image repels; he is ugly; life is the existential Other, a 'big orgasm', as Souza said in his autobiographical notes, it was 'like my father's. Then finished . . . I can never forgive him for having died just like that, and having left me in the lurch. I get into the church after that?'[1]

This is agreeable enough. The spectator's vision, wandering 'unframed' looking at the uncleft trees growing in the centre of the garden, is framed by the artist's personal history and acquires the same precision as that of the artist's vision. What the philistine is after is a somewhat illicit excitement: the sight of the painter, to have the 'tactile' tie in his praying soul and the aura of that uniqueness which accompanies the great artist. The expatriate provides this in good measure. And Souza understands what the searching eyes of his audience is looking for: the image of a suffering artist, the romantic saga suggested by his art. As every successful artist develops the actor in him, Souza shuns glory and fame and treats his art as so many predicates of his personality. And thus a myth is created.

At this point, plainsmanism of art takes over. The media machinery comes in to 'explain' art in the context of the artist's personal history. And most artists submit to the talk shows enacted for the benefit of the public. After all, the switched-on is the mark of celebrity although one is not sure whether an artist is really happy about these talk shows. Not at any rate artists like Souza's sensitivity. Souza will not allow the 'talker' to take over: he always talks back; his weapon is the weapon of argument. And the element of co-presence immediately comes into operation with his audience. 'It is surprising that at the age of 51, I can still pass as the *enfant terrible,*' Souza concludes his introduction to the catalogue. There is surprisingly no hint of his being a competing master with acolytes of different metropolitan 'avant-gardism': and for good reason because he is a proselytizing genius and always makes it a point to underline his responsibilities to the local art scene and these responsibilities count much more than the irrational belief in the metaphysical entity called 'art'.

POLITICS OF PROVINCIALISM

He lets out a big blast against the assumptions of provincialism implying that being a provincialist is no shame: a, provincialist cannot choose not to be a provincialist, and the native accents are all important for him. He speaks with the condescending rhetoric of the superiority of the role the Progressive Artists Group [PAG] aesthetic still plays in the art-making activities in India, attacking the 1890 Group artists as being in some kind of a satellite relationship with New York and other metropolitan art centres. Since the importance of the 1890 Group lies in the fact that they refused to bind themselves in a surrogate relationship with the art rhetoric of the Fifties – particularly the beginnings of modern art with the artists of the PAG. Souza divides the local [art] scene so that the focus of the endless talk shows, which came with the inauguration of his exhibition at the Dhoomimal's, continues even after he is back in New York. The premises of the attack are interesting. Souza says –

> Another lot who called themselves the 1890 Group which mercifully went kerplunk have also been taking swats at PAG, using pins and matchsticks on Gulliver, but could an anachronism named 1890 ever overtake progress which was the aim of hotshot artists of the Progressive Group? The answer is 'NOPE', particularly because the style these Lilliputians adopted is of the 1960s from the Royal College of Art, Kensington, London, itself borrowed from American pop art. They are illustrators who paint with 'illustrative paint', of the sort magazine illustrations, even comic strips, are made. American pop is the limp-wrist product of vulgar camp by fruits and faggots who were previously interior decorators, fashion designers and commercial artists and whereas their manifesto may not have been in the Queen's vernacular, they followed the words of Clement Greenberg to the extent that Tom Wolfe has pointed out in his book 'The Painted Word' (1975), the blowups of Greenberg's prose could well appear as exhibits illustrated with 'small illustrations' by the pop, hard-edge and field painters he helped to promote.[2]

Souza's attack on the 1890 Group should, of course, be dismissed as a light-hearted comment of an expatriate as unserious as the stated purpose of his visit: 'If you really want to know why I'm back after a decade, it's because I read an article in an American sexrag on the brothels of Lahore and Delhi.' Souza, it is true, never in his career played the surrogate to the art styles of metropolitan art. By choosing to leave India in 1949, he claims he had merely enacted the Gauguin journey in reverse. Gauguin was proud of being barbaric, to be amidst the unspoilt children of nature, while Souza lived in the West (since 1967 in New York, the imperial capital of metropolitan art) for enjoying the bourgeois logic of social status that accompanies fame and accolades; so he converted his modern Khajuraho mythologies into sweet money. Souza who had been a cardholding member of the Communist Party said goodbye to 'progressivism' before he left India. Gulley Jimson[3] and his endless suffering search for a studio has taught Souza that only millionaires are the true friends of art. He was to seek the good life of a bourgeois, not like Pissarro who said, 'it's a wonderful business being a bourgeois – without a cent!'[4] For him there was no hide-and-seek game against his middle-class credentials. Not for him the status of a moral god, which Gauguin sought and even acquired at a great price: his attitude towards the bourgeois is close to Picasso's – to fool him as much as possible by enacting deliberate crowd-pleasing

PATRIOT MAGAZINE

THE FALL OF MAN AND OTHER IMAGES

IT indeed is a fabulous show but not quite the show to match with Francis Newton Souza's genius. The enthusiasm it has generated is also not wholly unexpected. the provincial world of art has a special relationship with its expatriate artists, and for an expatriate there is a 'ready' and 'dynamic' audience which goes to his show with lewd veyeurist eyes. Of course Souza does not provide cleft trees but his 'garden' is laden with 'desirable'

By K. B. GOEL

fruits, big apple breasts and genitals, and there may not be much oral sin to 'devour' some of these with hungry eyes. And since Souza knows his audience, his Adam has only a passive role: he has been buried like so many irrational beliefs in the power of witches.

The Adam image repels; he is ugly: life is the existential Other, a 'big orgasm', and as Souza said in his autobiographical notes it was "like my father's. Then finished. I can never forgive him for having died just like that, and having left me in the lurch. How could I get into the church after that?"

This is agreeable enough. The spectator's vision, wandering 'unframed' looking at the uncleft trees growing in the centre of the garden, is framed by the artist's personal history and acquires the same precision as that of the artist's vision. What the philistine is *after is a somewhat illicit excitement*: The sight of the painter, to have the 'tactile' tic in his praying soul and the aura of that uniqueness which accompanies the great artist. The expatriate provides this in good measure. And Souza understands what the searching eyes of his audience is looking for: the image of a suffering artist, the romantic saga suggested by his art. As every successful artist develops the actor in him. Souza shuns glory and fame and treats his art as so many predicates of his personality. And thus a myth is created.

At this point, plain-man-ism of art takes over. The media machinery comes in to 'explain' art in the context of artist's personal history And most artists

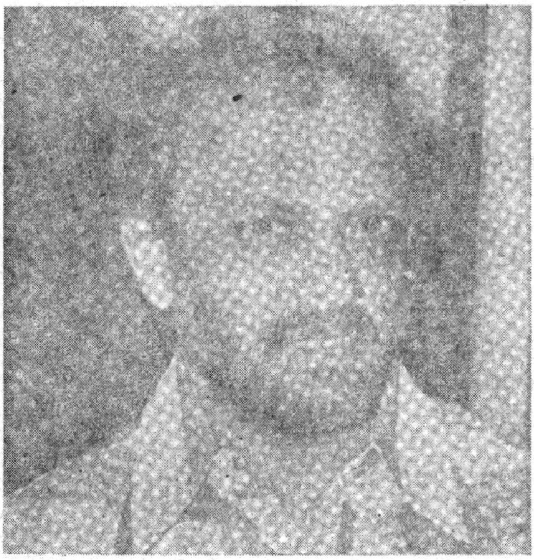

F. N. Souza.

taking swats at PAG, using pins and matchsticks on Gulliver, but could an anachronism named 1890 ever overtake progress which was the aim of hotshot artists of the Progressive Group? The answer is 'NOPE', particularly because the style these Lilliputians adopted is of the 1960s from the Royal College of Art, Kensington, London, itself borrowed from American Pop art. They are illustrators who paint with "illustrative paint", of the sort magazine illustrations, even comic strips, are made. American Pop is limp-wrist product of vulgar camp by fruits and faggots who were previously interior decorators, fashion designers and commercial artists,

fidently say that I am not influened by anyone and that I am not experimenting."

By implication Souza is drawing attention to the in-fighting among artists about patronage, and since Indian art has yet to evolve a firm support system, the Lalit Kala Akademi is the only institution to whip and rebel against. So what is wrong with Indian artists is the 19th century notion of middle-class ways being in conflict with the life style of an artist. Perhaps there is some truth in the contrary assumptions: the logic of art leading into one direction and the logic of social status into another. The Indian artist has yet to

cation with
periority to
ducts from
the metropo
provincialist
for ever co
tual talk-sh
were incapa
for Indian
provided by
Edward Lu
are to try
satisfactory
painting as
factory that
tiveness it i
sonal identi
painting nes
in it the u
which we h
for." There
tion this cri
the self is c
India."

This expl
ing acts, hi
to shock th
ence is rea
the next: ac
iroy and h
cantankerou

Souza's eg
ing superior
consciousnes
it were par
a centre w
to the new
bourgeoisie,
worried abo
tact with t
Souza's is th
above the
man conditi
remote from
divine Chin
Souza's orie
ment the b
are invisible
ern guru a
Humpty
ed by Poule
how can on
human iden
of movemen
is the disc
phic momen
itself in ord
invent itself
in itself, in
simulacrum

unconventionalities. And he [Souza] is proud that he sells. 'I am one of the few painters who live entirely on his art without resort to teaching or commercial portraits. As for my art I can confidently say that I am not influenced by anyone and that I am not experimenting.'

By implication, Souza is drawing attention to the infighting among artists about patronage, and since Indian art has yet to evolve a firm support system, the Lalit Kala Akademi is the only institution to whip and rebel against. So what is wrong with Indian artists is the nineteenth-century notion of middle-class ways being in conflict with the lifestyle of an artist. Perhaps there is some truth in the contrary assumptions: the logic of art leading into one direction and the logic of social status into another. The Indian artist has yet to sort out his confusion: while state patronage assumes that the artist is a member of the middle class, that is to say, the support for his skill is based on the assumption that he is a professional man, the artist behaves as if he is a member of aristocracy, and that is why he feels cut off from the mainstream of life. There is some truth in the artist's assumption that art-making is impossible in bourgeois culture and for 'being an artist' he has to pay a heavy price in terms of personal suffering. For this reason, he finds himself a prisoner of show business as it has happened in the West.

PROPHETIC

Souza that way has been prophetic: he knew as early as in 1947 that there was no escape from the bourgeois logic of modern art. The only escape from its octopus influence is to assume an aristocratic stance as Tagore did and to create art outside bourgeois values. So Souza and Raza decided to leave India: Gade, Husain and Ara stayed back and became decadent. The metropolitan initiative that came in the Fifties with abstract expressionism as the blast of internationalism, [had] the whole art scene in India go for it in a kind of provincial surrender. No doubt Husain and Ara kept their heads above the muddy aesthetic of internationalism but they were not even the minority as they were when Souza was on the scene. If some philistines still admired Husains, it was out of ignorance; the Gupta art paradigms of which Souza still provides a homogenized immutability to its development were no longer thought to be authentic, sustaining heritage. Trapped within the provincialist bind, Husain turned the form language of the Gupta art images into formalized conventions that reminds one as made up of some exotic formalist-modernist doctrine of the two-dimensional. Husain's cultural givens, no doubt, connect his images to some nostalgia for the past: what was lacking was the context which could be considered socially specific.

Souza could have provided for PAG an aesthetic basis for human communication with implications of cultural superiority to art's numerous optical products from the West. For it is clear that the metropolitan scheme of keeping the provincialist in surrogate relationship forever could be defeated by intellectual talk shows, which Husain and Ara were incapable of enacting. The reason for Indian art's provincial bind was provided by the *London Times* critic, Edward Lucie-Smith. He said:

> If we are to try to localize what seems unsatisfactory about contemporary Indian painting as we now see it – unsatisfactory that is, apart from sheer imitativeness, it is the lack of a sense of personal identity. Even their particular painting nearly succeeds; we fail to find in it the urgent egotistical statement which we have taught ourselves to look for.

There is another relevant observation this critic makes: 'Consciousness of the self is one of the European gifts to India.' This explains Souza's frontier-jumping acts, his extremisms, his readiness to shock the audience, and if the audience is ready for it, his readiness for the next: so his antics, the love of the irony and his Dali-like bluntness and cantankerous honesty. Souza's egotistical, almost condescending superiority exhibits the old kind of consciousness which is princely as if it were part of a throne, issuing from a centre without a margin. Compared to the new consciousness of the Western bourgeoisie – harassed, job conscious and worried about the results and in contact with the marginal subjects only – Souza's is that of an old king's which is above the common misery of the human condition, above time and as remote from the world as those of the divine Chinese Emperors. Compared to Souza's Oriental Buddha-like detachment the buzz-saw (because his teeth are invisible) consciousness of the Western guru appears very much like old Humpty Dumpty. This is well explained by Poulet (*Studies in Human Time*): how can one discover the principle of human identity amidst lineal sequences of movements? The self is obliged to the discontinuity of these typographic moments–

> Each time to forget itself in order to reinvent itself, to reinvent itself in order to regain interest in itself, in short, to effect a mocking simulacrum of continued creation, thanks to which it believes it will escape the authentication of its nothingness and out of its nothingness refashion reality.[5]

To escape from this time-structured consciousness, [James] Joyce embraced the modern spirit which he described as returned medievalism: 'The object of any work of art is the transference of emotions' and medieval art has 'emotional fecundity'.[6] Of course Souza, like Joyce, is medieval because India is medieval as Ireland is medieval and so the common symbolic mode of communication is medieval.

ART AS METABOLISM

Souza thus hates any kind of experimentation: the aim of his art is to compose uniqueness and his compositional logic is different; there are no attempts to fill the gap between appearance and reality. Souza says (and as much Picasso would have said about his art): 'I've made my art a metabolism. I express myself freely in paint in order to exist. I paint what I want, what I like, what I feel. "I wear my hat as I please, indoor or out," said Walt Whitman.'[7]

Like a medieval saint, Souza mythologizes his personal struggle against false consciousness. That is to say he is obsessed with the modern world's authoritarian dimension of conformity. Having to make art in the context of bourgeois culture, Souza reversed the role of narcissism and adopts a self-constructed negativity in opposition to its mirror image, positivism. Instead of narcissism and of perpetual conflict and its resolution where self confirms itself to itself, by the plain Hegelian dialectics the self goes through a circuit (that is objectifying itself by transforming the Other, annihilating it and making it a part of its subjectivity) of the objective world to discover itself while for the narcissist it is just a detour. Thus self-consciousness for Souza is a substitute for self-realization. Which is the aim of all great art: to provide a set of substitutes for reality. Souza's images of men and women seem still innocent because they have not touched the tree of knowledge, only the (non-existent) tree of life; they are more like after-images of a thousand memories.

Editor's Notes

1 'Nirvana of a Maggot', in *Words & Lines*, London: Villiers, 1959, p. 15.
2 F.N. Souza, 1983 exhibition catalogue.
3 The artist-protagonist of Joyce Cary's novel *The Horse's Mouth*, who 'exploit[s] his friends and acquaintances to earn a quid'.
4 John Rewald, ed., *Camille Pissarro: Letters to his son Lucien*, New York: Pantheon Books, 1945, p. 115 – from an 1887 letter.
5 Georges Poulet, *Studies in Human Time*, Connecticut: Greenwood Press, 1979, p. 87, quoted by Marshall McLuhan in *The Gutenberg Galaxy: The Making of Typographic Man*, Toronto: University of Toronto Press, 1962, p. 249.
6 Quoted in Arthur Powers, *Conversations with James Joyce*, The Lilliput Press, 1974, p. 95.
7 F.N. Souza, *Words & Lines*.

20

SOUZA OF THE FORTIES, DISCOVERY OF THE SELF

A reflection on F.N. Souza in a review of his 1982 exhibition of his earliest work, from the 1940s

'Complementarities', *Patriot Magazine*, New Delhi, 31 January 1982

The exhibition of F.N. Souza's paintings (representing the work of his years as a student at the J.J. School of Art and those done after his expulsion from the art school until he sailed for England in July 1949) are the best offerings of the season. Since the evenings are long, windy, cold and lonely, the best way to escape them is a visit to the Dhoomimal art gallery where the Souzas of the 1940s are displayed. It is undoubtedly *the* most important exhibition; I do not remember if any painter of Souza's generation has mounted an exhibition of the works of his formative years, which means the works done in the 1940s. What is the most unusual characteristic of the 1940s is the sense of visual exhilaration, the kind of which India has never witnessed.

The sense of visual exhilaration should be the oddest thing happening in a period which saw the invasion of the war-torn faces of young British Tommies and American G.Is. Also the long-lasting experience of the 1942 mass revolt which hastened the pace of our freedom struggle; it also represents the ugliest phase of modern Indian history, for the Partition experience was more painful, turning us all into beasts preying at each other's throats for the love of blood than the Bengal famine. Yet, Indian painting emerged into full consciousness to celebrate the role of the self in shaping a given medium of expression. This consciousness of the self as a shaping medium was first witnessed in the works of the Progressive Artists' Group which F.N. Souza founded in 1947. Witness the egoistical waggishness in Souza's assertion:

> We had clear-cut views on art, what it was and what it should be. We found Amrita Sher-Gil hybrid, biologically as well as aesthetically. George Keyt was also hybrid, biologically and aesthetically; he derived from Picasso as Sher-Gil derived from Gauguin. We dismissed both as unsuitable examples for the promulgation of our ideas in art. Santiniketan was too sentimental for us and Jamini Roy unsophisticated.[1]

This rationality of Newtonian prediction was a new voice in the 1940s; it was conscious of its astonishing power of competence and faith in itself.

This was a new experience to a mind which has been reduced to becoming all surface; it was a mind closed from inside so that every new gesture left it cold, a mind gone numb to react with feeling. Not surprisingly, therefore, the only people who lent ears to this voice were the communists which led him to become a cardholding member in 1946.

The first review of his work appeared in the *People's Age*, the English weekly party organ. Ramesh Chandra wrote (July 1948) about the exhibition of Souza's works: 'His (Souza's) colours are rich and striking, his style has the sweep of one who may well grow up to be a giant.' It was a prophecy come true when Souza founded the Progressive Artists' Group in 1947. It was the famous trio – Ara (born 1914), Raza (born 1922) and Souza (born 1924) – who originally constituted the PAG. Later, each one of them brought another artist: Souza brought Husain; Raza, Gade; and Ara, Bakre. Only Raza, Husain and Souza scaled the heights of international fame.

The works of the famous trio of Indian painting have this shared ground: their markedly developed individual consciousness. Between the Souzas and Husains there is this dialectical relationship: the Husains are like the comforting chair to relax on while the Souzas act out an emotion. In the Husains, the perception of the self is through the medium of his work while in the early Souzas, particularly those of the 1940s and the mid-1950s, we arrive at the correct perception of the work through the medium: the self. In the Razas, though sharing a common expressionist horizon, we have the vibrant colour of Indian miniatures; in lyrical weaving of the colour tonalities, the Razas surpass the Husains; as if by a conscious process, Raza has eliminated all traces of his self and yet they have a pronounced signature quality.

Souza and Raza are expatriates; Souza became a British citizen and Raza, French, but they are rooted in the Indian milieu, while Husain, who flies in and out of India as often as he changes his shirt, remains an Indian through and through. Living in New York since 1967, Souza has turned into a medieval saint; he has withdrawn himself from the daily commerce of the common world. Not for him the peddling of his ware in art's commercial market which gave rise to the rumour that he has given up painting. The Souza of London and Paris – open, outgoing, Byzantine, a caricaturist ('all the portraits look as if their subjects were unfrocked saints'),[2] aggressive and egoistical – is dead now. If the memories of the London Souza still survive, it is because Souza has long been identified as the heir of Nietzsche: reflecting the spirit of atheistic existentialism: '. . . and you there on the top, in a single furnished room, smoking, standing at the window expressionless, city man that you are, your suffering is far more complex than the obviously simple tortured expression of one crowned with thorns and impaled with nails',[3] he wrote of his London days. Now its memory is like some act of contract marriage, a past without any emotional hang-ups; the New Yorker Souza neither drinks nor smokes.

The role PAG played in shaping Indian sensibilities is a subject of PhD research now. But Souza himself, in my view, played Darwin in the Indian painting scene and succeeded in breaking up the sacralized Hindu universe of eternal sleep. In the process of his rediscovery of the self in New York, he has developed the intuition of Hindu consciousness. This was evident from his 1976 show at the Dhoomimal which qualitatively was very different from his previous work; in place of cerebral representations marked by elements of violence and satire, there was a religious quality about his work, 'a terrible grandeur which even Rouault and Sutherland have not equalled in this century' as one Western critic has rightly observed.[4] Like the Francis of Assisi, Souza saluted the world through his 1975 images as if it were an assertion of the Hindu animistic gods looking with fresh eyes, not with the open eye of the West: these are now half-closed, anaestheticized by doubt wrapped into themselves, meditating . . .

How important is the current showing of his work of the 1940s to Souza can be judged from the fact that his wife, Barbara and son, Patrick flew from New York to participate in its inaugural celebrations. But the Indian art scene, deficient in historical knowledge, remained unmoved. Of the local celebrities, only Swaminathan came from Bhopal to attend the inaugural function.

Editor's Notes

1 F.N. Souza, 'On Progressive Artists' Group', *The Patriot*, date unknown. Reproduced in the catalogue, *Souza in the Forties*, c. 1982/83, p. 9, in quotation by the journalist-critic Jagmohan.
2 Art critic David Sylvester, quoted in Souza's 1975 catalogue, *Souza 1975*, exhibition held at London's ARTS 38 Gallery.
3 F.N. Souza, *Words & Lines*, London: Villiers, 1959.
4 Edwin Mullins, *F.N. Souza*, London, 1962, p. 40.

21

EXPRESSIONISM, WORLDS OF HUSAIN AND SOUZA

A reflection on the art of two of India's best-known modernists and members of the Progressive Artists' Group: F.N. Souza and M.F. Husain

Patriot Magazine, New Delhi, 14 July 1982

F.N. Souza before leaving for New York last month showed his classroom work of the 1940s when he was a student of the J.J. School [School of Art, Bombay] and a communist activist. No doubt he still remains an activist, this time with a 'white' flag signifying peace but afflicted with the same messianic consciousness which showed itself politically in his association with the communist movement. His involvement with the larger causes helped him evolve a language which was characterized by the expressionist despair despite his lack of exposure to the expressionist works proper. While the painters of the Bengal school looked back for inspiration to works of Ajanta frescoes and miniatures, a flight from the hard angularities of the Second World War years, Souza and his band of artists at the J.J. [School] revealed a deep-seated will to revolt, to establish a style of art in keeping with the temper of the war, representing something of the catastrophe of self-destruction. The war phenomenon alone was enough to maim and distort a natural vision: not surprisingly, Souza painted pictures that have close family resemblance with the European style of expressionist pictures painted during the outbreak of the First World War. Had Souza not identified himself politically with the forces fighting the fascist hordes he would not have developed a common bond with the people, would never have been free from narrow nationalist vision – and India would not have seen the birth of modernist sensibilities. For Souza, cast in the messianic mould, to free himself from the oppressive backward-looking environment was as important a psychic release as to break loose from the 'fallen' conventional world.

Souza acknowledges that he has been an expressionist of a sort: his vision was transmitted to his fellow admiring band of students and they accepted it unknowingly as the impressionists accepted the role of light in building their beautiful outer surfaces without any inner substance. Painting a picture meant nothing more than expressing subjective feeling, working towards externalization of emotion in the belief that this was the only distinctive mode of painting. It was a new painting and it had nothing to draw upon in Indian tradition. If the pictures lacked depth, it was because they embodied an experience of a new artistic manifestation that did not presuppose a style but worked their way up guided by their own vision: this attitude is hard to come by as it has no historical analogue. Fantasy, rather than cheap sociological issues, was the prominent visual component, as distortion was which came as naturally to them as it does to a child learning to draw his first representational pictures. Besides distortion (or was it a deformation of the existing social image?), colour had an intensity which gave to the picture surface an agitation similar in effect to the one found in expressionist pictures: their loaded brush-work was naive and spontaneous. Souza's unfettered egomaniac attitudes combined with painterly qualities, characteristic of expressionist mythology gave an attention-calling armature to his images of suffering: these images had Christian iconography as a launching ground but the intention was unmistakably to discover truth within himself rather than in the outer world of Christian intellectual perception. Of course, he paid little attention to colour beyond emotive execution of a picture surface, for he was more interested in evolving a new order of images that had the same universality of appeal as we find in Van Gogh's (In fact, he could invoke Van Gogh's words to explain his painterly preoccupations: 'I want to paint men and women with that something of the eternal which the halo used to symbolize and which we seek to convey by the actual radiance and vibration of our colouring.')

Husain, who was Souza's discovery, his gift to Indian painting, since his joining the Progressive Artists' Group, has been an intensely chromatic painter: colour is upheld in his work as the life source of his art. In fact, colour tends to be moving towards abstraction conditioned perhaps by a desire for optical purity and intensity. Because colour plays such an enlarged role in his painting, he seems tradition conscious: influenced by a folksy way of applying it, he does not seek to subdue his pictorial forces but gives them a body through colour with a contained absorbed energy of the hue. The result is that colour almost has a mimetic function – as a coefficient of mood, for there is evidence of a perceptual delight in exaggerated colour as a component of a luminous beat. But in the Souzas of the Fifties there is a marked resemblance of method popular with expressionist painters: in his images of the bourgeoisie colour smacks of the orgiastic suffused as it is with overt sexuality. The Husains are cool Fauvist ways of arriving at the primaries and secondaries electrified to be the transmitters of volatile stimuli. While a Husain can be enjoyed from a comfortable easy chair, a Souza makes the spectator leap forward almost drunkenly. Putting it another way, a Souza of the Fifties 'acts out' an emotion, stimulates an empathy, while a Husain of the same period does not involve the viewer with the element of acting; the painting seems to arrive at by a logic of inner necessity, through the innocence and the optimism he has for his act of creation. In Husain, the perception of the self is through the medium of his work, but in the early Souzas, being inspired manipulations of line and colour, we arrive at the correct perception of the work through the medium of the self. This dialectical relation between Souza's and Husain's still holds true.

The likes of these two artistic manifestations, innocent beyond providing an honest connection with the past as well as the future, are hard to come by. The three post-Husain-Souza decades of deformation and decay are characterized by lengthening shadows of disbelief in the means of seeking after truth which does not conform to the established custom. There is thus absence of a promise of a milieu which can provide a unity of correspondence as it did to the painters of the 1940s.

With the transformation of man into a mass that accompanied the increase in industrialization and growth of material wealth, the creative potential and urge to discover self through the medium of a work of art has met with pessimism and got caught in a blind alley. The painters of the third generation seem to have been caged by a private language that they do not themselves understand. Though they may deny the fact that their primary concern is to seek the ground of immediate utility, this introduces an element of latent irrationality, which they seek to conceal behind the private language argument.

The private language argument for the young painter has the same charm and a depth of feeling which poetry evokes: as poetry is a technique of projecting inner feelings, painting is seen as a language game which presupposes and celebrates the hidden structures. The dadaists undoubtedly would have enjoyed their situation and showed them how futile their search for a private language is. Being enmeshed by the platitudes of self-expression, straining to discover his inner private self, the young painter finds himself alienated from his conscious personality. The private language argument is valid for him because it brings him to the sources of modernity which seeks validity of its self-image through subjective self-certainty. (The Cartesian self-evident truth – 'I think therefore I am' – gets him back to the familiar ground on which the modern philosophy is built.) There is this primitive appeal in the notion of a private language: as Wittgenstein has said, 'The individual words of this language are to refer to what can only be known to the person speaking, to his immediate private sensations. So another person cannot understand the language.'

Husain and Souza have never been interested in attempts at looking inside ourselves simply because the outer environment was dirty, nor were they interested in looking into the minds of other people as the *Place for People* painters are. They had what may be called libidinous interest in the objective outer world: how much the world has changed that the alienated painter finds his sources of libidinous energies dry and arid.

22
STUDY IN DISGUISES

Review of F.N. Souza's solo exhibition in New Delhi in 1992, examining the arc of the artist's career

'Artscape', *The Economic Times*, New Delhi, 25 August 1990

It was in February last year. Francis Newton Souza, who was returning from Pakistan where he had a successful one-man show, gave a small cocktail party to his friends at a five-star hotel in New Delhi. He was so overcome with nostalgia and afterthoughts that he withheld nothing. With a loving rush of blood, he raised a toast to Gaitonde's genius, '... wish I could paint like my friend Gaitonde'. Gaitonde had found beauty while he himself was still struggling to find it, he said. 'I've touched beauty, only touched her,' interrupted Gaitonde, gently correcting Souza. Both Souza and Gaitonde know their Baudelaire well. 'The principal and essential problem (is) to discover whether we possess a specific beauty intrinsic to our new emotions.'[1] This proposition of Baudelaire's has become one of the defining truths of modernism.

There is the possibility of our confrontation with this specific beauty; it is, to be sure, not possible at the optical level alone. Either it is there with us, or it is not. We had the same sensation of touching beauty, as it were, standing before the new works by Souza which are on view at the Centre for Contemporary Art in the capital. Some of these works we would like to possess, recognizing in them those specific features of beauty that live within us as a secret desire. But like some old reflex, an awareness is jerked within us and we transcend the desire for possession. We come to a pact with Souza.

Something in Souza has changed fundamentally. The tactile feeling is now more pronounced than ever before, with the role of the eye having receded to the background. Now, the general hand and its manual dexterities take over; painting is now more of an act of nature's dispensation. The Souza of the Fifties is there, though, and we still admire him. The new Souza now appears in fragmentary images and we do not view him as we used to earlier.

Souza's attention-drawing acts of modernism are there too, but they are in a small format. They tear us apart from the known horizons of taste. They are ironic reminders that an image is not a sacred object but belongs to a space of language. When these pictures of things, taken from glossy art magazines, are defaced and chemically altered, they achieve a new emotional and personal content, though we regret they suffer from formal laxity.

Done between 1969 and 1984, these fifteen works are in the same class of works that were shown earlier at the Kunika-Chemould gallery in 1969. Their closeness to print culture demanded that they be read as a self-apparent play of graffiti space. They also speak of how the artist's whimsies have transparent windows and how we ourselves enjoy looking through them to admire the compositional sense of how the game is played. It is the same old game Souza is adept at, one which allows him to break our inhibitions and undo our muscle-bound understanding.

His eight drawings – placed between Sartre's existential anxiety and the hippie's flight to a private heaven – are to be located in freedom's negative but beautiful reach. Seen independently, they provide amusement of the mind, and the famously naughty Souza is here at his best. Their power is the truth of affects, an alliance with risk, as they stand apart from the life of a solipsist mind.

The old Souzas that arouse voyeuristic feelings are part of our nostalgia; they now stand on the edge of our aesthetic habit. The new Souzas may appear as strangers to our world. With Redmonism[2] as a guide to action, Souza has arrived at peace with himself, having given up the priestly-seeming aspect of his personality.

It is like arriving at a historical terminus. The inside (the existential anxiety) no longer governs the outside (the play with colour). If there are still traces of a residual presence of the old anxiety syndrome, it is because Souza remains the subject of his painting. The new work has no reference to a world to which Souza can escape. For he is afraid to conform to a type. He remains an outsider.

That explains why he is self-consciously alone. Reality with him is personal; it is so private that its public face is an enactment of theatrical situations. But the recent signature on displayed landscapes does not come in the way of our old habits of seeing; the traditional attributes in his landscapes are still there, but, step by slow step, these have been pushed in the direction of abstraction – away from the pictorial subject, away from the references to topography and architectural forms. These landscapes do not carry an indexical relation to the symbolic land of a homeless, disinherited mind – as his earlier landscapes did. We rather confront them as we confront an artist painting in public where the act of painting is completed by the spectator. To view these landscapes is to see Souza giving a demonstration of painting, such as he gave at the last triennale. Here, as there, the maker and the spectator meet.

Mourning Man is the culmination of the new method Souza has adopted, which is successfully exploited in the creation of a new landscape genre. In this work, we are within hearing distance of the noise of paints. And let me assure you, there is no hidden meaning to this image of man. What is created is the image of the artist's self – a view of the self that can be remade at will. In the earlier images – I have in mind his work called *Six Gentlemen of Our Time* he painted in the mid-Fifties meaning had a transcendental property, misdirecting our attention from the images proper.

Mourning Man can be appreciated not as implying an ideal correspondence with meaning and symbol, but as displaying the artist's power to show how colour can be played. The image is a product of the environment. It is apprehended as a complex of evanescent emotions and transient moods. Our visual encounter, though personal, is with colour, with an interplay of action between figure and field, which forms the core of the Souza whom we will encounter in future.

23

SUPERBLY SELF-CONSCIOUS

Review of a 1990 solo exhibition of F.N. Souza in New Delhi

'Artscape', *The Economic Times*, New Delhi, 26 August 1990

It is a fabulous show: the season's first grand offering at the Centre for Contemporary Art. Francis Newton Souza is represented by seven large landscapes (oils), six small heads, twelve works in acrylic on paper, fifteen drawings bathed in chemicals and sixteen drawings, two of which were done in 1979. Our response to the show is characteristic of the poor tribes of eastern Brazil: whenever anthropologist Curt Nimuendaju came back after a sojourn in civilized parts, the natives wept at the thought of sufferings the ethnographer must have undergone away from their village – the only place where they felt life was worth living.

Of course the analogy is a vast exaggeration, we are no poor tribes of eastern Brazil, nor is Souza our imagined Nimuendaju. But bound as we are in a provincial relationship, Souza's status as an expatriate and knowing that life in New York for Souza is no bed of roses, we have our fears and sympathies and shed our share of tears. Souza is not an outsider as Nimuendaju is for the Brazilian tribal people: like James Joyce – who turned his back early in life on his native city and rejected his childhood religion but carried with him, wherever he went, the vision of his home and the emotion of his faith – Souza is our ambassador.

Now if Joyce represents the highest values of modernist sensibility (but had few followers) so is it with Souza. With him is born a painting rooted in the consciousness of the self, a gift of modernism to India via expressionism. The subject of a Souza painting is Souza himself and the expressionist sensibility gives vent to its emotion by spontaneously loaded brushwork. Souza does it with unfettered egomania, almost to the point of being blind to form: and yet there is evidence of rational control. His painting is a site of visual frenzy and yet it is marked by excessive stillness. His iconography is original: though Indian to the core, it does not suffer from the presence of the ethnic. His Christian iconography is far superior to anything produced in the West: it has the right mix of the medieval and modern sensibilities. Consider, for example, his *Last Supper*; the images here are delivered brusquely to the eye with a dramatic intent and what is remarkable is his drawing which is more readable than in others.

Souza's emergence was no odd happening given the revolutionary situation existing in 1942, the time was ripe for the coming into being of a painting which was a radical response to the age. And it did in the canvases of the young artists who formed the Progressive Artists' Group (PAG) immediately after independence. They celebrated - with their bruised, schizoid egos - the shaping of their medium of expression whose subject was the self, the painter himself.

Souza, of course, was their natural leader and egotistical. This rational Newtonian analysis was the representative temper of the PAG artists. The young painters, particularly Souza, showed not only faith in themselves but also astonishing competence. It was a new experience for a mind gone dead with cultural schizophrenia. Everything seemed a product of commerce, a form of colonial kitsch devoid of any aesthetic merit. But through the haze, they saw the presence of the ethnic, the revival of folk forms and embraced it as their identity.

Souza, in the West, turned a sexual voyeurist. It promised him not only liberation from his colonial self but also a ready market. Moreover, it was part of the expressionist ethos: lacking in any erotic tradition, the Western painter goes orgiastic with colour and in the process becomes the victim of sexual parasitism. Souza acts out the emotions associated with the worship of female fetish: female parts are exteriorized, breasts are the 'desirable fruits' and there is no sin committed in devouring these. His female images, rich in form, are as empty as mirrors; they are born out of inner necessity.

In the context of the ideology of the suffering flesh, Souza's sexual voyeurism has the touch of condescension. Sex is an escape from a time-structured consciousness: like Joyce who embraced the modern spirit which he described as returned medievalism, Souza goes medieval with Khajuraho as his Ireland, of which the landscape is the pleasure garden. In the six large landscapes, colour invents its own pattern as it does in Pollock: line and colour are woven into a psychologically active surface. The Souza landscapes exhibit a preconceived order; the visual logic of the eye is dominated by the discipline of the hand: a preference for what comes after meditation over the improvization and form over action. Souza is famous for his inflammatory treatment of heads. The iconography is morbidly personal, the distortion grotesque to the point of a neurotic edge; the image proper shows mannerisms played to the dark labyrinth of the psyche. Take, for instance, the group of six heads: these are the reworked images of the pen and ink work, *Six Gentlemen of Our Times,* he did in 1955. He repeats himself but retains a sensation of passion — too warm to be tragic, while the 1955 work was concerned with a tragic view of life.

Taken at face value, his prolificacy seems to have played out now. Old as he is and without giving up the sacred rage, how long can he be in a state of mental anguish? He continues to play the game of make-believe that he has played all his life - like in the last scene of the Antonioni film *Blow Up* where a game of tennis is being played: the court is there, the players are there, only the ball is missing.

24

THE GAME THEORY

Review of Krishen Khanna's recent works, including one of the Game *series, 1973*

Link, New Delhi, 9 December 1973

It was nice of Krishen Khanna to have arranged a private viewing of his latest paintings at his house last Sunday that he is exhibiting at a Bombay Gallery on 10 December. The show will include a large number of drawings, besides his famous painting on expositions of the war professionals and the Game theory. These canvases, because of their radical implications, certainly are not for decorating a middle-class drawing room. They are more like [George] Grosz's caricâtures of what they call in America, the Consciousness II people – people who rule society from their executive suites. Incidentally, they patronize the most extreme radical modes in visual arts and it is these people who buy the art that really condemns them, and in their taste they are the real avant-gardeniks. They seem to run society even if actually they are not running it. At any rate this is the general impression and to be sure it is a mere put-on. Behind the glass-and-metal desk there seems no one there: the executive suite is empty. And if there seems someone invisible running the office and looks very much like a man, he really is a representative of a man who does what the organization tells him to do. And he does what the representative tells him. His executive suite is more like a complicated machine, and he (or it) does not run it: he just tends it.

The 'representative' man is to plan profits like a great military strategist on the game board. The game-board image, indeed, does not surely recall any primitivistic association: it is the image of a monopoly house where everything is geared to a simple function – the promotion of the interests of the organization. The game-board expert is a devoted organization man who is at pains in convincing everyone that whatever he does has the sanction of law.

And he knows well that law, like his executive suite, is a grand abstraction: it is actually part of the property system because without the system's support, the law is an empty, hollow concept. So he is always attempting to draw your attention away from the real issue: that is the degree of power society grants to its citizens. But again the power is symbolized by the amount of money you have in your pocket, and so (as Marx said) money becomes the pimp between man and his values. The real arbiter thus is money, not culture, which used to be the case once upon a time in our society. The new painting has nothing to do with the old tradition, being part of the international art market. It is for this reason more experimental, forward-looking, progressive and 'avant-gardeish' in comparison with other arts. Painting can change hands as easily as money does.

This is not just to explain away Krishen's exposition of the Game theme: it is to draw a demarcation line between the working modes of two significant painters – Krishen Khanna and Bhupen Khakhar – and the similarities in their theme: the professionals in our society. Bhupen Khakhar, for instance, paints these days the professional classes like the watchmaker and the bank manager in the idiom of popular bazaar culture: and these people are painted rather stiffly as if they had posed before him and as they do before a photographer in Indian bazaars. These paintings have the same backdrop as we find in the bazaar photographer working in the open air. This gives a bizarre look but it has a positive hardcore sensibility of visual tradition, which is part of the cultural milieu of our less-sophisticated middle classes.

Unlike Bhupen Khakhar, Krishen Khanna makes rational but semi-surrealist images which have a fine art context: more than this context he is concerned with the message, the witticisms and the metaphors and these lack a general cultural environment that we find in Bhupen Khakhar's paintings. In a Khakhar painting, aesthetic and social assumptions have the same archaic quality while Krishen is essentially urban in outlook. As opposed to Khakhar's clownish peep shows, Krishen gives the impression of being metaphysically ponderous, and there is high seriousness in defining his viewpoint. Nevertheless, he succeeds in creating a state of mind which despite the fact that his main preoccupation is allegoric storytelling, is not altogether unusually well expressed perhaps also because he creates the evidence of real action. There are no illusive graphic symbols. One can read them as one does a Marxist text.

The images in Krishen's *Game* paintings are expressions more of a personal terror than of social comment – the terror of the 'firm' which has no regard for human values. They are also rich in literary allusions: one can read into them a bit of a modern Macbeth as interpreted by Mary McCarthy who translates the play into commercial images. General Macbeth, according to her, makes a good businessman, but a businessman who has no feeling for others and thus can be a good member of America's ruling military-industrial complex. This modern Macbeth in McCarthy's view 'is not even a monster, though he may yet breed monsters, thanks to his activities on the heath: he is timorous, unimaginative and a prayer he would like to say most fervently is simply "Amen".' The essay is not about Macbeth really: it is about the Pentagon, and the point she makes is that these nasty little men are not great men of sin and evil: stand up to them and they will fall apart. Krishen, however, leaves the interpretation for the viewer. He says –

> Do me the kindness of looking at them. . . . No, no you don't have to buy them, besides I know that you would not be able to live with them. . . . But you could spend a few minutes on something that has taken me quite long to do. For instance, you too could be participating in the Game even though the real participants are busy and don't have any time for you. You could at least try and outstare the hound who is there to keep you away.

He does not say, despite the strong literary content (which incidentally is a dirty word in the context of modern art), what these images are about except that he fears misreading of them. For instance, 'The vast majority of Indians', he says, 'thought I had painted Pakistanis and no doubt if the Pakistanis had seen these paintings (sorry, No Cultural Agreement, no seeing of my paintings) they would have thought that I had painted brutal Indians. I suppose I must be a poor painter in not being specific. . . .'

The paintings are no doubt very objective: there is hardly any visual complexity either, as they are a slice of life. The spotlight is always on the faces but they are hard to define, hard to separate one from the other. So the viewer is placed in a Kafkaesque situation: the characters occupying the executive table are like snakes, they look all alike. And recall the puzzled look on his face when K, the hero of *Trial*, enters a modern office and cannot make out which clerk he should meet because they all look alike – like snakes. Clearly, Krishen is making us aware of the indeterminate elements in our visual thinking and by fixing our own meanings on these images we are really making discoveries for ourselves. And since visual is only one aspect of an experience and each sensory organ records reality in its own way, these paintings awaken subjective images of our experience. That way Krishen's is a kind of perceptual realism.

The Grosz-like images have dadaistic implications also. It is doubtful whether Krishen is conscious of their dada fabric because the controlling element is not the intellect but the eye. And if dadaist Grosz comes to mind again and again it is because of the power of drawing and caricature. The references remain highbrow: no pop clichés for Krishen which are so much part of Khakhar's painting furniture. They could be monochrome studies, or portrait drawings in paint, but they are not, because of the effect of the dramatic composition. Putting it another way, the faces are etched in black and chiaroscuro on a coloured ground in invariably warmer hues, and to heighten the drama the surrounding areas are always painted in neutral shades. Then he employs the cross-cutting method of the cinema: the connecting lines of tension seem all very deliberately planned and all this within the confines of a single canvas which retains its flatness in all circumstances.

As far as his pictorial methods are concerned, he has no doubts about how to renew the power of images by purely pictorial means. Their aesthetic claims surely outweigh the considerations of their political content. Which is no doubt a tremendous achievement. He has borrowed much from the dada painters - particularly from Grosz but the principles of form are not from the dada sources: They are all his own, enriched by his past achievements as an abstract painter. There is certainly a grand union of the two elements.

The composition methods are repetitive and yet the composition allows interplay between mood and imagery. The surface is flat, rather excessively unemotive, and here again we become aware how much he has learnt from photography, the medium he uses most creatively. Indeed, the camera has taught him a good deal more than he might care to admit: the surreal, dadaist values of images. Similarly, the camera eye has no interpretative power; its image is highly malleable and it has a kind of emotional innocence that is the hardware of the photographic image. The colours have a searing intensity because of the passionate concern for spatial function they have been put to. Except the hard edges of the table which plays a prominent role in the composition, colours merge into shadows and in this way their effect is surreal. The narrative content is full of ambiguities that make perception quiver with anxiety. Perhaps it is a new language in which Krishen Khanna is speaking.

25

A MIRACLE OF CONSCIOUSNESS

Review of a 1993 solo show of the artist Krishen Khanna

'Artscape', *The Economic Times*, New Delhi, 18 December 1993

Krishen Khanna's exhibition of paintings opened at the Capital's Vadhera Art Gallery on 11 December and is on till 4 January. What is offered in Krishen Khanna's art is not what works of art normally offer. What is offered is the hint of a possibility of the completion of a long journey which started in 1947 – the year the Progressive Artists' Group (PAG) was formed.

He joined the group as an amateur enthusiast, conscious of the historical narrative of modernist sensibility which the PAG promised and worked for. The PAG artists were all men with a vision that was both transcendental as well as compelling. Transcendental because they defined themselves from their Archimedean point of vision, and compelling because they not only delinked themselves from their past but believed in a present that seemed to emerge out of nowhere. Let us not forget that the modern movement in Indian art was made by a few individuals, and Krishen had his share of distractions, history's cunning and the irreversibility of modernism's grammar. Grammar matters because the problem of modernism is one in which the question of value comes first as well as at the very end. It does not count where there is a tradition within which everything that counts does count; where the presence of the work of art is a felt experience, not merely known through mediation; where the genealogies are analysed, and a work of art gets placed within a historical sequence even if it leaves out the meaning of an individual work as part of its structure of subjectivity.

For Krishen, not the structure of subjectivity but the world of generals discussing war games at the conference table was the reminder of the Nietzschean truth: the world is not *what* it is, but *that* it is [emphasis author's], and which points to the facticity of the world as against its meaning. The presumed superiority of the objective world to the subjective became a new sensibility especially when 'pop culture' appeared on the art scene with its denial of the very possibility of interpretation. Under its influence, the basic unit for contemporary art was not the idea but the analysis and extension of sensation. And there was this new value: the value of free creation, the activity becoming its own end, rather without end and therefore without any need for justification.

To counter this, a tough conservatism became Krishen's visible frontier of consciousness. He was happy with pictures in which the moulding force was the brushwork and the hand was made to play hide-and-seek with the mind's unconscious inhabitants. No longer was the anxiety of influence there to trouble him and, unlike the expressionists, he did not make the mistake of equating men with flowers. But he did suffer from the anxiety of transition, of a 180-degree turn which he took with the *Bandwalla* paintings.

In these works, which he first exhibited in New Delhi, the empty space is cut up imaginatively, to open up linear tangles which he half covered: they satisfy the joy-evoked need for a song and its tactile sensation. What is not covered shows up as smudged traces of contour, acting as interconnecting elements within the net-like pattern. In order to obtain instant recognition, the net-like formations act as forms within a single form. Broad areas of colour, laid side by side, allow him greater freedom in the play with the mediations of colour application methods that contribute in developing a new sense of surface sensibility. This new surface in the present work is no more involved with the grammar of phrasing. He now addresses directly: the marginal stance is gone and so is the need for meaning and in keeping faith with modernism's expressionist grammar.

The presumed superiority of the objective world as he found it in daily life, too lost its referentiality. In its place, there is now a look of emancipatory consciousness: it is sportive and mutational; the colour has a retinal address, it interconnects and has a terrific binding power. There is openness and the appearance of insubstantiality which was first witnessed in the *Bandwalla* paintings. There is an airiness without those nagging problems of one area of colour having to balance another.

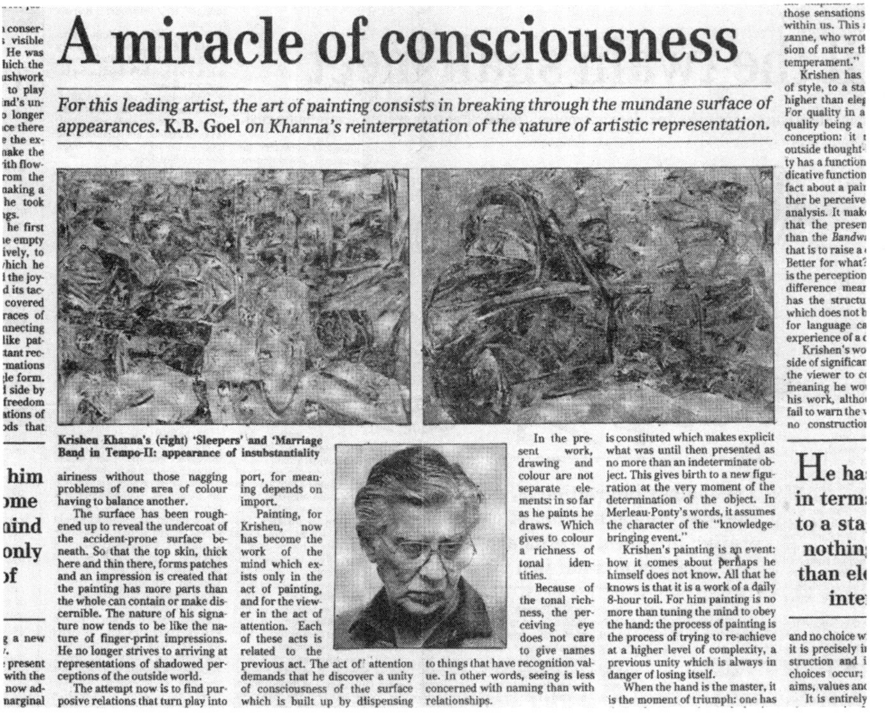

A miracle of consciousness

For this leading artist, the art of painting consists in breaking through the mundane surface of appearances. K.B. Goel on Khanna's reinterpretation of the nature of artistic representation.

Krishen Khanna's (right) 'Sleepers' and 'Marriage Band in Tempo-II: appearance of insubstantiality

airiness without those nagging problems of one area of colour having to balance another.

The surface has been roughened up to reveal the undercoat of the accident-prone surface beneath. So that the top skin, thick here and thin there, forms patches and an impression is created that the painting has more parts than the whole can contain or make discernible. The nature of his signature now tends to be like the nature of finger-print impressions. He no longer strives to arriving at representations of shadowed perceptions of the outside world.

The attempt now is to find purposive relations that turn play into port, for meaning depends on import.

Painting, for Krishen, now has become the work of the mind which exists only in the act of painting, and for the viewer in the act of attention. Each of these acts is related to the previous act. The act of attention demands that he discover a unity of consciousness of the surface which is built up by dispensing

In the present work, drawing and colour are not separate elements: in so far as he paints he draws. Which gives to colour a richness of tonal identities.

Because of the tonal richness, the perceiving eye does not care to give names to things that have recognition value. In other words, seeing is less concerned with naming than with relationships.

is constituted which makes explicit what was until then presented as no more than an indeterminate object. This gives birth to a new figuration at the very moment of the determination of the object. In Merleau-Ponty's words, it assumes the character of the "knowledge-bringing event."

Krishen's painting is an event: how it comes about perhaps he himself does not know. All that he knows is that it is a work of a daily 8-hour toil. For him painting is no more than tuning the mind to obey the hand: the process of painting is the process of trying to re-achieve at a higher level of complexity, a previous unity which is always in danger of losing itself.

When the hand is the master, it is the moment of triumph: one has

The surface has been roughened up to reveal the undercoat of the accident-prone surface beneath. So that the top skin, thick here and thin there, forms patches and an impression is created that the painting has more parts than the whole can contain or make discernible. The nature of his signature now tends to be like the nature of fingerprint impressions. He no longer strives to arrive at representations of shadowed perceptions of the outside world. The attempt now is to find purposive relations that turn play into recreations, for he does not take relations seriously. The play does not allow the player to behave towards what is being played as if it were an object. What interests him is the totality of surface and not its building up as an interplay of relationships among parts.

There is no attempt at composition either, for composition means representation and representation means import of a sign language which turns a work of art into a vehicle for some hidden content. An aesthetic surface has nothing to reveal other than itself: it has no import, for meaning depends on import. Painting, for Krishen, now has become the work of the mind which exists only in the act of painting, and for the viewer in the act of attention. Each of these acts is related to the previous act. The act of attention demands that he discover a unity of consciousness of the surface which is built up by dispensing with colour.

Dispensing with contour or outline means dispensing with representation: painting is now built up into space by a series of interlacing tonalities. Since drawing does not exist, its presence is felt in modelling, through which drawing seems to appear. There are only contrasts, not sculpted contrasts: they are built up step by determined step, stroke by stroke: the contrasts that give rise to sensations that are the outcome of the exact relationship of tones. In the present work, drawing and colour are not separate elements: in so far as he paints, he draws which gives to colour a richness of tonal identities. Because of the tonal richness, the perceiving eye does not care to give names to things that have recognition value. In other words, seeing is less concerned with naming than with relationships.

Everything connects with everything else. Call it a miracle of consciousness, but it is there; for Krishen, the act of painting consists in breaking through the surface of appearances. Yet the result is a new unity of the two distinctively separate worlds. He is able to achieve harmony with a new objective world the very moment it is sought to be destroyed.

Attention is focused neither on the associational nature of images nor on the return to itself of the thought which is already in control of its objects: rather, a new object is constituted which makes explicit what was until then presented as no more than an indeterminate object. This gives birth to a new figuration at the very moment of the determination of the object. In Merleau-Ponty's words, it assumes the character of the 'knowledge-bringing event'.

Krishen's painting is an event: how it comes about, perhaps, he himself does not know. All that he knows is that it is a work of a daily eight-hour toil. For him painting is no more than tuning the mind to obey the hand: the process of painting is the process of trying to re-achieve at a higher level of complexity, a previous unity which is always in danger of losing itself. When the hand is the master, it is the moment of triumph: one has then the sensation of having achieved something which the seeing eye could not imagine; it is the moment of having mastered the event - and all according to its own rules - and simultaneously one is gripped with a feeling of achievement, of having been liberated from the hegemony of all rules. I might describe this position as god-like.

In simple terms, it means Krishen's art should be interpreted as the process of making a picture (representation of thing) become a painting, (the process of making) the reality of which explains why the emphasis is on sensations - those sensations of art that dwell within us. This almost echoes Cezanne, who wrote of 'comprehension of nature through a personal temperament'.

Krishen has arrived, in terms of style, to a stage where nothing higher than elegance is intended. For quality in a painting is a lie, quality being a thought-language conception: it refers to nothing outside thought-language. If quality has a function, it has only an indicative function, a way of stating a fact about a painting that can neither be perceived nor subjected to analysis. It makes no sense to say that the present work is better than the *Bandwalla* series. To say that is to raise a different question. Better for what? What is relevant is the perception of difference: this difference means nothing, for it has the structure of subjectivity which does not belong to language, for language cannot express the experience of a difference.

Krishen's work is always on the side of significance: he leaves it for the viewer to construct whatever meaning he would like to give to his work, although he would not fail to warn the viewer that there is no construction without choice and no choice without a norm. And it is precisely in the work of construction and interpretation that choices occur; and with choice; aims, values and norms.

It is entirely legitimate for the viewer to give free rein to conflicting interpretations and evaluations as long as he respects his limitation that he has no access to meaning of a work of art: our knowledge of the meaning suffers from a subjective judgement, for meaning itself is mere fiction. Everything in Krishen is so tightly interlocked in terms of meaning and significance that the unlocking will never cease to be confused and one-sided.

What matters to Krishen is that any given plane of object must cling to his flat, two-dimensional pattern, and yet it should tilt sideways into an imagined three-dimensional space. For him the two-dimensionality of surface sensations – onto which all planes melt into one another – is all important: each plane, each little bit of it, knows every other bit, making the representation of his world irrelevant. Relevant is the intimacy of the inter-relationship between the parts, the inter-penetration of which is humanly incomprehensible. Krishen could perhaps declare like Oscar Wilde: 'It is only shallow people who do not judge from appearances,'[1] for his works are composed entirely of surfaces. They are impenetrable in the sense that they are opaque and without content; transparent in the sense that they harbour no secrets. It will be wrong to build expectations of a visual access to an interior form to lead us to an unseen force that may have formed the surface.

It is the self-sufficiency and opacity of meaning we admire in Krishen's handling of surfaces, which provides scarcely any sign of a body beneath them. It is a surface that consciously obscures and shrouds the image: the emphasis is on the apparent gulf between the open-endedness of his world of objects that passively fills the space, and the closed self-sufficiency of the surface. The surface alone is determined as permanent; the perception of its inner alternations through brushstrokes is a necessary condition of the perception of alteration itself. The presence of these strokes in different locations is what first yields to us an intuition of alteration.

Krishen's varied colour application methods make us aware of the distinction between a representation and the represented. He is, in other words, making it explicit that 'my representation (of my intended world) cannot be outside me, for that would be a contradiction'.

It could well be true that although the representation is within me, its object is, yet, without contradiction, outside me. It is a surface that consciously obscures and shrouds the image: the emphasis is on the apparent gulf between the open-endedness of his world of objects that passively fills the space, and the closed self-sufficiency of the surface. The surface alone is determined as permanent; the perception of its inter-alterations through brushstrokes is a necessary condition of the perception of alteration itself.

Editor's Note

1 Oscar Wilde, *The Picture of Dorian Gray* (first published 1890): 'It is *only shallow people who do not judge* by *appearances*. The true mystery of the world is the visible, not the invisible.'

26
HOWLAJI ARA'S WINDOW EXPERIENCE

An assessment of the art of K.H. Ara, one of the lesser-known members of the Progressive Artists' Group

Commerce magazine, New Delhi, 23–29 November 1988

Krishnaji Howlaji Ara, the painter who, along with Husain and Souza established the Progressive Artists' Group (PAG) and played a key role in changing our sensibilities in the direction of the modern, was perhaps one of the few contemporaries who worked in the tradition of genuine Indian aesthetics. He was a self-taught painter who expected little from his audience except joy in their eyes at seeing his work. He did not approve of the talk shows that his contemporaries put up along with their shows, he found the practice suffocating.

Art had a dialectical relationship with [for] him. He knew what he could do and what he could not and would not. For he found himself surrounded by a pictorial field, as it were, before a self-enclosed window experience that kept going some kind of intercourse between the self and the pictorial field. Often the background of this pictorial field is subordinated to a strong foreground. And the foreground has consequently acted like a reminder that identity in his art coincides with the window frame, and has no other immediate identity. Because of this, he remained as innocent as any art student.

He saw in the art student a fellow traveller. The window aesthetics of realism: that was his pole star, his guide and teacher, his compass, as he navigated the Indian aesthetic. To look at a painting as a window to see the outside world makes little demands on the viewer. Seeing here is equated with the thereness-thatness of experience. And, to be sure, the more pictures we see of the 'thatness' of the window experience, the more we see the world with Ara's eyes. The art categories, the classifications in terms of style and period and the name-giving impulse, cease to be our preoccupations.

Our preoccupations are all about the mediated language of art which defines our sense of visual exhilaration. Ara knew this as instinctively as we know what optical illusions mean. This was the advantage he gained from a sustained exposure to the window experience. He was led into what might, for want of a better description, be called visual thinking. The window in those moments was transformed into an interiorized mirror, the importance of which even the ideologues of photo realism tend to forget. Visual thinking enabled him to impregnate appearances with significance. This is perhaps an analogue to the window experience. For, without the understanding of the thingness of particular things - for example, appleness of apples - the relationship of particular forms cannot be signified. Cezanne's lesson of essences cannot be learnt. Ara never forgot Cezanne's lesson. What is involved in making a visual discovery through one's exposure to the window experience is the knowledge of registers, of difference. The point is best comprehended by comparing Cezanne's [painting series] *Mont St-Victoire* and the photographs of that mountain taken from the same vantage point.

In viewing Ara's work, it would be a rewarding experience to arrange objects in the same fashion that they appear in his still-lifes. That would demonstrate the relevance of the window experience. Photographs of these objects arranged in exactly the way they have been painted by Ara should demonstrate graphically Ara's particular vision of naturalist form.

Against many of the canons of the naturalist vision, the impressionists revolted. In the 1940s at the J.J. School of Art, F.N. Souza revolted. His close friend, Ara, too revolted. Both of them revelled in rebellion, thrived on it. Their rebellion might, of course, have had egotistical origins but they were artists with a basis of spatial generosity. They were not, like the impressionists, marginal men in revolt against patrons who did not know the nuances of light and its role in painting.

But marginal existence, nevertheless, it was. In Ara's art, it appears fresh, like the muted tones of reflected light in impressionist canvases, with a touch of rusticity and a mixture of mystic intuitions leading sometimes to a sense of bizarre misadventures. This is evident from the violence of the distortions sometimes employed. These are as unconventional as the highly individualistic acts of the PAG artists. They might be described, in the circumstance that obtained, as truly brave acts of a spirit that reached out to beyond everyday cares; they delineated Ara's distinctive capabilities.

But Ara himself was of course, never conscious of this. His work and his views were wholly rooted in personal 'motivations.' These seemed aesthetically closer to the point of view of the primitives. And like the other members of the group, he was a shaping influence on the plastic imagination of the Fifties. He made himself what he was without the totemic rationality of his contemporaries, particularly of Husain's and Souza's.

Indifferent to history, he did not like the revivalist rhetoric of the Bengal School. Unlike Souza, he did not work with a sense of history. Souza advocated with a semblance of intellectualism a radical elimination of history and its substitution by a myth rooted on the razor's edge of the present. Ara's was not a brave new world, more of a response which produced an aesthetic surface of modernism. But he painted in water colours and deftly managed to reach the effect of oils. He had little knowledge of the tactile and formal values inherent in the oil medium, unlike his contemporaries in the PAG. He was unaware of either of the crisis that his water-colourist contemporaries faced as the market for watercolours declined, or of the failure of water colourists to find equivalence for those effects which are particular to the oil medium. Yet, Ara did bring about a touch of the oil's effect into his water colours. This was no small achievement in terms of craft. His achievement in this was born of an individualism that had literally the dimensions of a myth though quite distinct from the existentialist's engagement with a medium such as Pollock's.

It was not speech within a format that Ara sought. He found the format intuitively in the spontaneous culture of the street. In this and in its expression, he was a true primitive. While his contemporaries in the Fifties became victims of art fashions, he remained with himself, delving into basic human emotion and motives without sentimentalism and without self-conscious intellectualism. He did not become a performer, nor did he rush to produce kitschy versions of what was the 'in' thing in Paris and London. Because of this, Ara's work matures with acquaintance: it is therefore, unlikely to become irrelevant.

27
GUJRAL'S IMAGES-69

Review of artist Satish Gujral's 1969 solo exhibition

Link, New Delhi, 30 November 1969

It is a new Satish Gujral that we meet in Shridharani Gallery. His fourteen paintings called Images-69 strikes us as pop bizarreries but such a view will be over-simple. No doubt, they belong to pop's sub-romantic environment; their meaning, however, is not totally dependent on environment. That, indeed, makes them difficult because the referents are not part of the environment but only mental quirks. In fact, as images they do not impress us as much as the new sensibilities which Gujral puts on them. The new sensibilities, to be sure, are translated in terms of the medium and not the image which only lays a false trap for the viewer. The subject matter, if there is any, is only accidental. No doubt about that.

NARROWING THE GAP

Rather it is a painterly obsession with the medium which, probably unconsciously, is aimed at breaking down the false barriers between painting and sculpture. That, indeed, is only so much of a guess for we know one thing for certain: they are not sculptures by any stretch of imagination. Then, is he operating within the tradition of easel painting? That is an open-ended question and difficult to answer because the motivating force again is not confined to traditional values of an easel painting. They look on the face like murals and the over-heavy decorative emphasis confirms this. Go and see the facade of Odeon cinema and the lines of association will be clear. What he has done at the Odeon is different and even in terms of technique is miles away from what he is doing now. If the two unconnected things look connected, it is because the total effect in both is decorative. Here one point needs clarifying; and Gujral himself is our best guide in judging a work of art. In simple terms, his advice is that one should ask standing before a painting or a sculpture whether the particular piece could have been done by the same artist a few years ago, say five years. Suppose his answer is 'yes', we can immediately formulate our reaction; we can say that the work lacks in energy and depth. So time becomes a carrier of aesthetic value.

And since values change within the lifetime of an individual (and perhaps in an artist's life they change faster), the time context gives a sense of urgency to the work of art. Clearly, then, the kind of mural that decorates the Odeon is not the kind of art Gujral is pursuing now; the line of communication is now more consciously social and cultural than it ever was. The present work in this sense is outward looking, less involved with formal questions and more with involving the viewer in its communication technology.

ENVIRONMENT, INVOLVEMENT

So, the fourteen images should be seen as products of his involvement with the cultural as well as the physical environment. As images, they have as much to be seen as read because seeing is not enough; that will lead us nowhere. When we say 'read' we mean it in the literal sense of the word 'read'. They are full of slogans and the most striking ones are; 'Mother Cow', 'Coca-Cola', 'Mao Thought', 'Vote Communists', 'Wanted a Virgin', 'Boy Going Abroad', 'Potency Back in Five Days', 'Ring 007', 'No Urination', 'Fly Pan American', etc. The implications of these slogans in terms of pictorial organization are negligible; they are intended to attack our cultural smugness and sloth. If the effect is a slight disturbance in the mind of the viewer then Gujral, to be sure, has indeed succeeded in putting them inside the pictures.

It is in this context that we call them pop bizarreries because like the pop artists who claim to get their lines of inspiration from life, Gujral too manipulates these slogans as a new form of visual language. The implication is that we not only see things but read them too and the urban landscape is plastered with slogans which are our media of communication. When these slogans are transferred into a fine art context, their shock capacity becomes enormous because they really become signposts of our culture.

The paintings with slogans, to be sure, are not the same as advertisement signboards where the medium serves both the literary and plastic purposes. In the advertisement signboards, words and images are interdependent; the two cannot be seen or read separately: in the Gujral painting the message of the slogan is only a Gujral whimsy because it is not the word but the letter which is used as a plastic device, in the same way in which painters from the cubists onwards have used them for the pictorial effects. His concern with the written word is purely calligraphic; the use of the written word can be justified on the ground that it is part of the urban landscape; we encounter the advertisement signs everywhere – on posters, billboards, shop facades and surmounting cinemas: they are part of the city landscape.

GUJRAL TECHNOLOGY

In fact, it is the new Gujral technology of media communication (borrowing slogans from cinema, advertising, newspapers and the radio) that makes these paintings so different from his earlier works. So it is necessary to draw a line between the aesthetic function the slogans play and the technological use they have been put to. Surely, aesthetics have little to do with communications systems; in the context of fine arts, communications systems operate on a much complex level. A Renaissance painting, for instance, reveals information both in the form of allegory and the physical picture of the world; it is another matter however that the illusionistic technique the Renaissance painters employed enriched our visual perception. A Masaccio or a Giotto does not have to depend on pure technology of pictorial organization, though painters since the Renaissance have spent quite some sleepless nights solving questions of technological nature. If that was not the case, the history of Western art would have been differently written much more on the lines Indian art geared its aesthetic ends, rejecting the technology of retinal painting.

The point we are making will be clear if we go back to Gujral's collage period to investigate why he gave up collage constructions. To be sure, the Gujral collages were super-folksy urban images; they were made perhaps under a false assumption that our popular culture is folk culture. This was rather blindly following the pop credo and using their standard tool – collage – rather unintelligently. Pop art is not involved with creating images; rather it is concerned with organizing the readymade images taken from the consumer ad-mass world. The aesthetic principle behind pop is not to create a new vision of the world or to provide new ways of looking at it but present it in a manner that the world looks absurd, which it really is. This existential involvement with the world leads them to imitate the gimmicks once indulged in by the dadaists. Though they call themselves neo-dadaists, they are part of the establishment's media landscape; in fact advertising and the display industry have gained more than the pop's by imitating the advertisement image. They ended up as visual technologists of sorts translating the mass-product images into another idiom. This translation of one media image into another has no aesthetic law; whatever is successful is art and moreover the market decides its aesthetic success. The pop artists failed, no wonder, to extend their aesthetics beyond the operations of the art market. So beyond accommodating the mass-produced images into a new pop context, they did not extend the range of their sensibilities.

Satish Gujral saw through it in no time and gave up collages because it did not lead him anywhere, although those collages were not the same as those produced by pop painters. He constructed images like the cubists did their collages; and not merely assembled them; these images differ from other pop images because they were not pieced together from the readymades. Since we do not have much readymade images turned out by mass media (perhaps because we are still generations behind in visual culture to the West), Gujral used coloured paper and folk images to create pseudo-pop images. But the experiment did not take off the ground.

ADVERTISEMENT IMAGE

Thus Gujral has returned to the advertisement image where the verbal and the visual are inseparable elements. But in the present context it is the image

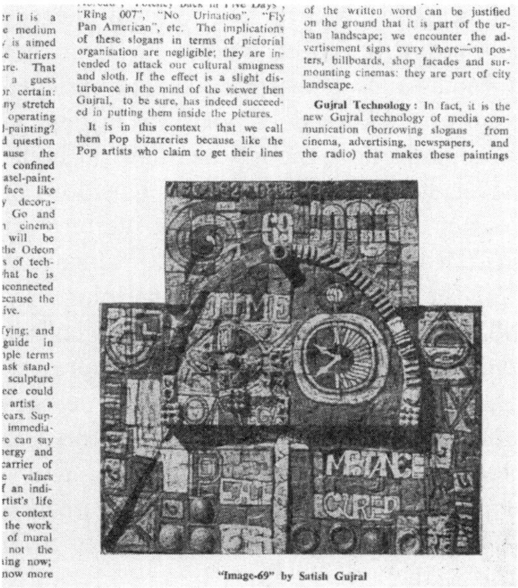

r it is a
e medium
is aimed
e barriers
re. That
a guess
r certain:
ny stretch
operating
l-painting?
d question
ause the
t confined
asel-paint-
face like
y decora-
Go and
n cinema
will be
the Odeon
s of tech-
hat he is
connected
ecause the
ive.

fying; and
guide in
ple terms
ask stand-
sculpture
ece could
artist a
ears. Sup-
immedia-
e can say
ergy and
carrier of
e values
f an indi-
rtist's life
e context
the work
of mural
not the
ing now;
now more

"Ring 007", "No Urination", "Fly Pan American", etc. The implications of these slogans in terms of pictorial organisation are negligible; they are intended to attack our cultural smugness and sloth. If the effect is a slight disturbance in the mind of the viewer then Gujral, to be sure, has indeed succeeded in putting them inside the pictures.

It is in this context that we call them Pop bizarreries because like the Pop artists who claim to get their lines of the written word can be justified on the ground that it is part of the urban landscape; we encounter the advertisement signs every where—on posters, billboards, shop facades and surmounting cinemas: they are part of city landscape.

Gujral Technology: In fact, it is the new Gujral technology of media communication (borrowing slogans from cinema, advertising, newspapers, and the radio) that makes these paintings

"Image-69" by Satish Gujral

with which he is involved; painterly problems are still his starting point – colour, form and space, and the dimensions of the canvas. The picture frame is visualized as a total image; that is why he uses irregular shapes rather than the traditional rectangular picture frame. In fact, the shape of the canvas determines the nature of composition and the organization of colours and forms. Everything follows from it.

The present exhibition establishes one thing: Gujral has moved away from the traditional notion that art should concern itself only with solving problems of form. This preoccupation had lasted well over a decade during which he no doubt turned out some good abstract canvases. But accompanying this success there seemed to be a feeling of emptiness. Clearly, he is not a painter content with formal exercises in pictorial innovations fiddling with shapes and tones till they seem right by some creative accident. Even when he was painting away pure abstract canvases, there were hints that certain things were more real than merely weaving the canvas like architecture, something that he felt was not a skillful piece of decoration but something more relevant and lasting. This something he thought could be achieved by cultivating a primitivistic attitude or going back to the rocking horse of his childhood. For sure, one just cannot become a primitive by choice. Little wonder he landed himself in self-contradiction though this was not of his own creation; primitivism had always been an obsession with artists since Gauguin. While for Gauguin, primitivism was a psychological necessity, with the artists following him, it turned out to be merely a trick of the trade.

That Gujral has moved away from the narrow aesthetics of primitivism is in itself a great achievement. The present work is forward-looking and public-oriented. If one reads into it hints of dadaism, it is because the time element is structured into the armature of the images; indeed, image is not the primary element but a construction device which carries the cultural load of symbolism on its lean shoulders. There is reason to hope that Gujral will not give us the easel painting but public art.

28

MYSTERIES OF BURNT WOOD

Review of Satish Gujral's burnt wood sculptures shown in New Delhi in 1988

Commerce magazine, 30 November–6 December 1988

Painter-sculptor-architect Satish Gujral never lets down his reputation. Each exhibition of his is marked by something new. For he does not set shop to promote this or that view about his own work: nor does he look for support from the academy artists. He is himself always with axiomatic certainties of geometry. He is not a devotee of the new – not in the sense of breaking new ground, which he invariably does with each one of his one-man shows. But this newness is cultivated in a way, conceptually related as it is to the local environment.

There is yet another aspect to Satish Gujral's show which is currently on at the Shridharani Art Gallery, New Delhi. Satish tends to locate his art-making impulse through a medium, and what is said, to be sure, has a spellbinding effect. It is easy to see; the work is addressed to the eye alone with this aim in view. It aims to create ground for aesthetic experience to blossom, something that is sought for as an end in itself. For Satish, working on a new medium and exploring its depths is knowledge itself, sought for and enjoyed for its own sake.

The medium is felt as an objective presence, its formal means dissolved into its highly expressive values. A thin line divides the impersonal values from the personal one, which is a new aspect of his sculpture. Art for cultivating a private corner of the self, as a means for creating beauty. Satish knows well that art is a difficult mistress to please, just as the poet knows that experience is a mistress of one who handles words well.

Art as a mistress cannot properly be pleased. Not with a commonplace gesture. She demands obedience, devotion; her obsession is to test the capabilities of her lovers. And given an order of rationality, something happens. Because of this, his starting points have never been the art styles currently in fashion in the art markets of London and Paris. Nor has he ever explored the nature of an art medium in art historical terms. With Satish, as with all major artists, the beginnings count. Beginnings in terms of the craft values, for instance, the shallow interior spaces have many optical roles, as diverse as do the organic movement of the exterior.

The organic movement of the exterior forms are perceived in the same way as the relation between a relief and its background plane is perceived. This depends a great deal on how the edges of forms meet the background plane, and they meet with an abruptness that is visually refreshing. This creates the illusion of standing before a sculptured wall. The whole surface of the wall itself is seen as pierced, undercut behind the forms. Harsh strong lines dominate and enhance the overlapping undulations of the ground which is brilliantly lit. It is cut up into spaces with a very strong sense of touch. On this subtle and plastic surface are projected forms in both convex and concave relationships. They give the impression that they are protrusions of frontality defined by the framing edges with a self-sufficient statuesque quality. Not only is the movement within the forms controlled by the tasteful use of the concept of frontality, it also enhances the impression of volume.

The creation of this illusion of depth in different degrees of spatiality is a familiar Gujral method. Recall the Gujral 1973 images show at the Ashoka Gallery and see whether the old memory images connect the present work to the kind of sculptural presence Satish always sought. Satish had called them images in three-dimension, and not sculpture. In the current show, Satish draws attention to the dominant view of the frontality. The frontal view has a presence of the third-dimension when seen standing against a wall.

A painting, too, has presence; it has a greater presence than sculpture. This is because three-dimensional objects on the wall alter the room space; they disturb our sense of space in a fundamental way. If put together, close to one another to create a mural space, they have an aesthetic function. They give off a kind of vibration. The third dimension makes them a live happening.

Satish Gujral has always been a muralist at heart, spellbound by the magic of the third dimension. And rightly so, for the third dimension, the element of physical reality that a work of art possesses is rich in tactile values. Their optical charm seems always a by-product. The physical reality of burnt wood, for instance, dictates a kind of sensibility that is possible only in the third dimension. This sensibility allows us to project forms and relate them to their linear transformations, which does not allow individual parts to distract attention from the totality of the composition.

The composition is best explained thus: the plane, the fundamental unit of painting as well as relief sculpture, are architecturally fused. This is done with great imagination, for on the surface it looks that he repeats his images, and in most cases they have a fixed projective function. They are container images, as it were, rich in surreal implications. They force us to explore another state of mind which can link mythic experience with the contemporary landscape.

But Satish does not link images in an obvious way; he does not like to link things as pop artists do: 'pop art is linking things,' according to Warhol. It is obvious that Satish does not link things, he builds images in a way that help him reach the darkest corners of the unconscious, to discover for himself the meaning of craft values. It is this which gives to his work a different context from that which defines the work of other artists. He has a streak of non-conformity, the drive to experiment and create without fear of failure or the thrill of success.

29
KULKARNI AND HIS ART: AN INTERVIEW

An early interview with the artist K.S. Kulkarni, 1957

Hindustan Times Weekly, New Delhi, 3 November 1957

K.S. Kulkarni's latest exhibit, a canvas of considerable magnitude, 12 x 4 feet, seen recently at the Delhi Shilpi Chakra, has aroused much interest, enthusiasm and controversy, not only publicly, but in the world of Indian art itself. Kulkarni's apparent apostasy, in the eyes of his critics, in his first use of the expressionistic approach, is not without reason or significance. But whatever its merits or demerits, this vital painting clearly establishes one factor that is of salient importance to the work of any artist, and that is that his past successes – much of Kulkarni's past artistic life reads like the typical success story – have had no petrifying effect, as so often is the case in such circumstances. Kulkarni, obviously, is not prepared to rest on his undoubted laurels or to let his art stand still. The urge to create, to seek and give expression to new forms dictated by the artistic ferment within himself remains the motivation of his work.

WHY THE TITLE

Kulkarni has called it *Composition 1957*. This title is singularly apposite but one that is generally misunderstood, as Kulkarni pointed out when I asked him why he gave a title which superficially seemed to convey no particular message, nor suggest a particular theme. 'In its overall effect,' said Kulkarni, 'it is intended to signify the chaos, the confusion, the fear and limitations, the specious and deceptive quality of power, no matter what paranoiac form it assumes [in] the motivations of life today and all that they connote in the context of our humanity.'

What was your source of inspiration and what circumstances led you to this almost revolutionary departure from your previous approach to art? Did you visualize or plan Composition 1957 *or is it the spontaneous outcome of purely plastic experimentation?*

I suppose I have arrived at this approach by stages, even though I was hardly aware of the evolutionary process of artistic gestation taking place within me – at least in the sense of its final implications and artistic conclusion, the changing sum of my aesthetic urges and emotional compulsions. I think I adopted it without conscious thought about it, since no planning whatsoever went into what I have called Composition 1957. Call it combustion, if you like, the spontaneous explosion of the idea, thoughts, fears and repressions seething within me. Nor do I think, I am alone in this reaction.

GROWTH OF TENSIONS

To me this painting looks like just another variation on the expressionistic theme that is so marked in occidental art today. Have you been particularly impressed or influenced by this trend – and how do you interpret it?

It is the evolution, of that form of expressionism which first became perceptible in the Germany of 1910 or thereabouts – the natural outcome of the artist's dissatisfaction with the pure objectivity of impressionism and similar art forms. You can define it as the inevitable need to express the emotions which took their source from the nervous tensions which were increasingly gripping man.

It was acute in the German climate of that day – Kaiser Wilhelm's Germany. A Prussianized Germany, inordinately ambitious and power-obsessed, the legacy planted by Frederick the Great, his Iron Chancellor, and the defeat of France in the Seventies of the previous century. The constant manoeuvering for power in Europe foreshadowed the cold war of today, foreshadowed the tensions of today.

Artists perceived that humanity wanted something more from art than the simple record or impression of human behaviourism, emotion, nature, life, as they were seen through the eyes of the artist. People wanted something not only seen but felt, felt through the very soul and being of the artist, transmitted to them or evoking a definite chord of response. That, if you like, was the foundation of expressionism, at least in my view.

FEAR OF WAR

You think those tensions have become universal?

Can you doubt it? The nervous tensions which worked up this expressionism in a country preparing and geared in every aspect of life for war have today seized upon all mankind, because today the preparations for and the imminence of war are far more acute – and the danger has been magnified a thousand times, because we all know that a war will not only bring devastation on an inconceivable scale but might also result in the extinction of the human race. These tensions are inescapable and their repercussions have made themselves felt in every corner of the globe. In Composition 1957, I have tried, obviously, I think, to give expression to those tensions; filtered, as it were, through my own aesthetic sentience and artistic personality.

Would you call this approach a final departure from the traditions of Indian art, or has there been any perceptible tendency towards such a trend in our artistic past of which most of us were unaware?

Each period in history cultivates its own aspects or interpretations of artistic expression, according to its climate and necessities. Indian art in the past was rooted in religious convictions and ideals and neither the people nor the artists attached any importance to individual experiences or individual emotions. They created an art which reflected their spiritual temperaments and ideals rather than the physical and material circumstances affecting their lives. The environment of their day made little impact upon their artistic sentience. They, accordingly, would have been incapable of feeling the tension, becoming involved in the conflicts or reacting to the frustration which grips all human race today.

ART AND NATIONALISM

Don't you think that this total departure from tradition will deprive your art – for that matter, all the art today – of its national character? After all, it is that which is held to be one of the qualities that give our art historical and cultural significance.

Talk of nationalism in art is meaningless, even crassly stupid. Art transcends both physical and intellectual barriers. It is universal. Humanity's sufferings, raptures, stresses and agonies, nobilities, fears, cannot be measured in terms of nationalism. There are no boundaries in human emotions. There can be no boundaries in art. All stresses and emotional tensions stem from social conditions and problems common to all mankind and not from religion or national traditions and environment.

So, in turning to this new approach, you have literally abandoned the limitations of which Indian art has been so replete and have acknowledged the impact of forces that are common to all humanity?

It is inevitable that Indian art will escape from the limitations of nationalism and seek an applicability and scope for itself that is international and stems from the very fact of living itself. In *Composition 1957*, I believe, the figures I have painted and deliberately and purposively emphasized, belong to no particular sphere of the earth. They are Man, Life, the World in which we live today. If I have exaggerated and stressed it is purposive. I have accentuated the futility, the overshadowing frustration in the human desire for power – irrespective of the shape and climate of that power. I have tried to depict the result of human exploitation, of rapacity – the frustration in man, for even when seemingly illimitable power is achieved, he remains chained and bound not only by his own humanity but by the external conditions governing all life. I have tried to show that power is full of frustration, incapable of surmounting the limitations of our humanity. It may sound a trifle precious, but I believe that art can do a great deal in bringing home to people not only the limitations of that humanity but in showing them to what heights humanity can rise. True art is as universal as life itself.

REASON FOR CHANGE

Then you discount a purely intellectual or a purely emotional approach in art?

I do not believe, as I have already indicated, that such things exist. Even if it is only subconsciously, the impact of any impression received is an impact upon the integrated whole that is the artist. At the same time, it is a truism that while the human mind may interpret nature and the life patterns in mental even more than visual terms, it is also the human mind that gives it precise design in expression. Insofar as there is a common humanity in all of us, in spite of, perhaps, an oversensitivity in the artist, a picture will always hold this quality of communication, even though an artist may be ahead of his time and the communication is only to the few. Today it may be the few; tomorrow it will be the many. We have had this demonstrated time and time again with the works of great artists like Van Gogh, for example, where recognition did not come until humanity had caught up. In order to achieve a universal communicability, it would engender a universality of mind on a level with that of the protagonist of art - in any medium.

Why does art undergo so much transition, so much transformation, change from age to age?

Obviously because life itself changes. Art that was placid, unhurried, calm, represented an age that was placid and calm. Art today represents and is symptomatic of the frustrations and uncertainties which enshroud our lives. We still seek fulfilment, and the search for that is what the artist depicts. All art is definitive of a particular day and stage of human evolution.

Should an artist seek publicity? Should he try to educate the public into an appreciation of what he is trying to say?

I see no purpose in an artist deliberately shunning publicity, just as I deplore him seeking it. If his work is worthwhile, it will get quite enough publicity without his going out of his way for it. As for educating the public, as you call it, I definitely feel that this is no part of his functions, as an artist says what he has to say. It is for the public to find out what he has said, if they have a mind to.

(Author: Parts of this interview are incomplete.)

30
TANTRIC PUT-ON

A reflection on J. Swaminathan's early tantra *works of the 1960s*

Link, New Delhi, 30 August 1970

We have many tantric devotees but only one Swaminathan who understands fully the etiquette of tantric innovation. Others are either purely derivative, or wholly imitative; there is none inventive enough to give to tantrism a touch of Indian avant-garde. Swaminathan alone can use his painting in the service of tantric rhetorics. It does not mean, however, that Swaminathan alone would have succeeded in developing the proper etiquette without an art historical background; it does not really matter, whether the established aesthetic precedents come from New York painters or India's indigenous traditions. If we assume for argument's sake that his style is wholly original, we might as well say that he really invented the art of tantric painting.

REDUCTIVE AESTHETIC

His art - or his role as tantric frontliner - makes more sense indeed if viewed in the context of minimal works and the current wave of eroticism in America. Significantly, it is critics like Clement Greenberg and artists like John Cage who have spoken highly of his art, and their appreciation means a lot, whatever the opinion of local critics. Whether Swaminathan is a tantric [artist] or its adulterated modern version is not the point of his art: what is significant in his paintings is the reductive element.

Reductivism, to be sure, is one of the most predominant qualities of modernist art, and it really does not belong to any style. Even Degas knew as much experimenting with unusual picture space; his friend Mallarme reminded him that the best poetry was made not by ideas but by words alone. So very dominant was the reductive aesthetics in those days that painting was cut down to a line or a square. Malevich's suprematism extended reductionism to such mystical heights that it was difficult to be level-headed. The contemporary avatar of reductivism is Yves Klein who displayed before his death in 1962 only all-blue paintings, perhaps to indoctrinate the public in one-colour aestheticism. He not only painted all his works in royal blue and patented it as International Klein Blue but publicized it throughout the world as IKB. It is arguable indeed, whether Klein's talent lay more in paint innovations or in qualities of showmanship. No doubt he was a highly original painter but he also knew how to stagecraft his originality. When he showed his works in a Paris gallery, he

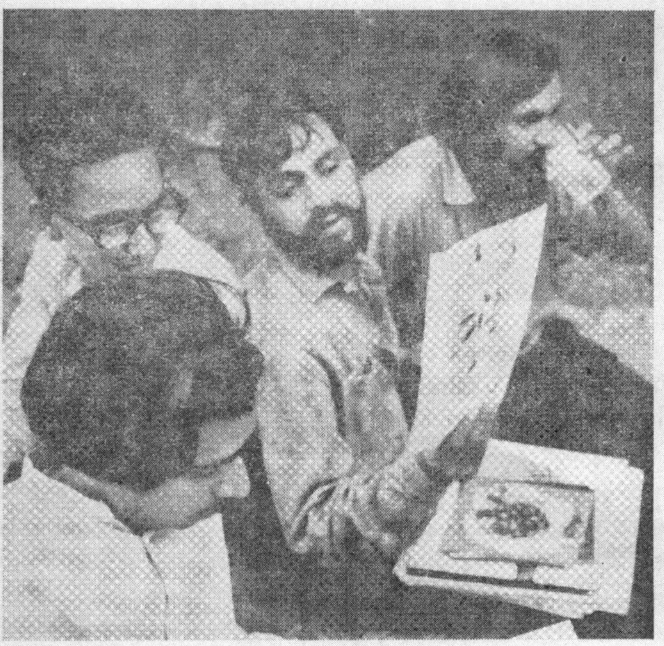

wards critics whc
hints of Minima
cult to discuss ai
trik devotees be
living in the nir
art was still in
and each master
only of colour sc
but a composite
are dedicated tc
else. They lool
audience with th
an aesthete. Wh
America and Eu
ing some kind of
case is that o
Reinhardt's, Pollc
sent the obsoles
which calls for a
tral nervous syst
believe that aest
ness and their
ness is their re
their natural su
aloofness is the
cal airiness, evei

Finally, even
reductionism is n
an accessory and
tool. Their aim
reductive methoc
tual or otherwis
tity of the artist
ment. This art-
produces art whic
a cultural decora
Dada joke is im
and audiences in
how to be really r
of the modern ar
modernism by fi

Swaminathan with members of Group 1890

made not by ideas but by words alone. So very dominant was the reductive aesthetics in those days that painting was cut down to a line or a square. Malevich's

nery to debunk his works, referring to them as ashes, The ashes were significant because they brought with them the rich experiences. "No matter what

completely redid its walls and served blue cocktails. Klein knew how to please the vanguard audience and build a career as spectacular as one in Hollywood. He kept his vanguard audience always guessing; sometimes arranging a show of nude girls dipped in IKB and then asking them to roll on the unprimed canvases, taking the imprints of their thighs and torsos for a future exhibition. Klein also burnt the surfaces of his canvases or simply exposed them to the wind and rain and then wrote poetry about them. A romantic neo-dada, he built up a reputation of living dangerously and often used dada's anti-art machinery to debunk his works, referring to them as ashes. The ashes were significant because they brought with them the rich experiences. 'No matter what one thinks,' he wrote, 'all this is in very bad taste, and that is indeed my intention. I howl it from the rooftops: "Kitsch, Corn, Bad Taste"; this is the new notion in art. And while we are about it, let's forget art altogether.'[1]

DADA DUST

This indeed is what is missing in Indian artists. Perhaps, one expects some dada dust from Indian tantric artists and what one gets is a poor, rather indifferent, quality of tantric ashes. Their intellectual pretentiousness is more put-on than take-off. What can be the reasons for their lollipop-sweet tantrism? One is that they have failed to recruit a sizeable vanguard audience, nor have they yet evolved an etiquette suitable for making art an entertainment medium. Rather they have their own underworld bohemia where their innovations and personal rebellions take shape, but this is too dark and campy. This does not make painting and sculpture a profession fit to be taught at universities.

So one expected more from Swaminathan. He did arm some painters with a few slogans and they produced a lot of noise and fury, but without a permanent vanguard audience and proper gallery support their energies got dissipated in personal quarrels. Take, for instance, Swaminathan's attitude towards critics who read in his new work hints of minimalism. Indeed, it is difficult to discuss art with the Indian tantric devotees because they seem to be living in the nineteenth century when art was still in the handicraft stage and each master was an inventor not only of colour scheme and its aesthetics but a composite style of his own. They are dedicated to art and to nothing else. They look down upon their audience with the contempt reserved for an aesthete. While the minimasters in America and Europe work for promoting some kind of eye culture (McLuhan's case is that, overall, paintings like Reinhardt's, Pollock's and Klein's represent the obsolescence of 'eye culture' which calls for a response of the central nervous system), our tantric artists believe that aestheticism is their business and their audience's insensitivity is their responsibility. Added to their natural superiority complex and aloofness is the attitude of metaphysical airiness, even of intimidation.

Finally, even their attitude towards reductionism is not contemporary; it is an accessory and not a fundamentalist's tool. Their aim is to augment, through reductive methods, the effects, intellectual or otherwise, disclosing the identity of the artist and his personal statement. This art-for-art's sake attitude produces art which is nothing more than a cultural decoration. Unless a bit of dada joke is imported into art, artists and audiences in India will never learn how to be really modern. No doubt, most of the modern artists have earned their modernism by fighting against the revivalistic rhetorics of the Bengal school. They however cannot become contemporary just by debunking a school.

Editor's Note

1 From Yves Klein's essay, 'Le Vrai Devient Réalité' (The Real Becomes Reality), Part 1 of his *The Monochrome Adventure*, available in English translation in *Yves Klein, 1928–1962: Selected Writings*, translated by Barbara Wright, London: Tate Gallery, 1974.

31
SCALING THE INVISIBLE WALL

Review of J. Swaminathan's solo exhibition held in New Delhi in 1970

Patriot Magazine, New Delhi, 29 March 1970

Contemporary Indian art has produced many Egyptians but few priests. Swaminathan by making the mystery of the art of painting is its head priest. His painting therefore is not addressed to the eye but to the mind; and it speaks in riddles and only the painter has its keys. Swaminathan did provide an opening, however, through the small but it makes visualization more enigmatic. He wrote in the tenth anniversary number of *Link*–

> It (the new art) requires, above all, that the artist stand in front of the canvas as the early Aryan stood facing the morning sun, and to understand as he understood:
> *Om Poornamadah, poornamidam*
> *Poornat poornamudachyate*
> *Poornasya poornamadaya*
> *Poornameva-avashishyate*
> *Om Shantih, Shantih, Shantih*

We need not bother about what the *shloka* means; we are impressed by the Egyptian priest's power of hieroglyphic knowledge. What Swaminathan is suggesting is, however, different; the Egyptian painters of India need not speak at all, whether pictorially or otherwise, because between the canvas and the painter, no historical dimension or human condition exists. What exists is the immediacy of his experience. If the visualization of the private experience is lacking in painterly qualities, it is because the mystery lies beyond the canvas and not in it. The canvas experience is not sensuous but merely a means for transcendental meditation.

ROMANTIC ATTITUDE

The mystic implications of modern art are not an exclusive Swaminathan discovery; it was part of the romantic philosophy. The recent spurt in the symbolistic painting industry merely vindicates what was so clearly seen towards the end of the nineteenth century by Robert Vischer in his theory of Einfuhlung or 'Symbolic Sympathy'. (Vischer, it may be added incidentally, belonged to the Kant-Hegel idealistic school of aesthetics according to which the artist's inner world is never satisfied with the invocation of nature; he creates his own world of forms, 'a handwriting that exteriorizes and clarifies his deepest feeling'. William Worringer, who set out in 1908 to criticize Vischer, merely landed himself in his idealistic trap. He concluded that certain civilizations tend to break away from 'nature in order to give the work of art the significance of pure thought or pure emotion which results in abstract art.') The substance of their rhetoric is that a work of art is a mystery of its own creation, a language peculiar to itself which cannot be translated into another media. Andre Malraux, thus, regards art as a constant metamorphosis. The Malraux brand of transcendentalism has found sympathetic echoes among the surrealists and the hard-edgers in New York.

It may be pure coincidence that Swaminathan too adopted the rhetorics of America's commodity culture exactly at a time when the latter began grabbing Indian miniatures and its archaic folk forms as found in Jain manuscripts. Swaminathan's interest in tantrism began with his success in the Delhi triennale. He has been experimenting ever since with variations on the same canvas. What he showed last year at the Kunika-Chemould was a repetition of the triennale canvas and now he has some colour sophistication to add at the Gallery Chanakya. It has the same dream screen of tantrism, the same love bird (the peacock) and the same scaffolding of mountain skyline and its mysteries. The only difference is that it shows a new use of space, which indeed is not so new because there were hints of its latent manifestation in the triennale canvas.

FEEL OF SPACE

In the new work, two things strike us immediately. Inside the overlapping mountain forms, Swaminathan creates an arbitrary colour area which both creates a feeling of space (not in the conventional sense of pictorial space which is defined as movement in and through volumes) and has a compositional function. The compositional device breaks down the monotonous symmetry of forms. This spatial experience is further defined by a stone-form mass which is seen hanging in the air as if some gravitational force other than the earth's is keeping it there. Thus a pyramid-like triangular movement is introduced; it has a fascination of its own. The intensity of our experience before such mystery is disproportionate to our capacity for conscious interpretation. The pyramid-like movement within the mountain forms makes us aware of another principle. We realize that the picture format itself is wholly illogical. This will be clear if we prevail upon Swaminathan to join all his eight canvases into a single panel. We can see then that the sequential movement of forms is independent of the picture format. Other aspects of the canvas like the surface values, colour and texture, will gain in richness of multiple imagery.

INVISIBLE WALL

This is indeed a mental construction, a way of explaining things which does not fit into any neat categorization. The indeterminacy of experience is an obstacle and Swaminathan enjoys this game of our trying to scale an invisible wall. His art, therefore, is not for normal commonsense perception. It presents the same old puzzle recently posed by America's single-colour giant-sized canvases covering the whole wall of a gallery; their enormous expanse forced the spectator through colour dynamics alone to feel as though he was inside the picture and yet conscious of the fact that he was outside it. This illusion of aesthetic distance finds a different expression in Swaminathan's recent work. The peacock painted in representational style reminds the viewer of other modes of seeing which of course are not apprehended with the naked eye but with the mind's projective subliminal vision. Its dream screen has a curiously undifferentiated space quality; this screen is as primitive as a child's undifferentiated vision.

32
THRO' COLOUR ALONE

An interview with J. Swaminathan

Link, New Delhi, 25 February 1979

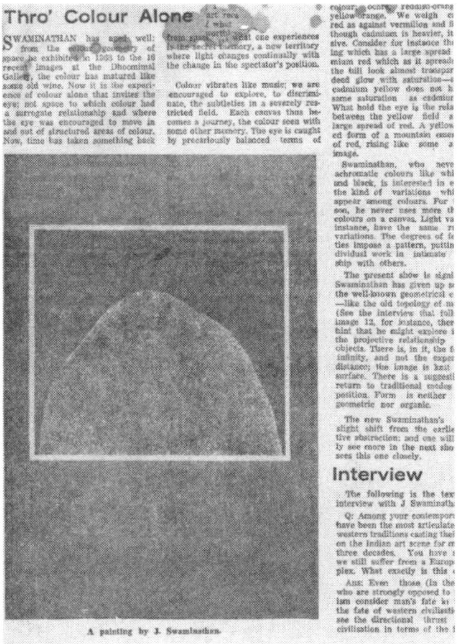

Thro' Colour Alone

Interview

A painting by J. Swaminathan.

Swaminathan has aged well: from the colour geometry of space he exhibited in 1968 to the sixteen recent images at the Dhoomimal Gallery, the colour has matured like some old wine. Now it is the experience of colour alone that invites the eye; not space to which colour had a surrogate relationship and where the eye was encouraged to move in and out of structure areas of colour. Now, time has taken something back from space and what one experiences is the secret memory, a new territory where light changes continually with the change in the spectator's position.

Colour vibrates like music; we are encouraged to explore, to discriminate, the subtleties in a severely restricted field. Each canvas thus becomes a journey, the colour seen with some other memory. The eye is caught by precariously balanced terms of colour: ochre, reddish-orange and yellow-orange. We weigh cadmium red as against vermilion and find that though cadmium is heavier, it is elusive. Consider, for instance, the painting which has a large spread of cadmium red, which as it spreads, makes the hill look almost transparent, indeed glow with saturation – although cadmium yellow does not have the same saturation as cadmium red. What holds the eye is the relationship between the yellow field and the large spread of red. A yellow textured form of a mountain emerges out of red, rising like some Aphrodite image.

Swaminathan, who never uses achromatic colours like white, grey and black, is interested in exploring the kind of variations which can appear among colours. For this reason, he never uses more than four colours on a canvas. Light values, for instance, have the same range of variations. The degrees of felt affinities impose a pattern, putting an individual work in intimate relationship with others.

The present show is significant as Swaminathan has given up several of the well-known geometrical categories – like the old topology of mountains. (See the interview that follows.) In image 12, for instance, there is the hint that he might explore in future the projective relationship between objects. There is, in it, the feeling of infinity, and not the experience of distance; the image is knit into the surface. There is a suggestion of a return to traditional modes of composition. Form is neither severely geometric nor merely organic. The new Swaminathans reveal a slight shift from the earlier reflective abstraction: and one will naturally see more in the next show if one sees this one closely.

INTERVIEW

Among your contemporaries you have been the most articulate critic of Western traditions casting their shadow on the Indian art scene for more than three decades. You have said that we still suffer from a European complex. What exactly is this complex?

Even those (in the West) who are strongly opposed to imperialism consider man's fate in terms of the fate of Western civilization. They see the directional thrust of this civilization in terms of the future of mankind. Happily, the present-day exponents do not suffer from the arrogance that the nineteenth-century thinkers suffered from. Speaking for myself, I do not think in terms of what is possible but what I consider to be desirable inasmuch as every man is naked inside. I do not find myself – in fact, for that matter, anybody in India flaunting the Western dress – superior to the naked tribal or a scantily clad peasant.

The desirable becomes possible only when you stop thinking in terms of social categories, and also are aware of the fact that whether mankind is wiped out in a nuclear holocaust tomorrow, or life on this earth becomes a paradise, you are living this life given to you. And it is not because you chose it that way. So what is desirable is to put some meaning into it. And it should be limited not to your own kind; the human horizon should include animals, the world of vegetation, also the sky, the sun, the moon, the stars, indeed the infinite space around. And in this context of infinity, the notion of progress becomes meaningless: no particular directional thrust can become solely relevant to the future of mankind.

Are they not the normal children of mankind?

When Marx called the Greeks the normal children of mankind, he was perhaps influenced by Darwin's thinking (in the sense that Darwin saw the evolution of man as the evolution of the species, man exhibiting the highest degree of the survival instinct as a member of the species). As an analogue to this, one might say that those ancient civilizations which could not survive in time had to be abnormal children. But if we give up the notion of temporal progression, then surely the people who lived and thought and worked, made love, created art, wrote poetry in the extinct civilizations nevertheless led full lives within the framework of their understanding of life.

Whatever sociological explanation an art historian may give of a human figure in an Egyptian sarcophagus where we have a frontal view of the torso and the face is in profile, such a rendering still surely has the power to fascinate us. If we were not to know that Picasso was living and working in our time, I wonder if any direct relationship could be established between perception in our time and expression in art. That a distortion by Picasso should be considered more significant than, say, by an Egyptian artist, is absurd.

If time is to be experienced as space, then the past will become as much present as the present when you are confronted by a work of art created in the so-called past. In those moments, you are fascinated and held by it as much as by a work which is created in the so-called present. The other day I was in the National Museum; and looking at pottery and earthenware from Mohenjodaro, I was in instant and living relationship with them.

Doesn't this happen when one is held spellbound by an object; time then stands still, turned into some kind of internal space, perhaps memory?
In my world, memory is as palpable and as uniquely real as the object of memory. That is to say, the experience of memory is not a second-hand experience of the object. Only thus art – I believe life also – is freed from the clutches of historicism. The fact that we cross distances by flying in an aeroplane does not make the mode of travel by, say, a bullock-cart any the less relevant. Moreover pace has its own consequences. Travelling by a bullock-cart in the countryside, passing through the jungle, arriving at a stray hamlet at night provides its own area of infinite experience. And travelling by air, one might remember only the pain in the back.

Do you think that the images of mountains in your present work has undergone some changes? Is it that memory has been playing tricks?
When I was doing these series of paintings, I suddenly found that the image of the mountain which in my previous work was, so to speak, rooted to the ground in order to provide levity to the rock had cut itself asunder becoming a free-floating form. It is as if the mountain becomes the rock and the rock a shard dug up from some ancient archeological site. I got a strange feeling that a magical transformation was taking place between nature as it exists and that which is created by man. The transformation has to be magical if it is to be real, palpable. I can assure you that this did not happen because I intended it. And another curious thing: the shard becomes an objectified image with its own independent existence when the civilization which created the pot exists no more. It has become a natural object. So it can become a mountain as well.

You think there is some development, evolution in art? Or, is all that we get from the defeated only a symbol?
Take, for instance, Chirico's example and his *Enigma* series. He was, you know, deploying the principle of the vanishing point or the concept of pictorial space as developed by Leonardo da Vinci and others during the Renaissance. He could be termed a reactionary, in the context of modern art's rejection of the mechanics of linear perspective as an outmoded concept. Or the return to the two-dimensional space by the modernists could be considered still more reactionary because they were going further back than the Renaissance artists. All the same, the *Enigma* series of Chirico constitutes a major contribution to the art of this century. I believe that while there is no going back to the past, there is no question of beating the past either. If you consider time as lived space, then as I said before, what was there in the past is there even now. And out of this encirclement you derive your unique expression. Indeed, every true expression in art is unique and that is why there is no repetition in art, but uniqueness does not imply progress: it implies change.

What about magical art? Was it not prior to religion? If out of art religion was born, without any art making would there have been any religion?
If we consider the magical art of the so-called primitives or even of the societies where religion was the dominant ideology, whether it be through collective efforts or because of an individual artist, the visual images created – whatever be their symbolic content – were uniquely expressed. It is only when we are not familiar with a tongue, that all that is said seems the same to us. A careful view of tribal, folk and religious art clearly establishes the fact of the uniqueness of expression.

For a man who is not familiar with the history of the modern movements in art, if a signature were not there on the paintings, a work by Picasso will not be distinguished from the work by Braque. So, while I do not accept the notion that the individual came into himself only in the age of reason or with the birth of capitalism or the break-up of the feudal system, I do believe that the lone individual that man has always been has become the lonely individual in the post-feudal society. In fact, the most important works in classical Indian sculpture are those which have surreptitiously departed from the norms given in the shastra. At the classical level any artist worth the name had to follow god's urge, and following this urge means upsetting, even if a little, bit the notions of man. In folk paintings – if we move from village to village and at times in the same village – we find that far from following a set pattern, the folk artist is always invariably inventive.

What role can an artist play in society where visual symbols have cut themselves loose from the shared ideology of that society?

Because artists in the so-called traditional societies were given the task of creating visual symbols befitting the ideology or the task of establishing rapport with nature or god, their art received easy recognition even if what they created at times was worthless in terms of art. I think that the artist now has to carry on the same function when society is inexplicable and inscrutable, art's iconic function still remains. In my opinion, this function was laid aside in the West ever since the Renaissance.

You mean that art's central core is its anthropomorphic transformations?
You see, what has happened during this century is this: we find that we are very near the beginnings of man. Has the reproductive function changed since the beginning of man? So, the need for man to express himself or what is called the artistic expression, for want of a better word, has not changed.

From the time of composing the colour geometry of space paintings, has the role of colour in your paintings changed much?
I have played havoc with the notions of colour in an extremely unobtrusive way. Take the painting with the tree as its central motif where green is a predominant experience and the painting in cadmium red, and see how one is predominantly a cool colour while the other is a warm colour. But the effect in both, as far as I can see, is one of quiet contemplation. If at all, it is the green one which is more disquieting. I believe that any colour could be made to function in a warm or cool manner. Here, I am introducing art as an extra-painterly statement: if in the process of painting, you happen to be in tune with what is seeking expression through you, then colour loses both its cultural connotations as well as its known retinal function. In other words, wavelengths pass through a stage of confusion and start behaving in a manner which the scientist did not ordain. Of course, colour is a function of light and therefore it cannot be freed from it but even though light rays travel in a straight line, they started bending with the coming of Einstein and between the Corpuscular theory and the wave theory, the artist is always left with the magical possibility of beating analysis.

You have given a new dimension to your painting by putting a frame on to the already framed paintings. It is intentional or for effect?
First, I want to clearly state that what hangs on the wall is a painting. Secondly, to emphasize the fact that the autonomy of painting does not lie in its becoming a natural object which it cannot become anyway, whatever be the claims to the contrary. Thirdly, by immediately suggesting the presence of a picture through the enclosing border, I build a bridge between the painting and the viewer. Here, he is not so much confronted with the unfamiliar as he is required to pass from the familiar to the

unfamiliar. The cubists at one stage introduced readily cognizable elements like a newspaper page and such objects in order to draw the viewer into their work. My object is somewhat different. As I do not unfold a new or a parallel reality, my object is to make the viewer see. This seeing requires no explanation and is born out of what is already seen. The reason why though my paintings are as much subject to analysis as any other there is no elaborative content in them. My intention – if there can be such a thing – is to make the viewer think or see not so much the world of the painting as the closed worlds inside himself. In our times, this is the nearest that one can aspire to do as an artist to reclaim his primary function in society.

33
THE PAINTER IN HIS LABYRINTH

A reflective essay on the artistic approach and work of J. Swaminathan

'Artscape', *The Economic Times*, 6 December 1991

The reply to a question like 'Am I still myself?' is difficult. But it presumably lies in the recognition of sociality which is at the heart of desiring – the desire for the 'other'. For, a relationship with the other empties me of myself and calls me into question. Under the other's gaze, let me confess, desire does not gratify but feeds new hungers. Or so it seems to me and, perhaps, painter J. Swaminathan, might not find it difficult to disagree with me.

For, the painter in Swaminathan is a peculiar animal. I have known it for nearly four decades and yet I cannot draw up its features. So I find myself in the same situation as that of Sonya Marmeladova in Dostoevsky's *Crime and Punishment*. She looks up to Raskolnikov in the hour of her despair. In summing up the scene, Dostoevsky speaks of the need for an insatiable compassion: it is as though compassion were a kind of hunger which the presence of Raskolnikov nourishes beyond saturation.

From personal knowledge, I can say that the desire for the other has always been there with Swaminathan, though it may have taken forms that we do not know. Let us go back, for instance, to 1963. Group 1890 was created in answer to a personal need. As a long-time trade unionist, he knew that man is a unity; he is many. So how could he fight his battles as a painter alone, in an unfriendly environment? He needed painter friends as his interlocutors. And since it is difficult to decide whether it is the painting that gives birth to a painting, it became necessary that he met his other as an interlocutor, someone to whom expression expresses in terms of signification: the contemporary as the interlocutor.

If not artists, their works certainly were. As artists, they were relatively unknown and so were in the same situation that Swaminathan was in then. But the anxiety of influence was more pronounced in their work. Theirs was a world purged of all ideology and, hence, they did not have the self-certainty of the artists of the Progressive Artists, Group (PAG) which was instrumental in forging the grammar of Indian modernist painting.

Sharing the troubled entrails of subjectivity of the PAG artists, they did not hold their egos as hostages. Rather, they sought to define themselves as individuals. Like the PAG artists, they were strangers as much to themselves as to their contemporaries. But, sure enough, it was this condition of being strangers that brought them together and in seeking the hand of understanding, they pledged to become each other's neighbours, as it were.

The tragic isolation of the painters of the PAG has driven this lesson home.

Swaminathan's main contribution was that he freed the minds of his contemporaries and encouraged them not to lock themselves into themselves. It was the only way to escape from the solipsist inwardness of the self-identical ego. His simple message: do not close the doors of your souls because these cannot be closed from inside. Swaminathan worked out its implications for the group. The idea of subjectivity, incapable of shutting itself up to the point of substitution, became a public platform with the launching of *Contra* in 1966. It was Swaminathan's little magazine. It was a new experience, qualitatively different from the political broadsheet he worked for until 1964.

In the columns of *Contra*, debate was welcome. Welcome in it were attacks relating to a linear conception of history; the distorted synthesis of cultural traditions; the Bengal School's attempts at translating cultural decadence and its projections into a national style in art; the utopian dream that humanity can be fulfilled in history through the coining into existence of a transparent society innocent of all social contradictions. The ideas discussed in the little magazine blazed up into a living torch. And the message was loud and clear – we are responsible for all the others, even if society regarded the artist (in the words of Octavio Paz) as the buffoon, saint and libertine.[1]

To Swaminathan, life has always meant responsibility, which has made him vulnerable in his post-1968, post-Jawaharlal Nehru fellowship work. The 'I' of Swaminathan is singled out by the convergence of many demands life has made on him: 'My responsibilities,' he might well confess, 'are never assumed. There is always more to them.' Because of this, he has several selves, each at peace with itself. He is father, lover as well as husband; a natural polemicist; a political activist; a public speaker who can put his audience to sleep with the music of his words; part-judge, part-lawyer and part-detective when he is in the role of a journalist; and, above all, a poet of considerable talent. As director of Bhopal's Bharat Bhavan, he brought all the coordinates of his personality into play.

But these seem inconsequential. The essential Swaminathan is a painter. His one and only involvement is with paint and, if one can speak of habit becoming addictive, the greatest of all addictions for him is painting itself – to its colours and their drying time; to paint in order to paint more. It is, thus, with some reservations that we speak of his beginnings which, no doubt, from today's perspective, look impressive. In their non-historical simplicity, they are absolutely unqualifiable. They are products of a sensibility which, far from signifying the intelligibility of experience, perpetuates the infantile within.

Swaminathan's early paintings of the Fifties seemed therapeutic in intent, as means for liberating them from their cultural presuppositions and to paint in a manner that enabled him to proceed directly towards meanings. He never was interested in paintings that tell a story, unless it is the fundamental story of genesis, of becoming – and to illuminate seeing painting that germinates in the manner of a dream allowing desire to represent itself as its secret truth.

These beginnings of Swaminathan were ignored. The ineffable went beyond common perception; it is not difficult to imagine that the ruling taste saw 'failure' written large across them. They were not the kind of images that are made for a drawing room. More, they lacked a known signature – that 'publicness' of a painting which triggers a look of recognition. Perhaps, Swaminathan was complacent about the privateness of his images. Delimiting them to a time of pre-culture and pre-aesthetic perception, however, did help accentuate curiosity.

The expected breakthrough came because by 1968 he had become a frontliner among the artists who were seeking reforms in the institutions connected with the patronage of art. In the first triennale, his work was singled out for honourable mention. This cannot be interpreted as a significant event in his life. It gave him a public that had money – not taste. The sublime, the painterly touch, though shrouded in its own mystery and its raw nature, pleased the public. For them, the sublime was the proper mode of experiencing the beautiful. Imagination supplemented what it had lost. It gained because imagination organizes theft of its own freedom.

The sublime is not to be found in nature; it is in us. For this very reason, the experience of the sublime is the effect of a subjective projection. Nature is used to give us a feeling of a finality of nature; we are encouraged to project our conception of the sublime into nature. Its presentation cannot be purely symbolic (in the Saussurean sense of the term which implies analogical resemblance between the symbol and what it symbolizes). Where the art is overtly symbolic, the content operates in it to the exclusion of form; content indeed renders form inadequate.

Swaminathan's colour geometry of mountains has a peculiar pictorial grammar. In them, the content becomes form. The mountain is defined by its magnitude – a feeling of largeness which seems incommensurable with the dimensions of an easel painting. The order of largeness is, however, made commensurable with the dimension of a bird that is, anyway, at much higher elevation. The bird, metaphorically speaking, transcends the largeness of the mountain; it appears absolutely large. Thus the content – the idea of mass and quantity – is presented not in terms of Albertian quantities of vision but as a noumenal agency of intuition. The truth, in the colour-geometric configurations of incomparable magnitudes, is simple to grasp. The sublime, in comparison with which all the rest appears small, proceeds intuitively and aesthetically through the imagination of the eye alone. Or, as Kant might put it: the evaluation of sizes of natural objects is, in the last instance, aesthetic – that is, subjective. The fundamental evaluation of size is subjective because the measure is the human body.

For about two decades, until his 1988 show at the Dhoomimal Gallery, Swaminathan played with the mental logarithm of the mountain-bird variables, structuring and destructuring the edgeless textuality in which was inscribed the metaphysical motif of the absolute referent of magnitude – the mountain. The gifted colourist that he is, Swaminathan managed to keep our attention focused on what he called 'colour geometry of space'. Every show of his during these decades was spellbinding and we kept looking for new sensations even though they were of the same order.

There were thrills, but they were never the upsetting ones. What seemed belonging to the fairies was that the most unconventional effects were achieved by conventional means. Swaminathan's colour application methods were conventional, but he achieved results that have made him one of the foremost colourists. He could translate volume and distance to a flat surface without denying the flatness of the canvas. This was achieved by substituting brushwork of comparable brilliance through distortion and geometrical simplifications. Such is his control of the brushwork that the paint looked rubbed on, giving to colour a new quality of 'paintedness'. The result was nostalgia for harmony which can be found only in mountains.

A 180-degree shift in sensibility came with the 1988 Dhoomimal Gallery show. With this, it seemed, Swaminathan returned to the point from where he had started. The position between the eye and the hand hardened into a resolve. The visible was received as it arose from the invisible with prayer and surrender. He said a final goodbye to the thinking eye that was rooted in the geometric graphic semiology of the mountains.

In the new paintings, the vision does not organize the visible, nor does it bestow meaning upon it, constituting it into a sign. The surface of the canvas ceases to be a two-dimensional support system upon which to represent a world, whether abstract or figurative. In the new mode, the surface becomes an arena within which to act and from which the creative act and its material world arise. The image in mind yields to the materials in hand. Intention gives way to surprise; the revelation is contained in the act of painting. The act is transfigurative; it is the birth of a world. In this world, the truth of seeing is acknowledged, not the truth of the visible. Seeing with the Swaminathan eyes, the other of Swaminathan is born. Delirious with new focal variations, this other of the imagination may not succeed in entering the

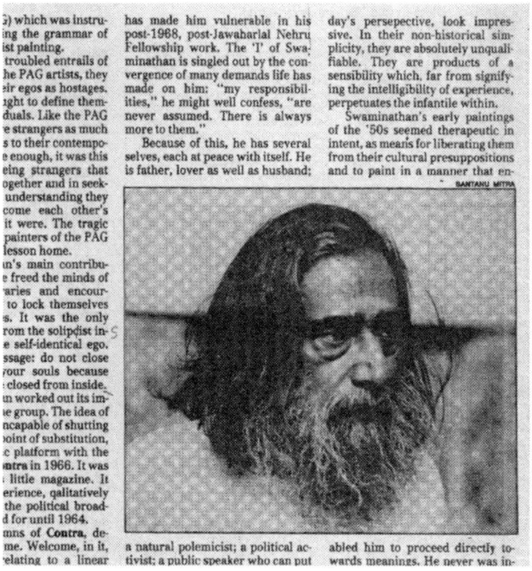
G) which was instru-
ing the grammar of
ist painting.
troubled entrails of
he PAG artists, they
eir egos as hostages.
ght to define them-
duals. Like the PAG
e strangers as much
s to their contempo-
e enough, it was this
eing strangers that
ogether and in seek-
understanding they
come each other's
it were. The tragic
painters of the PAG
lesson home.
n's main contribu-
e freed the minds of
aries and encour-
to lock themselves
s. It was the only
rom the solipsist in-
e self-identical ego.
ssage: do not close
your souls because
closed from inside.
n worked out its im-
e group. The idea of
ncapable of shutting
oint of substitution,
c platform with the
ntra in 1966. It was
little magazine. It
erience, qalitatively
the political broad-
d for until 1964.
mns of **Contra**, de-
me. Welcome, in it,
elating to a linear

has made him vulnerable in his post-1968, post-Jawaharlal Nehru Fellowship work. The 'I' of Swaminathan is singled out by the convergence of many demands life has made on him: "my responsibilities," he might well confess, "are never assumed. There is always more to them."

Because of this, he has several selves, each at peace with itself. He is father, lover as well as husband;

a natural polemicist; a political activist; a public speaker who can put

day's persepective, look impressive. In their non-historical simplicity, they are absolutely unqualifiable. They are products of a sensibility which, far from signifying the intelligibility of experience, perpetuates the infantile within.

Swaminathan's early paintings of the '50s seemed therapeutic in intent, as means for liberating them from their cultural presuppositions and to paint in a manner that en-

abled him to proceed directly towards meanings. He never was in-

SANTANU MITRA

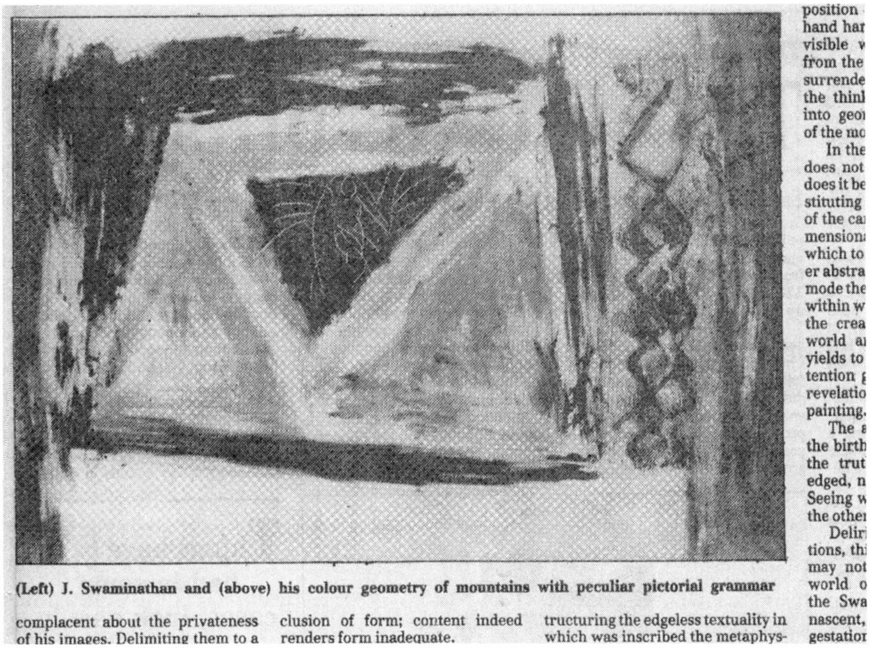

(Left) J. Swaminathan and (above) his colour geometry of mountains with peculiar pictorial grammar

world of Swaminathan. Because the Swaminathan world remains nascent, in a permanent state of gestation, it is like an apparition that never reaches the threshold of reality. It is like nature which appears to each one of us according to the pattern of relationship we have forged with it. The painting invites us to see the transformation of nature into a world – to see for ourselves how painting manifests the event of its appearing and to witness how a painting is born in us and, we in it.

The new paintings of Swaminathan appear nature-like. Every stroke seems natural as if the painter himself has become nature-like. Nature, when transformed into a world as it has been in these recent works of Swaminathan, haunts the visible while holding back the invisible for itself. This makes Swaminathan a romanticist for whom desire for the other was experienced as the desire to be a painter.

And the desire to paint and to paint more is at the heart of all desire. The desire for a world other than he was born into made him in his youth a utopian socialist, a trade unionist, a journalist. Did not Marx say: 'Philosophers have interpreted the world; it is time to change it.' But a desire for a self-made world led him to painting. Which, in the long years of struggle, became his other. The 'other' for Swaminathan has always been to paint a revolution which, in turn, revolutionized his painting.

Editor's Note

1 Octavio Paz, *Group 1890 Exhibition Catalogue*, New Delhi, 1963.

34

J. SWAMINATHAN: HIS ART AND CONTEXT

A brief synopsis of a book on J. Swaminathan that K.B. Goel was working on. The project was abandoned at Swaminathan's death in 1994

Lalit Kala Contemporary, no. 40, New Delhi, 1995

HISTORICAL

Harold Rosenberg in his *Tradition of the New* argues that the famous modern break with tradition has lasted long enough to have produced its own tradition. The prefix 'post' to modernism suggests that a second break too has become a historical fact. In order to lay our hands on the paradoxes of modernism, it is necessary to understand that the concept of modernity itself is not confined to the historical epoch of modernism. What distinguishes this European modernism is that radicalized consciousness of modernity abandons fixed historical references to the past but makes abstract opposition between tradition and the present.

As a subtext to this history of modern art, primitivism is considered a catalyst in the evolution of avant-garde art in Europe. For example, Picasso's *Les Demoiselles* (1907) is interpreted as a watershed in the development of modernism. Or take the concept of significant form. This is a gift from Roger Fry who, like the present day curators at the Pompidou Centre held up the 'primitive' as something abstract and indefinable.[1] Significant form shares this idea of spiritual quality with the discovery of the primitive. Fry's grand narratives were good currency until the Fifties. If the paleolithic and neolithic are followed by the art of the primitive peoples, then civilization begins its long march from Mesopotamia to Egypt, to Greece and Rome, to Renaissance, to French impressionism and post-impressionism. By making primitive art contemporaneous with the modern and claiming for it a continuous tradition which goes back to prehistoric civilizations, Fry opened up a way of legitimization of the present.

THE PRESENT

A distinction needs to be drawn between what is produced at the present moment and the totality of what is offered for interpretation. This distinction is a necessary condition of legitimization of the present. For legitimization needs support of tradition for the possibility of an affirmation of the present. Also, arguably, in place of tradition there would be the existence of the avant-garde or to narrow the circle of our reference, in place of nationalism, there would be the cosmopolitan; and finally, the place of universality would cede to pluralism. This is like Fry's throwback to prehistoric time, our history of the present. Now, the difficulty we face in positing this distinction resides in determining a specific semantic range for the term 'tradition'. Artist and art historian, Suzi Gablik suggests that tradition is what gives 'us' 'our' values, (*Has Modernism Failed?* 1984, p. 118). An intriguing element in this formulation is the use of the pronouns 'us' and 'our'. Lyotard talks of the interplay of interdependence between the unity of tradition, consensus and universality and asserts that it is the movement beyond a mere negative response to tradition that the avant-garde can be situated (*The Postmodern Condition*, 1984). Moreover, 'interplay of interdependence' is problematic; it cannot be accounted for within the terms set by a univocal tradition.

Post-modernism is an attempt to define value within a framework established by national identity. This means that tradition finds its ground of articulation in terms of the interconnection between the universal and the national. The linkage allows for critical exclusions or inclusions; it sanctions the promulgation of canon of 'national' artists. Nietzsche's *The Birth of Tragedy* is an attempt to join art and nation. The present for Nietzsche was a locus of loss, and in the rebirth of German music, he saw the 'rebirth of German myth'. A rediscovery of the essentially German would lead to an elimination of the foreign. (What the Bengal school in pre-independent India hoped for from the marriage of art with nationalism was a similar sentiment, using the national against the international.

The conception of nation is one whose tradition is unified; by eliminating the colonial implanted foreign elements [e.g. academic victorianism of the Bombay School] it was thought possible that the Indian spirit will return to itself.) The Nietzsche of *The Gay Science* speaks of the impossibility of such a rebirth, for the opposition between the nationalist and the modern is of a fundamental nature. The moderns are basically homeless, oppositional figures who have no sense of the nation (for example F.N. Souza and artists of a similar frame of mind. Souza incidentally provides the starting point for dialectical images of a Baudelairean dandy in his study of heads.) Nietzschian modernity is a concept of unity that refuses essentialism. The present, to use Nietzsche's term, is 'mixed racially' and, of course, culturally. The present is one in which there is always already a play of multiplicity of racial and cultural voices where the national and international exchange and interchange. But Nietzsche's European has no desire for either an exchange or a return; there is for him a plural present to be affirmed, for such plurality cannot accommodate the expression 'our cultural past'; it does not have a past in the sense the actuality of political nationalism may allude to the singular 'our' of the past.

SWAMINATHAN

As art-critic: Swaminathan belongs to the generation of the Fifties, modernism for us then spoke in the universalist language of existentialism. But he never viewed himself from the position of an exile as Souza does. Claims to universality by modernism are for him problematic positions imposed in the Fifties on Indian artists by contemporary Eurocentric culture. He reached out towards art that displayed non-Western art traditions only to regret the loss of innocence in them. He opposed the dominance of art-school ideology.

He has fought inside the Lalit Kala Akademi all attempts at canon formation by the interests of the more powerful among the artists; he argued, for instance, that no canon is properly representative. The charge that only a certain social group manipulates the canon is met by transforming the scene of conspiracy into a scene of representation. He is for liberal critique that works well in explaining disagreements within a homogeneous social group.

Art writing: Swaminathan's art writing does not involve much theory-testing. The distinction between experience (subjectivity) and interpretation is central to it, if we assume that tradition for him is not a univocal term. There is surely neither evidence of 'plurality' and 'locality' as major sources of meaning. It is free of bias. His proximity to works in the Western tradition is more reflexive – even marginal – than one of referentiallity. Nowhere does he ever seek conformity with the modes of thinking handed down as tradition. What stands out in his art writing is a unity of experience; meaning in art is linked to the unity of perception in relation to tradition of the present, the here and now of painterly practices. In focus here are the evaluative procedures of original import since interpretation involves construction of another's meaning.

Since Swaminathan had affinities with art's claims for universalist language, he has been a vocal critic of the Bengal School's ethnicity-based indigenism – ethnicity that works by positing contrasts, dividing humanity between 'us' and 'them'. For, if mankind was not divided by national identities, if there was one and the same ethnic group, there would have been no need for us to talk about ethnicity. He would be happier in the company of such identity erasures as Marcel Duchamp or Rauschenberg than Ravi Varma and Nandalal Bose.

As painter: Swaminathan assumed centre-stage visibility in the Indian art scene with the formation of Group 1890. In the formation of the group, he played the same role as is attributed to Souza in the formation of the Progressive Artists' Group. While Souza spoke of the radicalized consciousness of modernity claiming that modernism in India originated with his group, Swaminathan's contribution lies in focusing attention on the paradoxes of modernity. Modernity need not define itself as either the 'other' of national identity – appropriating the language of the avant-garde and making quality in painting a Western-art-dependent referentiality – or repudiating all values inconsistent with the concept of modernity itself. For him, artistic originality goes hand in hand with a seemingly visionary identification by the 'civilized' artist (a product of art's institutionalization or professionalization) with the forces of primitivism, the marginalized and the visionary attempting to go beyond a boundary. As with Souza, who defined modernism as men engaged professionally in the present as opposed to being representatives of a once-glorious past, so it is with Swaminathan: but with this difference that, for him, historical modernism simply makes an abstract opposition between tradition and present.

On the basis of an alliance with the perceived 'other' of modernist society, a modern artist is one who does not function as a subtext to the history of modern art, or as a catalyst in the evaluation of avant-garde to formulate his own aims. It is not the role, catalyst or otherwise, that he is concerned with, but the openness to the mythic speech of primitivism. He is suspicious of the modern because the discourse of the so-called modern primitivism effectively reinforces the separation of spheres of the modern and the primitive which significantly can be traced back to the Enlightenment. Primitive has served as a coded Other at least since the Enlightenment divided mankind into imaginary sets of opposition between civilized and savage, self and other, European and non-European peoples. Indeed, like anthropology, the history of European colonialism is in a way that knowledge of other cultures can be subsumed into the language of modernism.

What sets Swaminathan apart from his contemporaries is that he is a kind of iconoclast in its historical role of deconstruction. Most artists live in a prison-house of language; their horizons are limited by the high walls of their individually constructed prisons. There they exist in a prison and can only dream and not make themselves free. To such artists Swaminathan's example can work as a catalyst in the sense that he has worked out a conception of symbolism in which the symbol does not provide automatic access to the symbolized. Indeed, in his work, symbol tends to function as a non-referential sign.

The Sixties generation can be divided into two irreconcilable traditions: between J. Swaminathan and Bhupen Khakhar. For painters, who follow the Bhupen mode of representation of the sign, painting is emblematic of sign culture, within which art plays a privileged role. It is indeed in imaginary equation to the individual prison-house: they only exchange themselves among themselves; they only exchange themselves on the condition that they no longer exchange themselves with the real. There is no longer any access to a 'real' which is itself presented as an effect of the code or system. Even 'subversive communication' has to circumvent the codes and models. The difficulty with Swaminathan is that there are no obvious levels of meaning: there is indeed a continual level of signification – the primordial presence as otherness. The primordial as otherness and as the mark of difference is implicated by the surface's hidden order. Here, everything seems interconnected.

The 'other' as primitive is a Eurocentric construction. The primitive for Swaminathan is not even the figure of the unconscious – a figure constructed in modern art as well as psychoanalysis and anthropology in the privileged triad of the primitive, the child and the innocence. He is closer to Gauguin in thinking that modern artistic 'primitivism' is not antithetical to scientific knowledge.

Primitivism is a system of multiple beliefs. In Swaminathan, we have a counter-discourse to primitivism and it is posed by him on different levels, the destruction of racial or evolutionist myths, for example. For him, as for Edward Said, it is opening the culture to the experience of the other. And, as Said has said, it is 'the recovery of a history hitherto either misrepresented or rendered invisible'.[2] Rather than seeking to master the primitive as Eurocentric thinking tends to do, Swaminathan can be defined as the name of a primitive mode.

In no other Indian painter's work do we find involvement with the primitive mode in such an original way as in Swaminathan's. The quintessential Swaminathan is revealed in the painter's gestures that established his signature as a difference between gesture and signature. The signature plays with gesture and is included in the game: signature parodying, as it were, the question. Is naming the ultimate gesture towards translation of an unnamable structure?

Editor's Notes

1 'Significant form' was an idea put forward by Clive Bell. But both Bell and Fry spoke of the idea of the 'primitive' in art, drawing on the early twentieth-century interest in African art, and certainly impacted by the Othering 'noble savage' narratives of the art of Africa and other non-Western civilizations in the wake of Paul Gauguin's move to Tahiti and paintings of it.

2 Edward Said, *Reflections on Exile: And Other Literary and Cultural Essays*, Granta, 2001.

35

TANTRA AND SANTOSH

*Review of a solo exhibition in New Delhi of the neo-*tantra *artist G.R. Santosh*

Link, New Delhi, 30 December 1973

G.R. Santosh who showed his paintings last week at the Gallery Chanakya is a painter in the mystic tradition of *tantra* art. Also that he has a single theme (the interacting elements symbolized by *purusha* and *prakriti* and their sensual and suprasensual transformations into colour geometry) for his compositions which are as severely organized as any minimal[ist] canvas. Tantric forms have a primer-type armature which is self-contained, eliciting a sense of optical tension but held in a vivid suspension with a direct correlation between rhythm and intention. The total oeuvre of Santosh's *tantra* geometry amounts to an emergence of a new painting that has one basic characteristic – symmetry of parts. Actually, it is more of a symmetrical pattern with a kind of force which holds the parts together, pushing them simultaneously towards the centre of the canvas.

The relationship between the sensation produced by geometric forms and emotion generated by them is more intimate than one finds in the minimal canvases. While the minimal canvas stops at the optical, Santosh's always leads us back to the emotion, to something that only the mind can see and react to. Indeed, tantric forms are merely a new language mode of current geometric art: he makes use of them to express their identification with symbols that are buried in our racial memory.

Thus the geometric and the symbolic become analogous forms. That is why one should not read his paintings in terms of their *prakriti-purush* context: that would amount to separating content from form as if factors of significance are not logically part of the composition: rather the content should be felt as a quality.

QUALITY

Otherwise, critics should have helped improve our eyesight for painting. There is something odd when a critic dares point to a mystery called quality in a painting. It is indeed like seeing in the mind's eye; which is another name for imagining, a more complicated process than seeing, for it involves trying, which makes all the difference. Moreover, imagining takes time: it does not simply last over a period of time. When one is trying to imagine intention informing a particular painting, things just do not click into place: they are put into place. This means the 'seeing' of quality takes much longer time: indeed it spreads itself out over a period of time. So it is more proper to ask 'when did you start seeing quality' and not 'in which canvases did you see quality.'

The role of *tantra* mythology will thus seem out of context in Santosh's work although the critical rhetoric does suggest the relevance of tantric symbolism in his paintings as if Santosh's preoccupation is with solving the mysteries of life. Symmetrical patterns of geometry which have tantric associations are indeed his motifs and the theme is more painterly – to discover a logical destiny of these geometric forms in the process of abstracting them for compositional purposes: the exploration ends where it started from, that is painting originating with a virgin, uniform canvas and reverting to a plain uniform surface, which is mostly in dark colour. The *tantra* mythology would have been effective in the glorious days of the revivalist Bengal School when myth as an intermediary between art and material production had a more valid ground. A mythology coming from the same soil, the same people, the same cultural superstructure has not the same economic structure to support it. It is a mere bourgeois invention that mythology is valid in the works of art because the artist has transformed it into a kind of private religion. Myth, no doubt, did once play a part to express the forces of nature in the imagination but is no longer the case now: it is out of harmony with the empirical temper of our times.

PRESENCE OF NUMEN

Painters who dislike the role of a visual technologist do speak of the presence of numen, which they believe can be understood by means of symbols alone because they pretend they are concerned with making visible what is essentially invisible, what lies, that is, behind the phenomenal world. The nineteenth-century myth of artist as a magician (a parallel between the idea of god as creator fashioning man out of clay and man as an artist working in a similar medium) is still valid for a colonial mind who is unable to see the imperialist game behind attempts that seek to link the vogue for primitive art which was a nineteenth-century imperialist discovery with the modernist tradition. No wonder our artists are most happy when critics put a current work on the same level as primitive art because their works then acquire an instant prestige of timeless quality. The artist thus plays in the hands of bourgeois culture by devaluing his own history. As [Meyer] Schapiro, the influential Marxist critic of America noted that 'the preservation of certain forms of native culture in the interest of imperialist power could be supported in the name of the new artistic attitudes by those who thought themselves entirely free from political interest'.[1]

Religion has really acted as an opiate for the artists. We know how deeply religious Cezanne was, perhaps influenced by his sister Marie, a fanatic Catholic. Similarly Klee's naturalist philosophy was a diffusion of theosophical beliefs and more openly were Kandinsky's and Mondrian's attitudes. And compared with other contemporaries, they were no doubt largely unscientific minds but intensely aware of this claiming that in their aesthetic intuition played a far greater role than reason. Indeed, it will be some job if the role of metaphysical idealism in the modernist tradition was well documented tracing the association of mystical ideas with the crisis of rationality.

NEW YORK PAINTERS

The New York painters, influenced by the pretentious mysticism of Stael, Rothko, Gottlieb and Newman, have little faith in Platonic and Pythagorean mysteries. Their interest in religion is more a product of cultural and psychological conditioning, which is, [though], not true of Cezanne and Mondrian for whom the prior reality of nature was not an ego-dissolving psychological act. Mysticism, however diffused, had never been a source for motifs and forms; nor a justification for their humanistic ethic. The mystic gestures of these painters are merely self-elevating egoistic exercises.

This should be seen in the existential context of the late 1940s when abstract art became the dominant mode and it began to be justified in the mystic language of depth psychology and existentialism. Art historians and critics said that abstract art brought us a 'new awareness of the absolute' because it communicated more directly from artist to viewer. The makers of these 'non-objective' canvases believed in the existential whine about their work: they even contended that the forms and colours they employed were a priori and were charged with spiritual content. Not only that, they also were certain of their energies because they also believed that the gestural art not only produced a corresponding response in the soul of the viewer but heightened their sensory perception. Happily, Santosh has long ago shed that abstract expressionist cocoon.

Editor's Note

1 Meyer Shapiro, 'The Nature of Abstract Art', *Marxist Quarterly*, vol. 1, no. 1, 1937, p. 21.

36

REAR-VIEW MIRROR IMAGES

Review of a solo exhibition of the expatriate Indian artist P. Mansaram

Link, New Delhi, 20 August 1972

Few Indian artists desire the reputation of being hip as intensely as Mansaram does and the hip attitude is not a put-on but a genuine extension of his personality. Nearly six years ago, he left India to settle in Canada – the country of McLuhan with whom he has almost hip relations. The works he has brought with him on a recent visit to India were exhibited last week at the Dhoomimal Gallery. Called 'the images of the rear-view mirror' they were indeed translations of McLuhan mythologies. They were all small essays into mix-media (collage, serigraph and paint) compounding the message with the same complexity of metaphysical phrase which his guru, McLuhan is famous for.

What does the guru think about this business of translating the medium into its message? The first premise is simple: message is inseparable from the medium and the second follows from the first. The content of a medium, McLuhan insists, is 'change of scale or pace or pattern that it introduces into human affairs'.[1] And in the McLuhanian pictorial language it is 'like the juicy piece of meat carried by the burglar to distract the watchdog of the mind'.[2] Or is it merely a Gutenberg irrelevance?

CONSCIOUSNESS

Reading too much then into the latest Mansaram mixes will be a futile Gutenberg exercise: the critic should better shut his mouth because they are not for judging. If one insists upon judging them, go with a pair of big bifocals – one for reading the printed texts and other for seeing metaphors in good, close relationship of colours and their space geometry: they are, to be sure, not simple rear-view mirror images. They are playthings of a young McLuhanite mind. But Mansaram has his own differences with the guru. 'For me,' he says,

> 'The REAR VIEW MIRROR'[3] is the very basis of the forward progression of mankind. It does not merely reflect a dead past, for the past is never dead. And even if it were, its ghosts and angels would continue to haunt and protect. All that time obliterates is the logical connections. But the rear-view mirror reflects a vital collage, an indestructible organism, iridescent and resonant, seemingly formless yet above form, above logic, part of the great racial unconscious and therefore constantly beckoning the individual consciousness that once falls in tune with it.

Granted that the paintings have a conventional format, they are good colour and image decorations and very pleasing to the eye – and yet they are different. They have different psychic levels without a point of convergence. No one need quarrel with their multi-dimensionality for the simple reason that they are well crafted. One naturally does not understand them because the eye with a fixed point of view refuses to cooperate ('You wipe your glasses with what you know').[4] But one thing is certain that the galaxy of symbols have a 'high definition', because each one is transmuted into some glittering half-truth and all this by a process of colour alchemy and the technique of serigraphy. If some look like committing a sin of single vision – and these are surely the most lovely things on display – no man can transform himself into an electronic machine, although Mansaram thinks that he is like a machine.

BASIC ELEMENTS

What he strives for is a mosaic effect, the cubist simultaneity with this difference that he does not take a single object to peel off its layer. As he says, his work involves three levels of creativity. 'I use people directly or indirectly,' he says.

> In my films (experimental films in 16 mm) I create mix-media environments – people are part of it. My collage material is either handmade: manuscripts, paintings, drawings . . . or machine-made: printed matter, plastics and so on. Thus, in collages I use people indirectly through collage materials. In collages, films and environments – image, idea, humour, satire and colour are the basic elements.

The rear-view mirror images are not new constructions he has brought to India. At the Montreal world fair, the Indian pavilion was done up by Mansaram and the theme was 'Man and his World'. These were assemblages in the mix-media technique called the *Rear View Mirror Images*. The decorations received much critical acclaim and as one critic put it: 'In it one saw more than what the driver of the vehicle might see – one saw Mansaram's keen sense of perception and his ability to experiment with the unlimited possibilities of communicating with other human beings through his art'.

THE PROJECT

While in Delhi, Mansaram has done a lot of filming of old Delhi for the Delhi TV unit. But more than his paintings and filmmaking, his idiosyncrasies are full of future shock. He is currently working on a project which involves a bit of architecture and music. 'I can imagine,' he said about the project, 'a multi-storey house where all the floors are made of lens-like transparent material. One can see the activities on all the floors. One can focus on a particular floor if one wishes. Also one can tune in sounds from any floor one wishes to. This building can be used for studios or homes for artistic people.'

Editor's Notes

1 Marshall McLuhan, 'The Medium is the Message', in *Understanding Media: The Extensions of Man*, New York: McGraw-Hill Publications, 1964, p. 8.

2 Ibid., p. 18.

3 Mansaram's reference is to McLuhan's statement 'We look at the present through a rear-view mirror. We march backwards into the future' – in Marshall McLuhan and Quentin Fiore, *The Medium is The Message: An Inventory of Effects*, Penguin, 1967, pp. 74–75.

4 The quotation draws on James Joyce's words, appearing as a footnote in his novel *Finnegans Wake* in the form of advice to his readers: 'wipe your glosses with what you know'.

37
ART OF SUBSTITUTION

Review of Vivan Sundaram's 1972 solo exhibition in New Delhi

Link, New Delhi, 1 October 1972

Vivan Sundaram had almost given up painting and according to critic Geeta Kapur 'he had turned away from art with the feeling that it is not relevant in the society of our times; that there are far more urgent activities - political activities - that demand the entire attention of every variety of person.'[1] He was the one-man secretariat of the protest movement against the second triennale and the bureaucratic functioning of the Lalit Kala Akademi. It is almost after four years that he has come out with an exhibition of his works, now on view at the Kunika-Chemould.

POLITICAL

The deliberate turning away from art has been very fruitful, it seems, judging by what he has now achieved - an ideological position. Not any political ideology translated in fine art terms, but very nearly an art of substitution in which visual qualities have the experience value of daily speech; moving, that is, from one sensory experience to another. Or one might say he makes the new hobby horse the equivalent of the real one, as children do believing in the reality of the hobby horse because it can be ridden.

The theme of the current exhibition is the wide range of substitute images he provides to Pablo Neruda's poem, *The Heights of Macchu Picchu*, from his epic *Canto General*. Whether one sees them as substitute images or independently of the poem, they are an intensely gratifying experience and speak in a new voice relating a quality of sound (is not all good poetry a quality of sound?) to a visual impression. A good starting point - speaking in metaphors loaded with visual synaesthesia or translation of the poem in terms of syncretistic vision - is the child's way of seeing things and his art of the doodle.

Or, perhaps, it matches in vision to the syncretistic Picasso portraits, jumbled up details which have no convincing portrait qualities because there is no matching of detail to detail. What Picasso does is to take the entire person and not the face alone and somehow the jumbling up of details hold together and have a great spatial coherence. So, what the spectator should do standing before the drawing is to call up the child's syncretistic vision. They should not in any case be seen as illustrations, or read like the advertisement image.

The sophisticated response is not necessary indeed and has its dangers. One could see colour, for instance, in his lines and the purely surface qualities may lead him to imagine things which are not on the same plane of emphasis. The purely graphic construct of the images too are misleading: rather, each drawing should be seen in relation to the lines in the poem. A kind of gestalt view where reality appears as super-real and intensely plastic, and an awareness that these are substitutes related to the unconscious wealth of Neruda's fantasy. The drawings may attract attention for their surface charms, the play of light and dark woven into the graphic medium – they are for the eye. However, in relation to the poem they are emotionally packed icons directing the eye to the imagination. A pattern may emerge then which seems as whimsical as Neruda's images.

STRUGGLE

The Heights of Macchu Picchu is the best known among his poems. It is about the ancient Inca city, and the history of the town built into the lines comes out with elemental force. It becomes an act of pilgrimage for the poet, 'a venture to the interior of himself and the past of the Latin America' (Alan Bold in *Penguin Book of Socialist Verse*), who regards *Macchu Picchu* as 'one of the very greatest poems written this century'. Vivan begins with Section 10 of the poem with the line 'Stone within stone and man where was he?' What follows are the toiling images of the workmen who built the city and the life of meaningless, repetitive ritual drudgery. And finally his identification: 'Give me your hand out of the depths sown by your sorrow. . . . And give me silence, give me water, hope. Give me the struggle, the iron, the volcanoes. . . .'

To project such a landscape of images by the medium of drawing and its abstract patterning is equivalent of asking a man to go dreaming surrounded by the crude commercial reality of gallery art. Such images are for collective sharing even though they are intensely private.

Editor's Note

1 Geeta Kapur, in *The Heights of Macchu Picchu*, exhibition catalogue, 1972.

38
A SENSE OF DIRECTION

Review of a Vivan Sundaram solo exhibition of 1976

Link, New Delhi, 4 April 1976

Rarely do we come across work of such total commitment as Vivan Sundaram has mounted at the Lalit Kala Gallery. The fact that Vivan shows his work after four years of silent 'rumination upon himself, upon his taste, his intellectual interests, social judgements, the symbols that moved him' makes the exhibition an all the more rewarding experience. Three years before he painted the famous work, *Portrait of Mrs G*, one could draw a distinction between areas that were primarily sensuous (as a kind of presence with an element of mystery grounded into it) and those that were abstract and intellectually complex. Now, intellectual complexity has a symbiotic function; the concrete references woven into the surface have a sensuous immediacy. And if we look at them a little longer, we perceive a world which may be different from our own but which confers meaning and articulation.

This exhibition has a theme and Vivan calls it 'The discreet charm of the bourgeoisie'. And to make the intention explicit, he quotes American critic Harold Rosenberg to tell us how the role of historical self-consciousness is relevant to the painters of the third-world countries. To be sure with Vivan, painting is a professional activity which makes him conservative in the way he builds his canvas bit by bit like a devoted workman. What follows from this labour of love is an evolved answer. And there is no room in his method for creative accidents to happen and illuminate the work with the inner truth of feeling: rather he is committed to establish continuities, and in that sense, he almost lives up to the Rosenberg dictum: 'In our time each new work must constitute a decision as to what is living and what is dead in the painting of the past'.

If Vivan gives the impression of having appropriated much from the art of the Sixties, it is based on historical claims to necessity, perhaps, because the local bourgeoisie has modelled his value structure on the donor culture. These recent Vivans provide many paradigms of eclecticism of our dim colonial aesthetic legacy and this is presented with absolute authority. The concrete references to the world of Indian bourgeoisie have the charm of internal monologue: and they are of interest because Vivan's class origins make him a fighter from within. Little wonder that the works seem to be emotionally charged. Each work is conceived as a configuration of the outward symbols of the bourgeois so that it takes on a nature of sign. And this is what marks him out as a cool guerilla. Also we are aware all the time that beyond the sensuous surface there is violence and it is this that which gives his painting, power. A dialectical line of discourse is built with such logical cool that the sign is not allowed to collapse into what Levi-Strauss calls the status of a 'signifier without a signified'.

Vivan's new painting looks intellectually more complex, no doubt, than it really is. There is, hint of recognition between the world we know and the world of the Indian bourgeoisie which Vivan has constructed: but their distinct modalities are suspended halfway generating a dialogue. But Vivan does not trivialize; rather he points to a single line of dialectical enquiry leaving the spectator alone to build his own line of interpretation. One thing is clear: the spectator cannot remain indifferent, for he experiences a loss of innocence and the specificity of Vivan's images seems to him as built-up rationalizations of felt discontinuities. If there is presence of affluence, the spectator will also be impressed by the artist's humbleness towards his craft: and, there is no evidence to suggest the presence of a solipsistic ego to outdo his audience.

The starting point of Vivan's art is that painting is a constructed reality with its unique kind of ordered system of information. The additive procedure is built on a linguistic model: not the individual words but the whole sentence that makes a valid proposition. The Vivan painting may appear additive, its units can be seen separately from the whole, but it is in its completeness, in its final interlocked structure of the additive parts that the significance of image is felt. Such a painting is not the result of a growth but more of a demonstration of a fixed order. The painting is felt as an indivisible configuration: each work with a separate register; but the meaning always emerges from the same surface which draws us in first by its sensuous immediacy. There is reason to hope for a bright future for Vivan because there is a sense of inevitable direction in his work.

39

FORMS WITH A HIDDEN DIALECTIC

Review of an exhibition of Vivan Sundaram's installation art, 1992

'Artscape', *The Economic Times*, New Delhi, 9 March 1992

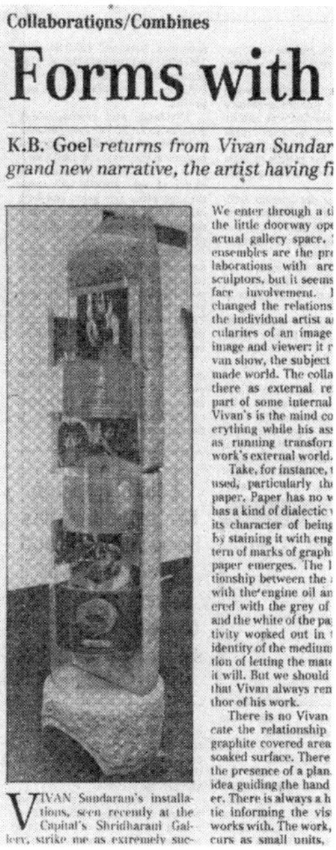

Collaborations/Combines

Forms with

K.B. Goel *returns from Vivan Sundar*
grand new narrative, the artist having fi

VIVAN Sundaram's installa-
tions, seen recently at the
Capital's Shridharani Gal-
lery, strike me as extremely suc-

Vivan Sundaram's installations, seen recently at the capital's Shridharani Gallery, strike me as extremely successful. For I have in mind the many installations at the fourth Havana Biennial and by comparison Vivan has done a good job. He has divided the gallery space neatly into sequestered structures and charged these with a strange sense of subjectivity, which is what makes an installation a phenomenological object.

The installations are intended to deny gravity as a factor of form. They are an attempt at constructing a public-private transference of art. We enter through a tiny gateway: the little doorway opens on to the actual gallery space. Some of the ensembles are the product of collaborations with architects and sculptors, but it seems to be a surface involvement. It has not changed the relationship between the individual artist and the particularities of an image or between image and viewer: it remains a Vivan show, the subject of his homemade world. The collaborators are there as external references, as part of some internal monologue. Vivan's is the mind controlling every-thing while his associates look like running transformers of the work's external world.

Take, for instance, the materials used, particularly the handmade paper. Paper has no weight, but it has a kind of dialectic which denies its character of being weightless. By staining it with engine oil, a pattern of marks of graphite and white paper emerges. The logic of relationship between the areas soaked with the engine oil and those covered with the grey of the graphite and the white of the paper is subjectivity worked out in terms of identity of the medium. It is a question of letting the material do what it will. But we should never forget that Vivan always remains the author of his work.

There is no Vivan map to indicate the relationship between the graphite-covered areas and the oil-soaked surface. There is, however, the presence of a plan, some vague idea guiding the hand of the painter. There is always a hidden dialectic informing the visual units he works with. The work, it seems, occurs as small units, the parts of which make a combination. When a certain combination is arrived at, it is treated as a unit. A sheet of paper is stitched to combine this larger unit with another paper, containing certain units in combinations. When the two papers are stitched, two units are joined. The result is a combination of many parts, units and then larger units.

The work can be taken in at a glance and one can enjoy exploring the relationship in terms of the complexities of ideas the random order implies. It is also true that one cannot find out what the whole drama is about at a single glance. But that does not mean that Vivan has a complicated message. That the presence of engine oil in his work came after the Gulf War should not tempt one to set up imaginary correspondence between idea and its execution. There is always a danger that these oil-soaked works may be misread as paintings. It is perhaps for this reason that a tray containing crude oil is placed at the bottom of the work. The *Combines* is so placed that these works have a theatrical presence. Theatricality establishes its identity, as opposed to painting, as an object. Yet it does not have the character of an object.

The nature of material used relates it to a surface that is ontologically that of a painting. What is it that a painting does not share with a physical object? A painting is all surface, nothing but surface. Whereas no ordinary object, however thin or flat (for example, paper), can be described as having only a surface and nothing else. Vivan's *Combines* defeats the theatricality of objecthood through an implicit appeal to the richness of their surface. In fact, what are combined are only surfaces which have an inward spread across the multiples of combinations, themselves made up of different visual units. A narrative of gestural directness connects the material content of these *Combines*. It is like working with sets, and sets are not the things that are represented.

In inventiveness, Vivan is a contemporary of the American artist Robert Rauschenberg. The Vivan of 1966, in retrospect, looks no less naughty than the Rauschenberg of the Fifties. When in the Fifties, Rauschenberg was invited to participate on the nostalgic subject of 'nature in art', his entry was a square patch of growing grass held down with chicken wires. The work was placed in a box suitable for framing and hung on the wall. He visited the show periodically to water the piece. Which is literally speaking, an act of a transposition from nature to culture.

A close look at Vivan's construction *Touch of Brightness,* which he showed at his first 1966 show in Bombay (and included in the current exhibition), will bring home the truth of the artist's uncanny attitude towards painting. The kitschy ritual objects are put into box enclosures; each is a separate unit and when joined together makes a single combine.

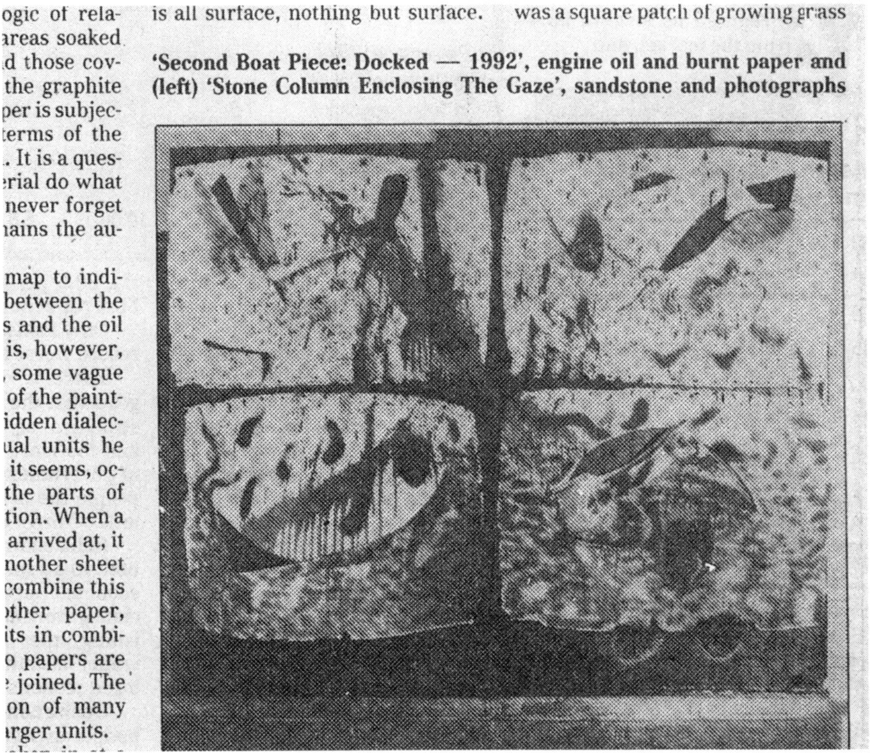

ogic of rela-
ıreas soaked
d those cov-
the graphite
per is subjec-
terms of the
. It is a ques-
rial do what
never forget
ıains the au-

map to indi-
between the
s and the oil
is, however,
some vague
of the paint-
idden dialec-
ual units he
it seems, oc-
the parts of
tion. When a
arrived at, it
nother sheet
combine this
ther paper,
its in combi-
o papers are
joined. The
on of many
ırger units.

is all surface, nothing but surface.

was a square patch of growing grass

'Second Boat Piece: Docked — 1992', engine oil and burnt paper and (left) 'Stone Column Enclosing The Gaze', sandstone and photographs

The hidden logic behind the work is what Leo Steinberg calls the allusion to hard surfaces such as table tops, studio floors, charts, bulletin boards, any receptor surface on which objects are scattered, on which information may be received, printed, impressed.

What is important, however, is that the flatbed ensemble has a distinct psychic address of nostalgia. And with the use of the symbolic vermillion, Vivan succeeds in producing a narrative the special mode of which is imaginative confrontation in which the portents and antecedents become increasingly recognizable. Little did Vivan realize in 1966 that the nostalgia mode is one of the theoretical grounds of post-modernism. The weight of the Hindu past and its memories in *Touch of Brightness* weighs 'like the nightmare on the brains of the living,' as Marx said in another context. And Vivan, of course, did not burn incense at the root of the work unlike Rauschenberg who went regularly to water the grass in his work!

The work is total pastiche. It mimics its original sources of religious iconography without the use of irony. Vivan then was too young to employ parody's ulterior motive. For the satirical impulse presupposes a latent feeling that there exists something normal compared to one in which what is being imitated is rather comic. In that sense, Vivan's 1966 pastiche was an engagement in producing blank parody: a parody that has lost its sense of humour.

A good parodist has to have some secret sympathy for the original. Vivan in search for his roots in the soil confronts us with the images of the Hindu pantheon, the kitschy character of which are mimic representations seen in the recent TV serials such as the *Mahabharata* and *Ramayana*. Vivan's *Combines* are a frank celebration of the aesthetics of kitsch. At another level, Vivan parallels in imagination to an old master like Rauschenberg who mimics in the language of blank parody the subject of his work, 'nature in art'.

A small digression is necessary to explain the relevance of Leo Steinberg's notion of the flatbed picture plane. The flatbed picture plane is pictorial surface that lets the world in. It is not the world that the Renaissance man knew; in his world he looked for his weather clues out of the window. Vivan's world is a place where men turn knobs to hear a taped message: 'rain or thunder accompanied by duststorm'. In this world the messages are electronically transmitted from some windowless booth. The flatbed picture plane, as employed for printing broadsheets, is for information and therefore for a consciousness immersed in the brain of the city. What Steinberg calls the flatbed is more than a surface distinction if it is understood 'as a change within painting that changed the relationship between artist and image, image and public'.

The flatbed is the ideal picture plane for what may be called 'denatured representation' (that is, representation of representation). It is the most suitable plane where images are layered and combined. Like words on a palimpsest, the images beg to be interpreted. This is well illustrated by another early work of Vivan's, also from 1966, *Bars Invisible* displayed at the exhibition. The work is an act of total appropriation of the language of pop and serial art of the Sixties.

Let me explain for the benefit of those who do not approve of appropriation of the images from the works of old masters. The famous artist Joshua Reynolds borrowed from Michelangelo images in his society portraits. In the late eighteenth century, he debated on the relative merits of Raphael and Michelangelo and advised his students to appropriate the images from the works of old masters as he himself did in his portraits.

In exploring the language of pop and serialization, this 1966 work *Bars Invisible* is an important signpost in Vivan's journey as an artist. There is the experience of the serial mode in it and also there is the anxiety about trust in seeing in it principally the pleasures of design. What is remarkable about the Vivan of 1966 is that he has not taken anything for granted; everything is to be tested against experience. The transparency between past and present has never been presupposed. It is built upon facts dealing with ontological questions.

Implicit in *Bars Invisible*, inspired by the conventions of serialized painting, is the tension between pictorial space and its relation to literal space. Pictorial space is a function of perceptual experience; it is fully

·wn with chicken wires. The ·as placed in a box suitable ·ning and hung on the wall. ·ted the show periodically to ·he piece. Which is, literally ·ig, an act of a transposition ·ture to culture.

·ose look at Vivan's construc- ·uch of Brightness, which he ·l at his first 1966 show in ·y, (and included in the cur- ·xhibition) will bring home ·h of the artist's uncanny at- towards painting. The ritual objects are put into ·closures; each is a separate ·nd when joined together a single Combine. The hid- ·ic behind the work is what ·inberg calls the allusion to ·urfaces such as table-tops, floors, charts, bulletin ·, any receptor surface on objects are scattered, on information may be re- printed, impressed.

·AT is important however is ·at the flatbed ensemble has ·ct psychic address of nostal- ·d with the use of the symbol- ·nilion, Vivan succeeds in ·ing a narrative the special ·f which is imaginative con- ·ion in which the portents

who mimics in the language of blank parody the subject of his work, "nature in art".

A small digression is necessary to explain the relevance of Leo Steinberg's notion of the flatbed picture plane. The flatbed picture plane is pictorial surface that lets the world in. It is not the world that the Renaissance man knew; in his world he looked for his weather clues out of the window. Vivan's world is a place where men turn knobs to hear a taped message: "rain or thunder accompanied by dust-storm." In this world the mes-

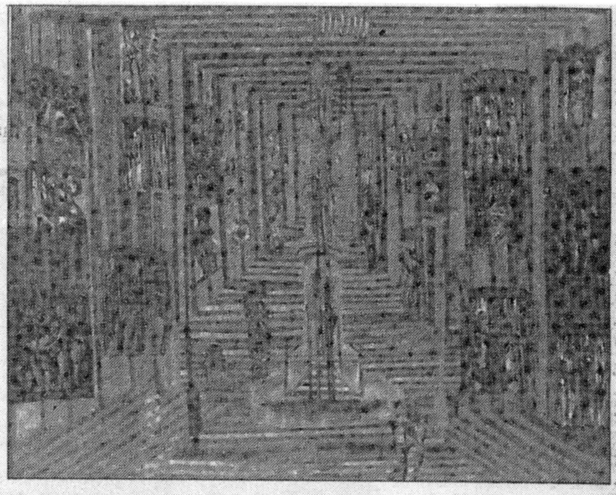

Vivan Sundaram's (below) 'Bars Invisible', 1966: appropriating the language of Pop art

1966 work: *Bars Invisible* displayed at the exhibition. The work is an act

ialisation came as a 180-degree shift in sensibilities. Serialisation is

cognitive. Literal space became a hotly debated subject when in the late Sixties serialization came as a 180-degree shift in sensibilities. Serialization is grounded on a simple premise: an image (or any visualizable idea) is, in principle, permutable. The rule of serial transfer are included in the terms of its presentation.

Paris-based Vishwanadhan's work, shown recently (October 1991) at Gallery Espace, well illustrates the pictorial truth where permutation involves shape as well as colour. Through serial transfers, Vishwanadhan builds up a range of melody in colour. The temporality of music implies that during transfers nothing material about the melody is changed. The experience of a serial painting is contrary to the experience of listening to a melody; there is the knowledge that a great deal in it will be changed. In front of a serial painting, there is the feeling that one is 'co-present' with the painting, that one shares the same space.

The current show, which Vivan calls *Collaboration/Combines*, is perhaps the beginning of a grand narrative. For, there is the apprehension that Vivan, it seems, has finally said goodbye to the traditional categories informing the art of painting. But would that not be a misreading of Vivan's intentions? What is interesting for me is to watch the way Vivan fights against the built-in theatricality when art exists for its audience. Vivan is a committed artist but more than that, his is a mind in love with itself, a mind in a permanent state of gestation.

40

WHEN ART ONLY LOOKS LIKE ART

Review of Vivan Sundaram's exhibition of 1993, in response to the pogrom following the Babri Masjid demolition of December 1992

'Artscape', *The Economic Times*, New Delhi, 11 December 1993

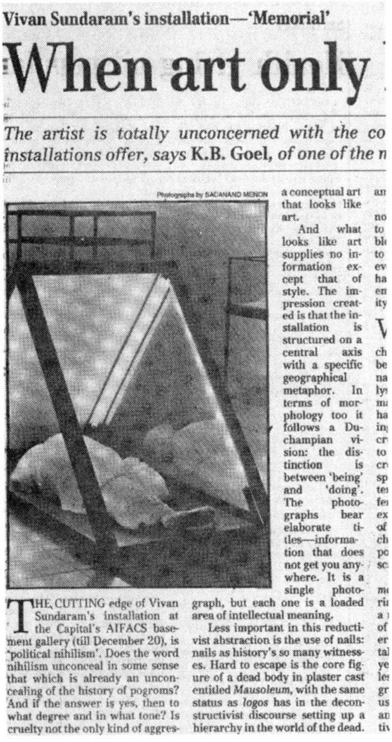

Vivan Sundaram's installation—'Memorial'

When art only

The artist is totally unconcerned with the co
installations offer, says **K.B. Goel**, *of one of the n*

Photographs by SADANAND MENON

THE CUTTING edge of Vivan Sundaram's installation at the Capital's AIFACS basement gallery (till December 20), is 'political nihilism'. Does the word nihilism unconceal in some sense that which is already an unconcealing of the history of pogroms? And if the answer is yes, then to what degree and in what tone? Is cruelty not the only kind of aggres-

a conceptual art that looks like art.

And what looks like art supplies no information except that of style. The impression created is that the installation is structured on a central axis with a specific geographical metaphor. In terms of morphology too it follows a Duchampian vision: the distinction is between 'being' and 'doing'. The photographs bear elaborate titles—information that does not get you anywhere. It is a single photograph, but each one is a loaded area of intellectual meaning.

Less important in this reductivist abstraction is the use of nails: nails as history's so many witnesses. Hard to escape is the core figure of a dead body in plaster cast entitled *Mausoleum*, with the same status as *logos* has in the deconstructivist discourse setting up a hierarchy in the world of the dead.

The cutting edge of Vivan Sundaram's installation at the capital's AIFACS basement gallery (till 20 December), is apolitical nihilism. Does the word 'nihilism' unconceal in some sense that which is already an unconcealing of the history of pogroms? And if the answer is yes, then to what degree and in what tone? Is cruelty not the only kind of aggressive-destructive behaviour towards the defenseless? Where is one to locate aggression focused upon specific enemies? Is aggression – man's ability to inflict pain and terror on others – an expression of baser instinctual drive? Or is it instinctual gratification in obedience to a blind law of the stimulus-response scheme? Or is aggression learnt behaviour?

Vivan's installation raises all these questions. I, for myself, believe aggression is learnt behaviour. Our class-based society is itself aggression-prone, though Marxism has committed itself to the old postulate that the human being is limitlessly educable provided we develop proper consciousness. Society is a mediating system, offering us the possibility of a differentiated understanding.

But the history of pogroms shows otherwise: it shows what has been done step-by-step to minorities, who are declared arch-enemies of a dominant group and put in danger of losing identity. Nationalism, of which fascism is the real face, masks the dehumanization process through cultural exclusivity: dehumanization is thus approved by a collectively shared distortion of judgement.

Vivan uses barricades that were erected at Ayodhya as self-referential interpretation of Duchampian 'facticity' (the subject-less art). They have what may be called phenomenological intent. The attempt is to indicate the ontological nature of the verbal problem inherent in Duchampian aesthetic – answering the problem of a conceptual art that looks like art. And what looks like art supplies no information except that of style. The impression created is that the installation is structured on a central axis with a specific geographical metaphor. In terms of morphology too it follows a Duchampian vision: the distinction is between 'being' and 'doing'. The photographs bear elaborate titles – information that does not get you anywhere. It is a single photograph, but each one is a loaded area of intellectual meaning.

Less important in this reductivist abstraction is the use of nails: nails as history's so many witnesses. Hard to escape is the core figure of a dead body in plaster cast entitled *Mausoleum*, with the same status as logos have in the deconstructivist discourse setting up a hierarchy in the world of the dead.

The figure demands that Vivan would have us accept that the discourse is open and not closed. The implication of this discourse is that in the bitter, long-standing enmity between ethnic groups with separate religious identities, we see cruelty liberated to a virtually incomprehensible degree. A reactive cruelty which can be inflamed in individuals or in a group or a nation when people are recklessly prepared for extermination of their opponents. It is an attempt to make us aware of our loss of empathy, our inability to step into another's shoes.

The steel-and-glass prism with neon light which houses the plaster cast from live body leads us to sandstone tiles and the brick channel with blood flowing: it is called *Cross*, symbolizing group cruelty and demonstrates the inability of the individual to defend himself against the destructive dehumanized belief of his society. The viewer finds himself as a resisting subject in the position of a strange, suspicious outsider, close to an enemy within. The totality of which is that one is confronted with the historic epidemics of collective cruelty. The individual moral structure against the destructive capabilities melts away, because the violence paralyses the senses.

The installation leaves little for imagination to allow moments of reflection when we stop observing human behaviour from the outside: we discover our self-deceptions, our shameless acts of bullying when we find ourselves at the bottom of the hierarchical pyramid. The normal attitude is one of not getting involved. As witnesses to the event, we watch in cold blood, too numbed and frightened to move. We all participate in such events with a certain disbelief of having experienced a process of emotional emptiness, of our inability to empathize with the helpless.

What is worse is that the whole administrative machine that Eichmann used has been employed. Vivan's use of nails point to the great need to analyse the extent to which society may be implicated because no one has the courage to point an accusing finger against the motivation of cruelty: our insensitivity in regard to the misuse of power has increased considerably. The gallery space, in simple psychological terms, is not the space that can offer an explanation for the human experience of pleasure in the pain of another human being. The psychopathology of society produces political consequences on a large scale; art is a small voice of protest.

Vivan calls his installation *Memorial.* The question arises: memorial to what? The establishment of a regime of terror, of the strategy of rebellion against the huge power reservoirs of bureaucratic totalitarianism? What happened last year, on 6 December, was nothing less than mass murder by some grand design: the fear of death was used by society as well as the state and the events representing reactive violence in Bombay were a warning to the majority to be prepared for a messianic mission of destructive aggression.

Auschwitz cannot be explained in our context. The obvious connection between the two events is the lack of guilt feelings and this seems to be the central message of Vivan's installation – as if people were commissioned to kill and maim fellow creatures. Where is then the question of guilt when one is commissioned to murder? 'Conscience,' as Freud has said in a different context, 'is at its root nothing more than social fear.'

And when society offers the license to kill, many an individual ego cannot resist the temptation to regress and act out fantasies of the early anal-sadistic libido organization; for, this pleasure is the pleasure of aggression and it is pleasure that goes hand in hand with the assertion of superior power. The cruelty-worker in a torture chamber has the upper hand. His conscience is intermittently silent, both during the act and after, because he is able to divest himself of that part of his personality. What the gallery space does is the same thing: the viewer assumes a multiple personality – with the same ease with which the soldier takes off his uniform.

Vivan could have said this of the victims of torture that they must continue to live with the memory of a terrible experience. Which apparently does not hold true for the torturer. Nazi murderers reintegrated with ease into the society of democratic liberal West: their conscience adapted to the new situation. These bureaucrats of cruelty are almost interchangeable in India. The secular constitution of India has clauses for defining the 'normality' of such acts of cruelty. Research on the 'My Lai' massacre has shown that participants did not see themselves as pathologically deviant members of their society.

Vivan is totally unconcerned with the conventional manipulation of the limits that art installations offer. He is rather conscious that photographs can be offered as counterparts to the four axial divisions of space. They exist at several removes from the original fallen mortal, these having been replaced by photographs. The photographs, too, seem an auxiliary effort: they

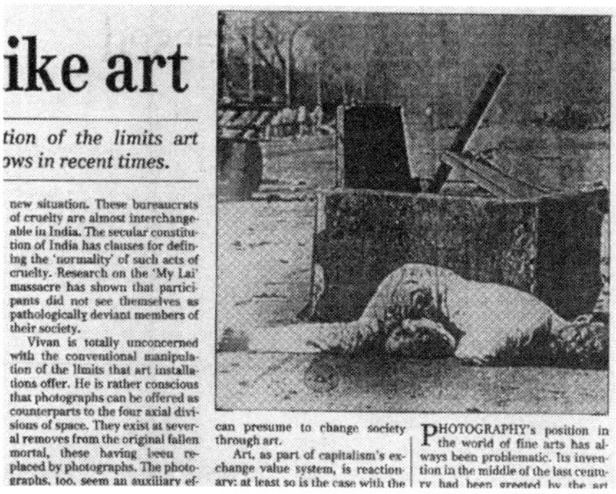

ike art

tion of the limits art
ows in recent times.

new situation. These bureaucrats of cruelty are almost interchangeable in India. The secular constitution of India has clauses for defining the 'normality' of such acts of cruelty. Research on the 'My Lai' massacre has shown that participants did not see themselves as pathologically deviant members of their society.

Vivan is totally unconcerned with the conventional manipulation of the limits that art installations offer. He is rather conscious that photographs can be offered as counterparts to the four axial divisions of space. They exist at several removes from the original fallen mortal, these having been replaced by photographs. The photographs, too, seem an auxiliary ef-

can presume to change society through art.

Art, as part of capitalism's exchange value system, is reactionary: at least so is the case with the

PHOTOGRAPHY's position in the world of fine arts has always been problematic. Its invention in the middle of the last century had been greeted by the art

have been erased just like Duchamp's readymades. The similarity to Duchamp's readymades may appear tenuous: the link is their repetition and virtual obliteration of legibility. The use of nails is not Duchampian at all.

Recall what the Nazis did to artists who mistook the art world for the real world. Vivan, in a sense, shares the same tragic failure as Grosz, who, facing impending imprisonment in Hitler's time, was defended by Dr Edwin Redslob, the Federal Arts Officer. An action for which Hitler had Redslob dismissed from his post. The world has not seen a more committed artist than Grosz. The chilly dictum of Tristan Tzara, the dada ideologue, bears repetition: politics of art is a tiny parody of politics of real power. Nobody, rather, nobody intelligent (in Duchamp's implied view), can presume to change society through art.

Art, as part of capitalism's exchange value system, is reactionary: at least so is the case with the French artist, Daniel Buren, who took the stand during the May 1968 students uprising in Paris that the artist is the only managerial interpreter of people's fantasies. In 1967, he put up about 200 billboards all over Paris and on the back of a sandwich man, parading outside the gallery, he put pieces of green and white striped cloth which, to the uninitiated eye, looked like an awesome canvas.

Safdar Hashmi did the same in theatre. He dared to disturb the peace of the bourgeoisie and paid for it with his life. If we have Vivan's installation as art, the conclusion is obvious: we cannot compete on level terms with the iconic influence of street theatre. An installation in a gallery is a small thing in comparison. Unless the artist takes to the art of the billboard.

41
A DETOUR WITH MODERNISM

Review of A. Ramachandran's solo exhibition in New Delhi, 1991

'Artscape', *The Economic Times*, New Delhi, 12 June 1991

It has been an old obsession of painter A. Ramachandran to give his art an indigenous dimension making it an expression of specific national disposition. Ramachandran showed his large-sized canvases, all entitled *Urvashi, Pururavas* and *The Lotus Pond,* at the capital's leading Shridharani Gallery some time back.

Not many painters have faith in the idea of a national personality as a condition of their art. The art of these painters has been in complementary relationship with and in mutually enriching exchange of modernism: they have avoided, rather consciously, the ground of the blood-and-soil rhetorics of cultural identity. Indeed, modernism in India came as an assertion against the all-pervasive cultural nationalism as represented by the Bengal school of painters in the pre-independence period.

Ramachandran too, was a rebel against the Bengal school variety of cultural nationalism. Being a student of Ramkinkar, who was less assertive of culture-specific ways of looking at art, he developed an enormous distance from what the Bengal school stood for. In fact, he claims that his art is an extension of Ramkinkar's, rooted as it is, not in unveiling some ideological meaning but in seeking an organic development of painterly values of which Ramkinkar is a historical ideal.

Ramkinkar was too strong a Dionysian to be undercut by any Apollonian appearances: he was too great an individualist to be bound by thematic demands. Nor did he suffer from any temptations of permanence; his whimsies represented the aboriginal truth of his art. Ramachandran, on the other hand, has always been in the grip of Ramkinkar's method of doing art. He seems now quintessentially fulfilling a historic mission. Since the creation of his *Nuclear Raginis* in 1976, the structural principle at work is to disrupt the self-assured individualism of Ramkinkar: the *Nuclear Raginis* show is the last link he had with Ramkinkar.

It would seem as though his show represented a return to the Ramkinkar method after a long detour with modernism. Prior to the *Nuclear Raginis* show, his work consisted of mere formal symmetries produced under the weight of the consciousness. The *Nuclear Ragini* series were marked by less subjective codes: they were a translation of his experience of living with the Gaudia Lohars, a nomadic tribe of Rajasthan. The code employed was derived from on-the-spot sketches: it was the same code that Ramkinkar employed; he lived with the Santhals of Bengal and they were the source of his inspiration.

But Ramachandran's relationship with the Gaudia Lohars is one which Levi-Strauss gives the name Bricolage. Since the modern artist is also a marginal figure in history, the focused interest of Ramachandran's is to establish a personal relationship between his life and the 'non-civilized', 'pro-literate' bricoleur and to study the analogical links between the artist as an outsider, and the life of nature that the tribals live. What these paintings draw attention to is a world of bewildering complexities and how the hapless tribals surrender willingly to the unfriendly environment on more than one level of simultaneity.

After the *Nuclear Ragini* series, Ramachandran was in possession of a new code: he learnt to manipulate the language of analogical thought. Ramachandran drew the lesson that the savage mind is the quintessential human mind operating in a mode not dissimilar to the mind of civilized man: the nature of both minds remains the same. The civilized mind is a fragmented one but as much a prisoner of its contemporary cultural codes structures: while the civilized mind seeks to overcome its experience of fragmented time through an imagined totality (Time past and time future/ Allow but a little consciousness) that art and philosophy offer, the savage mind aims to achieve it through myth. Since Ramachandran's is not as Europeanized a mind as, say, Souza's, and since the primitive man lies dormant in all civilized men, the next step Ramachandran took was the creation of the *Yayati* image: the mythical wanderer who is rooted as much in a particular and concrete present as in the mythical universe where movement from gesture to voice to hieroglyph had stopped.

Yayati, in terms of scale was not a painting but a mural (7ft x 60ft). It was commissioned by Ebrahim Alkazi, the owner of Art Heritage Gallery, where it was displayed in November 1986. It was an attempt to determine the limits of *Yayati's* absolute invisibility to its origins of visibility in every human heart. Its origins of presence have empirical determinants and in stylistic terms it was a reincarnation of Ramkinkar's ersatz magic. Of course, there was something additional: desire for achieving a natural perfection of style as a supplement of art education. As in the Nuclear *Raginis* (1976) and *The End of Yadavas* (1978),

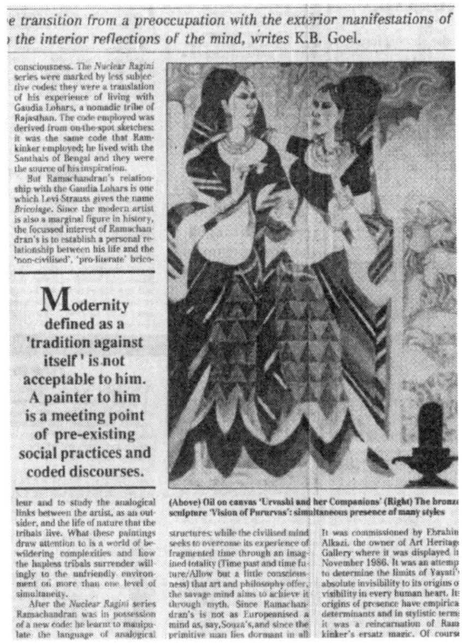
e transition from a preoccupation with the exterior manifestations of
the interior reflections of the mind, writes K.B. Goel.

consciousness. The *Nuclear Ragini* series were marked by less subjective codes: they were a translation of his experience of living with Gaudia Lohars, a nomadic tribe of Rajasthan. The code employed was derived from on-the-spot sketches: it was the same code that Ramkinker employed; he lived with the Santhals of Bengal and they were the source of his inspiration.

But Ramachandran's relationship with the Gaudia Lohars is one which Levi Strauss gives the name *Bricolage*. Since the modern artist is also a marginal figure in history, the focussed interest of Ramachandran's is to establish a personal relationship between his life and the 'non-civilised', 'pro-literate' bricoleur and to study the analogical links between the artist, as an outsider, and the life of nature that the tribals live. What these paintings draw attention to is a world of bewildering complexities and how the hapless tribals surrender willingly to the unfriendly environment on more than one level of simultaneity.

After the *Nuclear Ragini* series Ramachandran was in possession of a new code: he learnt to manipulate the language of analogical

Modernity defined as a 'tradition against itself' is not acceptable to him. A painter to him is a meeting point of pre-existing social practices and coded discourses.

(Above) Oil on canvas 'Urvashi and her Companions' (Right) The bronz sculpture 'Vision of Pururvas': simultaneous presence of many styles

structures: while the civilised mind seeks to overcome its experience of fragmented time through an imagined totality (Time past and time future/Allow but a little consciousness) that art and philosophy offer, the savage mind aims to achieve it through myth. Since Ramachandran's is not as Europeanised a mind as, say, Souza's, and since the primitive man lies dormant in all

It was commissioned by Ebrahin Alkazi, the owner of Art Heritage Gallery where it was displayed in November 1986. It was an attemp to determine the limits of Yayati's absolute invisibility to its origins o visibility in every human heart. It origins of presence have empirica determinants and in stylistic term it was a reincarnation of Ramkinker's ersatz magic. Of course the iconography was drawn from the character studies he had made of the Gaudia Lohars. The assumption was that 'any form of expression in art has to spring from the grassroots of its own culture which one knows intimately the moment one comes to this world'.

Yayati was a mixture of two codes which every painter knows intimately and manipulates as a limited variant of his or her style: working from life a la Ramkinkar, Ramachandran is a realist who favours, what may be called, 'objective' codes, and having been heir to modernity, his codes are subjective. Ramachandran is a modernist under a footnote: he separates himself from his contemporaries by his attitude towards the past. Modernity defined as a 'tradition against itself' is not acceptable to him; he abhors all forms of negative radicalism; nor is he in any way enslaved by the great tradition of so-called 'high art'.

The result is that he has got rid of the language of modernism. He is repelled by the kind of modernism, that variety, which is particularly self-referential and which most Indian painters practise as though it were a native phenomenon. That which seems a perfectly natural manner of painting to others is for Ramachandran an exercise in self-deception. A painter to him is not a product of an individual consciousness; rather he is a meeting point of several pre-existing social practices and coded discourses.

What has emerged now with his recent *Urvashi-Pururavas* show is the simultaneous presence of many styles: if the *Urvashi* image takes us back to Ajanta and the Kerala murals of the past years, the image of Pururavas is Ramachandran himself who discovered that he has lost everything, his localisms, their unique expressions and the capacity to say 'I'. The diminutive Ramachandran is reduced to a Picassoesque aberration, not only in moral terms but as a deviation from the normal look of man. The dwarf holding a mirror is asking himself whether what has happened is a result of his doings or a failure of the mirror.

The dominant culture of modernism grinds the ethnic identity to appear as deformed in unusually small statures. This is not to say that *Pururavas* in the diminutive bodily proportions looks man-like: rather the stunted creature in the German mythology is associated with the image of a craftsman and this is important. For the dwarf is an alienated craftsman who, by the oppositional logic of modernism, has lost touch not only with his land but has also been alienated from his own alienation in being so feeble and tongue-tied about it. In the symbolism of the dwarf, one can read a midlife crisis, marked by a moment of conversion, the psychological ramifications of which even Ramachandran himself is not aware. Dante sees in the experience of the midlife crisis a 'beginning of man facing death'. For Jung this moment of crisis means 'the reversal of all ideals and values'. For Ramachandran, it means growing up, becoming the father of his own self through a search for the internalized goals of the second half

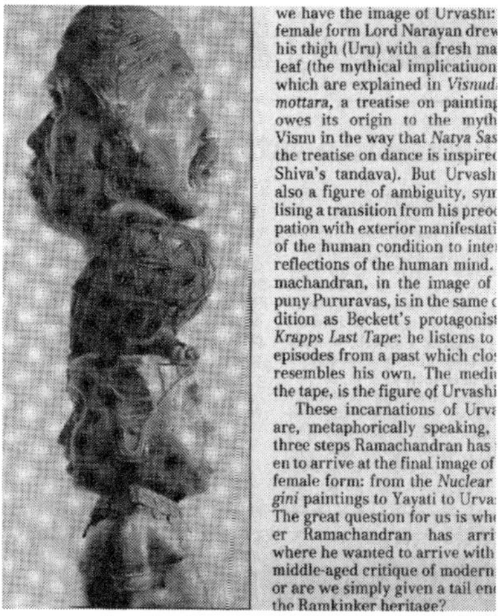

we have the image of Urvashi:
female form Lord Narayan drew
his thigh (Uru) with a fresh ma
leaf (the mythical implicatiuon
which are explained in *Visnud*
mottara, a treatise on paintin
owes its origin to the myth
Visnu in the way that *Natya Sas*
the treatise on dance is inspire
Shiva's tandava). But Urvash
also a figure of ambiguity, sym
lising a transition from his preo
pation with exterior manifestati
of the human condition to inte
reflections of the human mind.
machandran, in the image of
puny Pururavas, is in the same c
dition as Beckett's protagonist
Krapps Last Tape: he listens to
episodes from a past which clo
resembles his own. The medi
the tape, is the figure of Urvashi
These incarnations of Urv
are, metaphorically speaking,
three steps Ramachandran has
en to arrive at the final image of
female form: from the *Nuclear*
gini paintings to Yayati to Urva
The great question for us is wh
er Ramachandran has arri
where he wanted to arrive with
middle-aged critique of modern
or are we simply given a tail en
the Ramkinker heritage?

of his life and developing a kind of intuitive spirituality.

The midlife crisis is resolved by cultivating the available illusion of the permanence of art. That is why we have the image of Urvashi: the female form Lord Narayan drew on his thigh (*uru*) with a fresh mango leaf (the mythical implications of which are explained in *Visnudharmottara* [*Purana*], a treatise on painting: it owes its origin to the mythical Vishnu in the way that *Natya Shastra*, the treatise on dance is inspired by Shiva's *tandava*). But Urvashi is also a figure of ambiguity, symbolizing a transition from his preoccupation with exterior manifestations of the human condition to interior reflections of the human mind. Ramachandran, in the image of the puny Pururavas, is in the same condition as Beckett's protagonist in *Krapps Last Tape*: he listens to the episodes from a past which closely resembles his own. The medium, the tape, is the figure of Urvashi.

These incarnations of *Urvashi* are, metaphorically speaking, the three steps Ramachandran has taken to arrive at the final image of the female form: from the *Nuclear Ragini* paintings to *Yayati* to *Urvashi*. The great question for us is whether Ramachandran has arrived where he wanted to arrive with his middle-aged critique of modernism or are we simply given a tail end of the Ramkinker heritage?

42

JUKE-BOX ROUSSEAU

Review of Bhupen Khakhar's solo exhibition in New Delhi, 1970

Link, New Delhi, 1 March 1970

Bhupen Khakhar's Bazaar Pops, on show at the Kunika-Chemould Gallery, are difficult to come to grips with. Being highly original and intelligent they are difficult to categorize. The essential Khakhar is not what we imagined him to be on the basis of what we saw in the Delhi triennale and in this year's national exhibition; we wrongly thought him to be the latest pop avatar. That it was a misreading is clear from the present exhibition which is, in a way, as big a letdown as, say, Husain's popishly painted car. Painting for him is pure fun, a leg-pulling game, interesting, no doubt, provided its rules are followed without a single emotional slip – because at some point or the other, he is to be taken seriously, and his painting cannot always be reduced to a gimmick of the entertainment industry. A Khakhar buyer will naturally take him seriously. Will he not?

WEDDING ATMOSPHERE

Khakkar himself however does not take his paintings so seriously. Take, for instance, how he opened his exhibition; there was more of a *barat* (wedding) atmosphere with Khakhar acting like a bridegroom and his contemporaries (mostly from Baroda and Bombay) forming the marriage procession which was rather too large for the gallery to accommodate. All the same, the new rich painters, the switched-on ones mostly, were there with their Nikkormats and Bolexes, painter-young-thing Naseem [Nasreen] Mohammedi and critic Geeta Kapur in fancy dresses entertaining the *baratis* with jokes. The really go-go show with a big bang-bang painterly fireworks attracted even the Government of India's TV team which got on the job of collecting art trophies rather too greedily, too indiscriminately. Husain had spread out his Bolex on a tripod and was busy most of the time with his art footage exposures, taking now-painter Jeram Patel into focus and then moving on towards more 'attractive' celebrities but actually zooming around again and again to a painting called *M.F. Husain Near a Tonga after Visiting the Dargah*. Khakhar kept holding on to the mike – rather shy and self-conscious while cameras clicked. The supermarket gaiety seemed to be going well with the put-on attitudes of the art marketers.

The showbiz values, no doubt, are built-in elements of modern painting; only it was totally a new experience to us and more impressive because many painters came from outside to attend the Khakhar opening. And they behaved as if they were performing their roles in Khakhar's scene paintings. (Let us say Khakhar is a great narrative painter of bazaar mythologies and the supermarket painters are their essential components). Why did most Baroda painters come on the opening day? Is there anything more than meets the eye? Of course one can only guess; perhaps also admire the quality of publicity which has the overtones of New York's art market. One guess is that by pushing Khakkar to the frontline the 'established' artists want to use him for their own ends; if Khakhar in future becomes a giant-size painter they can look at him with patronizing eyes. It is a clever game; indeed nothing very clear either, come to think of it, in terms of art history because Picasso also played the same game with Henri Rousseau, modern art's first primitive painter. It was in 1908, the year when Picasso assumed leadership of the cubist movement with Braque that he picked up Rousseau as modern art's great find and threw a grand party at his rather dilapidated studio, the Bateau-Lavoir. At the party, everyone got drunk and the Douanier[1] Rousseau perhaps a little more than others when he told Picasso, 'Actually you and I are the two greatest painters: I in the modern genre, you in the Egyptian.'

POP READYMADES

When most Indian painters try to be consciously Egyptian, painting over-heavy abstract canvases which seem to be concerned more with problems of form, colour, structure and the so many fads of geometry (including, of course, the new wave of tantrism) an Indian version of Rousseau (which they have discovered in Khakhar) is professionally a big risk. More so because Khakhar is not only a painter in the 'modern genre' but has a pop dress. That is perhaps why Khakhar today is the object of so much attention and adulation even when what he is presenting us with is a peep show Rousseau; pop's readymades done with a primitivist's innocence. The total effect of his painting is thus deliberate archaism, indeed messy, as if he has no idea how a painting is made except that his products are slightly superior to glossy calendar paintings. So he plays down the design aspect of his painting to keep the subject matter in the foreground. The down-to-earth and the-matter-of-fact qualities of the Khakhar genre have a universal appeal; they are, besides, compositions illustrating our daily mythologies, which Khakhar cleverly surrealizes in the bazaar manner and not according to some aesthetic mantra relevant only to the aesthete.

PICTURESQUE

His painting is thus designed to be picturesque and it is towards this end that Khakhar selects relevant pictorial components from the nineteenth-century Company painting, using for picture format miniature painting's compositional devices. All these disparate elements are deployed in the most artless manner so that the first instinctive response is one of rejection as if what is present is not organic but transplanted onto the body of painting through some clever surgical tricks. The life of a Khakhar painting is thus uncertain, short-lived, being so very blatantly artificial. This lends to it a comic touch, a juke-box quality; the geometric formulae are most unimaginatively employed that they look unreal, lacking in any definable sensibility.

But a primitivist style is not measured in terms of sensibility but sentiments; underlying it is the sanction of modern art's intellectualism. So, either of the two things will be its resultant effect: the intellectual game might land us with an Indian variety of pop art in its nineteenth-century Company-art make-up or we may go back to folk forms which were dominant during the revivalist period of Indian art. Both alternatives, however, are dangerous because they lack the avant-garde edge so essential for modern art. A development of pop art on the Khakhar lines will be self-contradictory because pop art, as critic Pierre Restany points out, 'is a product of the megalopolis' and in India we do not have a super-city to inspire it. So, what is possible is only a juke-box Rousseau, a new kind of primitivism, and Khakhar provides a starting point. The only danger of cultivating such a genre painting is that it will mean our artists working in isolation; painting would be just another kind of entertainment and not the testing ground for intellectual theories of visual innovation.

Editor's Note

1 The French nickname for Rousseau, meaning 'customs officer', given his history of working at French toll gates and river ports/booths for many years before giving it up to paint full-time, braving the mockery that accompanied it.

43

POINT OF DEPARTURE

A discussion of the art of Bhupen Khakhar

'Artscape', *The Economic Times*, New Delhi, 27 June 1991

Provincialism in arts is a condition of the mind, an attitude of subservience which is externally imposed. I say externally imposed because the best of our minds has been defeated fighting against its imposed hierarchy of values.

I have in mind the works of Tyeb Mehta, Ramachandran and Jatin Das which do not suffer from provincialism's art historical reference: they treat figure as an element of their composition, one in which the medium retains its substantiality to become a sign for the intended meaning. That is to say, the more determinate is the meaning the less important the medium is held to be; indeed, some believe that when the communication is perfect, when the expression and the intended are seen as identical, the medium is wholly either transparent or disappears totally.

In Bhupen Khakhar, on the contrary, there is the over-determinate content, though the meaning in his work depends for self-definition on pop art's frames in which intertextuality serves as the actual border guards of taste. Which is to say that the narrative content limits the idea of context. Standing before a Bhupen Khakhar, the answer to the question 'which history is our history' is clear, because in the answer is implied the role of the agent who is claimed by tradition. Because of Bhupen, the Company Painting of the last century has become our contemporary experience; his painting has frame-referents of a miniature painting.

In the earlier Bhupens, there were imaginative combinations of the aesthetic and ethnic, which produced a simulation of floating unanchored images. His images herald the arrival of the contemporary as against the modern – that modern, self-critical by definition, is skeptical of the contemporary. Because the contemporary is modern, it is the provincial kitsch of tomorrow; it is suicidal in its very modernity. The contemporary (read provincial) courts what is fashionable and the fashionable is a version of kitsch, being part of art's current commerce. Kitsch produces saleable, instant art representing the triumph of the principle of immediacy. In supplying kitschy images the artist finds, he does not seek the coy falsity of content which is theatrical in intent.

Theatricality takes the form of exaggerated ambience, an awareness of and implied address to the audience. Recall the opening of Bhupen Khakhar's first one-man show in New Delhi's Kunika-Chemould Gallery.

There was more of a *barat* (wedding) atmosphere with Khakhar acting as if he were a bridegroom; his contemporaries formed the marriage party. The arrival of Bhupen on the Indian art scene with the first triennale field in 1968 represents a turning point in Indian painting's provincialist history. Another show which came almost unannounced, in marked contrast to Bhupen's in New Delhi and was simply called the Group Exhibition 1974, opened without any formal ceremony; the show was as significant as the Group 1890 show which Jawaharlal Nehru inaugurated in 1963. The works displayed seemed exemplifications of indigenism. The push of the roots-in-the-soil debate on indigenism of the Seventies towards provincialism seemed inescapably obvious; making good, original art right here was the declared intent behind the diversity of styles, for every painter seemed self-consciously dealing with problems of what identity ought to be. Theirs was a journey towards an outward look in order to open up extra-pictorial readings.

The show heralded Vivan Sundaram as a major painter; his portrait of Indira Gandhi, cast in the Egyptian scheme, was a political statement. Another Vivan was a triptych called *The Wall*. It was a bare wall, without memory and one which would not take any graffiti. The panel below the wall depicted in violent colours the mass of humanity; some nebulous human shapes suggested the presence of the world of misery and sorrow.

Indian art found in Bhupen an Indian version of Juke-box Henri Rousseau which presented Indian reality in a peon-show format, the total effect of which is the value-free response. There are visible elements of mimicry intended to enliven the narration: the story has the authenticity of a period culture. His images have the expendability of meaning; as against the opinionated pigheadedness of some of his contemporaries who believe that they could change the face of the world, his images look as belonging to the Sunday colour supplement.

In Bhupen Khakhar can be seen the first stirrings of a post-modern breakthrough; the return to the symbolic frame, as in Vivan's, would not have been possible without Bhupen's juke-box manner. The openness to embrace the impurity of the extra aesthetic, the priority of the theatrical over the self-absorptive mode of modernism, putting into focus the content rather than paying attention to the painterly aspects, have placed art in theatre's no-man's land.

Art has come to embrace kitsch and thereby the possibility of losing itself to ironic adaptations as in recent Vivan's. Or it can be as self-consciously naive as in Arpana Caur's. Or as provisional as the doodle; for what is important to the naive sentiment is the larger question of the human condition. It is a mode of painting in quotation marks, for it is a painting which inhabits us from an inner necessity of making a statement. No longer is such painting in need of representation of a world that is outside phenomenologically to the painter but is a pure sign of subjectivity.

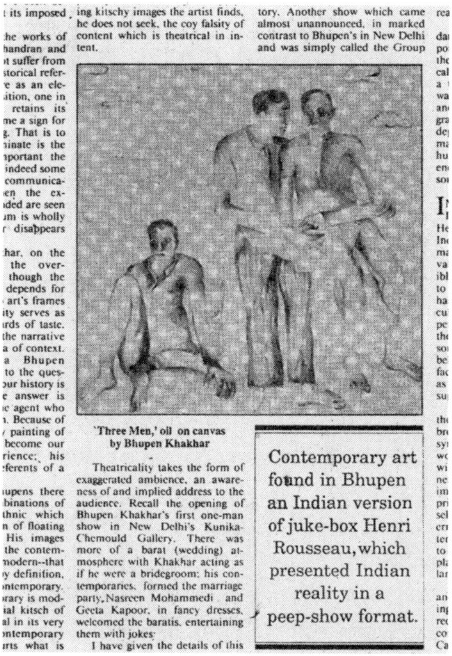

ing kitschy images the artist finds, he does not seek, the coy falsity of content which is theatrical in intent.

tory. Another show which came almost unannounced, in marked contrast to Bhupen's in New Delhi and was simply called the Group

'Three Men,' oil on canvas by Bhupen Khakhar

Theatricality takes the form of exaggerated ambience, an awareness of and implied address to the audience. Recall the opening of Bhupen Khakhar's first one-man show in New Delhi's Kunika-Chemould Gallery. There was more of a barat (wedding) atmosphere with Khakhar acting as if he were a bridegroom: his contemporaries, formed the marriage party, Nasreen Mohammedi and Geeta Kapoor, in fancy dresses, welcomed the baratis, entertaining them with jokes:

I have given the details of this

Contemporary art found in Bhupen an Indian version of juke-box Henri Rousseau, which presented Indian reality in a peep-show format.

The post-modern theory has given provincialism its voice in order to enable it to speak on its own terms and not as the ventriloquial echo of the other; as the work of Arpana Caur is a declaration that it is not about some potentiality to be developed but is wholly what it is. It claims the truth of being marginalized as women have been silenced to internalize the condition of marginality.

As Gayatri Spivak has pointed out, modernism as a cult of the global was a form of colonialism. The post-modern condition implies a vigilance patrol against the model of the centre versus the margin, against the provincialist bind to the art produced at metropolitan art centres and, moreover, against holding of what is called the international shows such as triennales. It is to reinforce the voice of the naive in its subjective formulations as other and voiceless.

The post-modern theory finds its voice in younger painters who are not hegemonic nativists as some of our old, self-conscious provincialists are. Madhvi Parekh is deliberately folksy while Arpita Singh is suggestively playful, little knowing that without de-centering, it is impossible to break loose from the provincial bind. Only Manjit Bawa manages to hold a balance between the acts of surrender and the will to freedom, between the forms that perpetuate the centre/margin hierarchies. He casts an almost flirtatious eye to remind his viewer that there is a need for misidentifications: his recent show at the Centre for Contemporary Art, Delhi, presented counter-identifying modes. It was an admission of the fact that the artist gives to the bourgeois what it wants: for Manjit, every level of reality is a perfectly plausible ground for a personal launch. The representational element in his work is also perspectival; it is as if to acknowledge the need of the existence of the bourgeoisie halfway. For, art is thoroughly bourgeois and Manjit acknowledges this in good measure.

44

TALK WITH CARL ANDRE

A reflection on the art of the American minimalist artist of the 1960s–70s, Carl Andre

Link, New Delhi, 14 February 1971

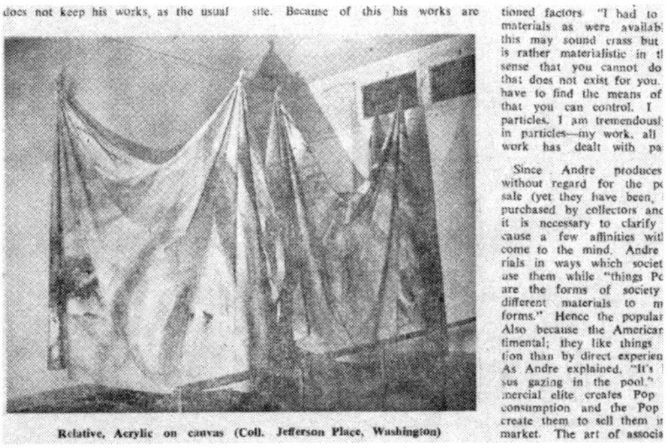
does not keep his works, as the usual site. Because of this his works are

Relative, Acrylic on canvas (Coll. Jefferson Place, Washington)

tioned factors "I had to materials as were availab this may sound crass but is rather materialistic in tl sense that you cannot do that does not exist for you. have to find the means of that you can control. I particles. I am tremendous in particles—my work, all work has dealt with pa

Since Andre produces without regard for the pc sale (yet they have been, purchased by collectors anc it is necessary to clarify cause a few affinities wit come to the mind. Andre rials in ways which societ use them while "things Pc are the forms of society different materials to m forms." Hence the popular Also because the Americar timental; they like things tion than by direct experien As Andre explained, "It's sus gazing in the pool." mercial elite creates Pop consumption and the Pop create them to sell them ir market. The art of associa

Carl Andre is obviously different. He does not look like the artist who has long ago arrived on the international art scene – and is as well known as Frank Stella, whose studio he once shared. He is different because he has identified himself with the people much more than a bourgeois artist can. So he dresses like them, like say, a railway worker more to remind himself perhaps that he too was once a brakesman and a conductor on the Pennsylvania Railroad between 1960 and 1964. Did he not 'resign', so to say, from the middle class during this period? Never to go back to his middle-class home again, never to take up a white-collar job. He has lived from then on the money he made from the sale of his work. Society offered him the chance of living like a king but he rejected it. As he put it, 'to become a big money artist and lead the kind of life with which the entertainers have been distrusting us for several decades now' – is not for him. He is happy doing the work he is doing and makes enough to support himself and his family. He wants little from society, only that much money from his work as he needs.

No false mysticism of the left either with him; he calls himself a worker and a Marxist – all the time stressing the fact that his work is inseparable from his lifestyle. Andre does not keep his works, as the usual studio artists do, taking a bourgeois interest in preserving and disseminating them. So, working where he finds a place to work with whatever is available at hand, he gives away the 'finished' piece to whoever admired it and wanted it. And when the work becomes too copious, he himself discards it. Since he has moved often and produced much, a great deal is lost. His friend, Hollis Frampton, seems to be the only man who has been keeping a photographic record of Andre's growth and development as a sculptor[1] – at least of those years when Andre was not so famous.

Incidentally, Hollis Frampton has collected a few photographs in the spirit in which T.S. Eliot collected Dante's shorter poems 'because', as Eliot said, 'they are by Dante'. But for Frampton's effort, we would have known nothing about Andre's earlier work except perhaps those which the international galleries have collected now. Frampton was convinced quite early that Andre is Brancusi's truest heir. 'The old Rumanian peasant stressed direct cutting in metal wood and stone . . . the young American makes direct cuts in gravity, mass, volume and density, the most fundamental properties of all sculpture, as of all matter' [Frampton, *12 Dialogues*].

PARTICLES

Andre does not believe that works of art should travel around the world. Rather the artist should be going round, to the site itself to create his work keeping with the environment and the conditions of the site. Because of this, his works are not limited to specific materials and specific environments. It is much like problem solving in a way: 'I have an imaginary graph or map upon which there are three vectors or three lines of force which create a point where the three converge.' The first is the artist's subjectivity, his condition, his history, talent and his needs. The second is the location, the objective factor, which also influences his sculpture, determining whether the piece will be placed outside or inside. Thirdly, the total economics of the operation affect the previously mentioned factors.

> I had to work with materials as were available at all - this may sound crass but I think it is rather materialistic in the Marxian sense that you cannot do something that does not exist for you . . . so you have to find the means of production that you can control. I always use particles, I am tremendously interested in particles - my work, all my mature work, has dealt with particles. [Andre, *12 Dialogues*]

Since Andre produces sculpture without regard for the possibility of sale (yet they have been, to be sure, purchased by collectors and museums), it is necessary to clarify things because a few affinities with pop art come to the mind. Andre uses materials in ways which society does not use them while 'things pop art uses are the forms of society but using different materials to make those forms'. Hence, the popularity of pop. Also, because the Americans are sentimental; they like things by association than by direct experience of them. As Andre explains, 'It's like Narcissus gazing in the pool.' The commercial elite create pop images for consumption and the pop artists recreate them to sell them in the same market. The art of association is the easiest thing to do and it is popular because the images of things are easily associated while the art of isolation is difficult: it has its own focus with a minimum association with things. 'I try to reduce the image-making function of my work to the least degree.'[2]

PLACE, NOT OBJECT

Andre's sculpture as shown in the gallery exhibitions in USA and Europe and various important museums is intended to make us aware of 'place' rather than of 'object'. He calls this sort of work a 'place' and explains:

> . . . A place is an area within an environment which has been altered in such a way as to make the general environment more conspicuous. Everything is an environment. But a place is related particularly to both the general qualities of the environment and the particular qualities of the work which has been done.

The idea of place is very important indeed: in fact this is Andre's distinctive contribution to the sculpture of the Sixties. Place is used as a kind of aphorism and its use is related to Andre's development as a sculptor. He started with sculptural form and shifted from form in sculpture to structure in sculpture, and finally ended with a place in sculpture. His starting-point was Brancusi, with form – or woodcutting essentially, that is chiselling the way as the master did. But soon he came to a structural position, the same as seen in neolithic work. The sense of place was discovered as it were through his admiration of neolithic work.

Most of his work belonging to the structural period is lost: 'They were discarded because of the peculiar condition of life early on in New York.' But if the choice was given to him for making them again, he would not make them. He might de-structuralize a few and turn them into particles, into modular units; that is to say change them in a way 'from a structure to what I call a place which is not based on structural principles. It's just place-making, let us say.'

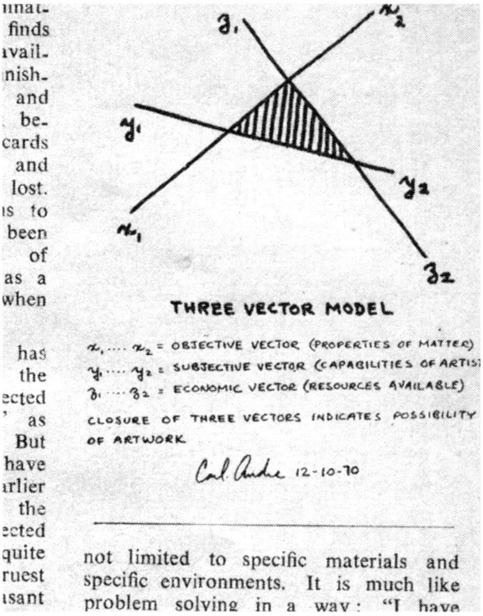

MYTH

Art does not have any special mean-ing, Andre says. Yet the meaning myth persists. People believe that art carries message like the telegraph. Andre has struggled hard to get rid of the burden of meaning which he has absorbed through culture – 'things that seem to have something to do with art but don't have anything to do with art at all'. He belongs to New York's Art Workers' Coalition group, and after the American attack on Cambodia and the killing of the four students of Kent university, most artists are searching their souls to give a concrete, visible political content to their art. So far, theirs have been a purely intellectual commitment: 'Most are inactive - even the super radicals and they have not yet aligned themselves with the radical movements'. What about him, we asked. 'As an art worker,' Andre said -

> My conscious identification is with the working class, that is the producing class rather than with the owning class, or the bourgeoisie. However, I cannot say honestly that in the class struggle my work is an effective support of the working class. On the contrary, my work is employed by the bourgeoisie. This is the kind of contradiction which haunts all artists in the so-called 'free world'. Some artists of the 'West' have overcome these contradictions like, I think, Jean-Luc Godard of France and Le Roy Jones of America.

The condition of the artists in America is no better than what it is in India - only the scale is different. Being an artist in America, he said, was like 'buying a lottery ticket. Only a few get the prize. And for the bourgeoisie this is the cheapest way to run the art world.' No sooner did Andre land in New Delhi to work on his sculpture for the second triennale that he found himself, as if by a reflex action, in total sympathy with the Indian protest artists. It is rather ironical of the current sophistication of art media politics that Andre, who has always been with one or the other kind of protest movement, in America - especially against the Museum of Modern Art which has sponsored him to participate in the triennale - should be part of the mix-up and rather prove by his example that even the most radical opinion can be to the service of the establishment.

Editor's Notes

1 Published in Carl Andre and Hollis Frampton, *12 Dialogues: 1962–63*, New York: CAD/New York University Press, 1980.

2 Kenneth Baker, *Minimalism: Art of Caricature*, Ann Arbor: Abbeyville Press, 1988, p. 138.

45
SKETCHING A METAMORPHOSIS

Review of a solo exhibition of Manjit Bawa

'Artscape', *The Economic Times*, New Delhi, 23 February 1993

When we look at a picture, we tend to identify our perspective with that of the picture. The result is that instead of looking at the picture, we end up looking at the object depicted. Not only is the painter annoyed with our way of looking at his work; we ourselves know that we have not done justice to the artist.

Take, for example, Van Gogh's famous painting, *Boots with Laces*, about which Heidegger has written a long essay. Now, when I look at the pair of old boots, a certain picture comes to my mind. The experience is so absorbing that the contemplation of states of consciousness and those moments of conscious enjoyment has a far greater value than if I had contemplated on the pair of boots outside the Van Gogh context.

This contemplation has an extra value which I am aware of in a subjective way, and it can be gleaned from the pictorial experience only if I attend simultaneously to the boots in the picture, and to Van Gogh's way of depicting them. Needless to say, Van Gogh offers such a powerful imaginative view of the boots that one can simultaneously attend to the objects depicted, and to the painter's brushwork.

A photograph, by contrast, will not give me the same aesthetic pleasure, primarily because photography as a medium is self-effacing; the physical surface of a photograph does not offer the extra aesthetic value a Van Gogh does. A photograph's aesthetic interest, if it has any, consists in making us aware of a depicted object and not of the physicality of the photographic vehicle. As a medium, the physical presence of a photograph has no value. Perhaps it was this ontological truth about photographs that led Erwin Panofsky to remark that the medium of motion pictures is reality itself.

Manjit Bawa's paintings, which were exhibited at the Centre for Contemporary Art, in Delhi recently, offer us that something extra that Van Gogh's *Boots* does. Or, to take another example, Manjit's cows and other animals, look analogously closer to the experience we have while standing before Matisse's dancing nudes, since both painters prefer spruced-up surfaces.

Our experience of both a Manjit and a Matisse alternates between an experience of attending to the use of brilliant colours, and an experience of seeing cows and nude dancers. The two experiences might alternate, occurring in sequence, but temporally they always coincide: one sees the paint at the very same time that one sees the cows and the dancers.

Standing before a Manjit painting, we retain this essential twofold experience – it is retained always in its purest form. That is to say, we switch rapidly back and forth between seeing a sign and the signifier. But we are not aware that this is, in fact, what we do. For, if the pictorial sign is the repository of meaning, then it is a mystery to us as to how we can ask it to disclose its meaning to us without our being aware of it. It is, however, a fact of our pictorial experience that we simultaneously attend to the music of colours and the resemblance-mediated representation of the depicted objects.

When I see Manjit's *Krishna Surrounded by Mythical Cows*, I see the cows in Manjit's work, like Krishna, being imaginary creatures. But being imaginary does not imply that they are not real objects in the sense that they are not present before my senses when I look at them. It is like looking at a person while also looking at his portrait. One has two experiences of the person, one of them being imaginary.

So, what is needed is not a twofold, but three-fold experience; an experience of seeing the canvas; an experience of seeing the model or the person, and an experience of those features that are iconic. Thus, in Manjit's work, one has more than a double-decker experience (of paint and cows). This something more in a Manjit painting is the painter's signature, his style. And it is this that immediately stares us in the face.

One can call this third element as constituting an omnibus experience; this experience has a unique picture relation to all the other elements, for, this omnibus experience is purely visual in that no structure can be imposed on it. It is this that warrants a previous knowledge of his work even though the experience offered is purely visual.

Pictorial experience being explicitly interpretative in nature, the experience of the purely visual is dependent for signification on my knowing Manjit's signature, which in turn involves my knowing its quality as also its stylistic significance. And, in the context of the Indian art scene of the 1990s, the signification of his signature is enormous, and its aesthetic picture higher than we are willing to concede.

You can measure the pitch this way: when the picture tells (and one is repeating the words used about Cezanne's apples) not only 'how apples can be depicted', but 'how they can be seen as though they are a Cezanne still-life'.[1] For, the whole point of the Whistlerian gambit is that it is possible to see nature as it has been depicted.

I am sure Manjit will not travel that far in claiming for his cows what Whistler claimed for his work. But he would surely like to make the point that although all pictures have some claims to exemplifying some content, he would remind the beholder that the main point in his work is not the picture's content, but rather how that content is depicted – the way it has been done and the colours used. It is no secret that the content in Bawa's painting is so commonplace that we are led to believe that it cannot be the point of his work to communicate that content to us. For it is not that he is trying to be informative; rather that a painting gives birth to a universe. And, what makes Manjit a universe is not the fact that these paintings were done by the hand of a painter called Manjit. What is important is that underlying the works is the 'Manjit structure', and it speaks the language of Manjit.

Manjit's structure is more or less the same that informs Cezanne's work. So what can be said of Cezanne's apples can be said of Manjit's cows, if we substitute cows for apples – 'look it is possible to depict them (apples) as spherical volumes and to compose the whole set of objects in such a way as to deny the viewer entrance into the space of the picture by raking the table and its contents up at an angle acute to the picture plane.'[2]

Much has been written about Manjit but not about those aspects that constitute the 'Manjit structure' and the essence of his style. It consists, in my view, of the mutations and transformations a sketch undergoes under the gaze of three-dimensional seeing. The sketch, beginning from the first sketches found in the walls of the caves, speaks to us and answers all the queries by metamorphoses in paintings. It embodies the painter's deepest heartbeats, his speech and style. It has enabled Manjit to bind his work in a tradition which he continues in the tradition he founds. It is the history of the sketch that puts everything in Manjit's present work.

In the life of the sketch, the present finds itself strangely co-existing with the past – the past of a painting. The sketch is seen in all its plastic gesture in painting, which is the authentic expression of appearances and their objectivity. Whether or not the structure is founded on a two-dimensional plane is a question, the answer to which can be found in the infallible recipes that Manjit makes for his works. Cezanne abandoned the two-dimensional perspective for the expressive richness of an apple. Similarly, Manjit observes the laws of perspective, but not in the way Cezanne does, for he is seeking expression through the sketch, and, unlike Cezanne, does not need to fill his canvas.

Manjit's mentor is not Cezanne but Matisse who said about the art of picture-making: 'If drawing is of the spirit and colour of the senses, you must draw first to cultivate the spirit and to be able to lead colour into the spiritual path'.[3] In a Manjit painting, eyesight is insight: drawing allows the artist to pay attention to the boundaries of the masses because three-dimensional bodies are bound by traditional two-dimensional surfaces, and the surfaces themselves are bound by one-dimensional borders – for example, by lines.

The lines constituting the structural core of an object are easy to grasp; one should draw in terms of contrast of an object's principal lines. And Manjit is a master manipulator of contrast. The principal lines of contrast are the edges which Manjit models into colour values to give the edge a fullness of being. By defining edges sharply he is able to achieve a two-dimensional effect, for edges always flatten an object and open its form to an interplay of shapes. Manjit consciously softens the edges to make the drawn object look soft and elusive.

Regardless of which angle from which we view the surfaces of a cow's body, it is an ideal surface to build a form that is contained by the juxtaposed shapes - the outer edges in a Manjit cow is modulated with care to bring into focus the dark and light configurative possibilities of the form. It is because - and Manjit is well aware of it - pictorial logic demands that the outer edge, where it meets with the negative areas, is seen to its best advantage when it contrasts with the adjoining surface.

Manjit's individualism is edgy. It is because he has acquired a notion of style to translate the relationship between sketch and painting. What he has been trying to do in his paintings is not the immediate self or its very nuances, but his style. He is one of the supreme stylists who arrived with a bang in 1978. Since then, he has been mastering his style as much in his painterly concerns as with its problems of articulation. The significance of his recent show is that now he speaks with his own voice, though the work has the same horizon as in the 1978 Dhoomimal show. There is evidence, however, of some internal movement. If Manjit is not able to discern these movements himself, it is normal: a painter is no more capable of seeing his work than a writer is able to read his.

Editor's Notes

1 Erle Loran, *Cézanne's Composition: Analysis of His Form with Diagrams and Photographs of His Motifs*, University of California Press, 1943.

2 Ibid.

3 From a letter Henri Matisse wrote to Henry Clifford, former curator of the Philadelphia Museum of Art. See *Henri Matisse Issue 2*, University of California Press, 1966, p. 7.

46
THE HUMAN CONDITION

K.B. Goel stopped writing c. 1998, the last date this volume of his writings too records in its title. However, post the 2000s, he wrote an article or two on request. This article, from 2017, to accompany the solo exhibition of Bela Gupta, was written in ill-health and is included here as a special addition to mark Goel's last writing. The article discusses Bela Gupta's work which references popular culture to comment on consumerism and social inequity.

Exhibition catalogue, 2017

Few artists these days have the capacity to surprise, perhaps because art has become a self-repeating enterprise. Those who do, command instant attention because veneration of the new has by now become a historical response. This is true even when the new turns out to be an empty gesture. Imagine the hurt and insult an artist will feel if he is introduced as the maker of some yesterday's dress! He has good reasons to fear any violent changes in style or content of his painting because what is achieved through sudden upheaval is difficult to keep up. Only the new should suggest that it has arrived with some speed.

Bela Gupta is an artist who is moved by the human condition and her art explores its irony, bordering on the absurd, of the human condition. The world of hunger and misery is juxtaposed against the hollow exuberance of modern society. And the two realms with all their glaring contrasts fuse in her art. Her show at the India Habitat Centre Gallery in New Delhi represents a quantum jump. To say so would be making room for high seriousness, a condition most unfavourable for art these days since this cannot form part of teatime prattle on art; what is required is a judicious mixture of seriousness and frivolity – a necessary condition to be successful.

Intuitively, she has worked out a complex relationship between language and visual imagery. The glittering models of *Victoria's Secret* are contrasted against emaciated bodies, warped by hunger and deprivation, which becomes a vehicle of expressing rage and pity as a manifestation against man's inhumanity. The paintings are not entirely illustrative in quality but have a definite pictorial merit. In her recent paintings, she is involved with surrealistic metaphysics. For the surrealists, the state of mind is a built-in condition, they rely on surprising effects by bringing incongruous objects together in unlikely situations. As an imagist, Bela employs their pictorial language, using photographs and images of mass culture made popular by Sunday glossies, the TV and the internet.

If her images look like representations of things that belong to the visible world, it is a mere device, an aid to allow us to enter the power of

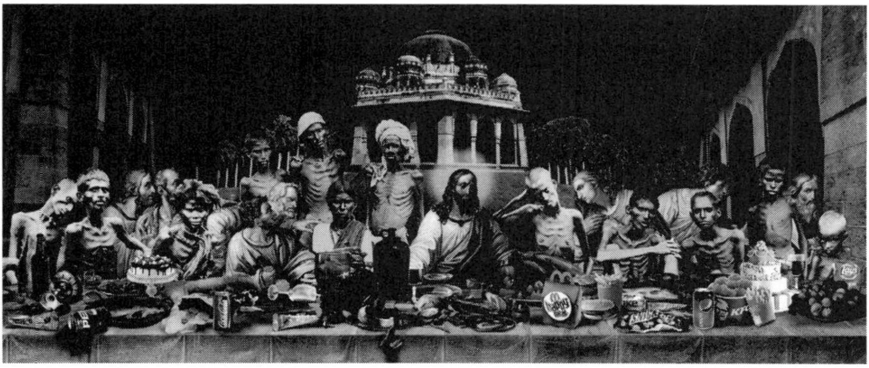

the works themselves where significance of one image can be understood in relation to another image. The images and objects depict ideas behind them, their presence has no obvious meaning or reality, they express a deeper reality/meaning which only a painting can express visually.

The viewer must seek meaning in the context of the images for Bela's art as more of an inspired activity, and thus to get at the true stuff is to go back to the gut response which the images create. They do transmit a certain feeling which we can share – a feeling of bitterness. The Dostoevskian perspectives and paradoxes are too pressingly alive in her work. Art here ceases to be merely an activity one associates with, like in Bela's earlier works, metamorphosing Cola cans into saleable art commodities. Art now means something higher than such activity, something closer to a religious experience, holding the possibility of release from suffering.

Art of such magnitude cannot be a mere vibration inside a museum: such art involves us with moral questions. The artist has either to play the moral role, protest against the pretended innocence of a corrupt value system, or quit practising art. Rather than quit painting, Bela has chosen art's essential role of shaping consciousness. Her art has acquired a quality of message that has overt political reference. It now appears to be closer to pop art, also to poster art, art with a message. Posters were used to express protest. They were bold, angry and schematized, a little exaggerated.

Although it should be added that Bela has managed to keep her narrative acts free from the constraints of a style, painting in a manner that stylistic features do not become too loud. In the works on display, what is sought to be communicated is the violence, the moment itself forms the all-round viewpoint, captured in harsh, bright colours that make her work more expressive than most of her contemporaries. The essence of her work, in a way, lies in bridging the gap between life and art by making us aware of the links between the artist and her universe via sensations: they are part of our environment and this is her theme and subject matter.

SECTION TWO

INSTIT

TIONS

ART INFRASTRUCTURE, POLITICS AND REFORMS

This section features K.B. Goel's writings from the early 1970s to the 1990s on the policies and functioning of institutions established in independent India tasked with the responsibility of creating an infrastructure for the arts. The state-run Lalit Kala Akademi, set up in 1955 as a national institution with regional centres, was mandated to be the governing and executive body in charge of developing the visual arts, professionalizing the field by hosting exhibitions, inviting, judging and awarding art, and nurturing the emerging art scenario. However, within a decade of its functioning, the institution attracted widespread criticism and large-scale protests by artists for mismanagement, partisanship, corruption and fomenting of art politics.

K.B. Goel's writings take stock of these aspects surrounding the institutions of art – primarily the Lalit Kala Akademi and to a lesser extent, the National Gallery of Modern Art. He also examines international art events such as the quadrennial Documenta and the exhibition held parallel to it by the Stoffwechsel group.

47
THE NEW PROTEST VOICES

An article taking stock of the snowballing strong protests by artists against the functioning of the Lalit Kala Akademi and the Triennale-India

Link, New Delhi, 2 January 1972

Art in India has not yet acquired the same momentum and speed as it has in the West. What was done in 1971,[1] for instance, remains still relevant for us, which is not the case in the West. Such is the speed with which art moves there. In the West, one never really speaks of the exhibitions held because they get dated the moment they are displayed and so discarded like yesterday's dress. The cult of the new has such a stranglehold there that an artist is forced to invent a new gimmick with every fresh exhibition he is planning to put up. So what remains relevant in the previous year's work are the hints and gestures expressed in art critical terms – not the works proper which are consumed as if they were nothing better than the industrial products of daily use.

But, in India too, the year that has gone by is in no way significant for exhibitions worth talking about in the new year except the fact that the young and lesser-known artists did produce a few surprises. The 'major' artists, the ones who dominate the art scene by hook or by crook, seemed rather too busy in art politics to pay attention to their studios. The protest movement, which was born with *Vrishchik*[2] and the open letter in its issue dated 10 November 1970 calling for the boycott of the central Lalit Kala Akademi by the artists, continued throughout 1971. The chorus of protests forced the Akademi to call a conference of the artists to consider the badly needed reforms of the Akademi. The conference ended as most conferences do with the establishment of a committee. It was hoped that the Akademi would present a revised constitution for the consideration of the committee. But the revised constitution of the Akademi was not ready yet and so the Committee of the Thirteen did not meet. The *Vrishchik* group seems to be active again, in the November issue [1971] it said –

> Time is running short and there are signs of impatience among those who feel strongly concerned about change in the constitution and policies of the Akademi, mainly because younger artists may find it difficult to continue the protest on a long-term basis as they have joined the movement of protest at the time of starting their careers.

PROTEST CERTAIN

The new year, it is now certain, will have a fresh spurt of protest, although it may be a diluted version of last year's and for a very short duration – lasting perhaps as long as the national exhibition stays on its walls. There are hints that the protest committee has already drawn up a plan of boycotting the forthcoming national exhibition. And if this happens, (which is very likely), the Akademi may be forced to call another conference of the artists where a new, revised constitution of the Akademi will be presented. It is indeed arguable that the revised constitution will be approved by the Committee of Thirteen, for the simple reason that time is very short, and the new general council of the Akademi is to be formed within a few months. If there is a deadlock, the new constitution cannot be adopted in time: the Akademi will be justified in going ahead with the formation of the general council according to the existing constitution of the Akademi.

The protest committee does not speak for the majority of the artists: the disenchantment of the younger, lesser-known artists (the *Vrishchik* defines a young artist as one who is below thirty) with the politics of the protest committee is well known; it dates back to the day when the Akademi appointed the Committee of the Thirteen which has no representation of the younger artists and they have been very vocal in demanding their proper representation. Besides, they have other grievances also and they are all about the way the art establishment functions in India, which is indeed no different from what it is in the West – like a private enterprise where the survival of the fittest is the rule. The welfare state, of which the Akademi is a part, has no plans to protect the defenceless young artists against the cruel, inhuman economics of the art establishment. Not without reason, therefore, they are demanding provisions of loans (like the FFC[3] has been doing for young filmmakers). Unless the new constitution of the Akademi has such a provision, it will not be acceptable to these young artists.

YOUNG ARTISTS

Curiously enough, the young artists are in majority while the 'senior', the so-called 'major' artists are divided about the future shape of the Akademi. The protest committee has not a large army of senior artists with them. It has only the painters of the Sixties who are unhappy about their lack of representation in the policy-forming councils of the Akademi. The protest committee, minus the support of the young unknown artists, has no voice except the known ambitions of a few artists of the Sixties. *Vrishchik*, which speaks for these artists, has a patronizing attitude towards the younger artists which hurts them the most. For instance, it wrote in the November issue,[4] 'We welcome these artists for their vocality and awareness (though belated) in spite of their curious definition of the "young" and slightly presumptuous stand'. After this admonition, the *Vrishchik* supports the demand of these artists for representation in the thirteen-member committee set up by the Akademi.

Here lies the rub. Will the younger artists watch with the same helplessness as they have done in the past the shadow-boxing between the bureaucrats of the Akademi and the so-called publicity-conscious protest artists? Will they follow them in the boycott of the coming national exhibition? The reports are that the smart ones among the younger set of artists have already entered their works for the national exhibition because they know that this is the time to cash-in as some of them did during the second Delhi triennale last year.

The biggest event of 1971, no doubt, was the second triennale which lasted for two months and occupied three galleries – Lalit Kala at Rabindra Bhavan, Shridharani Gallery and the National Gallery of Modern Art at Jaipur House. By the time the triennale exhibition folded up, the art season was over. Towards the end of March, Ambadas and Balkrishna Patel showed their latest ware producing very little impact against the loudness of the triennale. Jeram Patel's work signed with a blowlamp was quite an event for its critical superiority of whatever he has done in the past. Also memorable were Gaitonde's abstract, non-objective canvases, which he showed in New Delhi after a decade or perhaps more. The 1971 season ended with the Sankho Chaudhuri retrospective exhibition (1949–71) at the National Gallery of Modern Art which was perhaps the biggest event of the season.

Editor's Notes

1 The previous year, when the second Triennale-India took place.

2 An independent arts journal begun in Baroda and edited by the artists Bhupen Khakhar and Gulammohammed Sheikh, from 1968 to 1973. The journal was at the heart of the artists' protest against the functioning of the Lalit Kala Akademi, particularly over the administration and vision for the Triennales-India.

3 FFC – the Film Finance Corporation, set up in 1951 to finance individual film projects, which later became the National Film Development Corporation (NFDC). See Ashish Rajadhyaksha, *Indian Cinema in the Time of Celluloid: From Bollywood to the Emergency*, New Delhi: Tulika Books, 2009, p. 233.

4 *Vrishchik*, year 2–3, issue no. 12–1, November 1971, Baroda.

48

THE AKADEMIS: HAVE THEY HELPED ART, ARTISTS?

An assessment of the Lalit Kala Akademi, highlighting the reports of various investigating committees of the 1960s and early 1970s that were set up to look into its functioning

Patriot Magazine, New Delhi, 24 September 1972

Art needs its talk shows: the thousands of words written about them are welcome, perhaps necessary for a system which turns the artist into a movie star. Which makes him a bestseller: reputation indeed is necessary to give weight to his voice, and for spreading his influence. The artist as superstar needs commissions and cultural conferences, not a bare performance. Art is not the skill of the hand but a by-product; perhaps it is part of the myth of seeking art in states of alienation.

STAR PERFORMERS

True, the artist cannot live on what he produces: such a situation will be ideal indeed – an artist living solely on the sale of his products. To become a 'name' is easy, but it is not enough: one must over the years become a big name, say, a Husain. Then a painting fetches the artist Rs 20,000. If art today needs patronage, it is because it acts as an expedient. If reputation and patronage are in conflict, the artist will shun patronage. Reputation alone ensures gallery support and art merchants deal with it as if this was the buck itself. There is no limit to the artist's ambition: he has the Picasso ego and wants success on the same scale; the Lalit Kala Akademi comes poor, almost on ground level on this scale. Those times were indeed different when Lalit Kala's Rs 1000 award was considered something: the quality, signature painting then fetched not more than Rs 500.

BHABHA COMMITTEE

The Lalit Kala has functioned as a square, no superstar has ever lent it prestige and it has neglected younger artists. The big names refused to show their works at its annual exhibitions since 1958. One reason was that it has a very lean budget: a national prize of a thousand rupees is nothing when a Husain is fetching between Rs 10,000 to Rs 20,000, and a signature painting is sold at not less than Rs 5,000. The situation however changed overnight with the first triennale. To our surprise we discovered the senior painters represented in the India section. The first triennale brought a new wave of protest, and artists for the first time demanded that they should be the masters of the Akademi. With it also surfaced many ugly aspects of art politics, even reaching the Prime Minister, Indira Gandhi. The government appointed a reviewing committee in 1970 with Justice G.D. Khosla as its chairman. A review of the working of all three national Akademis – the Lalit Kala, the Sangeet Natak and the Sahitya Akademi – and also the Indian Council of Cultural Relations, was to be undertaken in the light of the Bhabha Committee[1] and its recommendations. Asked to present its report in six months, it took about two-and-a-half years to complete its work. The art scene has change and this is essential to know why the Bhabha Committee's recommendations were not implemented. The Khosla Committee mentions some of the Bhabha recommendations which were not acted upon:

> . . . Many of the recommendations were rejected, some were needless because they did not propose a change in the current practice, while others . . . were dropped because of lack of funds. In the circumstances, no startling change or improvement could be expected in the performance of the Akademis. . . . [T]hey have enjoyed almost complete immunity from the consequences of the corrective measures suggested.

It is a dismal picture and the report does not mince words. It notes that art activities are the exclusive decorations of metropolitan cities and even that too is seasonal and sporadic.

> There are very few theatres or concert halls in which dramatic or musical performances can be organized. Good picture galleries can be counted on the fingers of two hands. Artists find it difficult to hold exhibitions of their works unless they are willing to pay exorbitant reservation fees. The number of good museums and libraries does not exceed a single digit. There is no National Dramatic Repertory Company, no professional ballet troupe which gives regular performances, no national or regional opera company and no organized literary activity aimed at making the people aware of the traditional or the new cultural and literary trends.

FAILURES

For all these failures, one could hold our national Akademis responsible. The report too ascribes these failures largely to 'the incompetence, the lack of imagination and ignorance of those in charge of the administration of the Akademis'. Will the reforms recommended make any dent in the bureaucratic structure of these Akademis? Take, for instance, the constitution of the Lalit Kala Akademi against which the younger artists have been protesting for almost a decade now. The committee 's suggestions seem fundamental: it has adopted the principal recommendation of an electoral college of 200 members suggested by the protesting artists at an artists' conference called last year by Karl Khandalavala, the Lalit Kala chairman. But keeping all the other elements in the old constitution and substituting fifteen elected members (to be elected by the electoral college) in place of fifteen members which the Akademi adopted from various art institutions and organizations, is a farce. The artists' conference recommended 'a more substantial representation of artists, a smaller general council and the introduction of an electoral system for selecting 75 per cent of the members of the general council'. Their resolution passed in December 1970 says–

> With regard to the composition of the general council of the Akademi, its totally unrepresentative character will be evident from the fact that only 14 of its 56 members are representative of art organizations and institutions 'recognized' by the Akademi. Nine are eminent artists chosen by the Akademi. The remaining 33 are government nominees, state government representatives and what not.

ROLE OF SENIOR ARTISTS

Paragraph 5.25 of the report says:

> A complaint we have heard almost universally, namely, the concentration of attention upon the activities of senior artists, to the detriment and neglect of the younger elements. The paucity of funds provided to the Akademis was stated by an artist to be one of the reasons for their failure to act more purposefully . . . Some artists alleged that the members of the executive board and the general council had vested interests in the Lalit Kala Akademi, and they tended to benefit themselves in one way or another. It was also alleged that the autonomy guaranteed to the Lalit Kala Akademi by its constitution was illusory, because there was consistent interference by the government on the [grounds it] . . . provided the funds to the Akademi.

The committee is convinced that the root cause of the present dissatisfaction against the Akademi

> . . . is a feeling among the general body of artists, especially the young artists that their views and needs are not heard, and a cultural policy in which they have no voice is imposed upon them. We are satisfied that this grievance and the resentment occasioned by it are justified.

No doubt the arts will have more funds and a fair share from Rs 51 crores which the government collects each year by way of entertainment tax. The report says –

> . . . To use this money for purposes other than improving the quality of entertainment savours a kind of fraud upon the people who are required to pay large sums of money for poor intellectual fare. . . . A substantial portion of this tax . . . collected should be used to raise standards of cultural pabulum provided by private and public organizations.

The way out suggested is a fund system as it operates in Czechoslovakia – a cultural fund to which the central government contributes each year. It will support the Akademi's scheme, and 'obviate the compelling necessity of utilizing the allotted finances within the financial year to which they relate, and any amount left unspent will be carried forward to future periods'. If this system is adopted, the concerned ministries will also not be in a position to interfere in the working of the Akademis enabling them to undertake long-term planning: 'We wish to reiterate and emphasize the importance, indeed, the absolute necessity of long-term planning, if any worthwhile results are to be achieved by the Akademis in striving for the aims and objectives in view.'

The main question remains unanswered: who needs these Akademis? Clearly, the senior artists do not need the Lalit Kala anymore; if they do, it is because of its international art potential. On the other hand, it is necessary for the survival of the young, struggling artists who cannot live on what they create. The day the Lalit Kala stops arranging the triennales as recommended by the Committee, things would change. The senior artists may in consequence withdraw support and that will be good for the Akademi. The young painters will have a better market because they will be the 'official' painters. The Committee's proposal to give income-tax relief on purchases of works of art is bold. More employment opportunities will come the way of these artists if teaching of the arts – especially painting – is made compulsory at the school stage. One should be very careful, however, about what kind of art is taught in schools because painting has ceased to be an ordinary craft, handed down from master to apprentice. Instead, it has become a subject like philosophy and it should be taught that way.

AESTHETICISM

Holding exhibitions in schools and colleges will not help appreciation of art: so outdated has our art teaching become that in order to discover oneself, a trained artist has to unlearn all that he has learnt in school. The Lalit Kala should undertake a project to evolve an art course with emphasis on art-history consciousness. Let there be a debate first before more money is sanctioned for doing things with only imitation value. Like the great European academies, our national academy should have a cultural policy – to create an art consciousness for great art to flourish.

SANGEET NATAK AKADEMI

But there are difficulties, which the Akademi's critics mostly overlook. Take for instance the divergence of the reference points between the Lalit Kala and Sangeet Natak Akademis. Lalit Kala, for instance, has for long been a battleground between the modernist and the traditionalist values in art: its chairman, D.P. Roy Chowdhury, and secretary, Barada Ukil, had to go because their vision and sensibilities were found to be out of tune with modernist sensibilities.

Sangeet Natak is just the opposite: it has a great fund of inherited talent and the stress is not on modernity but on preserving the great traditions of the *gharanas*.[2] Its main task has been to give protection to the old, surviving *ustad*s [teachers] of these *gharanas* in the same way as they used to under feudal patronage. At any rate, this was the grand style adopted by its first secretary, Miss Nirmala Joshi, under whose stewardship many great musicians and dancers – particularly of northern India – became active participants in the Akademi's activities. She also provided institutional support to some *gharana*s. *Dhrupad*[3] for instance, which had almost disappeared, got a new lease of life with the Dagar Brothers joining the Bharatiya Kala Kendra. From Lucknow came Shambhu Maharaj with the opening of the Kathak Kendra, and the Kathak dance form could never have become popular without the Sangeet Natak Akademi's support and patronage.

BETTER PERFORMANCE

The report says, 'the Sangeet Natak Akademi has succeeded to a greater extent than the other two Akademis'. The Committee's conclusion is supported by the survey (conducted by the Institute of Mass Communications) of public attitudes towards the national academies. For the cultural enthusiast, the Akademi has provided an array of motifs he could identify with: he can feel the renaissance in the field of music and dance taking place before his eyes. Yet, the total impression is one of poor performance by the Sangeet Natak Akademi. May be the expectations raised were high. Take, for instance, the grants to the Akademi have increased from Rs 2.25 lakhs to Rs 25 lakhs within a decade but the achievements have not been proportionate. The grants have been given on an erratic and ad hoc basis since the Akademi has no inventory of cultural institutions in the country.

MODEL

> Many recipients of such small donations are quite undeserving of government support. For the future, a firm constructive policy aimed at fostering the best in the creative arts and promoting the development and dissemination of cultural values with the specific objective of achieving excellence should be adopted by all the Akademis. We suggest a system of selecting cultural institutions for central aid somewhat on the pattern of what is being done by the Arts Council of Great Britain.

This is indeed for the first time that a model has been suggested. The main function of the Arts Council, which is an independent body and so also the institutions it supports, is not the execution of any cultural policy but to create conditions that will enable the artists to have bigger audiences. The Council consists of twenty members, including the chairman and a vice-chairman and they are all nominated by the government. The Council appoints various committees and panels to assist it in matters of art.

The composition of the General Council is the Committee's main obsession. It agrees that government officials dominate the Akademis. 'Many members of the General Council,' one witness disclosed to the committee, 'do not possess sufficient knowledge of art to make any meaningful contribution.' The same criticism is true of the executive boards of the Akademis; they represent all kinds of vested interests. Why has the National School of Drama under 'the able and dedicated guidance' of Alkazi done so much better? The question is pertinent. A dedicated artist, Alkazi has few governmental trappings; that is to say, he is his own boss. The Committee has therefore recommended that 'the School should be freed from the tutelage of the Sangeet Natak Akademi and established as an independent institution with increased funds'. It wants a National School of Music and a National School of Dance to be established on the pattern of the National School of Drama.

Editor's Notes

1 Set up in 1960 to review the Lalit Kala Akademi's operations.
2 Traditional schools associated with individual styles in Hindustani music.
3 A traditional form of Hindustani classical music, differing from the *khayal*.

49

AKADEMI'S SENSE OF HISTORY

A reflection on the Lalit Kala Akademi's curatorial approach in the hosting of its permanent collection and its relationship with artists

Link, New Delhi, 30 June 1974

The Lalit Kala Akademi has put up a massive exhibition of award-winning works it has acquired since 1958 forming its permanent collection at the Rabindra Bhavan gallery. The national commissioner in his report has hinted as much and the art-loving public has been eagerly looking forward to seeing this rather historical exhibition. But could one have imagined that the Lalit Kala would have chosen an out-of-the-season approach for this exhibition? Who will brave the heat to visit this exhibition? Anyway, the arty set – the regular exhibition-goer – is not in town: the gallery almost wears a deserted look. Should the Akademi have treated this exhibition with such indifference? No catalogue is issued; neither has the exhibition been advertised. We learnt of it from a note sent to us. Curiously enough, the show opened on 15 June and the preview took place on 21 June: one New Delhi daily has already carried a review of it the previous day.

'This is a special exhibition,' says the Akademi note. And very appropriately, the Akademi chose a 'special' – summer heat at 43.5 centigrade – time for showing it. The Akademi, in a way, has done the right thing because the note tells us, 'some works (in this exhibition) which may have seemed outstanding at the time they were done no longer seem so important.' But this puts a new valuation on art objects – as if to say that artworks are no better than other commodities. They never have the same market value; when superior products arrive, the older ones get automatically devalued. The Akademi's new values has another element – the time scale, and it is time rather than art which is the source of all art values. So the old-fashioned art norms will not do. The Akademi has indeed become a forward-looking institution. Isn't the third triennale round the corner?

From the perspective of the Seventies, the displayed works offer little evidence of an Indian landscape ever present to guide our art perceptions. It may have been there in the Fifties when we thought that the Husain style was representative of the visual reality then obtaining in Indian painting. But since 1958 – the year from which these works began to be collected by the Akademi – the Husains have been declared out of date. From 1958 onwards, the visual reality began to seek for itself avant-garde features, turning the canvas itself into a 'landscape'. Several Pollocks were born in India as elsewhere and they chose to paint with their eyes closed favouring the secret, mystical energies of the abstract canvas over the decorative Husain girls; they painted as if the Indian landscape did not exist. And rightly, they claimed that they had penetrated the landscape to paint it from inside! Like Pollock they laid the canvas on the floor and walked into it as it were, turning it into a painter's landscape. Works of this genre in this exhibition carry the signature of the time – not of their authors. The reason is simple: art precedes reality.

The Akademi's note says as much:

> We see that some styles which obtained in the 1950s are virtually extinct – for example, the rather Indian decorative idiom, often in tempera (see Bihari Barbhaiya or Gautam Vaghela). Later on, we find a gradual change from figurative to abtract forms. Figures are distorted or attenuated and become separated into units of form (Ram Kumar, Biren De, K.G. Subramanyan). We see a rejection of subject matter or theme while painterly elements such as form and colour, line and texture become the sole subject of art. Thus we find that the art of the 1960s establishes a new freedom, each work expresses something unique and individual – and is not limited by the traditional past.

TURNING POINT

The Sixties were a turning point: for Indian artists, it represented a crisis of confidence, and for the Akademi, a new era of modernism. The Akademi, which had been under the domination of the Bengal School painters for the past five years, had new bosses – Mulk Raj Anand and B.C. Sanyal – who were sympathetic to modernism. Indeed, modern art became now an article of faith with the Akademi and works of art got surrounded by an atmosphere of unique belief. Since the Sixties, the commitment to modernism has enjoyed aesthetic credence; little wonder that art was seen and understood as a symbolic mode and its metaphoric models are best exemplified by the works of the [Group] 1890 painters. The entrenched orthodoxy of the revivalist painters, it seemed, was on the retreat; in 1959, some twenty painters held a protest exhibition at the Fine Arts Gallery and the boycott of the Akademi had begun on a permanent basis with serious implications for the revivalist groups as represented by the D.P. Roy Chowdhury-Barada Ukil team.

One hoped that under the painter Sanyal, aesthetic credence of the Akademi would become acceptable to the large majority of artists. But the 1960 annual show revealed that the situation had not improved. This was well brought out by the comments of the judges of the 1960 show –

> Out of 624 artists who have submitted their works 108 have been represented. This clearly shows that the general standard of entries is

below normal. Many students and amateurs seem to have entered the competition without realizing the exact nature and scope of the national exhibition.

In fact, the Akademi had never enjoyed the support and confidence of our major painters. What has come in the Akademi's way of enlisting support of these major artists was the protectionist status it has assumed since its formation. Besides, it seemed always in need of a psychic revival of an Indian version of modernism. The revivalists at least, were rooted in a tradition which acknowledged historicity valid in the Indian context anyway, while the pseudo-modernists had insufficient signifiers to relate their responses to products of modernism. They had narrow short-term projects and the more desperately they wooed the senior artists the more widespread became the discontent among the younger artists. The result was a package system of patronage distribution, perhaps a necessary adjustment because of the federal structure of the Akademi. The Akademi's collection, therefore, acts as a shop window to the shifting goal coalitions: things would not have been so bad had the Akademi been clear about its goals and imposed its system on the works it chose to award in its national shows; instead, it has become a tyrannical regime of a few vested interests who are more interested in personal power than in art.

As there is no distribution system operating in India, the Akademi is conscious of its power of patronage. The discontent among younger artists with the Akademi and the need of modern its structure has been admitted though by the Khosla report, no one has cared to examine the pile of dusty canvases it has collected since 1958. It is time the protesting artists took this up. It may mean a negative exercise but may lead to a fundamental re-orientation of art attitudes.

50

A NEED FOR INTROSPECTION

On the occasion of the publishing of the Triennale-India special issue of Lalit Kala Akademi's journal, Lalit Kala Contemporary, *a reflection on the successful international quadriennial art event, Documenta*

'Artscape', *The Economic Times*, New Delhi, date unknown, July 1991

Lalit Kala Contemporary-36, the journal published annually by the central Lalit Kala Akademi, needs a close look to initiate an informed public debate. It contains useful information regarding the six triennale shows the Akademi has previously organized. Much has already been written about the seventh triennale that concluded in March this year. The debate is necessary because it is almost a quarter century that we have been suffering from an inferiority complex caused by the import of internationalism through these triennales. The time has come not only for introspection and a critical assessment of the show, but to think of the alternate ways of either restructuring it or putting an end to this – art of the absurd.

We should ask ourselves why is it that the international exhibitions are today out of tune with the spirit of the 1990s. Internationalism is an attempt at self-representation of those tendencies in art which have interiorized, knowingly or unknowingly, the repressive narrative of progressive universal emancipation promised by the West. It seems as if the civilizing mission of the past is a psychological necessity of our post-colonial descendants. For, the strategy of these post-colonial aesthetes is to bring themselves from the margin into the centre. This they want to achieve not by applying deconstructive techniques of analysis to the dominant histories of the West but through neo-colonial arrangements that lie beneath their neutral and universalizing facades – such as the enactment of the Triennale-India.

They refuse to live on the margins and are therefore unwilling to see that most of the international exhibitions, for instance, the biennales (in Paris, Venice, Tokyo and Sao Paulo) promote only provincialists in the arts. They no longer promote the kind of art they were conscious of but promote an attitude of subservience to an externally imposed hierarchy of cultural values. It is undoubtedly a product of colonial history. Colonialism in the context of art should not be seen as a function of geographic location. For instance, the members of the art world inside New York too are provincialists in their work, attitudes and positions within the system.

Take, for instance, the history of Documenta, the four-yearly international exhibition held in the city of Kassel in Germany. It is perhaps the most important international show and its centralized organization speaks for the Teutonic rage for order. Yet, it is unable to hide the adversary space between commerce and art and tension between the German respect for social hierarchies and individual freedom. Despite being the greatest show on earth, it breeds provincialism.

Documenta was started in 1945 with the ideological support of the almighty American dollar and the indoctrination programme proved a huge success. This success encouraged American presence in the biennales held in Sao Paulo, Paris and Venice. The initial impulse was to control the mid-century abundance of art in Europe the Documenta offered for American museums and gallery men and art dealers. It was a heaven-sent opportunity to accumulate the artistic wealth of Europe.

The second Documenta represented the American presence not on the margins. It was too obviously a drive towards the centre, clearly to destroy the mainstream status of European culture through Americanization. The American superiority became evident with the projection of Pollock and Rauschenberg. The third Documenta held in 1953 was dominated by Werner Haftman.[1] Being a product of the high cultural mapping exercises, it turned out to be the embodiment of painterly values. It was the period of the discoveries of existential values in art of which Action painting in the Pollock mode became the painterly ideal: the ground was laid for the international launch of what is known as abstract expressionism.

The fourth Documenta demonstrated the power of the Leo Castelli-Virginia Dwan-Heiner Friedrich-Konrad Fisher coalition of dealers. They poured millions of dollars just to conquer their homegrown provincial inferiority in art. The new capital they accumulated, through their European contacts, had no rough edges. The Documenta was first in private hands, while in Europe it was state run and government funded. That meant that as against the aggressiveness and mobility of the American capital, the slower moving cultural bureaucracies of Europe were ready to surrender to make a fast buck.

Besides, the European museums were the seats of conservatism. No European museum is known for systematically collecting contemporary art. Alfred Barr, who has been connected with Documenta since 1949 – took up the cause of the institutional recognition of contemporary new art. He was a visionary and wanted to get history before history got art. As long back as 1938, he wrote that 'some of the younger of us had just left colleges where the courses in modern art began with Rubens and ended with a few superficial and hostile remarks about Van Gogh and Matisse'.

As director of the Museum of Modern Art, New York, he made the Museum a natural habitat of vanguard art. And for the American art dealers and museums the best of the vanguard gestures in art were to be found in Europe where the idea of the avant-garde had entered the continuous historical presence, in which the ideological polarities were resolved at least in matters of quality.

What was new in the art situation of the Fifties was that unlike the European art establishment, the American museums were eager to become the artist's accomplices. The result was a new permissiveness in the taste that European art never had. The newly discovered permissiveness in arts promoted a make-believe world.

The Documenta thus became the site of improvisatory blindness. It is not a place where art is shown but rather put on display. It is to remind us that the individual mythologies in art are conceived as a tribute to errant creativity that is beyond the reach of the category-dependent habits of the mind. The 1968 Documenta was exclusively an American affair. The worship of anything American in a client state such as West Germany came without any trepidation. German artists were committed to their own social iconography, but seemed provincial.

With the 1968 Documenta, the American artists had arrived as the role-taking avant-garde in world art. A central feature of the 1972 Documenta was the arrival of cold-war politics in the arts; it was dominated by the American style of photo-realism. Photo-realism was promoted as a global phenomenon; the intention was to prove that compared to socialist realism (which is a form of history painting), American photo-realism is the candid image of the camera's time-exposed reality. The Documenta authorities invited the Soviet Union to participate in the show, the main theme of which was realism. The Russians, however, did not oblige. Jean-Christophe Amman's [the commissioner] original aim was to put up a show providing contrasting viewpoints on realism. The contrast would have been a paradigm of the show as a whole. The ideological pairing was fundamental to the organizers' thinking. Communism and capitalism would have been seen standing behind these paintings. The assumption was that ideas function when one looks behind every meaning and understands it in terms of a work's genesis.

The attempt at the thematic control of the 1972 Documenta proved a failure, although it was financed generously. The 2,000,000 Deutsche Marks (DM) budget made it possible to work on a huge scale. In Paris, until the Sixties, each participating country selected its own contribution. From the beginning of the Seventies, an international committee was entrusted the job of selecting the works sent to its biennale with the result that some countries were not represented at all. Some countries were invited: for instance, China and in the last biennale, some Latin American countries. The idea was that the works from these countries should not be subjected to the critical standards demanded by the biennale committee because they represented a unique national style.

Similarly, the Venice Biennale selects the third-world countries for showing at its internationals while the participation for the Western artists is open and unconditional. The Sao Paulo Biennale which was organized in 1953 under the leadership of Mario Pedrosa, is a caricatured version of internationalism in art. A Brazilian government press release issued at the time of the sixth biennale said: 'Brazilian culture cannot afford to remain indifferent to the progress of present techniques and the evaluation of artistic creations.' The implication is that art is a mere technology and to fall behind the progress of techniques in painting would be equivalent to falling behind in electronics. Surely, it hurts one's national pride if a public admission is made of one's backwardness in culture.

India too cannot afford to make a public confession of its backwardness in the visual arts, of its provincialism, an example of which is that its request for a pavilion in the Venice Biennale was rejected. Mulk Raj Anand, who was the then chairman of the Lalit Kala Akademi, was not the man to suffer the humiliation in silence. The triennale was his response to the rejection of Venice although it was opposed by the artist community. The triennale exhibitions, which no one takes seriously except the local artists, are affirmations of our provincial connection with world art. The experience of the seven triennales have proved that they are counter-productive. They always divide the artist community. Many factional hosts that have taken residence in the Akademi have turned these triennales into almost scripted roles and have contaminated the whole atmosphere.

Editor's Note

1 German art historian who helped co-found the Documenta, and known for his early book on Paul Klee as well as the influential two-volume work, *Painting in the Twentieth Century*, California: Praeger Publishers, 1965.

51
STOFFWECHSEL: INTERPRETING MODERNISM

An article on the exhibition held parallel to the Documenta by the Stoffwechsel group, which visited India in 1991 to choose Indian exhibits for its next edition

'Artscape', *The Economic Times*, 10 July 1991

Between 10 and 17 August, Professor H. Attar, the leader of the project group 'Stoffwechsel' of the University of Kassel, Germany, will be in India to select a group of Indian artists whose works would be displayed at an exhibition parallel to the Documenta. The exhibition, which will be held in the city of Kassel from 13 June to 20 September 1992, is now historic. Founded at the University of Kassel in 1979, the project group, Stoffwechsel, has been holding parallel exhibitions to the Documenta that has come to represent the adverse commercial space and has caused a split in the artistic community.

Stoffwechsel literally means 'material change'. The group put up the first show in 1982: *Soft Material in Art* was the title of the exhibition in which 72 artists from nineteen countries participated during Documenta 7 International. At the time of the Documenta 9 in Kassel, the group will present its parallel show, titled *Scene Change*, in which 80 artists from eighteen countries are expected to participate. The artworks will not be chosen on the basis of a jury's verdict as is the case with most international exhibitions held in Europe. *Scene Change*, the theme of which is 'modern art in the non-European countries', will have about 8,000 square metres of space for the works of non-European artists. Which means that only the acknowledged manifestations of modernity will find entry into the show and not the traditional works of art, for the simple reason that modernity, in the context of non-European art, is not easy to define. It recalls attention to something that allows room for the non-aesthetic at the very heart of modernity. It is as if to say that the European face of modernism is different from its variations found in non-European countries; that modernity is explicated only through reference to those European works that have assumed an art-historical formative frame.

The question is: should one insist on the explication of this difference and forget the identity crisis of modernism? The project group's report says: 'We can see that the work of art in these (non-European) countries has to be more widely interpreted. We do not regard this as a form of manipulation but as a form of protection for individual freedom.' Which means that art for the European mind has both expressive and therapeutic functions, for 'the measure of freedom is the freedom of the individual'.

Implicit in the notion of freedom is the false camaraderie among those who think one can just strike up a conversation without needing a mediating third party because art speaks a universal language. Freedom generated false hopes in those who tended to dismiss the social barriers that kept strangers in silence.

The Stoffwechsel group insists on the title *'Scene Change'*: it permits two people not only to come together but encourages them to converse. One of the aims is to make the exhibition a subject for conversation where the artist can situate himself within the world of talk and profit from meeting some stranger by learning to talk to him in his own language. In conversation, we are not the master of our language since we do not wish that our partner be an echo of ourselves: what is more, we must also learn to listen. Any amateur can detect that the non-European artist is in need of a norm against which his strangeness is experienced.

Strangeness is the best possible face that modernity can borrow since the notorious difficulty in understanding the basic core of modernist art offers a bad start to a conversation. The unresolved question is the role of local traditions which are to be violated to produce instantly the effect of the modern. This is especially so in the non-European countries where modernism, as is the case in Europe, has not become a period style. That is why, for the non-European artist, modernism means celebrating the immediacy of an absolute present while current European art can look back from a distance to what post-modernism offers.

It is for this reason that the Stoffwechsel group insists on selection of the artists from the non-European countries, for it is aware that 'the kind of art we are concerned with is not supported in these (non-European) countries and has not yet found its way into the European scene'. They are not concerned with exploring the full range of implications of the statement, for it merely detracts us from the main question which is,

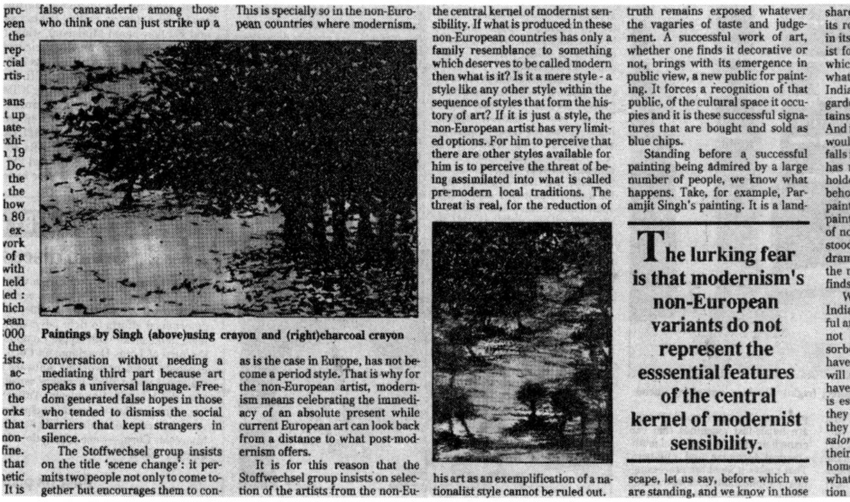
false camaraderie among those who think one can just strike up a

Paintings by Singh (above)using crayon and (right)charcoal crayon

conversation without needing a mediating third part because art speaks a universal language. Freedom generated false hopes in those who tended to dismiss the social barriers that kept strangers in silence.

The Stoffwechsel group insists on the title 'scene change': it permits two people not only to come together but encourages them to con-

This is specially so in the non-European countries where modernism, as is the case in Europe, has not become a period style. That is why for the non-European artist, modernism means celebrating the immediacy of an absolute present while current European art can look back from a distance to what post-modernism offers.

It is for this reason that the Stoffwechsel group insists on selection of the artists from the non-Eu-

the central kernel of modernist sensibility. If what is produced in these non-European countries has only a family resemblance to something which deserves to be called modern then what is it? Is it a mere style - a style like any other style within the sequence of styles that form the history of art? If it is just a style, the non-European artist has very limited options. For him to perceive that there are other styles available for him is to perceive the threat of being assimilated into what is called pre-modern local traditions. The threat is real, for the reduction of his art as an exemplification of a nationalist style cannot be ruled out.

truth remains exposed whatever the vagaries of taste and judgement. A successful work of art, whether one finds it decorative or not, brings with its emergence in public view, a new public for painting. It forces a recognition of that public, of the cultural space it occupies and it is these successful signatures that are bought and sold as blue chips.

Standing before a successful painting being admired by a large number of people, we know what happens. Take, for example, Paramjit Singh's painting. It is a landscape, let us say, before which we are standing, and we know in those

The lurking fear is that modernism's non-European variants do not represent the esssential features of the central kernel of modernist sensibility.

whether it is pretence to hide the truth behind the polemics of post-modernism. Because the underlying assumption is that what the group wants to show at the parallel exhibition to the Documenta 9 – it is the genuine article which has remained unchecked by familiarity with the original modernism that has its authentic predecessors only in Europe.

The lurking fear is that modernism's non-European variants do not represent the essential features of the central kernel of modernist sensibility. If what is produced in these non-European countries has only a family resemblance to something which deserves to be called modern, then what is it? Is it a mere style – a style like any other style within the sequence of styles that form the history of art? If it is just a style, the non-European artist has very limited options. For him to perceive that there are other styles available for him is to perceive the threat of being assimilated into what is called pre-modern local traditions. The threat is real, for the reduction of [sic] French painting became aware of this threat with eighteenth-century rococo art of which the classic example is the art of Francois Boucher. The connection between rococo and what is called modern art finds elaborate formulation in Michael Fried's book *Absorption and Theatricality* (1980). The following quotation, it seems, forms the central thesis of the book –

> It seems clear that starting around the middle of the eighteenth century in France, the beholder's presence before the painting came increasingly to be conceived by critics and theorists as something that had to be accomplished or at least powerfully affirmed by the painting itself; and more generally that the existence of the beholder, which is to say, the primordial convention that paintings are made to be beheld, emerged as problematic for painting as never before.

In short, this means that art does (not) exist for a beholder. That is what rococo is telling us. It is its fundamental truth about art. By implication, it also means that art ultimately ends up as decoration and answerable only to the beholder's pleasure. Most examples of successful translations of modernism in India have been manifestations of this fundamental truth. The truth remains exposed, whatever the vagaries of taste and judgement. A successful work of art, whether one finds it decorative or not, brings with its emergence in public view, a new public for painting. It forces recognition of that public, of the cultural space it occupies, and it is these successful signatures that are bought and sold as blue chips.

Standing before a successful painting being admired by a large number of people, we know what happens. Take, for example, Paramjit Singh's painting. It is a landscape, let us say, before which we are standing, and we know in those rare moments how nature turns into art for us by a mere act of gazing through the window. Not the physical window of the world, but a metaphoric one, and the metaphor becomes a representation of the real and the repudiation of nature in a way that determines the structure of our cultural history. The question then arises, is cultural history the sum total of a series of hidden and intuitively felt metaphors? Or is it the resultant aesthetics of fetishism which becomes part of our perceptual mechanism.

Paramjit Singh is not alone in turning us into voyeurs. Most successes in art betray the recognition in us of the truths of rococo art. And, to be sure, what art fears most is the recognition of its rococo fate: this threat art perceives for itself when it enters a bullish market and becomes a blue chip. The art life of the Eighties in India is the story of rococo achievements and failures; particularly achievements because they have created a new public for art. While the failures represent non-arrivals: art without a face value, for it is so tangled up into questions of quality, into the fruitless comparisons that people are always making between success and failure.

The success and failure measured in terms of the beholder's share, that is to say. If art existed in its rococo period for its beholder, in its modern period it does not exist for the beholder. It is the 'not' which in the long run constituted what is called the avant-garde. In India we never had a taste of avant-garde art because the negation contains art's possibility of failure. And in the colonial context, no artist would court failure: a painting that fails in our context is a painting that has no desire to exist for the beholder, if theatre is the name of the beholder. Outside the theatre, if a painting fails by failing to be a painting, it no longer runs the risk of not being art. It must be understood in some relation to the 'real' drama of the stage, a drama where the master term for the successful finds its form.

When Professor Attar comes to India and meets our more successful artists, it is essential that they do not allow themselves to be 'absorbed'. Whatever the price they have to pay: the reason is that they will not find the public there that they have here for their art. Therefore, it is essential for their survival that they not be absorbable: they should reject the international salon and prefer to be refuses in their own country. In their own home-made world of modernism, what looks like breaking with tradition does not betray its audience, nor in the present-day climate of post-modernist permissiveness, is it considered a betrayal of taste. For in India, one is always wrong about the Emperor. Remember Saint Saens, who said that the emperor had no clothes, was not an Indian. Moreover, the Philistine audience cannot afford to admit[1] that they do not know how the taste is governed: they are the lords of the art world.

Editor's Note

1 'Moreover the Philistine audience cannot afford to admit': the phrase, with reference to Saint Saens's comment, comes from musician and philosopher Stanley Cavell. The complete original statement is: 'The philistine audience cannot afford to admit the new; the avant-garde audience cannot afford not to.' See Stanley Cavell, 'Music Discomposed', in *Must We Mean What We Say?* Cambridge: Cambridge University Press, 1958, pp. 180–212, 206.

TRIENNALE-INDIA

In light and emulation of two and three-yearly inter-national art events in first world centres such as Venice and, by the 1950s, parts of the world deemed as 'developing', such as Brazil, the Indian art establishment initiated the Triennale-India in 1968 – an international art exhibition to be held once in three years, administered by the Lalit Kala Akademi. However, the Akademi's lack of vision for this event, its biases and what the artists saw as absence of real investment in the well-being of Indian art and its artists, and the expenditure incurred, led to protests from the art community from the very first edition.

K.B. Goel's writings capture the trajectory of the Triennales-India, commenting on the international and Indian art exhibited in each, and the politics over the invitation, selection and judging of entries. While he closely followed the Triennale-India, his available writings do not cover the fifth (1982) and sixth (1986) editions; the last one he covered being the seventh edition, in 1991. The Triennales-India have continued in fits and starts to the present day.

52

ARTISTS PROTEST

An extract from Goel's article on the first Triennale-India (1968), which appeared in Link *magazine. The original is lost and featured here is the brief excerpt which appeared in the special issue on the Triennale of* Lalit Kala Contemporary, *no. 36, 1990*

Link, New Delhi, date unknown, 1968

It was a protest evening. Almost all the artists gathered in the Delhi Silpi Chakra protested against the decision of the Lalit Kala Akademi to hold an international trienniale of art from 1968 in Delhi. Kanwal Krishna was in the chair . . . Tyeb [Mehta] read out a list of countries which have accepted the invitation of the Akademi to participate in the proposed trienniale. Tyeb said we cannot stop the Akademi from holding such a show, but we can definitely protest against it.

Krishen Khanna tried to emphasize the futility of such a venture on the grounds that Indian art would not gain anything by this trienniale since the countries which matter in the world of art have not been invited. Swaminathan said while no artist could oppose the idea of an international exhibition; as such, 'the sins of omission and commission of the Akademi with regard to its responsibilities towards Indian art and artists are so numerous that the triennale venture seems to be nothing more than another exercise in empty showmanship'. Swaminathan presented a long list of difficulties they are facing including shortage of colours and studios. 'The trienniale proposal, expected to cost about four lakhs of rupees', was 'typical of the Akademi's callous disregard of the real needs of the artists' in Swaminathan's view. He said he was not opposed to the idea. But to make it meaningful and comparable to such established international exhibitions as the Venice Biennale or the Tokyo Biennale, it had to be organized on a scale and with a budget which India just could not afford then. 'Moreover, the Akademi has not thought it fit to consult either the artists' community or other art experts in the country in this regard'.

The Akademi's Secretary B.C. Sanyal intervened to say that the proposal had already been carried too far to be reversed or amended. He said the Akademi wanted to provide a platform for the artists of the progressive countries of Africa and Asia to come closer and learn from each other's artistic experience. . . .

But nobody yet knows who among the Indian artists would be asked to participate or who will make selections for the purpose? Will it not be the Executive Board of the Akademi, seven of whose nine artist-members are no more working? And which once sat on judgement on and awarded 'certificates of merit' to Picasso, Braque and Guttoso in an exhibition organized by the AIFACS? Will the Akademi be able to do justice to a venture like holding an international triennale with an estimated budget of three to four lakhs of rupees when this sum would not be sufficient to insure even ten paintings worth the name while in transit?

53
SECOND TRIENNALE

An article on the second Triennale-India held in New Delhi in 1971, examining the featured art and the artists' convention held on the occasion

Link, New Delhi, 7 February 1971

The international art circus called Triennale-India 1971 has finally opened. It will be on for two months at three galleries – Lalit Kala at Rabindra Bhavan, Shridharani Gallery and National Gallery of Modern Art at Jaipur House, New Delhi. In terms of number and size, the show is indeed impressive with forty-seven countries participating: some 800 works by 360 artists are displayed, India alone contributing over 100 works. But more impressive was the silent demonstration by the protesting artists who stood like outcasts outside the main entrance of Rabindra Bhavan.[1] To the outsider, the protest spectacle must be confusing – as would a serious family quarrel to children. Art insiders, no doubt, will miss the works of the protesters sadly because what is exhibited in the Indian section in the triennale is truly a bureaucratic muddle, not even the pretence of a good provincial show.

ART POLITICS

The art politics of the triennale is by now an old story: everyone knows what happened during the planning for the triennale and how art bureaucrats have manipulated the selection of the works by their favourites which are now 'in' and how successfully they alienated those who should have been really 'in'. But the politics, it seems, has not been limited to the selection job alone: it has affected the judgement of the international jury also. Otherwise how can one explain the gold medal award to Ishwar Sagara? No amount of sympathetic explaining really can justify this kind of judging; and this is not our opinion alone. A contemporary wrote:

> The exhibit of Ishwara Sagara which has been awarded the gold medal also falls in the same category (weighed down by the decorative force). Such decorative works may appeal to foreigners. They seem to be created under the pressure of the world art market which has suddenly got interested in Indian iconography, symbols and tantric art.

The Sagara prettiness is typical of the Bendre art syndrome and since Bendre acted as chairman of the international jury, he must have forced his judgement on foreign colleagues. At least, such are the rumours. This is not to suggest that international juries are easily influenced. On the other hand, every award means hard bargaining - especially when the majority of the judges are from the underdeveloped countries - underdeveloped relatively in relation to the Western modes of vanguard art. So, an international award is part of cultural diplomacy; or, so it seems now because art in underdeveloped countries is justified on grounds of being an exportable item, a means of establishing one's cultural identity and to prove its supremacy. So, of the six awards only one goes to a Western country, France, and the rest are distributed among the Asian and Latin American countries.

NOT RELEVANT

Mulk Raj Anand's enthusiasm about the notion of 'open competition' looks so much misplaced when the awards were manipulated the way they have been in this triennale. Nor does the Delhi triennale prove that 'there is no monopoly of talent in the creative arts with any nation, race or country'.[2] Mulk Raj Anand justifies this costly art show (it means to the Indian tax-payer more than Rs 8 lakhs) on very specious grounds. Does it really matter that 'we have no pavilion of our own in the Venice Art City? And, in most international exhibitions,Indian exhibits are shoved into dark corners, through the competition for space?' Or will the Indian creative spirit be any the poorer if, not having enough foreign exchange, our artists do not travel often enough outside the country 'to see what is being done abroad?' Is all this really relevant? Of course for the colonial mind, it is in the same proportion, perhaps as the degree of intensity with which the cultural identity is asserted.

The fact that forty-seven nations are taking part in the second triennale shows perhaps that the West, which had so far been absent-minded about possible creative efforts of significance in the so-called 'underdeveloped' world has at last conceded an open mind about possible works of value in the most unsuspected quarters, against the closed mind of a generation ago.[3] If this is the intention for holding the triennales in India, the sooner we stop this nonsense the better. The superiority of cultural products, if such is the case, does not make a country developed or make it an equal of the so-called developed countries. Nor can it be justified on any economic grounds simply to prove that we produce 'possible works of value' when the proving game is played at a cost of more than Rs 8 lakhs. In Prime Minister Indira Gandhi's mind, the triennale's significance is however limited: because we discover 'world art through books or exhibitions' it seems necessary to have it at least for those artists who are 'prevented from circumstances' from going abroad and seeing with their own eyes the palpitating works of art in the countries of their origin.

A WHOLE WALL

Seeing original works is indeed not necessary as much as reading about them because, as Harold Rosenberg says, 'art has become a part of the "language"; it is a writing of sorts. . . . A painting now seems to belong in a book, instead of its hiding place on a ceiling or in the gloom of a cathedral.'[4] Take, for instance, the great avant-garde, environmental piece by Australia's Robert Hunter, aged 24, who came here to paint his piece directly on the off-white wall of the Lalit Kala. This is a large work and occupies a whole wall of the gallery: a kind of folksy arrangement of interlocking series of squares and rectangles stencilled in shades of grey and white acrylic. Those who will see this for the first time might not really take this as a proper triennale exhibit; this may be thought to be a decoration of the wall and this is really what it looks like. And suppose some take it seriously and worry about its permanence, it will be merely exposing art ignorance. The work will look quite familiar to those who follow Rosenberg's advice in matters of art. This is what [Australian art critic] Alan McCulloch wrote about Hunter's similar environmental piece in 'Art International' (20 October 1970): 'Apparently Hunter was exorcising his former absorption with Malevich's "white on white" but since his identical grey lattices joined with diagonals were stencilled onto the actual walls of the gallery (Pinacotheca [gallery], Richmond, Australia), they vanished like spring shadows with the next exhibition.' If art is to vanish like spring shadows, should we have the triennales which can be justified on the sole ground that they provide us with the opportunity of seeing the actual avant-garde works – something which permanently exists and not a whimsy to be protected inside the pages of an art book?

ARTISTS' CONVENTION

A well-argued, intellectualist criticism of the triennale came from the artist-brahmins among the protesting artists who held a two-day convention at the Gandhi Sangrahalaya (Rajghat) to discuss their problems. A whole morning was devoted to the discussion of the implications of internationalism in contemporary art. Critic Geeta Kapur's paper, already published in *Vrishchik* (10 January 1971) gave the intellectual direction to the debate which followed after Geeta had formally read it out like a professional radio commentator. The editorial reference to Geeta's paper in *Vrishchik* made it clear that it was intended as a reply to Mulk Raj Anand who, in one of his letters, has talked of one-world culture and the role of international exhibitions. (It is for this reason that we have given Mulk Raj Anand's arguments at some length – quoting not from the letter but from the preface he wrote for the catalogue to the triennale exhibition.)

Geeta Kapur quoted from Harold Rosenberg's book, *The Anxious Object*, an extract from a government press release from the sixth biennale at Sao Paulo, perhaps to caricature Anand's defence of international exhibitions. The press release said: 'Brazilian culture cannot afford to remain indifferent to the progress of present techniques and the evaluation of artistic creations.' Then Rosenberg's comment is added: 'To fall behind in the progress of technique in painting would be equivalent to falling behind in electronics. A nation that did so would be making public confession of backwardness.' No wonder the talk of international exhibitions promoting a climate for the development of a one-world culture is bogus. In reality, international exhibitions, according to Geeta Kapur, are a testing ground 'where different nations test their respective advancement – the underdeveloped ones with some anxiety following the criteria of advanced art set by the galleries and critics of the progressive West'.

Geeta made it clear at the outset that she was not against internationalism. But internationalism in art as it operates today has close links with cultural imperialism of the West and a 'cultural commercial mechanism' is developed which ensures through such value-packed notions as modernism, internationalism and progress to perpetuate the cultural supremacy of the West, and precisely through 'the manipulation of advanced technology'.

'INTERESTS'

She warned against such false gods as McLuhan[5] because the McLuhan notion of internationalism is based on 'optimistic assumptions' which no doubt 'tends to disengage media technology from its source and operators'. The McLuhan synthesis of different cultures through the effects of advanced technology no doubt 'anticipates a truly synthetic culture of the future', but, she argued, 'it must also be reckoned that these (attempts) carry the motives and values, indeed the wholesale ideologies of the operators who belong to particular cultures and class groups'. The boycott of the Akademi and the triennale, she thinks, are no doubt 'good in itself but attacking a bureaucratic body is a little like shadow-boxing when the basic issues, in which real interests may be at stake, remain unquestioned'.

The debate did not spell out what these 'interests' were. Most artists exhausted themselves in discussing those points which were already covered by Geeta's paper. Vivan Sundaram, the secretary of the action committee of the protesting artists, and Indu Jai Singh also read their papers. Vivan pointed out that international festivals like the biennales and triennales fostered 'reactionary art that had no contact with living reality and social environment'.

Indu Jai Singh came very near defining the areas of real interests at which Geeta hinted but it was expressed largely in sociological terms. The present ills of Indian contemporary art issued from the fact, she said, that artists have faced their problems on a personal level and have made much of the individuality of the artist, often playing into the hands of the ruling classes: 'the ruling classes in order to divide them (the artists) divest them of all social responsibility and thus make them the tools of the machinery of status quo'. The primary concern of the protesting artists then should be to 'reiterate a genuine principle of internationalism, striving to understand the cultures of the people's solidarity'. She asked the artists not to work in isolation of their studios but unite: 'What should and does unite the artist is his concern for humanity. This should be the underlying concern of any triennale or art show.' The triennale show which our officials have put up and as it is conceived by them, she said, 'is very much a product of the cultural imperialism that dominates the art world and which bases its headquarters in the USA and Western Europe'.

SICKNESS

Listening to the discussion, one got the impression that the artists were turning into social revolutionaries. Swaminathan quipped: 'Social revolutionaries or the artists are going to change the art scene?' Later, Swaminathan explained that the problems facing the artists cannot be solved in the context of known ideologies. It smacked of pseudo-revolutionarism when people talked of Sartre and Marcuse and forgot that nearer home the whole range of revolutionary thought is expressed between the polarities of Gandhi and Charu Majumdar. The West is attempting to universalize its own sickness and the triennales and biennales provide art modes and trends which are a product of this sickness. He admitted that these exhibitions did influence art trends but it is only the 'weaker artists' who are swept away by them. 'Surely, the weaker artists have no right to exist,' he added. He made a very interesting point about his art (including Krishna Khanna's also): between the easel painting done by Krishen Khanna and himself and the modes of decorations by folk artists or the creation of a ritual object by a tribal, no aesthetic principle should be set up for evaluation and comparison.

So, it is now easy to see the connection between the Australian artist, Hunter's tantrology, which is not an easel art and hence cannot be bought or sold in the art market, and Swaminathan's easel art which is still an art commodity. Maybe, Swaminathan is hinting at the new movement he is planning to launch – art without the art gallery.

Editor's Notes

1 The editorial in the November 1971 issue of *Vrishchik* reported the silent protest of the artists 'sporting large plaster cast medals printed in gold with "Boycott Akademi" inscribed on them'.

2 Mulk Anand Raj, prefatory note, Second Triennale-India, Lalit Kala Akademi, 1971, reproduced in *Lalit Kala Contemporary*, special issue on Triennale-India, no. 36, 1990, p. 28.

3 Ibid.

4 Harold Rosenberg, 'Art Books, Book Art, Art,' *The Anxious Object: Art Today and its Audience*, Horizon Press, 1964, p. 198

5 Media theorist Marshal McLuhan who spoke in the 1960s of the East and the West coming together, and anticipated the idea of a 'global village'. He, however, saw such internationalism in benign terms whose dangers those in the third world were more alert to, as the debates captured here demonstrate.

54
INSTRUMENTS-OBJECTS

An article on technological art from Italy and France on view at the second Triennale-India

Link, New Delhi, 21 February 1971

TRIENNALE

The exhibits from Italy and France, at Lalit Kala and Shridharani Galleries have many things in common. They are products of the highly charged experimental atmosphere of the Sixties offering visual stimulus ranging from eye-teasing optical puns to pop versions of Zen and machine art. The exhibits from Italy make up an exhibition of ideas rather than the traditional works of art: in fact, what is presented as art is not a rare collector's item or a cultural commodity for the privileged few. No eminent names either as much as certain categories of tendencies which sum up the best in the immediate past. Unlike the situational art by the American artists they have little futuristic appeal because they do not point the direction of the next few years. They are part of the media landscape, more as representatives of the now fully established internationalism of art which has spontaneously come up blurring all familiar national distinctions. This is of course largely due to the intense commerce of ideas between artists of different nationalities and partly the result of art's international market mechanism.

Machine Art: The impact of 'aesthetic operators' belonging to the formalized world of international gallery art is the greatest on Italian artists. The futurist machine has been resurrected, as it were, and unlike the old machine, the new one is full of strange love talk - most of which is pure culture shock - a kind of dada blankness that is. The Italian aesthetic operators celebrate the commonplaces of machine art and (in the words of the Italian commissioner) they 'aim towards the creation and diffusion of objects made in large quantities and of low cost having a proper specific and a precise finality'.

The art products are more like instruments for visual education. So their place is not the art gallery but the art departments of schools because they are models of a 'clear and distinct perception of images having their own structure and in some cases their own law of kinetic development'. They are cultural instruments tending to standardize everything into some form of apocalyptic geometry of the new aesthetic vision, cutting across all class barriers of taste and enjoyment. That is to say they are like 'the apparatuses of scientific laboratories' and so the art produced is no more

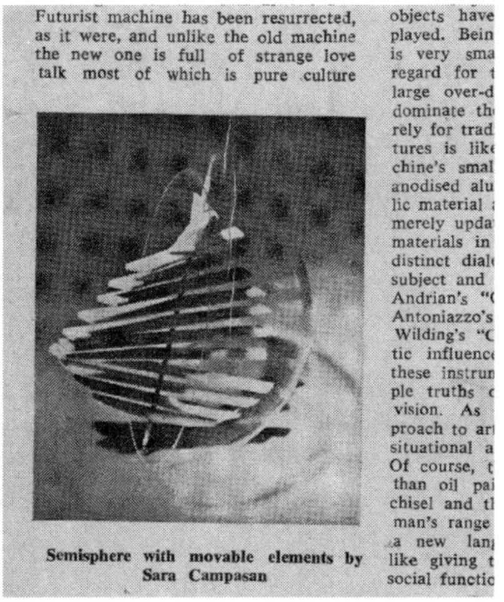

Futurist machine has been resurrected, as it were, and unlike the old machine the new one is full of strange love talk most of which is pure culture

Semisphere with movable elements by Sara Campasan

objects have played. Bein is very sma regard for t large over-d dominate th rely for trad tures is lik chine's smal anodised alu lic material merely upda materials in distinct dial subject and Andrian's "(Antoniazzo's Wilding's "C tic influenc these instrun ple truths c vision. As proach to ar situational a Of course, t than oil pai chisel and t man's range a new lan like giving t social functic

a 'commodity earmarked for the privileged markets or customers'. These instrument-objects come from Italy's Sincron, the biggest aesthetic operative centre and at the Delhi triennale they are 'shown not as the traditional works of art, but as didactical apparatuses for the formation of visual perceptivity and aesthetic experience'.

The pity is that these instrument-objects have not been properly displayed. Being instruments, their size is very small and without a proper regard for their cultural value, the large, over-dramatic Japanese exhibits dominate them. A visitor looking merely for traditional paintings and sculptures is likely to miss them as machine's smaller voices. The plexiglass, anodized, aluminium, polystrene, acrylic material and perspex sheets did not merely update us about the newest of materials in use today but present a distinct dialectic of relations between subject and object. Take, for example, Andrian's *Chromatic Composition, Antoniazzo's Op Cine Colour* and Wilding's *Cinetic N* and their hypnotic influence. What is presented in these instrument-objects are the simple truths of perception and human vision. As an interdisciplinary approach to art they are more valid than situational art from American artists. Of course, this art is more complex than oil paint and as tools – like the chisel and the brush – they extend man's range of expression and create a new language of art, which is like giving to the machine its proper social function.

BASIC ISSUES

The exhibits from France, no wonder, look a little peevish, old-fashioned compared with those from Italy. But they also are products of the psychological conditioning of the machine culture. It is the basic issues and the techniques they are concerned with, and not the specific French sensibility which presided over the entire modern art movement till the Second World War. In terms of tendencies, they belong either to op or minimalism. France, indeed, has taken the Delhi triennale this time more seriously and brought us works by such internationally famed artists as Victor Vasarely and Georges Mathieu, the artist who introduced action painting in Europe and made it an acceptable idiom through his writings and lectures. He is represented by his six works. But it is Vasarely, the Hungarian artist, now settled in France, who dominates the French show. Vasarely, a product of Bauhaus, has long been obsessed with two things:

architectonics and movement. So his art is most geometrical, strictly symmetrical and always non-representational. It is such a pleasure to see him indulging in the brightest and wildest colours because most of his earlier works which we have so far seen through art magazines has been on the theme of optical possibilities of black and white geometric shapes. The four colour serigraphs are eye-filling; the crazy polychrome checkerboard colour harmonies are stunning in terms of effects in colour vibrations. The only painter who comes close to Vasarely in colour technology is Morisson Philippe, who shows a minimalist work composed in poetic soft blues and although empty of visual interest because of the academic exposition of minimalism, it is beautiful because Philippe uses even emptiness in the service of his artistic intentions. The award-winning technologies of Jean Pierre are more like the instrument-objects of the Italian artists and intended to teach us the aesthetic relevance - or is it irrelevance? - of optical art.

55
THE SEMINAR

An article on the third Triennale-India held in New Delhi in 1975, reporting on the proceedings of an official seminar on the triennale organized by the Lalit Kala Akademi

Link, New Delhi, date unknown, 1975

The third Delhi triennale which has been on view at the Lalit Kala galleries and the Bhawalpur House annexe since February 7 [1975] will fold up this weekend. But this will not be the end of the controversies associated with it. The main topic of controversy, of course, is the jury report which has sought to place doubts over the very concept of triennales and biennales: even Prime Minister Indira Gandhi took note of it at the time of giving away prizes to the award-winning artists on 17 March at the Rabindra Bhavan lawns. 'The international jury has made some suggestions and due consideration will be given to them,' she said.

The international jury comprising Monroe Wheeler (USA), Walter Zanini (Brazil) and V.R. Amberkar (India) has called for 'fresh thinking', about the nature of these international exhibitions: in the opinion of the jury such exhibitions have ceased to be 'a living force' in the Seventies. There was some justification for holding such exhibitions in the Fifties because it was possible then to bring 'artists and public together in a particular centre'. The three triennales we have organized lacked any intellectual conception, limited as they were largely to a display of paintings, sculptures and graphics. This straitjacket approach – 'inviting several countries to participate, allocating space for each and awarding prizes to work selected by a jury' – to international exhibitions reduces the venture to a mere ritual.

ART VALUES

The last session of the two-day seminar on contemporary art values organized by the Lalit Kala Akademi devoted a whole afternoon to discussion of the third triennale. Critic Geeta Kapur initiated the discussion with her paper, 'Fallacy of the Triennales'. Perhaps, because of her personal involvement (she refused to serve as one of the national commissioners for the Indian section on ideological grounds), the debate that followed was marked by frequent interruptions and interventions. Most participants, their minds closed with their own artificial fixed horizons, opposed her and though they argued with some reasonableness, they hardly seemed interested in what she said, often missing the core of the issue. If the discussion was about the relevance of the triennales, the attempt has been on the part of those involved with the triennale not to force the issue to any intelligible conclusiveness.

STRATEGY

Or this looked like the strategy. V.R. Amberkar presented the audience with a relativistic construction of his own role: from such a vantage point the truth seemed no less a viewpoint. So the argument was made that the Akademi was willing to accommodate other viewpoints. Of course, no conditions hedged the proposal – the Akademi was even willing to accommodate the multiplicity of viewpoints and, if by overlap an opacity of purpose resulted, it fitted well with the notion of personal relativities.

The Akademi's theme song is, of course, the odds against which it has fought to make the third triennale possible. Richard Bartholomew was frank and honest in comments; he admitted that 'the triennale would not have taken place had the protest movement not been wound up'. He spoke as if he had faced some categorical constraints and these had played a large part in determining the shape of the third triennale show. Sankho Chaudhuri, the director of the triennale, hinted at the mirrorscapes of Larry Bell's box sculptures: 'whatever he wanted to say about the triennale exhibitions he has said in the article' (published in *Patriot's* Sunday Magazine of 16 March [1975]).

Behind such stereotyped replies, attempts were made to hide the truth of facts. And the plain truth is that too many factional ghosts and their ugly presences have taken residence in the Lalit Kala, and in almost scripted roles they have contaminated the whole atmosphere. R. Chatterjee, the former Akademi secretary, has now nothing to lose and hence the quotidian attempts to dust off the present cobwebs. The triennale committee did not discuss what should be the conceptual pattern of the triennales, he revealed. What the committee members were interested in most was 'stock-taking of the world art scene'. If the show gave the impression of being some kind of an international trade fair it, was beyond the powers of the committee to give it a meaningful structure because of the cultural restraints and the compromises the Akademi had to make: 'certain countries could not be ignored', he surmised. Another dimension was added by director, Dr L.P. Sihare the National Gallery of Modern Art. He took up the impossible role of justifying the dated image of art displayed in the three triennales. His rather flatly put argument was: 'Being an underdeveloped country we are not interested in the cake but a wholesome diet of ordinary bread.' This was for the simple reason that we wanted exposure to such art as reflecting some aspects of the vision our artists share. This functional approach ruled out any pretentious display of avant-garde attitudes which the Brazilian jury member, Zanini had pleaded for. Finally, the most significant thing that emerged from this triennale was that the seemingly irreconcilable differences among the artists have been forgotten in the euphoria produced by the triennale. What we should work for now, he pleaded, is an exhibition of 'quality' art informed by modernist sensibilities, and 'frankly speaking this cannot come from regional styles of Asian countries'. So never hope for an Asian triennale.

ARGUMENTS

Geeta's arguments against triennales on the pattern of world trade fairs remained unanswered: 'we did not get the best' (artworks) for the three triennale exhibitions we have organized, and 'objectively speaking, however hard we may try, we will never have them'. This was because there was hardly any possibility of sales of artworks. The motive force behind the enthusiasm for the triennale shows can then be traced to the psychology of competition – as if 'to make place for ourselves in the global roundabout of art' that has become of late a compulsive desire of our culture bureaucrats who do not like to be outdone by others, say by Australia. The artists too share this trivia and Geeta Kapur quoted an artist as saying, 'We must have a triennale of world art in India if we are not to be outstripped in the international arena by a far-flung country like Australia.'[1] Little wonder, 'at the bureaucratic level, the show is encouraged because this government is especially keen on window dressing'. More than the government, the artists who have reached the top are keener for such internationals as they 'find it hard to satisfy their vanity at a local level'.[2] As for the younger artists 'the triennale offers a coveted opportunity at two levels – the national and the international'.[3]

It is unnecessary to add that experience has proved that international exhibitions are counterproductive. This proposition was well argued by an unknown art teacher from Udaipur. The situation, of course, would be different if the receiving country has a sustaining authentic culture of its own: international exhibitions then would 'further strengthen bonds of goodwill and community feeling among artists everywhere'.[4] What is necessary in the circumstances is self-definition of the art situation. As Geeta has argued, this is possible 'if relevant questions are asked'. But she is pessimistic about its outcome because 'there are probably no answers at all and therefore no standard policy'. Artist B.C. Sanyal posed the same problem thus: 'If we have not been able to evolve a policy for our national exhibitions for these 20 or more years, how can it come about in the context of a triennale show?'

And it is a shame indeed that we failed to give a new pattern to the third triennale as the triennale committee 'comprises some of the most distinguishing artists and critics (such as Sankho Chaudhuri, K.G. Subramanyan, J. Swaminathan, Krishen Khanna, Richard Batholomew, L.P. Sihare).' She regretted the committee has 'done so little original thinking'. And surely this was the very occasion – considering a climate of awareness and protest had already been created – to formulate the premises of international exhibitions in India.

SUGGESTIONS

Since Geeta Kapur is the lone critic who has done her homework well and suggested some alternative patterns for organizing our future triennales, it is worthwhile listing these suggestions in her own words.

> Obvious suggestions come to mind. First of all, we should cut down drastically the size and the spectacle. The number of countries invited at a time should not exceed ten. Six, in fact, is a reasonable number. The grouping could be based on different criteria and those criteria could be successively tried out. Political categories like the "Third World" countries or the Socialist Bloc make one kind of grouping. Countries could be grouped also on the basis of culture-commercial inter-dependence as for example the US and Japan, US and Western Europe. Another year the basis of the exhibition could be a series of one-man shows, each of the six countries being requested to send a painter suggested by the Indian committee in charge of the exhibition. Another alternative would be to have theme shows based on major movements in the contemporary scene. With a given theme it would give one a chance to compare the variations of sensibility accruing from different cultural backgrounds, to see, for instance, how abstract expressionism or pop art or photo-realism manifest themselves across cultural frontiers. Such an exhibition being relatively small could be held in at least three big cities in the country. And since it would be conceived as a coherent show it could be followed up with exclusive seminars and discussions, very possibly with the participation of artists and critics from the respective countries.

Consider how interesting it would be to have a seminar on socialist art where USSR is brought face to face with countries like Poland, Czechoslovakia and Hungary. Or a seminar on art in the third world countries which have broken traditions and have a colonial culture as background. If it happened to be a theme show, a series of talks by experts who have been writing on that particular movement could be invited. And at the time the one-man shows are being held, hospitality could be extended for those artists to come and meet ours: a motley crowd of foreigners such as we get in our present triennales can barely make an impact or engage us in a meaningful discussion. Since the whole thing is conducted like a formal ritual in any case, a defunct father-figure like Monroe Wheeler gets to preside.

Editor's Notes

1 Geeta Kapur, *Patriot Magazine*, 23 March 1970, reprinted in part in *Lalit Kala Contemporary*, Triennale special issue, no. 36, September 1990, p. 55.

2 Ibid.

3 Ibid.

4 Report by the international jury on the second Triennale of 1973, *Lalit Kala Contemporary*, Triennale special issue, no. 36, September 1990, p. 50.

56
TRIENNALE

An extensive article on the third edition of Triennale-India held in 1975, reflecting on select international art on view and the Indian response

Patriot Magazine, 16 February 1975

> I send my greetings to the first triennale of contemporary world art . . . I would suggest the possibility of escaping from or even overthrowing the hegemony of Europe and North America in these matters. This hegemony is disastrous because whatever the personal feelings or ideas of individual artists or teachers may be, it is based upon the concept of a visual work of art as property. The historical usefulness of such a concept is long past; it stands now as a barrier to further development. The fight against imperialism and all its agencies is thus closely connected with the struggle for a truly modern art. I wish you clear-sightedness, strength and courage in your struggle.
>
> – John Berger, 10 January 1968

We recall John Berger's message to the first Triennale-India, not for his anti-imperialist rhetorics as some 'universalist' painters had characterized it, but to draw attention to a new development in European art: the notion of art as idea. True, we did not have any exemplification of it until the second triennale. As a serious critic conditioned by his experience of participating in several biennales and triennales, he had naturally assumed that the first New Delhi triennale would have a specimen or two of what is called conceptual art. It was not merely to put an 'emotional' discount on conventional easel painting, which is 'based upon the concept of a visual work of art as property'. Berger, no doubt, has a discerning eye for painting and had he come to New Delhi to see what we had received from the advanced centres of art, he would have been shocked. The first New Delhi triennale produced no less hostile a state of disbelief in Western art centres than our joining the club of the nuclear nations.

Berger hoped – and rightly indeed – that the introduction of conceptual art will enable our artists to see their own local art traditions with the perspective of this new post-studio art. There was also the hope that New Delhi triennales would insist on showing more of conceptual works and had we been true to our genius, to our communal vision of art and not the imported notion of art as property, the story of these three triennales would have been different. The participation of Europe's most leading conceptualists would have been instrumental in heralding a new movement.

The art's existing distribution system in the West, wholly controlled by the art galleries and museums, works against young artists who function as satellites to the few 'super stars', and the situation has been so structured that the young artist for reasons of survival has had to look for new solutions. The art galleries will not touch him because 'art as an idea', whatever its form, cannot be bought or sold like a commodity. The curator and art historian have their centuries-old mental prisons as they have been trained to see art as an object, and as in most professions they have their entrenched rules and criteria, and are unwilling to accept new metaphors and contexts unless these are pushed up by the gallery system as a new metaphysics of money exchange.

So, what is needed is the creation of a belief system and perhaps India would have been the ideal launching ground for this. Mind you, most of the well-known conceptualists have already become famous for their extreme styles, acting as avant-garde determinants of ideas. They also symbolize the crisis of the distribution system of Western art: for the simple reason that this new avant-garde has refused to transform itself into an agent of the art market. Had India invited these 'conceptualists' to its triennales, the result would have been a large number of this taste-making class coming to India as art émigrés. As Carl Andre, the famous militant artist of the Art Workers Coalition, said at the time of the second New Delhi triennale, India has lost an opportunity to strip bare the myth of superior Western culture.

MISSING

Berger, it seems, has overrated the intelligence of the first triennale organizers in responding the way he did. For, to put up the kind of international exhibition which would have become an escape from the colonial cultural matrix, if not a challenge to the hegemony of European art, it was necessary that the host country found its art on an authentic, sustaining culture of its own. But the surrogates of two cultures - national as well as international - more at home with art seen from a 'universal' standpoint - will have only a 'neutral' presentation of everything that has the status of art because such works conform to easily grasped formal conventions. And undoubtedly, these surrogates emotionally belong to a culture which is a pure mental construct and have wrongly exchanged it for their own indigenous culture. So, there is always the strong emotional need to have two nationalities and, since one negates the other, by the process of negation, they arrive at what is called the culture of the expatriate. Art, thus, becomes a means of seeking liberation from that part of their being that is rooted in decay, personal terror, degradation and savage property: art at this level represents utopia, of future promise with its minimum nucleus of security enabling a colonial artist to become a member of the white artists' club.

This is best illustrated by the then chairman, Mulk Raj Anand's comments on the neutral assemblages of what were called experimentations in the first triennale: 'Even a cursory look at the contributions from the various countries will confirm the impression that the large majority of artists of the world have gone on to an experimentalism which was, perhaps, implicit in the forces released by the machine civilization of the world'. In the Indian context, it is enough that we remember that in trying to do what the white masters do in their own lands, or trying to make European culture our own, we imitate and behave like spoilt children. As Anand said in the preface to the first triennale catalogue, the Lalit Kala's brainchild, the first triennale, 'will emulate the example set by Venice, the Sao Paulo, the Paris and the Tokyo biennales'. After hearing reports of what was collected in the first triennale, Berger never took any interest in the Indian experiment of organizing international contemporary art exhibitions. Enough to say that a blind, indiscriminate assimilation of the culture of the mother-countries goes on in India, giving birth to new culture colonies in the name of symbolism and surrealism.

Such international exhibitions of contemporary art in a country where the process of unqualified assimilation goes on at the slow pace of Indian time are bound to prove counterproductive, promoting a model of art making that will only make popular certain closed concepts of art. This became evident from the casual remarks by Karl Khandalavala, chairman of the Lalit Kala Akademi. When he saw a cement drainpipe lying on one of the lawns of the Akademi, he asked it to be removed immediately. Upon learning it was one of the exhibits (of the second triennale) he kept quiet and confessed that until that day he had not been able to understand why a seemingly utilitarian object like the cement drainpipe should have been granted the exalted status of a work of art. This explains why the third triennale is such a poor neutral presentation of art and can be thought of as an enriching experience only in a provincial situation.

Karl Khandalavala's cement drainpipe joke was actually meant to tell his audience that their provincial sensibilities would not be hurt because by a sleight of hand the Akademi has been able to keep out from the current exhibition those works which could at best be described as intellectual game-playing as, for instance, Australian artist Robert Hunter's avant-garde wall decoration in the second triennale. It was such works that Berger had in mind when he spoke of India escaping from the hegemony of Western art. The American section in the second triennale put up constructions by eight American artists, which in the words of the American Commissioner, Waldo Rasmussen, 'challenged the concept of the work of art as a discrete object for sale to museums and collectors'. He also reminded his Indian audience that 'for many of the artists, Indian thought and the Indian way of life have been special inspirations, and it seems particularly appropriate that five of the artists are creating new works for the triennale responding to the unique sense of place which India provides'. It is indeed curious that even advanced art of the nature we witnessed in the second triennale needed a kind of protectionist home in a museum, or to be presented as part of the international contemporary art show.

PRISONERS OF HISTORY

The kind of stress visible in the American exhibits is indeed no different from the uncertainties and fears about the avant-garde that bedevil the thoughts of the Akademi's bureaucrats. So, we have gone in for a rather detached kind of art certified by art history, as most of the exhibits from the advanced art centres belong to the art modes of the early Sixties. What seems a graver threat is that the Akademi bureaucrats have proved themselves to be prisoners of art history, wanting something that will meet with unquestioning acceptance the category of 'art', of which they have no clear notion except that it is a culture symbol. Gone are also those intellectualist criticisms of international exhibitions of contemporary art often heard in the heat of the second triennale, the 'boycott Lalit Kala' movement. It is indeed interesting that the artist protesting at the brutal cultural wash he received at the hand of the second triennale committee has won the award in the third triennale. No doubt, the glibness and the over-simplifications indulged in by these old protesters, who have now become the insiders of the Akademi, are part of the superstar's symbolic mechanisms that he needs for his psychic survival.

OPAQUE

The voices of dissent, angry protests, demonstrations and other publicity gimmicks have now given way to artful communication with the national commissioners of many participating countries who are in the capital, and the talks hinge on rational discourse, sophisticated theorizing, psychological probing, problems of unity of form and content, considered as a set of external references in relation to differing cultural landscapes. Membership to the Indian art circuit is secured by alienation from the self-contradictory local art scene, born of bad faith because it will not recognize its provincial status in relation to the metropolitan art centre, and by putting up a strong showing in international art exhibitions. So, the artists who gain most are those who are much talked about on a level coextensive with their New York contemporaries; their recognition coming in terms of their being the avant-garde. Of course, the rules of the avant-garde game are all made outside, in New York, and the role of these provincial avant-garde lie in the fact that they too easily institutionalize them and thus guarantee that the New York art scene decides what art games to play, how one plays it and who should win.

It is in this sense that the international art fairs, wherever they are held, in Paris, in Tokyo, in Sao Paulo or in Venice, have proved to be counterproductive. What is awarded, displayed and written about most in these art fairs is no doubt competent art, but created within currently fashionable art categories. They are invariably dull shows, as witnessed in the third Triennale-India: the evidence of localism in advanced countries like West Germany and Japan is totally absent. The accelerated avant-gardeism may look like a dazzling ballerina's display of skill but it is inconceivable that the New York audience will have the same reaction. The international exhibitions turn out, in the provincial setting of modern art, to be a demonstration of competence in putting up a brave show of national self-image – to prove how well the notion of competence itself has become commitment of a style. It is indeed a self-defeating exercise, the provincial artist paying exaggerated homage to his metropolitan master and acknowledging at the same time his own limitations of the local scene. Thus, he is always unsure of himself, his performance tested against the performances of closely similar selves and it is at this level of self-construction of reality that he realizes that it is stupid to speak of his art product as the work of his hands: he verbalizes, speaks with arrogance that suggests authoritarian, anti-social accents.

'emotional'
el painting,
oncept of a
ty": Berger
ing eye for
New Delhi
from the
must have
Delhi trien-
ile a stare
rt centres
the nuclear

y indeed—
ceptual art
their own
ne perspec-
art. There
Delhi trien-
ng more of
we been
unal vision
l notion of
colonialist
these three
have been
stic partici-
ding con-
have really
ing a new
end to the
matters of

tion system
ed by the
ns, works
no function
stars', and
ctured that
of his sur-
utions. And
artist who
metropoli-
sixties, but
hout a sup-
es will not
a whatever
r sold like
nd art his-
old mental
ined, to see
nost profes-
ched rules
not willing
s and con-
l up by the
aphysics of

creation of
as religious
would have
ground for

ti Dave

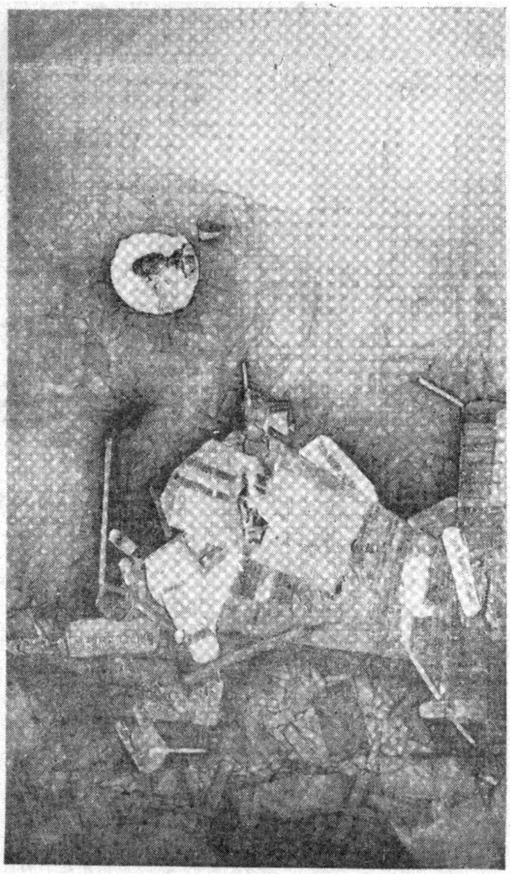

What is awarded and displayed and written about most in international art fairs is no doubt competent art but created within currently fashionable art categories. They are invariably dull shows as witness the third Triennale-India at Rabindra Bhavan, New Delhi

this. Mind you, most of the well know conceptualists have already becom famous for their extreme styles, acti as avant-garde determinants of ideas what is good taste. They also symboli the crisis of the distribution system Western art; and for the simple reas that this new avant-garde has refus to transform itself into an agent of t art market. The result would have be had India invited these "conceptualis to its Triennales, that a large numb of this taste-making class would ha come to India as art emigres. As C Andre, the famous militant artist the Art Workers Coalition, said at t time of the second New Delhi trienn India lost an opportunity to strip ba the myth of superior Western cultu

MISSING

Berger, it seems, has overrated t intelligence of the first Triennale or nisers in responding the way he d He "wished" clear-sightedness a courage: and these two things were sin larly missing, for to put-up the kind international exhibition which wou have become an escape from the co nial cultural matrix if not a challen to the hegemony of European art was necessary that the host count should have founded art on an authe tic, sustaining culture of its own. E the surrogates of two cultures—natio as well as international—more at ho with art seen from a 'universal' sta point will have only a 'neutral' pres tation of everything that has the sta

(Continued on page 4)

The split in the art-making activity is the product of bad faith, the self-construction of a subjectivity that has no relation to the artwork produced, utterly false and consciously put-on: subjectivity becomes the dream content because style is not the way to discovering his self-identity but merely a performance act whose historical constituents he has never tested in terms of ideology: rather he is surrounded with several duplicates of ideology. He operates only on a level of self-awareness, and this is structured around some axiomatic beliefs and unquestioned assumptions about the notion of the artist: he is convinced that, what he creates is art because what he expresses is something that has never existed before.

What these international exhibitions in a place like New Delhi prove is the special aura that surrounds the work of an expatriate artist: his presence is immediately felt in the same way as his absence missed. This complex historical role of the expatriate is a vindication of the belief that the provincial art depends for its justification as valid and significant art on the works of the expatriates and not on those who are representative of the local scene. This has been our experience that once the expatriate decides to come back home losing contact with the metropolitan art centre, he is regarded only as a local celebrity: and if he stays long, the seminal impulses that characterized his art as belonging to the metropolis fail and he does not know how to work out his change in style within the framework of the local art world. He is no longer considered the celebrity and he is as confused as others in the provincial setting. He would think himself lucky if his new native accents are recognized and thus he is able to find his feet again. Or, if the metropolitan art scene has changed completely where he has no chance of getting a foothold in new art's emerging power structure, he is sunk. He tenuously keeps to the minority group identifications as crutches: the only door open for such an artist is the outlet through some international art exhibition. By implications that are not difficult to work out we have the international show, currently the third Triennale-India, for this expatriate so that he can again make it in a big way.

57

IN BONDAGE TO NARROW SELF

An assessment of the Indian art exhibited at the 'Kala Mela' alongside the fourth Triennale-India held in 1978

Link, New Delhi, 26 February 1978

For the last two weeks the capital has seen so much of art that it need not have art for a whole year: it has become virtually a festival city. The Kala Mela, organized as an adjunct to the fourth Triennale show, is the biggest art carnival ever enacted in the capital: it has attracted more than a thousand artists from all over the country. There are about 130 stalls of which forty-five are devoted to one-man shows: put up at the Bhawalpur House complex and for a period of three weeks, the mela provides the right conditions for viewing art objects. Absent in the mela is the external clown – we mean the so-called art critic – who comes in the way of artists and their audience: what is enacted is very close to spontaneous theatre where participation is the rule of the game. Not like the experience one has inside Kafka's castle, housing art objects from forty countries, projecting a construction of reality that has a limited human base, being in the nature of a contractual agreement as reached by the hero of *The Castle*. Putting it in another way, it is more like a house of consciousness where what is called personal time is at the service of a higher historical time which is built on the premise that man with his narrow reason and vision is not allowed to be free but in constant bondage to his narrow self. One does not have to grope in the dust to recognize the contours of this castle: its opaque, dense nature conjured up in a different form was given to us a little more than a month ago by the *Pictorial Space* exhibition (between 14 December and 3 January) put up by critic, Geeta Kapur.

It was no doubt for the first time that we had the experience of a theme exhibition: it provided us with a singular level of perception where the secret of a work of art was sought to be disclosed in a transparent language. Surely, it was not an exercise in the reductive use of pictorial language: the job was to present a model exhibition of spatial paradigms. In the absence of felt correspondences between visual observations and pictorial records (which has become evident in painting after Cezanne replaced it with graphic signals), it is evident that a grammar of one kind or another is necessary for understanding this new painting. This new approach to exhibitions, which seeks to provide necessary platforms to make recognition implicit in any encounter between the work of art and its public, was indeed a welcome development. And we looked forward to the real thing and its important implication, for we were promised that the fourth triennale was to be structured in terms of a concept with emphasis on the humanistic values in art. 'The fourth Triennale-India', we were told, 'proposes to bring together and project such abiding tendencies in world art which refuse to be submerged by the widespread, faceless, cosmopolitan trends that have passing retinal appeal or are merely formalistic'.

In other words, what was to be projected was the independence of the dialogue between the works of art and their public. This is not to deny that art is not a special kind of language: the language-like nature of the arts has not put us off, certainly when the supremacy of the dialogue – and not an art which is 'merely cerebral, coterie inspired, formalistic, made-to-order or experimental merely for the sake of experiment and innovation' [catalogue] – was offered in the dialectical sense for us to participate in. And since we are what we are lacking, the melody of experience has become the exclusive preserve of the arts. The show promised us experience of becoming, of emergence, of participation between the 'I' and the 'Other' – the two poles of tension we sought to converge through this invitation to the works embodying human values, an art promising us a dialectical transformation of our stale patterns of perception. That grand vision now is ground to dust. There is so much mud on the canvas.

SIX PAINTERS

Take the case of [the] six painters who declined to show at the triennale. Their exhibition at the Kumar Gallery (Hansalaya branch) is in the nature of protest and 'to express their solidarity in opposition to an act of chicanery by the organizers of the fourth triennale – the triennale committee, and the general council of the Lalit Kala Akademi.'[1] They were among the twenty-two artists whose work commissioners thought represented new emergent trends in the Seventies. By electing to show in a group of six artists and not involving other painters and sculptors who were selected by Ramachandran,[2] they have unwittingly played into the hands of their detractors. In fact, the real issues as emerged

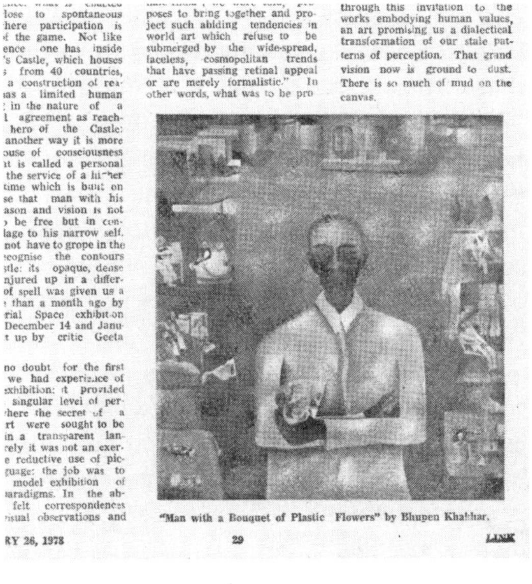
lose to spontaneous
here participation is
f the game. Not like
ence one has inside
's Castle, which houses
s from 40 countries,
a construction of rea-
as a limited human
in the nature of a
l agreement as reach-
hero of the Castle:
another way it is more
ouse of consciousness
it is called a personal
the service of a hi-her
time which is built on
se that man with his
ason and vision is not
be free but in con-
lage to his narrow self.
not have to grope in the
ecognise the contours
stle: its opaque, dense
njured up in a differ-
of spell was given us a
than a month ago by
rial Space exhibition
December 14 and Janu-
t up by critic Geeta

no doubt for the first
we had experience of
exhibition: it provided
singular level of per-
here the secret of a
rt were sought to be
in a transparent lan-
rely it was not an exer-
e reductive use of pic-
guage: the job was to
model exhibition of
aradigms. In the ab-
felt correspondences
nsual observations and

poses to bring together and pro-
ject such abiding tendencies in
world art which refuse to be
submerged by the wide-spread,
faceless, cosmopolitan trends
that have passing retinal appeal
or are merely formalistic." In
other words, what was to be pro

through this invitation to the
works embodying human values,
an art promising us a dialectical
transformation of our stale pat-
terns of perception. That grand
vision now is ground to dust.
There is so much of mud on the
canvas.

"Man with a Bouquet of Plastic Flowers" by Bhupen Khakhar.

RY 26, 1978 29 LINK

from Ramachandran's resignation [and that of the other commissioners] have been distorted by lending to their work an unwarranted loading of authority. The exhibition has divided the artists who were in the original list. Or is there more to it than meets the eye? But however exceptional their gesture might seem, it is a necessary exhibition to bring to public notice the rigged-up nature of the national section in the triennale show. Only such a committee could have done the trick of mounting an exhibition within a couple of weeks.

Not without reason, the preface to the Indian section is silent about the 'primacy of the image' theme of the triennale. Whether the Indian section represents the 'well-reasoned and well-conceived cross-section of Indian art' is for the public to judge. As against the disapproval of more enterprising art which the works of twenty-two artists represent, an addition of works by another five dozen artists represents the conspicuous virtue to err in favour of the majority and thereby expose themselves to the charge that our art culture is what our culture lacks. If nostalgia has meaning for artists, our memories go back to the strong showing that the Indian section made in the first triennale. In an almost as-if way, many of our artists whose work remains un-assessed are willing to bind themselves into a surrogate relationship to the art of the signature painters. And these artists are not asking for a larger portion of the cake the Akademi offers: they would willingly withdraw to a kind of rationalized regionalism only if they knew that the regional alternative would not suffer from the inbuilt unfairness of art's hierarchical structure. They must be seen making their contribution to the art scene, this is the crux of the issue.

JURY

The international jury has seen the significance of the regional styles as an agent of change in the Indian situation and the award to Nandagopal's *Ritual Image* will go a long way in strengthening local traditions. Of course, those who are in the habit of seeing art in terms of significance and quality – the terms which have implications of superiority – will be disappointed. Painting, like any other creative activity, is a conditional enterprise, even existential, in the sense that one's visual culture cannot be seen existing independent of the conditions of visibility in a local art scene. In that sense, the award to Nandagopal should be seen as a setback to that section of critical enterprise which encourages formalism as a constituent of contemporary trends.

The Indian art establishment, presided over by the Triennale Cell, owes to Indian artists an explanation why a few months ago the *Pictorial Space* exhibition was forced on us; the radical posture of giving to the fourth triennale a perspective of human values seems merely a gimmick. Was it a deception that every image is the coincidence of dialectic between illusion and idea? The *Pictorial Space* exhibition was an exercise to define the exclusively visual nature of illusion in painting and give to the idea part of the dialectic the certitude of an ideological proposition. No doubt, the triennale concept does not suffer from the limited position of formalism as *Pictorial Space* exhibition did. But the kind of show that emerged finally gives the impression that formalism covers a very wide area; indeed, it seems to encompass all painting including the misleading coherence implied in the ideology of cultural convergence.

BHUPEN KHAKHAR

The only artist who perhaps would not find the picture we have drawn, banal, is Bhupen Khakhar who, in his art, celebrates the thingness of a thing; his art does not admit such critical fabrications as manufacture or handicraft as opposed to production as creation. Not given to dreams, his work in essence is the work of labour. 'Why are all my reactions to art polluted by history, culture and friends?' he asks. Perhaps because his paintings are not very different from picture postcards, calendars, which, he says, are not 'part of an artistic heritage: they are pure, untouched and objective'.

Art in the West (and in India also, it being still a colony of the West) has reached a stage of mechanical redundancy that no amount of critical analysis can save. The entire superstructure of the Western art world has become part of the repressive decadence of the late capitalist era that 'cultural criticism' in the words of Adorno 'even at its best with Valery sides with conservatism'.[3] Indian contemporary art too has become an inseparable limb of bourgeoisie, a form of 'property which is stable and independent of stock-market fluctuations'.[4]

Editor's Notes

1 'Six Who Declined to Show at the Triennale', catalogue text. The six artists were Gieve Patel, Laxma Goud, Bhupen Khakhar, Vivan Sundaram, Mrinalini Mukherjee and Gulammohammed Sheikh.

2 Artist A. Ramachandran, one of the three commissioners of the fourth Triennale. The other two were sculptor Nagji Patel and art critic Pranabranjan Ray.

3 Theodor Adorno, 'Cultural Criticism and Society', in *Can One Live After Auschwitz?: A Philosophical Reader*, California: Stanford University Press, 2003, p. 150.

4 Ibid. Adorno's statement references conservative cultural critic and poet Paul Valery, whose 1919 essay, 'The Crisis of the Mind', opened with the statement, 'we later civilizations . . . we too know now that we are mortal', reflecting the sombre European mood in the wake of the First World War. Adorno's statement reads: 'If cultural criticism, even at its best with Valery, sides with conservatism, it is because of its unconscious adherence to a notion of culture, which during the era of late capitalism aims at a form of property which is stable and independent of stock market fluctuations. This idea of culture asserts its distance from the system in order, as it were, to offer universal security in the middle of a universal dynamic'.

58

SEVENTH TRIENNALE: SIFTING THROUGH A CRAFT MELA

Review of the seventh edition of the Triennale-India held in 1991

'Artscape', *The Economic Times*, New Delhi, 11 March 1991

The experience of the works displayed at the seventh triennale is disappointing. Going through the two galleries of the Lalit Kala Akademi and a makeshift gallery in the Bhawalpur House is in no way different from going through a crafts bazaar. The disappointment verges on frustration because it lacks what one expects - one fails to locate a single referential dimension one looks for in a show which claims to present world art.

In purely statistical terms, the show is impressive. The international jury has considered about 600 works, comprising nearly 300 paintings. There are about 200 graphic prints and drawings and 73 sculptures. In qualitative terms, the works are so poor that it will be wrong to call it a provincial show. The Indian section is a nightmare and for this, the Akademi bureaucrats are to be blamed. The Akademi laid down a fresh rule under which artists who had exhibited their works in the previous two triennales were not eligible to participate. Consequently, most senior artists remained out of this triennale. And all this, courtesy the art politics which has turned the Akademi into a Kafka-like castle. In the novel, *The Castle*, it is difficult to locate the sources of authority. So is it with the Akademi.

That the seventh triennale is the poorest is borne out by the fact that out of the ten awards, two were withheld. Out of three members of the international jury, two were Indians: Anand Dev, a painter and also the vice-president of the Akademi and the 76-year-old sculptor, Chintamoni Kar. Mikio Soejima, a Japanese art historian, was the only foreign member of the jury. The truth behind withholding the awards is pernicious. They were withheld, according to some authoritative sources, because the two foreign jury members - Llilian Llanes (Cuba)[1] and Augusta Monferrini, (Italy, art historian) could not come in time for judging. Llane did come but by that time the judging was over.

Since the jury said nothing to explain why the two awards were withheld, the inference is obvious: either because these awards were reserved for the countries the two absent jury members came from, or because the exhibits were not good enough for the awards. Which reading of the situation sounds more probable is not the point. What is disgusting is that India is happy with having bagged two awards, especially for works which do not substantiate that judging at the international level involves some irrefutable time-tested norms. It appears to be lackadaisical: every award perhaps was a bargain.

The seventh triennale therefore stands exposed. The two awards (one for Abbas Batliwala's painting, *Nostalgia* and another for two of Prayag Jha's etchings called *Bachelor's House* that India has collected, mean nothing in the context of the observation that in this triennale the works in the Indian section represent a kind of kitschy aesthetic for which there are no buyers in the art scene of the 1990s.

Kitsch acquired legitimacy in the context of the supreme value we put on the aesthetics of the new. The aesthetics of the new has converted art into an industrial commodity: art now can be compared and contrasted as if it were another commodity which would not suffer any loss of elegance when seen the way it is seen today. The Sao Paulo biennales support this proposition. Since the aesthetics of the new turns a contemporary practice of a given mode of art into the kitsch of tomorrow, the new bourgeoisie can have only kitsch for appreciation because it comes as a piece of yesterday's merchandise. Besides, he is not required to refer his pick of art to any established modes of taste. For, good taste belongs truly to the world of imagination, always treating art as its raw material. So all our critical judging – whether at a national or international level – is merely an expression of a given condition of taste which provides the artist a culture space in which to operate with some feeling of stability.

The situation is different when art is seen as an enterprise seeking stability in the material world as does good taste in the world of the imagination. The merchandized art is never an independent, autonomous art object, but merely an aspect of art: for, it does not take place in its own setting; as it always refers to the future it has no meaning in the present, being one of the modes of merchandized operation. And the rejection of this meaning of art is the point of art's basic enterprise. Pop works, for example, really never exists fully anywhere since, pop by definition lacks in specificity, in fullness. The artist's individuality, his work, is nothing: only a sign, an instance of what constitutes the history of merchandise. For, the pop image is located in its first usable forms in the world of advertising and the entertainment industry.

The art we get from foreign countries for display in our triennale internationals is art within quotation marks, an exportable item seen as a means of establishing one's cultural superiority. The triennale is not the place where India can hope to establish its cultural superiority: no developed country takes our triennales seriously because it is not the place where reputations can be made – in a country which could never manage to show its works in the Venice biennales. Japan, for instance, has won a prize in every triennale (except the fifth one) and has presented category-grounded variations on what has been the currently popular piece of merchandise in New York. If Japan has had a strong showing in all our triennales it is because it has proved that America is in its bones: the commodity culture has no national soul. Besides, the yen has acquired a fine art context in translating, with an obsessional rigour, the interconnections with the mass media, the urban landscape of waste and alienation.

In Miran Fukuda's five works (acrylic on panel), we have this collage-like eye-catching visual information system that has an externality of reference without a hint of interiority. Technique-wise they are superior and more experimental – more radical than anything seen in the works of similar modes from other countries. Hers are the true advertisement images with a vulgar blend of past and present: they are like despair putting on a mask.

This mask is off in Luigi Ontani's work called *Shivalandohanuman-drogins*. For, in India, Ontani is doing what the Indians do to engage themselves for a breath of life from the mythical god Pygmalion. If the god is pleased and the boon granted, the epiphany grounded in the work may come alive and become an event of real life. For the artist Ontani, it almost comes true. His is the largest work displayed, measuring disproportionately 140 by 3,600 cms, decorating the whole wall at the entrance point of the Lalit Kala gallery. The work is good theatre: it is intended to ridicule the old distinction that theatre always seeks to hide – the distinction between appearance and essence, and between surface phenomenon and profound, real processes – without the knowledge of which the dualistic Western worldview cannot be comprehended. This happens just as in good theatre events unroll themselves. What interrupts the horizontal spread are the photographs of the artist in various theatrical guises: seen in some as Shiva, in others as Krishna, Durga or Hanuman.

Ontani was in India between 1975 and 1976, the years of the Emergency. Since then, he has become an India convert, producing works soaked in personalized myths. The images appear as apparitions which are lost to the unattentive eye – the image of the Sagittarian which Ontani calls his own, a composition of two bodies – a man and horse; or the Shiva image transforming itself into Kali because both have numerous arms – all emerging from the bust. Such is Ontani's involvement with India that at the 1978 Venice Biennale he turned up dressed in Indian silk with a turban on his head.

This montaged variety of confessional art is what has become the quintessential image of the Western participation [in the triennnales] of which 50-year-old Gareth Sansom from Australia is the true representative. Sansom came to India with a view to producing work for the seventh triennale. And according to the Australian commissioner, Terence Maloon, he tried to produce one watercolour a day in his stay of four months; what if they do not hold our attention the way Ontani's Indian ethnicity does. Similarly, British painter Gillian Ayres makes a collage of colourful kites and runs away with a prize.

It should not be a matter of regret if the West does not take our triennale seriously: no colonial slave should ever dare look into the eyes of his former masters. That is not in keeping with the style of a true comedian, whether he is Quixote or Sancho: the limits of fallibility should never slip out of our sight.

Editor's Note

1 Llilian Llanes: art historian and, later, curator of Museo Wilfredo, Lam, Havana. The Havana Biennial for which the commissioner of the Indian section was K.B. Goel was also held in 1991, the year of this review. See pp. 375–79 of this volume for Goel's curatorial note on the same.

SECTION THREE

ART AN

IDEAS

Concepts and ideas stimulating art practice were central to K.B. Goel's interests as an art critic. While his primary mode remained the art review, using an exhibition review as occasion, he frequently dwelt on aspects of art raised by the art on feature. Included in this section are Goel's reflections on contemporary trends, styles, movements and social/cultural concerns – from minimalism, pop art, socially responsive art, the Bengal School style, technology-driven art, neo-realism, to an assessment of John Berger's position as a critical voice on art or wider cultural concerns such as growing communalism in the country and the artist's response to it as a political being.

59

POP OR ADVERTISEMENT ART?

On pop art and its close affinity to advertising

Link, New Delhi, 11 July 1965

Now and then, just as piano keys have to be tuned, clearing the decks becomes necessary for they get cluttered up easily with the unnecessary. But things get difficult when the decks are cleared without a single fight; or when the piano-tuner sits for days and months, without a tune being played. One gets exasperated, sick and finally indifferent. This is exactly what has happened to modern painting – especially to painting of the post-Second World War period. Cubism, more than impressionism, was all right; it not only cleared the decks totally but fought a last-ditch battle with literary subjectivism, which dominated painting since the Renaissance.

A WAY OF PROTEST

Even after the brilliant success of cubism, the fight went on for causes which, though unrelated to visual arts, voiced the general anguish, pain and uncertainties of our times. It was part of the general cleaning up in the arts, beginning with philosophy and the movement against metaphysics. The logical positivist Wittgenstein performed the burial ceremony. He said: 'The philosophical discussion should lend to show that philosophical discussion is a mistake. His attempt was very much like that of Karl Barth who wrote some 15,000 words to discover that theological discourse was impossible. The linguistic philosophers further purged philosophy of its literal nonsense, particularly of Wittgenstein's quest for purpose. A group in France cut the hero-world out of fiction, and in the theatre, Brecht jettisoned much of Aristotelian sentimentalism.

It was a way of protest which continued well into the mid-1930s – until the outbreak of the Second World War. After the war, the means became the end; the act of clearing the decks was confused with fighting or winning a battle. The subjectivism of the painter became a means of escape; art, instead of being a critical discourse between man and man, became a therapeutic exercise. Emotion became the mainspring of visual arts, an element against which stood the whole movement of modern art.

For nearly two decades, the decks were loaded with the rubbish of this subjective emotionalism until, in the 1960s, pop artists came and swept it off. Groomed by dada and formed by cubism, they indulged in a kind of shock therapy. It was the same kind of treatment that was once administered by cubists and dadaists but in a new form. Their paintings are violently theatrical, more stunt than anything else, with almost a funhouse atmosphere. There was more noise than sense in what they said. The point of this noise was an art which involved the artist the least; he stood as far away from painting as a consumer does from the advertisement image of a product he wishes to buy.

THE ADVERTISEMENT ART

For many good reasons, pop art is regarded as a superior relation to advertising art. It has the same directness and non-involvement with the product. It utilizes all those means that advertisements do. Likewise, it is also didactic. It is a brand of realism which had cut itself off long ago from all ties with social realism, photographic naturalism, and the dull academicism of the nineteenth century. While the advertisement image has no attitude of its own to share with the consumer, the pop image of the same object is a comment. It exaggerates reality to the point of making it look absurd. The result is that this exaggerated image excludes the viewer's sympathy. He stands cool before a pop work without any personal emotion. This non-involvement is the essence of pop art. But few pop artists can claim to have achieved this detachment. Even artists like Jasper Johns and Rauschenberg, painting as no one has ever done before, have failed; their works do involve the viewer. So does the desert-stage imagery of [Philip C.] Curtis and the frontality of [Wayne] Thiebaud's figures which outdo the Sphinx.[1]

MARCEL DUCHAMP

Only the grandfather of pop realism, Marcel Duchamp, 78, (famous for his *Nude Descending a Staircase*) was really an uninvolved painter. He started as a follower of Toulouse-Lautrec, picked up fauvist manners and cubist vocabulary and finally gave up each to arrive at the devastating conclusion that chess playing was a more fruitful activity than painting. Between 1913, the year he painted the famous *Nude Descending a Staircase* and 1923, the year he abandoned painting finally, he experimented with many things, all of which were aimed at showing that art could be made of anything, just as earlier painters since Gustave Courbet demonstrated that anything could be a subject of painting. There was no end to the gimmicks he played with man and machine-made objects. He once hung a snow shovel and said it was a 'readymade' work of art, whimsically titling it *In Advance of a Broken Arm*. His *Why not Sneeze?* was nothing but a bird cage filled with lumps of sugar. He exhibited a urinal in 1917 and called it *Fountain*.

He abandoned oil painting because it was old hat and he was too much of an intellectual. 'I gave up painting,' said Duchamp, 'because I felt it was too retinal. It didn't go beyond the eyes'. In saying this, he was demanding a redefinition of visual arts. The proof of a good painting, according to him, was not the pleasurable sensation it evoked but the amount of intelligence it disclosed. Surely, little intelligence is needed to paint abstract pictures; even domestic animals can do it. It is strange that, when so much has been mined from Duchamp's paintings (once considered too naughty) by pop artists, they seem to have missed the point of their message. Duchamp certainly detests involvement but he is sick of advertisement art that most pops tend to become.

Editor's Note

1 Philip Curtis created a large number of works broadly within the landscape category inspired by the desert and landscape of Arizona in the 1940s. Featuring Victorian figures and tropes in the desert setting, his works created a magic realist and fantasy world as opposed to representing the desert unlike some contemporary artists, and they form the highlight of the art museum at Phoenix, Arizona. A significant pop artist, Wayne Thiebaud is known mainly for paintings of brightly coloured confectionery and everyday objects in the 1950s and landscapes of (largely) rural America. Said to have influenced painters such as Edward Hopper with his style of neo-realism, Thiebaud's human figures possessed a marked frontality that K.B. Goel here remarks on.

60

THE ART OF THE REAL

Reflections on the movement of minimalism emerging in contemporary art in the 1960s

Link, New Delhi, 15 June 1969

Modern art seems to have reached the end of the road. Otherwise painters would not have abandoned the trail and taken to making objects – objects which are so much canvas and so much paint and which have no message and no emotional referents. These objects are necessarily big because scale is their content and theatrical presence their form. They are often bigger than the space they occupy, otherwise they would not make the intended impact, nor would they appear out of place. The scale and theatricality (out of place-ness), indeed, are basic to these objects which are described as pieces of minimal (also literal) art. Some art historians prefer to call them exemplifications of some sort of macrocosmic art because these giant objects keep the spectator forever at bay and set up a wall – most intractable and brutal.

MINIMAL OBJECTS

We have yet to see in India these objects which have become quite commonplace in the world's important art centres. Not even in the Delhi triennale were we treated to a single minimal object, although many Indian painters have become aggressively minimal-minded. Eric Bowen's recent exhibition is an instance, although his paintings are by no means influenced by the minimal wave. Of course, being unit composed, they can easily be blown up to minimal [ist] dimensions. Our excitement is natural: we read such a lot and see minimal objects in reproductions so often in art magazines. And there is no hope of our seeing them actually because minimal objects cannot be transported easily because of their size. There is also the fear that the technological finish may quite likely be damaged in the process of transportation. The third reason why these objects will never come to India is that we have no idea how to present them in a gallery. We do not have a gallery to fit them in. Even such an established gallery as the Sonnabend Gallery in Paris found it a job handling minimal works by the Californian artist, John McCracken, who exhibited his seven coloured planks there. Five of his planks were about seven and a half feet high. Each of McCracken's one-colour plank was exhibited in a single room with spotlessly white walls.

The McCracken planks had no support of their own and were put leaning upright against the wall as if they were a magical intrusion. Now, the Sonnabend Gallery did not have seven rooms – each room had to be totally empty where a single plank, quite alone, was to lean against the wall in an all-white space. But the exhibition in Paris was a craze and the gallery did manage the McCracken planks – only god knows how. However, the colour reproductions were very charming, very pretty, though there was hardly anything there to distinguish one plank from another except that one was blue, another mauve, the third green and so forth.

Actually, the McCracken plank does not represent the proper minimal size which is far more macroscopic and gigantic. For instance, Ronald Bladen's constructions well exemplify the importance of scale in minimal art. The construction called *Scale as Content*, a painted wood piece, was 22 feet wide, 26 feet long and 14 feet high. Shaped like an X, it almost reached the ceiling and looked very much like an abstract giant.

VISUAL GAME

In other words, minimal art will never reach India for a gallery show. And unless it is shown, its local adaptation is also highly unlikely because our painters simply do not know how to play the visual game with rules of their own invention. Then there is another reason against our not going in for minimal creations; which is that minimalism is a product of electronic technology which is absent in India. So many of our self-styled minimal-minded painters must have read with great interest the debate which the minimal exhibition has given rise to among London's art critics. Organized by the New York Museum of Modern Art, the exhibition at the Tate Gallery is called *The Art of the Real*. The exhibition, which ended on June 1, was not so well received as it was hoped; most critics found themselves at a loss when at the time of press view (April 24) things were not ready and in shape. The organizers had clearly not realized the difficulties of hanging, because to make the minimal objects look [like] works of art they have to be put in a theatrical situation, which is clearly not an easy thing. In fact, there is a clear rule of hanging: the simpler the works the more precisely they have to be hung.

The main point of the debate among the London critics was not about the quality of the works they were confronted with but the semantic tease indulged in by American art critic E.C. Goossen who had written a brief introduction to the exhibition. Firstly, he had taken for granted possible British ignorance of minimal art which he thought was America's special contribution to modern art of the Sixties, just as abstract-expressionism was thought to be in the Fifties' America's great leap forward in the art world. So, the introduction warned British viewers that they should not expect this exhibition to be an exhibition of realism. The introduction said, 'Today's real makes no direct appeal to the emotions, nor is it involved in uplift, but instead offers itself in the form of the simple, irreducible, irrefutable object'. Goossen's game did not impress anyone. A critic even said rather ironically –

> One may as well join in (the game) and deny straightaway that they are either irreducible or irrefutable. They would all be much closer to irreducibility if they were ground to dust and the act of grinding them down would constitute a gesture of refutation. One needn't, in any case, have any qualms about destroying them.[1]

NICE CARPET

He did not stop at that but suggested, instead, that in case these objects were at all considered functional (and it is claimed that minimals are functional) at least some could be put to better use. For instance–

> Robert Morris's white slab could certainly be used as a platform; if Donald Judd's painted wood cube is hollow, one side of it could be cut out to turn it into a bicycle shed, but it's so execrably painted that it would spoil the look of any suburban garden; Carl Andre's 144 pieces of aluminum laid out on the floor of the Tate to form a large square would make a nice metal carpet for people who could stand its squeaking every time they walked across it, and any collector who owns one of McCracken's coloured planks could put it across a couple of trestles whenever he wanted to whitewash the ceiling.[2]

Goossen arranged the exhibition historically and used his arbitrary judgement to exclude many of the more important American painters who, it seems, did not influence the minimal object-makers. What principles of selection Goossen observed were not clear but the works of some of the painters he included gave a clue. A few works by Pollock, Morris Louis and Newman showed that Goossen thinks that the freehand, semi-automatic abstraction was a forerunner of minimalism. Here, too, he is wrong because minimal literalism does not have history and its godfather is Marcel Duchamp, and not the abstract expressionists. In fact, what the London critic we have just quoted has said about some of the minimal works which can serve a practical purpose was, in fact, caricaturing Duchamp's comment on Rembrandt which he said can be used as an ironing stand.

Goossen too has borrowed some of Duchamp's rhetorics. For instance, he says that the art of the past was concerned with fobbing us off with symbols instead of giving us facts. He, therefore, included in the show some paintings where the paint has soaked in and become part of the canvas. What he wanted to prove was perhaps this: a canvas is more real than paint. It is indeed difficult even for knowledgeable critics to say what actually the American minimal movement is about. Critic E. Devling who attempts a definition in an anthology of American art criticism published by Studio Vista last month, makes it so broad that anything that happened in America's post-abstract expressionist period can be included as part of the minimal movement. He says –

> The minimal artist is only interested in a totality or whole and not in an interplay and relationship among parts of the work of art, and not at all in composition. In order to get rid of all compositional effects very simple primary forms are used which have neither parts nor relationships but just form an indissoluble whole.

Definition apart, is such an art possible? Can anything be created which has no parts but just a whole? A painting can be without subject matter, without any brushstrokes used, but how can one do away with composition? A canvas can be empty – just pure white or painted in any single colour – but the moment it is hung against a wall, it gets a compositional definition. If this is not so, there is no point in calling them either paintings or sculptures; they are just 'objects' painted blue or white or some other colour – but colour without surface values, texture or tone. And they exist because they take up quite some space in an art gallery. Outside the gallery, they have no existence, no meaning.

Editor's Notes

1 Catalogue text of the exhibition when it was mounted at MoMA, New York, prior to the London exhibition. E.C. Goossen, *The Art of the Real: An Aspect of American Painting and Sculpture 1948–1968*, New York: Museum of Modern Art, 1968.

2 Ibid.

61

BERGER, ART AND PROPERTY

An assessment of the key ideas and art criticism of John Berger

Link, New Delhi, 21 September 1969

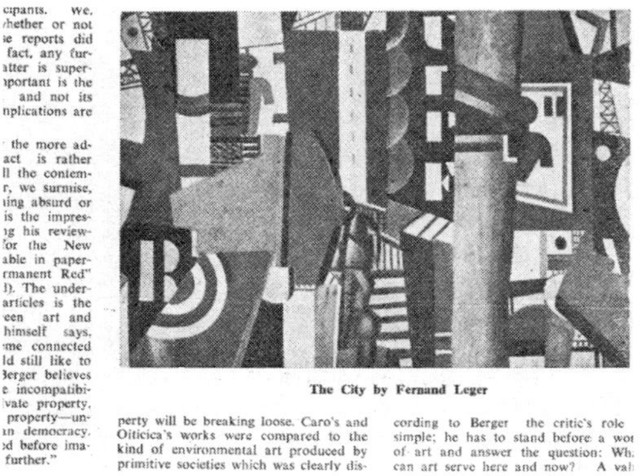

Painting has reached a point where the spectator seems to have acquired a totally irrelevant role. It very much looks as if painting now exists solely through what is being said about it. This surely must have been the assumption when two young Argentine painters enacted a 'happening' where nothing actually happened. But the painters did send reports of it to the press accompanied with photographs and statements of the participants. We, however, do not know whether or not an interpretation of these reports did appear in the papers. In fact, any further probing into the matter is superfluous because what is important is the nature of the happening and not its consequences. Its larger implications are simply frightening.

ART AND PROPERTY

How the more advanced critics would react is rather difficult to say. But of all the contemporary critics, John Berger, we surmise, will hardly find such a thing absurd or depressing. This, at least, is the impression we got after reading his reviews, mostly written for *The New Statesman* and now available in paperback under the title *Permanent Red* (Methuen, London, 12s 6d). The underlying theme of these articles is the disastrous relation between art and property. And Berger himself says, 'This is the only theme connected with art on which I would still like to write a whole book.' Berger believes that 'there is an absolute incompatibility between art and private property, or between art and state property – unless the state is a plebian democracy. Property must be destroyed before imagination can develop any further.'[1]

This is one way of arguing, though a little indirectly, that art criticism has no other function, whatever the critic's opinion, except to serve the art market. A humanist critic has certainly no place in the art market; what is demanded by such a market is criticism which is less interpretative and more descriptive. As a result of it, descriptive criticism has developed its own Wittgensteinism. So, we are not surprised when in 1968, Berger feels that he has changed a lot since he wrote criticism in the 1950s.

> As I re-read the book today I have the impression that I was trapped at that time: trapped in having to express all that I felt or thought in art-critical terms. In some respects, I would be more tolerant today. . . . I am more tolerant of those artists who are reduced to being largely destructive.[2]

In other words, Berger admits, though he does not say how, the art market laid the traps for him.

DESTRUCTIVE ART

In fact, since these review articles were written some ten or fifteen years ago, art has become more and more destructive; neo-dada and much of what passes in the name of environmental art is clearly opposed to aesthetics of permanence. The two recent exhibitions in London of the [sculptor, Anthony] Caro and [Helio] Oiticica environments clearly establish Berger's view that with art gaining more and more destructive postures, the relationship between art and property will be breaking loose. Caro's and Oiticica's works,[3] were compared to the kind of environmental art produced by primitive societies which was clearly disposable. The art object in its environmental setting was not for possessing; it was created primarily for totality-experience, out of human life, for enjoyment. The environmental art object has thus its own validity no doubt, but it is like the fetish symbol of primitive communities, of use so long as it served its purpose and later discarded when it was supposed to have lost its potency.

It is difficult, therefore, to judge what Berger thinks about this new development in painting; the new aesthetics of impermanence, he might say, has nothing new in it, the perishable art object of environmental art has, no doubt, its place in art commercialism and it plays a part in the environment of capitalism and industrialism as adjuncts of personal wealth and status. This is just a guess and which, for all we know, perhaps is a wrong one, because Berger does not talk either about surrealism or dadaism – neo or old – except for saying that surrealism is decadent. Which is indeed saying very little and therefore a pity because an art critic's education is hardly complete if he has not devoted himself seriously to a study of surrealism and dadaism. We assume then that Berger perhaps did not find any good opportunity to write about the surrealist painters.

MARXIAN CRITIC

This is, to be sure, not a quarrel with Berger because as a critic he is a class by himself; his art critical terms are related to the Marxian world view and not confined to any narrow aesthetic theorizing. In the introduction to the book, he defines what he thinks art criticism should be. According to Berger, the critic's role is simple. He has to stand before a work of art and answer the question: what can art serve here and now? A valid work of art should 'help or encourage men to know and claim their social rights'.[4] In other words, what Berger is suggesting is that art is born out of hope. The Berger criterion – whether or not art helps men to claim their social rights – implies that there is no such thing as the unchanging nature of art. 'Here it is essential to remember,' Berger tells us, 'that the specific meaning of a work of art changes – if it didn't, no work could outlive its period, and no agnostic could appreciate a Bellini. The meaning of the improvement, of the increase promised by a work of art depends upon who is looking at it and when. Or, to put it dialectically, it depends upon what obstacles are impending human progress at any given time. The rationality of a Poussin first gave hope in the context of absolute monarchism; later it gave hope in the context of free trade and Whig reforms; still later, it confirmed Leger's faith in proletarian socialism.'[5]

HISTORICAL CONTEXT

Such a long quotation is perhaps justified because it is necessary to show how Berger aesthetics operate in relation to the changing context of history – that is to show how two totally unrelated painters such as Poussin and Leger get related in their revolutionary vision, even when their historical contexts are different. This is also relevant in terms of current hysteria; the artists today deny their present and choose to live in a futuristic make-believe world where they think 'they'd be right'. Because his criticism was not involved with rigid Kantian aesthetic imperatives, being more history-oriented, Berger was able to adopt an attitude of 'belligerent wariness'.[6] He attacked the greatest Olympians of the art market such as Klee, Picasso, Pollock and Henry Moore. In fact, when he attacked Moore (reviewing one of his London exhibitions in the Fifties he said that the exhibition revealed a fall-off from his earlier achievements); he got into serious trouble; but for the support and friendship of the late Kingsley Martin (then editor of the *New Statesman*), he would have lost his job as art critic. His review kicked up a hysterical protest; the British Council which organized the Moore exhibition, even apologized to the artist for 'such a regrettable thing having occurred in London'. The vested interests of the art world all joined in for Berger's head. Mind you, Berger then was a nobody; he was in his twenties, feeling his way as a critic. He not only survived as a critic of sizeable influence but brought about re-evaluation of many leading artists. The respect which Leger commands from neo-dadaists in New York today is due largely to Berger's efforts.

LEGER

But before we discuss Leger – and Berger's view that Leger was the artist of the future – we make a few passing observations on Picasso, although what he writes on Picasso in this short essay has already been blown up into a thick volume, *The Success and Failure of Picasso* published in 1965. He has called Picasso the painter of today belonging to the first half of this century and not to the future, and it is for this reason – and many others too – that it is impossible to salute him for his achievements. But Berger's one observation (which incidentally has not been mentioned in his book on Picasso) is most significant. No other critic or art historian as far as we know has made it so forcefully as Berger.

Picasso's art, Berger argues, 'must turn many of our (critical) opinions inside out'. Because, Picasso's major innovation was to import the art of 'foreign' cultures (chiefly African) into the mainstream of European culture and art, and its significance has not yet been understood, nor a close study made. But if such a study were only to show the effects these foreign influences had on European art, it will be a pity. As Berger rightly observes, 'The real importance of Picasso is that he has taught African and Asian and Latin American artists to see the connection between their own traditional art and the discoveries of the twentieth century.'

And this brings us to Leger who besides Picasso gave to European culture a new aesthetic vision – the discovery of the machine, not as a love object as it was the case with the futurists. 'Every day, modern industry creates objects which have an uncontestable plastic value,' Leger wrote (*Modern Art in Advertising*, Art Institute of Chicago, 1945). Leger even anticipated the technique of pop art in his film *Ballet Mecanique* (1924).

> To isolate the object or the fragments of an object and to present it on the screen in close-ups of the largest possible scale. Enormous enlargements of an object or fragment give it a personality it never had before and in this it can become a vehicle of entirely new lyric and plastic power.[7]

Leger remained a classical cubist although his style is closer to some pop painters, particularly, Lichtenstein although the two artists are miles apart. Shall we say then without any hesitation that the later half of the twentieth century will be dominated by Leger and Duchamp? Berger has produced a much discussed documentary for BBC on Leger. Now let us hope he will write a book on him also.

Editor's Notes

1 John Berger, *Permanent Red: Essays in Seeing*, London: Methuen, [1960] 1969, Preface, p. 7.
2 Ibid.
3 Anthony Caro was a noted sculptor known for his assemblages created with found industrial junk. The aesthetic and choice of material posed a direct challenge to classical sculpture of

stone or wood and their proportionate contours and smooth surfaces. Environmental art or Land art gained ground in the 1960s as anti-art gestures that could not be appropriated by the museum-gallery art establishment and culture, or were anticipated to resist it. Brazilian artist Helio Oiticica was a significant early Environmental art proponent, and the works shown at London's White Chapel Gallery in 1969 referred to above, which were showcased as an 'experience', included his installations *Eden* and *Tropicalia*. The two works were shown in 2017 as part of the Oiticica retrospective held at the Whitney Museum of American Art, New York.

4 Berger, *Permanent Red*, Introduction, p. 15.

5 Ibid., p. 18.

6 Ibid., Preface, p. 9.

7 Fernand Leger, 'A New Realism – The Object', *Little Review*, 1926, reprinted in Lewis Jacobs, *Introduction to the Art of the Movies: An Anthology of Ideas on the Nature of Movie Art*, New York: Farrar, Straus, [1960] 1972, available at https://www.flickeralley.com/a-new-realism-the-object-its-plastic-and-cinematic-graphic-value

62

ART IN THE AGE OF RISK

On the art critic Nicolas Calas's collection of essays, Art in the Age of Risk

Link, New Delhi, 15 February 1970

Nicolas Calas is legendary because he belongs to the generation of Andre Breton who liked being legendary above everything else by cultivating his own legend. An ardent champion of the new and a product of the 1930s, associated closely with the polemics of surrealism, Dr Nicolas Calas, a Greek now settled in America, went there during the Second World War along with several surrealist and avant-garde artists of Europe. He became famous with the publication of his first book of essays, *Confound the Wise* (1942) and his slogan – 'Let us change the past and transform the future! Let us fill them with images of our desires!' – became part of the surrealist mythology. His art writings in *The Village Voice* have now acquired the status of critical documents. As a writer-critic friend of Andre Breton, his advocacy of surrealism, surrealist criticism, its myth, memories and psychoanalysis have been a source of inspiration to criticism in America. If he did not occupy the front seat in the Fifties dominated by the abstract expressionist movement, it was because he did not fit in with the new role of the critics who seemed to be writing copy for the painter's publicity.

ART OF THE FIFTIES

So his new collection of essays, *Art in the Age of Risk*, published by Dutton Books, New York, dealing mostly with the art of the Fifties is very timely. Besides his attacks on the pop cult and happenings, there is a lot more in them which we should not only be listening to but critically examine. The Indian devotees of the pop cult should read these essays and the wide area of their investigation. Introducing these essays which are from the first instalment in a projected series of volumes called *Documents in Modern Art Criticism*, painter, American art critic, Gregory Battcock, says, 'Calas has consistently sought to reveal the larger implications of art and the deepest meanings held within the art statement.' The Calas brand of criticism does not lend itself into easy categorization. In the twentieth century, humanist criticism was the first casualty because criticism became more formal expressing one or the other variant of the doctrine of art for art's sake. So in the essays, one running theme is the attack on formalism. In a commemorative write-up on Andre Breton (1966), Calas says 'Breton is no more responsible for this turn of events (the young American painters adopting automatic writing to serve the aims of pure art) in the destiny of surrealism than Lenin is responsible for the nationalistic character of post-revolutionary Russia. What nationalism is to socialism art-for-art's-sake is to humanism.' Except perhaps Berger, few critics show this kind of social awareness with a sharp political edge. The other humanist critics like Wilhelm Worringer (the famed author of *Abstraction and Empathy*) and T.E. Hulme[1] did not succeed because they were not fortunate enough to be working with the surrealists, who opposed capitalism, but followed Freud.

ROLE OF MUSEUMS

The most interesting passages therefore are naturally those concerned with the defense of surrealism. 'Art historians and critics measure the surrealist contribution in terms of a retreat from cubism or an advance toward abstract expressionism; they are involved with development of style.' For this reason he finds museum curators more guilty of misleading art than the historians or the critics. The art museum is no longer the depository of revolutionary art, Calas warns us, because it is both academic and establishment. Reviewing the exhibition *Dada, Surrealism and Its Heritage* put up by the Museum of Modern Art (1968) he wrote:

> The Museum of Modern Art is a repository of major works of the twentieth century and as such is invaluable for the artist and the scholar, but like all official and semi-official organizations, it harms more than it helps when it thrusts its weight around. In the age of technocracy we take for granted that managers of museums disregard intellectual problems. The programmes of museums have become as meaningless as those of the political parties; they are but advertisement slogans.

For practical reasons, history-oriented criticism (and museums, to be sure, nurtured it) played a vital role in promoting many of the modern art movements; without a historical perspective much of their formalistic polemics would not have made sense.

RIGHT TO BE WHIMSICAL

The main essay 'Art in the Age of Risk' is more stimulating, packed with new lines of enquiry which can easily be expanded into a volume. We come nearest to a debate here and fire its first brilliant shot as the following: The artist's right to be whimsical is granted as it is by now part of the mythology of modern art, but the point is how much of his whimsies [is acceptable]. Like scientists, artists too claim that they are exploring the unknown, and in this they should have the surgeon's freedom from responsibility, the surgeon's immunity also when accidents occur in the course of performing their duties. In other words, what the artists, since the cubists, assured the public was a certain level of performance and in return demanded freedom from the responsibility of complying with what was expected of them. The problem is well illustrated by what Braque said, 'How could I have made a mistake since I did not know what I wanted?' Thus, art was reduced by the cubists to mere play and they worked, as Calas puts it, like a player risking the loss of his knight in capturing a pawn for the sake of improving his strategic position. 'The risks taken in games played according to rules are very limited when compared to the risks a painter can take in an age when art has been turned into a wide open field of experimentation.'

So one should not ask such inconvenient questions as what the painter would have lost if instead of a curve, he had put a straight line; the answer to this is the famous remark by Picasso, 'when I run out of blue I use red'. This is how Calas explains this remark, 'It is as if Picasso were saying that art is the art of substituting substitutes as well as being a substitute for reality.' (To explain the point further, cubism, by stressing structure at the expense of imitation, paved the way for artists to substitute structure for imitation.) Modern art dealing with structures and abstract shapes has been a problem for interpretation; the critic has yet to discover a method by which the artist substitutes to determine whether he is playing according to his own rules or not. It is for this reason that formalist criticism became such an important industry of the commercial art galleries. Critics like Calas are needed if an alternative to the neo-modern tyranny is to be found. As Calas has shown us, pop, even in its neo-dada dress, is not the answer; and a new revolution is needed. Otherwise art's anti-game will go on inventing its own gimmicks. So Calas warns –

> To the artists who assume all risks to court success one might oppose those who have of art an anti-art concept. To the game of winning and losing on the canvas by substitution they oppose the knowledge that winning is impossible, because ultimately that which is being attempted is impossible.

Editor's Note

1 English critic, philosopher, translator and poet working in the early twentieth century, who was greatly influenced by and wrote on the philosopher Henri Bergson – many of whose works he translated into English from the French. Said to be a significant 'imagist' poet – describing images in simple, focused language – Hulmes is seen as an important influence on modernism in poetry.

63
ANTI-MUSEUM ART

Response to an exhibition of American art in New Delhi with a premise of challenging the notion of museumization

Link, New Delhi, 14 February 1971

Doubts have been raised about the usefulness of international exhibitions but no one has so far told us why. The eight American artists exhibiting in the Delhi triennale provide the answer. From what these American artists present, one thing is clear that the art we know and respond to as art is not the art the American presents us as art. According to Waldo Rasmussen, the American commissioner, 'They (American artists) have challenged the concept of the work of art as a discreet object for sale to museums and collectors.' This is rather a baffling statement coming from Rasmussen who is one of the directors of the Museum of Modern Art, New York, and the exhibits are selected and brought to the triennale by him under the auspices of the museum's international council. It is illustrative of the cultural permissiveness of the Western art world that a museum is presenting us works which challenge the very basis of museum art.

For the ordinary visitor, the American exhibits will produce some form of an anxiety response. The reason is that his old aesthetic notion – a thing of beauty is a joy forever – is demolished and replaced by a new notion, that art is not always a thing of beauty, nor is it intended to last forever, which is so far the case with museum art. It will appear to him more as a show to prove a point and when the point is proved the exhibits, let us assume, will be folded up perhaps: the materials either sold away or disposed of as yesterday's cultural waste. This is only a guess yet and we do not know what the Akademi will do to with these American 'art' structures and how the Museum of Modern Art will treat them when the exhibition is over. A clarification to this from either of the two institutions will naturally be of great value, for we can then safely adjust our aesthetic notions accordingly – but only when we have learnt what will be the fate of structures such as [that] stand in the lawns of the Akademi building. For instance, Allan Saert's [sic] structure of bamboos which the artist has still to complete on location.

The American exhibits are indeed an unusual sight – not so unusual perhaps in the New York context where such art is a common sight. What is surprising, however, is that the Americans did not bring this kind of 'new art' in the first triennale. Had they done so, we are quite sure, some of our advanced artists would have laid out their own Epicurean gardens and we would not have found the sight so disengagingly hopeless. The process of expanding our consciousness (which is the principal target of the American exhibits) would then have come naturally. But the shock of first experience is too disturbing for us 'to make us more truly human'. Surely no quarrel is possible with Rasmussen's thesis: 'The artists shown here try to expand the ways in which this (expanding our consciousness) can be done by touching more of our senses and by making this experience in itself a work of art.'

The Museum of Modern Art deserves all our grateful thoughts in giving art which is more like an energy food package for starving Indians. We endorse Norman O. Brown's view also who sees 'art as food going right through the body'. So we now know why art is experience. No sooner does it reach the body than it is taken in and becomes waste product and unsavoury. This sounds too simplistic but John Cage too implied as much when he said in an interview (*The New York Times*, 17 March 1968): 'We aren't having art just to enjoy it. We are having art in order to use it.' He made it clear, lest we miss his meaning, that using art really meant using it up literally and then getting rid of the remainder. The remainder, he said, is the work of art itself, the waste product. The Cage rhetorics did not end at this. He asked, 'You wouldn't ask me in the case of a steak which I ate ten years ago somehow to regurgitate it and eat it over again, would you?'

So, art is an activity as simple and inconsequential as eating and its value is wholly in the doing. Once the thing is done and devoured by our senses, it becomes like the emptied milk bottle to be got rid of, like other consumer litter. Culture is only its by-product. When art is not a thing of beauty and a joy forever, then by logical extension it is also not a badge of personal sensibility and of intimate experience. This is like death to bourgeois art – perhaps a necessary artery to nourish the city culture where man has become an island in himself. It is of course as true of New Delhi as of New York.

64
THE SENSE OF REALITY

A reflection on the constituents and import of technological art which the Lalit Kala Akademi sought to bring to India via a curated exhibition

Link, New Delhi, 16 April 1972

The Lalit Kala Akademi is currently looking for a new secretary to work on a project it has circulated among its executive members. The project envisages a Pavlovian approach to art,[1] which is no doubt highly sophisticated technology. Some of the bright ideas of the project are summarized below.

TROJAN HORSE

The Akademi visualizes an exhibition of non-situational art, not like the situational gimmick one American artist put up in the lawns of the Akademi at the second Delhi triennale. The American artist's bamboo scaffolding was a mere protest against technology. The Akademi is not against technology because technology is after all a means - not an end; the technological instruments being extensions of our ideas. It aims at putting a soul inside the machine and puts the Trojan Horse on sale to whoever wants it - the Trojan Horse, that is, with a tantric soul ticking the cosmic time.

The Akademi is advised to enter into a collaboration [ive] agreement with the American Rishi, Maurice Tuchman. This will be a fitting reply to the National Gallery [of Modern Art, New Delhi] which, by mounting the International Computer Art Exhibition in collaboration with Max Mueller Bhavan and IBM (India), has stolen the show while the Akademi believes it can always do better than what the National Gallery does. What matters in today's art are the labels and names: and the Akademi has too many of them. The project will surely put the Akademi on its feet. Only Maurice Tuchman, the museum man who created the 'Art and Technology' movement[2] in America should cooperate. Imagine then that he sends none other than James Turrell,[3] the artist who walked out of the A&T[4] experiment at Los Angeles to assist the Akademi in its plans to mount the technological show. Turrell has been saying all kinds of things - including technological fascism which he says is coming - and will be a reality in our lifetime. Take, for instance, experiments with perceptual psychology. Yes these experiments are the most welcome for artists who themselves are experimenting with colours and tantric geometry: the tantric art no doubt belongs not so much to art history as to scientific investigations into human perception.

THE PROJECT

The visiting American artist wants that the Akademi build a room heavily insulated against outside noise and [be] non-reverberant. This will be what he called an anechoic chamber – a chamber into which sound and visual stimuli could be introduced for the purpose of testing human responses to various sensory phenomena. The project is entitled, 'Working With Non-Verbal Experience'.

> This project, we believe, is an extension of our work, just as our work is an extension of some mainstream of modern art. A problem may arise with this project in the minds of the art community who may regard it as 'non-art' – as theatrical, or more scientific than artistic, or as being just outside the arena of art. Although it is a strong alteration as far as methods, means and intent we believe in it as art, and yet recognize the possibility of redefinition needed to incorporate it into the 'arena'.
>
> The necessity of this statement stems from the fact that this project will ultimately be dealt with by the art world, not so much the scientific world, though this might not be unwarranted, and therefore we are held to the dialogue of the art community and are subject to its reviews and criticism. Thus we feel we must make our position clear, that we feel our project is not inconsistent with what has come before (how can it be?).
>
> If we define art as part of the realm of experience, we can assume that a viewer looks at a piece she leaves with as art because the art had been experienced. We are dealing with the limits of an experience – not for instance with the limits of painting. We have chosen that experience out of the realm of experience to be defined as art because by having this label it is given special attention.
>
> In short, the purpose of the project is to make clear that art making was the viewer's responsibility because it is he who makes the art. What the project intends to accomplish is to bring the viewer to an awareness or perception, 'of perceiving yourself perceiving, pressing the information against the senses – making the sense of reality a sense of the senses.

NON-OBJECT SITUATION

The tantric avant-gardes are all cooperation for the project because nothing of the kind has so far been attempted by art – that is to say, art reducing reality to a sense of the senses. As the American guru later explained in a TV discussion with our artists – 'instead of placing our images on an object, we will define a non-object situation as setting up the boundaries of experience to be perceived. . .'. No doubt the artist sets up the boundaries of experience when he creates an art object but the trouble is that he never gives the experience itself. Between the art object and the spectator, the artist acts as an interpreter: the role of the interpreter was abolished when the abstract expressionists painted non-object canvases. The canvas became thus the thing itself. The pop artist extended it to include the media images as these are part of our consciousness.

Now Blake's 'If the doors of perception were cleansed, everything would appear to man as it is, infinite'[5] says more to the art audience: Look, don't go to see paintings for learning how to see. There is nothing in those all-over colour paintings which you don't already have within you. Just look within and learn the only lesson the colour-field painting teaches you, that the experience is formed within. That it is he who forms the experience [that] gives it substance. It is like the drug experience, the effect of the anechoic chamber, which the Akademi will be constructing outside its lawns if ever our new secretary is appointed.

ANECHOIC CHAMBER

The chamber experience will also demolish the old wall between the art and its public. A layman entering the chamber will have the same unique experience (which is the true function of art) as the artist has while working on his non-object, all-colour canvases. On entering the chamber, he will feel as if he is drugged: he will not be able to hold himself back from any kind of stimuli, will not refuse experiencing the new as he did in the normal state attempting to correlate the new to something already known. In short, the chamber experience will bring to him the truth that 'all art distinctions are meaningless . . . there is no such thing as modern art, there was art done then, and art that is done now, art is equal'.[6]

The Trojan Horse is really lovely. The art world will naturally be ever divided between the square and hip artists and the Pavlovian approach to spirituality will be dismissed unless art or technology becomes a religion, maybe this stuff (anechoic chamber, for instance) will start getting more exciting. As Turrell said: 'There's got to be an Art and Technology Christ. . . .'

Editor's Notes

1 The term comes from Ivan Pavlov, an early twentieth-century psychologist who worked with psychological conditioning and conditional reflexes through experiments on his dog. The dog, on repeated introduction of a bell before being presented with food, began to salivate at its sound, associating it with expectation of food. Human behavioural response to technological intervention - termed Pavlovian - has followed in its wake, including in technology-driven art.

2 Maurice Tuchman became, in 1964, the founding curator of modern art at the Los Angeles County Museum of Art, and of his initiatives, he is best known for the programme of 'Art and Technology' that he ran from 1967 to 1971. In this 'A&T' programme, he brought together avant-garde artists such as Claes Oldenberg, Andy Warhol and Richard Serra, and technological corporations such as General Electric, Lockheed Martin and Disney as research partners to collaborate on artworks that used technology. It led to a landmark exhibition on the theme titled 'Art and Technology', lasting four months in the city of Los Angeles in 1971.

3 One of the participating artists, known for his work with light and space, who worked with Robert Irwin in collaboration with Garrett corporation as part of the A&T programme to build an 'anechoic chamber'. Turrell withdrew from it and the work could not be completed, but he has gone on to become an avant-garde artist in the present day – known for creating a unique perceptual experience for the viewer with light projections made with the aid of technology. Incidentally, as the next paragraph shows, it was a similar if not the same 'anechoic chamber' that Turrell sought to create for the Triennale-India the same year.

4 The Art and Technology programme and exhibition referred to above.

5 From William Blake's 1793 poem, 'The Marriage of Heaven and Hell'. Writer Aldous Huxley famously used 'The Doors of Perception' as the title for his account of the psychological trip in response to taking the drug Mescaline as a scientific experiment (medically administered by a psychiatrist at Huxley's request). The book itself inspired the name of the rock band, The Doors.

6 Robert Irwin in *Artforum*, possibly issue dated October 1965. See his *Notes Toward a Conditional Art*, edited by Mathew Simms, Los Angeles: Getty Foundation, 2011, p. 38.

65

FASCIST ART GAMES

A reflection on technology-mediated art in America in the 1970s, being used to further statist fascist agendas

Excerpted from *The Patriot Magazine*, New Delhi, 23 April 1972

The last closing scene of the great film *2001: A Space Odyssey*. The space traveller returns home but it is the image of a plastic man returning to a plastic house. Everything is expensive looking: perhaps it is a hotel, not a house, and the room is as good as an interior of a spaceship: there is nothing in it. Nothing he could do with his hands, no work and nothing that asks for a reaction. Nothing to which he can relate himself: no sense of time, place or change.

Of course, it is a science-fiction image of the technological man, or the new man of the technological age – the man who has permitted himself to be dominated by science so much that he is now a smooth-down man. Another image of this new man comes from John Barth's novel *End of the Road*. The image of a young couple who understand each other so well that they are able to see right through each other. There is no mystery or contradictions in their lives, no corner of privacy where they can retreat as individuals, everything is open and functional like modern architecture which denies man's artistic need to elaborate his surrounding by carving images that suggest the unknowable.

US STUDENT REVOLT[1]

It is in the context of these images that America is debating technology. All agree that America is becoming fascist as a result of its long adaptation to machine. But the debate is not about this. It is about whether American fascism is real or not A Harvard intellectual has said America will be living under 'real fascism . . . before three years are over'.[2] Herbert Marcuse, on the other hand, thinks that American fascism is rather incipient and already the forces are working against it. As far as he was concerned, he said in an interview, 'one can speak with complete justification of an incipient fascism'. Prof Slater of Brandeis poses this choice: 'Liberals will be given the choice during the next decade or so between participation in some way in the new culture and living under real fascism.'

The American universities have no doubt felt the teeth of American fascism earlier than other institutions: radical student activists and teachers charge each other with behaving like Nazis. Caught in a crisis, the university intellectuals have turned to Weimar, which, today is more

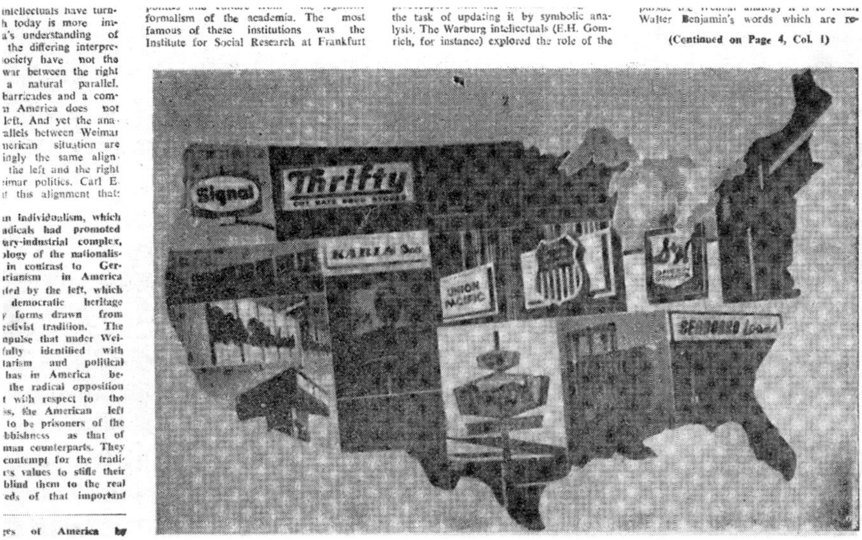
formalism of the academia. The most famous of these institutions was the Institute for Social Research at Frankfurt

the task of updating it by symbolic analysis. The Warburg intellectuals (E.H. Gombrich, for instance) explored the role of the

Walter Benjamin's words which are re-

(Continued on Page 4, Col. 1)

important for America's understanding of itself. No doubt all the differing interpretations of Weimar society have not the same tone but the war between the right and left offers a natural parallel. Except the campus barricades and a common fear of fascism, America does not have any organized left. And yet the analogies and close parallels between Weimar society and the American situation are real: there is strikingly the same alignment in America of the left and the right as witnessed in Weimar politics. Carl E. Schorske says about this alignment that:

> Here republican individualism, which the [German] radicals had promoted against the military industrial-complex, serves as the ideology of the nationalistic right. Again in contrast to Germany communitarianism in America has been assimilated by the left, which is enriching the democratic heritage with participatory forms drawn from the utopian collectivist tradition. The communitarian impulse that under Weimar was most fully identified with nationalism, militarism and political authoritarianism has in America become a part of the radical opposition of all three. Yet with respect to the great middle class, the American left intellectuals seem to be prisoners of the same urban snobbishness as that of their earlier German counterparts. They also allow their contempt for the traditional middle-class values to stifle their sympathies and blind them to the real psychological need of that important stratum which in the end will probably determine the fate of all of us.[3]

The urban snobbishness is the result of the outsider as a cultural operator in America and Weimar culture was also created by the outsiders of the pre-war Empire – Jews, democrats and socialists. The outsider by evolving a counter-culture, became an insider because there was no other political way to function as an insider under the Weimar. The Weimar intellectual-outsider gave the world the international style in architectural, expressionist art and poetry, symbolic and iconographic analysis in the arts, depth psychology, existentialist philosophy and atonal music - and they were all conceived as the counter-culture of Empire.

WEIMAR ANALOGY

The counter-culture under Weimar was less bohemian and more organized. Semi-autonomous cultural institutions were established for research to liberate German politics and culture from the legalistic formalism of the academia. The most famous of these institutions was the institute for social research at Frankfurt established by independent Marxists. The radical thinkers of this institute who migrated to America include such internationally famous names as Herbert Marcuse (philosophy), Walter Benjamin (literature), Erich Fromm (psychology), Leo Lowenthan (sociology) and Theodor Adorno (musicology). Warburg Institute at Hamburg, unlike the Bauhaus school, was preoccupied with the classical heritage and the task of updating it by symbolic analysis. The Warburg intellectuals (E.H. Gombrich, for instance) explored the role of the myth in the culture of the past.

Because of the outsider character of Weimar culture, such opposites as Bauhaus architecture and expressionism could co-exist and in the Bauhaus rationalist architects and expressionist artists both embraced each other's work as complementary. The German avant-garde was a prisoner of the pre-1914 counter-culture which could not develop a politics capable of dealing with the return of the repressed in the German middle class. The American avant-garde similarly is a prisoner of the media world and the big industry which controls it.

The attitude of the American avant-garde cannot surely be prophesied by the analogy of the Weimar experience. It is however relevant because technology has politicized art as fascism did under Hitler. But surprisingly, no American artist has ever admitted this truth. If we should pursue the Weimar analogy, it is to recall Walter Benjamin's words which are relevant to what fascism and technology do to art. He said:

> *Fiat aspereat mundus*, says Fascism, and as Marinetti admits, expects war to supply the artistic gratification of a sense of perception that has been changed by technology. This is evidently the consummation of *L'art pour l'art*. Mankind which in Homer's time was an object of contemplation, for the Olympian gods, now is one for itself. Its self-alienation has reached such a degree that it can experience its own destruction as an aesthetic pleasure of the first order. This is the situation of politics which fascism is rendering aesthetic . . .

Avant-garde's inhuman aesthetic is not a new development and its extreme is well illustrated by the rhetorics of the futurists.

m Page 1, Col. 4)

ascism and technology
d: Fiat arspereat mun-
, and as Marinetti ad-
to supply the artistic
ense of perception that
by echnology. This is
mation of "L'art pour
which in Homer's time
contemplation for the
w is one for itself. Its
reached such a degree
nce its own destruction
sure of the first order.
on of politics which
g aesthetic..." Avant-
esthetic is not a new
s extreme is well illus-
rics of the Futurists.

AVANT-GARDE

of the European avant-
the elitist status, and
de has been pro-tech-
he spokesman of the
art. Unlike the Euro-
which had a sense of
rican counter-part de-
sciousness of belonging
nor to the future but
or sense of transition.
s also unique: a work
ished but always "in
peculiarity of the
de is that it is a-poli-
the European avant-
home in America has
iance with aesthetic ra-
radicalism.

heticism of Abstract
ituational aesthetics of
erican avant-garde has
oad of psychological
ecame simply a cons-
game which, in the
peings' guru, Kirby,

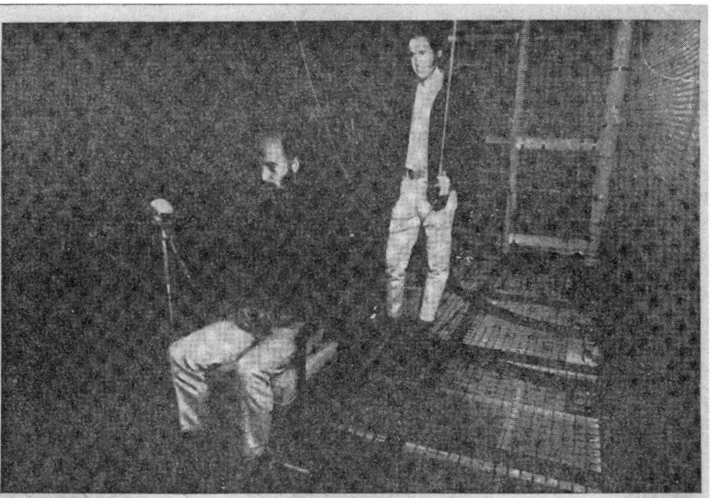

Turell and Irwin inside the anechoic chamber

ing an equal status the avant-garde is
dead. American art scene is now a long
way from the age of the avant-garde.
The new artist, like the new man of
technological society has no quarrel with
society, nor does he think in terms of
forming an alternative culture. Art, in

geois. Two possible escapes from the
bourgeois are, 1) aristocracy and 2) in-
tellect, where art never thrives too well.
There again I'm talking as if I want to
create art outside b. values. Perhaps
this can't be done, but why should I
crime which it requires some courage

ing in. But every one is going to get
pushed in, or jump in finally. It doesn't
make any difference. There are forces
which are about to push us in.

"All this is very Pavlovian. You are
not really asking much of the person

AMERICAN AVANT-GARDE

In America, most of the European avant-gardes were given the elitist status, and since the avant-garde has been pro-technology, it became the spokesman of the new technological art. Unlike the European avant-garde which had a sense of tradition, the American counterpart developed a new consciousness of belonging neither to the past nor to the future but to an eternal crisis or sense of transition. Its sense of time is also unique: a work of art is never finished but always 'in progress'. Another peculiarity of the American avant-garde is that it is a political in orientation. The European avant-garde which found home in America has given up its old alliance with aesthetic radicalism and social radicalism.

From pure aestheticism of abstract expressionism to situational aesthetics of the Sixties, the American avant-garde has travelled a long road of psychological conditioning. It became simply a consciousness-expanding game which, in the words of the *Happenings* guru, Kirby, 'enables us to live more accurately and therefore more successfully'. So art became a mixing of genres in intermedia that make use of dance, films, painting, electronics providing a particularly exciting enlargement of the domain of art. Kirby's book *The Art of Time* has a long essay on the American avant-garde where he cites many common attitudes between avant-garde artist and scientist reducing art to a theory: art as sports. No wonder *Happenings* are mind-expanding atheletic events, including the too-frequent warm-ups, the working of chance, errors, fair play and foul play. Kirby's electric circuitry has a manipulated time sense that is indeed dizzying.

ELECTRONIC THEATRE

Pop art is really the great dividing line between art as history and art as sports: it also means a complete change of heart – an attitude of critical irony and mockery towards both abstract art and the throwaway iconography of the commercial culture. This also means the underlying affinity between art and non-art, between aesthetic experience and common experience of the industrial environment. Pop's slogan that it closes the gap between art and life when translated into the art gallery terms means closing the gap between fine art and commercial art. This was on the same level as minimal sculpture losing its identity finally in the direction of industrial design and the art-and-technology movement openly aspiring to transform the visual arts into a form of electronic theatre. With the artists and engineers occupying equal status, the avant-garde is dead. The American art scene is now a long way from the age of the avant-garde. The new artist, like the new man of technological society, has no quarrel with society, nor does he think in terms of forming an alternative culture. Art, in short, is another entertainment industry, a form of bourgeois sentimentality. Oldenberg's book *Store Days* (1961) summarizes the American art situation thus:

> If I could only forget the notion of art entirely I really don't think you can win. Duchamp is ultimately labelled art too. The bourgeois scheme is that they wish to be disturbed from time to time, they like that, but then they envelop you, and that little bit is over and they are ready for the next. There even exists within the bourgeoisie values a code of possibilities for disturbance, a certain to do but which will eventually be rewarded within the bourgeois scheme. Bourgeois values are human weakness, a civilization built on human weakness, non-resistance. There are many difficult things to do within the bourgeois values, but I would like to find some way to take a totally outside position. Bohemia is bourgeois. The beat is bourgeois – their values are pure sentimentality – the country, the good heart, the fallen man, the honest man, the gold-hearted whore et cetera. They would never think, for example, of making the city a value of good. Possibly, art is doomed to be bourgeois. Two possible escapes from the bourgeois are 1) aristocracy and 2) intellect, where art never thrives too well. There again I'm talking as if I want to create art outside bourgeois values. Perhaps this can't be done, but why should I crime [sic] which it requires some courage even want to create 'art' [sic] – that's the notion I have got to get rid of.

Oldenburg was the presiding superstar of the Art and Technology exhibition (held at Los Angeles between 10 May and 29 August 1971) and had put a huge illuminated billboard across the street saying ART SHALL HANG. He believes that technology has already swallowed up art. Art, he said, was basically a 'matter of childhood' while 'technology concerns adulthood'. The exhibition was the culmination of the four-year project 'to effect a practical [word missing] of the corporate industrial society'.

It was indeed a surprise that the artists cooperated with the big industry. First, they were participating with 'war-oriented' industries and secondly, most artists who were once influenced by the systems-conscious attitude had come to realize its corrupting influence through the collaboration. Technological art (particularly the one which employs systems philosophy) has a great potential for subliminal coercion. Systems of information aesthetic is indeed another name for fascist game. James Turrell was the only artist who walked out of the four-year art and technology project. He said in a three-way interview (with engineer Wortz and artist Irwin):

> I have found out (largely through the collaboration) that you can order people's experience, there's really a lot that you *could* control in making people confront something. . . .
>
> You could make this thing (art and technology enterprise) historically significant if you want to, I have the feeling that whatever is happening here is a symptom of something that's going on – but I think – I hope – it's going to be overshadowed by the thrust of the things going on independently.
>
> We are going to have to work through this time of ego and of separating artists form all those around them. . . . We are very involved in our roles as individuals right now. The thing that happens with technology, or (something like) [the] Manhattan project . . . in which people put their energies into a cause where they have to forget themselves . . . people are afraid to devolve themselves into any sort of human cosmic consciousness; we are standing next to a swimming pool, a little bit frightened about jumping in. But every one is going to get pushed in, or jump in finally. It doesn't make any difference. There are forces which are about to push us in.
>
> All this is very Pavlovian. You are not really asking much of the person or yourself. And all you can watch are surface responses. People were often interchanged between artists and members going through a dance with you. . . . Then (the project) began to change and move into sensory interaction, where the senses influence one another. And then into alpha conditioning, which is sort of taking a Pavlovian approach into spirituality. It has no end. . . . Technology isn't anything outside us. . . . We just go about it very clumsily and very wastefully because we have to actually *make* all these devices. We have to go to the moon, we can't see the cosmos in a rock, we can't meditate without having this thing strapped on us.

The project in which Turrell, and Irwin were engaged was to built anechoic chamber (a room insulated against outside noise stimuli and thus non-reverberant). The project was aimed at studying human responses to special environmental situations. Indeed, it was to study all 'information where man's sensual awareness were tested with conclusions of degrees of awareness-human prowess' and 'basic necessities for maintaining sanity'. First, it was thought that the structure will be displayed at the exhibition. The anechoic chamber, no doubt, was completed but was not displayed. The artists who began with their own observation in the chamber, felt the horrific results of the alpha conditioning in the chamber so nerve shattering that they gave up probing into the experiments further.

An equally horrifying experiment was one of Wesley Duke Lee's: it was called *The Birth Capsule* or *The Suspended Pneuma of Los Angeles.* The structure was a plastic box 3x3x3 metres (a cube) in which the observer with his space suit adjusted his air helmet from which he breathed and received the special smells of blood-shit-sea-forest and heard the sound of a heart beating, plus the blood running through his vessels. About the experiments of *The Birth Capsule,* Lee said:

> The farther away we go in space, the more frustrated we become; going to the moon has to do with power, it's a political power play. It's already boring essentially. I'm trying to deal in fast processes of communication; something that could shorten all the fears we have of getting together. And I think we only do that by full examination of our structure, and this is what the Capsule is about, I have an idea which is not mine: it comes from a lot of reading in psychology and my admiration of Freud. If you could re-enact the birth process and your whole life seen with the adult's eye, you would have at your disposal a life-power which can be used to live with your fears. So my dream was to invent a machine so that man could be exposed for a short period and would be so shocked by the experience that he would automatically start to revise himself.

MECHANICAL WOMB

Later, he wrote about his findings of the experiment to the museum director Maurice Tuchman that –

> Your exhibition exposed me to a complete situation. Through the process of 'building the birth capsule' I trapped myself (naturally with a lot of help from Acapulco Gold) into seeing the 'sin' I was committing. First to myself, through deviating from my natural and best ways of expression. Second, against nature, you don't build a mechanical womb! As in the same way you don't take heaven by assault!

These are two exemplifications of the ugly face of fascist aesthetic produced in liaison with big industries. Aside from the political implications of the project, it is noteworthy that the big industries included the Garnett Corporation (designing high-performance jet engines) for military aircraft; General Electric (which has its own thinktank called TEMPO which runs seminars on nuclear weapons) Hewlett-Packard Company (radar, guided missile control) Jet Propulsion Laboratory and Litton Industries (build submarines, amphibious assault ships and advanced guidance and fire-control systems); Lockheed Norris Industries (a major ordnance manufacturer since World War II), North American Rockwell and The Rand Corporation. A rogue's gallery of violence industry no doubt. As artist Richard Serra, a participant in the show, observed, 'technology is what we do to the Black Panthers and the Vietnamese under the guise of advancement in a materialistic theology'.

The big industries and corporations which financed the project had their own selfish motives. Jet Propulsion Laboratory, for instance, wanted to move out of space exploitations and devote larger funds to environment research. Other corporations did not conceal their business motives either: most were involved in the project to promote a particular product. For example, Cowles's Xography or Garnett's life sciences products – they all sought to be better known through the collaboration. Similarly General Electric wanted to present a more modernized image. The smaller companies joined the programme for publicity. In short, the companies were not interested in a project which produced works of poor productive value. The meaning of corporate patronage of art is that art is superfluous unless it has an immediate commercial value.

Editor's Notes

1 A possible source for the then gathering concerns of fascism in the Unites States is a 1971 article in the *New York Times*, 'Six "Big Lies" About America' by Arnold Beichman, available at https: www.nytimes.com/1971/06/06/archives/six-big-lies-about-america.html. Many of the quotations in this article by K.B. Goel appear in the *New York Times* article, and it is possible that he read the article at the American Center library and used its source material to discuss the imminent threat of fascism that technology-mediated art suggested.

2 Ibid.

3 Carl E. Schorske, 'Weimar and the Intellectuals: II', *New York Review of Books,* 2 May 1970, p. 22.

66

CONTEMPORARY TRENDS IN INDIAN PAINTING

An outline of the historical development of Indian modernism and current trends

Patriot Magazine, New Delhi, 14 January 1973

It has always seemed inevitable to begin with Amrita Sher-Gil. Everyone admits that modern painting in India began with her, and not with the Bengal School. No doubt it is with the Bengal movement that we saw for the first time the emergence of an Indian type of painting, and that is a significant fact. But we do not care much for the Bengal school experiments in evolving an Indian style which is radically different from painting done in the West. The products of the Bengal movement are more exotic than Indian and as Amrita Sher-Gil observed –

> . . . it (the Bengal movement) cannot claim to have captured the spirit of the Indian art of bygone ages. In fact it has about as much in common with it as the Omar Khayam illustrations [of *The Rubaiyat*] of Edmund Dulac. The work of the Bengal school is in fact entirely illustrative in quality, and depends for its popularity not on pictorial merit, but on romantic appeal.[1]

The Bengal movement died the day India became independent and that is now a universally accepted fact. So we begin with Amrita Sher-Gil because she brought the modernist sensibility to India. She not only fought against the decadent, revivalist Bengal movement but against the academic naturalism of the Bombay school, which did not liberate the imagination but sought to limit it to art's representational tasks. She thought it was foolish to speak derisively of the modern art of Europe because such people were ignorant of 'the innumerable points of contact' which the modern art has with the best of Eastern art.

> 'Were our artists,' she wrote, 'to seek inspiration from modern Western art – just as the [Western] Moderns discovered a new means of self-expression through the study of Eastern sculpture and painting, not only would they infuse new life into Indian painting but it would help them really to understand the underlying principles of the ancient art of their own country.'[2]

Her role in shaping the Indian sensibility towards modernism is very much like that of Cezanne's. Like Cezanne, she knew what she wanted to do. And this is what marks her out as a genius. Cezanne knew that there was something wrong with Delacroix and he set about correcting it in his work. That is to say he knew what was right and what was wrong about Delacroix, and it is this knowledge which is really important.

AMRITA SHER-GIL

What Amrita Sher-Gil in effect was saying was that art is a system. Her work affirms that paintings owe more to other paintings than any wishful theorizing about art. This can be illustrated with the example of Constable who saw the English landscape in terms of Gainsborough, but what about Gainsborough himself? The answer is simple: he saw the lowland scenery of East Anglia in terms of Dutch paintings. One can ask, from where did the Dutch get their inspiration, their vocabulary? One can go on like that explaining one thing in terms of an earlier one which again needs the same type of explanation. It is such type of questions that lead us to assert that art has a history and why its history developed in one direction rather than another.

In the revivalist climate it might have looked perverse to think that the study of Western art would help us to understand, as Amrita Sher-Gil was preaching, 'the underlying principles of the ancient art of their own country'. We all know with what passion she studied the art of Gauguin and above all it is because of Gauguin's influence that she decided to return to India. 'Modern art has led me,' she wrote to her father from Paris, 'to comprehension and appreciation of Indian painting and sculpture. It seems paradoxical, but I know for certain, that had we not come away to Europe I should perhaps have never realized that a fresco from Ajanta or a small piece of sculpture in the Musée Guimet is worth more than the whole Renaissance!'[3] This is not an instance of misplaced enthusiasm. The quarrel between and eventual separation of Van Gogh and Gauguin is also relevant here. Gauguin saw colours flat as we find them applied in Indian miniatures for instance. Amrita Sher-Gil learnt the Gauguin lesson well and in the last years, she painted, bringing in the colours of miniatures and their multi-perspective compositional methods in her work. In this she touched upon the vital source of 'India's magnificent art heritage'.

Like Gauguin, she simplified her forms and the outline of figures. *Brahmacharis* is the best representative of her discovery of Indian miniatures through the eyes of Gauguin. She painted for a very short period and the conventions of life she had learnt in Paris seemed too powerful for her to easily overcome. Still her paintings, like the *Brahmacharis*, brought a new message for Indian painting.

We have discussed Amrita Sher-Gil's role – her achievements and discoveries at such length because it has now become fashionable with most artists to speak about Indian art with an anti-West stance as if Indian painting is not part of the main current of modern art. All comparisons with Western aesthetic attitudes as a means of gaining deep insight into Indian painting is considered an insult to the Indian painter's genius. They prefer, on the other hand, the psychologizing whine of existential criticism, the bad poetry written in the name of art criticism. Feelings generated by historical conditioning of works of art are denied. Seeing a work of art in terms of art history as a method of clarifying the intent of the artist is out of fashion. Like the innocent eye, criticism should also be innocent.

DISTRUST OF WEST

Some kind of in-built distrust of the West, its analytical mode, its reliance on historical method, its preoccupation with techniques and formalism has always come in the way of our drawing proper lessons from Amrita Sher-Gil's example. No wonder she is found today in Vakil's Greeting Cards. The painters of the 1940s for instance did not learn anything from Sher-Gil. These painters did not work in the wash technique much favoured by the Bengal painters: they took to tempera which was the colour the miniaturists favoured. For reasons of national identity, the nostalgia for folk art became the rallying point. Kalighat *pats* were revived by Jamini Roy, and the image painted in flat colours with thick bold outlines and against a lifeless background became painterly obsessions with these painters. The painters of the period of transition to modern art (the most prominent among these are Hebbar, Chavda, Sanyal[4] and to a lesser extent, Sailoz Mukherjea) sought in folk art the validity of their personal styles. Their influence continued in the Fifties even when the world of painting had gone international by the worldwide acceptance of the gestural art of abstract expressionism. [A.A.] Almelkar, Badri Narayan, K. Sreenivasulu and Sunil Madhav Sen were the products of the folk-oriented tradition.

The 1950s also saw a curious blending into the folk style such related influences as Jain illuminations, Rajasthani miniatures and even a few elements of commercialized aspects of modern art. In the hands of painters like [Gautam] Vaghela, folk art acquired the illusionistic features of fine art. Can folk art be grafted to modernist sensibilities? The answer is very clearly, no. Folk art is a poor way out of Bengal school romanticism and as a style, expressing the collective consciousness of India; it runs in an opposite direction to modern art which is individualistic. No original style by way of folk art is possible because of its ritualistic nature and use of symbols. Matisse, for example, gave it up after a short period of flirtation and turned away from the romanticism of his teacher, [Gustave] Moreau. So very overpowering was its influence that even a painter like Husain acknowledged his debt to folk inspiration. He said in 1955: 'My paintings, drawings and the recent paper work has been directly influenced by my experience of traditional Indian dolls, paper toys . . . shapes galore. The

seemed inevitable to
ımrita Sher-Gil. Every
modern painting in
her, and not with the
› doubt it is with the
that we saw for the
ıergence of an Indian
and that is a signifi-
/e do not care much
:hool experiments in
a style which is radi-
·om painting done in
roducts of the Bengal
ɔre exotic than Indian

. B. GOEL

her-Gil observed, "it
nent) cannot claim to
: spirit of the Indian
s, in fact, it has about
ɔn with it as the Omar
ıns of Edmond Dulac.
: Bengal school is, in
trative in quality, and
ɔopularity not on pic-
on romantic appeal."
ment died the day
ependent and that is
, accepted fact.
ɪith Amrita Sher-Gil
ht the modernist sen-

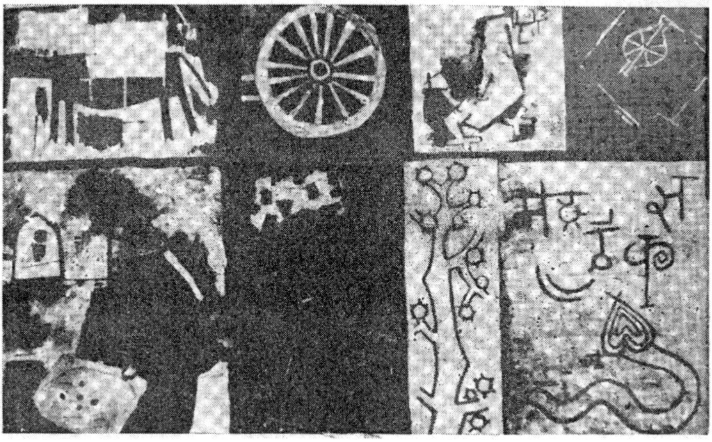

experience of being with them and the inspiration to create them are inseparable.'

The weight of tradition or the assumptions of power of the middle class which forces painting to have links with the past, to become the collective psyche of its people to impose upon it a coherent, stable, unequivocal and an entirely decipherable universe – has always come in the way of Indian painting, arresting its growth and natural development. Even Clement Greenberg, the high priest of formalism, considers such paintings useless as are not exportable. That is to say, paintings done by Indian artists should have the unmistakable imprint of Indianness. As another, equally influential Western critic, Ludwig Goldscheider has said:

> An Indian artist . . . cannot merely study the Ajanta and the Tanjore wall paintings and imitate them on a smaller scale – this would not make him a modern master: he has to go through the school of world art. But to become a genuine artist he is not allowed to forget or suppress his racial and national way of seeing and shaping – he has to be an Indian artist or nothing at all. In the end, his painting will be as different from all European art as the thinking of India, Upanishads and Buddha, is different from European thought. (No true message without that difference.)[5]

WEIGHT OF TRADITION

The culture of the folk is heady stuff and its fancy dress has an exotic appeal for the city sophisticates. Even in the late Sixties the international commercial art institutions find a great exploit in Indian folk specimens. In 1965, George Butcher, a British critic, spent twenty-eight months in collecting material for the *Arts of the Commonwealth Exhibition* at London's Festival Hall. British critics found the Indian paintings not at all exciting. They said they were the weak echoes of the work being done in Europe and America. The folk art collection, according to them, was enormously itself. Both the fine art and folk specimens were exhibited as a unity 'each helping to explain the qualities of the other'. The paintings selected by Butcher supposedly shared the same aesthetic belief as reflected in Indian folk art. Philip Rawson, the critic and art historian, whom J. Swaminathan never tires of quoting, was among the admiring British critics moved by the heroic struggle of Indian painters to find their feet. He wrote:

> Amongst the sophisticated artists there were many surprises, and deeply impressive work. It does really seem that some Indians have re-established at last a consistent and valid artistic language of signs and symbols and thrown overboard both conventions, the phony revivalism and the pretty-pretty pastiche of abstractionism, that have plagued India for so long. It is a very hard and unrewarding job, to kick out against deeply entrenched conformism, to be yourself, explore the logic of your own style without paying lip service to any accepted conventions. But it is being done, brilliantly, and often at great personal cost to the artists. They deserve our highest respect.

The artists whose works were included in the show suffered, according to Rawson, because they learnt 'the real virtues of their art' from Western art. The *London Times* art critic has another view of this struggle. He wrote:

> They are the product of a struggle which is cruel enough – a struggle to find a way by which the Indian artist can reintegrate himself with an India which industrialism must slowly but surely transform. Instead of the prince, he finds the bourgeois; in place of the despotic patron, the bureaucratic one. And in place of submission in the artist we discover a disturbing self-consciousness. . . . If we are trying to localize what seems unsatisfactory about contemporary Indian painting as we now see it – unsatisfactory that is apart from sheer imitativeness – it is the lack of a sense of personal identity. Even where a particular painting nearly succeeds, we fail to find in it the urgent egotistical statement which we have taught ourselves to look for.

NO PUBLIC GALLERIES

Indeed the egotistical statement, the personal identity in the art product was the only thing that brought into existence, immediately after India won freedom, the Progressive Artists' Group of Bombay. And this was at a time when art appreciation was limited to the few and there were no public galleries where their works could be exhibited. It was truly a Victorian India where art sensibilities found stunted expression either through academic realist art or the romantic mythologies of the Bengal painters, and in the name of national identity, the Bengal revivalists dominated the art scene. With the formation of the Progressive Group, the Bombay painters became more dominant because they were more aggressive. The painters of the Progressive Group did not produce any manifesto as it had become customary in Paris in the 1920s. The common thing that united the Progressives was their hatred of India's so-called glorious past. Each of these painters followed a personal road for solution of their pictorial problems. They were loud, however, in the declaration that they were not imitative or drew inspiration from the European masters.

Theirs was not a revolt against Bengal school revivalism: They did not have this negative attitude. On the other hand, what was positive in their attitude was that they sought to identify their own personal statements with attitudes and styles in Europe. Every young painter, for instance, accepted Picasso's post-cubistic achievements. Of these painters, Souza was inspired by Picasso, and his Goanese Christian background found an outlet through Picasso's violently aggressive style and his images of that period are the most valuable achievements of Indian painting. In Souza's paintings, we find the first signs of expressionist style. Later, when Souza left India (he found the Victorian atmosphere of India suffocating) to settle permanently in England, he found in Francis Bacon's work quite a parallel development. But the expressionist idiom of his paintings remained very much his own. The personal statement of Souza and Francis Bacon, though analogous and sharing the common idiom of expressionist art, were as different as the temperaments of these two painters.

Gaitonde and Mohan Samant modelled their work on Paul Klee's style and they sought a complete identification with it, and never attempted to dilute it with anything remotely connected with Indian aesthetics. It liberated their imagination and they achieved beautiful lyric effects in colour and line through symbolic configurations of an inner landscape. Klee's influence became widespread because of the achievements of these painters. Those who imitated Klee had seen nothing of the master's original works, so they accepted the Gaitondes and Samants as representation of the European master's art. The complete identification of these artists with alien modes of expression did not produce any loss of identity: on the other hand, they realized their talents fully through the European tradition.

LANGUAGE MODES

The language modes of modern art are not bound to any national borders: it is an eclectic formal language in which there is no possibility of language-meaning dichotomy affecting an alien relationship. The total alliance with Western art by the painters of the Progressive Group resulted in the acceptance of judging art by Western standards. The group soon became a minority institution, and it was subject to all kinds of pulls and pressures. The members often quarrelled amongst themselves and the talk shows went on past midnight hours and ceased only when they had tired themselves out by too much talking. These painters – Husain, Ara, Bakre, Gaitonde, Samant, Raza and Padamsee – constituted the avant-garde of

Indian painting. They faced the same hostile public which the European avant-garde must have faced. They accepted the hardships and public neglect willingly: as an institution of counter-culture working in the name of art, it seemed a necessary sacrifice. The consequence of this group's ideological polemic was that the work of these painters became the testing ground of innovations of their contemporaries. They never surrendered their vision to either the requirements of nationalism or exchanged their painting for dollars producing works that sold in the market then.

This does not mean that they did not have patrons. The three patrons were all wartime exiles from Germany and Austria. These European émigrés not only bought their works but helped them in making available, through reproductions and discussions, examples of European art. Dr Walter Langhammer, himself a painter influenced by Kokoschka, Rudi von Leyden, an art critic and advertisement consultant and Emmanuel Schlesinger, the buyer of their works, were their friends, philosophers and guides. The Progressive painters were the true heirs of Amrita Sher-Gil. Husain, for instance, could not have developed the way he did without Amrita Sher-Gil. And of the early avant-garde painters Husain alone acquired the legendary status and his works became a safe investment for the Indian bourgeoisie.

The Progressive Group painters realized soon that they could not work in the suffocating art climate of Bombay: Souza, Padamsee, Raza and Laxman Pai migrated to Paris and settled there permanently.[6] Only Husain stayed in India; his first visit abroad was in 1953 and it had a marked effect on his work. By now, recognition also had come and the cultural bureaucracy comprising the intellectual city elite patronized him and the newly established Lalit Kala Akademi honoured him with an award. He had now 'superstar' value and the possession of his work in the Indian bourgeois homes became a status symbol. He represented Indian avant-garde painting abroad.

LIMITED ACHIEVEMENTS

It will be wrong to say that no modern stylistic language existed in India. Amrita Sher-Gil and George Keyt attempted in their paintings to synthesize East and West in artistic terms. Sher-Gil was the first painter to attempt psychological interpretations of the Indian people, as she herself said that she wanted to paint – 'those silent images of infinite submission and patience, depict their angular brown bodies, strangely beautiful in their ugliness; to reproduce on the canvas the impression their eyes created on me'.[7]

George Keyt, who assimilated in his language the formal elements of distortion used in post-cubist painting in the 1940s, painted a wholly personal style which reflected the sensuous voluptuousness of Ajanta and Indian sculpture. His was, no doubt, a limited achievement but it was a bold one and provided perhaps the best solution to the problem of creating a modern Indian painting outside the context of Western values.

So, Husain discovered the beauty of Mathura sculpture through the eyes of Keyt and learnt from Amrita Sher-Gil to compose them in a dramatic psychological setting. But it is Picasso and other European painters who influenced him most, although it is not without danger to say this in definite terms because he was able to metamorphose them to the extent that they became part of his style. But one thing is very clear, and this separates him from Amrita Sher-Gil: his assimilation of Western art's pictorial language was visual, and not intellectual as was the case with Sher-Gil and Keyt. Husain's painting has never had any intellectual content: it is addressed to the eye alone. No doubt he shares many of the beliefs and intentions of the European expressionist painters – the black outline, almost fused, and part of the violent colour-application methods. But his brushstrokes are more articulate.

Unlike his other contemporaries of the Progressive Group, Husain is very reticent in speaking of the foreign influences, particularly of Picasso. He has, however, admitted after his first visit abroad in 1953 that he became interested in the works of Bernard Buffet and Marino Marini. But it is not clear how far these artists had influenced his paintings done between 1953 and 1957, his most productive period. His image language was now mature, which has no references to any Indian sources, either folk or fine art traditions. The dominant is colour which is boldly applied and well woven into the pattern-making language of his images. Even though it is an eclectic language it is best understood in terms of its own conventions, so much has it been personalized. He is indeed the tallest Indian master who forces us to see his work in the Husain way, with Husain's eyes. This independence, this self-reference in his work, both setting up personal conventions of a style and becoming later its prisoner, is not seen in any Indian painter who followed and imitated him; the painting scene of the Fifties is dominated by him.

The other painters who influenced the painting landscape of the Fifties are Satish Gujral, Ram Kumar, Samant and Gaitonde. All these painters were influenced by the trend in Western painting and there is nothing in their works which can be related to Indian pictorial sources. The creative autonomy in their works is established by the strength of their personal styles. Satish Gujral and Ram Kumar are significant because of the social content in their works although by the close of the Fifties they had given up their socially-oriented styles in favour of purely formalistic abstract painting. Satish Gujral's portrait studies of Nehru, Indira Gandhi, Krishna Menon and, above all, poet Ghalib and his paintings depicting the agonies of partition in the pictorial language of Mexico's Orozco and other European expressionist masters and Ram Kumar's pictures of the depressed alienated youth without any hope or escape routes was a new idiom in Indian painting.

Of all the European masters, Klee's influence on the major painters of the Fifties is sizeable and the works of Samant and Gaitonde showed how a totally foreign influence can be assimilated into the Indian context. The use of symbols is central to the Klee syntax but the painting composed in that syntax had no local identity either in terms of Indian mythology or to any archetypal images; it is no doubt a most lyrical, evocative and poetic landscape composed in the universal language of symbols.

The influence of Klee had continued till the mid-Sixties and the metaphoric language derived from the primitive sources of the Indian psyche that was developed and explored by the second generation painters who had graduated from the corrupting influence of gestural art can also be traced to Klee. The pictorial language of these younger painters (and the most prominent among them are Swaminathan, Ambadas, Jeram Patel, Gulam Sheikh, Rajesh Mehra and Balkrishna Patel belonging to Group 1890) in the earlier stages of their career was borrowed from Klee. But the works of Swaminathan after a short spell of what he called the 'colour geometry of space' have freed themselves from any visible foreign sources and the world of metaphors is now self-referring. Since 1969, Swaminathan has moved so far in his pictorial language that the metaphoric images tend to be iconic. He has reduced the elements of pictorial language to the minimum of three symbols - mountains (representing the metaphor of higher consciousness), the *tulsi* plant or the lotus flower (possibly standing for female or male principles in the realm of the numinous) and a bird (*mynah*, peacock or parrot) which in the metaphoric language may mean love and the freedom of the soul. The connection between *Vaishnav* poetry and painting, which has a long pictorial tradition in Rajasthan and Jain miniatures, is re-established in Swaminathan's work. But the total effect of his paintings is tectonic, involving both the mind and eye.

SECOND GENERATION PAINTERS

The Sixties had also witnessed the invasion of pop art which has been as pervading an influence as the abstract expressionism of the Fifties. While in the West, the pop pictures refer to the comic strip clichés and consumer culture images and were conceived as archetypes with self-conscious identities and memories and produced in the straightforward manner of a simple, craft-based activity, the Indian version of pop has the calendar god and goddesses, national leaders and other wayside icon-images, including the Western hippies. Bhupen Khakhar, a self-taught artist, is the only painter who has put a grand, self-consciously aesthetic perspective on these images. His recent paintings are very different from what he showed, some three years ago. Now he paints the modern archetypes, like the clerks, the watchmaker and other men of professions. Similarly, Krishen Khanna has given up his early painterly paintings and paints now the generals and pictures with a social content.

Only in Khakhar's paintings have Indian pop images, the popular visual culture of India, found an aesthetic which is full of humour and satire.

He is considered, not with reason, as the new avatar of Henri Rousseau, giving to his images a magical quality. He has created a new pictorial language and the sources are Jain illuminations, Rajasthani miniatures, and the overpowering landscape space which gives to his human figures a strangely lonely diminutive look. The paintings are other-directed in the sense in which pop images are. For the first time we have an art idiom where the viewer and the artist share the same language. Khakhar's influence is very wide indeed and the third-generation artists, the new painters of the Seventies, are all influenced by him. He is also responsible for giving birth to a new style, a purely indigenous school in which the art of miniatures is re-established as a living contemporary idiom.

Editor's Notes

1 Amrita Sher-Gil, 'Indian Art Today', *The Indian Listener*, 19 August 1941, in *Amrita Sher-Gil: a self-portrait in letters and writings*, introduced, annotated and edited by Vivan Sundaram, vol. 2, New Delhi: Tulika Books, 2010, p. 731.

2 Ibid. p. 737.

3 Amrita Sher-Gil in a letter to her father, as cited by Salman Rushdie in the Foreword to *Amrita Sher-Gil: a self-portrait in letters and writings*, p. xi.

4 Artists K.K. Hebbar, Shiavax Chavda, B.C. Sanyal.

5 For one source of the text, see its quotation in K.C.S. Paniker, *Chitram Ezuthu: A Publication on Art and Letters*, [1969] 1979, pp. 12–13.

6 Both Akbar Padamsee and Laxman Pai returned to India in the 1960s.

7 Amrita Sher-Gil, 'Amrita Sher-Gil – The Talented Artist', *The Indian Ladies' Magazine*, vol. X, no. 1, January and February 1937, in *Amrita Sher-Gil: a self-portrait in letters and writings*, p. 325.

67

THE MATHURA BUDDHAS

On the aesthetics of the fifth-century AD Mathura sculpture and its strong influence on M.F. Husain

Patriot Magazine, New Delhi, 20 January 1974

M.F. Husain's discovery of Mathura sculpture in 1948 had the same implications for his painting career as Polyclitus's [also Polykleitos] (the fifth century BC Greek sculptor) view of the ideal equilibrium which Indian sculpture exploited to luxurious enhancements. French sculptor, Aristide Maillol, has sought, through his sculpture, the Polyclitus harmony and its enhancements in Indian sculpture. Like the Mathura sculptors of the Gupta age he sought in sculpture architecture and volumes: 'sculpture is architecture, balance between masses and tasteful composition', he has said. Polyclitus's has by now become a natural pose (the weight resting on the right leg, the left bent as if to move [the contrapposto]), a mere symbol of desire. But for Indian sculptors it was a revolutionary compositional device: without disturbing its frontal composition it achieved a counter-balancing movement in the upper part of the body in which the thorax and shoulders tilt in the opposite direction to the hips. A set of contrasting rhythmic curves are achieved in a more natural way making the one side long and the other broken and more forceful.

Husain absorbed all this, and much more: the language of sculptural form which he translated in painting giving rise to a new composition – movement of forms in space. The internal structure of Mathura sculpture is everpresent in his painting and through the medium of paint he makes explicit the operation of these internal forces: the changes in the surface are connected through the line which defines both volumes as well as their surfaces. There is another aspect to the Husain aesthetic which one cannot miss in Gupta sculpture: the linear feature which in the sculptural language is called 'modelling lines'.

MODELLING LINES

This needs explaining because it seems odd that in a three-dimensional art, modelling lines are necessary for clarifying three-dimensional forms. In a sculpture that cannot be viewed from all sides, such as in relief sculpture, high degree of intelligent visibility naturally depends on the clues in the two-dimensional projection. Most recent sculptural idioms share the aesthetic of archaic Greek and Indian relief sculpture: in such sculptures, the frontal view is complete in itself. A close look at a Husain painting, for instance, will reveal that the contours modelling the interior forms are frequently broken and at different depths: they do not form a continuous outline. In no other sculptures of the world - this must be said - are modelling lines used as intelligently as in Indian relief sculpture.

Some might think that because the wall and niche sculpture cannot be walked around, it might be lacking in a fuller three-dimensional structure. This is a mistaken notion. Why are we interested in showing that the relief conception has deepest roots in visibility? It is because Indian sculpture by and large is relief sculpture, and it has achieved greater maturity than the West ever did. To make this point explicit, we quote L.R. Rogers:

> The main function of the interior lines is to clarify the movement of surfaces and enhance the impression of volume. They are not mere decoration. Indian relief sculpture, even more than Greek, places its emphasis on sculptural methods. The figures are almost always undercut and detached visually, if not actually from their background and almost everything is subordinated to the impression of volumes. Although the background plane is often concealed under a profusion of detail, it is always implied and is never carved into an illusion of spatial recession. Partly because of the volumes, Indian figures are divested of all the surface anatomy that is present in Greek sculpture and partly because their drapery and ornaments are laid tightly over the volumes so that they do not break the continuity of their surfaces, the outlines of Indian reliefs tend to be simpler and more continuous than those of Greek reliefs . . . Indian relief sculpture aims like Greek at clear visual presentation from one viewpoint; but even more than the Greek, this desire for the visibility is pursued by Indian relief without loss of tactile qualities. In fact, if the idea of a sculpture strong in tactile qualities has any meaning at all it is perhaps more clearly exemplified in Indian sculpture than in any other style. The volumes have the fullness and all-round self-enclosed completeness and palpability of fruit.[1]

This overlong formal view of Indian sculpture is necessary because most books on Indian sculpture are written in the dead language of archaeology. We are told that Indian art belongs to the past and the manuals of aesthetic procedures have no relevance, as if all life in the good old past was given over to religion. That art was the expression of the life of gods and not the creatures on earth. That art is merely a history of so many confusing myths and symbols, and to understand various periods of Indian art it is essential that one understood the structure of Indian metaphysics. In the name of Indian art, we often get a kind of intellectual commentary on the sources of Indian myths and their pattern of symbolism. So far no one has written why Husain reacted the way he did after seeing a few examples of Mathura sculpture, not even those who have written monographs and books on Husain.[2]

INDIGENISM

The Mathura school today is more important for the debate now on among artists about indigenism: it can clarify many issues if it is studied with the perspective of the Seventies. Of the many available images of the Buddha, why is the image of the Buddha from the Mathura school thought to be an authentic Indian prototype? why were those new forces that inaugurated a new epoch in Buddhist iconography distinctly Indian and classical while the local tradition that burst into bloom at Mathura had much in common with the pre-Aryan traditions as represented by the stupas of Sanchi and Bharhut? Why do the Mathura Buddhas have more vitality of gesture and realism than the Gandhara Buddhas?

In answering these questions, we ask the same questions which our artists are asking today, although in a different context. Gandhara and Mathura represented two traditions which were diametrically different, and the two traditions continued along its old native, lines. Mathura sculpture reached its perfection, no doubt, in the Gupta period during the fourth and fifth centuries AD. The terracotta figures, particularly the terracotta statuette now in America's Boston museum, found near Mathura, have been classified as pre-Mauryan and iconographically closer to the traditions originating in the Indus Valley period. The Boston statuette we are told, 'has the same flatness and frontality and the same emphatic display of the attributes of fecundity, the heavy breasts, and enormously exaggerated pelvis that are characteristic often of a far earlier representation of the mother goddess found all over the ancient Near East.'

The statuette is regarded as a far more superior example of terracotta art than anything produced during the Indus Valley period. Surprisingly enough, we are told that it is a more vital image, not art-wise but in terms of its anthropomorphic aspect. What is significant about this image is the additive method of making it: and incidentally, this has been the technique of Indian sculpture in all its periods. The additive composition of the body is not conceived as representing a counterpart of a human model but built part by part, each part having metaphorical implications. So, the Mathura School traditions have roots in the Indus Valley. And from the end of the Indus cities to the rise of the Mauryans, over a millennium lapsed and we have no evidence of the surviving artworks of the Mathura school.

It is necessary to examine in some depth the conflicting traditions of the Gandhara and Mathura schools. What is called the Indian type of image of the Buddha was first created at Mathura in the early centuries of the Christian era. Most early European scholars are of the view that the first images of the Buddha were created by Gandhara sculptors, though some recent experts have their doubts. Most Indian authorities, however, are of the view that Mathura has the honour of having produced the first original images of the Buddha. Through Mathura, the style of sculpture associated with the Gupta period developed, and this is more significant than the purely chauvinistic dispute whether the first images of the Buddha were created at Gandhara or Mathura. Indeed, Mathura could be regarded as an outgrowth of the ancient Indian school. As a centre of religious art, its history goes back to 200 BC, and stylistically it was as advanced as the Barhut and Sanchi sculptures.

KUSHAN PATRONAGE

The conflicting styles produced at Gandhara and Mathura were largely because of the nature of the Kushan patronage. At Gandhara, the Kushan rulers created a school of sculpture by employing foreigners, mostly journeymen or craftsmen of the Roman east who practised a provincial Greek art in the service of Buddhism. The Gandhara School lasted as long as the dynasty of Kanishka – for about 150 years and all Buddhist art in Gandhara came to end with the invasion of the Huns.

The Gandhara style found a new life in Kashmir later and a few Buddhist establishments in Afghanistan. Why did Kanishka employ foreigners and not bring sculptors from Mathura, his southern capital? There are good reasons why Kanishka, with the support of a foreign culture and by adopting a foreign religion – Buddhism – wanted to advertise his faith and his cultural roots in India. The synthetic character of Kushan art and culture is evident from the Kushan coins. On them are found such strange deities as the Buddha, Siva and many divinities of Iran and Greece – and all identified in inscriptions of corrupt Greek letters!

There never had taken place any real fusion of the Indian and Greek aesthetic perhaps because of Gandhara's geographical remoteness which has put it at a distance from the main cultural stream. Even the later Aryan Vedic literature does not mention Punjab and the North-West area of Peshawar, and wherever a mention is made, it is with some contempt – the land where the Vedic sacrifices were not performed. Moreover, in the Indian context, the Gandhara style was considered a mere imitation of an imitation and so, wholly unoriginal. The translation of Buddhist iconography into available provincial Greek pictorial idioms was like the attempts of our tantric painters translating the *tantra* mystique into the geometric idioms of the New York school.

So at Gandhara, the attempts to translate the master into human form underwent the same process of rejection as it took place in the formation of early Christian art. The earliest Gandhara images of the Buddha remind strongly of the Greek Apollo images. This was exactly the same way the earliest representations of Christ were done in Europe – Christ with the head of the Greek sun god and dressed in the garb of the teachers of the ancient world. The soft, effeminate Apollonian type of representation of the Buddha lacked the iconic power of a symbol: it was perhaps the mask-frozen face of a man called Sakyamuni. Much more inventive than the Buddha image was the Bodhisattva type of images, and their portrait-like character suggest that they may have been representations of donors - a parallel development to be seen in Cambodia where the Khmer rulers are shown in the guise of Hindu or Buddhist deities. For instance, the Gandhara Bodhisattvas are shown wearing turbans, jewellery and muslin skirts - which certainly was a literal adaptation of the actual dress of the Kushans.

Take, for instance, many portraits of Kanishka and his predecessor, Wima [alternately, Vima] Kadphises and Chashtana, the Kushan governor of Sind. These representations are not done realistically although they are quite different stylistically from the native techniques of Mathura. They are, incidentally, the only examples of portrait sculpture known in ancient India. Kanishka's statue (identified by an inscription below it), gives a stronger impression of authority and power than any effigy of an Assyrian king or Roman Caesar: it has an idol-like rigidity of form and though the relief does separate itself from its background, there is no hint of the three-dimensional. Art historian Rowland says about these Mathura statues of Kushan rule: 'One is left with the feeling that the primitive and crude quality of these portraits is perhaps partly due to the Indian workman's complete unfamiliarity and lack of sympathy with this form of art: without the systems of proportion and tradition that determined his operations in carving Buddha images, he could produce only the crudest ideograph of a portrait.'[3]

LOCAL TRADITIONS

The Mathura sculptors, in carving the first Indian representations of the Buddha, had local traditions to fall back upon; they drew inspiration for their Buddha images from the Yaksha figures of the earlier centuries and the Jain traditions - the many images of Jain Tirthankaras. Unlike Mathura sculptors, Gandhara artists had no such local traditions: the only models they had were the gods of the Greco-Roman world.

It was indeed a very demanding job; the nature of the subject was such that the Buddha - who had passed beyond nirvana - should assume in the image that iconic aspect of divine perfection that bestows an awe-inspiring hieratic visualization of the great teacher. Besides, the Buddha image should incorporate all the *lakshanas* [traits] and thirty-two major signs of superhuman perfection that show him in the final yoga state of inner peace, making evident the *abhaya* mudra, the gesture of reassurance. Among the signs of his spiritual perfections are included the *ushnisha* [a topknot-like cranial protuberance on the Buddha's head] on the skull and the *urna* or tuft of hair between the eye brows: his body described as that of a lion, the legs like a gazelle and on his feet appear two shining wheels with a thousand spokes. So that human form was to be a translation into stone metaphorical signs, and this surely was a difficult task.

The achievements of Mathura sculptors can be fully comprehended by comparing the images of the Buddha from the Gandhara school: the Gandhara images were a curious mixture of abstraction and realism but the result was mask-like and lacked the spirituality one associates with the Enlightenment. In contrast, the Mathura Buddhas were a product of the sculptor's self-imposed abstraction. No wonder the artists in the ancient days were thought to be yogis themselves who were capable of identifying themselves with their subject through the yogic self-induced trance. It was in this state of trance that the image appeared in their mind. The Mathura Buddha reveals the intensity of the artist's realization of the same state of bliss which he sought to communicate through its sculptural realization in stone. The icon was never intended to be a likeness of anything on earth: it was an expression of a definite spiritual attainment.

The Mathura Buddhas do have human features but these never interfere with the primary concern of the sculptor to create the solid volume of the whole: there is a suggestion of expansive inner force which is achieved totally by compositional means. The head becomes a collection of interlocking swelling planes, from the curve of cheek and jowl to the related curvatures of eyelids and brows. It seems that the Mathura sculptors under the Kushan patronage have, with the creation of the Buddha images, outgrown the archaic styles of the past. Perhaps the Mathura school, in an indirect way, had learnt much from the innovations at Gandhara.

RELIEF SCULPTURE

At Mathura, relief sculpture made a far greater advance than the production of the Buddha images: the panels carved at Mathura do not have the illusionistic depth as in Sanchi reliefs. Here, the sculptors have combined the two contrasting traditions of Barhut and Gandhara. The creative vigour of the Mathura school found a new energy and expression in the period of Gupta supremacy: this was indeed not a revival of the school but a continuation of several Kushan traditions, including a complete absorption of the Greco-Roman art of the Gandhara school. Take any of the Buddha images carved from the fourth century onwards at Mathura workshops and what has been achieved in terms of technical virtuosity and a majestic serenity of expression have been seldom equalled in any other school of art.

There is now total coalescence of the Mathura and Gandhara traditions. The sharp definition of planes in the Gupta Buddhas from Mathura remind one of the hard precision of the Gandhara Buddhas but the Mathura type does not have the Gandhara's mask-like coldness of expression. The individual features are composed in the metaphorical language of the archaic sculpture of the Kushan period but they are additive – the swelling roundness of the interlocking planes are fused in a geometric manner that radiates a feeling of warmth and fullness, unlike the organic life-like methods of the Gandhara school. The Buddha images of the Gupta period are extremely moving: the fully realized sculptural mass becomes an expression of spiritual dignity of form. The feeling of plastic volume dominates, though the additive method is still present and one can read the Buddha image as separately as to say that the eyes are lotus form, the lips have the fullness of the mango, the hair represented by the snail-shell convention and so on. One distinguishing feature of the Mathura Buddhas is the carved haloes consisting of rings of floral patterns. The abstract conception of the body in smooth and unencumbered planes has a plastic feeling of volume that is a means of communicating the spiritual state of being in which the body becomes immaculate, purified.

Editor's Notes

1 L.R. Rogers, *Relief Sculpture: An Appreciation of the Arts*, Oxford University Press, 1974.

2 Richard Bartholomew and Shiv S. Kapur, in their 1971 book, *Husain* – the first major scholarly work on M.F. Husain – mention the Mathura influence on the artist but do not explore how it came about. In her 1978 work, *Contemporary Indian Artists*, critic Geeta Kapur briefly discusses Husain's response to the Mathura sculptures, and also to the Khajuraho forms (tenth century, Chandela dynasty), as they evolved in his body modelling. This comment, made at the time of the article's writing in 1974, has interestingly, remained largely true. The Mathura origins and the nature of the impact on Husain's art have never been explored deeper by any Husain scholar, and K.B. Goel remains perhaps the only critic to note its importance with much insistence.

3 Benjamin Rowland, *The Art and Architecture of India: Buddhist, Hindu, Jain*, UK: Penguin Books, 1953, p. 93.

68
ART AS A WEAPON

On social realism in art, on the occasion of the publication of an eponymous volume, Art as a Weapon

Link, New Delhi, 16 June 1974

The most 'in' thing today in painting is the art of social comment. Pop art, for instance, has changed the whole painting scene of the Sixties by appropriating things from real life and given them another meaning. Neo-dada pop artists are the social realists of the 1930s. We have social realist painters too, like the Group 74 Baroda painters, who produce the art of social comment, no doubt, but not the social realist debate about its proper iconography and imagery. Nor have they succeeded in generating any dadaist noises. One can speak of a parallel growth of social consciousness about art's involvement with the social problems, but the volume of debate has been far less than in America, perhaps, because the Left in India is indifferent to art's revolutionary potential. Social realism has never been able to influence the central - decorative - tradition in India. Nor do we have any influential group of artists who consider themselves revolutionaries. No doubt, some Baroda painters have emerged recently with a Marxist approach to iconography but is based on emotional appeal. In other words, their art forms do not reflect their ideological contradictions.

The social realists in India now have a document (*Social Realism: Art as a Weapon*, edited and introduced by David Shapiro and published by Frederick Ungar Publishing Co., New York, 12 dollars) about the social protest painting which emerged during the Depression years of American capitalism. The movement lasted for about a decade but its anti-bourgeois stance still survives and in the Seventies scene of American painting it has become a dominant issue. No doubt, parallels exist between the American art scene of the 1930s and the present-day art scene of India. The Armory Show, for example, had introduced abstract art of Europe to America and like Indian painting, American art produced only the derivative canvases, though done in modern techniques as were in fashion in Paris of the 1930s. The wealthy collectors and museums largely ignored their homegrown experimentalists and bought only the European masters. The Depression made the 1930s a frightening experience forcing the local bohemia towards the Left.

MIDDLE-CLASS CULTURE

Little wonder, Stuart Davis, a well-known abstract painter, has painted the Depression years in bleak colours. The American artist of the 1930s, as Davis saw him, worked within the framework of the middle-class culture. His art was in keeping with the middle-class taste (for instance, the American Scene paintings), perhaps from being forced by economic circumstances to 'become a part of respectable business-oriented society'.[1] Working through the channels set up by the middle class, he was 'badly exploited by art dealer and patron alike'. If his work was accepted by an art gallery, it was on the basis of consignment only, the dealer deducting thirty to fifty per cent of the sale price as commission when a painting was sold. The artist, in addition to the commission, paid for the cost of a catalogue, advertising and mailing which amounted to a further cut of thirty per cent. What he was left with was not even what a worker got after a day's work. No wonder, he chose to become an employee of the Federal Art Project because he believed that as a union man he would 'develop as an artist through development of a social human being'. The atmosphere, in Oliver Larkin's phrase,[2] resembled a 'grotesque carnival'.

The situation of the Indian artist is not very different; the only difference is that the economic situation has not forced him to revalue his art beliefs: his faith in the art's future profit still remains. Perhaps, it was not economics alone that made the American artist of the 1930s adopt a protest stance: the looming horrifying spectres of fascism and war appeared to be more deadly menaces. If our painters seek inspiration in the protest art of America's neo-dadaists, it is because of their disgust with imitating Western art forms which are totally alien to their environment.

COMMUNICATION

The Depression years, though produced an art created wholly outside the studio, lacked the revolutionary fervour of the Mexican mural movement. A more positive feature of social realism was its involvement with the American cultural landscape. Social realist movement did not produce a style, but only a new attitude that saw a decaying mining village or shacks along the railway lines as part of the cityscape. Every canvas produced during the social realist wave had the human figure dramatized to focus attention on the indignity and pathos in the lives of ordinary poor people and the inhumanity of the capitalist system was its subject matter. They painted people in slums, not soaring skyscrapers; they painted scenes of industrial suburbs and not the glory of mountains or the pretty side of America's village life. Their paintings told a story, pointed a moral or created an emotion in the onlooker – the emotion that should lead to militant social action.

The Depression years produced a new artist, a union man, for whom art had a moral significance. Today the artist, whether of America or India, has a totally different conception of his work: now the end use of his work is exhibition, criticism and sale although he is beginning to realize that his limited ambitions have resulted in his selling himself to the dealer. Take, for instance, Artists Equity, a national organization in America devoted to protecting the interest of professional artists – now more or less defunct because of petty internal disputes. The survival of National Equity does remind one of the trade union ethics of the Depression days.

MORAL SIGNIFICANCE

That art has moral significance is today beginning to find a place in the consciousness of young artists – especially those belonging to the Art Workers Coalition and the National Art Workers Community [NAWC] which came up in the late Sixties, their dynamic leadership provided by anti-war artists. The NAWC has opened its door even to commercial artists: working with the youth movement and in confrontation with the establishment for the first time since the 1930s, the NAWC artists were recently in news for dumping cockroaches on the Metropolitan Museum's banquet tables. Despite an impressive mailing list and radicalism of these two organizations, they have failed in creating a force at the centre capable of uniting the younger professional artists against the establishment.

For the unemployed, little known young artist, the WPA (Works Progress Administration) Arts Project is something of a dream: it was brought home forcefully by the letter a young artist has written to a prominent critic to enquire if there was in existence any programme like the WPA to assist her financially. The WPA project gave employment to over five thousand artists; but more importantly, the project became a training ground for art. The artists worked as salaried employees and accepted willingly the rules and regulations and even the tyranny of the supervisors. What they objected to was the pauper's oath they were forced to sign for qualifying themselves for employment.

Summing up the creative role the WPA played in training artists for their job, we quote [sculptor] Louise Nevelson's interview (published in *Art in America* magazine in 1964) because of its immediate relevance to our art situation. 'When I came back from Germany where I studied with Hans Hofmann, and also did some movie picture work at the studios, I got on WPA. Now that gave me a certain kind of freedom and I think that our great artists like Rothko, de Kooning, Franz Kline, all these people that have promise today and are creative, had that moment of peace to continue with their work. So, I feel that was a great benefit, a great contribution to our creative people, and very important in the history of art'. Should we not have an Indian WPA project?

Editor's Notes

1 Stuart Davis, 'The Artist Today: The Standpoint of the Artists' Union', *Magazine of Art*, vol. 28, no. 8, 1935.

2 Oliver Larkin, art historian and 1950 Pulitzer Prize winner for his book *Art and Life in America*. He wrote on leading avant-garde and anti-fascist artists such as Stuart Davis who formed a part of the Artists' Congress.

69

SOME WOMEN ARTISTS

An assessment of the work of leading women artists of the day

Link, New Delhi, 7 September 1975

One hardly wishes to deal with women artists as rarities or birds of some special plumage; at the same time, to be a professional woman artist today bespeaks emancipation on more than one front. To be a woman artist (and not merely a craftsman) as a profession, was not a common feature till recently. Devayani Krishna, a self-effacing, modest and conscientious worker, would say, 'But it just happens that I am a woman; that's all. One works anywhere.' This is true if we measure feeling with action, and thought by what is expressed. But there still remains the element of struggle in a world where the presence of a woman has raised not a few eyebrows. And no one can ignore the strides art has taken with the contribution of the work of some of these artists.

Some, like Amrita Sher-Gil, have actually heralded an entire genre and style in painting. (To say a school of painting raises a difficulty in that her imitators have been usually superficial, taking their cue from the surface motif, rather than having understood the basis of her art). Some have taken her work as a point of departure and progressed further to 'third states' of expression where they have found their own idiom. But her impact has remained. Others have ventured into fields not before much experimented in, as Mrinalini Mukherjee with her textile hangings. Devayani Krishna, along with her artist husband, Kanwal Krishna, was among the first artists in the country to have taken an active and growing interest in the graphic arts, and to make a significant contribution through her experiments in printmaking. Others like Anupam Sud, Arpita Singh and Madhvi Parekh have worked with the figural motif. Nasreen Mohamedi's work in pure form is unique. And these are only a few of the themes.

DISCOVERIES

Certain artists have included vast numbers of experiments in their repertoire which is the richer for it, both in content and in style. Stylistic progress is accompanied by probings in subject matter and this is true of most artists who have chosen to experiment and discover. Devayani Krishna's work would seem to be a case in point. In her ceramics, her paintings, and her enormous graphic output, there is constancy; we see the same translucency through the glazes in her ceramics, the stained-glass effect in some of her paintings and in the waxed and watered effect of some of her graphics. In all, the statement is firm: constant questioning of states of mind, and a positive spiritual experience that runs like an undercurrent through all her work, surfacing, when it does, with brilliance. Devayani began drawing and painting in the 1950s. Her work of this period carries folk elements, animal and bird motifs, and the stylized human figure in simple, unequivocal surroundings (*Mask* and *Peacock*). These become more complicated and then progress into abstraction with time. Her large earlier drawings as *Abuse of Power* (1 and 2) are part of the transitional phase, where concern for form is obvious; the animals and small figures have long since given way to a world where entire cities tumble in a deluge, or a holocaust, swallowed up in sweeping arabesques. Where Devayani's paintings done at this stage are more concerned with form, those done later display an increasing interest in the inclusion of graphic effects. But the introduction of this new element which would seem a technical and stylistic departure, do not interrupt the subject matter, which continues (*Man of Power, Petal of Peace*).

These graphic effects are in evidence in all her paintings and in fact her prints and graphic work are a stylistic advancement on these paintings. Of her graphics, the *Allah* series and the *What and Where?* series contain elements of all that is most significantly representative in her work, marking a high point of refinement where the earlier imagery is developed and spun into the finest whiteness. That Devayani and Kanwal Krishna have broken ground in the field of printmaking is a point that cannot be too strongly stressed. Its impact has had an effect on a number of graphic artists.

FORM

Most art concerned with form or its purely formal aspects, suffers in one way or another, impairing its 'purity'. (Meaning that the artist does not achieve what he has set out to – not having carried his particular kind of expression to its fullest realization, allowing it to absorb figurative and symbolic elements in a superficial way, therefore being neither truly abstract not truly realistic). Of the few painters who have chosen to study and work with form, Nasreen Mohamedi's work demands attention, both for clarity and experimentation. Nasreen has worked consistently from the 1950s through to the 1970s. Her earlier work included collage and ink drawings, with compositional integrity as its chief intention. This regard for and desire to achieve purity in form has left her to work in a fine, measured style, with a map-like precision in the laying down of lines and planes. Some of her earlier collages had included colour in some instances, but most of her subsequent work uses black, white and grey tones, sectioned off, woven and webbed into intricate grid patterns – even when they seem to be 'simple'. And perhaps it is when she is most simple that she is most complex – with line and space assuming the tautness that comes from constant discipline.

Nasreen's propensity for spare economy has sustained itself with a curious and exceptional regard for structural exercises, with an even curiouser disregard for any recognizable motif in her work. This may disturb one, as the desire to identify remains among one's most natural impulses. But it is this very singularity – and, most of all, the ensuing quality that such determination ensures – that merits applause. The process of identification is a recurring factor both in life and in art, which is itself significant, as it abjures any differences between the two. The art of image shows the human figure either as the protagonist or uses the figural as a point of departure. Often, this results in work of no small ferment.

Anupam Sud's early paintings and more recent graphics are part of such an experience. Having graduated from the Delhi College of Art in '67, Anupam joined the influential Group 8 and began working in graphics. Human anatomical detail and the figure are positioned as part of an architectural setting (*Human Museum*), or shown burgeoning through a seed-pod; the figure in motion dances, taking on the mobility of an acrobat, and in some examples as *Co-existence*, the man–woman relationship lies latent. *Life, the Revolutions*, shows people at a crossroads, in what is a symbolic representation of a basic conflict. Anupam's graphics, done while she worked as commonwealth scholar in London (1971–73) show concern for technical finesse and compositional strength. In her more recent work, textural effects are seen to advantage, and her firm association with printmaking underlines her own involvement in a relatively new medium in this country. Anupam's work poses the human factor as chief arbiter.

FIGURATIVE

Arpita Singh has taken the identifiable world as a step to grow from. As with many artists, Arpita's interest in figurative work began with her observing Indian miniatures. About 1963, she did a number of small drawings related to her new interest. The human figure, although furnishing the point of interest in her involvement with representational themes, did not become a focal point in her work until much later. In her early work, the figure possessed a cardboard-like stiffness, like those seen in playing cards; Arpita's work of this phase has been labelled 'naïve'. The figures in these paintings carry a peculiar air of mystery about them; they are part of a large charade that includes other objects that surround them in their closeted interiors, with their distorted perspective – as bottles, apples, chairs, a vase of flowers. Her later paintings, shown in the group exhibition in '74 [Group 1974's exhibition] show the human figure in an unfamiliar and hostile landscape, anxious and at odds with an environment that undergoes seismic upheavals – and always at large. This idol-smashing and dissembling carried elements of her present work – the striations, hatchings and loose brushworks developing in the objectivization in her new drawings and paintings, with their pre-occupation with form.

These drawings and paintings, with their light, hieroglyphic wanderings into areas sometimes thick with paint, sometimes finely washed over, concentrate upon graphic impressions. From the earlier representational work to the present drawings and paintings, the change came gradually, as with compositional experiment. The introduction and assimilation of the new dimension has entered, changing and moving, and for that reason, vital and constantly creating.

Difference in vision may be the only truly unadulterated factor in experience, especially if it is left to grow and acquire its own perspective. Madhvi Parekh, too, paints and presents a human world. But it is like that of no other viewer, and no other artist. It has grown, unknowingly, from a deep cache of memory-images into a bright and moving world of cadence, humour, mirth and fire. Madhvi, initially encouraged and taught by her artist husband, Manu Parekh, had no formal art education. Having perhaps unconsciously, absorbed village painting motifs, scratches upon the walls, the flamboyance of village textiles, fairs, temples – Madhvi has constructed a throbbing world of drama where little people, animals, humanoid creatures with fins like puppets animate entire landscapes, or hang like microcosmic men against vast spaces, in an empty field, or against a wall. This private world of knobbly people and animals crawls with activity and life, it seems, marches on. Her *Village Opera*, exhibited at the recent triennale, is fine evidence of all that is representative in her work.

Madhvi started painting in 1969. Until then, she did black and white and coloured drawings, using ink and felt pen. Her paintings are done in pastel and oils on canvas. The early drawings carry much of the expression that is enlarged, revised and finds maturity in her later paintings. The point is that Madhvi's work, while being figurative and full of symbols, is completely different to work that is generally referred to as representative. An overt folk motif has been transformed into a moving and modern metaphor. This transformation of the common into a complex diagram of event and movement sets Madhvi's work apart. It remains a human world, intense and precipitate; its strength stems from its belief in a life of growth, nourished and nourishing. It is representative painting, with an optimistic and joyful involvement in the ordinary things of life. And it is for that reason unique.

In the field of sculpture, it will be seen, women have been few. The reasons for this may be as much the domain of the sociologist as of the psychologist. Among the few sculptresses in this country, Piloo Pochkhanavala's work merits attention for its variety and numbers at least. The vast body of her sculptures ranges from smaller objects to large monumental designs for environmental purposes. Much of the sculpture in our country has taken Western models to study from, as has Pochkhanavala's. Her technique is as varied as her materials, and the scope of her matter ranges from abstractions of images to lessons in pure form.

A new medium, or an old craft put to new use, as that of the textile hanging, or woven sculpture, is the language of Mrinalini Mukherjee. Using varieties of fibres, ropes and other materials that lend themselves to non-loom weaving and knotting, Mrinalini has created hangings that take plant and vegetable forms as their basic theme, and flute and curl off into tangible yet mysterious objects with a sculptural feel in their roundings off and textural effects. This medium poses an endless company of possibilities, and environmental wall surface design is only one of them.

There are other women artists, too numerous to name, whose work too follows suit. The truth remains, that the woman artist is now much less the serious dilettante and much more the dedicated workman of a section of our society today where women are not required to remain anonymous. The presence of women artists should encourage further ideas on advancement in the art scene today so that emancipation is not merely a thing of the time spirit, but also more tangibly of the mind and of values. In this, art will have reached out to life, and having touched it and found reassurance, will turn back to renewed expression.

70
PAVLOVIAN LINKS

On Western technology-mediated art shown in India, particularly early 'computer art'

Link, New Delhi, 27 April 1980

'IT'S LIKE MAGIC' was the comment of the viewers who were exposed to French artist Jean Dupuy's tech-art optical constructions. And the success of his work lay in the fact that the work was susceptible to misinterpretations; that indeed constituted the core of its meaning: the idea (as Duchamp had postulated) that the art work is completed by the spectator's apprehension of it. That is to say, the art work in itself contains no meaning and Dupuy has turned this Duchampian truism into a working aesthetic. Dupuy makes boxes, seemingly anonymous, which reveal their content through peep-hole lenses. 'I use technology only to show the things that are invisible,' says Jean Dupuy. And this is how Alan Moore, a critic has described the Dupuy mystery:

> They (Dupuy's boxes) must be physically encountered, each lens inspected in turn. Among the many drawings and collages Dupuy has made that relate to his boxes, one especially preserves the evidence of this anticipatory contact. In *Table Periscope*, spectators look through a lens stuck in a sheet of paper marked by the accumulated sweat of many foreheads, and accompanied by two tiny photos of the pieces in use.[1]

METHODS, MODES

In simple language, art is what methods make of it: there is thus no predetermined end to it. What is predetermined, it seems, is the absolute methodology – the ways of looking at a work of art: either the pictorial content belongs to the artwork or it belongs to the eyesight. So we get paintings that concern themselves with paintings alone and not to the eyesight, paintings that are beyond experience – that is to say, the experience of looking. And if method is all (since criticism rests on unverifiable experience), the computer can do better than the artist. And not only better, with such speed that it is beyond the imagination of an artist. Besides, the computer is more accurate, never indulges in errors as it has no memory, and produces works more complex and artistically more satisfying.

TECHNOLOGY

This is merely to assert that the technological competence of the computer is definitely superior to that of the artist. But the computer can never hope to do better because a computer does not have the multi-level feedback capacity of a human brain. But the artist today has taken to working with the help of the computer because the high pressure, market-oriented art world, given to the celebration of the new, has compelled the artist to innovate at a speed which only computer technology can provide.

The artist working out his problems with the help of the computer has given rise to a new art movement called the art-and-technology movement. The *Happenings* guru, [Michael] Kirby provides the aesthetic framework for this success-oriented art in his book, *The Art of Time*. Kirby's one ambition is to transform, through the art-and-technology movement, the visual arts into a form of electronic theatre.[2] And since the artist, particularly, the American avant-garde interested in making another dollar as fast as the computer's operations, is no longer an outsider, he has no quarrel with society even though he may advertise his membership of a minority subculture. It is not long that technology will swallow art, for as pop superstar [Claes] Oldenberg has observed, art is basically a childhood while 'technology concerns adulthood'.[3]

OPEN, FUNCTIONAL

Technology to be sure is not outside us; not for an artist seeking to adapt himself to the demands of art's new technology. This is, in a way, extending the Pavlovian approach to matters spiritual. Much of it, no doubt, is science fiction, but the relationship between the computer and the artist is something close to the image of the young couple John Barth has drawn in [his novel, 1958] *End Of The Road*. This young couple is well adjusted inasmuch as they are able to see through each other, resulting in no mystery or contradiction in their lives: in fact, they have no private corner to go back to as individuals, for everything is open and functional like modern architecture.

Only with a few artists, the see-through relationship with the computer is reached: most artists treat the computer more as playfield on which any number of games are played out. Any game that the human imagination is capable of defining with critical awareness of the elements of design. 'A world without gravity' game can be invented where bodies float. Or a playwright can, with the help of the computer, singlehandedly write as well as produce his plays that do not admit any limitations. There are many such science-fiction games the compulsive programmes play out.

Why, the sky is the limit, for the game indeed is the thing, detached as it is from the real world as any imaginable abstract game is. More like the game of chess, perhaps with rules that have nothing to do with the world of living. If errors are made – and many errors are made which cannot be explained by pointing to some empirical facts – they are made unknowingly; a bad move is a bad move, for the knowledge of experience with the rules of the game could not falsify the bad move, or ensure a better one. 'The physically determined bounds on the electronic and mechanical events internal to the computer have no significance whatever with respect to that game, no more that is, than it matters how tightly a chess player grips his bishop or how rapidly he moves it over the board,' as one scientist has explained. The game is regulated by ideas, through a set of perceptions and the range of innovation is as boundless as the limits of human imagination.

ART OF REWORKING

Thus, the game can be defined as producing art from the reworking of previous art: that is to say, the name of the game is – 'art about art'. This is closer to the theory of poetry as original and provocative as Harold Bloom's take, for instance a few samples[4] (and if you substitute painting in place of the word 'poem' you are very near the computer art game) –

> 'Every poem is a misinterpretation of a parent poem.'
> 'There are no interpretations, but only misinterpretations, and so all criticism is prose poetry.'
> 'The best critics of our time remain [literary critic, William] Empson and [G.] Wilson Knight, for they have misinterpreted more antithetically than all others.'
> 'Criticism is the discourse of the deep tautology . . . the art of knowing the hidden roads that go from poem to poem.'

PURE PAINTING

Empson and Wilson Knight can be read in the context of painting as Clement Greenberg and Michael Fried, and the picture is complete. For instance, Greenberg seeks to dissolve all Empsonian ambiguities with Kantian rhetorics: he, indeed, is so clever that painting need not have any authorship now because it attains purity and autonomy comparable in cerebral status to the logical categories which only Kant knew how to employ. Greenberg does not appeal to any conventions as other critics do. Fried has modelled himself on Greenberg except that his variations on Greenbergian rhetorics do not have the logical severity of Kant: there is only a shift of mode. For Greenberg, to give one instance, pure opticality is the core of a painting, while Fried underplays opticality and the major formal factor in a painting for him is shape – 'a new mode of pictorial structure based on the shape rather than on the flatness, of the support' is the goal of modernist painting.[5]

As the computer has no lay audience around, so is the new dematerialized art of the Sixties and Seventies: if this new art admits the presence of critics they have a simple role: their job is descriptive and not prescriptive. Like the computer artist this critic, a devotee of dematerialized, serial art, ignores the presence of the lay audience. As Lucy Lippard, the critic who has inherited the mechanically ordered universe of Greenberg and Michael Fried, has observed: 'originality not only can be but should be a basic criterion for aesthetic judgement'.

Painting, whether produced with the help of computers or with the painter's mind enacting logical tautologies, has been conceptualized with Duchamp, [photographer, Eadweard] Muybridge and Joseph Schillinger [composer] and his Mathematical Basis for [of the] Arts [1943] providing the historical justification. The current ruling aesthetic of this new art is to 'create directly from principles without the intercession of reproductive reality'. The new criticism has made computer art not only respectable but invulnerable to any attack by dissociating it with sensuous sources. Has the ultimate zero point been arrived at?

Editor's Notes

1 Alan Moore, critic and artist, quoted from his article, 'Jean Dupuy', *Artforum*, October 1974.

2 Michael Kirby is associated with Happenings through his book, *Happenings: An Illustrated Anthology*, New York: E.P. Dutton Publishers, 1965.

3 Claes Oldenberg, *Store Days: Documents from the Store (1961) and Ray Gun Theater (1962)*, New York: Something Else Press, 1967.

4 Harold Bloom, 'Manifesto for Antithetical Criticism', *Anxiety of Influence: A Theory of Poetry*, Oxford University Press, 1973, pp. 93–96.

5 Michael Fried, 'Shape as Form: Frank Stella's New Paintings', *Artforum*, vol. V, no. 3, November 1966.

71

THE PROVINCIAL BIND

An assessment on the debate begun in the 1960s–70s on 'provincialism' in international art and its presence in Indian art

Design magazine, New Delhi, April–June 1986

> Provincialism appears primarily as an attitude of subservience to an externally imposed hierarchy of cultural values. It is not simply the product of a colonial history; nor is it merely a function of geographical location. Most New York artists, critics, collectors, dealers and gallery goers are provincialists in their work, attitudes and positions within the system. Members of the art world outside New York – on every continent including North America – are likewise provincial although in different ways. The projection of the New York art world as the metropolitan centre for art by every other art world is symptomatic of the provincialism of each other.
>
> – Terry Smith[1]

How does one recognize the face of provincial-ism? As a possible culture, does it not suffer from internal contradictions? Which is a provin-cial style and which is not? Terry Smith might have answered: go and visit the triennale which India mounts. Because, according to Smith, 'a commitment to art in terms of styles' is the fate of every provincialist as his notion of style is worked out in the metropolitan centre. This makes provincialism a negotiated environment; one cannot exist without the other.

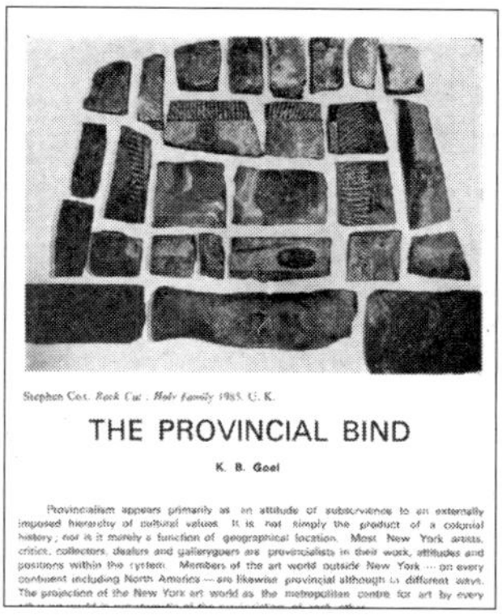

Stephen Cox. *Rock Cut : Holy Family* 1985 U.K.

THE PROVINCIAL BIND

K. B. Goel

Provincialism appears primarily as an attitude of subservience to an externally imposed hierarchy of cultural values. It is not simply the product of a colonial history; nor is it merely a function of geographical location. Most New York artists, critics, collectors, dealers and gallerygoers are provincialists in their work, attitudes and positions within the system. Members of the art world outside New York — on every continent including North America — are likewise provincial although in different ways. The projection of the New York art world as the metropolitan centre for art by every

We mount international exhibitions every three years to affirm our provincial connection; our desire for a strong showing in these international shows is evidence of our surrender to what is called mainstream tendencies in art. As one Akademi official put it: the triennale is a three-yearly 'stock-taking of the world art scene'. Now stocktaking is one thing; trying to place one's achievements in art in the context of world art is another. If we fail to make a strong showing in one triennale we try to do better in the next.

More important than making a strong showing, the worry of the provincialist is about his self-image. His main worry is whether or not he has made the right impression on his metropolitan visitors. He knows his local audience, but by definition of his situation, he should be seen as a significant artist in terms of metropolitan art critical standards. If he fails to impress the visitors, his reputation at home is at stake. No geographical isolation for him, because he knows, as a good provincialist always knows, what is 'in' and what is 'out' in terms of style in the New York world of art.

He is not alone: he knows that the works exhibited from what is called the advanced centres of art suffer the same fate as his, for they stand in a provincial relationship to the art produced in New York. New York, to be sure, depends as much on the inputs of the provincial artists because it is the mutual dependence that guarantees the perpetuation of New York's accelerated avant-gardeism. Imperialism is inconceivable without its colonies.

This explains the status that an expatriate enjoys in the local art scene. How come S.H. Raza who left India thirty-six years ago and has lived in Paris since, became India's nominee as a jury member of the sixth triennale which concluded in Delhi last month? Raza's projection as an artist who has broken the provincial bind by making a strong showing in the Paris art scene should be taken to mean as a provincial construction of reality, a fact which is universally shared by Indian artists. The provincial submission is so deep-rooted that not a single critical voice was heard against the decision. The reason is simple: just as most of the artists working in New York find themselves in a satellite relationship to a few stars, similar structural hierarchies have their surrogate parallel in New Delhi.

What divides artists in India is the system of satellites which circle around their respective competing superstars. If F.N. Souza complains of neglect by the Akademi, having not been invited for participation in any of the six triennales India has hosted, is it because he does not have enough followers at home who are in satellite relationship to him? Given to enacting exciting talk-shows, Souza ought to have been the leader of provincial artists, for the substance of metropolitan art is talk: art there subsists more on words than on picture. Take, for instance, the work of three Japanese artists who are bound stylistically to the old cliché of what is called post-studio art, which in the provincialist language is translated as environmental/earthwork art. These grand gestures of avant-gardeism have a local environmental analogue natural to most primitive societies. But the Japanese commissioner, Hideki Nakamura, thinks that such is not the case: the problem of what he calls post-modernism, though based on the Western European/American cultural context, is to look for a deeper level of self 'within the blend of native and Western contexts'. And this, according to him, is 'likely to be one of the most probable future trends'.

Japan should not take up the metropolitan initiative, for it is bound to the art scene of New York in the same provincial relationship as any other country. What is presented is an art of place-making and not the conventional art objects. In the late Sixties, the art scene of New York was dominated by happenings and environmental art – gestures aimed against the all-powerful museums. All of which was authentic in the context of the politics of those times: it was a heroic attempt to construct a mirage-like experience, for art's ultimate aim was to provide an intimate experience, believing in the illusion that meaning is a put-together experience. Such experience is arrived at alone, for the mind has no reference point outside the projection of its own epicurean garden.

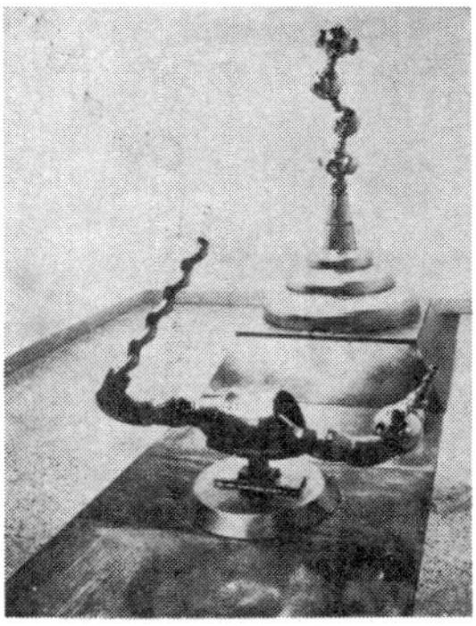

Viseux Claude. *Naga's Birthright*. France

The projection of a future promise of art, as laid out by the Japanese commissioner was, unfortunately, not shared by the triennale's jury members. Had it been so, and the existence of the epicurean garden were to be universally shared, Ranjana Thapalyal ought to have bagged an award for her garden called *Encloser* (in ceramic mix-media). If Japan could run away with an award for a similar kind of work, on what grounds is Ranjana denied it, especially when hers was the only entry in the environmental mode? Perhaps she is a sculptor of the future working today - and within a limited space. And space is what is important for a place-making artist. Perhaps, the complex of metropolitan-provincial relationship is valid only for countries like Japan.

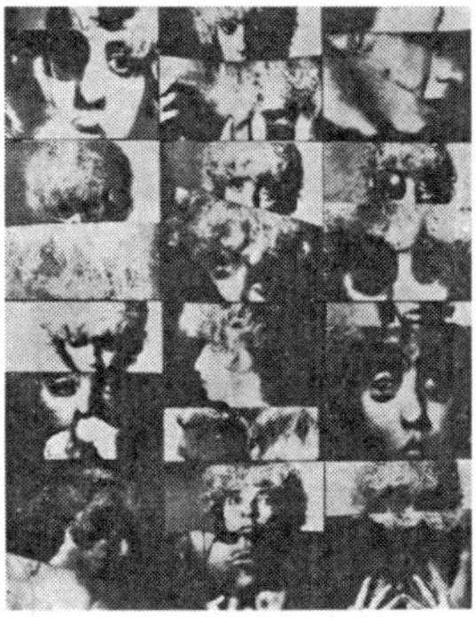

Isabella Gustowska. *Untitled*. Poland

As we said earlier, the triennale show presents a negotiated environment with a well-defined principle of closure. Which means that there are issues which should not be raised; provincialism's point of view is not one among many. The attitude of surrender implicit in the provincial situation admits of no other perspectives on art. We can explain the issue of the provincial bind from Roland Barthes's observation: 'What makes writing the opposite of speech is that the former always appears symbolical, inverted, ostensibly turned towards the occult side of language, whereas the second is nothing but the flow of empty signs, the movement of which alone is significant.' The provincialist is always attracted to art's occult side while metropolitan art, like the written word, belongs to the public information system.

The last of the painters whose art did not belong to the information system was Rothko, a picture for him lived by 'companionship, expanding and quickening in the eyes of the sensitive observer'. Those who have eyes for native accents in art still hold on to the Rothko truth. They are in a minority now; yet they hold on to their truth against the unfeeling acts of translations of these accents into an informational grammar.

Art's chances of survival in India may be linked to the condition of its under-nourished millions, its neglect of comparative and historical information, its economic under-development which permits the fullest feedback from the native vision. If in India art should survive, it would survive with the tribal people. Even they seem too eager to learn the mysteries of the written word. In their art is preserved the virtue of the first person and on a conversational level.

As all tribal cultures are threatened by the ideology of modernism, the art experienced on a private conversational level is threatened by international exhibitions which demand a continual conscious participation. Which means that those who have chosen to work outside the mainstream tendencies of art are forced to work in oblivion. Which means that if they persist for long in doing art the way they know art is made, the incorporation of their art in the mainstream of their country is no longer assured. Their risk is higher; the provincialist by comparison is a sly worker operating on the art scene with a remarkable degree of flexibility.

The experience of six triennales has proved that the international exhibitions are counter-productive. The situation would have been different if we were less committed to modernist ideology and more to our authentic traditions of art making; if we were truly a socialist state and not competing culturally with the culture of free-enterprise. The modernist ideology of art is based on free-enterprise ethic and will thus not permit a self-definition of our art situation. We wish a Nandalal Bose was among us to fight this modernist ideology: we look forward to K.G. Subramanyan and J. Swaminathan to play that role.

The self-definition of our art situation is a distant horizon. As B.C. Sanyal put it: 'If we have failed in evolving a policy for our national exhibitions for all these years, how come we can deliberate on the art situation in the context of a triennale show.' The fact is that too many factional ghosts have taken residence in the Akademi and have turned it into a Kafka castle; in almost scripted roles they have contaminated the whole atmosphere. We have embraced many distortions of the Victorian spirit of which we are not even aware. And to remedy this, a 180-degree shift is needed.

Because of the ideology of anti-elitism, the situation of utter despair prevails: it reminds one of Kafka's allegorical tales *The Next Village* – the traveller never gets to the next village even if the journey is broken into the smallest parts, not taking into account the small, insignificant, wholly incidental undertakings. From the perspective of this, travellers to all the international exhibitions that India has hosted had the same frame, the same aura of international participation as witnessed in Venice biennales which are as old as modern art itself. Venice biennales represent a certain nostalgia for the art of the past. In a truly colonial city that is New Delhi, with its foreign architecture and bureaucracy as its residue, the triennales cannot have hoped for the aura of Venice.

Editor's Note

1 Terry Smith, 'The Provincialism Problem', *Artforum*, September 1974.

72

PANTOMIME EXPERIENCE

On the aspect of 'theatricality' in art as argued by key Western artists and art critics in the twentieth century

Commerce magazine, New Delhi, 3–9 October 1988

A modernist painting can be judged by asking two questions: what constitutes the art of painting? And, what constitutes a good painting? The answer to the first question should merge or increasingly tends to merge with the second. Literalist sensibilities, have an answer: develop a good audience for art. It will decide 'whether a particular work can stand [in] comparison with the painting of the past whose quality is not in doubt',[1] and unless this comparison 'compels conviction, as to its quality, it is no more than trivially or nominally a painting'.[2] But like film experience, art experience too, having become wholly conventional and circumscribed, comes as a postal stamp; which is as it should be when it is experience alone that matters. This has become the condition of art; experience alone secures a painting's identity as presence. The notion of presence implicates a situation as in a theatre. Like epic theatre which by definition includes the audience as part of its enactment; everything exists on the Brechtian stage in its substantiality, not in a surrogate relationship with the world: everything visible, that is, in the exposed light where nothing is hidden from the audience. The actor, for instance, has nothing to hide – only a role to play since he is his author's character. In playing the character, he is playing the role. He knows this as much as the audience, for he does not identify himself with the character he is playing. Brecht's is the anti-illusionistic theatre; whatever its nature, it exists for its audience, as all forms of theatre do – in a way other arts do not.

ART INTO THEATRE

And this is what pop art sought to do: to turn art into theatre and to provide for art its secure audience. It succeeded, with a pile of accolades, with a permanent bullish market for its images, creating an audience in love with its superstars like Andy Warhol. As with theatre, the audience decides what art should be: it exists for the individual alone. As in a happening where art is what is happening to its spectators: a Happening gets its structure as it gets going, its temporal order improvised according to the whims of the audience; the result is that room becomes space in the sense when something is said to be in the individual's space.

The art object is in the same room as him/her: it is so placed that he/she cannot ignore it. Since an art object is an objet manqué, it has something, and this something exists for its audience:[3] this experience is accessible to everyone as film experience becomes accessible to all. As accessible as the billboard: for the billboard has an audience like theatre and one of J.C. Lipchik-McGarry's ostensible aims is to project, at the American Center where her works are on display, that face of the literalist theatre that lies on the borderline between art and non-art. This is done more convincingly by Kendall Baker, the sculptor whose works are displayed at the same venue; sculpture for him provides the sensual analogue of the experience of the literal, with its form and content in absolute dualism.

With Lipchik-McGarry, the sensual is the labyrinthine detail: the juxtapositional game of adjusting the one with the other provides a kind of pantomine experience of the literal in art. The element of presence in her art, as in theatre, is conferred by the billboard format, by the technique of frontality which makes the pierced edges of the picture plane the surrogate parts of the billboard: indeed, the surrogate itself is made real. Which is what theatre does to reality where art itself degenerates as it approaches the condition of theatre.

The artist is saved, though narrowly, because, as she says 'using a figure in its multiples reduces the importance of the subject'. In pop and minimal art, theatre is the content of art, and McGarry does well by eliminating the subject. With the subject gone, the eye comes to rest on the edges that lie outside the frame; then it journeys back, on a fresh detour; this time probably for exploring the details of a figure's make-up rendering all empathetic attempts largely irrelevant. Irrelevance not of response, but of the subject itself: which lends to her paintings a certain complexity: this spatial complexity may be wholly unintended.

Everything being equal and of the same weight, everything is in space with itself: one is a textural correlate of another. There is thus more to look at in the Lipchik-McGarrys, as the mind is held by swiftly changing details: as on a road where something is seen as a mapped-out experience, something that needs a frame, something that has yet to find expression in art.

Editor's Notes

1 Michael Fried, *Art and Objecthood*, Chicago: Chicago University Press, 2011, p. 169.

2 Ibid.

3 The idea is traced to the philosopher Monroe Beardsley in the 1950s: 'Aesthetic objects . . . are all, so to speak, object manques' that lack something that keeps them from being fully real. See Monroe Beardsley, *Aesthetics: Problems in the Philosophy of Criticism*, New York: Harcourt, Brace & World, 1958, p. 529. Also see Allan Shields, 'The Aesthetic Object as "Objet Manque"', *The Journal of Aesthetics and Art Criticism*, vol. 30, no. 2, Winter 1971, pp. 221–27.

73
ART'S DISTORTING MIRROR OF CONSCIOUSNESS

On the reception to current trends in Indian art in the late 1980s

Patriot Magazine, New Delhi, 15 August 1989

It is almost banal to say that art's experience is always from the inside while for the artist it is available both from the inside and outside. The artist operating from the inside knows the limits of communication from the outside. But the presence of the new in art is not always from the inside: the artist knows intuitively what is new about his work because it is something which he cannot explain, something he has not felt from the inside. The new in his work remains unframed in terms of his vocabulary of art.

He is in the same situation as the viewer when it comes to explaining the new element in his work: in fact, there is some kind of an epistemological muddle that he finds himself in. He cannot say that something is impinging on his consciousness when he knows it is not there; nor can he pretend that the new is there for all to see: pretend 'as though the thought of making the new appear betrays the presence of intention'.

This is a form of imagining, placing himself thereby into an 'as if' situation. This helps us to understand the nexus between imagining and projection. The distinction between imagery and projection enables us to decode the meaning of the visual image. While projection is entirely subjective, a matter of one's whimsy and predilection, imagining is not – for imagining calls for a one-to-one correspondence with reality.

Projection, on the contrary, has the element of free play: the element of arbitrariness is more pronounced. For example, the statement about the meaning of a work by a critic is actually a statement about his subjective understanding, about his personal perspective on art and the world. All projections are relative to the viewer's situation in art historical terms, for understanding involves projection which is indeed a search for meaning: projecting a meaning upon one's perceptions is arbitrary in that the meaning is not contained in the perceptions themselves.

This Husserlian insight[1] into the ways of seeing, of understanding an object as a perceptually given something, finds its correlative projection in the experience of the art of three-dimension. When we say, for instance, that we are never able to see all the sides of an object at once, we are not exaggerating our difficulty: rather, we are admitting the fact that we see each side as a side and anticipate the third-dimension of the object in our perception. This is not to deny that all acts of perception are intentional, that is, meaning-giving acts of projection: there is no pure seeing or pure hearing, for perception is always impregnated with meaning. Which is to say that projection of meaning in perception is always on the basis of a partial experience of it: we are always inclined towards a particular meaning, coloured as our eyes are to see what they want to see. We are prejudiced this way or that depending on our mood and inclination, but we are not conscious of this. For, on a conscious level it is difficult to fight one's prejudices: we do not know how they operate upon our judgements and modes of perception. Neither do we admit that prejudice is another name for the colour of our subjectivity; it comes to us naturally, like our second nature, like culture, forming the very structure of our involvement in this history of seeing.

We understand a Shakespeare text as our predecessors have understood it; Shakespeare as a text of our culture has been incorporated into our understanding of the whole tradition of Shakespearean criticism. Likewise if something shocks us in modern works of art, it is because of our lack of involvement with the tradition of modernist sensibility: the shock capacity of much contemporary works is contingent upon the traditional expectations it obstructs. What we believe as something belonging to our art tradition is grounded in what the previous generation has formulated for us: our predecessors' ways of seeing becomes our inheritance which works on our consciousness as an operative force.

We can thus say, the works of art represent our effective history; they are the operative forces of our tradition. Both the interpreter and the critic are subject to the hold of this effective history, to the way, say, a Husain is understood in the context of our tradition to which it belongs. Putting it in another way, we can say that the act of understanding, though subjective to its core, is not subjective after all: it is conceived rather as an aspect of our effective history. This effective historical consciousness is like some distorting mirror; the self-reflection of the individual is only a flicker 'in the closed circuits of historical life'.

The new in art does not necessarily represent a break in tradition, nor a breakthrough in terms of the new. For the simple reason that the perception of the new implicates the presence of a mainstream tradition - or what constitute the sources of our current prejudices. However, a breakthrough, since it cannot be conceived outside of what constitutes the mainstream tendency, is of historical significance.

Towards the end of the nineteenth century, for example, when the dividing line between painting and sculpture was being erased by the bursting of limits as a result of avant-garde painters taking to sculpture, the first breakthrough came with collages of Picasso that he executed between 1913 and early 1914: Picasso cut out a paper guitar onto which he glued and fitted other pieces of paper and four taut strings. This, according to the critic Clement Greenberg, is the first work of revolutionary significance.

Perhaps as revolutionary as Picasso's experiments with the cube and its interplanar study into form and volume.

With this breakthrough the emphasis has now shifted to highlighting the economy of physical substance which, in pictorial terms, means reducing everything three-dimensional into two-dimensional objects. The emphasis is now on expressing the two-dimensionality of the thing painted or sculpted in lines and surfaces that define space but do not occupy it. This way, the anti-illusionist element in a picture gets exposed in its stark literalist aspect. This is well exemplified by cubist pictures where a three-dimensional object is reduced to two dimensions while in constructing collages a two-dimensional picture is given a sculptural space. This historical breakthrough in sculpture, which Picasso's friend [sculptor, Julio] Gonzalez called 'the art of drawing in space', became the mainstream tendency in the Sixties of which the work of David Smith is a fine example. 'Creative art has a better chance of developing from coarseness and courage than from culture,'[2] David Smith in a different context said in 1953.

The only breakthrough that India witnessed in the Sixties in painting was tantric art's esoteric bizarrerie that ingested the tantric symbol itself. When seen against America's minimal reductive art they seem inauthentic. As subject-matter for the minimal reductive tendencies which, in essence, were purely optical, tantric art got mixed up with our wish to catch up with the West, to show that we too are capable of a mutual co-existence: its success seemed a turning point for Indian painting. Tantric art, though, was not an organic growth; it was imposed on Indian painting by the West's discovery of the sitar. A mass demand for the esoteric *tantra* turned our painters into competitive manipulating mandarinates of art: as performers they did very well, and this was their finest hour.

A tantric painting is the best example of art's alienation from itself: art is as meaningless without its roots in reality as economics is without money. That is to say tantric symbols without reference to their ritualistic use value are a meaningless painterly gimmick: it has become, in the hands of its mindless practitioners, a kind of topographical symbol representing the position of India on the world map of art. Tantric symbols that were to free man from his bondage to everyday reality have themselves become the sources of bondage.

Indian artists after their success of tantric bizarrerie in the West, turned expatriates in their home producing art that is bound in a provincial relationship to the metropolitan art centres. The result was that they found themselves always at the crossroad, working out a path for themselves without the knowledge of what lay ahead of the road. They were not true to their local obligations because few of their localisms could be wedded to some advance style in the West.

Their culture, a pure mental construct, lacks in coarseness of speech and courage; their surrogate relationship with modernism forecloses for them the possibility of liberation: liberation from that part of their being that is rooted in decay, personal terror, degradation and savage poverty. If they suffer from a sense of crisis it is the crisis of identity, their refusal to own the truth of their historical prejudices. They wish to have two nationalities: one at home where art is pursued as a utopia, full of future promise, and another for a place in the metropolitan landscape of art in the West. They long for residence in the West for reasons of personal greed, for seeking liberation from poverty at home, and for having a romantic kick in face of the collapse of traditional culture. Their work tells a story of defeat, full of violations of expected continuities that have an ironic look.

As opposed to these expatriates-at-home, the Bengal School painters before independence were better placed: they had a well-defined place in the social structure as they had identified themselves with the freedom struggle. Until independence, the support system of the arts was not as faceless as it is today. They were in close contact with the sources of patronage and for this reason did not suffer the indignities of cultural Darwinism. There were no Kafkaesque castles then to fight against; nor was there money in painting. Working within a tradition for them meant working within the framework of prejudice. Negatively speaking, prejudice means a judgement given before all the elements that determine that a situation have been finally examined; it gives rise to expectations, allows us to project without any fear of contradictions.

Editor's Notes

1 Edmund Husserl, philosopher, often considered the father of phenomenology. Husserl evolved the science/realm of enquiry and philosophy known as phenomenology as based in (individual) perception. It has influenced, via different thinkers and followers, the idea of subjectivity lying at the heart of phenomenology.

2 A sculptor, David Smith's writings and this quotation are available from multiple sources – prominently, his 1960 text, 'Memories of Myself'. Another good source is his collected writings: *David Smith: Collected Writings, Lectures and Interviews*, edited by Susan Cooke, University of California Press, 2018.

74
COMPANY ART: ON A COMEBACK TRAIL

On the art that emerged in nineteenth-century colonial India termed 'Company Art', which brought together visual traditions of the West and of India

'Artscape', *The Economic Times*, New Delhi, 2 July 1990

What is called the Company Art of the mid-nineteenth century India was an alien presence; we never had a window view of the world, of which easel painting is one of its allegoric representations. That original window which was conceived as a hole in the wall disappeared with the modern tradition, becoming a universalist aesthetic. With the coming of the cubists, the window was bricked up. Painting since has become a mere sign and its visual signifiers get related to other signified units as sense and reference, as contexts, frames and focus. A painting can now be understood as a system of signs, but with this difference that it implicates a private space between the viewer and itself, which language does not. The notion of private space came under attack in the Seventies: with the popularity of story art, it was necessary to structure art's discourse on the fundamental disparateness between the world and the self. The result was a new internal interrogation of modernism's closed world pre-suppositions, which led again to the opening of the window on to a world that is electronic in essence.

The relaxing of the authoritarian uniformity and denial of all frames that subsist on the division of the aesthetic between high and low arts, have opened up a process of cultural externalization which promises to bring into visibility all those gestures of local popular culture that once had a life of marginality. It has brought into focus the Company Art collection of the late [art critic] Jaya Appasamy, the show of drawings held last year at the CMC Art Gallery, New Delhi, from the collection of artists and collectors, Jagdish and Kamala Mittal.

In 1985, E. Alkazi, the owner of the Art Heritage Gallery, New Delhi, published three portfolios of prints on the Company Art period of the British Raj; these have now become collectors' prints. Two British artists have been included in the collection, who came to India to secure commissions for portraits, which was most lucrative for the lesser-known artists of the West. Colonel Robert Smith's collection of watercolours is about the India that lives only as a picture postcard reality. They present scenes of his journey down the Ganga. Smith loved India, and his works, picturesque as they are in approach, are of great charm.

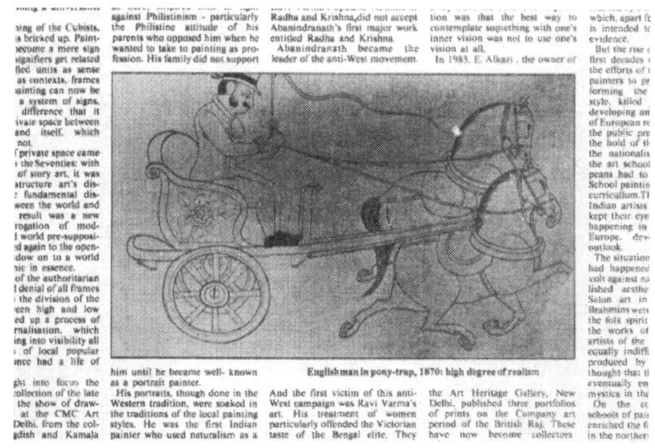
against Philistinism - particularly the Philistine attitude of his parents who opposed him when he wanted to take to painting as profession. His family did not support

Radha and Krishna, did not accept Abanindranath's first major work entitled Radha and Krishna.

Abanindranath became the leader of the anti-West movement.

tion was that the best way to contemplate something with one's inner vision was not to use one's vision at all.

In 1983, E. Alkazi, the owner of

Englishman in pony-trap, 1870: high degree of realism

him until he became well- known as a portrait painter.

His portraits, though done in the Western tradition, were soaked in the traditions of the local painting styles. He was the first Indian painter who used naturalism as a

And the first victim of this anti-West campaign was Ravi Varma's art. His treatment of women particularly offended the Victorian taste of the Bengal elite. They

the Art Heritage Gallery, New Delhi, published three portfolios of prints on the Company art period of the British Raj. These have now become collectors

Colonel James Skinner is better known for his portrait studies. He is also known for building a temple, a mosque and a church in India.[1] The last of the three portfolios deal with plants, birds and animal studies from an extensive collection of natural history paintings. These were made by local artists and supervised by the Company surgeon, Dr William Roxburgh, who was in India as the company botanist between 1789 and 1793. These are marked by a high degree of realism which, apart from its artistic merit, is intended to serve as scientific evidence.

But the rise of nationalism in the first decades of this century, and the efforts of the Bengal School of painters to present their work as forming the core of the national style, killed the hope of India developing an indigenous version of European realism. So strong was the public pressure that the art schools run by the Europeans had to include the Bengal School painting as part of their art curriculum. The result was that the Indian artists who ought to have kept their eyes open to what was happening in the art capitals of Europe, developed a myopic outlook.

The clever Brahmins were successful in killing the folk spirit that once informed the works of Jamini Roy. The artists of the Bengal School were equally indifferent to the images produced by folk artists. They thought that the folk artists would eventually end up the way the mystics in the past did. On the contrary, Rajasthani schools of painting influenced and enriched the folk styles of painting in the northern regions of Jammu, Kangra, Garhwal and, to some extent, Sikh painting. The Rajasthani painters, who worked in the Mughal court ateliers, moved away from the court art and supplied to the Mughal painting what it lacked in poetic background. The best of its traditions were to flower into the Kangra School.

Editor's Note

1 Popularly known in India as 'Sikander Sahib' in his time, James Skinner is also known for the cavalry regiment he raised in 1803 called Skinner's Horse, till date a part of the Indian army. His Persian books, *Kitab-Itasrih al-Aqvam*, a social history of Indian castes and his *Tazkirat-al-Umara*, biographies of noblemen, feature rich illustrations in the Rajput and Delhi miniature styles.

75

A DISCIPLINED JOURNEY

A reflection on the early century revivalist art style known as Bengal School

'Artscape', *The Economic Times*, New Delhi, c. 1990s

We have recently had two historic exhibitions which did not receive the critical attention they deserved. Critics wrote about them as if they were another set of exhibitions. No attempt was made to make explicit the context to bring out the meaning behind their historic frames. The exhibition of the works of Asit Kumar Haldar, mounted by Lalit Kala Akademi, was in the nature of a homage. It was put up as part of the artist's birth centenary celebrations. In the Haldars, we find the disciplined progress of the Bengal School. At the CMC Gallery were mounted more than 70 works by Abanindranath Tagore and Gaganendranath Tagore. Abani Babu [Abanindranath], the founder of the Bengal School, sought to translate in his paintings the mystic vision of E.B. Havell and A.K. Coomaraswamy. He produced images which are not born of feeling, the core of which is personal experience, but with a strong colouring of nationalist feelings. His younger brother [Gaganendranath Tagore] was more experimental and, therefore, a rebel, and let his mind indulge luxuriantly in the Western formal styles such as cubism.

The Bengal School wash painting has a geisha-like charm and that was its supreme value. That also became a condition of taste in a cultural climate which made everything Western untouchable. As members of the landed aristocracy and being free of economic cares, the Tagores became fond of Mughal miniatures which were first introduced to Abani Babu by his guru, Havell. As an expression of taste, the miniatures represented the crux of the problem of style to be developed. When Abani Babu first saw Mughal miniatures, he realized for the first time, 'what treasure lay hidden in the medieval art of India'. And when Havell retired in 1905 and Abanindranath became the principal of the Calcutta School of Art, he resolved to recreate out of Mughal miniatures, a national style.

And the Bengal School became a national style until the arrival of Amrita Sher-Gil. But she failed to effect a separation in taste. The Bengal School images have a certain aloofness and an unconcealed consciousness of superiority while the Amrita Sher-Gils seemed to belong to an alien land. She lacked those 'deep and spiritual impulses'. The nationalist bourgeoisie could appreciate the art which spoke the revivalist language of the gods of Hinduism [and] had become enmeshed with the semantics of nationalism. Mughal painting got an emotional edge when the Hindu gods were depicted as vivid national realities [in the adaptation of Mughal miniatures in the Bengal School style].

One may argue that good taste belongs to the imagination: self-evident truth needs no elaboration. It goes without saying that mind treats art as its raw material and for this reason judging is thought to be a mere critical activity expressive of a given condition of taste, which provides for the artist a cultural space in which to operate with some feeling of stability.

Little wonder then that the Bengal School died when art sought to be merchandized. The statement was true until the advent of post-modernism. Since 1984, when the French philosopher Jean-Francois Lyotard's book *The Human Condition* was published in English, post-modernism has become a vogue word. While modernity resorts to great narrative scenarios (beginning with the French revolution to the Marxist promise of a transparent society), the post-modern suggests the possibility of a return to the small, provincial ethnic world with its own paradoxical narration. Primarily because, unlike modernity in which the succession of the historical stages are completely determined, post-modernity has nothing to do with any kind of stage theory of evolution. Being historical and value neutral, post-modernism gives the impression of being amusingly kinky.

And who can be more eccentric than the gurus of the Bengal School. The Bengal artists, in their search for the indigenous roots of their visual grammar, sought to return to the past, which fulfilled two very different needs. In the past could be located the possibility of a true national art; and since in the 1920s, the freedom from the British rule seemed remote, in cultivating the great historical themes was the promise of overcoming despair. 'Why have none of you painted a picture with sunshine?' The answer Abanindranath gave in 1924 was revealing:

> It is because we Indians do not see the sun. Suppose you look out on a clear blue sky and then you are told about somebody who is killed. At once you find the sky grey and the landscape dark. We Indians do not paint things as they are; we paint from the feelings which possess us and paint ourselves. We are never glad – there is no smile in India – the children do not play in the streets; they do not even smile. We carry the darkness in our soul.

When one finds the sky grey and the landscape dark, the inside of an artist knows the limits of communication from the outside. He pretends that the new is there for all to see as though the thought of making the new appear betrays the presence of the intention. Through individualistic insights, the Bengal School of painters projected a wholly Indian version of European easel painting: the invented manner resulted in a painting, the beginnings of which were rather eclectic. But problems of eclecticism did not worry them because they knew that it was a mixture of such diverse things as

Indian miniatures, frescos, scroll and *pat* paintings. Mind you, there was no European outfit for this painting; rather what was good in Persian and Chinese wash techniques was adopted.

Undisguised despair and shrinkage from reality were also the characteristic of the national movement for freedom. The Bengal painters were like the romantics who could not move a single brick of the 'naturalistic' prison in which the painting before the impressionists found itself. In the context of the collective failure of the Bengal School, the causes of Abanindranath's failure seem purely psychological. If style must express the artist's personality, the style must be a man: and if there is no personality there is no possibility of art. If the personality make-ups of Abanindranath and Jamini Roy are investigated to find out why the Jamini Roy survives and why Abanindranath has failed, we can understand better the conditions which produce a strong national art.

In the continuing post-modern debate on ethnicity and the shifts in our myths of concern, we fail to attribute any meaning to our understanding of conditions which produce a strong national art. Jamini Roy, whose role as a painter can be seen in making us conscious of the need to bridge the gap between folk and fine art, has become a post-modern contemporary. Placed against the majestic achievement in narrative art, his art represents the magnitude of neglect. The important thing is in freeing ourselves from the prejudices of modernism which has played strange tricks on our value to get rid of the monster of revivalism of which the high priest is Abanindranath Tagore.

76

WIELDING A CRUSADER'S BRUSH: ARTISTS AGAINST COMMUNALISM

On Indian artists taking a stand against communalism in the early 1990s

'Artscape', *The Economic Times*, New Delhi, 22 May 1991

India's appalling misery and its ever-increasing poverty seem to belong as inherently to the Indian landscape as the consumer culture does to the dollar affluent societies. In such a society, it is shocking to be making art for art's sake. But the Greenbergians among the artists, with a fatal illusion, argue that making works of art has nothing to do with either eradication of poverty or alleviating the culture-consciousness of the people.

Greenbergianism in art is associated with content-free art; there is the primacy of the optical values over all other elements in painting. It has a well-developed Kantian formalism in which the task of self-criticism came to be associated with a purging from painting all effects that might conceivably be borrowed from other arts. The Indian art scene of the Fifties and Sixties was influenced by Greenbergian aestheticism. Only in the Seventies did there emerge a new breed of artists, of artists as precursors. The cult of the artist as precursor means that you substitute a prospective with an imaginary relationship between present and future. For it is good to remember that the traditional focus of culture tends to treat the present (the living contemporaneity of experience) as the culmination of the past.

But the role of the precursor artist is different; it frees the artist from the process by which the past feeds into the future. By pushing art into a direction it does not know, the precursor turns the artist into a historical expedient whose role is less to be than to assist the labour of becoming. The precursor, that is to say, frees the artist from the parenthesis location between the dead past and the unborn future.

The exhibition, 'Artists Against Communalism: Images and Words', currently on in the capital, is in the nature of preparing the participating artists for the role of a precursor. Gone are the days when one could talk of the past as a well-etched, harsh, black-and-white image: it now has stark hieroglyphic features. Only those who look for their roots in the past find the experience as luminous as the colours in a stained-glass window. The artists who fight against communalism assume the role of precursor and act as a kind of scouting party that goes ahead of the main force. In some cases, they initiate a skirmish but have never really taken a decisive role in the battle. They belong to a class of artists about whom the Utopian

Wielding a crusader's brush

The artists are a kind of scouting party that goes ahead of the main force but never takes a decisive role in the battle, writes K.B. Goel *of the unusual protest in the Capital.*

INDIA'S appalling misery and its ever-increasing line of poverty seem to belong as inherently to the Indian landscape as the consumer culture does to the dollar affluent societies. In such a society, it is shocking to be making art for art's sake. But the Greenbergians among the artists, with a fatal illusion, argue that making works of art has nothing to do with either eradication of poverty or alleviating the culture-consciousness of the people.

Greenbergianism in art is associated with content-free art; there is the primacy of the optical values over all other elements in painting. It has a well developed Kantian formalism in which the task of self-criticism came to be associated with a purging from painting all effects that might conceivably be borrowed from other arts. The Indian art scene of the fifties and sixties was influenced by Greenbergian aestheticism. Only in the seventies there emerged a new breed of artists - artists as precursors. The cult of the artist as precursor means

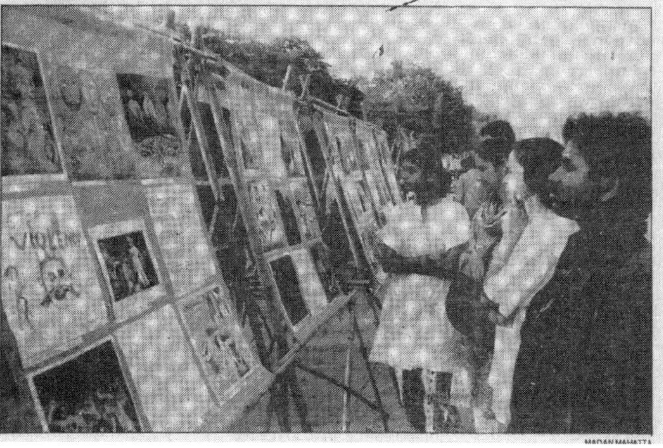

socialist, Saint Simon, in his book *Opinions Litteraires*, talks affectionately: in an imaginary conversation with the scientist, the artist asserts that 'it is we, the artists, who will preserve you as avant-garde.' Such an artist claims for his work 'a priestly function'. 'The power of the arts is, in fact, most immediate and most rapid: when we wish to spread new ideas among men, we inscribe them on marble or on canvas.'

Most artists fighting communalism believe that art can fill that role. But unlike Gustave Courbet, about whom it was said that he was a 'terrible' socialist at the head of 'a band of conspirators',[1] there seems nothing threatening about their art. They [Indian artists] could not save Bharat Bhavan despite their brave, confrontationist noises.[2] J. Swaminathan's warning to the Indian artist community, of the likely consequences of the BJP's (Bharatiya Janata Party) takeover of Bharat Bhavan is relevant. Swaminathan resigned as life trustee of Bharat Bhavan in protest against the fundamentalist intervention in Bharat Bhavan of Madhya Pradesh's ruling party, the BJP.

No longer can painting claim the possibilities of social threat and intellectual disturbance that it possessed during the mid-nineteenth century. Art in India, to be sure, does not act directly on politics the way it did during the Weimar days in Germany. The Weimar experience has become a model of dissent representing a fusion between radical art and radical politics. Similarly, there is a lesson to be learnt from the failure of the Russian avant-garde who wanted to change the art scene of their country after the October Revolution. They were interested in creating not just a style but a new rational man. They were snuffed out by 1930 by Stalin.

The Bauhaus movement in art and architecture sought to create an international style, a chief characteristic of which was what is called functional rationalism. It gave birth to a severe geometric design and brought about a new respect for materials. With the rise in popularity of Nazi ideology, the school was forced to move out from Weimar to Dessau. Conditions were created that led Walter Gropius, its first director, to resign. He was succeeded by Hannes Meyer, who too was replaced by Mies van der Rohe.

Recalling the Nazis and what they did to the artists who had mistaken the art world for the real world, brings painter Grosz's tragedy to mind. When George Grosz was threatened with imprisonment, Dr Edwin Redslob, the Federal Arts Officer, appeared in the court to give testimony. Since his testimony was in favour of Grosz, Hitler refused to shake hands with him and saw to it that he was dismissed from his post. The world has not seen a committed artist equivalent to Grosz. Tristan Tzara, the famous dada ideologue, may be right and his chilly dictum needs repeating: the politics of art is a tiny parody of the politics of real power. Or the Beuys truth: nobody, or rather, nobody intelligent (in Duchamp's implied view) can presume to change society through art.

Art, as part of capitalism's exchange value system, is reactionary: at least so is the case with the French artist, Daniel Buren, who took the stand during the 1968 students' uprising in Paris that the artist is the only managerial interpreter of other people's fantasies. His solution for taking art to the people was simple. In 1967 he put up about 200 billboards all over Paris and on the back of a sandwich man, parading outside the gallery, he put pieces of green and white-striped cloth which looked to the uninitiated eye exactly like an awesome canvas.

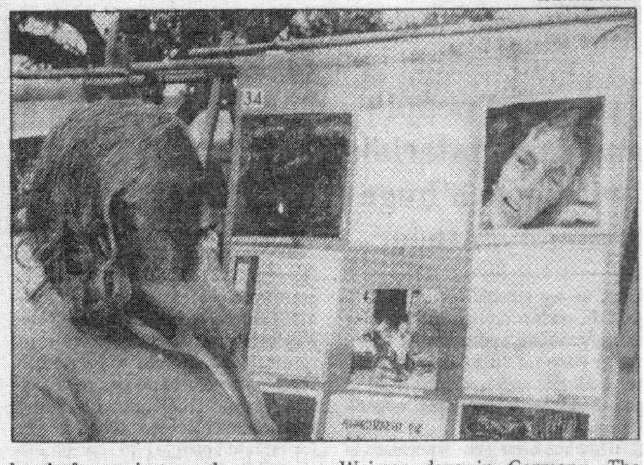

ing against communalism
ı 'Words and Images': of
ıjective importance

ıs luminous as the colours in
ɛd-glass window. The artists
ht against communalism
the role of precursor and
kind of scouting party that
ıead of the main force. In
ıses they initiate a skirmish
'e never really taken a deci-
e in the battle. They belong
ss of artists about whom the
socialist, Saint Simon, in
k *Opinions Litteraires*, talks
nately: in an imaginary con-
ɔn with the scientist, the art-
rts that "it is we the artists
ill preserve you as avant
Such an artist claims for
k 'a priestly function'. "The
ɔf the arts is in fact most im-
and most rapid: when we
spread new ideas among
'e inscribe them on marble
ınvas."
t artists fighting communal-
lieve that art can fill that

MADAN MAHATTA

band of conspirators, there seems nothing threatening about their art. They could not save Bharat Bhavan despite their brave, confrontationist noises. No longer can painting claim the possibilities of social threat and intellectual disturbance that it possessed during the

Weimar days in Germany. The Weimar experience has become a model of dissent representing a fusion between radical art and radical politics.

Similarly, there is a lesson to be learnt from the failure of the

Buren's solution for taking art to the people is analogous to what Safdar Hashmi did in theatre. He dared to disturb the peace of the bourgeoisie and paid for it with his life. If we have over 350 artists, poets and writers who have come together to commemorate the tragedy of Hashmi, it is indicative of the fact that painting or poetry cannot compete on level terms with street theatre, which is far-reaching in its iconic influence. For painting is a small thing compared to theatre unless the artists fighting communalism take to billboard art a la Buren.

The paintings and poems, as they were displayed in a 3 x 3 feet format, the total exhibits comprising thirty-five panels with nine works on each panel, seemed to be obsessed with nuances and spoke in muted voices that had no objective importance. In the context of power politics, of which communalism is a fascist manifestation, it does not matter what art says. What matters is how many battalions are there behind the statement art is making. For, it needs to be remembered that art is not even a religion to evoke a stock response from the lay public.

Of course, art is serious business as its essential role is to enlarge the arena for free thought and loosen up regimented feelings. It is for this reason that art has come to represent the voice and conscience of the middle class. For this very reason oligarchs dislike art's intervention in politics because art creates a new class of elites, splitting the audience into those who understand it and those who do not. The cleavage runs along political lines. For instance, art is seen as providing an opportunity for being used by the celebrities as a container for fame: art is either Husain, Amitabh Bachchan or nothing. Which is to say that art, when seen on the roadside, is never art: it is just a gathering of individuals and has the potential of becoming a movement.

Editor's Notes

1 See 'Institutional Theory of Art' in the section 'Catalogues' in this volume, pp. 383–90.

2 Bharat Bhavan, an autonomous cultural centre for multiple art forms set up by the Madhya Pradesh Government in 1982, envisioned as a secular and liberal space for free, creative expression. Its unique museum, Roopankar, housing modern, contemporary and folk/tribal art, was established by the artist J. Swaminathan.

PHOTOGRAPHY

Within the visual arts, photography was an area of great interest to K.B. Goel. He wrote on it extensively, making him quite unique among his generation of Indian critics. Presented here is a brief selection of his writings on photography that trace its history and reflect his interest in its technical aspects, via a discussion of contemporary Indian and international photo-graphy. The subject is also explored at some length in an essay in the 'Catalogues' section.

77
FROM IMAGE TO ICON

An early article on the Indian photographer O.P. Sharma, and his technical innovations

Link, 18 May 1969

Photographer O.P. Sharma treated us to his latest experiments with photographic emulsions at a private show in his studio in Modern School, New Delhi. There is nothing very exciting about these experiments except that they are photographs only by a loose definition of the term. They are a kind of graphic creation closer to monoprinting but, in effect, look like works in tone separation process (posterized prints)[1] and a few, like lithographs. The resultant image is a pure accident – something of the kind the abstract expressionists have achieved in their play with colours. Just a beginning, Sharma, if he is serious, has to do still more work to give them a proper status of photographs. Because these are mere darkroom paintings produced with photographic emulsions, not camera images, it is necessary to touch them with the camera's cautious approach.

No doubt some eyebrows were raised and not everyone seemed satisfied with what they were being treated to in the name of photography. But one thing was clear: this was the farthest photography could go abandoning camera on the way. Darkroom photographic materials, emulsions and chemicals were then Sharma's working tools and studio. What Sharma intended to prove, however, is simple: no longer should we make the old distinction between a painter and a photographer. Now photographers too can 'make' pictures rather than 'take' them. Ever since the camera was invented, photographers did not like the idea that they only took pictures and not made them.

NEW MEDIUM

This surely is not a mere verbal difference: the difference between the connotation of 'take' and 'make' has raised a creative issue of a new order. Many still ask and not without reason: How can a mechanical, mindless device like a camera produce pictures that can be given the status of a painting? Then there are the casual snapshooters who use the camera for fun and entertainment alone. And this precisely is the trouble with photography: thousands who practise it have no allegiances to break, are in fact hardly aware that the new medium has artistic possibilities. They have nothing in common with the pictorialist-experimentalist photographers: they have no traditions to break, no training to bind them into any discipline of an academy or a guild. They are not aware of each other's work. To them composition, light, shade, form and texture are so many catchphrases. Anything that attracts their attention, whether a visual field or a face, gets focused in their camera and for the fun of it a shot is taken.

Pictorialists are different: they are the ones who turn a casual snap into a photograph, can produce things which apparently seem most un-camera like. Because they are a connection between the art of painting with that of photography, which is as old as cubism. Picasso himself is a great admirer of the camera – especially the photo-montage technique. He compared, for instance, the painter to a magician or faith-healer who keeps a normal distance between himself and his subject's reality and the photographer to a surgeon who 'operates directly on the tissues of reality'. What Picasso established was this: the painter's image is total; the photographer shows 'a multiplicity of details coordinated according to a new law and resulting from an intensive penetration of reality'.

The movie, by sheer speeding up of the mechanical, has shown the truth of Picasso's observation. No longer is the camera image bound to the world of sequence; it is a new world of creative configuration and structure. Photography no longer means mere documentation; it is becoming an icon-obsessed art. Pictorialists, to be sure, do not just take pictures but make them by playing up plain contradictions, dimensions of different patterns of light and textures in dramatic conflict.

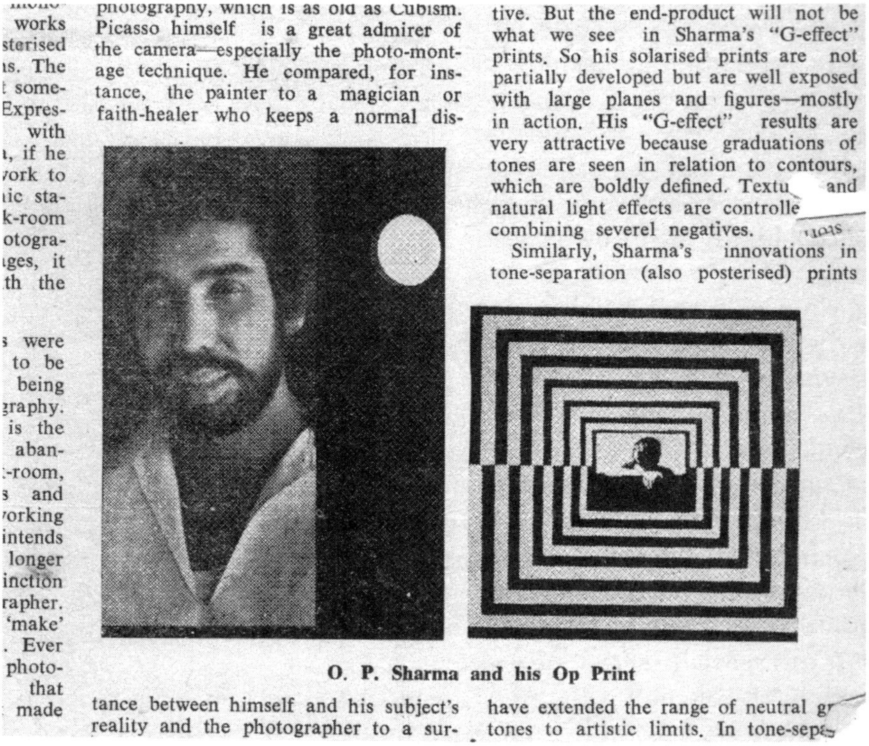
works
sterised
is. The
t some-
Expres-
with
, if he
vork to
nic sta-
k-room
otogra-
ges, it
th the

s were
to be
being
graphy.
is the
aban-
-room,
s and
vorking
intends
longer
inction
rapher.
'make'
. Ever
photo-
that
made

photography, which is as old as Cubism. Picasso himself is a great admirer of the camera—especially the photo-montage technique. He compared, for instance, the painter to a magician or faith-healer who keeps a normal dis-

tive. But the end-product will not be what we see in Sharma's "G-effect" prints. So his solarised prints are not partially developed but are well exposed with large planes and figures—mostly in action. His "G-effect" results are very attractive because graduations of tones are seen in relation to contours, which are boldly defined. Textu and natural light effects are controlle combining severel negatives.

Similarly, Sharma's innovations in tone-separation (also posterised) prints

O. P. Sharma and his Op Print

tance between himself and his subject's reality and the photographer to a sur-

have extended the range of neutral gr tones to artistic limits. In tone-sepa

SOLARIZED

Sharma's innovations are many and the best known among them is his 'G-effect'. He has written about this technique and demonstrated in public discussions the stages through which a negative passes in the darkroom. 'G-effect' is obtained with multiple, solarized negative placed off-register around a centre of rotation. 'G-effect' or multiple solarization prints are not Sharma's inventions; he has added a few things of his own so that the prints have a distinctive Sharma flavour. Solarization seems too much like technical photography which it is not. If a negative is partially developed and is exposed to white light (during development) and then developed to normal it will produce a pseudo-solarized negative. But the end-product will not be what we see in Sharma's 'G-effect' prints. So his solarized prints are not partially developed but are well exposed with large planes and figures – mostly in action. His 'G-effect' results are very attractive because graduations of tones are seen in relation to contours, which are boldly defined. Textures and natural light effect are controlled by combining several negatives

Similarly, Sharma's innovations in tone-separation (also posterized) prints have extended the range of neutral grey tones to artistic limits. In tone-separation, the shades of grey are what count because these grey tones give the photograph volume and a painted look. The current work which Sharma is showing at Palghat [a town in Kerala] is either abstract-expressionistic produced without the aid of lens and entirely inside the darkroom on process film, or, optical prints done under the influence of op art. The difference between op painting and op photograph is not very wide, and a photographer is at a disadvantage while working with pure geometrical structures. But Sharma's op geometrical prints are nearer op painting than photography.

Sharma has held several one-man shows trying to establish the truth that photographs should have their place alongside other works of art. While in more advanced countries photographs have entered the art museums, in India they are still miles away from their journey's end. In fact, Sharma's development, like the history of photography itself, has been less a journey than a growth.

Editor's Note

1 Monoprinting is a process that allows for a single impression or print to be taken from a block, which might be reprintable, like a woodcut, etching or lithograph block or matrix. It involves creating a unique image on the printmaking matrix through painting, collage or with changeable elements, so that the print taken is unique, with no duplicates. Tone separation in the darkroom involves creating contrast between adjacent tones in black-and-white photography, to create a (tonally) rich image bearing different areas of tones and a gradation of them instead of just a flat (and seemingly single-toned) surface. Posterized prints/posterization – used extensively to create and print analogue posters – involves the breaking up of a continuous area of image, whether colour or black-and-white, into distinct regions of tone or colour, drawing attention to each.

78
GRAND EXHIBITION

Review of the photographic exhibition, 'The Photographer's Eye', brought to New Delhi by the Museum of Modern Art, New York

Link, New Delhi, 4 October 1970

In judging an art object, the healthy, critical approach is to judge it in isolation without taking into consideration the intention subsuming it. This is the most precious lesson Duchamp taught us. According to him it is not the intention or the capacity for making art objects but the artist's power of choice which is far more important. In fact, a work of art is the product of a series of choices; that is to say, to single one thing out and to affirm loudly that this is art and surprisingly enough becomes that object what the artist wishes it to be. Isolating things is indeed very important, and this is truer in photography than in other arts, including the found objects (which Duchamp transformed into art by simply placing them inside an art gallery). Of course, the old way of judging art is still relevant and the safer rule is to match the art object to the intention. But the rule has not been working satisfactorily over the years and more and more of recent art seems to frustrate it. The reason is simple: the thing that we see before us is not the whole work of art, some bodiless idea or a set of ideas are also part of its structure. So it is difficult to isolate the object from the circumstances of its creation.

SELECTION

A photographer, claiming for his time-exposed camera images, the status of art is placed in an enviable position because he does not claim to be making any art object, he merely isolates it and gives it a frame. The frame indeed is more important because this represents the photographer's area of choice. The photographer, unlike the artist, does not 'conceive but selects' and 'the edges of his film demarcate what he thinks most important'. He works very much on Duchampian lines, selecting 'ready-mades' for the camera. The artist, on the other hand, reveals himself more in his power of choosing than in his power of creating physical things. By separating objects from their environment and seeing them meaningful in themselves make them shed their Humpty Dumpty existence in the world of objects. These objects thus get the power of the Sphinx capable of giving us the right answers.

A challenge to the photographer is making Humpty Dumpty an enigma. Some two hundred variations of this enigma were displayed last week at

Lalit Kala Gallery at an exhibition mounted by the Museum of Modern Art, New York. The exhibition, called 'The Photographer's Eye' was educative. It presented photographs with the thesis:

> . . . to know, understand, and appreciate the photographic form, one must consider the medium's fine art tradition and its functional usage as intimately interdependent. This exhibit is an investigation of what photographs look like and of why they look that way. It is concerned with photographic style and with photographic tradition: with the sense of possibilities that a photographer today brings to his work.

GRAND DISPLAY

Delhi has never seen such a grand exhibition of photographs, some as old as photography itself. The exhibition followed John Szarkowski's system of photograph classification which he deals with fully in his book, *The Photographer's Eye*. So the exhibition turned out to be a demonstration of Szarkowski's ideas. Better ways of classifying photographs are there but that is indeed another matter; they came too late when the Museum of Modern Art had already accepted Szarkowski's system. The exhibition suffered to the extent that it was an exposition of Szarkowski's ideas. Was this because Szarkowski is the director of photography attached to the Museum of Modern Art?

The exhibits were grouped (about 30 each) into five sections: 'The Thing Itself', 'The Detail', 'The Frame', 'Time' and 'The Vantage Point'. Szarkowski himself had doubts about making such rigid categories but if they are taken together to probe the history of the photographic medium, his method does indeed makes some sense. Independent of historical context, they do not define anything concretely. Indeed a better system of looking at photographs is to categorize them in terms of effects, such as mechanical, optical and compositional.

In 1853, more than a hundred years ago, *The New York Daily Tribune* estimated that some three million daguerrotypes were made that year. Since there is no academy and tradition to govern the work of a photographer, sensibility is a question of personal taste. The result is that much of the skill, knowledge and invention that inform a camera product is of little artistic value. If ever a photograph reaches the limits of art it is just by accident or luck.

Because of Szarkowski's loose classification, a large number of photographs were included to prove a point. Of the thirty photographs included in the category – in 'The Thing Itself', for instance, only a few were of recognizable merit. The point that photography dealt with the actual could be demonstrated with equal weight with fewer prints than were displayed. Another section, 'The Detail', showed about thirty pictures which were hardly necessary because the camera's preoccupation with the actual and the immediate also included the consideration that the actual should look real. The detail in photographic terms means that the actual - the thing itself - should be recorded with compelling clarity. The point was well illustrated by the famed Second World War photographer Robert Capa: 'If your pictures aren't good, you're not close enough.'

79

THE ARTIST AND THE CAMERA'S EYE

Examining the two dominant movements in photography: realist and artistic photography

Patriot Magazine, New Delhi, 17 January 1971

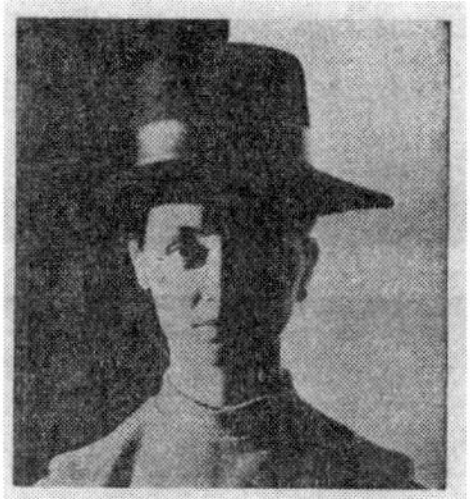

Portrait, David Manuel

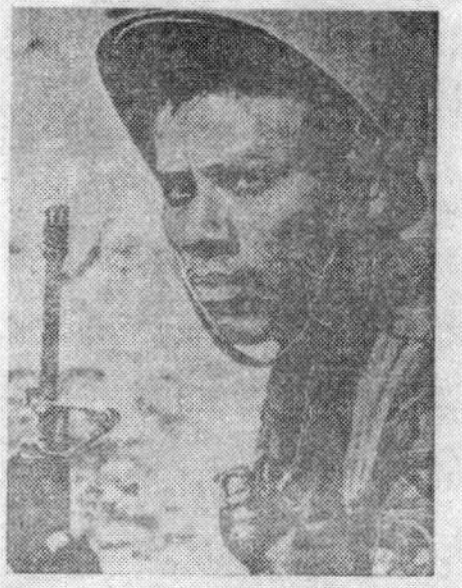

The soldier, Tran Dai Quang

Competition is for horses, not artists. But photographers are an exception: they must compete with painters to prove that their creative freedom extends to the limits of their imagination. Of course, this is ridiculous because a photographer works best within the limitations of his medium. And whether photography is an art medium or not is still a controversial issue because the minimum requirement is to produce prints which should follow the realistic principle under all circumstances. Photographers of whatever mode and conviction must devote themselves to the text of nature, that is to say, to represent significant aspects of physical reality without trying to overshadow that reality and the resultant effect should leave the raw material focused upon both intact and transparent. If the free compositions of experimental photography threaten to divert our attention from the limits of its medium, it will not be in keeping with the true photographic spirit.

If experimental photographers' creative products fail to maintain the limits of the medium, it will be better to consider such products as a special genre of graphic arts than photography proper. For instance, photograms or rayographs which dispense with the camera image altogether, and photomontage, which has very thin affiliations with the camera actuality, are some of the instances of this special genre of photographic art.[1] Such products are clearly not records. As James Thrall Soby[2] once said, they do not 'wear well when hung as pictures'. The dadaists, the surrealists and the Bauhaus masters used photographs as part of the visual grammar of their respective aesthetic beliefs. They never bothered about the sacred limits of the photographic medium. Laszlo Moholy-Nagy is a case in point who took to photography to liberate it from the 'narrow rendering of nature'. His plea was that we should consider photography as an 'ideal instrument of visual expression'. The Bauhaus slogan was: artist-photographers don't take pictures as much as they make them. Similarly, Man Ray brought photography to a creative level where through the peculiar sensitivity to light of the photographic material it reached the 'poetry of nature'. These artists never suffered from any obligation to record nature in the raw which most photographers did; for them, photography's function was not reproduction but expression and that being the case, any artifices and technique could be combined to bring to bear on the raw material 'subjective experiences, our personal visions, and the dynamics of our imagination'.[3]

This implies that the issue (the limits of subjectivity in photographic expression) is not yet settled. The history of photography is itself a great conditioning factor. When photography came to France it coincided with the spread of positivism which aspired to a faithful and completely impersonal rendering of reality. The positivistic syndrome is well expressed by Taine who said: 'I want to reproduce the objects as they are, or as they would be even if I did not exist'.[4] Thus, the subject matter of the artist's imagination was not considered as important as the unbiased objectivity in representing the visible world. This was not only true of literature; in painting, too, a simultaneous movement developed and pictures became plein-air, devoid of any romantic colouring.[5] Photographic realism became the idiom of the day. The camera was hailed as an ideal instrument of recording nature.

It had an overwhelming effect both on painting and graphics. When J.M.W. Turner saw the first daguerreotype he said with great resignation: 'This is the end of the Art. I am glad I have done my day.' Of course, it did not mean the end of art and more pictures were painted since the invention of daguerreotype; only the artists took to the camera and use of photographs as copy material. Delacroix, for instance, used photographs for his portrait studies, while lesser painters painted on the photographs themselves for reasons of pictorial precision and to save time. This was no doubt gross materialism, and if artists argued for or against the new machine it was because their livelihoods were threatened; the most affected were the miniaturists and portrait painters.

Photographers, too, imitated the painters – all those effects in portraits which the camera could not produce. It became fashionable with the commercial photographers to imitate what is called 'Rembrandt lighting' and to produce portraits as sweet as romantic painting and aesthetically as satisfying as the academic idealism of Ingres and his followers. Disderi[6] set the pattern for this kind of portraiture. The daguerreotypists were fond of soft-focus pictures. Imitating the works of the popular contemporary artists, they often retouched the features of their less attractive clients. Julia Margaret Cameron[7] went to such extremes as to employ very poor lenses so that she could get only the 'spirit' of the person portrayed, leaving out the incidental details which seemed to interfere with the intended effect. The pictorial beauty in fashion those days was a blend of the real and the artificial.

So the pictorialists are as old as the invention of the daguerre and the allegiance naturally is split between those committed to the camera truth and those who thought that the truth could be sacrificed to beauty. The peculiar properties of the photographic medium were debated from positions of vested interests and since properties of a medium cannot be defined with any convincing clarity of definition, what happened was that the practitioners since the beginning of photography determined dogmatically, and quite in advance, what was or not the nature of the medium. So the starting points of the aesthetic analysis were never clear and when something seemed to define itself in historical terms of revolutionary photographer came up to upset all the previous calculations about the nature of the medium.

There were, however, a few areas of agreement. The ideal photographer was thought to be the very opposite of an unseeing lover, like an indiscriminating mirror who saw identical to the camera lens. It is thus not wrong to say that photography is the product of alienation. But its one-sidedness is obvious, and all this is in keeping with the credo of the nineteenth-century realist, according to which a photograph holds a mirror up to nature. News photos and television pictures are still considered as products of an alienated photographer who merely records and does not metamorphose.

But the objectivity in the sense of a realist manifesto is a myth because the camera does not record nature but reveals it. About this again there is no disagreement, it is built-in in the medium itself: a photographer selects motif, frame, lens, filter, emulsion and grain according to his sensibilities; that is to say he selects in order to transform the given requirements, because nature just does not give herself up to him. Yet, Proust is right and a photographer remains in a state of alienation because he is not working with hands but with the mechanical box.[8] So what counts in the end is the right mixture: of realistic loyalities and formative tendencies. Lewis Mumford sums up the case thus: the photographer's 'inner impulse, instead of spreading itself in subjective fantasy, must always be in key with outer circumstances'.[9] This precarious balance is to be seen in the works of such early artist-photographers as [Felix] Nadar, David Octavius Hill and Robert Adamson in whose portraiture we see 'the dignity and depth of their perception'.

A good photograph is like a surrealist object; a faithful reproduction of nature but its actuality expresses the creator's feelings. So the artistic creation in photography meets with the demands of the medium only when it creates a surrealist picture. The experimental photographer is thus the best surrealist artist and in September this year [1971] we shall be meeting the best of them when the biggest international salon of experimental photography is held in New Delhi. It will be the first exhibition of its kind, put up jointly by New Delhi's Foto Arte Group and Ahmedabad's F11 Camerealists. The only international photography salon was held in India in 1954 but it was more of a traditional character limited to only monochrome prints. The coming exhibition, it is claimed, will be truly representative and show in addition to black-and-white prints, colour prints, slides and nature prints.

Editor's Notes

1 Photograms are photographic images that are created without using a camera – a technique used from the advent of photography by inventors such as William Henry Talbot. It involves creating a light-sensitive paper surface (by coating it with light-sensitive salts/chemicals) and then exposing it to light, which forms latent images on the paper. Photograms became quite popular in the 1920s; photographers adopted the process, creating images by placing objects directly on photographic paper that was light-sensitive. The photographer Man Ray tried out some of the first of these by placing objects – such as springs, screws and other curvaceous objects that partially let light pass through them – directly on photographic paper, interested in the tonality and shadows they produced, and termed the photograms he created after himself, as Rayographs. Photomontage is the technique of bringing together multiple individual photographic images to create a new composite one with individual images juxtaposed or interacting with one another.

2 James Thrall Soby was a critic, collector and writer who worked with the Museum of Modern Art (MoMA), New York, for decades (from the 1940s to the 1980s) in various significant capacities. A bulk of his personal collection is available with MoMA, which also holds his papers.

3 Statement attributed to the experimental photographer Leo Katz, from his essay, 'Dimensions in Photography', *The Complete Photographer*, vol 4, issue 21, 1942, p. 1354.

4 Quoted originally in Gisele Freund's work, *La Photographie en France au dix-neuvieme siècle: Essai de sociologie et d'aesthetique*, Paris, 1936.

5 *Plein-air* is a process of painting in the open air, popular among realist painters in Europe in late nineteenth–early twentieth century. Many of these painters created works, in fact, with considerable 'atmospheric effect'. The quotation '*plain [plein]-air*, devoid of romantic overtones' is from Siegfried Kracauer's celebrated book, *Theory of Film: The Redemption of Physical Reality*, New York: Princeton University Press, [1960] 1997.

6 Disderi, first name unknown, an early photographer in France known for his portraiture work.

7 Early British photographer known for her portraits of celebrities as well as themed work, largely on heroic and legendary subjects.

8 The reference is to Proust's celebrated work, *The Remembrance of Things Past/Swann's Way*, where the narrator muses that in the presence of the photographer, with his camera, he was able to see the physical changes that had overcome his grandmother which he, blinded by love for her, had never noticed previously; that it is the distance and alienation created by the machine (camera) that allows a photographer to capture 'reality' otherwise unnoticed by those living it.

9 Lewis Mumford, *Technics and Civilization*, New York: Harcourt, Brace & Co., 1934, p. 339.

80
THE MAGICAL BOX

An article on the American photographer Jerry Uelsmann, a major pictorialist

Link, New Delhi, 18 July 1971

Jerry N. Uelsmann is not very well known and in India only a few may have heard his name. It is also rather difficult to decide whether he is a good photographer or a good teacher. Or is he good at both? As Associate Professor of art at the University of Florida, USA, he has long been exploring new possibilities for photography. He is currently on a grant from his university to work in the darkroom for a year. As a photographer he belongs to the darkroom, and this is what sets him apart from other photographers: 'I like the freedom that darkroom manipulations give me'.

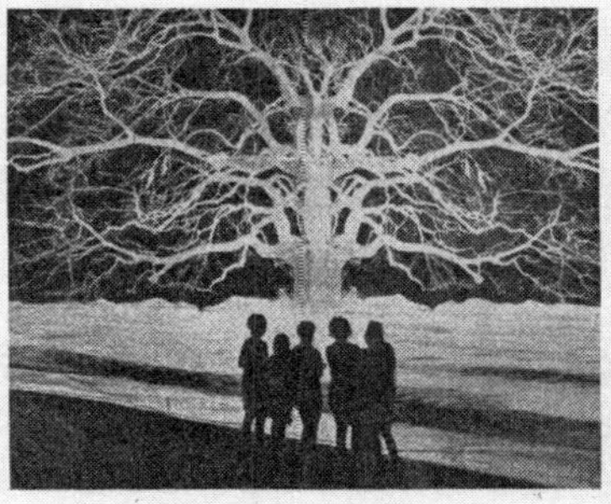

'Apocalypse 2' by Jerry N. Uelsmann

wings. Likewise a good photograph becomes a theatre of the self, "a very private performance" and all this with the little magic box. With this magic box we just stop looking at what we see; instead what is required of us is participation as a viewer and we are to keep all the options of viewing open. It goes beyond the perceptual mechanism of ordinary seeing and this indeed is what modern art has taught us the most.

A photographer then works like a painter or a sculptor and like him he does not begin with a fully-conceived canvas, but allows things to happen. This sense of the unexpected image is the result of the in-process discovery venting a vocabulary at the same time as he is making use of it. Because in photography the technique provides the vehicle for the image: and it is in full knowledge of the technique that a photographer creates the image which is not a mere record of the camera. It is in the darkroom that he can see how things really resolve themselves, how they look with the change in the context of the image and what new things happen with such a change.

METAMORPHOSIS: Uelsmann has learnt this the hard way, for he did not begin with the darkroom but the camera's "straight tradition". But he was lucky to be a Minor White's student who always used to remind his pupils:

The over heavy makeup of the darkroom at the expense of the camera truth has made him a controversial photographer. Critics have said that his work is not photography. Such criticism indeed hurts him the most. It has led him to write a paper called 'Post-visualization', published in 1966, where he defined his attitudes towards photography. So far, the dominant aesthetic of photography has been called pre-visualization, which means that the camera image, its actuality, is time exposed and anything done to alter the time breakdown of the image is indeed to interfere with the camera truth. A photograph is truly the mirror image of nature and this is what distinguishes it from all other arts.

RIGIDITY

But Uelsmann looks at the photographic medium with different glasses: for him photography is a medium 'capable of providing a means by which many individuals can more effectively relate to the world and themselves'. So what interests him is this humanizing aspect of the medium. He rightly questions the rigidity about procedures that come in the way of an open dialogue with the material and process. 'Often, confident that we have the right answers,' he says, 'we fail to ask enough questions, and thus our smug confidence fogs our vision and the inconceivable remains truly unconceived'. Of course the common notion about the photographic image is that it is easily readable and we have been conditioned to see it that way by the popular picture-magazine culture. A complex photograph looks an oddity of the medium and yet we have complex photographs; and it is these which the museums collect and the artists talk about. This is indeed to believe in angels.

> But there is a great deal that happens in human relations that goes beyond very literal, very specific kinds of fact. This is the thing which I think is most important about teaching photography, that photography can enable people to relate to the world in some very poetic and some very beautiful ways.[1]

HAPPENINGS

The angels as they go up in their hierarchy get more wings. Likewise a good photograph becomes a theatre of the self, 'a very private performance' and all this with the little magic box. With this magic box we just stop looking at what we see; instead what is required of us is participation as a viewer and we are to keep all the options of viewing open. It goes beyond the perceptual mechanism of ordinary seeing and this indeed is what modern art has taught us the most.

A photographer then works like a painter or a sculptor and like him he does not begin with a fully conceived canvas, but allows things to happen. This sense of the unexpected image is the result of the in-process discovery and as far as Uelsmann is concerned, this takes place in the darkroom which is truly capable of being a 'visual research laboratory, a place for discovery observation and meditation'. Photography today is indeed not what it had been with the nineteenth-century masters who first discovered the art of photography. Like painting it has moved from the outer-directed to the inner-directed, from art that was history-oriented expressing the attitudes and ideas of a given culture of society, to art that is personal and very individual.

A new inter-relationship between the technique of photography and images in photography has developed and like painting, photography too has made the medium its message: often the techniques dictating the image. A photographer, according to Uelsmann, is confronted with the problem of inventing a vocabulary at the same time as he is making use of it. Because in photography the technique provides the vehicle for the image: and it is in full knowledge of the technique that a photographer creates the image which is not a mere record of the camera. It is in the darkroom that he can see how things really resolve themselves, how they look with the change in the context of the image and what new things happen with such a change.

METAMORPHOSIS

Uelsmann has learnt this the hard way, for he did not begin with the darkroom but the camera's 'straight tradition'. But he was lucky to be Minor White's[2] student who always used to remind his pupils: 'Once you photograph objects, not only prove what they are but for what else they are'. That is to say that a literal photograph is not enough, that the aim should be to produce the kind of metamorphosis so that the image would acquire other qualities which could allow it to transcend the literal subject matter. So Uelsmann discovered much quicker than others that what his teacher Minor White was telling him in effect was that the photographic technique was much closer in the image-making function to the technique of assemblage in art, where various things were brought together for creating the image which was in the artist's mind.

This led him to experiment with the 'negative sandwich' technique, where two negatives were put together one upon another in the enlarger to produce the effect which is much similar to that of double exposure. Working on the technique, Uelsmann discovered a grammar of visual metaphors. Now he began to work on a new idea exploring the near-far duality of space, a kind of new pictorial relationship in which image could be read at two different levels. That was the most exciting period of his career; his images during this period dealt with young people trying to understand their lives. He also worked on self-portraits, one of which was published by the Museum of Modern Art, New York, in its calendar of the year. Then for two years he devoted himself to exclusively photographing interiors. Of the most famous photographs of that period is the one entitled 'Room No. 1', about which he said: 'This particular photograph puzzles me in a way, and I am excited about it. It seems to me that there is a renewed effort in art today to restore mystery, to restore enigma'.

Currently, he is occupied with the creation of archetypal images making use of laws of symmetry the way psychedelic art does, and in photography its effect is the creation of the most unexpected image because it is also the most unanticipated.

Editor's Notes

1 Jerry Uelsmann.

2 Minor White was a significant and influential American photographer and teacher who started out with the first generation of pictorialists such as Alfred Steiglitz, co-founded the *Aperture* magazine, and was known for his 'mystical' themed photography through the 1950s and '60s. Uelsmann, who studied with him in the 1950s, became one of his more prominent students and frequently speaks, even in the present day, of the idea of the relationships between images that White drew his students' attention to.

81
O.P. SHARMA

An article on the photographer O.P. Sharma as a significant Indian pictorialist

Link, New Delhi, 17 October 1971

O.P. Sharma is a photographer who has been recently awarded the associate membership of the American Photographic Society. A rare honour, indeed, for Sharma who has already won several awards and fellowships: only two years ago he was elected a member of the Royal Photographic Society of England. The RPS and APS [American Photographic Society] members are so few in India that you can count them on your fingertips. Which means, in other words, that we have not many outstanding photographers who can compete with the best in the world of photography. Snapshooters are many, in thousands indeed, but photographers are few and, fewer still, the pictorialists. Let us then be clear about the three types of camera users. The snapshooter is easy to identify: he is a product of the old Kodak slogan: 'You press the button: we do the rest.' And these friendly infiltrators are hardly aware that they are trespassing on anybody's preserve: they indeed have not even heard the name of pictorialists; so how could their preserves be trespassed? They are merely enjoying the treasured delights of a mechanical age.

HORDES OF KODAK

Now with the invention of built-in exposure, the snapshooters have upgraded themselves as photographers because the manufactures' techniques have helped them to put on that air of superiority which earlier was a characteristic of the photographer – the one who knows many techniques of photography and is always proud to soften the sharp focus when it suits his artistic ends, uses filters to intensify or reduce the tone massing of his pictures or sometimes breaks them by screening or restricts by separation.

All these small satisfactions of a photographer which once distinguished him from a snapshooter have now been taken away from him, having today little chance to innovate: the electronic techniques have replaced such old-fashioned photographic techniques as high contrast, solarization, superimposition, negative images and distorted colour: these – once considered innovations of high aesthetic value – can now be achieved instantly by the tweak of a knob in the control room where formerly they were achieved with much labour in the darkroom. Both the snapshotter and the photographer have benefitted by the progress in camera technology.

PICTORIALISTS

The recent advances in improved camera technology and processing methods have put an end to the age-old controversy among camera users which divided them between the mere takers and the exalted makers. The difference between the connotation of 'take' and 'make' which has been a creative issue since the invention of the camera is no longer of any interest today. But the movies, by speeding up the mechanical, have shown that the camera image is not only bound to the world of sequence: it is a new world of creative configuration and structure. So a photographer now properly belongs either to the movies or to pictorial journalism. Photography as hobby is now the exclusive preserve of the snapshooter; all the refinements in the manufacturer's techniques and processing innovations are addressed to him.

Who, then, is a pictorialist? Among the photographers he is surely an oddity flaunting the 'old hat' of yesterday as the hippie gear of today. Talking to O.P. Sharma about the pictorialist's hippie gear was satisfying: it was like reviewing the whole history of photography. Because of the peculiar properties of the photographic medium, he said, the debate on its artistic possibilities has been carried from positions of vested interest. The properties of the medium at the same time cannot be defined with any convincing clarity of definition. 'And why should one attempt to define it? Do artists ever bother about the medium?' Sharma asked rather agitatedly and seemed lost, his speech dry, but he spoke with a measured, self-assured voice. 'You see, the photographer is indeed a very cunning individual. He has been so ever since the invention of the Daguerre. He determines dogmatically, rather quite in advance, what should be for him the true nature of the medium.'

How was one to distinguish a pictorialist from a photographer? Sharma was hesitant at first to say anything, to clarify. He came up finally with a rule which seemed workable enough. A photographer mechanically records, like an indiscriminating mirror. Or call it a mode of seeing identical with the camera lens. A pictorialist, on the other hand, does not merely record but metamorphoses.

> The camera never records, it is pure ignorance to think so, to limit the camera to the recording task. The camera always reveals; this is built-in in the medium and no disagreements about it. Because a photographer always selects; his motif, his lens, his filter, emulsion and gain – and all according to his sensibility.

Sharma was emphatic and attacked those who sought to limit the camera to its realist loyalties.

> He selects and therefore he transforms. But transforming should not show, because whatever the inner impulse of a photographer he cannot go the same length a painter can because his intentions cannot just spread out in pure subjective fantasy but must always be in key with outer circumstance.

His tone changed suddenly as if to say that such sophistry was meaningless small talk. 'You see, art does not need pictorialism. . . . It is there with the artist.'

In another way, he was saying that pictorialism's greatest asset is its intangibility. And like heaven it is there right inside a man's mind and so it means many things to many people. Pictorialism is present when a photographer treats his products in the spirit of amateurism because it has been nurtured in the spirit of amateurism. A pictorialist, for instance, will never put the mechanical eye in place of his own. 'This is the best way to define a pictorialist if you need defining him at all,' Sharma said. 'The pity is,' he added, 'that no matter what was the aesthetic impulse of a photographer, the camera did not share it. That is why a pictorialist has always to return to the darkroom trying to adapt the aftermath of mechanization to the enthusiasm of human perception'. So he experiments tirelessly with after-exposure techniques in the hope that he may be able to wash out all the mechanical traces of the recording lens. He is never satisfied because what he gets is never the work of his own eyes and hands. Perhaps it is this dissatisfaction with his experiments that a photographer calls himself a pictorialist and not an artist.

One thing became clear, however: that like other photographers a pictorialist was not in the hands of others for carrying out his aesthetic idea. He did all his processing himself, although not as fortunate as the early pictorialists who contrived their own media from calotype collodion, albumen and platinum to manipulating gums, bromoils and bromoil transfers.[1] He now depended for materials on the manufacture of any photographic material worth working on. Even in the West there is a general scaling down of standards in the production of photo materials. After the Second World War, Sharma said, one could have a good selection of manufactured bromide: some forty and fifty choices to suit a worker's individual preferences. Now the choices are very few, even in the West. 'The time has come when a photographer has to make his own material, otherwise he'll be no better than the snapshooters.'

How much has his own work suffered from the non-availability of photographic material? Or how far a photographer's artistic conception was restricted to the scope of the material he was using? Replying, Sharma sounded a little bitter. 'A photographer cannot surely be innovative beyond the limits imposed by the medium – and the photographic medium is dependent on the skills of others.' The artist-photographers are not needed because society needs only the recording task from the camera, and for the Sharmas it is almost a lost battle. Pictorialism in India is in danger of dying still-born.

PHOTOGRAPHIC MATERIAL

[Indian] Pictorialism indeed was born with Sharma's taking to photography, one might say and this would be no exaggeration because hardly anyone did the kind of experiments Sharma is doing though he did not innovate anything revolutionary. But the quality of his work is such which made other photographers take note of his experiments. For instance, texture printing was being done before Sharma started doing it but it didn't have his quality. He invented what he calls the 'G-effect' or multiple solarization.[2] His 'G-effects' experiments are indeed very attractive because a graduation of tones are seen in relation to contours which are boldly defined. Texture and natural light effects are controlled by combining several negatives.

Similarly, Sharma's innovation in tone-separation (that is solarized) prints have extended the range of neutral grey tones to artistic limits because the total effect is to give to photographs a new graphic quality. Recently, Sharma has been working on what he calls the *Ghost* series, and the hard core of these experiments is to load the negative with as much subjectivity as it can take without destroying the very character of the medium. The end product is like a surrealist object which has the dignity and depth of Sharma's perception. His candid work is also enormous but it is never the product of an alienated, unseeing photographer. The personality of the photographer is all-important which may be because of several factors including the superb print quality Sharma is famous for. The citation of the American Photographic Society award said that Sharma has given to his photographs a personal touch which, indeed, is difficult to achieve.

Editor's Notes

1 The calotype is the first photography process invented by Henry Fox Talbot, which involved coating paper with light-sensitive salts and exposing to light via a *camera obscura* – the exposed areas created a negative image. Bromoil printing is a variation of an early photography process called oil printing, which involved coating a paper with a gelatinous substance and creating a contact print by placing a negative over it; the print is then painted over with an oil-based ink which sticks more to the hardened gelatinous areas. Bromoils are variations of this process that permit enlargements. Bromoils were very popular with the pictorialists for the soft, pastel-like quality they gave to the images – due, perhaps, to the oil in the inks.

2 In basic terms, solarization is an effect that involves the reversal of tones in a negative on extreme or overlong exposure to light, first observed in images of nature, including the sun. In the darkroom, too, the tones of a negative or a print can be reversed to make dark areas appear light or vice versa.

82
THE WALL

Review of an exhibition of photographs by Raghu Rai, capturing life around a wall in Old Delhi

Link, New Delhi, 3 March 1974

A still photograph has greater power than the moving image: perhaps stills have more memory, and unlike the TV images which come and go each erasing the preceding one, still images are more like objects to which one can return again and again. And these images have a context of feeling and an attitude is established which defines their zone of meaning. Perhaps because of their moral context the recent photographs of Raghu Rai at Shridharani Gallery were different: those which have the wall – the one that connects Daryagunj to Jama Masjid – as their subject.

The wall provided Raghu Rai with a large canvas: 'Here was a stage, set for life's little ironies, its comedies and tragedies. For hours did I linger on this scene as a change from the crises that news photography offered me', he says. A clever device indeed, and the wall gives to his images a continuity, almost a narrative quality. Otherwise, the camera images remain arbitrary frames – where anything can be separated from anything – a series of unrelated anecdotes, that is. The wall acts like a painted surface and because of this there is much understanding, and less of fantasy.

The reality of the wall is established not so much through the images as in their interpretative function: that is to say, these photographs have the same function as paintings and drawings have. The images thus are not a mere slice of space or that of time: they are visual statements. And they awaken a kind of moral feeling, as they get more specific, more individualistic. Perhaps it is beyond the power of photographic images to create a moral feeling, but in defining anxieties of urban life they reinforce a moral position. The graffiti, the political slogans on the wall, are in as sharp a focus as the image proper. The images that way acquire a narrative dimension. We tend to ask that if this is the surface of reality, what the reality will be like beyond it.

Perhaps these images are about suffering: they wound, and some feelings go dead and we grieve for them because of the many images of suffering we have seen and have long been anesthetized by them. The tragic aspect does not register on the mind being worn off with the repeated viewing: their misery, their privations and injustices they have suffered look ordinary, remote. It is the wall that gives to these images a new dimension: it is its meaning context. And that is why these photographs have more memory than those which are about demonstrations and acts of public violence, which Raghu says are the images of 'extreme situations'.

The photographs having the wall as their subject are more innocent, and hence more authentic because their relation to visible reality is not in terms of the formal statement of a camera truth: it is about time itself which has been recorded. So in their innocence they look like artless Polaroid images which Raghu seems to have used as a form of note-taking. Here, he is not haunted by obscure rules of news photography or by imperatives of tastes or by aesthetics of pictorialism: he is concerned here with keeping the emotional charge of the images in a high key.

83
GRAPHIC IMAGES

Review of an exhibition of photographs of natural formations and landscapes by Raghu Rai

Link, New Delhi, 18 February 1979

Raghu Rai's prints (at least in the gallery context of viewing) always look more than photographs. It is because he never repeats himself (show a photographer who is not repeating himself) and comes up with a one-man show only when he has something fresh to show. The prints on view at the Shridharani he calls earthscapes, they are landscapes of a kind where discovering their literal truth is not the point why he took them. There is no personal statement of the author and so we can only hazard a guess about the intention.

No doubt Raghu has the highly developed sensibility of an artist and so uses the camera technology for transforming the actual into something which Klee might have called a cosmological consciousness. This is especially so in the two prints No 17 and 19, all taken from a great height. These are demonstrations of a new Raghu universe brought to light with the near-impossible mixing of micro and telescopic images. Or so they seem like. The prints have such high contrast, a quality of texture that they may pass as engravings. They are attempts at a painterly iconography of the natural world, and it is for this reason that they excite our imagination.

This heightened awareness of detail is not given to the eye: it is the property of the lens which when activated by the power of light is much superior to human vision, to the average sight. This extra sensitivity to detail when married to the evocative structures revealing an individual way of seeing has come to be identified with Raghu's style. Because he reveals something that is not given to ordinary seeing, we have the illusion of experiencing cosmic phenomena (in the Kleean sense of cosmology). The magnified pores of stone make it an object of false consciousness. Thus, they have the status of an artifact with the same immobility, stillness of pattern as revealed in the prints where the isolated parts of a furrowed field have been blown up. They have a hieratic freezing quality. And wherever he resorts to frontality in composition, he achieves, rather effortlessly, a definitive modernity, a more striking achievement [in] photography because the medium does not allow enough room to the 'taker' to manipulate the sequential levels in a landscape.

This handicap looks almost insurmountable if a photographer is a devotee of the decisive moment credo, and in such photographs 'form

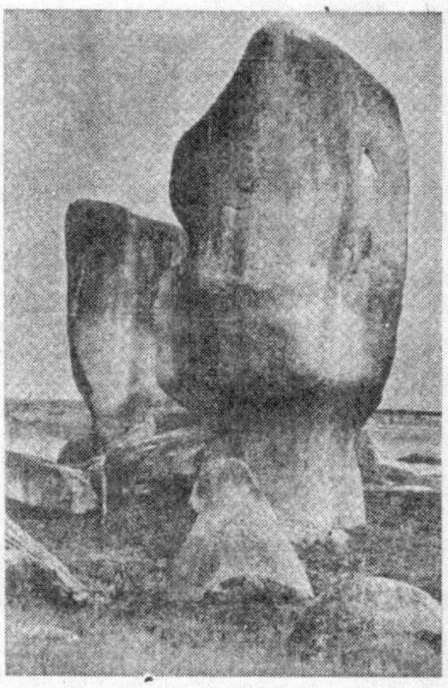

A recent photograph by Raghu Rai

is reluctant to become content' as some critic has observed. But Raghu's ability to manipulate his sophistication in the use of camera angles and his talent in playing variation on focal grammar is superb. Because of this, his way of seeing -which no doubt consists in truthful recording of the visual world - becomes our way of seeing also: if there is a meaning to his images it is that they intensify the normal perceptual operations in a viewer and turns photographs into pictures.

This needs some explaining because Raghu hates to play darkroom tricks with the photographic medium. Because of the mechanized nature of the medium the aesthetic experience is freed from the constraints of tradition, taste and history . . . [illegible] . . . [binding] us in an instantaneous response. A photographic image either moves us at first sight or it does not; and to judge . . . [illegible] . . . [value] in such an image we have to have another go at it again after an interval of time, and on this second viewing if the image gains in depth it has the quality of surface as we meet in a painting: another viewing merely converts the instantaneous response into a reflective recognition. These photographic images are in the nature of their response closer to the actor's and he moves us instantaneous[ly], of course, but some of his gestures are the memory that are worth re-experiencing for their own sake a second or third time. More often, the decisive-movement photographer surrenders the pictorial act to the optical, remaining a slave to the automatic nature of the medium and that is where he meets his defeat. No doubt, a photographer's control on the medium has several unpredictable, unforeseeable components, and since he can never construct an object he can only report [that] the production of photographic images has several levels of devices - mechanical, optical and compositional and these are largely the products of the trial and error method. It is because of this that the camera products are characterized chiefly by their malleability: they are subject to contradictory interpretations, that is.

But the Raghus are more perceptive given to reflective constructions of the mind. Above all, they are extremely graphic given to a low range in exploring the intermediate tones with an all over-contrasty [sic] effect. In that sense they have a shared paradigm tradition with pictorial art.

84
PURE PHOTOGRAPH WASN'T TRUE ENOUGH

A reflection on the alteration and otherwise manipulation of the photographic image in early Indian photography as an extension of the Indian pictorial aesthetic – as opposed to maintaining the 'purity' of picture-taking

Portrait Magazine, New Delhi, 9 September 1982

> Question: Can a photograph be a work of art?
> Answer: A photograph is a disposition of sensible matter and may be so disposed for an aesthetic end but is not a human disposition of sensible matter. Therefore, it is not a work of art.
>
> Question: If a man hacking in fury at a block of wood makes there an image of the cow (say) has he made a work of art?
> Answer: The image of the cow made by a man hacking in fury at a block of wood is a human disposition of sensible matter but it is not a human disposition of sensible matter for an aesthetic end. Therefore, it is not a work of art.
>
> – James Joyce, *Paris Notebook*

The two excerpts from Joyce's *Notebook* (both dated 28 March 1903) show where Fox Talbot failed and why in his failure he became an artist. The Talbot machine was no camera - a mere machine for accumulating energy: it took him more minutes than instant thousandth of a second to make images. Photographic art for him was an act of long deliberation, and if this is a valid criterion for art his camera products were surely works of art. If his means betrayed him - and he fought against all odds, experienced those heartbreaks known to every artist since Plato and with slow fabrication of his images worked and prayed for windless days one is free to infer whatever aesthetic ends these images served. Perhaps a made-up fiction they pointed to; for the camera is an instrument no more or no less human than the typewriter. Talbot did not fail: whatever he did produce had an aesthetic end.

As the camera technology evolved becoming almost electronic with the imminence of a revelation, the photographer lost touch with his intuition called time: it is now Cartier-Bresson and his tribe, the trigger happy snapshooters, their, what is called, thousand decisive moments and a million photo images that seem to be mapping time back upon space. As Susan Sontag says, the split second time-exposed camera images are the inventories of mortality. The photographic document is not an evidence of life preserved in the act of living but life 'trapped' in a moment of time.

The nineteenth century Indian photographer who worked at the image-making machine, as archaic as Talbot's, erased the traces of time, didn't seize them. He had no conception of what is called a pure photograph: he was least interested to capture the mood of the sitter in a particular moment of time. What he was surely interested in was his subject's ontological status representing for him not as he was on earth, but as he was in himself.' That is to say, he was interested in bringing out the sum total of the human essence of his sitter. So a photograph became in his hand not a mere camera product but as in a painting, a systematic structuring of parts; an ordered system of information.

In New York recently, at the prestigious International Centre of Photography, an exhibition, called, 'Through Indian Eyes', of the works of the nineteenth century Indian photographers was held. Alongside these photographs were shown miniatures to bring into focus the similarity of aesthetic approach, between the two contrasting modes of representation. The exhibition mounted seventy photographs taken between the 1850s and the 1920s and more than a hundred miniatures explicating their influence on the photographs which were acquired by Judith Mara Gutman, historian and scholar of American photography. It was a labour of love covering a period of six years. Mrs Gutman's travels and the catalogue of these exhibits was financed by the Smithsonian Institute. For mounting this show, New York's International Centre of Photography received $196,000 from the National Endowment for the Humanities. It was the 'largest budget the ICP has ever had, twice its normal budget for most exhibits,' an ICP member said.

There is the good news for Indian photographers: these photographs will eventually be housed as a permanent collection at the National Centre for the Performing Arts, Bombay. But Dr Narayana Menon, director of NCPA, says: 'We have not even begun discussions as yet. . . . It is bound to be a long process. We have yet to approach the government for a grant for this project. In any case, the project is expected to be complete, if it is followed through, only in 1984–85.' For the former curator of ICP, Bhupendra (Karia) the good news has a touch of sadness; for, according to him, 'the documentation of its core collection is forever tainted by ersatz scholarship'. So whenever this project comes through and whoever heads the Tata Centre for Photography, Bhupendra contended in an interview to an Indian correspondent stationed in New York, will have inherited a problem.

> And that's no way to start an institution. A new institute should be engendered by a well-defined curatorial premise; here the premise itself comes from outside which may or may not have relevance to India's

> needs. But aside from that, the premise itself is being questioned on all sides, and there are gross factual and historical errors. This is the perfect example of doing the right thing (the starting of a center for photography) for the wrong reasons.

The Judith Mara Gutman premise stands up to any critical scrutiny: the nineteenth-century Indian photographs she has collected are a representation of a reality which is essential Indian. And the Gutman premise is well supported by no less an authority on Indian art than Dr Stella Kramrisch, curator emeritus [emerita] of Indian art at the Philadelphia Museum of Art: 'With an unconscious compulsion the Indian photographer reduced his photographic space into a flat plane. That is what looked right to him . . . the picture field in a classical Indian painting is a conceptualized space with no necessary relevance to any part of the physical world.' And what Mrs Gutman (who I met last year at a photographic meet organized by New Delhi's Foto Arte Group where New Delhi's top photographers were present) says about her nineteenth-century photographic collection is not very different.

> People do not have to look like specific persons. Nor do buildings and terrain serve as models. Usually filled with several 'pockets of interest' across a flattened picture field, a painting's rhythm does not necessarily lead to a single dominating subject as in a Western visual representation. Everything in the picture happens at once, and in an idealized space over a timeless eternity.

Photographers do not share any idealized space now; they behave as seasoned quarrelsome lovers do towards each other's work as if each one is locked into a space where doors are neither precisely open nor completely closed. They have never experienced the kind of personal terrors as Talbot had: time is the substance of which theirs are made. Not much has been written about the relation of time to photographic art. For example in the film medium it is the human consciousness that is at work in ecstatic time: we are presented with such perfect illusion that we often give in to its spell as if we have had our cake and eaten it too.

Early photographers, both from East and West, accepted the assumption that true art must be 'built' from ground up. As opposed to the notion of 'built' art another attitude became popular around the 1920s as symbolized by the generation of Strand and Weston. Their notion of a self-generating work, sufficient in its own immanence and only nominally connected to an invisible or anonymous maker was an extension of the nineteenth-century aesthetic of naturalism. In Indian photographic vision, there were no such pressures as that of naturalism in Europe, nor has it been subjected to the ruthless determinism of historical time. No other object imported from the West has been looked up as more alien to Indian sensibilities than the camera; yet this image-producing machine was devoured, rather Indianized. If it did not yield the images that did not suit their vision they altered them. That way they never treated the camera as a machine yielding images, with only pressuring of the button: they performed skilled labour; for, a picture was a built thing - object making assumption they borrowed from painting now applied to the new medium of photography.

Compared to their work, today's photographer looks more like a butcher: he uses knife to produce edible meat. The metaphor of knife does explain the true nature of photographic medium as it evolved at the hands of Paul Strand and Edward Weston until the Second World War when Cartier-Bresson came on the photographic scene. With Cartier-Bresson and his decisive moment credo, the photographic act became more like a 'cut' in space and time and thus the camera images became dimensionless, anonymous and functional; in short, real machine products.

85
PHOTOGRAPH AS INDEX, PERSONAL IMAGE

On the essential indexicality of the photograph, as also of the photographic image being a system of signs

Portrait Magazine, New Delhi, 13 October 1982

> Painting after all is an inferior way of making likenesses, as ersatz of processes of reproduction. Only a photographic lens can give us the kind of image of the object that is capable of satisfying the deep need man has to substitute for it something more than a mirror approximation . . . The photographic image is the object itself, the object freed from the conditions of time and space that govern it. No matter how fuzzy, distorted, or discoloured, no matter how lacking in documentary value the image may be, it shares, by virtue of the very process of its becoming, the being of the model of which it is the reproduction: it is the model.
>
> – Andre Bazin, 'The Ontology of the Photographic Image'

Photography since the Sixties has become a necessary component of visual arts as evident from the popularity of the recent styles like photo-realism and the conceptual art. Of course the absence of photograph in the Indian painting styles is largely because of the media-based mass culture in India being limited to the pre-eminent experience of the cult of film heroes and heroines. The only image that has mass dimension is that of Amitabh Bachchan. Torn from the context of internally generated meaning, it represents not a fact of social image but the reiteration of his physical presence representing for the younger generation an aspect of their own narcissism. That fact is indicative of the arrival of mass culture in India. His recent illness brought to us the power of the photographic image: those recent images of Amitabh Bachchan, we looked at with the same attentiveness that we encounter in a painting. How, in what way, an image is different from the visual picture, its photographic surrogate, we learnt recently.

Or, take for instance, the third World Exhibition of Photography, concluded last week at the Rabindra Bhavan Gallery organized by the German magazine *Stern* in cooperation with 367 museums and 52 countries. Another exhibition which opened on 9 October at the same gallery called the *Family of India* mounts the works of 132 photographers: it represents the labour of love of photo-artist Ajoy Dey of Calcutta who has collected more than 400 photo images. This plethora of images which we confront everywhere elevate the commonplace, the trivial and in some cases, the isolated as if it were the real component that makes up India's many faces. Most images are indeed incidental – if not the work of snapshooters, amateur candid photographers – incidental because there is absence of the careful rendition of tonal values and the balancing of masses. Or putting it another way, the displayed images make us aware of the age-old problem of the candid photographer: the problem of resolving the contradiction between artistic intention and the mechanical nature of the medium. Rather, we notice that calculated composition, representing the intention of photographer, has given way to the overriding snapshot value much favoured by the 'decisive moment' photographer. The aesthetic credo of the snapshooter is based on the logic that 'the photographic image is the object itself, the object freed from the conditions of time and space that govern it'. And Bazin's ontology is based on the sound premise: form in photography is reluctant to become content.

So, the meaning of a photograph has the same status as that of a shifter in language, the shifter's need for captions, the need for a physical referent as a supplier of meaning. Thus, photographic form has come to be defined as 'image plus' caption; its rather too obvious manifestation is found in the photographs reproduced in newspapers and slick magazines where the photographic image is a decorative component of its written text. How is a photograph completely dependent upon caption? In what relation does a caption stand to the image proper?

Imagine yourself standing before a mirror and a camera recording the encounter between your private self and the mirror. In this situation if you talk to yourself and do not address the mirrored image of yourself, it is the 'I' situation reflected in the mirror. Now imagine yourself being addressed by the mirror image: the addressee is the image, you are the person addressed. And as the hidden video camera is recording the monologue, the constant shifting and slipping between the self and the other, between I and YOU, builds into an extended performance of narcissism, the drama of the shifter in its regressive form.

So, the shifter is that category of linguistic sign which is filled with significance only when through denotation it points to an empty place, waiting to be invoked, for its referent to be supplied. This denotative use of the shifter in everyday language is clear when the words this is applied to, say, a chair or a table: we say pointing to the object – this table, this chair and if there is something on the table to which we want to draw attention, we say not that, this. . . . Similarly, I and you are also shifters: in a conversation when I am the referent of I, that is when I am the one who is speaking, and when it is your turn it belongs to you. The distinction between the self and the other, between the use of I and you, is acquired early on by a child when he learns a language, but this is one of the last things he masters. At the pre-linguistic level, the confusion for the child between self-identity and identification of the self provides a theoretical model for understanding the nature of photographic meaning.

The shifter, like the photographic image, is suspended between two genetically separate conditions sharing the features of two distinct types of signs - the symbol and the index. Unlike the symbol, the index for its meaning, depends on explication of physical relationship with its referent. Through the photographic medium, a form of selfhood is experienced at the 'decisive moment' when the shutter is pressed: the physical presence of the object photographed stands in a narcissist relationship to the photographer. As the territory of index is defined by the empty space - the empty signs whose meanings are eventually supplied by the physical or literal presence of the object - the photograph is a similar territory within the world of visual signs or icons. Rosalind Kraus tells us:

> At this point in time it is not just the heightened presence of the photograph itself that is significant. Rather, it is the photograph combined with the explicit terms of the index. Everywhere one looks at the Seventies' art, one finds instances of this connection.

For instance, in Dennis Oppenheim's *Identity Search* we are shown a blow-up, a thousand times the size of a thumb print, its explicit index, and the meaning of work is definitely a new visual presence of its index. The implication is that there is convention for meaning independent of the physical presence. As Rosalind says, photography is no longer the minor art it has been so long: it is coming into its own with an entirely separate sign system of its own, 'one whose nature is to resist an internally generated means of symbolization and which is now recasting the relationship between the work of art and its system of producing meaning.'

86

KISHOR PAREKH'S LENS: A RETROSPECTIVE

A reflection on the photography of noted photojournalist Kishor Parekh, on the occasion of his posthumous retrospective in New Delhi

Portrait Magazine, New Delhi, 9 September 1983

The retrospective exhibition of photographs by Kishor Parekh which opened at the Lalit Kala Gallery on Monday is not just another exhibition of photographs; it is an event. One can live these photographs while one is seeing them, for they grow on us little by little and like some germinal experience, open a nerve of memory. We think of Kishor Parekh the man who has given birth to these images and is no more with us: he died last year with camera shutter unwounded for the next frame.

One remembers well with photographs, and this way of remembering teaches us the simple truth that remembering really belongs to the past, and photographs connect it up with memory as no image does, for they act on the mind like memory; they are the expression of a long, long ago feeling. But Kishor Parekh, his ways of seeing, his images, do not belong to the past; it's not a nerve of memory they open. They open new horizons and some very relevant truths about the photographic medium.

The photographs on display at the Lalit Kala Gallery are the expression of his voice; standing before them we can hear him as if he is there with us, talking to us through these images. All this takes place as we listen to silent speech within and, filled with nostalgia, even given expression to it. He was the first photo-journalist who brought the discipline of the darkroom to the snapshooting casualness of news photography. Kishor has never been a snapshooter, shutter-happy egotist as most news-photographers are as if the camera was a substitute for a gun. One would say that Kishor knew what it was to work with a mechanical eye, and for sure he knew it from the inside. Putting it another way, he knew what it meant to see three-dimensionally; in what way the three-dimensional character of the photograph was different from the three-dimensional seeing as one experiences standing before a sculpture. This is three-dimensional seeing as though through a stereoscope, if one can see photographs. And in those moments the picture lives for him while he is seeing it. Kishor Parekh had this natural faculty of seeing things in the round. Compare his knowledge of the medium with his powers of seeing three-dimensionally and one is very close to unveiling the mystery of the Kishor ways of seeing.

Kishor Parekh had said that he is not interested in making pictures. What he meant was that he was not interested in the photographic medium the way the pictorialists are. The photographic image, has the character of a sign and he was not interested in the code switching activity the pictorialist indulged in. The photographic image, however striking it may be, is not valuable for its own pictorial qualities. The photographic image has an indicative function which is the issue of a sign; it has the character of a poster in the sense that it suggests the presence of something that is not present. Or more like the mirror image. It has nothing beyond its appearance and the photographic image is a mode of representation in the manner of a mirror having the function of identification as in a photograph on a passport.

So does it matter really that the photographs displayed are not made by Kishor Parekh himself? It does. Knowing as we do, what it meant to him to be doing his own thing, for there still is this feeling that in some way the prints exhibited do not measure up to the Kishor sensibility. This is a subjective assessment and is better left unelaborated. He was an artist, and naturally pictures came to him before he released the shutter when he was viewing the outer world through the viewfinder. As evidence, I quote what he said about a photograph he took during the Bangladesh war.

> As a press photographer, I have never tried to indulge myself in pictures. I never control or arrange my photographs, I like to present bare facts in my photographs. While covering Bangladesh war, I was a keen observer that the 'enemy shoe' lying in a Dacca street might be an insignificant thing to a passerby, but I saw it there. I lay down on my belly, and used a wide-angle lens to exaggerate its size and took the photograph, there was no question of arranging the frame.

The photograph Kishor Parekh is talking about is a matter-of-fact shot; but it has insides, as that of picture. Beyond the pure indicative function of a sign, the image of the enemy shoe has the essence of a symbol. The photograph stands halfway between the function of a sign and that of a symbol. That is to say, the shoe does not disappear behind its pointing function: it holds the attention by making one linger over its meaning. It does point to something that is not present, being an important ontological part of a soldier's uniform. Thus the image of the shoe is equipoised halfway between a sign and a symbol and its representative function is neither a pure pointing-to-something nor a pure taking-the-place-of something.

Of course no war photographer ever had the time to arrange the frame. The enemy shoe lying in the foreground heightens the drama; it is indeed the focal point of the photograph, setting up a situation which compels us to see and read the image the Parekh way. There is an as-ifness character. The same kind of situation that we are transported to while reading fiction and we see relationship between the visible parts, which are purely subjective. In short, the importance of the photograph is this that, it represents the quintessence of the Kishor Parekh method.

His method is actually the subject of foreground and the historical role it has played in the development of photographic image. Not much attention was paid to the nearest parts of the scene before the invention of the camera. The painter's neglect of the foreground has a long history: they always looked beyond whatever was very close choosing a point in the middle plane to fix the limits of his foreground The photographer, on the contrary, chose to record whatever was near his feet, perhaps because the photographic medium allowed him to record the immediate foreground on a larger scale. The photographer broke the nineteenth-century convention that it was the middle distance and not the nearest part of the scene where the real picture was located. Painters learnt quickly the value of composing in the frontal plane, if not dividing the picture in terms of the perspectival representation, and the very near objects of the scene began to be included in the pictures. Inclusion of the foreground as an important visual unit was the beginning of a new pictorial grammar.

Why did the old masters almost neglect by not paying much attention to the foreground? The answer is simple: they knew that by giving importance to the objects that were nearest to the scene it would be impossible for them to control the relative sizes of the objects; if they had the near objects as the local points of their pictures a vast difference of scale in objects threatened the very unity of the picture.

With photographers one of the rules of taking good pictures has been: 'you must include the foreground object'. The wider use of the wide-angle lens even today speaks of the power of the older myth of composition. This is because most photographers do not know to what degree the photographic scale differs from that of the human eye. The eye, for instance, does not – indeed cannot – see all the scales at one time in equal distinctiveness. Moreover, the human vision is very selective; although it does register the scale of far and near it keeps each scale in its own separate view or plane.

Kishor Parekh joined [the newspaper] *The Hindustan Times* in 1961 and made pictures that made us aware of the value of the foreground. It seems he took photographs to dramatize the foreground of the scene but they were never freakish; they appealed to the cultivated taste for there were echoes of the painting surface. The photographs were infused with the individuality, with their daring, unconventional startling camera viewpoints. It was this quality of his photograph that sent his reputation up as a great news photographer. His photographs stood out because they looked unlaboured, unpremeditated and spontaneous. 'I wanted to be a poet with the camera, but only when it came to appreciation of the beautiful in life,' he said once. He covered a long road since this statement (appreciation of the beautiful in life) reaching the central truth of his vision when he realized that 'The day-to-day life struggle and pathos of human life have their own charm and beauty. . . . If I cannot record the significant depths of this human world what is the use of my medium?'

87

HUMANIST EYE-VIEW

On the work of the well-known photographer S. Paul

Link, New Delhi, 16 May 1990

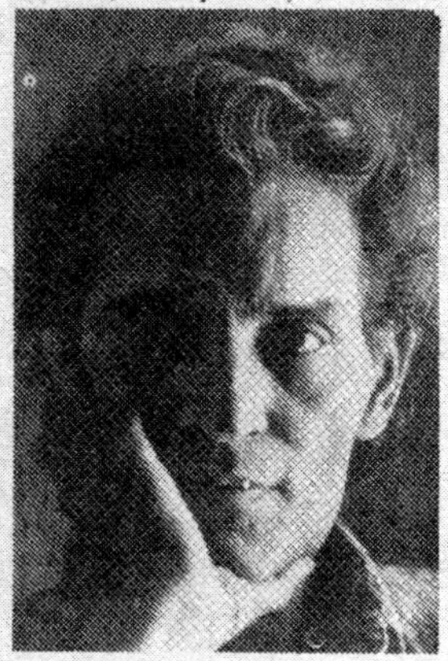

the character of an individual eye; seeing them as Paul sees.

They are cultured, educated eyes such as we find only in good painters: educated because they take in the whole space, each plane falling into a pattern; and cultured because, like a painter, he fixes his solid and another airy and then the two are weighed visually to decide which is the higher tonewise. It is by this previsualisation and weighing of the tone that Paul decides the vantage point: the visual balance is always right.

It is not easy to weigh the tone difference in black and white photography: it varies in a different ratio as the light varies in intensi-

S. Paul's photographs on view at the Max Mueller Bhawan, New Delhi, offer more than a window of reality; they have a feeling tone that blunts the edge of technical virtuosity. They stand apart, not for their underlying technical virtuosity, but for a quality of visual awareness, that affective tone which gives to his framed impressions the character of an individual eye; seeing them as Paul sees.

They are cultured, educated eyes such as we find only in good painters: educated because they take in the whole space, each plane falling into a pattern; and cultured because, like a painter, he fixes his solid and another airy and then the two are weighed visually to decide which is the higher tonewise. It is by this pre-visualisation and weighing of the tone that Paul decides the vantage point: the visual balance is always right.

It is not easy to weigh the tone difference in black and white photography: it varies in a different ratio as the light varies in intensity. Perhaps because of our awareness of the difficulties in accurately reading the tone values we are reminded of a remark by Zola, the foremost ideologue of naturalism; 'In my view', he declared after 15 years of amateur picture-taking in 1901, 'you cannot claim to have really seen something until you have photographed it.' Which is to say that camera is not a copying machine. Nor is a photograph a journey into nostalgia; it is an experience which only those who have looked through the camera's viewing window know. It is like looking through the viewing window and to exclaim; so that is what it looks like.

Understanding Paul's photographs is like understanding a piece of music; and being able to judge the tonal music of sights. Or like opening oneself up to innumerable impressions and self-consciously reflecting upon

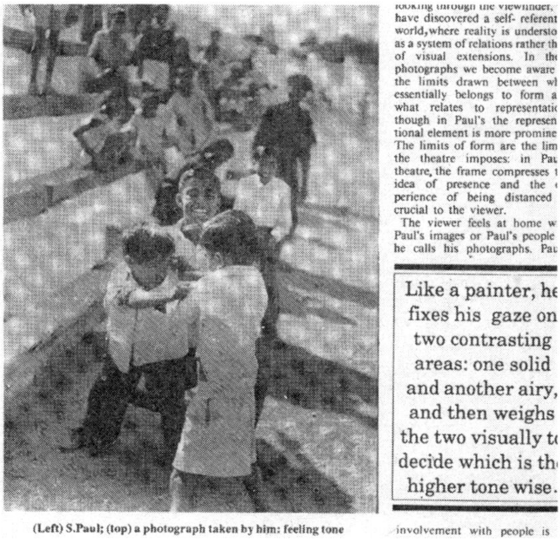

looking through the viewfinder,
have discovered a self- referent
world, where reality is understo
as a system of relations rather th
of visual extensions. In th
photographs we become aware
the limits drawn between wl
essentially belongs to form a
what relates to representati
though in Paul's the represen
tional element is more promine
The limits of form are the lim
the theatre imposes: in Pau
theatre, the frame compresses t
idea of presence and the
perience of being distanced
crucial to the viewer.
The viewer feels at home w
Paul's images or Paul's people
he calls his photographs. Pau

Like a painter, he fixes his gaze on two contrasting areas: one solid and another airy, and then weighs the two visually t decide which is th higher tone wise.

involvement with people is

(Left) S.Paul; (top) a photograph taken by him: feeling tone

the transition from one plane to another in a personal way that you can claim is only yours. This is the meaning of Paul having an individual eye; with him the photographic image is a vastly complicated affair.

It is a complicated affair because looking at the world from the viewing window of the camera, one cannot separate the instrument of perception from perception; what we see is something like a copy. But that too is not true; rather the reality has an as-if character which allows even for a war photographer, time to arrange the frame. And the frame sensed is essential for understanding Paul's picture; he sees the world either through the window which has a horizon in an allegorical sense, or the world appears to him as an experience of a mirroring of reality.

What is relevant in Paul's photographs is that we see in them something distinctly different from what we see with naked eyes: as if looking through the viewfinder, we have discovered a self-referential world, where reality is understood as a system of relations rather than of visual extensions. In these photographs we become aware of the limits drawn between what essentially belongs to form and what relates to representation, though in Paul's, the representational element is more prominent. The limits of form are the limits the theatre imposes: in Paul's theatre, the frame compresses the idea of presence and the experience of being distanced is crucial to the viewer.

The viewer feels at home with Paul's images or Paul's people as he calls his photographs. Paul's involvement with people is existential and this is borne out by the absence of the newsmaker's photograph; he is rather a humanist photographer. With him photography is not the fragmented time counted in terms of frames exposed: it is about the long journey he undertook 40 years ago: and the image now reaches out for universals in their metaphoric equivalences.

SECTION FOUR

REV

EWS

As an art critic, K.B. Goel wrote primarily in the review mode – in newspapers and magazines. Over his long career from the late 1950s to the late 1990s, he covered solo and group exhibitions – of Indian as well as international art. His reviews of solo artist exhibitions appear in the section 'Artists' in this volume. This section features his reviews of group exhibitions and one book review – of Ernst Fischer's celebrated work, *The Necessity of Art*.

88
ENTER: THE MODERN PRIMITIVES

Review of Group 1890's first and only exhibition held in New Delhi in 1963

Mainstream, New Delhi, 2 November 1963

The artists belonging to the newly-formed Group 1890 are modern primitives who, abandoning the established attitudes to painting, attempt like Don Quixote to conquer the world anew. There is a touch of romanticism in whatever they do, reading into the artist a magician and a man possessed. They carry with them the legacy of archaic man. They represent a metamorphosis of taste in the plastic arts in India. Their creative impulse is compulsive and what they call a good painting is a built-in world, apart and self-contained, existing in its own right.

NO SONG FOR MAN

In their manifesto released at the opening of the exhibition at Rabindra Bhavan, Lalit Kala Akademi, they reject art that is born out of a preoccupation with human condition. They refuse to sing for man or be messiahs. The function of art, they maintain, is not to interpret and annotate, comprehend and guide, smells [sic] of false heroism.

> A work of art is neither representative, nor abstract, figurative or non-figurative. It is unique and sufficient unto itself, palpable in its reality and generating its own life. The image proper describes itself inevitably through the creative act. It is neither the translation of an experience, feeling, idea or act, nor the objective organization of form in space.

Having thrown out form, space, feeling, experience and history, one wonders with what means 'the image proper defines its own space, delineation, colour and composition'. The total impression of declarations is one of nothingness and their forms express nothing. This attitude leaves a yawning gap between the work that merely appeals to our taste and one whose autonomy reassures man's own freedom. The group does not 'advocate any specific mode or manner in art', but their works are pale derivations of manners and attitudes prevalent in the West. But I'm perhaps wrong in pointing to these ugly facts as I should know that we are living in a world in which art museums have no walls and reproduction has brought the wealth of world art at our doorsteps where styles have replaced schools.

A FEW FORMAL ELEMENTS

Most of the painters of this group regale in colour and its possibilities for a formal statement of form. Like the primitives, they have a few formal elements which pervade the canvas and the pictorial image with the rigidity of the ritual. The pattern is stable, being made up of well-defined elements. Technique overrides vision and their sweet little world of textures, which they mistakenly call images, is eclectic. Their whole approach seems to consist in the declaration that 'no animal could have done what they have done'.

This is all about their manifesto and the attitude to painting. My quarrel with them is the lover's quarrel and not for a moment do I deny them sincerity or competence. I only wonder whether all the members understand the significance of the words in the manifesto, let alone base their attitudes on them. Within the group there are many tendencies without any meeting ground. Rajesh [Mehra] and Jyoti Bhatt represent the two opposite ends of belief; Ambadas and Gulam Mohammad [Sheikh] have affinities, so have Himmat Shah and Jeram Patel but they are temporary.

It appears that these eleven painters and a sculptor, by coming together and forming themselves into a group, have found a platform to allow themselves to make individual statements. They have no programme either that could shape the group into a movement. Raghav Kaneria's sculptures are a treat. He is in the tradition of great sculptors pursuing the principles of geometric constructivism. Junk in his hands becomes the stuff of dreams; by the negation of its concreteness, he builds a form by wielding the discarded rubbish into a structure that has no volume. The wholes bring the outer space into the inner form and open up the surrounding landscape.

WOOD BURNING

Jeram Patel's recent exhibition of his works at the Kunika Art Centre showed that he is now in complete command over the technique of wood burning, making poetic landscapes out of the burnt surfaces of wood. He has in fact achieved a facility of expression that is organically constructive. His art is often termed merely a technique to shock people and this being his third show in this genre, voices are heard that he has come to the end of his technique. This point needs to be clarified. No technique can be a substitute for form and Jeram is a disciplined painter with a feeling for form. He has by his experiments in wood burning enlarged the vocabulary of painting – true at least of India.

89
A MARXIST APPROACH TO ART

A book review of Ernst Fischer's The Necessity of Art: A Marxist Approach, *which first appeared in English translation in 1963*[1]

Source and date of publication unknown, c. 1964

The publisher's blurb says that it's 'probably one of the most influential books on art to be published since the war'. Probably, this is true, though it's a tall claim to make even after allowing a large margin for exaggeration. If it doesn't look so very exaggerated, it is because of Fischer's reputation and the high regard in which he is held by European intellectuals. Fischer's intellectual capital is large, comparable among the Marxist theoreticians to [Georg] Lukacs. Unlike Lukacs, Fischer is not a fundamentalist and therefore less difficult than other Marxists; being essentially a poet (and a translator of Baudelaire), his strong point is lucidity. A non-Marxist reader feels at home with him; and in his writing the magic of words is compelling and a reader is held spellbound even when he knows his writing.

The magic of words in the chapter 'Art and Capitalism', for instance, reveals he has little to say which is original, if one knows one's Marx, Caudwell and others well. But the way he analyses bourgeois art (of course, in Marxist terminology) and the general dehumanization in painting and depersonalization in poetry is brilliant and perceptive. It is due to Fischer's advocacy that Kafka is 'rehabilitated' and considered now a novelist of an alienated world speaking of social reality in parables. He brings a freshness of approach to such (rather over-discussed) subjects as romanticism, impressionism and naturalism. It is undoubtedly a best first introduction to Marxist aesthetics and even to modern art and literature, films, drama and music (both serious and 'pop').

The arts of the twentieth century are individualistic and the Marxist explanation is of interest. Alienation is the key concept; it has influenced the writings of Kafka, the music of Schoenberg, the painting of the surrealists, the anti-novelists and anti-dramatists, Samuel Beckett's farces and the much-discussed poetry of American beatniks. Kafka is the best representative of the spirit of our century, of alienation and of Taylorism (a system which visualizes the total transformation of the worker into a machine part on a conveyor belt in the mass production age). Industrial society dehumanizes: we speak in statistics, of price trends, of stock exchange prices; personal relationships become work relationships, and in the bureaucracy which is the mode of power in an alienated society, a man becomes a 'case' (the pity is that the junior representative won't treat him even as a case but as a 'file'). About these bureaucrats Kafka says in his *Castle*, 'How am I to know one of you from the other, the only difference between you is your names, otherwise you are as alike as . . . two snakes.' Nihilism was the logical end (the idea that there is no sense at all is pathological) and the theme of existentialism is the meaning of existence and the nihilist idea that an individual is 'thrown' into his times.

The end result of this is fragmentation, an inability 'to see things in their proper size'. The Romantics did speak about fragmentation between man and his world; but it was on a different level and is well expressed in modern poetry through associative, disjointed imagery, its intellectual irrationalism. It is the very core of the poetry of Rilke, Benn, Ezra Pound, Eliot, Auden and Alberti and others. Hemingway represents this fragmented reality in escapes – from boredom, from all obligations to society and ideology – and the mode is speed, a holiday 'somewhere in the midst of the unknown, a flimsy tent where it will be brighter inside than it is in the outer darkness'. The colossal entertainment industry acts like a drug for vast masses of art consumers. Kafka is aware of this when he says that 'only a party to a case can really judge but being a party, it cannot judge. Hence there is no possibility of judgement in the world but only the glimmer of a possibility'.

Lukacs offers a method of judgement, though he too recognizes the limitations of his method. It can be summed up as follows: man is uneasy in the world of his ego, desires to refer to something that is more than 'I' and wants to be a whole man. He can be a whole man by sharing the experience of others and make it his own. This potential includes 'everything that humanity as a whole is capable of . . . and art is the indispensable means of this merging of the individual with the whole'. But the plan is beset with difficulties: this means that the understanding of reality is conditioned by our understanding of the whole and the understanding of the whole is conditioned by our understanding of the parts. This leads to intellectual despair because when an individual is trying to grasp the parts, he is worried about the whole and when he is trying to grasp the whole, he is not sure where to stop. Isn't this obscure richness? (Incidentally, Lukacs's ideas are developed a stage further by Lucien Goldmann in his recent book, *The Hidden God*, published this year by Routledge and Kegan.)[2]

At this point, it is necessary to point out Fischer's debt to Lukacs who has been called the Marx of aesthetics. It is surprising that Fischer, having drawn so heavily on Lukacs, doesn't mention his name even once. One can explain this lapse on the ground that the book was first published in communist Germany where Lukacs was in disrepute. Just as one can explain away that the most political chapter of the original, 'Problems of Transition', has been omitted because the English reading public has no use for a discussion on the relationship between the communist party and the artist.

But, this should not be taken to mean that Fischer has borrowed everything from Lukacs. There are some important, even fundamental, differences. To point out only two instances of their differences - Lukacs is much concerned with objectivism: good art, for him, is an objective reflection of an objective reality. Fischer keeps a balanced attitude. Again, Lukacs believes in the total unity of society: society remains a whole in his philosophical system whatever the quality of fragmented individual experience: one might even say that its unity continues to be intact despite, and indeed, through the fragmented understanding of reality. Fischer is, on the whole, in disagreement with this view; he agrees with [philosopher, Ernst] Bloch and it is discussed in the chapter 'The Loss and Discovery of Reality' of the book. On the question of outlook and methods in socialist art, he differs with Lukacs. Lukacs sees method and outlook as interrelated, aspects of a single reality, while Fischer separates them and thus undoes his own distinction between naturalism and realism. But this has given to his arguments greater flexibility. The result is that he looks at romantic art with sympathy and understanding while Lukacs's running it down bores.

Art then, for Fischer, is a 'life substitute', a means of arriving at social unity. 'The permanent function of art is to recreate as every individual's experience the fullness of all that he is not, the fullness of humanity at large.' Fullness in Lukacs's system makes sense; but in Fischer's formulation it is unclear. Let me quote him in full:

> In the first collective period of human development art was the great auxiliary weapon in the struggle against the mysterious power of nature. Art in its origins was magic, essentially one with religion and science. In the second period of development, and the beginning of every kind of social conflict - art became the chief means of understanding the nature of these conflicts, of what it was, of overcoming the individual's isolation by providing a bridge to what all men shared. In the late bourgeois world of today, when the class struggle has become more intense, art tends to be divorced from social ideas, to drive the individual still further into his desperate alienation, to encourage an impotent egoism, and to turn reality into a false myth surrounded by the magic rites of a bogus cult. And in the socialist world today art tends to be subordinated to special social requirements and to be used as a simple means of enlightenment and propaganda. But when the third, communist, period is reached when the individual and the collective are no longer in conflict, when classless society exists in an age of abundance - the essential function of art will consist in neither magic nor enlightenment.

The passage needs no comment. But one feels like asking: After Rome, what. . .? Of course the main thesis that art provides 'fullness of all that he is not', is undone and thus the magic of it. Fischer's confusion about the role of magic in art is felt throughout the book. Art springs from magic, he argues, because man is magical, because he made the tool and thereby also created an artifact and a whole world of art. But art springs from the magic of the primitive collectivity, and when Fischer persists in calling the art of advanced society, magical, he simply doesn't know what he is talking about; and surrenders to the metaphor. But this is not to deny the practical insight of the proposition. Fischer's contribution lies in connecting sexuality with the economics of totem and taboo. George Thomson has admitted that Fischer has taken his work still further.

Fischer has two things to say on the subject of magic: one is the necessity of the magic for art – the art of all periods and the other is that art is spellbinding. He seems to have read [philosopher R.G.] Collingwood, [anthropologist Bronislaw] Malinowski, [anthropologist Claude] Levi-Strauss, and knows what magic signifies to them.

> The primary function of all magical arts is to generate in the agent and agents certain emotions that are considered necessary or useful for the work of living. . . . Magical activity is a kind of dynamo supplying the mechanism of practical life with the emotional current that derives it. Hence magic is a necessity of every sort and condition of man and is actually found in every healthy society.

But this is certainly against the Marxist grain and opposite of what rationalist anthropologists like [E.B.] Tylor and [James] Frazer put out.

Fischer's explanation of the evolution of the hunter in close parallel to the development of his prey is both interesting and attractive. He says that primitive man confused his animal world with woman, as exemplified by the common practice of suckling of animals by woman – 'The woman suckles the animal, the man kills it; thus many hunting tribes come to believe in a mysterious bond between their women and their prey, with all the contradictions and fears that this implied.' The sexual intercourse and preying blended in the minds of primitive man; the spear outside the hut became his symbol of the phallus, and hence the sexual excitement before a hunt and the sexual rites which were performed before the work on cave paintings began. The book is full of insights and the following is worth a lot.

> . . . [I]f we bear in mind that the primitive hunter's attention was totally concentrated upon the prey – not upon the specific or individual features of any particular animal but upon the essential features of the species he set out to hunt; that, in other words what mattered to him were the contours of the animal and not the manifold details of its appearance – we shall, I believe, have found an adequate explanation for the works of art of the Stone Age.

There are other very many insights like these, and the book is indeed a must for anyone who wants to know the state of modern art and the tragic sense of our age.

Editor's Notes

1 Ernst Fischer's original German book, *Von der Notwendigkeit der Kunst*, was published in 1959; K.B. Goel reviews here its well-known English translation, of 1963. The review is undated and the source of publication is missing, but it appears to have been written the following year, in 1964.

2 Lucien Goldmann, in his 1955 work, *The Hidden God: A Study of Tragic Vision in the Pensees of Pascal and the Tragedies of Racine*, translated by Philip Thody (Routledge and Kegan Paul, 1964), draws on Lukacs's book, *History and Class Consciousness*, translated by Rodney Livingstone (London: Merlin Press, 1967), to examine the idea of the 'tragic vision' in European thought as influenced by Hegel and Marx.

90
EXHIBITION OF BRITISH PRINTS

An abridged review of contemporary British printmaking exhibited in New Delhi in 1970

Link, New Delhi, 20 September 1970

It is perhaps natural to be looking around for signs of an avant-garde, for without its existence it is as good as not having the arts at all. This is truer of painting because its modernist tradition is inseparable from the concept of avant-garde. For almost a hundred years now, the avant-garde has been the high fashion in the plastic arts, creating its own 'academy' which is, a contradictory thing but that is the irony of modernist art. It is a vogue word and its loose application has confused the public so much that it now looks upon it with great suspicion. Every market catching shift in style is shown to be avant-gardeish, whether deliberately or in sheer ignorance.

To say, therefore, that the current exhibition of 120 British prints at Lalit Kala Gallery is for us the first physical manifestation of avant-garde art is like giving to the public a used bus ticket for a journey to this exhibition. However the exhibition should not be missed. It will be an experience, to be sure, and as thrilling and spellbinding as having the first knock on erotic love. For many good reasons, it is beneficial to be a little romantic about this exhibition.

CLASSLESS IMAGE

First about the artists most of whom are under forty. The great majority of these artists came into prominence at about the same time when London went swinging with cultural hijackers like the Beatles, the rock and the mod-cinema people. Their art was the manifestation of the classless image which was very different from the BBC image of London. It shared its notions of culture and art with what was projected in the colour supplements, creating a false illusion of leisure and good life. There was a sense of visual exhilaration which was a natural development when art became an expression of the colour supplements and a sub-romantic area of admass culture.

The artist who, in the Fifties, was living in isolation, in the world of high bohemia, was too readily absorbed in the pop spectrum of society: now he was no longer dangerous to society, nor did he put any distance between himself and 'them' and thus prided himself as artist. He was no longer an outsider. Unlike the pop artist in America who is still an outsider trying to come to terms with his environment, creating from just the art side of the demarcation line the [Marshal] McLuhan world of media as message, the British artist takes the other world for granted and sleepwalks through it as if he were born into it. However, unlike his American counterpart, he is operating in a narrow circle, limited to London's mod inhabitants while the American artist is more dada because he is fighting the whole industrial military complex which not only dehumanizes the arts but seeks to turn the living into the dead.

MIX MEDIA

So, the London artists are part of the media landscape and work in easy and close relationship between the arts and the popular media in London. The London artist is now a tamed animal, he has thus a larger manoeuverability than the pop artist of America. Two institutions played a vital role in getting the artists involved with the admass world – the Institute of Contemporary Art's Independent Group, where some of the first investigations of popular culture took place and the Royal College of Art's magazine *Ark* which concerned itself with the cinema's image of London city as long ago as 1956. The Beatles, no doubt, prepared the ground for the permissiveness and freed the artists of the immense pressures which they were once subjected to. The London artist's preoccupation with media landscape has made him aware of the new possibilities in communication techniques of mix-media art, as artist Richard Hamilton wrote in 1964. 'Mixing idioms is virtually a doctrine . . . less perhaps to change pace than to preserve the identity of different sources; though a diversifying of language is, I like to think, a mutual object.'[1]

So, the one thing that is a shared sensibility among all the artists is to exploit the communication system for its own sake, to decode the communication codes employed by the admass world. The British artists' preoccupation with the technology of communication has made a vital contribution to pop culture, and a new technology may arise out of their experimentations. Their influence is already felt on the systems of communication because these artists analyse the existing systems of communication and translate them into a fine art context. Thus, a new responsiveness has been established by a pattern of feedback and cross-fertilization. This will certainly inaugurate a new renaissance, evident in the newer print mediums of silkscreen printing and vacuum forming.

Editor's Note

1 Richard Hamilton on the artist R.B. Kitaj in the Hanover Gallery catalogue, 1964, quoted in *Richard Hamilton*, New York: The Solomon R. Guggenheim Foundation, 1973, p. 32.

91
AVANT-GARDE OR KITSCH?

Review of Australian printmaking exhibited in New Delhi as part of the 1971 Triennale-India

Link, New Delhi, 19 December 1971

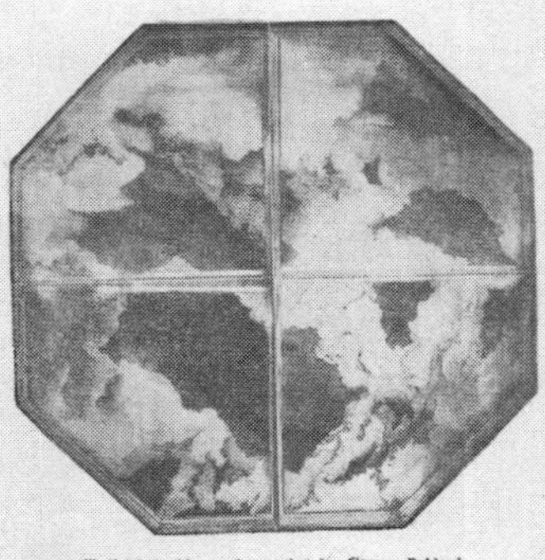

'Skylight' (etching and aquatint) by George Baldessin

We were first introduced to the Australian avant-garde in this recent exhibition, the second Delhi Triennale, via Robert Hunter's work occupying a whole wall of the Lalit Kala Gallery. Hunter's was not an art object, a mere stencilled drawing transferred on an actual wall painted white; the drawing had no colours, only a non-colour celebration of [Kazimir] Malevich's *White on White* and the grey lattices which joined a configuration of squares joined with other squares by diagonals. The Hunter wall acquired a certain optical relevance because of its scale: indeed, scale was its content as was the huge bamboo structure by an American artist which outside the gallery context would have passed as a stage for a miracle play. The Hunter evocation of Malevich's non-art disappeared from the wall the moment the triennale was folded up: the Hunter wall was redone in toned yellow and the avant-garde art vanished like yesterday's city waste.

PICASSOIDS

One could hardly believe one's eyes that this could have come from Australia, a country which was discovered only two hundred years ago. This also underlined the fact that Australia is a country of white settlers who created urban enclaves around the coastline – it is the last outpost of the old European culture. The criminal-settlers, who were its first white inhabitants, brought ruthless devastation as more settlers came, to the natural flora and fauna of the coastal landscape. The coastlanders were the literal reflectors of London's culture, their original home; so it is even today – literal reflectors of London's pop culture of the Sixties.

Art consciousness came late to Australia; indeed, it was as late as the end of the Second World War when many European artists migrated there. These were surely not the frontline European avant-gardes who had chosen America for settlement; they were mostly either teachers or

'Picassoids' – that is to say the artists who lived by imitating the art of their contemporaries. As Australians, their involvement with the international styles of painting and sculpture was more natural because they had hardly any local tradition of their own to fall back upon. The language shared was not their own either: it was a hybrid of English and American; [they evolved] a truly developed colonial art which spoke with a metropolitan arrogance, its mecca being located either in London or in New York. Art historian, Owen Spurway is right when he says (in the catalogue to the exhibition of Australian prints which is on view at the Lalit Kala Gallery) that 'Australia has always been a highly urbanized country'.

And this is central to their visual ideas. The Antipodean identity is reflected not in the bushman's innocence of European culture, but as [Australian] artist [Albert] Tucker[1] said, the Antipodean is one of 'the paranoiac outsiders of the extremist international fashions'. An artist – without having to look back upon the art of the past and a self-elected priest of television culture, a natural beneficiary of America's cultural imperialism – is a born avant-garde, although in the context of London and New York, he is pure Australian kitsch. But the kitsch in New Delhi has the glitter of the original: Has the Hunter wall in the Delhi triennale not merged totally in the anti-art hellfire enacted by the American Museum of Modern Art?

DIRECTIONS

This long introduction to Australian art would have been unnecessary but for the fact that our contemporaries have mistaken kitsch for the original avant-garde gesture, as if these were the specimen of an easily recognizable Australian style – a claim which Owen Spurway himself denies. 'There is no easily recognizable Australian style as such, but rather a diversity of interpretation about similar concerns. This exhibition simply attempts to indicate directions being explored by some Australian artists today.' The catalogue has a few words on Australian printmaking, too, which is more explicit: 'Although there is as yet little particularly Australian identity and the various influences of Europe are apparent (no doubt due to our short cultural history) many Australian printmakers have been included and have won prizes in important international print biennales'. This indeed reflects perfectly well what the colonial mind seeks in art – international recognition from places it looks up to for cultural inspiration.

It is a pity that the exhibition does not have prints by the artists who are outspoken critics of Australia. Take, for instance, the prints by Noel Counihan, the leader of social realism in Australia. The five prints by him have all the skill and aggressiveness of his style, particularly the print, *Boy in Helmet*, marked by its fiendish look, the innocent face brutalized by the experience of the Vietnam War. Another print, *Boy*, is a variation on his now famous painting, *Man in Combat Dress*, which has the mask-like face of aggression.

AUSTRALIAN WARHOL

Another artist who makes a deep impression on us is Brett Whitely who is regarded by many as the Australian avatar of Warhol, although he does not make films, nor is he a pop artist. Indeed, he is a pop-style parodist and his bas-relief of a Rembrandt *Self-Portrait* won him last year the Captain Cook Bicentenary Awards (second prize). His logical following of Duchamp has brought him very close to renouncing painting as an art. (After the award, he told a critic that 'the world's in a terrible bloody mess . . . and art has let us down'.) For Whiteley, painting as painting is long dead but drawing as drawing is still alive and given all professional consideration in his hands. His two lithographs, both done in 1966, do not represent his genius fully and missing from these prints are the typical Whitely concerns, particularly his anti-Vietnam war drawings which represent him as an artist who participates in social upheavals and who is a caricaturist of respectable art. Of course, even in these two feeble prints, we have the evidence of his Duchampian fervour and a fine sense of observation. Look at his *Hyena* print and what powerful lines form the animal.

John Brack's bizarrerie are powerful whimsies no doubt. He too is a Duchamp follower but has not renounced painting: it is a tool of expose and he uses it with great skill and insight to satirize the ritualistic incongruities of urban subculture. His etching, *Scissors and Mirrors,* surrealizes with the child's simplicity of vision on the human condition and the metaphor he uses is the cage which urban culture has built for man. For enacting an original surrealist environment, we should, however, look at Jan Senbergs's screen print, *Love the Stage*. Indeed, the stage is the world gone topsy-turvy and its burlesque is a hanging plate-form – objects, planks and curiously odd things. The ensemble is given an illusory unification by colour and the common chemical processing that binds its entire range of hues. But composition also plays an equally powerful role in bringing the separate, fragmentary configurations into a relationship with the whole. He is a prophet of doom believing that industry has set on a disaster course that nothing could [can] check. His aesthetic sensibilities of the disaster image are graphic, even inspiring. It is a pity that his surrealist outfit has only a formal dress and does not bite as hard as Noel Counihan's does. His is a pure technology of compositional devices and a highly original use of colour.

ART AS TECHNOLOGY

Technology itself becomes art in George Baldessin's etchings and aquatints. Baldessin, who is better known as a sculptor, gives to his printmaking processes the objectivity of metal sculpture. Indeed, the printmaking is an extended activity of his sculptural innovations. There is little to distinguish them as two distinct art forms, because the prints can be looked at as a form of sculpture, of the two-dimensional variety that is. Whatever the

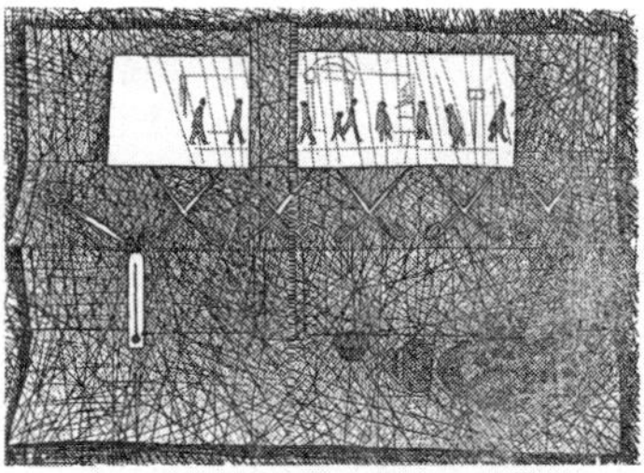
'Scissors and Mirrors' (etching) by John Brack

value of the new in these prints, in Baldessin's hands technology becomes an aid to plastic expression which has rarely been better demonstrated as in the silvered surface of *Skylight* in aluminium, a material used overmuch these days in sculpture. 'In viewing this print,' Spurway tells us, 'the spectator is placed in the awkward position of looking at an image, on a wall, of something which would normally have to be viewed from below.' He is cool and clinical, reminding us perhaps of the fact that a print is actually a plate. And so it is.

The National Gallery of Victoria, which has brought together this exhibition, has surprisingly in its collection the drawings of Captain James Cook, the first artist-settler in Australia two hundred years ago, which marks the discovery and annexation of Australia. These are a record of Australia's topography and coastline. But they now have a contemporary relevance because these drawings by Cook are very similar to those done by Christo, the wrapper-artist,[2] and they too were exhibited recently. This coincidence of similarities between the Cook doodle and Christo art is central to contemporary tradition in Australia.

Editor's Notes

1 A significant post-war artist, Albert Tucker, was one of the chief members of the 'angry penguins' avant-garde art movement in Australia in the 1940s, known for his excoriation of post-war Australian white society in his highly expressionist, dark paintings.

2 Artist Christo has worked with 'wrapping' – in ordinary fabric and rope – a variety of objects ranging from tin cans, furniture to bicycles and trees, and, famously, oil barrels, changing the familiarity of an object to its mysterious silhouettes and, through it, setting up novel ways of protest. In 1969, Christo and his fellow-artist Jean-Claude wrapped about 1.5 kilometres of Australian coastland of rocky cliffs southeast of Sydney for a period of ten weeks. The massive Environmental art project, titled *Wrapped Coast – One Million Square Feet*, used erosion-control fabric and ropes, and saw the participation of mountain climbers, architecture students, artists and teachers over a period of four weeks. It was self-funded, drawing attention to the shapes of the coast – the rocky cliffs – by altering their viewing and perception through the act of wrapping.

92
GROUP 1974

Review of the exhibition of the artist collective Group 1974, formed that year, in New Delhi

Link, New Delhi, 10 March 1974

The current exhibition of works by the younger generation of painters who came to the Indian art scene in the late Sixties may prove to be as significant as that famous exhibition of 1963, which displayed the works of the Group 1890 painters and was inaugurated amidst great fanfare by Jawaharlal Nehru. The show comes in marked contrast to the 1963 drama almost unannounced: it is simply called the Group Exhibition 1974 and opened without any formal ceremony.

Except Gulammohammed Sheikh, the old 'old-timer' of the 1890 Group, the others are under forty and came to the scene after the tidal wave of tantra and its geometricism had swept the Indian consciousness. It is significant that none of these artists was caught up in that treacherous current. Their works during the tantra wave had only a neutral context working from outside the known stagnant categories. Because of our habit of looking in terms of blanket categorization, these artists remained in comparative obscurity. Working outside the transcendental realm of formal values, they did not surrender their vision to an inward-looking art; on the contrary, they were occupied with the task of evolving an imagery that sought to narrow down the distance between their work and audience. Little wonder, these artists went almost unnoticed. The only exception perhaps is Bhupen Khakhar.

On the face of it, these painters do not look different; rather they seem as much idiosyncratic, staying outside the fence of the lyrical art of the Sixties and thus willingly choosing isolation. In a

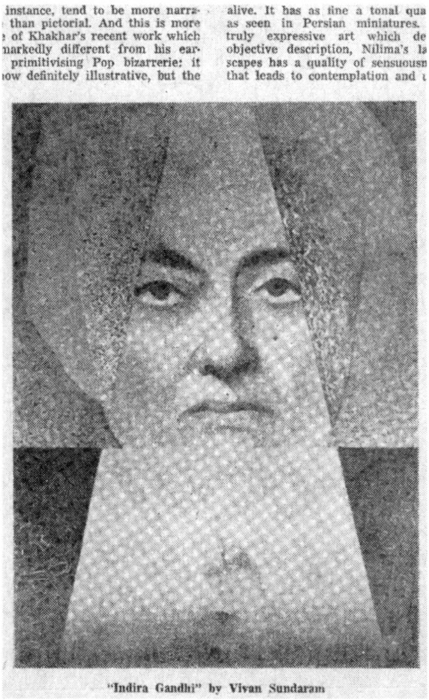
instance, tend to be more narra-
than pictorial. And this is more
of Khakhar's recent work which
narkedly different from his ear-
primitivising Pop bizarrerie: it
ow definitely illustrative, but the

alive. It has as fine a tonal qua
as seen in Persian miniatures.
truly expressive art which de
objective description, Nilima's la
scapes has a quality of sensuousn
that leads to contemplation and

"Indira Gandhi" by Vivan Sundaram

way, their work can be seen as so many aspects of the indigenism debate that started with the painters of Group 1890: they, it seems, have definitely pushed that root-in-the-soil debate into the Seventies, although their works arrive from the specific context of their trivial individualism.

So, there are no hints of a collaborative vision nor of a conflict between local obligations and aestheticism; perhaps, there is a tidal pull towards a definitive ideology. Or perhaps, more than ideology, there are those compulsions of imagery that has a predominance of informational elements. In other words, no mythical status for their art objects; theirs is a journey from an inward to an outward look, their art, increasingly opening up to extra-pictorial readings. Still the presiding value is the old obsession: the autonomy of the painted surface, and this has no 'inscape' interiors to be sure. On the other hand, there is the attempt of an open discloser [sic] of the surface as is evident in the works of Sheikh, Khakhar, Nalini and Laxma Goud.

Their works have a specific context and the imagery has an intentional space stated with such directness that we can share and discuss it across the table. Khakhar's and Vivan's works, for instance, tend to be more narrative than pictorial. And this is truer of Khakhar's recent work which is markedly different from his earlier primitivizing pop bizarrerie: it is now definitely illustrative, but the illustrative is presented in a stylized form. Gieve Patel's work has a different surface; his attitudes and anxieties expressed in metaphors are literal, while Vivan's imagery, his metaphors, spring from a different anxiety. But the current anxieties in their works are accelerated to such densities that they get a well-defined political level. While Gieve could be casual, Vivan has the Mexican vision.

The only painter who seemingly looks detached from such preoccupation as filling the canvas with content and message is Nilima Sheikh. Her work is expressive, but of a different kind: it is about silence – in the sense Malraux speaks of voices as the voices of silence.[1] In her work the surface is sensuously alive. It has as fine a tonal quality as seen in Persian miniatures. A truly expressive art which defies objective description, Nilima's landscapes have a quality of sensuousness that leads to contemplation and ultimately to communion: one becomes aware of a co-presence; put in another way, the individual consciousness and the aesthetic surface for a moment become one: there is near complete coalescence and the objective landscape dissolves into pure consciousness of feeling.

Vivan's *Indira Gandhi* tells us so much more about his politics than is possible to construct it through a medium of visual statement. Geeta Kapur, in the catalogue, puts Vivan's message in perhaps extreme radical terms:

> He has done a portrait of Indira Gandhi in the mould of an Egyptian empress. But there is no pageant to proclaim her power, only a crazy destitute who has walked a long distance away from her . . . and as spectators we cannot

> turn away, not until she sinks into the horizon like a gigantic obelisk and the old woman finds her way across the ruin and rubble.

If the portrait could be read with the verbal clarity of a book – and Geeta surely seems to think that it can be read like a book – its intellectual construct has poor pictorial value because a truly expressive work is the least communicative. What is unique about this portrait of Indira Gandhi is not its dramatization into a billboard image but in conceiving an image that fits well into the Egyptian schema. This is what Gombrich calls 'making' an image and then matching it with the observed reality.

Vivan has conceived the portrait in two panels: the upper panel shows the blown-up face of Indira Gandhi lit by a beam which splits the monolithic granite-textured planes to reveal the magic personality of what the unsympathetic call the image of an empress. The next panel is indeed a picture within a picture which shows the subjugation of a people mesmerized by her populist politics: one could read into this landscape a condition of perpetual contradiction, which is what populism actually is.

But Vivan's more successful work is the triptych called *The Wall*. It is not an invisible wall; it is a bare wall, without memory and it does not admit any graffiti. But its bareness has a definite intellectual context and this registers on the mind when we attempt to analyse the rather stage-set situations: the panel above this wall shows a green spread, a golf ground and a barbed wire running across horizontally separates the sports world of the bourgeois from the everydayness of the general human condition. The panel below the wall depicts in violent colours (reds, pinks, blues and other related hues in between them that shock us with their sensuous immediacy) the mass of humanity, and some nebulous human shapes suggest a complex configuration of the world of misery and sorrow.

Here, no doubt, a painting could be read like a book and its intellectual content emerges without destroying the unity of the work; in this work we do not read things which are not there. No doubt several levels of meaning are admitted, and the movement between the levels of meaning in the painting is reflected in the movement from one panel to another. Each area sets up a pattern of tension which can be related to another section of the painting and the meaning at each level contributes to the structure of one that is placed either above or below the wall.

Like Vivan, Gieve Patel, too, is a politically conscious painter and their common starting point is the photographic image. While Vivan's social realism is slightly diffused, allegorical and even metaphysical, Gieve Patel's is more specific, for he has been painting members of the ruling class with 'a deadpan irony' for a long time. There is certainly a great illusionistic potential in the game of shadows he sets up which has the same spellbinding power as in a Chirico. The real people are composed with directness of iconic symbols, and the form and meaning in the political drama merges in the silences of the shadows. What is left with us finally is a dark atmospheric distance of Kafkaesque terror. Gieve has developed a highly complex pictorial syntax for expressing his political pantomimes.

Laxma Goud is by far the most powerful graphist to have emerged in the Seventies: and to be sure, we are all familiar with his bizarrerie. He dramatizes the dark fears of an inner life in terms of the jungle and his imagery and pictorial vocabulary has taken a definite form where object and metaphor function in a mimetic animation. He has the old surrealists' obsession with nature and art.

Nalini [Malani] and Arpita [Datta, later, Singh] offer us two different worlds as contrasting as the world of guilt and innocence. Nalini paints in the expressionist idiom and is closer in painting methods to Francis Bacon. Her subject is self-exposure: the images of women in their sexual struggle with man. But this goes beyond the biological level. The velvety strokes of flesh-tinted colours form an urgent image, but their twisted anatomies have no vulgar grotesque look. In her painting, flesh becomes a metaphor, 'a defying force that struggles for resurrection'.[2] It is no doubt difficult to deal with every artist's work in a review. For instance, Arpita has emerged from this show as a sizeable talent, but her painting mode is so full of surprises that we are not sure how long she will keep the current hotline with narcissism open.

Editor's Notes

1 *The Voices of Silence* (New York: Doubleday, 1953) is Andre Malraux's collection of essays that discusses, among other things, the idea of a 'museum without walls' – where, via photographic reproduction (in books), a viewer can behold an artwork of any period and from anywhere in the world without having to behold it physically, creating thus a museum 'without walls' or a virtual museum, extended today to accessing art from numerous collections on the internet.

2 Geeta Kapur, in her introduction to the exhibition catalogue.

93
LANGUAGE OF PRINTS

Abridged review of an exhibition of prints of well-known Western artists at the National Gallery of Modern Art, New Delhi

Patriot Magazine, New Delhi, 17 February 1974

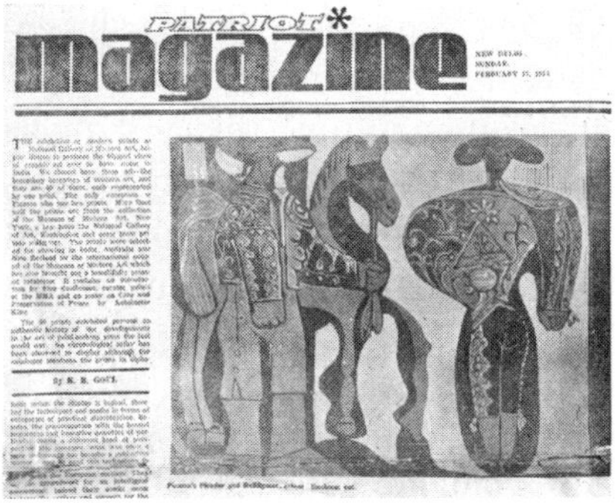
PATRIOT* magazine

The exhibition of modern prints at the National Gallery of Modern Art, Jaipur House, is perhaps the biggest show of graphic art ever to have come to India. We almost have them all – the legendary inventors of modern art, and there are forty-nine of them, each represented by one print, except Picasso who has two prints. More than half the prints are from the collection of the Museum of Modern Art (MoMA), New York, a few from the National Gallery of Art, Washington, and some from private collectors – to be shown in India, Australia and New Zealand. The catalogue contains an introduction by Riva Castleman, curator of prints at MoMA and an essay on care and preservation of prints by Antoinette King. The 50 prints exhibited present an authentic history of the developments in printmaking since the last war. Beside the preoccupation with the formal sequences and inventive densities of a particular media, a different kind of perspective also emerges: what was once a pure technology has become a subjective matter, to read which is to begin with the European masters.

Most of them represented in the show use lithography, whose interest in it, the catalogue introduction observes, led to its revival. And which impacted silkscreen printing's dominance in the Sixties. Chagall's *Arabian Nights* print, from his illustrations, is made with the help of a master printer: their translation into lithographic technology gives to his colours a vividness achieved by overprinting transparent pastel inks. Masson too, like Chagall, did not work directly on the stone. Unlike most lithographs which require a separate stone for each colour, hisis printed from a single stone, the image conceived in separate coloured areas with gestural strokes of crayon as if he was painting directly from nature.

Picasso's *Owl on a Chair* is a rare print as it has no people. Spending many months underground in Fernand Mourlot's lithograph workshop in Paris during the Second World War. After it, his experiments led to

Picador and Bullfighter, where he cut all the colours successively from one linoleum. Braque's lithograph, *Leaves, Colour, Light* (1953) offers a different kind of colour sensitivity: the first lithograph of such a size with innovative use of the medium. Equally impressive is Jean Dubuffet's *Carrot Nose* with a textural richness seldom found in lithographs. His 234 prints, using direct methods like heated resin, mixtures of water and turpentine, made up the collage *Phenomena* series, from which arises the present print.

VERVE

Other lithographs that attract attention are Pierre Alechinsky's combined with aquatint, Hans Hartung's *Brown Composition* with negative and positive elements so reversed as to have flat-edged strokes appearing scraped into a solid ground. Antoni Tapies creates a new sensitivity by collage and embossing, translating the tactile qualities of material into lithography, while Willem de Kooning's *Minnie Mouse* (1971) extends his gestural painting techniques. Action painter, Sam Francis's *Untitled* lithograph has the verve and spontaneity associated with action art. Fine tonality of colour in Josef Albers's *White Line Square IV* reminds of his famous painting, *Homage to the Square,* the only printmaker to have produced prints with the help of computer-activated machinery. Edward Ruscha's lithograph is a technological feat: the abstract image of the work *Adios* is like liquid colour dripped on paper. Jim Dine's work uses the most complicated print technology, having undergone the presses at least thirty-two times: the litho press, the screen printing frame, gluings of collage, individual block printings and hand writing.

Rauschenberg's colour lithographs, *Lawn,* combine two opposite modes of painting – abstract expressionism and pop art clichés. He says: 'The image that is made by a printer's mat, a metal plate, a wet glass or a leaf plastically incorporated into a composition and applied to a stone, stops functioning literally within its previous limitations. They are an artistic recording of an action as realistic and poetic as a brush stroke.' The subject is chosen rather randomly, so the green graph becomes the environment which holds together many images, brush strokes, palm and newspaper prints, and magazine images of violence and sports. We are forced to read these images as if it were a screen; the narrative becomes more nostalgic the more we understand the significance of the cultural signs used. Rauschenberg is the ideal of William Ivins's aesthetic who saw prints as means to reach a wider public and a technological approach to problems of picture-making.[1]

LITHOGRAPHY

Before lithography's invention, commercial engraving resulted in producing only the copies of copies: the draughtsman for the engraver copied in black and white what the painter had painted and the engraver rendered the draughtsman's drawings. Lithography soon became a favourite,allowing the artist to print from his drawing as there was no reworking by another hand. The formalism that interests Indian printmakers will no doubt find encouragement because the exhibition presents only one side of the picture – at least in terms of the history of print technologies – with no traces of the trauma of photographic invention which had upset the settled universe of the nineteenth-century artists. According to Ivins, printmaking is older than the invention of the Gutenberg technology. Without prints, the development of science would not have been that rapid because these illustrations were the only means of communication. He saw how prints can shape technological forms:

> Until a century ago prints made in the old technique filled all the function that are now filled by our linecuts [sic] and half-tones by our photographers and blueprints by our various colour processes, and by our political cartoons and pictorial advertisements. . . . It becomes obvious that without prints we should have very few of our modern sciences. . . . Far from being merely minor works of art, prints rate among the most important and powerful tools of modern life.[2]

AURA

In the age of mechanical reproduction prints are regarded as works of art perhaps because of the fact that their production processes are hand-based and have that quality we call aura absent in the purely mechanical arts like photography. An artist's print, not intended to be a reproduction of anything, is considered an original expression and thus has the aura essential to the cult of the original work. For much of their indisputable aesthetic merits, the prints in woodcut, etching, engraving and other media cannot be looked at from the point of view of general idea and particular functions. Ivins asks to 'think of them as conveyors of information and on us as receiver of information'.

This brings us back to Rauschenberg, the lithograph stone for him is just 'a surface, a billboard or a projection screen and this has close associations with the flatbed stone of the printing press'. Critic-historian, Leo Steinberg, thinks that the flatbed picture plane is the characteristic picture plane of the 1960s, with 'symbolic allusion to hard surfaces such as table-tops, studio floors, bulletin boards – any receptor surface on which objects are scattered, on which data is entered, on which information may be received, printed, impressed – whether coherently or in confusion' – a significant insight indispensable for a correct viewing of the prints by Rauschenberg, Warhol, Jasper Johns, Paolozzi, R.B. Kitaj, Roy Lichtenstein and Sol LeWitt. Prints become means of documentation and information, but the painted surface is no longer the analogue of a visual experience of nature but of operation processes, the shift from nature to culture registered by screenprinting.

Rauschenberg is the only painter who in this century has invented the most since Picasso, famous for his erasing of a de Kooning drawing and exhibiting it as *Drawing by Willem de Kooning erased by Robert Rauschenberg.*[3] This was more than a psychological gesture, as Leo Steinberg has noted. 'He was changing – for the viewer no less than for himself – the angle of imaginative confrontation, tilting de Kooning's evocation of a world space into a thing produced by pressing down on a desk.'[4] To him, printing media is preferable as 'the work becomes a product or a witness' of the artist's own personal involvement.

WARHOL, LICHTENSTEIN

As opposed to Rauschenberg's images of personal involvement, Warhol's and Lichtenstein's represent a 90-degrees shift – the shift from personal, inward and aggressively aesthetic imagery to imagery of the opposite kind: anticipated earlier by Jasper John's flags and targets. Its extraordinary exemplifications are to be in Warhol's and Lichtenstein's prints: they are impersonal, public and aggressively commonplace. Warhol's notorious images of film star Marilyn Monroe, his subject matter for five years – from 1962 to 1967, were conceived in mechanistic terms, in the tradition of minimal seriality.But they were significant not in terms of current pop art aesthetic but pop culture: they represent the trauma of popular consciousness which her suicide evoked. His interest is in the 'deteriorized image' which is far removed from the image of the real Marilyn. The isolated elements of her portrait are printed in garish poster colours to emphasize her artificiality: her lipstick, her eye shadow, her hair, her collar stand out, and they are distortions of the real translated through the silkscreen medium into art. Thus art of the Sixties takes a U-turn: from representing something of an act taken against the world, the artist has turned to address his audience, both their object and subject.

Lichtenstein and Warhol rejected the current mode of expressing the cultural point of view by autobiographical means: by elevating printing methodology to an aesthetic level. Roy Lichtenstein's print (*Sweet Dreams* in colour serigraph), for instance, retains the edge of comic book style. In fact it is nothing more than an act of switching the image from one channel (printing) to another (screen printing). The comic book style is absorbed completely, including its cultural clichés, which not only form his style but also determine its meaning. Lichtenstein retains the impersonal or the commercial while Warhol is mechanical at a cottage-industry level. Warhol's repeated image lends ambiguity while Lichtenstein's is a single holistic image.

Following in the opposite direction, Kitaj and Paolozzi's imagery has a common source of inspiration: Wittgenstein's theory of information. Kitaj, for instance, does not mind if his art has the touch of 'the illustrative and the vulgar' but it is not created in anonymity. Literal and political, his single ambition is to forge a great figurative style. So his pictures and prints are impregnated with a mixture of political convictions, social interests and literary tastes, but not a well-defined ideology. He is not pop either, although he uses pop clichés and its stylistic conventions. Many of his silkscreen prints are published in the series *Mahler Becomes Politics, [Beisbol]*[5] (the print displayed comes from this series), *Struggle in the West – The Bombing of London,*[6] and most recently a fifty-print edition called *In Our Time*. Like him, Eduardo Paolozzi too treats printmaking as a kind of journalistic activity. His print *Conjectures to Identity*[7] has a random but well-arranged imagery chosen from parts of illustrations of machinery, machine parts, a photograph, patterns of checks and lines, and all these elements are pasted up as in a commercial advertisement.

The prints by these pop artists remind us again of the revolutionary shift in sensibility: art turning its back on nature and becoming a consumer product and as commonplace as any other commodity. This shift is of such magnitude that it is too early to graph its direction. But no other media except in the screen-printing medium do we find a proper documentation of this shift. Future historians looking for evidence in the screen prints of the Sixties will find Ivins's insights dazzling.

Editor's Notes

1 William Ivins Jr. was the curator of the prints at Metropolitan Museum of Art, New York, from 1916 to 1946, and built its core printmaking collection, writing several books on the subject.

2 William Ivins, 'The Tyranny Broken', *Prints and Visual Communication*, Harvard University Press, 1953, introduction, p. 3.

3 The work is now in the collection of the San Francisco Museum of Modern Art.

4 Leo Steinberg, 'Reflections on the State of Criticism', *Artforum*, March 1972, reprinted in Joseph Brandon, ed., *Robert Rauschenberg*, 2002, p. 29.

5 Now in the collection of Tate Modern, London.

6 A print, each, exists in the collections of Tate, London and V&A, London.

7 Also in the collection of Tate Modern, London.

94

NEW CONCEPTS LACK SUPPORT OF TRADITION

Review of an exhibition in New Delhi of ten British landscape artists

Patriot Magazine, New Delhi, 27 July 1983

> Tradition is not something a man can learn; not a thread he can pick up when he feels like it any more than a man can choose his ancestors. Someone lacking in a tradition who would like to have one is like a man unhappy in love.
>
> – Ludwig Wittgenstein

The ten British painters, all of them young with new approaches to landscape painting shaped by the aesthetics of photo realism of the Seventies, whose works were displayed recently at the Lalit Kala Gallery, seemed to be men who have given so much to their art and are therefore unhappy because they have got so little in return. They are without reference points to their supposedly new conceptions of landscape painting. It is not a lack of a tradition that ails them really; at the root of it there is the confusion – their failure to distinguish between the function of aesthetics and the technology of communication, for, aesthetic problems have no relevance to communication systems.

But why display this confusion – in a third world country? Is it because vulnerable as we are to the seduction of new technologies in art – having fallen for minimalism the way we did in the Sixties, naming this West's yesterday's dress as tantrism – we may adapt to this new fashion in photographic realism too? And it is not unlikely that we might; for the impact of minimalism on the Indian art scene of the mid-Sixties was unmistakable and its art historical terms in the context of Indian transcendental aesthetics came to be translated into old archaic forms of tantric art. Most practitioners of tantric art would however deny – and rightly – that their variety of minimalism had no traffic with the technology of communication. But their products had the same appeal as the advertisement image. The Indian version of minimalism also failed to distinguish an important aspect of the minimal aesthetic: minimalism was a closed system of energies while the admass images like the technology of communication is part of a process of recreating from the transmitted sensibility a wholly original language.

Take the technique of illusion built up during the Renaissance. The perspectival landscape, besides conveying information about the physical world, has a message that is coded in the form of allegory. Although foreshortening, chiaroscuro and the evolving techniques of perspective had become recognizable components of the sophisticated code of visual informations these were incidental to the main preoccupation of the Renaissance masters like Masaccio and Mantegna; the core of their search in this new landscape of fact was 'that kind of landscape which is entirely occupied with the tame delineation of a given spot'.[1] The artist not only produced a visual record of the scene as does a photographic image but was involved with evolving a code of graphic equivalent for everything he saw. By the end of the seventeenth century, it was a mechanistic universe: the artist being concerned less and less with the effect of light and the sky and more with topographical reproduction. Not that the artists of those time as topographers willfully suppressed their interests in the beauty of atmosphere or that they were too occupied with meeting the demands of their patrons: they sank to the condition of industrious topographers because their patrons did not demand something more than information from the landscape that would raise it to the condition of art.

By the time the Turner landscape became the in-thing, the landscape of fact as 'a tame delineation of a given spot' had ceased to have the same patronage as it had in the two preceding centuries. The importance attached to what Constable called 'chiaroscuro of nature' in the context of early nineteenth-century art was the result of the popularity of aesthetics of camera lucida. The term chiaroscuro of nature is not enough to explain the whole drama of light and shade; the keynote of feeling that this drama plotted out for the viewer is left out by the term even though the artist pretended to nothing but imitation of nature. Constable recognized the truth of the artist's mission: his only job was to translate that single dominant idea representing the core of his naturalistic vision which he could expand, enrich but would never lose sight of.

A Constable landscape is defined by the truth of impressions received from actual objects that constituted the scene: these infinite sensations of visual data of landscape were built up and simplified to a single idea. 'Perhaps no other painter (except Rubens) has succeeded as Constable did in subordinating the infinite visual data of landscape to a single idea,' Sir Kenneth Clark has said. 'Later painters have either killed the idea by enriching it or offered the first sensation without daring to build it up.'[2] The Constable example is to illustrate the historical importance of the code even when it is still in the process of evolution. This code when it becomes part of art's closed system of historical consciousness tends to impose itself on taste. The taste, like a sense organ, operates in visual arts in an instinctive, and assuredly, negative way. For, only in a negative reaction, the taste registers its presence; taste, needless to assert, seeks not what is tasteful but what does not offend it.

The works of ten British artists record journeys with photography but not the land routes of taste. They look more like projects with the same appeal that scientific probings have because of their intricate methodologies. What appears to be merely a 'palette' of things the artists have collected (perhaps because of their protean genius) is of as much interest as anything lying unnoticed outside the window and which suddenly gets transformed into a structure because the attention is focused on something intriguing. The Seventies gone, what the British sell as avant-garde gesture of the decade is actually a period style. The death of the avant-garde is announced by the BBC itself: and this is the thesis Robert Hughes's book, *The Shock of the New.*

> By 1979 the idea of the avant-garde had gone. This sudden metamorphosis of one of the popular clichés of art criticism into an unword took a great many people by surprise. . . . By 1976 'avant-garde' was a useless concept: social reality and actual behaviour had rendered it obsolete.[3]

Editor's Notes

1 Statement attributed to Henry Fuseli, professor of painting at the Royal Academy, London, who cautioned his students in 1799 against the perils of painting such a landscape, distinguishing it from mere topography. He went on to say that the masters, from Titian to Reubens to Rembrandt, all 'spurned' such 'map-work' in their landscapes.

2 Kenneth Clark, 'The Natural Vision', *Landscape into Art*, London: J. Murray, 1949, p. 150. Art historian and museum/gallery director Kenneth Clark is best known for his pioneering television documentary series, *Civilization* (1969), accompanied by an illustrated book on Western art, architecture and philosophy. It was the first such TV programme which inspired many others, most notably John Berger's landmark BBC series, *Ways of Seeing* (1972) and later, Robert Hughes's *The Shock of the New* (1980). Berger's series and book emerged as a distinct counter to Clark's grand narrative of European painting, which Berger complicated as inherently multilayered, political and not as one received story, so to speak, radically altering how people learned to view art.

3 Robert Hughes, *The Shock of the New*, New York: Alfred A Knopf, 1980, p. 365.

95

AMBIVALENT TERRAIN

Review of an exhibition of works on the themes of nudity and nakedness

'Artscape', *The Economic Times*, New Delhi, 3 September 1990

The space between the naked and the nude was the subject of images mounted by the Art Heritage gallery at its low-profile summer show. The 'naked' in art historical terms is vulgarity, and as Kenneth Clark has observed, 'to be naked is to be deprived of our clothes and the word implies some of the embarrassment which most of us feel in that condition'.[1] This view is definitely not shared by Latika Katt, who self-consciously seeks to hurt our Victorian sensibilities. The naked for her is the emblematic sign of the male-dominated parasitical culture: naked as opposed to sublime, organs exteriorized as opposed to a veiled defenseless body.

[R.B.] Bhaskaran's mapping of the space between the naked and the nude is rather conventional: his is a body viewed as the central focus in the life class of an art college. The body in this life class does not involve memory and, therefore, there is no inscription of the body's nervous system on to the canvas or paper. The body is remade as folds of a plane, as shapes that form volumetric statements. They are images of the human body peeled open where the mind is on its way to be exteriorized, the mind that is innocent of the difference between the naked and the nude, and innocent of seduction. Bhaskaran has obviously not learnt to give up petty prudence. He is not allergic to the self-deception which fills the life class either: those shapeless models employed by art schools for students to draw and turn them into an illusion.

Akbar Padamsee joyfully identifies himself with these bodies and thus makes room for hope. He is at the opposite pole of Bhaskaran. The naked moves up to empathy, to the illusions of a presence we call the nude; the naked becomes a point of departure for a work of art, and the history of the nude's visual narrative is presented without a drapery of shame. But we perceive them as parts of a design, not as a living organism with a nervous system, as the key cultural principle of spatial contiguity. As studies, these are archetypal nudes, realist to the point of escape from the subjectivity of voyeuristic involvement.

Only [A.] Ramachandran, it seems, is free from the nude's language of power relations: his *Girl with Watermelon* and *Girl on a Stool* under the banana tree are the opposite number of what we associate with sexual voyeurism. One is never tired of looking at them even though they look so much alike. Indeed, the more one looks at them the greater is the pleasure in discovering in their minute transitions a world as rich as Indian classical music. They are *abhisarikas* and their 'play-power' is spellbinding. The *abhisarika* in our times is close to the concept of a woman dropout, a woman on a love hunt. Her image [in the works] is decorative without a suggestion of literalness which would turn it into a biological illustration.

Or like Manet's *A Bar at the Folies-Bergere*: the image of a barmaid facing us with her reflection in the mirror, in a position inconsistent with the frontal view. The barmaid, in soliciting our gaze, is turned into an *abhisarika*. T.J. Clark treats this image as a play on the illusory nature of the self; where we look into an impossible space, one where 'we are left no place . . . least of all the place we are allotted on the mirror'.[2] For Clark, it presents a scene of capitalist alienation. For us, it is a new kind of space where we encounter the age-old question of existence and reality. It is not the portrayal of the degradation of a 'fallen woman' Clark claims it is in a Victorian phrase.

Standing before Manet's image of the barmaid we experience a kind of instantaneousness: a single brief instant seems long enough to experience the work in all its depth and fullness. The experience persists in time; we are hardly conscious of duration because every moment of the work is wholly manifest. It is this image of the barmaid that a photographer, who calls himself a pictorialist, has in his mind when he photographs a nude. His objective is not to photograph a naked body but a body that is archetypal. We have [Victorian era photographer, Oscar] Rejlander's nude photographs in mind. It is as if the Rejlanders were exemplifications of John Berger's cryptic comment: 'men act' and 'women appear'.[3] Perhaps, because women 'watch themselves being looked at' and this determines not only 'the relations between men and women, but also the relation of women to themselves', for 'the surveyor of woman in herself is male: the surveyed female. Thus she turns herself into an object – and most particularly, an object of vision: a sight'.

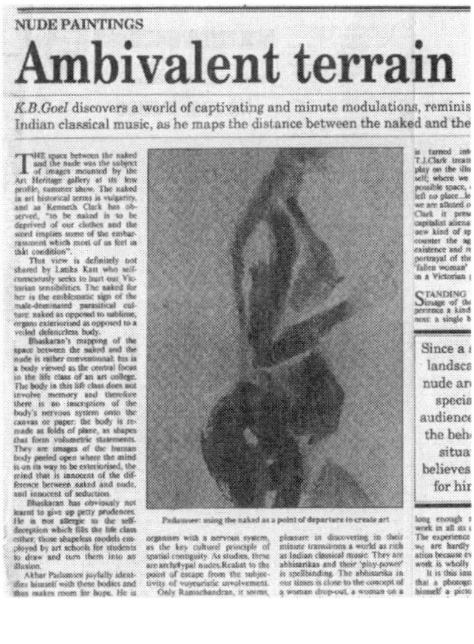
NUDE PAINTINGS

Ambivalent terrain

K.B.Goel discovers a world of captivating and minute modulations, reminis
Indian classical music, as he maps the distance between the naked and the

THE space between the naked and the nude was the subject of images mounted by the Art Heritage gallery at its low profile, summer show. The naked in art historical terms is vulgarity, and as Kenneth Clark has observed, "to be naked is to be deprived of our clothes and the word implies some of the embarrassment which most of us feel in that condition".

It is only in the hands of Matisse that the naked becomes a nude and reveals both the visible and the vision itself. The nude of Matisse is a sight that opens a new horizon. The body's contours become its structural filaments. And the line is no longer a device: it is a modulation of a pre-given spatiality both in relation to meaning and art. The Matisse nude is a live body, one which is situated. It is erotic in all its creative aspects of signification. It is a nude which is energy at rest, quiescent, provisionally conserved, inscribed. It is a metaphoric operator which transfers, transforms and inscribes libidinal energy. It is not energy in stasis, but energy that transforms the subject.

After Matisse, the nude has declined to stillness: it became a self-conscious subject, which drew attention to itself, became aware of being watched. And this was against the very grain of modernism, for modernism defines itself by the theoretical project of an absolute self- absorption. It is oblivious of its beholder. That which is theatrical is not modern, because theatrical implies the presence of the beholder, while modernism demands complete absorption of the beholder in the painting. The success of the modernist enterprise consists in defeating theatre. For, theatre has an audience – it exists for one – in a way the other arts don't. In fact, more than anything else, this is what modernist sensibility finds intolerable in theatre generally.

Since a still-life, a landscape of a recognizable terrain, and a nude are pictures somewhat special to the audience, such representations put the beholder in a situation that he believes is created for him alone (even if he is not alone in the work). A picture of a nude has a special relationship with a beholder: the body is displayed in a manner that the man looking at the picture feels that it is made for him; made to appeal to his sexuality. For this reason, even artists begin to question the very premises of a nude study. If the nude as a subject still exists today, it is as a parody of the aesthetics of seduction.

Editor's Notes

1 Clark's words on nudity here are from his book, *The Nude: A Study in Ideal Form*, New York: Pantheon Books, 1956. He goes on to say, 'The word "nude", on the other hand, carries, in educated usage, no uncomfortable overtone.'

2 Quotation untraced. See T.J. Clark, *The Painting of Modern Life*, 1984, for a discussion of the work. Manet's well-known painting is now in the collection of the Courtauld Gallery, London.

3 This and further quotations in this paragraph are from John Berger, *Ways of Seeing*, London: BBC and Penguin Books, 1973, p. 47.

96

SUGAR-COATED SUPERFICIALITIES

Review of nineteenth-twentieth century colonial prints exhibited in New Delhi

'Artscape', *The Economic Times*, New Delhi, 23 October 1991

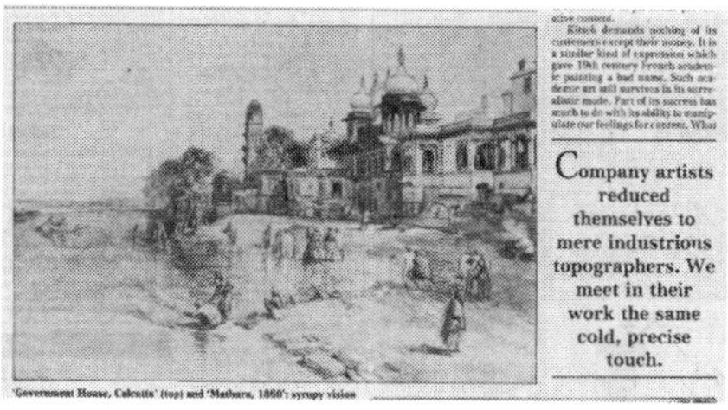
aive content.
Kitsch demands nothing of its customers except their money. It is a similar kind of expression which gave 19th century French academic painting a bad name. Such academic art still survives in its surrealistic mode. Part of its success has much to do with its ability to manipulate our feelings for content. What

Company artists reduced themselves to mere industrious topographers. We meet in their work the same cold, precise touch.

'Government House, Calcutta' (top) and 'Mathura, 1860': syrupy vision

The season had opened at the Alkazis' Art Heritage in New Delhi with a display of about 50 prints, all reproductions using the technique of engraving and lithography which were the most popular modes of illustrations and decorative arts in the nineteenth century. Most of the prints displayed dated back to 1847. The rare prints filled us with nostalgia - nostalgia for pastiche. Whether such pastiche is collected for sentimental reasons we do not know. What we do know, however, is that the Alkazis have been collecting these Company [period] art prints for more than forty-five years. How else can one explain the sentimental value attached to each of these prints?

About twenty-six plates come from the Harding collection. Earlier, in 1984, the Alkazis published three portfolios. *The Tranquil Eye* and *Between Battles* (17 x 12.5 inches) have now become collector's items. More history-oriented is the *Wellesley Collections* (23 x 17 inches). Robert Smith's works, some of which are reproduced in *The Tranquil Eye*, are realistic representations of the artist's journey down the Ganga in the first decade of the nineteenth century. Smith was an amateur painter who worked as ADC to Sir George Nugent. The drawings and landscapes in watercolour were actually made to please Lady Nugent, who was an avid collector.[1] At the bottom of each landscape are inscribed detailed notes on the circumstances, natural setting and the vantage point from where the works were executed.

Colonel James Skinner's album, *Between Battles*, contains pictures of the countryside. Famous for the 'Skinner's horse' (named after him), Colonel Skinner was a professional soldier born of a Scottish army officer and a Rajput mother. His collection is now in the India Office Library. The Marquis Wellesley Collection comprises drawings by Indian artists employed by the Company officers. They were employed to record faithfully and draw from life the natural history of India as well as the birds and animals collected by Wellesley's personal surgeon, Francis Buchanan [Buchanan-Hamilton]. Wellesley collected about 2,600 drawings, quite a few of which bear the signatures of their authors. The artists belonged to families of hereditary painters whose genealogy can be traced to the fifteenth-century Lodi Sultanate.

These three portfolios contain the best works in the Alkazi collection: they speak of the taste and judgement of their collectors. But what we missed in the exhibition at the Shridharani Gallery were the works of the Indian artists employed by the Company. The Indian artists almost spontaneously adapted to the kind of Western realism that the Company officers exposed them to, yet adding something of their own which became their specific signature on the genre. The difference can be seen to the best advantage when their works are put alongside those produced by British and European artists.

What these British and European artists produced has the sweet smell of colonial kitsch at the root of Western realism. Kitsch is a particular variety of bad art, some of which is sweet because it is made to meet some specific demands. The syrup just gets thicker with respect to pastiche, which is a form of obsessive historical nostalgia. Under its influence, kitsch becomes saccharine sweet and acquires heuristic value: nostalgia for bygone artistic periods competes on equal terms with the artistic value the works those periods produced. More telling examples of this kind of kitsch are the sugary, oil-on-canvas religious images produced by the painter Ravi Varma. In them the best emotions seem to become the worst.

The prints look kitschy saccharine because they were made to meet the demands of their patrons, the nineteenth-century nouveau riche. As a class, it has money but not taste. The taste – it is comfortable with is the good old aesthetics of provincialism. It wants art only for decoration, as an ornament for the drawing room. The formal and refined aspects of art do not interest it. It does not matter, therefore, that kitsch lacks in form: the object of attention is its particular provocative content.

Kitsch demands nothing of its customers except their money. It is a similar kind of expression which gave nineteenth-century French academic painting a bad name. Such academic art still survives in its surrealistic mode. Part of its success has much to do with its ability to manipulate our feelings for content. What is more, it looks for the one-dimensional purity of emotion: it sees only the 'beautiful' in art.

The European and British artists who came to India during the Company rule, painted from the sketches they had made here, in studios located not in India but in the countries of their origin. That explains the popularity of these landscapes in Britain which itself had a rich tradition in landscape painting. But, to meet the demands of their patrons, these artists reduced themselves to mere industrious topographers. We meet in their work the same cold, precise touch. Beneath the skin, nothing breathes. The drama of light and shade does not touch them: reality, for them, was merely a question of likeness. They resemble present day hyper-realists, stopping the flow of life with their freezing gaze.

It may be misleading to expect, therefore, from these landscapes a single and linear route of taste leading us to masters like Constable. Blinded by our period's taste, the best we can say about these landscapes is that they present to the viewer a post-modernist's appetite for sweet kitsch. Like post-modernism, kitsch too is manipulative. Standing or walking in front of these landscapes, the blame could be placed on the viewer: for a moment or two, one feels that life is sweet. We can say that there is need for kitsch because genuine emotion has become so rare. The desire for it lies dormant and there is need for artificial stimulation. It is the same need we have for religious kitsch: it seeks to elicit religious devotion without an encounter with any spirituality within. Or, for the erotic kitsch: it provides the sensations of love without the presence of someone with whom one is in love.

What the Art Heritage exhibition has given us is kitsch that fills our hearts with historical nostalgia for a past when it was possible for art to be beautiful and nothing else. The value of the exhibition is its emotional bonus. Pastiche in the absence of the real is a thorough-going involvement. Call it an infatuation for the superficial, but it has its uses because it is usually short-lived, often casual. It is useful because nothing is at stake, for nothing is invested. This reminds me of Kundera who has written about kitsch in another context. He said recently: 'Kitsch is the translation of the stupidity of received ideas, not the language of beauty and feeling'.[2] The banal and unoriginal ideas of a perspectival landscape painting as translated by the Company artists tempts us to moments of self-indulgence and binds us sentimentally with a past that never was.

Editor's Notes

1 George Nugent went on to become the commander-in-chief of India in 1811–14; at the end of her stay in this country, Lady Nugent authored a first-hand account of British colonial rule under the title *Lady Nugent's East India Journal*, first published in 1839.

2 Milan Kundera, 'Jerusalem Address', in *The Art of the Novel*, New York: Grove Press, 1988.

SECTION FIVE

CATAL

OGUES

GROUP EXHIBITIONS

Through his career as an art critic, K.B. Goel mostly wrote reviews of exhibitions. But much like art writers elsewhere, particularly newspaper reviewers of art who are seen to have some influence on the art-reading public, he was occasionally enjoined upon to write for catalogues of exhibitions and these, expectedly, form the smaller part of his writings. Featured here are the introductory texts he wrote for catalogues of group exhibitions.

97

SPACE BETWEEN THE ARTS

Curatorial text for the Indian section at the Havana Biennial, 1991; K.B. Goel served as the commissioner for this section

Catalogue text, 1991

The Indian section of the fourth Havana Biennial is represented by six painters – M.F. Husain, Krishen Khanna, K.G. Subramanyan, J. Swaminathan, Vivan Sundaram and D. [Dakoji] Devraj – one painter-architect-sculptor, Satish Gujral, and one young sculptor, N.N. Rimzon. They are all among India's frontline modernist artists.

Seventy-six-year-old M.F. Husain, who is more popular than a prime minister, is one of the founding fathers of Indian modernism with a background ideology of progressive thought. The discipline and tradition of this were forged in the fight against the ideology of the nationalistic Bengal school of art. The encounter with a Husain painting is thus necessarily an explication of the history of modernism in Indian art. It is also an acknowledgement that it takes its form from an appropriation of the contemporary in India's artistic heritage.

The works of the other artists are significant in relation to issues that are usually set up for 'modernism'. I put modernism within quotation marks advisedly – to remind myself that Indian painting – since the formation of the Progressive Artists' Group (PAG) in 1947 – does not have to brick up the Albertian window[1] in the way the cubists did. Since in India we had no tradition of easel painting, the Albertian window seemed then a painterly irrelevance. Its bricking up by the cubists,[2] however, that always opens up the recent memory of modernism's provincial context. This produces a deeper understanding and an acknowledgement of the irrelevance of the Albertian window. So also is the realization with Husain that the past is not a past; the colonial experience does not constitute a deeply historical past. It is, for Husain as well as for the other painters (whose works are displayed here), their own past because they have witnessed its movement within themselves.

This is perhaps the prime reason why there seems no vantage point from where either art historian or the modern Indian artist might look upon a continuity-providing past: the vantage point had to be discovered by each artist for himself. The process obviously cannot but have been painful, involving, as it did, the tearing out of mores that were rooted in the artist's entrails. The artists belonging to the PAG [Progressive Artists' Group] discovered this for themselves.

Distracted from the necessity of authenticating their art practice, they fell into a characteristic parent-children relationship, the fathers threatening to run away from home. Some did and became expatriates. The 'broken homes' admitted a completeness of the father's isolation. In this situation, in the midst of onslaughts on identity, the children of the 'broken homes' discovered the concealed 'I' within themselves as a device for locking themselves into themselves. They went out in search of an 'America' in themselves - which was not a place; where they eventually landed was a setting, a theatre with its backdrop of some kind of destiny. Inside, the theatre of their imagined discovery of an 'America', it came as a shock to them to find themselves in total privacy, with the self as audience. There were no children, no homes, no identity conditions: each was ranged existentially against the other and the circle of social and historical arbitrariness seemed without exit.

F.N. Souza, a contemporary of Husain, now living in New York, epitomizes the conditions in which the runaway fathers live, isolated but speaking with godlike authority: the ego, unbound and untamed and without the constraints of an internal 'other', expanded sometimes monstrously, at other times, sublimely. The expatriate, alienated from an environment with which he was integrated inseparably, became a figure of tragedy - the tragedy being that he could not or would not conceive of the present as growing from the past.

It was as in theatre: drama demands a continuous attention to what is happening. Everything of significance is seen to occur in the present. There the past is made present. Likewise, the past as past is absent in the culture of the expatriate - a culture which, to be sure, dominated the Indian art scene of the Fifties: everything that solicits our attention emerged in the mould of the 'Schools of Paris'. The works of Husain and Krishen Khanna are soaked in the anxiety of influence of the art-critical logic of 1950s Paris. But what is authentic about them is that they are predicated on a denial of theatricality which one associates with the works of expatriates. In the art scene of the Fifties, there is the presence of tension between the impulse towards novelty and the silent anxiety of rootedness, between the desire to see painting as painting and the obvious fact of a work's origin in history. That was an era of modernism's aesthetic romanticism.

This variety of modernism had by the beginning of the Sixties acquired a perceptible level of coherence; radical changes had come into play with the world's art capital moving from Paris to New York, as it were. The works of the Indian painters of the Sixties, led by J. Swaminathan, reflect this change. Modernism is experienced by them, not as a sign of alienation and cultural despair, but as an end to cultural provincialism. The painters associated with Group 1890 (formed in 1962, introduced by poet Octavio Paz and inaugurated by Jawaharlal Nehru) reacted differently to the 'Western presence in Indian painting'. In a manner of speaking, they seemed too conservative to recognize that the dust and heat of history had put the time out of joint, clouding vision.

Central to their vision was the debate on and exploration of the artist's relationship to history – history being, for the group, the reality that was perceived as shaping individual intention; whether for or against, history did not allow heroes or hero-worship. In this sense, the group might be described as the first decolonizers of modern Indian art. In the Seventies, the Baroda group of painters, taking a cue from Group 1890 and bringing into focus an Indian version of pop art, rediscovered nineteenth-century India's Company Art in the work, primarily, of Ravi Varma – in a sort of peep-show manner. A shift was taking place from the margin to the centre, as it were.

The political significance of this shift left the Indian artist in a state of demystified surrender to the internationalism of pop culture. The discovery of the arrival of a new culture in the Indian art scene was made at the first triennale of world art held in New Delhi. By implication, the significance of the event was that we had entered the post-modern age – if one were to define post-modernism as a return to theatricality. Theatricality in pop art takes the form of exaggerated ambience, an awareness of the spectator, an implied address to an audience.

For the first time, the threat of pop culture is construed as a threat theatricality. The threat itself bears not on the painting but on the stage, which places the viewer in the situation of a voyeur. The voyeur, like Baudelaire's dandy,[3] is happy with anything that looks like 'art' and is 'interesting'.[4] In the context of pop art, voyeurism is another term for the extra-aesthetic: it must be understood in relation to the drama on the stage. And good drama is, to be sure, the master term for a successful painting – which makes for art of another kind.

This raises the question of legitimacy – legitimacy in art. Standing before a pop painting, one is led to ask two questions – what constitutes the art of painting? What is a good painting? Under normal circumstances, the answer to the first question should more or less merge with the second. According to traditional criteria, however, a good painting is one that, among other things, is predicated on a denial of theatricality – in other words, a denial of the beholder. The beholder is mastered and drawn into its frame; the painting does not allow him to see itself as an object. It cancels the distance which theatre assumes as essential to the presence of the spectator.

New York, the fount of pop culture, acknowledged the economic virtue of the spectator and thereby promoted uncertainty of response. The reason was that American kitsch absorbed modernist clichés. There, like the film experience, the experience of art too became conventionalized; its experience came like a postal stamp. Which is as it should be when it is experience alone that matters: where experience alone secures for a painting's identity as presence. And, needless to emphasize, the notion of presence implies a situation akin to theatre.

And this is what pop painting sought – to turn art into theatre and gather for itself a secure audience in a way that painting does not have and all other arts do. The Eighties in India were marked by a boom in colour magazine cultural journalism which projected pop images as neo-colonialism's radical plinth. In their reach into culture, they can be interpreted as attempts to bridge the gap between life and art. Such is the appeal of new cultural journalism that books and 'the cow-on-the-grass' variety of paintings no longer seem relevant. In India's urban culture, it is the TV screen that is becoming a socially dominant medium.

The works of the eight Indian artists going to Cuba come from a home-made world. Local obligations to their past mark them out. This is true of the Ganesh (one of India's popular gods) images by painter-sculptor Satish Gujral; true also of a contemporary reading of the part-mythological and part-historical images of India's past in K.G. Subramanyan's work. The images are the works of the minds which luxuriate in their self-reading of history, minds which are not part of any definite social processes and therefore beyond incorporation in any particular period. Such minds belong to the metaphysical term 'world', which is a supplant of the older conventional term, society. The breaking of the known, apparent historical bonds gives to these works a typical modernist edge; we are led to believe that modernist painting entails a desire for re-evaluation of India's great art of the past. The encounter with these works is, therefore, necessarily an acknowledgement that a healthy art takes form from what could be described as appropriation of the great works of India's past.

The works of Swaminathan bear the weight of the radical rupture with the past lightly. They are the products of a mind which, in the ultimate imaginative reach, is capable of finding itself wherever it looks, even if it is to find itself only in division against itself. For it, nothing originates in history. It belongs to a symbolic order and is hence untouched by the mode of historical becoming. It is, in essence, purely structural, purely visual. The prime appeal of the visual is not limited to symbolism; it is built on a present that affirms nothing but risk; we have no choice but affirmation within, or without, Indian history. There is no other way of experiencing Swaminathan's work.

N.N. Rimzon, who emerged on the Indian art scene in the mid-Eighties as a sculptor of considerable talent and promise, presents situations of sorts, but these do not share theatricality of objecthood, the presence of which the spectator encounters, as in installations. The situations are not empirical but grammatical – explorations of self-relation within a gestalt. His works can stand comparison with those whose quality is not in doubt; and might be treated with the respect due to them.

Vivan Sundaram's drawings make explicit the role of chance and therefore of a large element of risk. But the drama is realized at no stage: the heaping up of intricate, cognitive details and a search for effects that infectious chance offers expose to view romanticism's substitution of the simulation of control and release. One has to get close to the works to appreciate their tonal quality. Vivan is a self-conscious modernist and therefore part-lawyer and part-judge in a country where a successful painting or drawing is one which is in no way a gamble.

It will not be an exaggeration to say that the sensibilities informing the works of these eight Indian artists are at war with theatre or theatricality: whether it is the theatre that employs the stage of provincialism or the abstract threat of theatricality, implied or demonstrated by the success of what Michael Fried has called literalist sensibilities. Fried's warning against perversion of art by theatre is now more than two decades old; it has yet to find its partisan-believers.

The works in the Indian section of the biennale demand close attention. They are somewhat old-fashioned exemplifications of an era of aesthetic romanticism which was a gift of the West to India. That romanticism has become outdated in the West. India's commitment to modernist sensibilities has brought its art at the interface of many theoretical disruptions; it has transformed the entire way we see paintings and sculptures. What is unique to these works is a sense of composition, something that seems no longer relevant to the modernist enterprise. For, composition is a device: it makes the action of both making and viewing seem oppositional in intent. Such a limited proposition now looks irrelevant in a world where theatre has gone 'absurd', painting is either minimal or narratively pop; and sculpture, mere installation. It is a world where art and life have come so close that fraudulence today is a real threat to serious art. It is not for me to formulate in words and make a judgement on the position that the works in the Indian section occupy. They show what they say – on a rectangular plane.

Editor's Notes

1 Scholar Leon Alberti and his three-volume, 1495 work, *On Painting*, published under London Penguin Classics (2005), discussed a fixed perspective in Western art and how a painting (framed and, usually, a rectangle) should be seen as a window to the world. This thought has been foundational to Western classical art in its focus on illusionism and 'realism', triggering rebellions against it in the modern period, centuries later. K.B. Goel frequently makes this reference to the Albertian window in his writings on the avant-garde in the West and in the Indian context, with artists rejecting this view in the 1960s for that of a painting as a 'wall'.

2 The reference here is to the 'bricking up' or closing of the Albertian window – the concept that easel painting promoted of the painting as a window in the wall, the illusion of looking on to a 'view'. Cubism fundamentally changed that illusionistic idea of painting by breaking up visual planes and providing new perspectives and angles from which to view the image.

3 Discussed by Charles Baudelaire in *The Painter of Modern Life and Other Essays* (1863), translated by Jonathan Mayne, London: Phaidon Press, 1995.

4 While he keeps himself uninvolved or at a remove but distinctly giving such an appearance. Source: ibid.

98
NINE CONTEMPORARY ARTISTS

Introductory text for 'Exhibition of Paintings and Sculptures by Nine Indian Contemporaries', held in New Delhi in February–March 1991. The featured artists were: Arpita Singh, Bal Chhabda, Himmat Shah, J. Swaminathan, Jeram Patel, M.F. Husain, Manjit Bawa, Paramjit Singh and Ram Kumar

Catalogue text, 1991

The works by the nine contemporary Indian artists on view here are a braid of several traditions, some of which go as far as the beginnings of modernism in India. Modernism in India came enmeshed with the Pygmalion myth – the Pygmalion who makes a statue that comes alive – like the child who plays with the stick and it becomes a horse. To the Indian artist, modernism did not mean a break with the Albertian window. Since the window was not there, it meant dismantling the Havellian pedestal on which were mounted the Bengal School painters; it meant playing trains without having seen a real locomotive engine. The distinction between a substitute (playing the game of trains) and the thing itself (the locomotive engine) did not disturb his otherwise probing mind. This had far-reaching implications. The modernist painter did not suffer from the anxiety of influence. The mythical Pygmalion produced a representation and it became an identity-seeking act. He was free to choose his roots from among cultures and traditions that were considered alien. What was borrowed was modified. Without any definite break with tradition, modernism in India produced its own tradition. And this tradition has as many faces as there were modern movement makers, for it was made by individuals who had in their works an unmistakable sense of Indian presence.

This is true of the M.F. Husain's mode of iconography and his use of the language of gesture of Indian classical dance: Husain's is the most authentic Indian variety of modernism. Many of the expressionist conventions he has metamorphosed by the use of his modelling line have the same degree of visibility as we find in the Indian relief sculpture. Next to Husain stands J. Swaminathan for his inventiveness in developing a purely indigenous iconography. Like Husain, who came to be identified with the multi-dimensional symbolism of the horse motif, Swaminathan's colour geometry of space and the mystic overlaps of mountains and the bird motif became his signature. Which he erased in the mid-Eighties: he gave to the erasure a surface that is built on epiphany. It is as if he had discovered a sacred wall which is in perceptual effect something very close to what [Mark] Rothko had achieved in his colour-soaked canvases.

Standing before a Swaminathan canvas our perceptual mechanisms come to a stop. A similar kind of 'unthink' is experienced before a Jeram Patel colour blotch. Here, the perceptual densities of colour are explored to a degree until they suggest a transformational interface between painting and sculpture. The spectator is invited to share the undifferentiated space of the colour blotch as a corollary space of the real world. This has the same effect as entering a maze: once inside it, the created spatial movements completely take over; we go in and out of it unaware of the maze's limitless configurative conning.

Ram Kumar's landscape, similarly, draws us in as if its topology is made up by the mind's private mirroring act: as the mirroring process gets more subjective, we explore the landscape as one explores a fragment of music the counterpoint of which exists elsewhere. The referentiality of this land is three-dimensional and we drift there with pauses and detours until the resulting images become the product of our encounter. Paramjit Singh's is not a landscape in the conventional sense of the term: it is a pre-formed anticipated picture. The brushstrokes, applied as thickly coloured mass, are the life of his pictorial mode: the physical movement of the strokes becomes its representational element and the signature of the artist. In his work, the role of the hand determines the quality of his signature, not the eye which controls the hand.

The eye determines all in Manjit Bawa's painting. The image fills the picture frame as sculpture confronts the viewer with its material reality. It energizes the space within which is seen with a mode of stillness specific to Manjit's form-making manoeuvres. They turn the viewer into a voyeur: the longer one looks at them, an increase in desire is felt, one lingers before them a little longer. Colour acts as a coordinate to the pleasurable sensations which are close to those where a woman is subjected to the male gaze: the voyeurism within the viewer sees himself being seen and seeing.

Arpita Singh's topsy-turvy world of make-believe invites a seductive gaze, for this world is without a centre, without focus, and without any referentiality. The images have denotative reference, but their objective correlatives need connecting on a different plane: they are signs which have lost touch with their significations. As with Arpita, so it is with Bal Chhabda. But Bal's formal world does not suffer from a lack of focus, for improvisation is the soul of his method. The disjointed fragments get their sense as the painting process gets into stride and the truth of the effects of colour on the mind is discovered. In his work, risk is transposed into a sustained vision.

The presence of vision in Himmat Shah's sculptures is an instant experience: it is a dialogue between the maker and the viewer because Himmat's metaphors are self-referential. His is a world sensitive to the force of symbolization in which the metaphors mirror the ambiguities of a reality beyond the reach of reason. The focused gaze of his heads allows the eyes to become conscious of seeing as well as of being seen by a mind. It is not to any past achievements of Indian art that the works of these nine Indian contemporaries draw our attention: it is the present of a future to be that gives them a force of a tradition, a present where everything is to be made anew. The present is the ultimate sign which is that of the artist's presence in the work.

99
THE INSTITUTIONAL THEORY OF ART

Abridged introductory text for an exhibition held to inaugurate the AIFAC's Regional Centre at Panchkula, Haryana, November–December 1995

Catalogue text, 1995

The Romantic exalts the artist who does not give a material form to his dreams – the poet ecstatic in front of a forever blank page, the musician who listens to the prodigious concerts of his soul without attempting to translate them into notes. It is romantic to consider concrete expressions as a decadence; a contamination. Mario Praz is most eloquent in putting across the case of romanticism.[1] He might have done even better had he included in his review Marcel Duchamp whose irreverent eccentricity explodes the conventional source of meaning – the convention which allows art to be 'only art'. After Duchamp, art's presence is substantial, not virtual: after him, the modern period comes to a final break with tradition. The break represents a transition from vision to the perceptible thing. It was Picasso, according to Octavio Paz, who discovered how to say yes to the age, but it was Duchamp who resisted the age, who taught us how to go against the grain of movement itself. A master work by Duchamp, Paz argues, is 'an open space that provokes new interpretations and invokes, in its incomplete state, the void on which the work depends. This void is the absence of the idea'.[2]

Romanticism, by contrast, asserts the presence of the idea, the priority of vision; indeed its autonomy is exalted. Duchamp, being a single-minded apocalyptic visionary, is the first painter to warn us that a celebration at the altar of pure vision can only lead to pure, aesthetically destructive silence. Duchampian sensibility has always claimed to be engaged in defeating the idea of a centre or focus towards which forms point. If there exists an ideal space prior to experience, waiting to be filled, it is the space art occupies inside a museum. Outside a museum a Duchampian object has no desire, perhaps because nothing that the artist says about it can bring it to life. The implication is that art is a historically situated set of social processes and not a basic human orientation.

The other Duchampian insight is that modernism, above all, is about the collapse of what is called the canon, or what art historian Gombrich calls the schema [schemata].[3] The schema-governed art created tradition which refers back to the canon. Modernism undermined the canons of taste; for it was very much about the unintelligibility of experience as it was actually felt to occur, a result of the split between experience and knowledge. This is why it is not always easy to evaluate the works of a contemporary; for knowledge based on experience is like the owl of Minerva which flies at dusk.[4] That is, knowledge can be gained only when the event is over: the very relationship between knowledge and experience is determined by the various structures of understanding and interpretation. Even our conceiving the opposition between experience and knowledge has its origin in particular knowledge structures.

On these grounds, Steven Connor argues that modernism 'must be grasped henceforward . . . in terms of its own modes of self-understanding – the ways it thought it was experiencing itself.'[5] The point is that the subject should be free from a narrowly restricted context and move about at will. Which means the aesthetic erasure of the symbolic and the ability and eagerness for discovering precise methods of displaying the negativity of experience, of which minimalism, conceptualism, earthworks, happenings, graffiti art and all forms of erasures are good examples: these movements represent a kind of collective blush of cultural embarrassment.

Emerging after the First World War, it was the self-promoting vision of oppositional positions of the avant-garde that determined the terms of modes of understanding the modern. But after the 1968 Paris student protests, it is the cultural forms, including advertisement, TV and the mass media that replaced the canonical avant-garde and supplanted themselves as the central focus. In the absence of the avant-garde, institutions have become the seats of power as dominant forms of interdisciplinary discourse. As forms of control, they have succeeded in destroying individualism by convincing the individual that his personal experience is invalid. They asserted themselves as places of difference, plurality and instability by the newly discovered vehicle of post-modernism: the post-modern debate itself can be seen as various attempts to master the field, coercing into, as it were, 'intellectual performativity'.

It is a new world from where the intellectual figure – such as Sartre was – has vanished. Thinking now tends to be looked upon as synonymous with quixotic aspirations, one of the irremediable faults of which is the imagination. The Sixties are famous for acts of negative heroism. Despite the violence of the critique mounted against the academy called modernism and despite a prodigious expansion of culture through the social realm, the images, styles and representations of the period remained what they were before: promotional accessories to economic products. What seemed to have changed was that they were seen as the products themselves, seeking the same functional equivalences between the consolidation of a system and the fostering of plurality within it.

Art is now a small thing compared on level terms with TV images; it no longer matters what it says. Earlier, avant-garde not only offered newness and confrontation but came to represent the idea of a fusion between radical art and radical politics. About Gustave Courbet, for example, it was said that he was a 'terrible socialist, at the head of a band of conspirators'.[6] No longer is such a thing said about an artist; painting no longer contains possibilities of social threat or any form of intellectual disturbance. Saint-Simon claimed for art a priestly function: 'The power of the arts is in fact most immediate and most rapid.'[7]

Now, TV images [in the 1990s] are more vivid, farther-reaching in their iconic influences than the images of visual arts. Pop art in the Sixties sought to revive the myth that painting might recover the same stature it had enjoyed when it projected itself as the avant-garde. But pop art never claimed for itself the kind of seriousness as the nineteenth-century avant-garde. Pop art's only fancy-dress intellectual rival is religion (for, both define themselves as the consciousness of the Western middle class). Religion, like art, first divides: it splits its audience between those who understand 'the message' and those who do not. The cleavage runs along political and class lines. Since most Sixties pop artists came from advertising they did what a good advertisement does: flatter people, inducing them to believe they have something in common with the artist, and the consumer is a rare discriminating connoisseur of sensations.

'All art is reactionary': this is the implied view of Duchamp since nobody intelligent, he thought, should presume that art can change society. This should not be taken to mean that he subscribed to the McLuhan ideology which claims that the medium is the message.[8] Pop art worked to eliminate the oppositional ground which the moderns cultivated, with little attention to worrying details. Art's claims to seriousness were given away by pushing art to the reactionary position.

This position is well put by French artist Daniel Buren when he says the artist is '"beautiful" for others, "talented" for others, "ingenious" for others'.[9] In other words, art became a container for celebrity and the idea of the Courbet-like artist has now been consigned to its social parody: an alien, unless a celebrity, to the world of fashion, promotion and commercial manipulation. The structure of this world is self-consciously that of fashion: art's goal, like fashion, is only to disappoint the meaning that it luxuriously elaborates.

The result is that modernism has surrendered its prized space of autonomy; signs are relieved of their function of referring to the world. The new world of post-modernism does not need those grand narratives we associate with modernism; instead, the fragments of modernism's well-known texts are reshuffled. Under post-modernism, the reification has become a fact of life: as the reification intensifies, the referent moves further away from what it was supposed to be referring to. When a sign is relieved of its function of referring to the world we know that we have retreated to a realm of ideas where we can comprehend Nietzsche's idea of an 'eternal recurrence of the same'. Here, the emphasis is on experience, and not on any formal or intellectual way of looking. The rejection of the past and the future makes me more aware of existence and my relation to the rest of the world.

This explains why in the Eighties the metaphors of primacy, of genetic history and the concept of the will to power, of the self, have been under attack. The new theology has become the epistemological ground for defining the role of intention. For example, Pollock requires a different ground of intentionalist approach from that of Van Gogh. The survival value of the intentionalist aesthetic can be ascribed to the dilemma presented by the existence of private worlds and to the existentialist notion of homelessness of the self. It is linked to the notion of the Husserlian transcendental ego: between the transcendental world of spiritual apprehension and the rationality of man is situated a position which governs both Western institutions and myth.

One cannot decide because interpretation is a dissimilative force for the production of new meanings. Whether here or in the Christian West, the process of canon formation has always been determined by the interests of the more powerful groups. These works reflecting the social position and beliefs of the elite and its ideological inclinations occupy the centre stage of a sensibility. Outside the elite groups, one can never hope to have an evaluation of a work, though liberal critique admits the possibility of an argument that a canon may not be properly representative, and entertain the fairness of a charge that only a certain social group manipulates the canon. By such guile, it transforms a scene of conspiracy by a scene of representation. This is the historical process by which certain works have become canonical. The liberal critique works well in explaining disagreements within a homogenous social group. Where it is forced to revise a concept of aesthetic value, it has failed; it is by cunning that a new concept is smuggled in, and works which have been [previously] excluded come to be acclaimed as canonical. Otherwise, the liberal critique is committed to the erection of separate canons for different social groups: regarded as separate but not equal.

The word of god and faith in reason are like the two gods of the Christian West (the god of Abraham and the god of Aristotle). They blend and fuse into a single unifying idea of a romantic artist: it is also the favourite hobby horse of romantic humanism. If the world is worthless or meaningless, the artist is called up to give it meaning and worth. Even Nietzsche pins his faith in the miracle-making powers of the artist: 'It appears to us a laughing matter if man were to take upon himself to invent values which would surpass the value of the real world.'[10] He reminds us, it is not god who created the world for man in his own image; rather it is we who have invented god as the creator of the world.

The death of god – which, in Duchampian discourse, can be called the death of painting as a mode of representation – is this a new referent? With it the 'interpretation of sign' is born. A sign can only be interpreted: it can neither be given in advance nor be defined or coded. A text, Nietzsche reminds us, does not say that 'this is not the text, it is an interpretation'. It is always a net of relations, the implied nexus of plurality of interpretations. The view of modernism presented here is not one which foregrounds a text; it is deconstructed both from the 'inside' and the 'outside', by framing it into a system – the system based on the analysis of Duchamp's *Fountain* which allows me to read modernism outwards, from text to context to context-of-context. The revival in the faith of graffiti, on other hand, gives me the reference point of reading modernism with an 'inward' movement: from context-of-context to context-to-text.

The Duchampian 'found object' presents us with the transcendental site of truth about art objects, the final destiny of which is residence in a museum. Duchamp christened a mere porcelain urinal as a work of art and proved that artistic baptism is analogous to Christian baptism. The baptizing ceremony must have for its background the institutional setting either of a church or of a museum. The message is loud and clear: it is impossible, conceptually, to create an artwork independent of the context of an art institution. This is indeed a bleak pronouncement and goes against the conventional belief: whether a work of art is created will depend upon the person who created and christened it. What is often forgotten is another truth about art: an object is an art object only under interpretation and for this reason no object would fail to be a work of art if exhibited in a well-known museum or an art gallery. What is essential for a work of art is that the status conferring has taken place in an institutional setting.

Nearer home, we have an example of almost Duchampian denotation. Last year in February, Vivan Sundaram exhibited a painting he jointly did with the less-privileged children of Mangolpuri. Vivan's signatures decontextualized their presence: the context depended on was what came from the 'outside' – Vivan's signature and its transcendental truth for the world of gallery art. Or, one might say that the performative-collaborative work depended for its effects on what could be said to exist 'outside' the work proper. The children of Mangolpuri occupy only an empty corner away from the public realm of art. They are like Rousseau's noble savages, and to bring them into public focus is to violate the unwritten rule of civilized behaviour, to ask questions that are sure to embarrass the patron and must not be asked – similar to the question raised about Swaminathan's placing of his contemporaries' work alongside those by nature-bred tribals.

Modernism's aesthetic theories have no answers: only an anti-aesthetic account of art such as provided by Duchamp can give a more convincing answer. If the Eskimo is, say, in New York, will he be tempted to mimic those involved with the illegal acts of graffiti? Perhaps not. This is to say that he is an alien to the New York ambience, to that world of art to which artists like Duchamp and Warhol belong, although for him graffiti may be the natural mode of expression. Today, graffiti enjoys the high status of fine art; those who practise it have formed a corporation called the United Graffiti Artists, with a manifesto authored by the novelist Norman Mailer. They exhibited their rude ware in New York's Razor Gallery. There is 'standard graffiti', different from ordinary run-of-the-mill graffiti and there is much to be said in favour of art's permissiveness that something considered public nuisance has been embraced as art. The questions raised reveal the hypocritical nature of New York's devotion to avant-gardism: what entered the gallery space was art; the rest was variations on vandalism.

After the Razor Gallery show, another exhibition of graffiti art was mounted called *Post-Graffiti*. Sidney Janis announced in the introduction, the death of graffiti, for, according to Janis, graffiti is in the tradition of pop art. That is, indeed, the establishment's way of appropriating graffiti. The claiming of its death was as much a spoof as converting graffiti into an art commodity; designating it as a form of folk art is the invention of both nostalgia and currency. As a 'bouquet from Latin America' (in Oldenberg's words),[11] graffiti for Mailer represents 'the impulse of the jungle to cover the walled tanks of technology'.[12]

It was not a matter of racial associations with graffiti when Rauschenberg erased de Kooning's drawing and converted the erasure into art. Rauschenberg's erasure was not graffiti but only the assertion of a name: a saleable product. 'We can even erase Rauschenberg's erasure, get the artist out of it altogether, and it is still art,' Mailer would like us to believe. But Mailer is smart; he reminds us that the 'world is turning inside out'. We are also told that, as a record of the act of protest, graffiti is 'not a political but a symbolic act'.

Since the point of the institutional theory of art is to deny that there is anything beyond the correct rules and conventions of aesthetic behaviour, the only universal criterion would seem to be social authority of the art world. This implies that those invested with the power to confer art status are bonafide citizens of the art world. Otherwise, what Duchamp did could have been done by a salesman selling plumbing material. Duchamp knew what constituted the epistemic break with tradition in the art world of the First World War. His warning was illuminating: 'The "blank" force dada was very salutary . . ."don't forget you are not quite as blank as you think you are".'[13] It is a reminder that a Duchampian object is a work of art under an interpretation. And in interpretation, what is left as residue is the unwarranted signs of truth. *Fountain* is a mere sign; it has no intrinsic meaning to it; Warhol's *Kennedy* and *Marilyn* are signs, too, where meaning is both present and absent. Such signs - which have historical reference - are necessarily ambiguous and cannot be constituted in advance. And in the context of Duchampian romanticism, interpretation is inseparable from the interpreter.

It is this return of the subject that gives to post-modernism its epistemological ground. In focus are the evaluative procedures of the original formulations since interpretation is the construction of another's meaning. Foucault sought to outlaw another's meaning and supplant it with autonomous discourse. Discourse, according to him, 'is not the majestically unfolding manifestation of a thinking, knowing, speaking subject but, on the contrary, totality in which dispersion of the subject and his discontinuity with himself may be determined.'[14] Much of what passes as art does not please us: constructions, collaborations, installations and such projects where the presence of the subject is foregrounded demand of us an attitude that is closer to the innocence of children: to be experienced without interrogating their presence.

Editor's Notes

1 Mario Praz, Italian art critic and teacher of English literature, who wrote a book titled *The Romantic Agony* (Oxford University Press, 1970), discussing the erotic and morbid/death-focused Romantic literature of the eighteenth and nineteenth centuries.

2 Octavio Paz, *Marcel Duchamp: Appearance Stripped Bare*, translated by Rachel Phillips and Donald Gardner, The Viking Press, 1978, p. 79.

3 Gombrich, in his influential work, *Art and Illusion: Study in the Psychology of Pictorial Representation* (New York: Pantheon Books, 1960), termed 'schemata' at the heart of artmaking as something the artist begins with – an idea or a scheme, and not a visual impression. The artist adjusts this idea to fit the landscape or object or person before her or him, which Gombrich terms 'making and matching'.

4 The Hegelian idea expanded in his *Philosophy of Right* (London: G. Bell, 1896) – 'The owl of Minerva spreads its wings/takes flight only as the dusk begins to fall.' Minerva is the Roman word for Athena, goddess of wisdom and philosophy associated with the owl. Hegel's statement means that philosophy understands reality/history only after the latter's end or its passing. The famous reference also reflects in the Hegel Society of America naming its journal *The Owl of Minerva*, still operational since its inception in the late 1960s.

5 Steven Connor, *Postmodernist Culture: An Introduction to Theories of the Contemporary*, Basil Blackwell, 1989, p. 4.

6 A belief about the nineteenth-century painter Gustave Courbet that gained popular credence from his bid to create art in defiance of the conventions around him and the unsettled responses to him. The quotation itself is attributed to Urbain Ceulont, one of the models who sat for Courbet, who cites this rumour about Courbet in a letter to the artist's sister: quoted in Claire Moran, *Staging the Artist: Performance and the Self-Portrait from Realism to Expressionism*, Routledge, 2017.

7 Henri de Saint-Simon, *Opinions Litteraires, Philosophiques et Industrielles*, Paris: Galerie Bosange, 1825.

8 Media theorist Marshall McLuhan wrote the phrase 'the medium is the message' in *Understanding Media: The Extensions of Man* (Boston: MIT Press, 1994), explaining it thus: 'The personal and social consequences of any medium – that is of any extension of ourselves – result from the new scale that is introduced into our affairs by each extension of ourselves, or by any new technology' (ibid., p. 7). That is, the 'medium' or the technology was the message by how it impacted human world, and not by the content it carried – and as examples, he discusses the electric bulb, clothing and print technology, while later mass media such as television and the internet too have been understood along the lines of his theory. Discussing his much misunderstood thought, he explained in later years that it was the 'environment that changed people, not the technology'.

9 Daniel Buren in an interview to *Galerie des Arts*, no. 50, February 1968, quoted in Lucy Lippard, *Six Years: The Dematerialization of the Art Object from 1966 to 1972*, University of California Press, 1997, p. 41.

10 Friedrich Nietzsche, 'Our Note of Interrogation', *The Joyful Wisdom*, New York: The Macmillan Company, 1910; subsequently, London: Edinburgh Press, 1924.
11 Claes Oldenburg, formerly a graffiti artist himself, writing in praise of graffiti art in the subways of New York city in 1973, mostly made by men of Latin American descent. He writes: 'You're standing in the station, everything is gray and gloomy and all of a sudden one of those graffiti trains slides in and brightens the place like a big bouquet from Latin America.' See Margo Thompson, *American Graffiti*, New York, NY: Parkstone International, 2009, p. 15.
12 Norman Mailer and Jon Naar, *The Faith of Graffiti*, Harper Collins, [1970] 2009 - an essay that first appeared in *Esquire* magazine and later in book form with the eponymous title.
13 Duchamp uttered these words famously in a 1945 interview with MoMA's curator, John Sweeney, that was to have led to a monograph but appeared instead in part form in different times, first in 1946 and later in Pierre Cabanne, *Dialogues with Marcel Duchamp*, Cambridge, Mass.: Da Capo Press, 1987; *The Writings of Marcel Duchamp*, Cambridge, Mass.: Da Capo Press, 1989; and in Dalia Judovitz, *Drawing on Duchamp and Company*, Minneapolis: University of Minnesota Press, 2010, and other works.
14 Michel Foucault, 'The Formation of Enunciative Modalities', in *The Archaeology of Knowledge, Parts I–II*, English translation, New York: Harper & Row, 1972.

100

A CONTEXT FOR ABSTRACTION IN PAINTING

Abridged introductory text for the exhibition 'Major Trends in Indian Art, 50th Anniversary of India's Independence', held at the Lalit Kala Akademi, New Delhi, 25 September–12 October 1997

Catalogue text, 1997

The emergence of the Progressive Artists Group [PAG] in 1947 was significant in relation to the automatic presumption of knowledge in whatever the artists chose to say about their work. But in the provincial climate, the exhibition space in India was deaf to the voices of these articulate artists, with the result that many of them chose to go abroad. These and many expatriates among them, are significant in relation to the issues that are usually set up for modernism, for modernism opened up recent memories, of their art's provincial context. They, however, maintained it was the formal elements alone that art should be concerned with.

Not knowing the difference between the picture plane and literal surface of the painting, they held to self-criticism as their way, their works echoing Picasso: 'At the beginning of each picture there is someone who works with me. Towards the end I have the impression of having worked without a collaborator.'[1] The presence of this collaborator was real and it made their self-criticism subjective. And so they believed what was significant in their art must begin inside the artist as each individual creator is different. For self-criticism in phenomenological terms means questioning the way in which one perceives one's consciousness and knows that he or she is thinking in a particular way. If we take painting as the subject of our consciousness and question it, we can know what is ours and what belongs to the collaborator. The background acknowledges the presence of the interlocutor, the 'other' who cannot be captured in any representation; nor is it possible to work out the solution of one's problems without the active participating presence of this other; perhaps because the internal relations which are established by grammar could not be examined without this analytic other.

The PAG had no local tradition to draw upon for guidance in establishing a relation either to visual grammar or to the past which could act as the common space of viewing and by extension, of discussion of art. They were given no style in the sense of an authoritative way of working that is received and then asks to be recreated. Style, in this sense, is available only to the abstract artist. And since most of the PAG artists were schooled in the Amrita Sher-Gil tradition of representational art, it was difficult for them to undo it. The most obvious area left where common 'problems' can arise – problems which can stimulate and challenge their imagination – seemed that of art's abstract, formal values. And these were problems internal to painting itself. Representation has to adopt itself to style, to a formal impulse. If concentrated upon and made an issue of, the given pictorial solution can evoke a new problem and hence further development. The concentration on purely pictorial problems became more intense and self-conscious. Whatever reference there was to the world of the 1940s had been abolished. The visual coordinates of a picture's literal flatness – and the enclosing shape – became the sole determinants of their art.

In the early Husains and Souzas, line is the final boundary of an expressive presentation. Line and, finally colour, become the primary expressive agent with them and Raza. As representational painters who were not alienated from their own traditions, they found abstract painting empty, their own style modern in a significant way. Their 'modernity' however is positively expressive, for it derives a sense of style from representational styles of the past; that is, from representation's own tradition, although, let me add, the availability of modernist art is not of this kind. To them, modernism has come naturally, organically, because their chosen styles lend themselves to modernist grammar.

This saved them from a provincial bind.[2] Provincialism is primarily an attitude of subservience and is not the product of a colonial history. Or, perhaps, this is one among many ways of defining the different situations they are in; the provincial artist sees his commitment to art in terms of styles of art, of competing notions of art's history – all determined in the metropolitan centre. Artists like Husain and Souza, however, did not swallow the formalist-modernist line in whole. They refused all invitations to join the mainstream of art history. They neither attempted making works which conform to easily grasped formal conventions, nor did they ever subscribe to a crude set of rules which hinted at how to 'innovate' within those conventions.

Talking of conventions, M.F. Husain, for example, absorbed the grammar of Mathura sculpture and sought to build a syntax of a perceptual subject in his painting. Standing before his mid-Fifties' images of dancers (which Kant might have read as deferred messages addressed to our faculty of feeling), we wait a while to be able to understand how the 'felt sensible' changes into the 'feeling sensible', into perceptual awareness of movement of form into space. As in the Mathura images sculptured in high relief, the changes in the surface are connected through the line which defines both the undercut volume as well as their surfaces; but the presence of the modelling lines cannot be erased. Perhaps, visual presence is the only aim of these paintings of Husain. Not the presence of a dance gesture, but form, which our mind goes digging for in the visual field – does the figure – present itself. But it is 'form', its secret organization, which in reality presents it, without presenting itself. As Lyotard would say, form hides itself in the figure: 'Any artist knows that visual isn't visible, as sonorous isn't audible.'[3] What then is that which forces the mind to guide the eye towards it? Form, or that 'something' that brings to a halt all interruptions and intercessions?

That 'something' is movement of form in space; its presence in itself is nothing. Achieved form, said Cezanne, is when colour is at its perfection. Because colour makes a feeling, a sense before the mind does; a mind which has given up its own self for colour. And Husain's colours have a presence, the felt presence such as a vowel has. So Husain's colour is a vowel without voice and as we all know, one does not talk with vowels. Only a line can saturate colour, and drawing in a Husain is as good as colour.

The Fifties' painters - and those who were influenced by them, and they were many - were formalists at heart. In those times of abstract expressionism it was natural that it seemed synonymous with visual exhilaration. But what is dirty about formalism associated with the aesthetics of post-painterly abstractions is that it treats all frames as value neutral; the kind of experience they provide is valuable in its own right. They were, all of them, children of Cezanne and this naturally led their painting towards abstraction.

The difference between the pre-modern and modern is stated in terms of transparency - transparency is pre-modern and opacity, modernist. The figure of transparency converts a picture surface into an immaterial plane - according to the usual metaphor, windows render visible what lies beyond them. In contrast, the figure of opacity suggests that a picture surface retain an undeniable materiality. Thus we can say: whatever physical 'reality' the transparent picture possesses must belong to the external objects it represents, whereas an opaque picture holds 'reality' within its surface. Transparency facilitates vision while opacity impedes its course; its materiality invites touch. The two senses that are involved in the practice of painting, the eye's vision, and the hand's touch - vision corresponds to transparency and distance, touch to opacity and proximity. Every picture may seem to possess both transparent and opaque features in a modernist work. A painting such as Gaitonde's, however, is created by touch, performed piecemeal touch by touch, through repetitive action.

Jasper John's comment, as quoted by Grace Glueck in 'The 20th Century Artists Most Admired by Other Artists' (*Art News* 76, November 1977), on Cezanne's *Bathers*, claimed Cezanne's touch captures the look of an object in such a way that the depiction conveys the object's tactile properties and also has a tactile physicality of its own. That is to say, it recognizes the properties of the medium rather than using the mastered medium as an instrument to reach beyond itself. As Swaminathan has said about his work of the latter period: 'It is as I work, as the work develops, it is through the course of the picture: that itself begins to have an effect on me.' Vision itself acquires the force of touch. Having acquired material identity, the space of a painting imposes itself on the viewer. 'For Rosenberg every touch becomes the equivalent of a completed picture.' [Art historian] Richard Schiff explains:

> This entails a certain cutting, not of the picture itself, but of its claim of signification. Like a fragment of handwriting under the graphologist's eye, each gestural mark simply refers a viewer back to the originating artist as an independent actor with an identifiable character.[4]

Each gestural mark, that is to say, having its own identifiable character, refers to three aspects of a painting and its process. First, touch is a gesture; it deposits the painter's mark as an imprint or impression and has the character of the indexical sign of the gesture. Second, touch is the applied paint mark itself in its capacity as a visible form, and, third, touch is the tactile sensation the painter actually experiences while making such a mark. Each mark could be regarded as the representation of a moment of sensation and experience; it represents the artist's personal signature. Rosenberg suggests that it has brought Cezanne's kind of modernist representation (by touch) to an end, for he defined what he termed *action painting* as non-representational.

The non-representational, self-referential or gestural function [in Indian art] was a dominant mode even after Group 1890's formation and the popularity of the narrative style. The current scene induces a sense of product proliferation and artists enjoy a high-profile projection in the existing system of information handling in the arts. The exchange value of art is today a source of prestige, not the one that carries with it a hint of corruption as it was in the Sixties. The art world now can be viewed as shifting coalitions; it is not as animated as it was when polemicists like Swaminathan and Richard Bartholomew were there to provide an instant commentary beside written criticism.

The Sixties was a brilliant decade, and the artists associated with the Group 1890 did not suffer the way their predecessors did by a slower development in the evolution of their individual styles. Consider, for example, the Washington show which was curated by Richard Bartholomew as part of India's silver jubilee [of independence] celebrations. Patricia L. Raymer reviewed it in the *Washington Post*: 'The works are too much alike. The show includes a lot of abstract oils and acrylics – the types one sees daily hanging in antiseptic offices and passes by without a glance. . . .'

There is yet another tradition of the modern to which we have had no exposure until the second triennale in New Delhi and which has still to develop its grammar in India. This tradition is based on the notion of the sublime; its best intellectual critique is to be found in the critical writings of Michael Fried. Theatrical art, as Fried has termed it, denies that making art requires artists; rather, any object can be made into an artwork provided someone having the genius of Duchamp, is able to sell it in the art market. Since any object can be contemplated in this fashion, Fried believes that all that the theatrical artist had done is call public attention to something that was art to begin with which is made no more intrinsically interesting by being put into a recognized art context. As part of theatrical art, a new aesthetic, a new world had emerged. Here painting has come to mean panels of pleasant wallpaper paintings, such as Miss Raymer condemned as decoration.

Fried reminds us in his book *Absorption and Theatricality*, that rococo tells a fundamental truth about art and this truth is that it exists for a beholder. So, painting fails by failing to be painting, by being some other art. And theatricality is not so much about painterly failure as it is about painting's destination. Or its destiny where the end of the story is in agreement with its beginning, and its story repeated in a thousand ways including that of the historian. But painting, such as Gaitonde's, seems to deny that any presence (or theatricality) has a hold over it. Painting's . . . surface, writes Lyotard, 'has been prepared in order for lines to be traced on it, for words to be written on it. So read them, try to understand, decode the diagrams, think about it.'[5]

This article is an attempt to suggest what kind of painting does not imply the presence of a beholder, by asserting equivalence between 'modernity' and the kind of consciousness in philosophy called 'critical'.[6] Touch, or the mind's exertions, is the point of such a consciousness and it lays bare what has been there all along and appears to itself when it is at home. If the risk of staging a work is that theatrical representation, however brilliant, is artificial, it is because if we write the history of art, our idea of what art is, it is itself the outcome of history – the point at which history is forever open.

Editor's Notes

1 Christian Zervos, 'Conversation avec Picasso', *Cahiers d'art*, 7/10, 1935, Paris.

2 See K.B. Goel's extensive discussion on the theme in the article 'The Provincial Bind', in the section 'Art and Ideas' in this volume, pp. 277–80.

3 Jean-Francois Lyotard, 'Presence', in *The Language of Art History*, Minneapolis: University of Minnesota Press, 2011, p. 21.

4 From Richard Schiff's essay, 'Cezanne's Physicality: The Politics of Touch', in Slaim Kemal and Ivan Gaskell, eds, *The Language of Art History*, Cambridge University Press, 1991, p. 34.

5 Lyotard, 'Presence', in *The Language of Art History*, p. 13.

6 Developed by Brazilian pedagogue Paulo Freire, critical consciousness 'focuses on achieving an in-depth understanding of the world, allowing for the perception and exposure of social and political contradictions . . . [it] also includes taking action against the oppressive elements in one's life that are illuminated by that understanding' (Wikipedia). See Friere's landmark work, *Pedagogy of the Oppressed*, translated by Myra Bergman Ramos, Continuum International Publishing Group, 2000.

101
SIGNATURES, COUNTERSIGNATURE

Abridged introductory text on the concepts of signature and counter-signature as espoused by Jacques Derrida, discussed in the context of the doodle and graffiti in art, written for the 68th Annual All India Art Exhibition, New Delhi, 18 January 1997

Catalogue text, 1997

> Exactly, because I consider, in effect, that if someone, any genius, were living in the heart of Africa and doing extraordinary paintings every day, without anyone seeing them, he wouldn't exist. To put it another way, the artist exists only if he is known. Consequently one can envisage the existence of a hundred thousand geniuses who are suicides [sic], who kill themselves, who disappear because they didn't know what to do to make themselves known, to push themselves, and to become famous.[1]

Marcel Duchamp said this when he was asked to define the spectator's role in the evaluation of a work of art. Take, for example, [Picasso's] *Les Demoiselles d'Avignon*. The public came to know its value and place in the history of Western art only thirty years after it was done. There were other works that Picasso did in those years which he thought were more important, yet *Les Demoiselles* is thought to be the first real modernist work. There is to be had in it a distinct sort of experience; in it theory triumphs which is used as a key element to account for what happens when we see it. In it is to be found the first move towards abstraction in a different way: the extension of sheer surface of areas of colour to provide, in the words of Clement Greenberg, 'an equivalent of the space' of the old masters. In the context of *Les Demoiselles,* we return to the focused truth of Duchamp's assertion that 'the artist exists only if he is known'. That is to say, an artist is known by his signature.

> The signature is regarded as the effect of presence that is there as something more than the work. For example, the use of impasto in Van Gogh: when you see a Van Gogh, the effect of the presence of impasto, the body of paint, is felt immediately. One is haunted by the body of Van Gogh: the body makes up part of the experience of the work. What haunts Van Gogh's works is the very body of the artist: it is this body, violently implicated and involved in the act of painting that relates Van Gogh in terms of his signature: Signature not in the sense of attaching his name but in the sense that he signs while painting.[2]

By my experience of the signature of Van Gogh, I give it a presence. This presence is made possible if I myself countersign. That is to say, while I countersign it I become involved bodily. I countersign an original Van Gogh because the work is in a museum: it waits for me. Here, talking of a Van Gogh's residence in a museum, forget the politico-institutional problem involved: the signature of a work cannot be countersigned, that is to say attested as signature, unless, as Derrida tells us –

> There is an institutional space in which it can be received, legitimized and so on. There needs to be social community that says this thing has been done – we don't even know by whom, we don't know what it means – however, we are going to put it in a museum or in some archives; we are going to consider it as a work of art.[3]
>
> Without that political and social countersignature it would not be a work of art; there wouldn't be a signature. In my opinion, the signature doesn't exist before the countersignature, which relies on society, conventions, institutions, processes of legitimization. Thus there is no signed work before the countersignature. That goes for even the most extraordinary masterpieces. Michelangelo, for example. If there is no countersignature the signature doesn't exist . . . the countersignature precedes the signature.[4]

So, there are no non-signed works because in the conventional sense the work itself is the attestation of a signature – an attestation on the basis of recognition as work of art. 'If we don't recognise it, if we say that it is not interesting and we toss it . . . there is no signature. Thus it all starts with the countersignature, with the receiver . . . The origin of the work ultimately resides with the addressee, who doesn't yet exist, but that is where the signature starts'.[5] 'In other words,' Derrida says –

> When someone signs a work, we have the impression that the signature is her or his initiative . . . But that signature is already produced by the future perfect of the countersignature. . . . When I sign for the first time that means that I am writing something that I know will have been signed only if the addressees come to countersign it. Thus the temporality of the signature is always this future perfect that naturally politicizes the work, gives it over to someone else, that is to say, to society, to an institution. . . . And with that we move from the private to the public. A work is only public: there is no private work.[6]

Is drawing a private work? Consider, for instance, Van Gogh's drawings, especially his early ones of Borinage peasants, and the later landscape drawings made often as substitutes for paintings where a range of texture plays the roles of brushstrokes and colour. In contrast, drawings in Oriental countries are different, made for purely aesthetic purposes. For instance, Riza-i-Abbasi's drawings those from seventeenth-century Persia, but they were made to meet the demands of his patrons. Similarly, the drawings in the Far Eastern tradition – consider the influence of Ku K'aichih (CE 345–406) and his treatise *On Painting the Cloud Terrace Mountain*. These drawings were made solely for the aesthetic impression they could convey to the spectator; not in subordination to any outside requirement but only for the sake of communicating refined experience. Neither did any forms of representation, iconography, record nor moral elevation ever enter the mind of their patrons.

Is drawing a vehicle for the artist to externalize and give form to internal experience? Admittedly, equivalents acquire some form of ontological significance. Because drawing is seen as some sort of 'external' equivalent, the Western patronage puts such a high value on the artist's first thoughts or, in terms of their aesthetic significance, on the studies which the artist meant for his own eyes alone. The Western patron believes that the artist neglects nothing. The epitome is Poussin's drawings who was capable of carrying his final pictures to a density of structure unparalleled in other arts: he alone was able to capture in his drawings the 'presence' of a truth to feeling which is not present in a worked-on painting. The artist in the Western tradition struggled to the limit of optical finish, or even conceptual completeness. Drawings of such artists present an aesthetic, more uncompromising than that of other artists.

Both word and image may be gathered up in the idea of conceptual image – a leitmotif in E.H. Gombrich's path-breaking book, *Art and Illusion*. In it, we find that the images that are not perceptual (that is, simply imitative or naturalistic) must be conceptual. Illustrative of polar oppositions are Wolfflin's 'linear-painterly', and Riegl's 'haptic-optic' [tactile/optic or visual] general scheme of styles.[7] The history of representation of nature in Western art is plotted as a chain in the development of representation moving between the poles of the conceptual and the perceptual.

Conceptual image is the frontal planar, non-spatial, hierarchically proportioned image which is widely associated with non-Western archaic and children's art in art historical writings. Also that conceptual images are images of mental concepts whereas optical images are images of percepts. That should not be taken to mean that we form images in our mind that are frontal planar, non-spatial and hierarchically proportioned out of what we see. We have actually mental images in mind that are like what we call conceptual images; they are different from optical images in that they very nearly correspond to the verbal definition of a thing and thus rooted in the Saussurean ambiguity of the verbal-visual notion of concept.

The 'conceptual' image, in the Saussurean world of signification, suggests that the icon also functions at a metaphorical level as the 'higher' icon, since Saussure treats the notion of concept itself as a mental icon. In old philosophical language, it made perfect sense to talk about 'invisible form'; that is one can describe the 'essential' and 'invisible' in metaphorical terms of the visible 'forms' to be 'seen' by a higher faculty of mind. E. Panofsky justifies such habits of thought by projecting them as the art of making the higher reality visible.[8] A long metaphysical tradition is there to uphold the notion that the word is established and validated by a mental icon, the concept. According to this tradition, 'impressions' are in effect 'icons' standing in a relation of resemblance to their object and serving as substitutes for them. In being natural signs, impressions were opposed by Aristotle to words which are conventional signs.

These natural icons are rooted in nature and are therefore universal. Thus, we share the same concepts of the same things although we do not understand one another's language. Western naturalism in painting has been based on the assumption of a relation between image and thing represented, comparable in one way or another to that between word and concept. In the Western tradition, an image is understood as something that first of all refers to something else by resemblance and may therefore be the record of a visual experience. But Gombrich in 'Meditations on a Hobby Horse' maintains that the simplest conceptual images, on the other hand, are primarily substitutive and do not refer by resemblance. Naturalism begins to develop when the notion of the image as a 'record of visual experience' is separated from the substitutive magical image. The earlier substitutive image, Gombrich argues, has become the schema adjusted by progressive comparison to appearances of things. Making comes before matching. The demand for substitution, to which 'making' first responds, arises from deeper demands than those of a child at play to make a stick serve as a hobby horse.

The spaces of use of the image derive from the reflecting of the eye by the image, for the opacity of the image comes about as a result of being approached. How in a drawing, the seeing principle becomes the visible is a mystery. Jean-Francois Lyotard describes the mystery of this seeing principle:

> An artist, a postmodern writer, is in the situation of a philosopher: the text she writes, the work she accomplishes is not in principle regulated by established rules, and they may not be judged by means of a conclusive judgment, by application to the text to the work of known categories. These rules and these categories are what the work or text seeks. The artist and the writer work without rules and to establish the rules of what will have been made or done. Thus it is that the work and the text have the properties of an event, and thus also they come too late for their author, or what comes to the same thing, that their selling down begins too soon.[9]

In other words, style hides the man. As [Saul] Steinberg puts it in his Cogito drawings: 'I think, therefore Descartes is,' one creates not oneself but another. Being is in the act. A Steinberg drawing presupposes the kind of visual resemblance that it seeks to interpret. Because the viewer binds himself in the dual world of look; not only does he find himself inside it but discovers that the visible is tinged with the invisible; he is invited to feel beyond seeing in the very act of seeing. The inter-subjective exchange is analogous with the experience of the doodle.

Doodling or acts of graffiti have a kind of 'thereness' which is not subject to a set of analysable semantic elements. An event takes place, and thus there will be a signature every time an event occurs, every time there is the production of work. Naming takes place only once and so there is a signature for a doodle or graffiti. Its 'thereness' is a singular event; it cannot be repeated: it is there even if it does not mean anything, it is there in addition to all that it means. And this excess obviously provokes discourse of a countersignature: the idea of a work represents a type of countersignature. The idea is a kind of remainder that cannot be assimilated by any discourse. Two examples of such a work are Rabindranath Tagore and his doodle where one does not know what separates the doodle and its many transfigurations, and J. Swaminathan and his use of graffiti to deconstruct its cultural metaphoricity.

RABINDRANATH TAGORE

Meaning is what separates poet Rabindranath Tagore's doodles from that of a child's. There is a work there – I, Rabindranath Tagore, affirms it, and 'I' countersigns it. In Swaminathan, the relation to and the desire for the other is what excites the imagination. There is something of a tonal differential, an effect of differential vibration that at the same time interrupts, prevents access and maintains a distance. Criticism is ineffectual in whatever way you read his graffiti. It is a record of the act of protest, not so much political symbolism, as much as the fact that it is also an act of self-transcendence, the exit point of the last romantic hero.

Rabindranath Tagore, for whom picture making is synonymous with dreaming, is our first 'modern' painter. Interestingly, his work is about the collapse of the schema but in the context of the doodle-based art of Klee and Miro, it was very much an act of keeping faith with the tradition of the modern. Familiar with the work of Klee, its conventions of doodling and free use of geometrical forms and their abstracted style of figuration allowed Tagore's art to be 'only art'.

The doodle was therapeutic in the sense that it was easier to secretly communicate the illusion that the internal world of the poet-painter was real; one with no intermediate space between the experience of 'me' and 'not me'. In keeping with the mystic mode of his poetry, doodling too is a mystic act. One may say that it was a vehicle for entering, as it were, a state of mind, in the midst of which, in its particular mode of encountering, he discovered himself. Old age had opened for the poet-painter a universe of articulated understanding. The only answer to be found was in the notion of temporality and its mode of extension. Tagore discovered this extension in a distinctive way – in the child doodle and its dependence on mood and of a state of mind.

The doodle did not represent some real experience; rather it seemed to be a kind of as-if experience: an experience of imaginary awareness of one's empirical self in the making process itself. The doodle is a way of giving oneself over to the one-dimensional as-if world, free from the constraints of a style. It is free because it is innocent of any methods of known organization of manual movements which define form. For this reason, the doodle does not duplicate experience: it has no private content because form in a doodle is incidental and meaning cannot be read independently of form.

The dominant Klee paradigm helped Tagore acquire the schematic basis for his doodling. This in turn became the prime effect of meaning. That meaning we have missed and because of it his kind of doodle still remains unassessed. His physical powers had declined and his tactile imagination had sharpened and this certainly did not need any mediation through words. The aesthetics of cultural relativism – which is the protein diet on which provincialism in art has thrived – has come in our way of recognizing the 'true' origins of modernism in Rabindranath Tagore's doodle. If there is a relation to be discovered through Klee and Miro, it is one of similarity and not of identity: for similarity implies difference – the difference between what the doodle actually means and the interpretation of its fictional construction and implied suspension of disbelief.

J. SWAMINATHAN

Graffiti as drawing, of which the oldest surviving forms are to be found in Egypt, goes back to 2500 BCE. But it is very different from the graffiti we admire – which Dubuffet romanticized as art in the Fifties. What he admired most was the freedom of the child doodle and still more interesting was street graffiti: it soiled the environment and was thought to be a vulgar manifestation of low taste. The intense subjectivity of street graffiti came to constitute, over the years, the basic protein of his art. Made of junk-tar and sand material, it presented the effect of a mud-like pigment on to which he scratched shapes resembling human figures, mostly the aggressive Paris women. With street graffiti he found low cultural value – potential existential material for farce. The result was his famous painting, *The Cow with the Subtile Nose* [MoMA collection]. The cow is the most unheroic animal: a symbol of ridicule of the Picassoesque tradition of heroic metaphors of minotaurs and horses. And with this painting, graffiti graduated to gallery art; its farcical intent produced admiring glances from the existential crowd. His doodle-based art could shock the bourgeoisie but the effect was wholly unintended. What he wanted to say was this: his art was driven by a dedication to total liberty from all rules and conventions of representation.

For Swaminathan, the context is graffiti's innocence of message. Like electrons, his graffiti cannot be observed from the outside without change as the behaviour of the doodle changed. It is a form of *ecriture*, an anonymously arrived-at structure, an image without symbolist context that might enable us to read it. *Ecriture* is not just a discernible trace of the brush; it is a mark of self-identity and one stands before it silent and confessional in the way that Rousseau is confessional. As if he had absented himself to write, hiding himself to show himself. As a brush mark, as graffiti, as an attempt at articulating space through line, as a scratch on the wall that is still virgin space, it is a mode of self-presence for the absent self. But this should not be taken to mean that we look for this absent self in the doodled world of graffiti. Rather there is nothing to hunt for beneath images. The symbol does not reveal any idea; it merely breaks away from the world of sign, a central truth of which is that there is nothing to understand which can be understood.

Swaminathan's doodled play with graffiti is at heart about this doubling process of me and not me. The Swaminathan doodle seeks accommodation inside an objective reality, for there is no area of experience in the doodled play of graffiti images where the realm of the I and the objective reality exist separately, an accepted convention in the West. But the phenomenon is described as the aesthetic realm where graffiti is considered dirty in the sense that it is inscribed in the wrong place. It entered into gallery space because of the success of Dubuffet's love of graffiti. Inside the art gallery's formalized world of aesthetics, it meant the artist's signature where it invented for itself a self-conscious intentionality. With Dubuffet, this received an ironic stance and in association with pop art, it extended itself to billboard images and various forms of advertising gimmicks, comic strips, logos and commercial calligraphy.

What helped graffiti to enter the formalized world of gallery art was success at an international scale of abstract expressionism such as no art style has ever enjoyed, coming to be absorbed by the pop artists. The Sydney Jaris Gallery in New York opened its 1983 show under the banner: *Post-Graffiti Show*. Does it announce the death of graffiti as art? Could Swaminathan's approach to graffiti image minus-its-symbolization context be an answer?

Editor's Notes

1 Pierre Cabanne, *Dialogues with Marcel Duchamp*, Cambridge, Mass.: Da Capo Press, 1987.

2 The idea of signature and countersignature here and over the next paragraphs quotes Jacques Derrida from 'The Spatial Arts: An Interview with Jacques Derrida', in Peter Brunette and David Wills, eds, *Deconstruction and the Visual Arts: Art, Media, Architecture*, 1994, pp. 15–16, 17–19.

3 Ibid.
4 Ibid.
5 Ibid.
6 Ibid.
7 Wolfflin and Riegl, with Panofsky, are often seen as the founders of modern art history. In his book, *Principles of Art History: The Problem of the Development of Style in Later Art* (Dover Publications, [1915] 1950), Heinrich Wolfflin distinguished between what he termed the 'linear' and 'painterly' styles of Renaissance and Baroque styles. 'Linear', he defined as a style of painting with all the figures and important forms clearly outlined, while 'painterly' meant to him a style of painting with the figures not discrete but fused together, with variable levels of visibility in the forms. Riegl discusses the use of space in ancient art and examines the objects observed as if at arm's length, similar to comprehension through touch; hence his use of the term haptic (tactile). This, he sees in contrast to 'optic' art, which, as he characterizes late Roman art, for instance, is the opposite of tactile comprehension with its three-dimensional relief sculptures. The optic is more linked to the mind as opposed to the haptic, whose connection is more bodily or sensory, making the art and its reception more intimate.
8 Erwin Panofsky, *Meaning in the Visual Arts*, University of Chicago Press, 1955.
9 Jean-Francois Lyotard, quoted in Brunette and Wills, eds, *Deconstruction and the Visual Arts*, p. 84.

SOLO EXHIBITIONS

K.B. Goel wrote catalogue texts primarily for exhibitions of artists he felt a close artistic affinity with, and who came to be his close friends – whether J. Swaminathan, Krishen Khanna or Vivan Sundaram, or when he was formally commissioned to write such texts for group exhibitions. Presented here are the significant introductory texts he wrote for catalogues of solo exhibitions.

102
REVOLT

A brief monograph K.B. Goel wrote on J. Swaminathan in 1975, reprinted in the catalogue of the artist's 1988 *exhibition titled 'Swaminathan '88'*

Catalogue text, 1988

The Sixties were critical years for Indian art: it was discovered that the secure landscape of the Fifties and its well-established hierarchy of cultural values were merely a projection of the colonial mind. The heroes of the Fifties, it was admitted, were after all provincialists. To escape from the provincialist climate of Bombay, for instance, Souza, Padamsee and Raza migrated to Paris to settle there permanently. As expatriates, they became instant successes, significant painters in the Indian art context which had always looked for foreign inputs to stay modern. And within the currently fashionable art categories of the Fifties, they were also identified as avant-garde. The local artists naturally sought to adjust their vision with the advanced art rhetoric of these expatriates whose art works appeared as so many vindications of what was acceptable in the art markets of London, Paris and New York. After all, these artists have made a strong showing at the new art-making metropolitan centres.

The revolt against this axiomatic superiority of the expatriate artist came from J. Swaminathan as one of the founders of the Group 1890 which held its first group exhibition in 1963 inaugurated by Jawaharlal Nehru. The revolt actually was against machine-minded Western art historical values and not so much against those mechano-artists who, after importing the Western engine, constructed it with a refined sense of mechanical knowledge: they could even make the engine run and, with the help of expatriate Indian artists, could even check on the engine's working. When this engine collapsed and was declared beyond repair by the Western technologists operating in the metropolitan art centres in the West, our provincialists did not accept the fact of the engine's decomposition: instead, they got down to the task of repairing it. The result was the deathlike repetitions of abstract expressionist modes. Instead of building a new engine, they hugged the fragmented parts as brilliant, perceptive personalization of what in the West is represented as advanced art.

The Group 1890 painters had no ideology when they revolted against the colossal entertainment industry set up by the mechano-painters of the Fifties. Some of the artists of the Group projected their artware as products of the 'whole' man. Their brave attempts did not make the kind of impact they had imagined; and for the simple reason that they had themselves been working within the system which set up such false categories as 'advance', 'new' and 'significant' art. What was significant in their art-making rhetorics was the belief that the writing of provincial art history through their local accents was as much an important historical constituent as building a wholly indigenous 'engine'. They had the know-how and experience and they succeeded in constructing a reality as convincing as that of the expatriates. And within the framework of the local art world, they made a place for themselves, which provided a foothold in art's emerging power structure of the Sixties. They were, in short, recognized as a minority group. The result was the questioning attitude towards the exaggerated homages paid to the art styles created in the metropolitan centres of world art. And this was a healthy way of evolving the rhetorics of indigenism.

In this context, Swaminathan's show at the Kunika-Chemould Art Centre in February 1969 was significant: it was a big leap forward from the earlier space-geometry work he showed some two years before: for its justification as valid, significant art one looks to duplicates of Western ideology and optical concepts of art. But they were a piece of intelligent grammar within the category of space geometry of colour. But the ranges of exploration were conventional in the context of international art. What was provincial was the presence of the Indian sun and the unsentimental demonstration of its power. Swaminathan's geometry has connections with very ancient archetypes. One can even quote Greenbergian rhetoric to lend them the prestige of metropolitan art: they were exclusively two-dimensional, optical and in their purity of the optical were resolved 'all conflicts between nature and art' and there was the perceptible shift towards art rather than nature.

And sure enough, the new device being more pictorial allowed Swaminathan to enact a balancing act, to build a symbolic schema, that is, which may equally be applied to the phenomenal world. In other words, he was able to cohere things related purely with the processes of the mind and those related by the senses. As Swaminathan noted in his catalogue of the 1969 show: 'But if I had an artist's scruples in politics I perhaps brought something of the revolutionary's ruthlessness into art'. The ruthlessness was evident in the native accent of colour which in the Western art historical terms represented a kind of rationalized regionalism. He was still a prisoner of the category of crutches: the certainties offered by the geometric mode of art-making continued to be the ruling values of his pictorialism until the show of 1969. In this work, there is freedom from his earlier fascination with the purely optical colour [that] is not tied to a formal order of a composition but is in the direct nature of expression itself. The substantiality of the mode is established in the nostalgic: the logical form of his earlier geometry-based constructions have given place to what may be called feeling forms; now the personal response is central. The work being true to itself achieves its own standard.

Perhaps the mode is significant in the context of Swaminathan's total commitment to art. But for this commitment it would have been impossible for him to shed the geometric vision of optical purity. Or, perhaps, it was all a result of his long experience of measuring the correct size of mountains where he set down to work on the tedious explorations of multiple focal points and the creation of many centres in his compositions. He applied the Chinese wisdom of landscape composition: your centre is always where your sight-line is. So the geometry, since his 1969 show, became actually diagrams of his own relationship with mountains. These had necessarily an abstract format because these were private images, images that were the result of meditations and perceived at a given moment of time. Thus, there was no place for the outside viewer who merely saw these as so many geometric manifestations of some advanced art. He allowed the spectator the freedom to formulate his own relationship with nature. Only a complete devotion to intuition, the intuition of the self, that is, formed the basis of colours. Put another way, the composition was arrived at objectively being a geometric diagram of man's relationship with mountains and revealing the existence of multiple focal points while colour was a servant of the unconscious, a product of intuition, of thinking eyes and it has the same power as mantras have in relation to the mandala.

At this point, it is relevant to quote what Swaminathan wrote in the tenth anniversary number of *Link* (15 August 1968): 'It (the new art) requires above all that the artist stand in front of the canvas as the early Aryan stood facing the morning sun, and to understand as he understood: *Om poornamadah, poornamidam / Poornat poornamudachyate /Poornasyapoornamadaya Poornamevavashishyate.*[1]

For, the canvas is a mystery of its own creation. Swaminathan for the first time set out to conceal all traces of what can be called craftsmanship: the new canvas is not constructed bit by bit: it is arrived at in a moment of time. By implication Swaminathan reminds us of the futility of what is called an art object and its property value in the context of gallery art. Colour is thus fused with the ground of the canvas as if the random passages of colour areas have no particular value. Yet, they form beautiful configurations as patches of colour. The nostalgic images of vedic life are clearly etched out but they seem to be accidental effects and not premeditated compositional properties. Their sensuous impact is stunning, the way these have been weaved into the semi-opaque tone of the canvas. The result is that surface has no independent structure and colours seem to have been soaked into the fabric of the canvas, images glide in and out of these inert but luminous patches of colour surface: they are bound by atmospheric colours.

The work has freed Swaminathan from the need for any kind of verbal rhetoric; perhaps he has achieved a sensuous use of colour as no Indian painter has and his powers of colour application are supremely displayed, and in the emotional sense they are absolute and self-evident. His vision now does not need a private map of mountains because he can now manipulate symbolic elements through a play with colours to evoke a mystic mood in a very high degree of concentration. This is an art of substitution: the hard-edged, objective canvas has been exchanged for a dream screen which is closer to the primitive man's undifferentiated awareness of the mysteries of nature.

Editor's Note

1 See 'From the Whole, Whole is Said', in the section 'Catalogues' in this volume, pp. 404–07.

103

AFRICA OF THE RATIONAL MIND

Introductory text for J. Swaminathan's solo exhibition, 'Swaminathan '88', shown at Dhoomimal Gallery, New Delhi, 1988

Catalogue text, 1988

The Canvas a Body Dressed in its own Naked Enigma.

– Octavio Paz, 'To my friend Swaminathan, the Painter'

What the eye registers the mind transforms: J. Swaminathan's old geometry, mapping different orders of landscapes and their subjectively determined magnitudes, has now been given a 180-degree jerk. As if these were some ordinary stones that have been arbitrarily pushed out of focus: also, it looks as if the old complementarities of the parts have lost their edges: parts of that famous reified bits of colour geometry of space, Swaminathan's being and becoming, that stood to each other in a relation of complementarity.

And in the span of two decades it has become his signature the personal bird, signifying ethereal dimension to Swaminathan's arrival on the painting scene of the Sixties. Its presence was felt as is the presence of anything that escapes the mechanical laws of gravitation. Some saw it as constitutive of nature's gestalt, the transcendental point between the mind and nature, their mutuality implicated to each other, parts of that geometry seen as necessary for the meaning of each: to take away from it any part or to add to it any part was to kill the soul of that metaphorical bird the representation of which embodied the gestalt truth of Swaminathan's compositions.

The bird is now lost to Swaminathan: what has stayed with him is the dark nature, the Africa of his rational mind, which sets the limits of his pictorial language: that nature, if commanded, must be obeyed. Now, Swaminathan labours, as his less fortunate contemporaries labour, solitarily; for whatever dimensions there are to his labour they have acquired an insomniac fuzzy edge; for the act performed does not seem to be the relevant act, since relevance shares a mental screen of the stereotyped gesture that a successful style demands.

What we, all of us, ask is: what is at the tail end of the style that has middle age? The answers vary according to how you look at it. For those who look at paintings as pictures, the signature matters: it turns a mere picture into art; whether seen horizontally as a link in a chain of developments, or seen vertically, in depth, in its relationship to the transcendental act of experiencing quality, the signature matters.

The only radical development in Swaminathan now is to deconstruct the text his signature implies: and Swaminathan has done just that - refusing to discover any personal truth in the pattern, the syntax and grammar of the language of the mountains. That is one aspect of the painter's truth; the other is to reject the apparatus. As Brecht has phrased its tragic implications, the apparatus has features resembling those that identify it with Kafka's *The Castle*: it controls the creative artist. And such is its hold on the arts that it processes a work to fit its own requirement, and this is to a general habit of judging the work by its suitability for the apparatus without ever judging the apparatus by its suitability for the work. Swaminathan could see how the *Castle* has become art's meaning and it has imposed itself as it were incognito. And this was what McLuhan said: the medium is the message and the ersatz reality of that darker truth is a pointer.

It is easy to see now how the ugly aspects of the McLuhan truth has affected the balance of our visual culture, emphasizing expendability as against the permanent: art itself has become something for uncritical consumption which the apparatus produces daily, now more open to monopoly or official direction than ever before. The present tendency to merge the visual and the literal is an illustration of the point where McLuhanism has obscured everything by its misapplication of the term 'visual'.

No longer does a purely visual song make sense to Swaminathan; nor is he concerned with fobbing us off with the old symbols in a new language. Earlier, the paint soaked in and became part of picture's life: now, the canvas has a life of its own. It is more real than the paint application methods. Similarly, Swaminathan's concept of totality in which parts were all fitted into what is called a composition has gone: now, colour implicates not only surface values, texture and tone but the responsive echo of the presence of the other, the ontology of the symbol and its acts.

The act germane to the new aesthetic is the act that commands spontaneous assent sharing the dark secrecy of the soul. And, in the present mode to strike that echo is to confront the image: to see in it the distillation of its own awareness. Like the situation of a mirage: the feeling of loss is there for there is no getting away from it as there is no way to find one's way about inside Kafka's *Castle*; for Swaminathan, with considerable intuitive freedom, now mistakes the mirage as real as the novelist mistakes fiction's fictionality, its forms of reality, the window itself, as the reality. Now colour is deployed as colour should be - with the innocence of a child, as if painting has no formal units: one colour has not to adjust against another, or the large area of it against the small. While symmetry seems to be the governing principle in some, there are obvious marks of struggle, even disquiet and tension, in others.

Happily enough, at the moment he is not limited by the constraints of a style that can impart epistemological insight to his mystic search into the being of the symbol. Each is an independent frame of experience; each is a frame of violence of internally felt fear, its experience of angst, since Swaminathan does not find himself in what might have been a controlled encounter with the image proper. The new painting is not addressed to the eye but to the mind: it therefore speaks in riddles. He is back to where he started from: to unlearn all, to kick the ladder underneath away, to explore the Africa within - not through the known cultural symbols: mountains, the *tulsi* plant or a lotus flower and a bird or a peacock. The clock, if the calendar has any meaning in arts, has been put twenty years back. Or we might say not quite; for something has happened: it is a leap anyway.

But the beginning counts; it should, for the great beginnings are always problematic and therefore important: they are never false as under no circumstances are they borrowed. In going back to his pre-*tulsi*, pre-mountain-and-bird period, there lies the peril of being lost, since Swaminathan, who will turn sixty this year in June, cannot travel back in time. If Swaminathan fails, it is the artist who alone dares fail. He has arrived at a stage where what is important is the mode of arrival and the quality of involvement and not whether what he is doing has future promise, whether he is seen as a success or failure, if over the years you have known the old Swaminathan. The passionate affirmation of his exploring self: the poet who disappears behind his poetry; the possibility of a pure music of vision and the importance of that possibility in the new painterly mode - these define Swaminathan's current engagement, his beginnings: and in a way, they also define the limits of his new painting.

104
FROM THE WHOLE, WHOLE IS SAID

Introductory text for J. Swaminathan's solo exhibition, 'Swaminathan 60', held in March 1990

Catalogue text, 1990

Om poornamadah, poornamidam
Poornat poornamudachyate
Poornasya poornamaadaaya
Poornameva avashishyate
Om Shanti Shanti Shanti

This one-man show by Jagdish Swaminathan can be inaugurated with the chanting of this mantra (which in English translation reads): *That is the whole; this is the whole; from the whole the whole is said; from the whole is taken the whole, and what remains is whole.*

Or perhaps, standing in front of his new work one may ask: is the whole the sum of all things? Or putting the question in another way: is it the formal unity of that sum which is not an element of that sum? For a tentative answer, we should accept that it is the principle of formal unity seizing the moment of unity discovered as the whole, as the lived experience of form. For whatever the nature of linguistic analogue to this formal unity, it is a unity as abstract as the sum of its constituent elements, which is by definition invisible, though in the self-evident visibility of form it is the painting's apparent world: the 'true' world is the construct of imagination, erected as a logical necessity to cover up the contradictions of the apparent, actual world.

For, painting is always as it is, whatever the interpretative acts to reconstruct it as an intentional object. Even Picasso had to invoke god to see it the way he saw it: 'We ought to be able to say that such and such a painting is as it is, with its capacity for power, because it is touched by God.' This is one way to admit the presence of the whole in a painting which is what it is; the whole, like god, remains invisible; the sum of its elements makes painting what it is; it is its apparent world; and the whole, as a principle of unity to human experience, is accessible only via painting or poetry.

Pure painting that is. Swaminathan, for several years, has engaged himself in ruthless self-criticism, purging from painting what did not belong to it. He gave up everything he loved; he staked his signature; and after a long remorseless process of purification he arrived at something, the essence of which is the absolute self-identity of the aesthetic surface. Or the self-identity of painting about painting. That is: 'a picture – before being a warhorse, a nude woman, or some sort of anecdote – is essentially a surface covered with colours arranged in a certain order'. That was Gauguin's friend, Maurice Denice in the manifesto, *The Definition of Neo-Traditionalism* in 1890. This is modernism's canonical truth: the commitment to upholding the coherence of the two-dimensional surface. Modernism demands an intense self-consciousness of what one is doing, to know that what it is his art depends upon. If the modernist artist does not have any a priori criteria for defining a painting, it does matter that he realizes that the criteria need to be discovered. Swaminathan has been, ever since he gave up political journalism, on the road to the discovery of such criteria.

The discovery of the 'thing itself' in art: the aesthetic surface which is an experience of co-presence. It shows; it says nothing; it has no voice; it is sensuously alive, animated, and it quickens our life of feeling. It is frontally oriented; what is emphasized is the presence of the frontal plane. Because of this the relationship between flatness and depth remains undifferentiated; in fact, there is no suggestion of depth, for the surface is not cut up in terms of 'figure' and 'ground'. There are no windows; only a frame enclosing the surfaces, and it is the frame in relation to the physical space of the viewer that is the key factor. For, within the frame the surface has variations; in some, there are frames within frames, a picture within a picture, with perceptual pushes and pulls that animate the direction of the perceived movement.

The syntax of the painted surface is built on epiphany: the disclosure of the sacred wall, a personal self-discovery, as it were. It is a metaphoric mode of self-presentation: self understood as quasi-self, for it has no perceptual components. The presence of the wall is sheer because the perceptual components are woven into the surface: what we are exposed to is the phenomena of sheer surface in which is included the neutral white space of the canvas inasmuch as it is part of the woven layers of colour tonalities. Within the relatively quiet frame there is intense activity; obviously, the energy made visible is controlled, and one has to watch closely the expressive visual modulation of colour into which are woven interlocking planes which are so thin that they may go unnoticed.

I am the wall, Swaminathan may as well paraphrase the Pollock statement, 'I am nature'. The wall is illuminated as it were, by an entirely expressive affective surface, but it never gives itself away as external sign. It confronts us as the Other; it is the Other, rich in privacy and inwardness, though, phenomenologically speaking, it has no interior. While the other has its inalienable inferiority we cannot grasp this from within; there is no privileged access to the Other's 'inscape'. But it lives out its psychic acts, immediately and simultaneously.

The Other is the imposition by our imagination; for Swaminathan hides nothing; has no interior to be revealed. We meet the Other rather indirectly, inferring the meaning of its inner acts through a network of indicative signs; lines, doodles scratched on the surface, the grapheme of the alphabet, animal forms entwined with human physiognomy. For, the surface is apprehended as an intentional, not an actual, object, because the aesthetic surface is not a point of transition but something essentially intransitive.

The presence of the Other is not necessary for Swaminathan; it is so because the phenomenal surface of art and myth differ from that of language; language does not engage our attention as language. Language as vehicle is suppressed by the meaning conveyed by the vehicle. While looking at a work of art our attention is riveted directly on to the phenomenal surface; what we are looking at happens on this surface, not beyond or behind it. It is felt as inherent in the phenomenal surface. The linguistic model has distorted our understanding of painting; we demand standing before a painting that it should reveal itself in terms more appropriate to verbal expression; we look for a hidden meaning not presented in what we call the aesthetic surface.

Yet we look for a hidden meaning, for we believe that the world as it is constituted is in some way relative to the language – as if inside the linguistic world, we are placed in an environment as animals are placed in theirs. Similarly, we look at play as pretence and give it purposes, for what is a mere play is not serious. But, for Swaminathan, play is what matters: he paints as if painting were a play and he is lost to the game; the movements are without a goal, for it is the game that is being played. The game is building a surface: a literal surface, as it were, rich in physical tactility. His occupation is watching the tactile values in the moment of their becoming; it is like watching the waves: gentle breezes play on them and the gravitational pull sweeps them away in the direction of the wind.

Because of the involvement with play, there is repetition and this helps sustain our interest; for, repetition enables us to experience the logic of identity and difference: repetition, moreover, is tied to the concept of the return of the same – the surface identified with Swaminathan's fingerprints. Which means that play power is organically linked to the concept of a private identity. Only in Gaitonde's work, besides Swaminathan's, do we have the presence of this private identity which manifests itself as surface. But Gaitonde's surface effects do not haunt us the way in which Swaminathan's do: in Swaminathan's, the surface is the manifestation of the aesthetic of reductionism. Swaminathan sets up the game of repetition which establishes the supremacy of the picture plane: it tends to heighten our awareness of the absence of the parts. But the repetition does not suffer from stasis because the surface is full of atmosphere, of that mood which is the result of listening to good music.

The Swaminathan painting now has become the act of the mind: a painting mode given to repetition which is essential for memory: the memory of surface values remain with us whether we are looking at his painting or not. When the painting is not before us, the recall sensations stay with us: the interaction between repetition and recollection has already become part of the memory. What stays in the memory is not so much the repetitive nature of the surface but the sensations one had of it.

Such a painting represents an immense shift in our sensibility: the intensities of the sensation are more acute since the visual field is organized on the basis of frontality. Frontality appears as a principle of formal rationality as against the substantive rationality of the keyhole aesthetic which Indian painting has to shed if it has to free itself from the inferiority complex of having a position of marginality. Because we have experienced art only in the margins, we find ourselves not only alienated but alienated from our own alienation: without doubt, we speak in a feeble tongue.

105
DRAWINGS

Introductory text for Krishen Khanna's solo exhibition, 'Drawings', shown at Gallery Espace, New Delhi, November 1990

Catalogue text, 1990

This is Krishen Khanna's first one-man show of drawings though earlier he has shown his drawings in group shows, the most memorable one being the 1964 group show held at the Shridharani Gallery. The drawings [of the present exhibition] have the same terms of visual analogies that informed his paintings he showed last year at the Centre for Contemporary Art [New Delhi]. There is a clear relationship of complementarity between what constitutes the true painterly mode, both in painting and drawing, and what is experienced as graphic forms and their realities. Forms that are kinesthetic, tactile and sensuous have recall values in Krishen's work. The values of recall and their dependence for explication on the external time make possible for us to enter a world that looks familiar and is at the same time beyond the reach of the meaning-hungry mind.

For the mind has the tendency to look for analogies between two analogized forms. Thus, it will be wrong to claim that one understands these drawings through a process of analogizing; if you understand, if analogy is your mode of looking at the world, so much the better for you; keep it to yourself. But as a friendly warning, let me tell you that it is wrong to identify the subject matter of a drawing to what it depicts. That is a wrong way to grasp what a drawing truly means; for it is not important that you are aware of the dialectics of difference between the apparent image and its notional referentiality to an outer reality and what is given to you through the perceptual mode which displaces the model for its representation.

Meaning, of course, is contextual: it is simultaneous with the act of seeing. Indeed, it is one of the commonplace assertions of linguistic philosophy that meaning and context are synonymous words. To apply this insight in visual terms, we can say that standing before a Krishen Khanna is to discover what context one brings to his act of viewing. And one of the many contexts that makes sense to me is the invisible armature: it is the ground plan of Krishen's drawing; it is there like his 'first thoughts'. And like his first thoughts it remains nebulous and it is a function of the whole which represents a system of relationships based on the truth of interdependence between the system and the visual units through which it finds expression. Whatever the structure of an image, however complex its armature-contour setting, the limits to lines which may rise, swoop, plunge or float, the bonding elements are visual units; these visual units embodied in the drawing method relate to one another at the level of generality.

For Krishen, this level of generality is to be located in the act of play: play within and around visual units; to set up enclosures as the director erects a stage to enact a play, the meaning of which is pure performance, its expression. Such is the situation of a figure for Krishen: it is contained within a contour, is the ground where the play is enacted – the real world is the world of visual units, and not the outer world of which the figure is a mere referential expression; it has no truth of its own to disclose. What interests him (and what should interest us as well) is the variety of surface into which is woven the positive and the negative white of the paper: white is a natural given for Krishen, the white offers opportunities for apparent spontaneity.

Charcoal is the natural medium for achieving spontaneity; it can build up the depth of dark, useful for invoking a pattern: a pattern which displaces the model and gives to the hand a temporal command, the authority to say 'I', prior to the act of seeing the trace of its reflection. The 'I' of the hand that is aggressively hostile to the machination of the psyche. Which means that when the hand is the master, it sees the mind breaking out of the body's constraints. Charcoal is a supplement to this hand. A line drawn with charcoal establishes itself three-dimensionally and in Krishen Khanna, it is exploited with a surgeon's concentration.

106
LONER

Introductory text for Krishen Khanna's solo exhibition held at Vadehra Art Gallery, New Delhi, November 1993

Catalogue text, 1993

In Krishen Khanna's art, what is offered is not what works of art normally offer. What is offered is the hint of a possibility of the completion of a long journey which started in 1947, the year the Progressive Artists' Group (PAG) was formed. He joined the group as an amateur enthusiast, conscious of the historical narratives of modernist sensibility which the PAG promised and worked for. The PAG artists behaved as if they were apostles, no less intense in their faith than Father Abraham. They were all men with a vision that was both transcendental as well as compelling. Transcendental, because they defined themselves from their Archimedean point of vision; and compelling because they not only delinked themselves from their past but believed in a present that seemed to emerge out of nowhere.

Let us not forget that the modern movement in Indian art was made by a few individuals, and Krishen had his share of distractions, history's cunning and the irreversibility of modernism's grammar. Grammar matters because the problem of modernism is one in which the question of value comes first as well as at the very end. It does not count where there is a tradition within which everything that counts does count; where the presence of the work of art is felt, not merely known; where the genealogies are analysed and a work of art gets placed within a historical sequence even if it leaves out the meaning of an individual work as part of its structure of subjectivity.

For Krishen, not the structure of subjectivity, but the world of generals discussing war games at the conference table was the reminder of the Nietzschean truth: the world is not 'what it is' but 'that it is', and which points to the facticity of the world as against its meaning. The presumed superiority of the objective to the subjective became a new sensibility especially when pop culture appeared on the art scene with its denial of the very possibility of interpretation. Under its influence, the basic unit for contemporary art was not the idea but the analysis and extension of sensation. And there was this new value: the value of free creation, the activity becoming its own end, rather without end, and therefore without any need for justification.

To counter this, a tough conservatism became Krishen's visible frontier of consciousness. He was happy with pictures in which the moulding force was the brushwork and the hand was made to play hide-and-seek with the mind's unconscious inhabitants. No longer was the anxiety of influence there to trouble him, and unlike the expressionists, he did not make the mistake of equating men with flowers. But he did suffer from the anxiety of transition, of making a 180-degree turn which he took with the *Bandwalla* paintings.

In those works which he first exhibited in New Delhi, the empty space is cut up imaginatively, to open up linear tangles which he half covered: they satisfied the joy-evoked need for a song and its tactile sensation. What is not covered shows up as smudged traces of contour, acting as interconnecting elements within the net-like patterns. In order to obtain instant recognition, the net-like formations act as forms within a single form. Broad areas of colour, laid side by side, allowed him greater freedom in the play with the mediations of colour application that contributed in developing a new sense of surface sensibility.

This new surface in the present [body of] work is no more involved with the grammar of phrasing as it was in his *Bandwalla* series. He now addresses directly: the marginal stance is gone, and so is the need for meaning and in keeping faith with modernism's expressionist grammar. The presumed superiority of the objective world as he found it in daily life, too lost its referentiality. In its place, there is now a look of emancipatory consciousness. It is sportive and mutational; the colour has a retinal address; it interconnects and has a terrific binding power. There is openness, and an appearance of insubstantiality first witnessed in the *Bandwalla* paintings. There is an airiness without those nagging problems of one area of colour having to balance the other.

The surface has been roughened up to reveal the undercoat of the accident-prone surface beneath. So that the top skin, thick here and thin there, forms patches and the impression is created that the painting has more parts than the whole can contain or make discernible. The nature of his signatures now tends to be like the nature of fingerprint impressions. No longer does he strive for arriving at representations of the shadowed perceptions of the outside world. The attempt now is to find purposive relations that turn play into recreations, although he does not take relations seriously. The play does not allow the player to behave towards what is being played as if it were an object. What interests him is the totality of surface and not its building up as an interplay of relationships among parts. There is no attempt at composition either, for composition means representation and representation means import of a sign language which turns a work of art into a vehicle for some hidden content. An aesthetic surface has nothing to reveal other than itself: it has no import, for meaning depends on import.

Painting for Krishen now has become the work of the mind which exists only in the act of painting, and for the viewer in the act of attention. Each of these acts is related to the previous act. The act of attention demands that he discover a unity of consciousness of the surface which is built up by dispensing with contour as it was in his *Bandwalla* paintings. Dispensing with contour or outline means dispensing with representation: painting is now built up into space by a series of interlacing tonalities. Since drawing does not exist, its presence is felt in modelling through which drawing seems to appear. There are only contrasts, not sculpted contrasts; they are built up, step by determined step, stroke by stroke: the contrasts that give rise to sensations that are the outcome of the exact relationship of tones. In the present work, drawing and colour are not separate elements: in so far as he paints, he draws, which gives to colour a richness of tonal identities.

Because of the tonal richness the perceiving eye does not care to give names to things that have recognition value. In other words, seeing is less concerned with naming than with relationships. The consciousness is tuned to its own affinities with the outside world – the affinities, that is, between the relationship of form and colour. Everything connects with everything else. Call it a miracle of consciousness, but it is there; for Krishen the act of painting consists in breaking through the surface of appearances. Yet the result is a new unity of two distinctively separate worlds.

Because of it, he is able to achieve harmony with a new objective world at the very moment it is sought to be destroyed. The attention is focused neither on the associational nature of images nor on the return to itself of the thought which is already in control of its objects: rather, a new object is constituted which makes explicit what was until then presented as no more than an indeterminate object. This gives birth to a new figuration at the very moment of the determination of the object. In Merleau-Ponty's words, it assumes the character of the 'knowledge bringing event'. It transforms everything; meaning, though still in its nebulous state, emerges to clarify the event: it is the motive and not the cause of the event.[1]

Krishen's painting is an event: how it comes about, perhaps, he himself does not know. All that he knows is that it is a work of a daily eight-hour toil. For him, painting is no more than tuning the mind to obey the hand: the process of painting is the process of trying to re-achieve at a higher level of complexity a previous unity which is always in danger of losing itself. When the hand is the master, it is the moment of triumph: one has then the sensation of having achieved *something* which the seeing eye could not imagine: it is the moment of having mastered the event – and all according to its own rules – and simultaneously, one is gripped with a feeling of achievement, of having been liberated from the hegemony of all rules.

I might describe this position as god-like. A kind of seeing 'I' blocks the vision of the normal seeing 'eye'. Not only does this seeing 'I' engage itself in theory-making, making the event comprehensible, the painter too gains in knowledge of himself, his intricate sense of what he is like. In other words, the mind is allowed to bypass the impressions of the seeing eye and pick up information of the event direct[ly]: or some might describe this as intervention in the external physical process by the seeing 'I'. Call this seeing 'I' mind-power, if you like. But one thing is certain: such mind-power includes much more than what we know through parapsychology – that is to say, meditation, yoga and all forms of spiritual make-beliefs.

I call the seeing 'I' god-like. It is a gloss on Merleau-Ponty's reading of the birth of a 'creative genius' –

> When I contemplate an object with the sole intention of watching it exist and unfold its riches before my eyes, then it ceases to be an allusion to a general type, and I become aware that each perception, and not merely that of sights which I am discovering for the first time, re-enacts on its own account the birth of intelligence and has some element of creative genius about it: in order that I may recognize the tree as a tree, it is necessary that, beneath this familiar meaning, the momentary arrangement of the visible scene should begin all over again, as on the very first day of the vegetable kingdom, to outline the individual idea of this tree.[2]

The implication is that Krishen's art should be interpreted as the process of making a picture (the representation of a 'thing') become a painting (the process of capturing the moments of making), the reality of which explains why the whole emphasis is on sensations – those sensations of art that dwell within us. This almost echoes Cezanne when he wrote of 'comprehension of nature through a personal temperament'. By personal temperament he meant that, if each shape in a painting produced a different sensation in Cezanne, he had to find the right hue and right value for each brushstroke; the resultant effect was to be, not to convey his own sensation one by one to the viewer but to harmonize them, which implies that we can never reach 'correct' results or that we can never be objective.

Objective in the sense of representation: what is a possible availability is the Nietzschean perspectivism. And to be honest, some perspectives can be shown to be better than others. This is precisely what Krishen is telling us: a perspective that is the best of all is not a perspective at all. A unified synoptic picture that satisfies all perspectives is not possible, although, it is true, that in a trivial sense all our perspectives are directed upon 'the world'.

Krishen has arrived, in terms of style, at a stage where nothing higher than elegance is intended. For, quality in a painting is a lie, quality being a thought-language conception: it refers to nothing outside thought-language. If quality has a function, it has only an indicative function, a way of stating a fact about a painting that can neither be perceived nor subjected to analysis. It makes no sense to say that the present work is better than the *Bandwalla* series. To say that, is to raise a different question. Better for what? What is relevant is the perception of difference: this difference means nothing, for it has the structure of subjectivity which does not belong to language: and language cannot express the experience of difference.

The perception of difference is possible if we have access to the painter's meaning where meaning is determinate: that is, it is self-identical in order for it to be shared and the object of a valid interpretation. But admittedly there is always a vast gulf between the meaning of the work and its significance for the viewer. Significance, being context-dependent, is all wrapped up in ambiguity. Since content and context are two different things, 'significance' designates the relevance of content in a painting beyond itself, as it is a function of publicness of a painter's signature and values and norms associated with it. The reason is that understanding, to be sure, is not a validating, self-correcting process; it is always polemical. The logic of the separation of meaning and significance would require that the painter's intentions be a case of 'meaning-for-another'.

Krishen's work is always on the side of significance: he leaves it for the viewer to construct whatever meaning he would like to give to his work, although he would not fail to warn that there is no construction without choice and no choice without a norm. Our knowledge of the meaning suffers from a subjective judgement, for meaning itself is mere fiction. Everything in Krishen is so tightly interlocked in terms of meaning and significance that its unlocking will never cease to be confused, and one-sided.

What matters to Krishen is that any given plane of an object must cling to the flat, two-dimensional pattern, and yet it should tilt sideways into an imagined three-dimensional space. For him the two-dimensionality of the surface sensations onto which all planes melt into one another is all-important: each plane, each little bit of it, knows every other bit making the representation of his world irrelevant. Relevant is the intimacy of the inter-relationship between the parts, the inter-penetration of which is humanly comprehensible. Krishen could perhaps declare like Oscar Wilde: 'it is only shallow people who do not judge from appearances' [*The Picture of Dorian Gray*], for his works are composed entirely of surfaces. It will be wrong to build expectations of a visual access to an interior form to lead us to an unseen force that may have formed the surfaces.

The self-sufficiency and opacity of meaning is what we admire in Krishen's handling of surfaces which provide scarcely any sign of a body beneath them. It is a surface that consciously obscures and shrouds the image: the emphasis is on the apparent gulf between the open-endedness of his world of objects that passively fills the space, and the closed self-sufficiency of the surface.

The surface alone is determined as permanent; the perception of its inner alterations through brushstrokes is a necessary condition of the perception of alteration itself. The presence of these strokes in different locations is what first yields to us an intuition of alteration. Krishen's varied colour application methods make us aware of the distinction between a representation and the represented. He is, in other words, making it explicit that my representations (of my intended world) cannot be outside me; to admit that it is otherwise would be a contradiction. It could well be true that although the representation is in me, its object is, yet, without contradiction, outside me. Or else, the representation together with its object is in me. The argument is that the inner experience requires intuition as well as the representation 'I am'. Thus, he employs a more complex surface to suggest the division of ways in which the self is presented, making explicit the two-fold distinction between the experience of time in relation to his own representations, and the knowledge of his own self as a being determined in time. We take the form of representation in time as meaning the successiveness of all representations in time. For Krishen, this constitutes the manifold of the inner sense of which time is nothing but the form. It is a gambler's experience of time and its temporal location is an externalized present that is experienced always as transitional. That makes him a loner.

Editor's Notes

1 Maurice Merleau-Ponty, *Phenomenology of Perception*, translated by Colin Smith, Routledge, [1945] 1962, London: Routledge Classics, pp. 35–36.

2 Maurice Merleau-Ponty, quoted in Henry Pietersma, *Phenomenological Epistemology*, New York and Oxford: Oxford University Press, 2000, p. 143.

107
RIVERSCAPE

Introductory text for Vivan Sundaram's solo exhibition, 'Riverscape' (1992–93), shown subsequently at the Birla Academy of Art and Culture, Calcutta (1994), Sakshi Gallery (1995) and British Council Art Gallery, New Delhi (1995)

Catalogue text, 1993

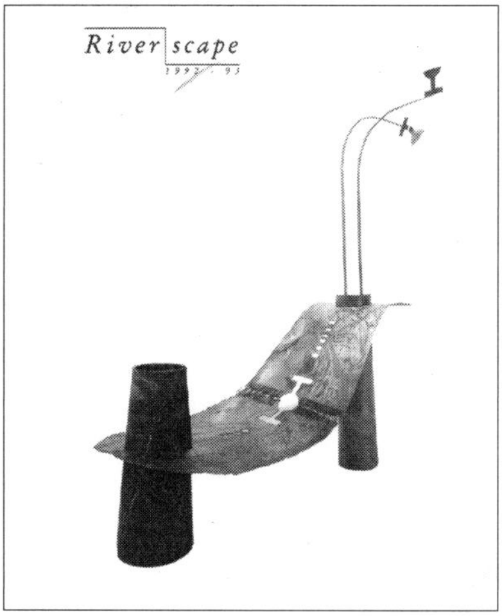

Conceptualism, in the Kantian sense – especially that part of it which is radical – has sought to exclude the art critic and art historian. As a practitioner of 'vanguard' art, Vivan Sundaram may not subscribe to such a strongly stated position. Nor would he want to commit himself to a position where his art is described as non-conceptual: no art, theoretically speaking, no matter how alienated, ever aspires to be 'against' anything: it is always 'for' something.

Unlike the conceptualists, Vivan has not rejected the artwork – either as 'art' or as 'object': certainly not its secondary sources – photographs, interviews and all other available forms of documentation, as supplants of the primary 'things'. What he has rejected, presumably, is an intellectual asseveration, which tends to act as reference. Also rejected are the much used contemporary modes of fabrication made according to art historical rules. If he has used a photograph seen at his last year's show (called *Memorial*: an installation with photographs and sculpture, 1993), it was as a naming device; as a documentation act – such as the one used in the courtroom. Its concern is less with history's index card, more with expression of human existence; in other words, as a form of anthropomorphic projection of pain. The various versions of this single photograph were mounted, in a manner which minimalist artists reserve epistemologically for the square, seriality and the monochrome.[1] With a great deal of hesitation, Vivan, I believe, does not want us to infer that what is being seen is 'art'. The denial is necessary lest it be construed as art. It is used as token of both interiority and exteriority. The intention is to show how time is taken to cut across subjectivities. For, the use of nails is intended to show how temporality as an existential condition made possible the securing of meaning against time.

The nailed photograph is at the same time both literal and metaphorical, its pointed reference is obvious: that the notion of subjectivity is strategic, in that it makes it possible to secure meaning by allowing it a transcendence on the viewer's side. This should not be taken to mean that Vivan is interested to set up dialectic between site and non-site; nor is it the case that such transcendence offers a way of arriving at meaning or a concept of it. What is offered is a way of conceiving the relation between the presence and absence of meaning.

The mode of relation is Duchampian. Vivan, like Duchamp, forces us to confront the limits of intellection that trap us in a hermeneutic game. Recall that Duchamp too once nailed a hatrack on the floor, designed, like his work in general, to trip people up.[2] To trip people up is to counter Judd's statement: All a work needs is that it be interesting.[3] For me, as for Vivan too I presume, all a work needs is to be *uninteresting*: uninteresting seems a necessary condition to avoid the attributed meaning; for, theoretically, interesting would imply the attributed meanings. The proposition that all a work needs to be is that it be uninteresting involves a contradiction: the statement can be interpreted to mean that interesting is uninteresting. And this interpretation makes sense: *uninteresting* is no longer uninteresting. In simple words, it makes sense to interpret 'uninteresting' as meaning that which is normally thought to be uninteresting or that which avoids attributed meanings.

'Duchamp demonstrates' – Pincus-Witten argues convincingly (in his essay on Bruce Nauman, *Artforum*, December 1971) – that 'the ultimate basis of meaning in art is linguistic and not formal, whatever the formal properties his work may possess'.[4] The implicit logic raises another problem – relating to the meaning of 'interesting': interesting comes very close to objectification or to being a substitutional equivalent of 'quality'.[5] If this is what interesting means, Vivan is justified in arguing that he wants his work to be uninteresting. The point is that the criteria used in this way are wholly arbitrary, as are all criteria for quality perceptions in general.

Let me remind you that for Vivan the world is a place of meaning and not the fabricating subjectivity of the artist; for, meaning is what makes his world the site of significations, conceived inter-subjectively as the relationship between presence and absence of meaning. Meaning, to be sure, has always been the central question for modernist painting since its cubist era: how the actual means and substance could be disclosed. To answer this question is to set up a historical task of self-definition. 'A bridge to imaginary shores,' well illustrates Vivan's answer. It offers the possibility of freeing pictorial space from within and allows the spectator to enter it. Rather, he tempts the viewer that such a feat is possible.

The temptation is not without logic: pictorial space, as it occurs in paintings, is something optical rather than literal, and one, therefore, enters it alone. In its distinct privacy, this also accounts for the fact that the viewer as subject, as the bearer of a consciousness, does not come into consideration until pictorial space itself becomes problematic in painting.

The problem which modernist sensibility has not been able to solve is to show how temporality, as an existential condition, has made possible the securing of meaning against time. It is only Vivan who has so far been able to address this problem - both directly and successfully. In his installation *Two Old Boats and a Plan for an Oil Rig* (1993), an effort is evident to specify certain ways in which meaning can be made - and made in such a manner that it persists as meaning. As Michael Fried has argued, the survival of modernist painting was assured when its 'actual' nature was not taken to be its literal nature. Once this change in attitude is admitted, there can no longer be the sense that innovations within painting alter the 'actuality' of the terms of painting, thus posing afresh the modernist problem. In contrast to his earlier work, *Sailboat and Oar Resting Against Tent* 1992, it seemed less of an innovation within painting when it was made to share the ground plane of the gallery. It was wholly subjective as it consisted of a compilation of related images, each composed of one continuous movement, as it were.

The concept of meaning arguably first appeared with the juxtaposition of tokens of inferiority and exteriority in his 1992 show. The non-sites seemed literal and metaphorical at the same time, as exemplified in *Stone Column Enclosing the Gaze*. The optical mix is assimilated by the eye instead of being interpreted by the mind. Subjectivity itself is a strategy; it allowed - indeed, made it possible to secure - meaning by allowing it a transcendence on the viewer's side. What was offered was not the dialectic of site and non-site, or a way of arriving at meaning, but a move that represented a change in the value of meaning. In other words, was it a suspension of the question of whether, or how, one sense of meaning ought to be weighed against another? Or, alternatively, if the disclosure of the conditions of meaning is the task of modernist sensibility, then the bare phenomenal appearance of signification could seem to have the same equivalence of meaning. That is to say, the conditions permitting the appearance of meaning finally revealed themselves as the conditions of the presence of the world. By making the intensity of the experience of himself as a subject, Vivan exposed aesthetic meaning to time. By this demarche, Vivan simultaneously seemed to threaten the very entity of meaning. How can one experience [of] interiority [act] as a mediator between concept and process when images invite a comparison in terms of its presence and absence? Context places one in the embarrassing position of not being able to escape the loss of intimacy and meaning.

Take for example Vivan's *A River Carries Its Past* (1992) - the work moves into private space. But going into that space we discover that it lacks that quality which would have truly defined its value as private space - an opacity to the gaze of others. True, Vivan's imaginary landscape is a critique of power relations. It presents to us a human world 'which is biased towards, is promoted by and exerts influence upon particular sets of social relations. By accepting such premises, it becomes easier to see how appropriate they are to manipulation of the powerful in society'.[6] The work has been interpreted as a demonstration of a grand joke on representation. As with Duchamp, Vivan continually uses contradiction to undermine the meaning of his work. Like Duchamp's *Fountain*: it both is and is not a fountain; is and is not a 'real' urinal, is and is not 'art': here negativity is creativity for Vivan who shows that an artist's oeuvre is purposely fragmented. Because, in Vivan, we find that the breakdown of the boundaries of 'art' and 'life' are part of the assault on language: his work cannot be defined in any clearer way than the object within them, words no longer 'fit' when we encounter a world in which objects, experiences and works of art have become 'unnameable', in an 'as-if' way.

As I said in the beginning, I do not see Vivan as belonging to, or influenced by, the conceptualist movement. Nor is he interested in defeating criticism and art history by incorporating subjectivity as a source of sensibility. That criticism stands in the relation of art, of reaction, of subjectivity, to painterly action, does not imply a political, regressive or inferior connotation of the word 'reaction'. It means that art discourse is not confined to any surface articulation: the discourse is merely the working out of a particular form of knowledge.

What Vivan's recent concerns are can be summed up in [Joseph] Beuys's words: The activity capable of liberating humanity into socialism is art, but first art must be expanded to include every kind of 'creativity'; then (so I infer) we can tap the wellspring of each person, (who) newly aware of his/her creativity will participate in democratic reform/revolution.

True, Vivan is our version of Beuys, although he is aware of the limitations of his modes, skills, and he moves with a quiet self-assurance. He is the opposite of what Robert Morris calls 'the artist as a journalist anti-hero', who has replaced the Romantic artist who would draw his art out of himself as he resists absorption by either nature or culture. This new personality cuts across the need for a responsive discourse not only because he frequently uses language itself as a means but because he does not produce transcendent objects in need of language's mediation.

In other words, a new artist has emerged - the professional artist - and his success is his undoing. And Morris thinks that the notion of 'professional artist is a contradiction in terms for any avant-garde position'. What seems most tragic is that he has lost much of his political power such as the romantic artist once commanded. Vivan, in a way, is a romantic artist with this difference, that the material itself generates a surface - a surface which is the ground for differentiation. His work is both a critique and an appropriation: as a critique, it provides reflexivity between America's present and Europe's past. Art, all art, clusters around centres of power, and

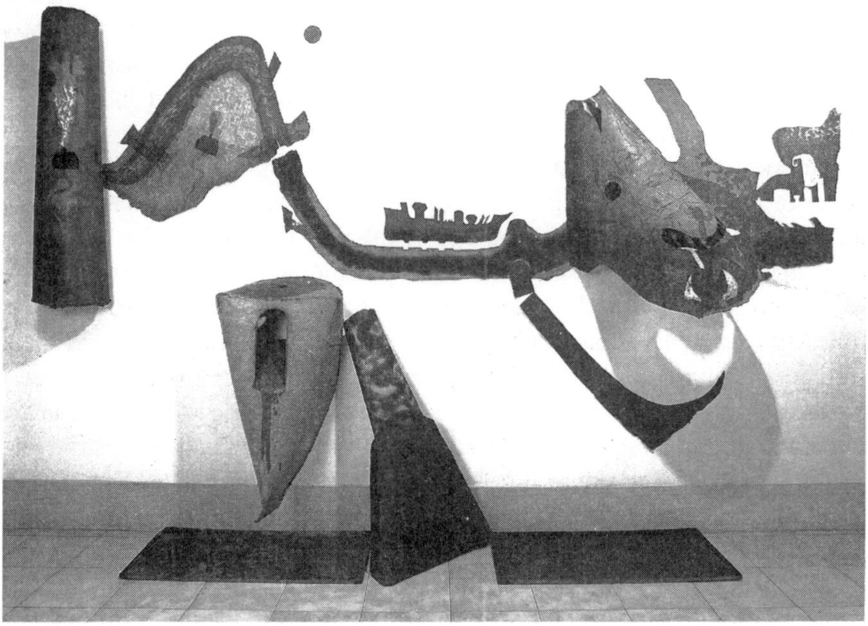

has always been imperialist in that it makes the vernacular of one region serve as a universal code. Vivan is aware of this contemporary situation which has made, in more than one sense, European ethos disinherited. By turning his art into a prism through which to consider the implications of our post-colonial bind, Vivan insists that we learn something from it.

I do not know of another artist who has the authority of a leader, who has the freedom of a man unburdened by followers, and who is concerned with art world's hierarchies and their historical correctness. It is not that Vivan refuses to be influenced; he rejects the implication of power and control implicit in hierarchies of clearly traceable influences. But these aspects seem almost visible. For, he is an engaged artist without being political. Vivan has always been extremely problematic in the sense that he does not accept the need for separation of the visual and the verbal. That is why he never indulges in putting a theoretical straitjacket around his work. Nor does he seem eager to play the meaning games. What interests him most is that the world viewed remains non-referential, for his world is about the nature of its own existence. Essential for this world of Vivan is the grounding notion of art as model [with] which man maps himself into the universe and the universe into himself. It allows us to view his world as if the meaning of a work is only a step away. The easy access is based on the premise that the distinction which one draws between oneself and the rest of the world is only provisional, more a matter of habit and preference than fact. His work is meant to be completed by the viewer.

I have not dealt with the presence of literal space which plays a very crucial role in Vivan's recent work since literal space is a completely different medium – a medium that is deeply affected by the issues of the documentary mode. The experience of a break in the wall allows us to read it as a window frame. Yet, the window itself is intersected by the plane of the picture; so that if we were to mentally complete the window it would exist entirely in our space. The device of the window underlies the sense of picture plane as an interface between two territories which are mutually complete and completing: the one pictorial, and the other literal. To write about pictorial space and its relation to literal space in Vivan's recent work calls for a full-length study: the whole discourse built around the disjunction between the two spaces is there and discoverable for a viewer who is aware that the categories of pictorial space have changed fundamentally. Vivan knows this, as should a critic whose job it is to understand and respond to the change.

Editor's Notes

1 The three aspects that came to be associated with minimalist art. Seriality evolves from the repetition of a single image or something possessing a sequence. A significant minimalist artist, Sol LeWitt, for instance, defined a serial composition as 'multi-part pieces with a system or series of regulated changes'. Another, Mel Bochner, wrote: 'Seriality is premised on the idea that the succession of terms within a single work is based on a numerical or otherwise predetermined derivation from one or more of the preceding terms in that piece.' See Gregory Battcock, ed., *Minimalist Art: A Critical Anthology*, University of California Press, 1995, p. 100. Both the mathematical basis of much of minimalist art and the properties of the square lend themselves to easy spatial multiplication, repetition and balance, and thus made the square a staple of minimalist works. The monochrome came to be adopted from the minimalist mandate to 'pare down' and simplify.

2 In 1917, Duchamp nailed a coat rack/hanger to the floor, impelled by the frustration of continually tripping over the coat rack on the floor that he never got around to hanging up on the wall. Duchamp named the work *Trebuchet*, French for 'trap', deriving from its homophone *trebucher*, which is a chess move to trap the opponent – the projecting coat rack trapping the unsuspecting visitor to Duchamp's studio. Soon after, he created another *Trebuchet*, of a hat rack with projecting prongs that he hung from the ceiling of his studio with strings and which made eerie shadows as it swung. These first experiments with readymades led him to create the now famous *Fountain/Urinal* in the same year. See John F. Moffitt, *Alchemist of the Avant-Garde: The Case of Marcel Duchamp*, New York: State University of New York, 2003, p. 233. The chess reference is not incidental, as Duchamp grew increasingly obsessed with the game from the mid-1920s and gave up art to play chess, continuing till his death in 1968.

3 Donald Judd, 'A work needs only to be interesting', quoted in 'Specific Objects', *Arts Yearbook 8*, 1965, in Thomas Kellein, *Donald Judd: Early Work, 1955–1968*, New York: D.A.P., 2002.

4 Robert Pincus-Witten, 'Bruce Nauman: Another Kind of Reasoning', *Artforum*, February 1972.

5 The phrase is Bruce Boice's, from his *Artforum* article, 'The Quality Problem', October 1972, where he discusses Pincus-Witten's above-mentioned article on Nauman, available at http://allanmccollum.net/allanmcnyc/textpdfs/quality_problem.pdf.

6 The quotation is from J.B. Harley, a seminal cartography scholar and pioneer of 'critical cartography' who critically read into the map's associations with power. See J.B. Harley, 'Maps, Knowledge, Power', in *J.B. Harley: The New Nature of Maps: Essays in the History of Cartography*, edited by Paul Laxton, Baltimore: Johns Hopkins University Press, 2001, p. 53.

108
JERAM WAY OF SEEING

Introductory text for Jeram Patel's solo exhibition at Gallery Espace, November 1996

Catalogue text, 1996

When sign is relieved of its function of referring we know we have retreated to a realm of the ineffable. The ineffable makes one's relation to the world problematic: what is experienced are the limits of rejection of one's past as well as of future. One is metaphorically speaking enveloped in *now* time. Which implies dualism: between the experiencing self (the 'subject') and that which is experienced as reality. It all happens within – a kind of game within oneself, in a make-believe world where one functions as part of an interconnected whole of a communication system. A mysterious mosaic code sends out messages, and one fails to relate them to anything outside the system. Richard Bartholomew, an old art critic-friend of Jeram Patel, once asked –

> What is all this imagery about? What is the purpose of the artist in presenting these images which do not refer to the facts of worldly experience? Man and nature seem to be absent from Jeram's work. Then what is the feeling or the sensation he wishes to establish? The incredulous viewer might ask, what is the significance of this vision.[1]

My answer is: get as close to the work as you can and stay there for as long as you have the moments of sensations of self-absorption to be able to know what is foreign to you and what is familiar. Catch the play between work's orientation and its foundations. Orientation here means work's articulate principles of presence, and by foundation is meant that which leads us to make lyrical self-celebrations in the midst of critical climate. The situation is similar to that ancient Hindu philosopher who, when he lifted the veil from the god, saw: 'It was me in him and it was him in me now, and it is that which reviews the vision.'

The point is, where do you find yourself: inside or outside. From the outside, one can claim that the (Jeram's) world is not mine and yet I find myself inside it, perhaps because of the agency of the gaze, or through the acts of anthropomorphism which casts these visible images into endless circulation, the act of transfiguration being part of the seen.

It is for these reasons that we have the promise of substantially more useful dimensions of a role for the arts, because the anthropomorphic changes require locating values in a world in which the master narratives seem no longer valid. They are no longer the basis of interventionist polemics. Because the seen is actually the historicization of the aesthetic – its inside is admittedly less contaminated by or mixed with what is enframed as outside. This is admittedly for the simple reason that the idea of an artwork as a medium, as sign or a communicative token is put into play beneath the surface of art history. Meaning then is predicative with respect to a beholder's subjecthood. But Jeram's power of enframing is such that interpretation, in the context of a certain individuating gaze, cannot be construed as the lifting of a veil or rendering transparent of what seems opaque.

Call this *presence*, this opacity of image: it is enigmatic in the context of Jeram's placement of anti-aesthetic in relation to the aesthetic. Since the work is enframed leaving unfocused the anti-aesthetic elements, the situation is open to interrogation in conceptualist terms. The image is a gift which springs, as it were, from a certain feeling of graciousness. Implied in such a gesture is a conscious attempt, rather a manipulation of desire, to name something which belongs to the traditional context of representations.

From 1961 onwards, Jeram has not changed; rather has been consistent in conception and execution. Perhaps to the point of single-mindedness. Besides being compelling, his work as it is detached from time and place, refuses to surrender itself as an art commodity. Between these approaches, there is an obvious link: the fascination for the force that the centre holds. In traditional painting, the emphasis on the centre of the canvas organizes the depth of field; in Jeram's, as in a typical Malevich, image is the thing, and the whole canvas is tilted away from an unstated centre. The painterly problems have always been of what to put here and there, and how to make it go with what was already there and these became more and more difficult to solve. Solutions to these problems are difficult to come by except where determination of a centre is made to seem totally arbitrary, to the extent that arbitrariness becomes a centre for intense visual expression. Painting, in the hands of Jeram, becomes a Nietzschean process, not because of the artist's will to power but because Jeram knows all that wills to justify power. The result is that each of his works is marked with the inescapable traces of an individualizing intelligence testing its own capacities to elaborate its provisional centerings.

Jeram's signature is pathbreaking. In 1963 he, alongwith J. Swaminathan and Ambadas, founded the Group 1890. His works then were in a traditional breakaway gesture from easel painting. The seductive appeal of classical colour harmonies has been overthrown long ago; he was at that stage seeking to define an alternative structure of tonal difference. There was a self-asserting presence of colour with a playful decompositional force. Colour echoed and transformed – aggressively. It was ultimate and literal; it involves the richest textural examples. On such things we must dwell more and more to set up interpretive predicates making incursions upon that which they allow us to name. We look for the distinctions between inside and outside; they may be there, intensified by negative space, because each colour, vivid in differential force, defines its own set of containing contrast. Tonally, colour seems perversely incompatible, and the way it tilts away from its closest primary it achieves a balance depending upon how much tension it can manage to work together.

If we look very closely at these colour relations we find a great deal of indeterminacy – in terms of possible or imaginary spatial relations. These are, however, countered by the quite unambiguous overall flatness of the picture. Indeterminacy, to be sure, helps undo identity of effect, and does not allow one plane of colour to slip under any other. The result is a careful refusal of a collage effect. One is tempted to describe this as the principle of adjacency so fundamental to modernism. Adjacency for Jeram, more often than not, is not a synthesis: it consists simply in a struggle against negative space that energizes all the edges of colour and makes them function as irreducible despite their differences.

Jeram's drawing, as in minimalist art, is meant to undo the limit between art and the rest. Like [Brice] Marden, Jeram considers himself a painter rather than an artist; for drawing needs no adornment other than itself: drawing is capable of expansion without limit. Besides, drawing is full of non-conceptual pleasure because it leads us back to an inside wherein it is the outside that appears purposeless. Within it is born a movement of interiorizing cutting us loose from what we seek outside. The play associated with freedom, a lawfulness without a law, and a subjective harmony of the imagination without an objective harmony – all this is possible only in a Jeram drawing.

'To make seen what makes one see, and not what is visible'– that is the task that Lyotard assigns to painting after Cezanne.[2] Translating it into simple terms this means that which causes there to be seen an eye that does not see itself. This is what Jeram teaches us: what is proper to art is merely an approach by which the seeing principle becomes the visible. The seduction of form falls back into a failure of form itself, and if art is approached from the point of view of a limit, art is made into a question – questioning not its presence but its presentation of a failing through which it offers itself. In short, Jeram never sought in his art something surpassing art itself. The image in his work refers back to the experience of the subject and the offer of limitlessness that is made to it in the very limit of the work.

Editor's Notes

1 Richard Bartholomew, 'Jeram Patel', written as catalogue text for the Sao Paolo Biennale, 1977, in *The Art Critic*, New Delhi: Bart, 2012, p. 556.

2 Jean-Francois Lyotard, *The Inhuman: Reflections on Time*, English translation, California: Stanford University Press, 1991, p. 102.

109

THE HIDDEN TEXT IN PHOTOGRAPHY

Introductory text for a solo exhibition of the photographer O.P. Sharma

Catalogue text, 1998

In the class of Hollis Frampton, one of North America's better known and perceptive grammarians of the photographic medium, a girl stood up, threw up her hands and said in great agitation: 'I'm giving up photography, I'm weary of it'. Asked what she would do instead, whether she would go back to painting with which she had first started, she said, 'Good God, no. That would be even worse'. After a short pause, she added, 'Anyway, all photographs are beginning to look alike to me, like pages of prose in a book'.

Why is it that photographs have that same look even though they have been 'made' by different persons? The question has dogged photographers for the seventy odd years since the use of the 35mm camera. It is true that around the 1920s with the generation of Paul Strand and Edward Weston, the photographic image-maker was finally able to make something coherent of it and a continuum of understanding was achieved.

In O.P. Sharma's works, Strand's and Weston's texts find a new spacing: the voice separates it. And what separates it is something of a tonal differential, and yet one is aware that the true nature of this tone is inaccessible. All that one can say is: it is beautiful, it exists somewhere beyond, has an effect of the transcendental. Perhaps because it is not consumable as true works of art are not. There is a predominance of the 'I' (or the eye!) in his vision. His photographs inaugurate something, a type of work which was not possible without his signature, a work that has a life of its own. Sharma's signature since the 1960s generates a desire of greater fullness of being: it is powerful, self-reliant, tough. They are delicate,

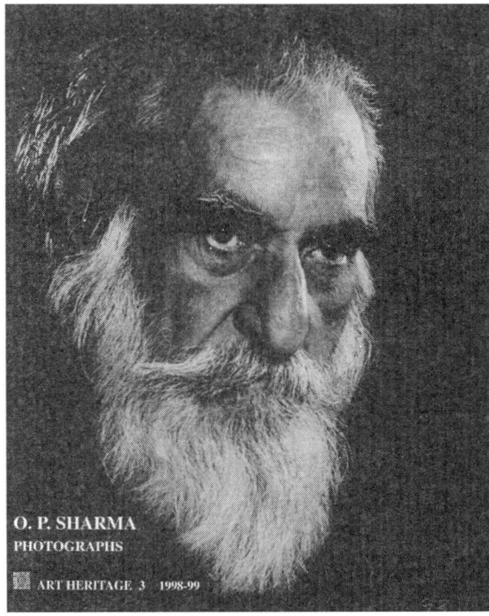

carefully dusted fine spots for the forms to become content. His more famous contemporaries still wait for some content in order to shape themselves accordingly.

The differential is replayed through the tone and the gradation of tonality: this tone differential evidently constitutes the essence of his signature, something not exhausted by its meaning. Nearness to this tone differential allows us to distinguish between a diagram of possibility and its enactment. What is not sought for is the content; what defines it is the tone; since tone is never present, it is felt differentially, and Sharma never allows himself to be confined to a single interlocutor or a single moment. He is never overwhelmed by the beauty of the pictorial because the effect of the beautiful is the presence of the signature: there is always a certain presence of the artist.

A photographer's relation to discourse is very complicated. For pictorialists are different. They are the ones who turn a casual snap into a 'photograph', and often produce things which apparently seem a most uncamera-like image. Also because, there is a connection between the art of painting and that of photography, which is as old as modernism in visual arts. Picasso was a great admirer of the camera technology, especially the photomontage technique. He compared, for instance, the painter to a magician or faith-healer who keeps a normal social distance between himself and his subject's reality. The photographer, he thought, worked like a surgeon, 'who operates directly on the tissue of reality'. Sharma's credo, however, is this: the painter's image is total: the photographer shows 'a multiplicity of details in accordance with a new law and resulting from an intensive penetration of reality'. The movie, by sheer speeding up of the mechanical, has brought forth the true content of Picasso's observation. No longer is the camera image bound to the world of sequence; it is a new world of creative configuration and structure.

Photography no longer means, and is no longer limited to, documentation. The photographic image, however striking its effect on the mind, is not valuable as a picture, for the essence of the picture is not exhausted by its indicative function. The indicative function in a photographic image is similar to one that characterizes the image in a poster. It is, therefore, more of a sign that points away from itself and implicates the presence of something that is not present. In photographs such as Sharma's, in which a sign becomes a symbol, the tone differential turns them into pictures and forces us to linger longer than one does on something that has only an indicative function. It is then more than a photograph and its sign character retreats into the background. Such photographs are closer to tone values of pictorialism.

How is one to distinguish a pictorialist from a photographer? A photographer, unlike the snapshotter, records fusing the intention with the mechanical mode of the camera. A pictorialist, like Sharma, does not, record inasmuch as he works towards metamorphosis of the mechanical: the mechanical disappears behind the intentionalist coda. A pictorialist would argue his case something like the following: the camera never records, it always reveals. A pictorialist pays more attention to the picture in the mind: his lens, filter, emulsion and grain, are all in accordance with the sensibility and the intention, spreading out and manifesting itself in pure subjectivity, although it must always be in tune with its outer circumstance. Its greatest asset is its intangibility, like the idea of god. Like a god, a pictorialist-photographer tries to pick just the right instant to appropriate it; the subject itself can be interpreted in the darkroom.

'To make seen what makes one see, and not what is visible'. That is the task Lyotard assigns to painting. It is as well for a pictorialist like Sharma. In the photographic medium, this paradox is resolved by the subjectivity of the eye; outside of its field of vision nothing can be seen. The seen is thus the space experienced in films as there is no stopping the image through its dispersal of the trace through which the image in the mind escapes, by such negative devices as, 'no, that doesn't work', 'the light isn't right', or, the 'the light isn't enough', or, 'the angle isn't right'. Yet, the mind is a participant in all the framefolds in the fictional decisive monuments while the silent lens draws figures out of them. For, the principle of visibility means that the eyes never stop framing images. But the nature of the photographic medium is such that it leaves little room for variability of representation: what varies does not belong to the subject and therefore there is no subjective aspect to the photographic process. We can say it is intended to be a window to the modern world: Descartes looks out at men with a mechanical eye, unmoved by all fluctuations of sense and sensibility.

Yet Sharma does not suffer from Cartesian doubts. The photographic medium, and the progress he has made in four decades should have been the focus of this essay but there are only hints and suggestions about his development. The work of vision strutted with portraiture and an undisclosed subjectivity began to dominate the visual process. How does the truth of the sitter show itself? Is the essential truth to be different from what comes-to-appearance? These questions troubled him; was reaching out to one he had focused his lens on, the beginning of a mystical experience? And vision for an instant was transformed, with no loss of contact with everyday reality.

It is this experience, when it is enframed, that invites us to what might be called the photgraphic discourse. Since it was illuminated from within, it seemed inevitably subject to cultural definition. And since the photographic utterance is incomplete, being a message without a code, it depends on some external matrix of conditions and presuppositions for its readability. That is, the meaning is necessarily context-dependent. There is, however, a hint of some hidden text. Sharma's text should be read alongside that of such masters as Edward Weston and others. In accordance with the sensibility and the intention, spreading out and manifesting itself in pure subjectivity, although it must always be in tune with its outer

folds in the fictional decisive monuments while the silent lens draws figures out of them. For the principle of visibility means that the eyes never stop

essential of the truth to be different from what comes-to-appearance? These questions troubled him. Or was reaching out to one he had focused his lens on.

The Bridge of Life 1989

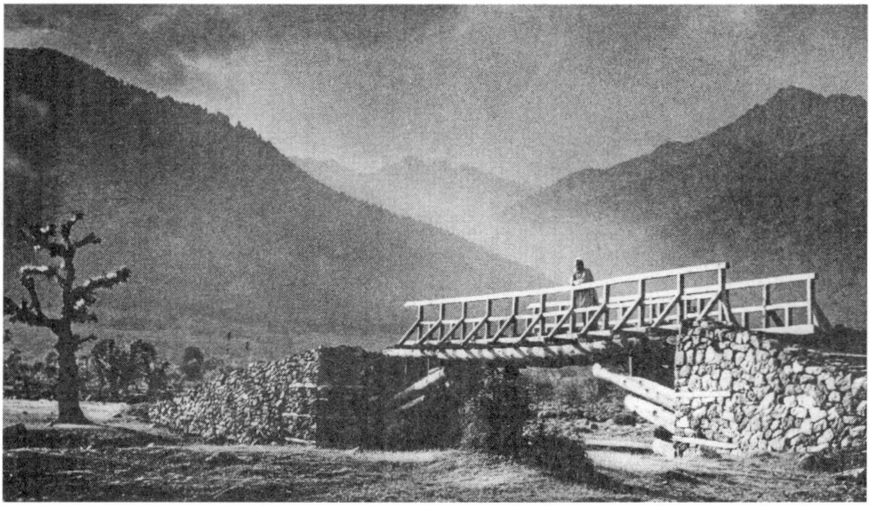

India, there have been photographers like J.N. Unwalla, H.L. Syed and R. R. Bhardwaj among others, who gave to the photographic medium its own language, something that is 'beyond speech', in short, a universal and independent language.

Where Sharma excels is in the fact that his photographs derive their semantic properties from conditions that reside within the image itself. His discourse is of course, the outcome of a culturally determined relationship, but the equal formalist notion cannot be overlooked, for, it is the tonal differentiation that is the vehicle of his voice. The terms of his photographic discourse have a primitive core of meaning devoid of all cultural determinations. A meaningful encounter with Sharma's photographs must necessarily occur at the level of connotation: it is to render the medium transparent.

ARTIST INDEX